JOHN G. LAKE
The Complete Collection of His Life Teachings

Compiled by
Roberts Liardon

ALBURY PUBLISHING
Tulsa, Oklahoma

All Scripture quotations are taken from the *King James Version* of the Bible.

John G. Lake
The Complete Collection of His Life Teachings
ISBN 1-57778-075-2
Copyright © 1999 by Roberts Liardon Ministries
P. O. Box 30710
Laguna Hills, California 92654

Published by ALBURY PUBLISHING
P. O. Box 470406
Tulsa, Oklahoma 74147-0406

DEDICATION

Lovingly dedicated to Pastors Les and Sheila Bowling and the congregation at Eagle Rock Ministries for your leadership, integrity, and wisdom. You are a never-ending source of inspiration, true friends, and a great help to my ministry, staff, school, and church.

ACKNOWLEDGMENTS

Reverend and Mrs. Wilford Reidt, John G. Lake's son-in-law and daughter, who graciously provided a tremendous amount of material for this publication.

John G. Lake III, who offered a wonderful foreword and gave us some rich background information, especially regarding the photographs.

L. G. Jack and Ruby Lake, John G. Lake's son and daughter-in-law, who added to our research and took time with us on the telephone.

Wayne Warner and the staff of The Flower Pentecostal Heritage Center (Assemblies of God Archives) who were always ready to help in whatever way they could, doing additional research and supplying text for this publication.

Ricki Wright, for helping us to build our photo library and add to our research. We appreciate your dedication and expertise regarding the life and ministry of John G. Lake.

CONTENTS

Section Two: Undated Material Arranged by Topic

What gave my grandfather, John G. Lake, his power?

FOREWORD

That was a question asked of me in a letter from a friend several years ago.

I came upon the letter recently while sorting and packing to move across town. As I thought about the question I kept coming back to the same conclusion. Grandfather had the power of God in his life because he was utterly consumed with the prize: A closer walk with Jesus Christ and a better, clearer, more personal understanding of the nature of God and the purpose of man's journey through this world.

The reward for his focus on the prize was the gift of healing he operated in so strongly. As he remained single-minded toward the goal of eliminating the barriers between the physical and spiritual realms, the power came to him, though it never took over as his focus. Grandfather was not overawed by the power to heal. It was a good gift, but his life goal was still not healing. His goal was still a closer walk with God.

As with healing, Grandfather was also never overawed by wealth, although he was an incredible businessman and had an ability to make money. He did not turn his life or ministry toward getting rich or making others rich. In fact, toward the end of his life, when the Great Depression pressed down on him and having enough money to live became a real issue, Grandfather's prayer life centered not on himself but on finding a message of hope, power, and direction for His beloved people. "God," he prayed, "give me a message to show before the faces of Your people."

This selfless quality was what empowered Grandfather to live in total obedience. My grandfather's life was dedicated to finding the will of God and fulfilling it wholly. Much of Grandfather's power came from simply being where God wanted him at the time God wanted him to be there. That was certainly true in South Africa where, forty-five minutes into Grandfather's first sermon, one hundred Zulus were filled with the Holy Spirit. These one hundred then went out and started a major revival. The following eight years of ministry in South Africa would see nearly one million people come to God.

I believe the testimony of Grandfather's powerful ministry can be summed up in the book of Daniel: "The people who know their God shall be strong, and carry out great exploits." (See Daniel 11:32.)

Keep your eyes on the prize.

Sincerely,

John Lake III

John Graham Lake

John Graham Lake was a man of prayer and commitment. You will better understand the quality of his life and his consecration to God by reading his sermons, diary entries, and other writings.

A BRIEF BIOGRAPHY OF JOHN GRAHAM LAKE

John G. Lake was born March 18, 1870, at St. Mary's, Ontario, Canada. While John was still a child, his parents moved to the United States. At the age of twenty-one he became a Methodist minister; however, he chose to start a newspaper instead of accepting a church ministry.

When his wife entered into a prolonged serious illness, she was miraculously delivered under the ministry of John Alexander Dowie in April 1898. This experience forever altered the direction of John G. Lake's life and ministry.

Lake is probably remembered best for his missionary work in South Africa, but his ministry in the United States was also powerful. One-hundred-thousand healings were recorded in five years at the Lake healing rooms in Spokane, Washington. Dr. Ruthlidge of Washington, D.C., called Spokane, Washington, the healthiest city in the world as a result.

What he accomplished as a result of his intense regard for the Word of God is an example to all Christians of what is possible for any person who will believe and act on the Scriptures.

THE HEALER: DR. JOHN GRAHAM LAKE

*T*he man whom Gordon Lindsay declared was, in his opinion, "the greatest missionary that has appeared since the period of the early Church," was also a man who profoundly impacted the Northwest District with the message of Pentecost — even though he himself was never a member of the Assemblies of God. His name was John G. Lake.

John Graham Lake was born at St. Mary's, Ontario, Canada, on March 18, 1870. When yet a small boy, he accompanied his parents to the United States, settling at Sault Sainte Marie, Michigan.

Editor's note:

The following biography of Dr. Lake is taken from *Let Light Shine Out: The Story of the Assemblies of God in the Pacific Northwest,* by Ward M. Tannenberg, Ph.D.

In October 1891, he was admitted in the Methodist ministry in Chicago and appointed to a church in Peshtigo, Wisconsin. He finally decided against going there and instead went into the newspaper business. In the town of Harvey, Illinois, he founded the *Harvey Citizen.* (This town was named after D. L. Moody's brother-in-law.)

In February 1893, at age twenty-one, he married Miss Jennie Stephens of Newberry, Michigan. Three years later, she was pronounced incurable of consumption by several physicians who had given her the best treatment then possible. They advised Dr. Lake to take her north. On that advice, they returned to Sault Sainte Marie. Five years later on April 28, 1898, she received an instantaneous healing under the ministry of John Alexander Dowie. In Sault Sainte Marie, Lake opened a real estate office. As a salesman and contractor, he remained there until 1901. During this time, together with George A. Feris, he founded the *SOO Times,* a local newspaper.

In 1904, he moved to Chicago and bought a seat on the Chicago Board of Trade with money borrowed from a friend. During this time, he handled Jim Hill's western Canadian land and made a long-time personal friend of this great railroad financier.

The first day he opened his office, he made $2,500 on a real estate deal. At the end of twenty-one months in the real estate business, he had over $100,000 in the bank, a $30,000 paid-up life insurance policy, and real estate valued at $90,000.[1] He traveled to New York representing the Chicago Board of Trade. There he met Tom Lawson, together with Mr. Harriman and Mr. Ryan, all celebrated financiers. He was employed by Ryan to further his negotiations, amounting to $170,000, in an effort to form a large insurance trust between the New York Life, Equitable, and Mutual Insurance companies. He also represented Mr. Lawson on the New York Board of Trade.

About this time, a huge scandal erupted in New York in relation to insurance companies. Dr. Lake, together with several others, organized the People's Life Insurance Company of Chicago. He was appointed manager of agencies and wrote a million dollars worth of business in his first year. He had received a guarantee of $50,000 a year to continue in this business, but it was during this time that God dealt with him in such a way that the course of his life was definitely altered.

A number of years had passed since God had healed his wife, Jennie. During this time, he had continued practicing the ministry of healing. Every answer to prayer and miraculous touch of God created within him a greater longing for the deeper things of the Spirit.

During his business life, he made it a habit of speaking somewhere practically every night. After the services, he was in the habit of joining with friends who, like himself, were determined to receive the baptism in the Holy Spirit as they believed the early disciples had received it (Acts 2:1-4). His prayer was, "God, if You will baptize me in the Holy Ghost and give me the power of God, nothing shall be permitted to stand between me and one hundredfold obedience."

Sometime after this, he accompanied a minister to pray for an invalid lady who had had inflammatory rheumatism for ten years. While the minister talked with the lady, John Lake sat at the opposite side of the room deeply moved in his spirit. He testified that he suddenly felt as

---

[1] Gordon Lindsay, *Sketches from the Life and Ministry of John G. Lake* (Shreveport, Louisiana: Voice of Healing Publishing Co., 1952), p. 14.

[2] Ibid., p. 15.

though he had just passed under a deep shower or warm tropical rain that fell not only upon him but through him. His whole being was soothed into a deep stillness and calm. An awe of the presence of God settled over him. After moments passed, he seemed to hear the Lord say, "I have heard your prayers, and I have seen your tears. You are now baptized in the Holy Spirit." Then Dr. Lake testified to "currents of power" that began to rush through his being, increasing so greatly that his entire body began to vibrate intensely.

At this time, the minister friend asked him to join him in prayer for the woman. He found it difficult to walk across the room — the presence of the Lord was so intense. As he touched the sister's head with his hand, her clenched hands opened and joints began to work. The woman who had been an invalid for so long arose from her wheelchair and was perfectly healed![3]

As a result of this baptism, Dr. Lake testified to seeing mankind through "new eyes." He had a great desire to proclaim the message of Christ and to demonstrate His power in the world.

In April 1907, he closed his office door for the last time and disposed of his bank account by giving to various religious and educational institutions. Fred R. Burr of Winamac, Indiana, who was his financial agent, assisted him in disposing of everything, including his real estate holdings.

Dr. Lake started out in independent evangelistic work with a single dollar, being absolutely dependent upon the Lord — along the faith lines of George Mueller of England and Hudson Taylor of the China Inland Mission.

During the next several months, he preached each day to large congregations with outstanding results. Many people accepted Christ as their Lord and Savior, others were healed of diseases, while still others received the baptism in the Holy Spirit. While in a meeting in northern Illinois, the Lord spoke to him and directed him to go to Indianapolis to prepare for a winter campaign. He was instructed to acquire a large hall, and then he was told that in the spring he would go to Africa.

---

[3] Ibid., p. 16.

On April 19, 1908, he left Indianapolis, Indiana, for Johannesburg, South Africa. He needed $2,000 for expenses but had not one cent. In answer to private prayer in his own room, an unknown donor from Monrovia, California, a place he had never visited nor known of anyone living there, sent to a friend four $500 drafts. He told the friend that God had urged him to send Lake $2,000. It was needed for a special purpose, although that purpose was unknown to the donor.

So God supplied the expenses needed.

ARRIVAL IN SOUTH AFRICA

He arrived with his missionary party in South Africa, on May 15, 1908. Before he could come ashore, it was necessary for him to place $125 with the immigration department. He, again, had not one cent. As he stood in the line of people who were making their payments, awaiting his chance to explain his dilemma to the immigration officer, a man walked up, tapped him on the shoulder, and called him out of the line. He handed him a traveler's check for $200 and said, "I feel led to give you this to help your work."[4]

On arrival at Johannesburg, he and his family had nowhere to go. They were strangers with no friends or acquaintances there. As they stepped ashore, Mrs. C. L. Goodenough, an American missionary and a complete stranger, walked up to Dr. Lake and said, "While in prayer last night, God told me to meet this boat and that there would be upon it an American missionary with a family of nine, consisting of two adults and seven children, and that I was to give them a home." At three o'clock that afternoon, the Lakes were living in a furnished cottage in Johannesburg that God had provided for them.[5]

Some time later Dr. Lake went on an exploring trip in the Kalahari Desert. He returned to Johannesburg to find his wife dead. A sudden stroke had instantly killed her. She had no other illnesses.[6]

Early in 1909, Dr. Lake met Bishop Furze, the bishop of the Church of England for Africa. At the bishop's request, Dr. Lake arranged a

---

[4] Gordon Lindsay, *The John G. Lake Sermons* (Shreveport, Louisiana: Voice of Healing Publishing Co., 1952), pp. 12-13.

[5] Ibid., pp. 18.

[6] In *God's Generals*, Pastor Liardon goes into more detail. Due to the strenuous demands of ministry, Jennie Lake was exhasuted and malnourished, which probably caused her stroke.

series of meetings for the Church of England ministers. He was to teach them along the lines of divine healing. These meetings resulted in the establishment of the Emmanuel Society for the Practice of Divine Healing by the ministry of the Church of England in Africa.

As word of these meetings and the work of the society continued to go forth, a committee from England came to examine and report upon Dr. Lake's work. He later accompanied that committee to England and conducted similar meetings in London under the direction of Bishop Ingram.

This conference authorized a committee to further visit other healing institutions in England and Europe. In the company of this committee, he visited healing institutions in London and went to Lourdes, France. There, they visited a Catholic institution where healing was reputed to take place by the waters of Lourdes and where they maintained a board of two hundred physicians whose business it was to examine all candidates and report upon them.

At Lourdes, they were privileged to visit the then greatest hypnotic institution for healing in the world. This institution sent its representatives to demonstrate their methods to the Catholic board of two hundred physicians, and hearing of the committee, they were invited to go along. Dr. Lake agreed to take part if he were allowed to make the final demonstration.

The committee selected five candidates who had been pronounced medically incurable. The hypnotists tried their various methods without success. Dr. Lake then had the five candidates placed in chairs in a row upon the platform in view of the audience of physicians and scientists. He prayed over each one of them separately. Three were instantly healed, a fourth recovered in a few days, and one passed away.[7]

Dr. Lake returned to the United States for six months, holding evangelistic crusades in Chicago, Portland, Oakland, and Los Angeles for the purpose of recruiting missionaries to take with him to South Africa. During these crusades, he acquired eight men but needed $3,000 for their expenses. While in Portland, praying alone in his

---

[7] Ibid., p. 20.

room, he received assurance that the answer was on the way. Four days later in Los Angeles, a letter arrived at his hotel from George B. Studd of Los Angeles.

> Dear Dr. Lake: There has been a windfall in your favor today. A person who does not wish to be known gave me a draft of $3,000 saying, 'God wants me to give this to Lake of South Africa.' I am sending you, enclosed, therefore a draft for $3,005, the $5 being my personal contribution.

In January 1910, he returned to South Africa with his missionary party via London, where he preached in Dr. F. B. Meyer's church and spoke in G. Campbell Morgan's weekly Bible classes.

He remained in South Africa for several years, during which time he founded the Apostolic Faith Mission with headquarters at Johannesburg. He was elected its president and continued for years after that to be its honorary president. During his ministry, he organized 125 white congregations and 500 black congregations.

In 1920, the African fever ravaged the area in which he lived, and in less than a month, one-quarter of the black and white populations died. Agencies of every description were called into action to combat the epidemic. Dr. Lake worked there with several assistants, four of whom died of the fever, but he never had a touch of the disease.

Later in Johannesburg, he was invited by Louis Botha, premier of Transvaal, to visit the Transvaal Parliament, where resolutions were passed recognizing his services during the severe epidemic.

Due to the strain of overwork with the Apostolic Faith Mission, he ultimately gave up his ministry in South Africa to return to the United States. There, he met and married Miss Florence Switzer of Milwaukee, Wisconsin, on November 27, 1913. In addition to the seven children born from his first marriage, five more children were born into his second union.

John G. Lake was on hand at the organizational meeting of the Assemblies of God on April 2, 1914, in Hot Springs, Arkansas.[8] He did not become a member, however, neither at that time nor at any time later.

---

[8]   Irwin Winehouse, *The Assemblies of God A Popular Survey* (New York: Vantage Press, 1959), p. 31.

That summer, Dr. Lake met Jim Hill while walking along the street one day in St. Paul. When asked about what he was doing, Dr. Lake replied that he was simply trying to gather his health and that he was preaching wherever he went.

Mr. Hill invited him to his office and gave him complimentary passes that were good over all of his railroad lines.

Dr. and Mrs. Lake began traveling, stopping at Spokane where he was invited to open a healing room. He accepted the invitation and ministered to the sick for about six months. Thus, he was to begin the ministry that was really the climax of his life's work.

The Healing Mission in Spokane

Dr. Lake's entire ministry had been profoundly affected by his exposure to John Alexander Dowie. Dr. Lake had been an elder in the Zion Apostolic Church when Dowie was at the height of his power. Thus he, together with various other persons exposed to the Dowie approach to Christian living, became dynamic disciples and missionaries of the Gospel of Jesus Christ, coming west through the Dakotas, Montana, and into Washington.

Dr. Lake had made no preparation or study that prepared him for missionary work, nor was he particularly trained in a theological perspective, as were most ministers. But he was a man of strong and forceful personality who seemed to make his way to the forefront in whatever situation he found himself.

His ministry had its weaknesses as well as its strengths. It was believed by some that his failure to properly anticipate the heavy responsibilities his wife had to carry was an unfortunate mistake that contributed to her untimely death on the mission field. This fact, plus the responsibilities he now had in order to care for a large family, was one of the primary contributing factors to the close of his ministry on the mission field. However, his days of glory were not yet finished.

His early ministry in the city of Spokane became a demonstration of the power of God that resulted in more than one-hundred thousand healings being reported during a period of five or six years. Some declared that Dr. Lake, through his ministry of divine healing, had made Spokane the healthiest city in the world. This, of course, was similar to a documented report that came out of Washington, D.C., some years earlier regarding Zion, Illinois, during the peak days of John Alexander Dowie's ministry.

His activity in Spokane had such impact that the *Spokesman Daily Review* carried full-page advertisements each week regarding his ministry and the miraculous acts of documented healing. The full-page advertisements in the *Spokesman Review* were often as follows:

The Church at Spokane

John G. Lake, Overseer

Divine Healing Rooms, 340 Rookery Building

Open each weekday from 10 to 4.

Personal interviews and ministry

Through prayer and laying on of hands.

Public services on Sunday at

The Masonic Temple at 11 a.m. and 3 p.m.

Our ministry is private and confidential. Persons desiring to

Give public testimony must arrange with the ministers in advance.[9]

Then would follow letters of testimony from those who had received healing and/or their physicians, as well as articles by Dr. Lake.

In a general letter published Saturday, February 8, 1919, in the *Spokesman Review*, Dr. Lake indicated that they ministered to an average of two hundred people per day in the healing rooms. He stated that over sixty thousand personal "ministrations through prayer and laying on of hands" had taken place during the previous twelve months. In addition, calls for prayer and the ministry came by telephone, telegraph, letter, and cable from all parts of the world.

Ministry to the sick in their homes was another phase of work accomplished by the use of two motor cars in which ministers were conveyed from home to home, praying for those who were unable to present themselves at the healing rooms. Dr. Lake indicated that at least one-hundred thousand people were ministered to each year either by car, telephone, telegraph, letter, or cable.

---

[9] *The Spokesman Review*, May 19, 1918.

Thousands of people would attend the Sunday services held each week at the Masonic Temple. Dr. Lake always liked to make a point of emphasizing that he did not spend money building church buildings and "sepulchers for the dead." Funds given to the church at Spokane would be used to send forth the Gospel message into the world, according to Dr. Lake. There were no fees charged for any of the ministry, and the entire project was supported by means of love offerings. An especially appealing story was published on September 20, 1919, in the *Spokesman Review*. It was testimony shared by Walter J. Williams, science department chairman of an eastern university.

In the article, he told about two of his friends in the East who had traveled to Spokane and received amazing healings. This scientist-educator was very adverse to anything savoring of what might be called the supernatural, but he journeyed to Spokane to gather first-hand information. He visited several persons who professed to have been healed under Dr. Lake's ministry. Then he visited the man himself. After an extended interview, he was invited to stay and see for himself what God was doing there.

Dr. Willliams did.

> I saw them come, hundreds in a day. I talked to them, asking them questions — the lame, the poor, the rich, the uneducated, and the intellectual. Were they healed? Yes, they were. Was I convinced that it was God? Indeed, I was. The presence of God was there and I left Spokane inquiring if I was true enough to God to be trusted with His power as Dr. Lake and his associates were.

> I have listened to some of the greatest teachers on earth, both secular and religious, but I have never heard such revelations of life or such a revelation of God as I heard and witnessed at the Healing Rooms in the Rookery Building in Spokane.[10]

LAKE AND DIVINE HEALING INVESTIGATED

One summer, Dr. Lake and his staff were waited upon at their healing rooms by a committee of the Better Business Bureau of the city of

---

[10] *The Spokesman Review*, September 20, 1919.

Spokane. Their duty was to investigate the truthfulness of the public announcements that were continuing to appear in the city papers. For some time, Lake's staff had been publishing many of the testimonies of healing through the power of God that had taken place in the course of their ministry.

These testimonies were so astounding that complaints had reached the Better Business Bureau to the effect that the testimonies must certainly be untrue. The Better Business Bureau immediately undertook an investigation of the Healing Rooms' ministry and Dr. John G. Lake.

The committee examined eighteen witnesses whose testimonies had appeared in public print. Further names of persons who had received healings within the city were given to the committee so that they could go personally and investigate for themselves whether or not these things were so.

Dr. Lake suggested to the committee that on Sunday, June 23, at three o'clock in the afternoon in a public service, he would present one hundred cases of healed persons for their investigation. He invited them to form a committee composed of physicians, lawyers, judges, educators, and businessmen who could render a verdict. During the intervening period between the interview in the healing rooms and Sunday, June 23, the committee continued their investigations. On Friday, June 21, Dr. Lake received a letter from the committee assuring him that they had no desire to interfere in any way with the good being done and had determined that their appearance at the Sunday meeting would not be necessary. Two members of the investigation committee spoke privately to Dr. Lake and his staff and said that the committee was astounded. They had found out upon investigation that "the half had not been told."

One of the committee members visited at Davenport, Washington, and found printed announcements advertising a meeting Dr. Lake was about to conduct in the area. He inquired as to why these announcements were being made and the manager of the store replied:

> The whole countryside 'round Davenport is aflame with surprise at the marvelous healing of a girl in this community, well-known to me, and, I believe, well-known to

yourself, Miss Louise Reinboldt, daughter of Mr. Jack Reinboldt. About three and a half years ago, Miss Reinboldt and her sister were operated on for what the doctors thought was appendicitis. The one girl died as a result of the operation. Louise came out of it unable to speak. She was taken to throat specialists, who pronounced her case absolutely incurable. Recently she was taken to Spokane to Dr. Lake's Healing Rooms and ministered to for twenty-six days.

On the twenty-sixth day she startled her mother and family and, in fact, the whole countryside, by calling her mother on the long distance telephone and announcing to her in plain words the fact that she was "healed." While preparing for her daily visit to the Healing Rooms she heard herself whistling and said, "Well, if I can whistle, I can speak also," and thus discovered the paralyzed condition of her throat was truly healed.[11]

After the Better Business Bureau committee backed away from further investigation, Dr. Lake announced that there would be no change in the program. He indicated the meeting would take place as announced, and if the Better Business Bureau would not take their place, he would appeal to the public for its verdict. Thousands of people attended that afternoon in the Masonic Temple, while hundreds were refused admittance due to lack of space. Testimonies by ministers and lay people alike of significant, documented healings were given throughout the remainder of the afternoon. The publicity of this meeting was tremendous and was perhaps one of the high points in the sometimes controversial, but always unique, ministry of John G. Lake.

In May 1920, Dr. Lake moved to Portland, Oregon, to establish a similar work to that of his church in Spokane. Within a few years, this ministry in Portland was making a similar impact in Oregon as had

---

[11] Gordon Lindsay, *Sketches from the Life of John G. Lake,* Op. Cit., pp. 107-110.

the church in the Inland Empire. One of his converts in Portland was Gordon Lindsay, who later became an independent Pentecostal evangelist of some significance and forerunner of the present Christ for the Nations ministry headquartered in Dallas, Texas.

Dr. Lake's ministry was unusual — to say the least. He possessed a remarkable ability to create faith in the hearts of his hearers. Gordon Lindsay was no exception. Having followed Dr. Lake's ministry with deep respect and admiration, he one day had need of the great man's faith. He was stricken with a critical case of ptomaine poisoning and for days hung between life and death. Dr. Lake offered prayer for Gordon, and although deliverance did not immediately come in a visible manner, he professed confidence that indeed the Lord had answered prayer. Mrs. Lake brought Reverend Lindsay some of the typewritten sermons her husband had recently given, and while reading these messages, faith suddenly sprang into his heart. He arose from what many thought was a deathbed, instantly healed.[12]

While he was in Portland, Dr. Lake entertained hopes for raising up a chain of healing missions on the order of his works in Spokane and Portland. However, though he was not yet advanced in age, he had lived with an intensity that had taken its toll. A decline in the strength and vitality that had characterized his earlier ministry became apparent. He seemed unable to match his spiritual vision with the physical strength that was required to bring it to pass. In Houston, Texas, he had some initial success in the founding of a church, but was called away to the side of his eldest son who had suffered a serious accident that almost took his life. He never returned to Houston.

For awhile, he ministered in churches throughout California. However, the dynamic touch that he once had was lacking. He later returned to the city of Portland, where he pastored for a time. Afterwards, he returned to Spokane. There he pastored until his death.

On Labor Day 1935, Dr. and Mrs. Lake attended a Sunday school picnic. He came home very tired and after a hot supper, lay down to

---

[12] Ibid., p. 9.

rest. A guest speaker was at the church that evening so Mrs. Lake prevailed on him to stay at home. She went to church in his place. When she arrived home, she found that he had a stroke in her absence. He lingered for about two weeks, unconscious most of the time, until September 16, 1935, when he went to be with his Lord.

His ministry was summed up in the brief testimony of Reverend B. S. Hebden who spoke at the memorial service:

> Dr. Lake was a strong, rugged character of loving and winning personality, and he has left his mark indelibly upon the world of Gospel Truth.
>
> Dr. Lake came to Spokane. He found us in sin. He found us in sickness. He found us in poverty of spirit. He found us in despair, but he revealed to us such a Christ as we had never dreamed of knowing this side of heaven. We thought victory was over there, but Dr. Lake revealed to us that victory was here, a present and possible reality. We regarded death almost as a friend, but Dr. Lake came and revealed to us the Christ, all-glorious and all-powerful, that is triumphant, compassionate, and lovely, and our night was turned into day and despair was turned into laughter. A light shone in the darkness and we, who found Christ at last as He really is, only have words as the words of Thomas, who said, "My Lord and My God."
>
> How I thank God that Brother Lake came to Spokane! How I thank Him that I ever contacted that man, unique, powerful! I will never forget the day in the Hutton Block when I was sick with several chronic complaints and I heard that message of Christ, that His arms were under me, and I kept it and the message kept me and instead of my being long and long ago, gone and forgotten, I am here rejoicing and thanking our brother, Dr. Lake, who brought that message to me. Friends, he should still speak in me, not by the pen but by the Spirit that is in me, by the Light that is in me, by the regeneration of Jesus Christ

that is in me. Let us, friends, not go and squander it by
hiding it in a napkin, but let us keep it by giving it out.[13]

(NOTE: Much of the additional information came from conversations with various persons who knew him and from some of his
mimeographed messages.)

---

[13] Ibid., pp. 11-12.

ohn Graham Lake

Birth Date:

March 18, 1870

Birth Place: St. Mary's, Ontario, Canada

Height: 5'11"

Weight: 190 in 1935

Eyes: Grey, wore bifocals on occasion

Marital Status: February 1893 married Jennie Stephens who died in Africa. On November 27, 1913, married Florence Switzer

Date of Death: September 16, 1935

Place of Death: Spokane, Washington

Place of Burial: Riverside Memorial Park

JOHN G. LAKE
Personal Glimpses

Editor's note:

The following personal interviews are taken from the book, *Anointing Fall on Me: John G. Lake Personal Glimpses,* book four of a ten-book series on Dr. Lake, written by B. Alan Wyatt.

CLARK PETERSON INTERVIEW

As I recall, most of his preaching was about how great our God is. What He is able to do in His healing. John Lake just commanded an audience. In faith, he'd build up faith in you to believe what God can do and what He will do.

Lake was a wonderful man. He commanded respect. It was just his nature. What he had to say people took it 100 percent because of his ability to speak and convey what the Lord was speaking to him. He was magnificent.

He would take on anyone, anytime, anywhere I understood. He took on the *Spokesman Review* and so forth, and he was natural because he was an editor himself. When it came to that they couldn't trip him up or anything else.

I believe in someplace it talks about how he was trying to find out something about the Spirit by some machine. They had a machine of some kind and they wanted to test him to see something about the Spirit. He'd just say, "Bless the Lord," and then he'd say, "Bless the Lord." That machine would go so high it just couldn't go any higher — just getting the "radiation of the Spirit." They tested it on neutral but when he started to bless the Lord and then go deeper and deeper that thing couldn't register it.

He wasn't a man especially for show, but if you really needed a proof of the real thing, he would never back down. He would come out on top, because he was a man of faith.

He was a man of means at one time but he gave that up. Lake was a man of education and so forth, so he was well in command of his vocabulary and he put things across and he had no fear. He was like a lion.

Meeting Place... it was the Rookery Building and the entrance came in from Sprague Avenue. There was Fogwell and Westwood. Westwood was one of the main ones about that time. And they set up what they called the Healing Rooms and they had church there just about all day, continuous, and the people would come in that were sick and needed help. Lake had one and Westwood had one.

If people were not familiar with divine healing it would depend upon how urgent their condition was and how they felt about getting into the Spirit. God would heal them and they just kept coming back every day or whenever they felt like it. Those rooms were open and men were praying for them and there were others who took over, and between praying for them, why they had services there, teaching them faith, and were able to get them healing.

We had a large orchestra, and we sang songs like "All Hail King Jesus."

I remember when they were downtown and were having meetings at the Masonic Temple, and we were going down there. It was a big building there and you entered it from Riverside. It was very large. Many people came to the meetings and received their healing through the ministry. Whenever someone needed help, Lake was there to help them. People aren't as pessimistic when they see that they can get help. Then they are ready to bend to do what it takes to get their healing.

I remember Lake telling a story of a native preacher in Africa named Letwaba. Letwaba had come to a place where he needed to cross a river, and he just found himself across the river doing the work of the Lord. They asked him how he got there. He didn't know. He was translated. He had to cross the river and the Lord took him over to the other side.

Oh yes, there have been great amounts of people brought to Christ through Lake's ministry.

I tell you, the things that man had to go through; he was stubborn and strong. Naturally, he had a strong spirit. God really picked a man that had something that was not wishy-washy — not up one day and down the next. It was just something in his character. He could up and give everything away. When he went to Africa he didn't even have enough money, but God sent him that far, so he had faith. The fire of God burned in his soul, praise God.

In the early days, boy, you couldn't talk about anything Pentecostal, speaking in tongues and so forth, without having people fight you for it.

All my Christian learning is based on the foundational teachings of John G. Lake. I started when I was only eight years old and I am 82 now. So I had been under a lot of teaching, so have my family, my wife, my children, and her side of the family.

We have been in many dire positions many times, and God has come through and answered prayer. The impossible, God did it. Praise God, hallelujah.

John Lake was a man who was able to stand up. He could speak intelligently to the forces — the enemy. He could speak to the people in papers and editorials and in fact, he enjoyed it. He himself put editorials in the paper quite regularly. He had a lot of opposition, but he put them in. When you get isolated out in a field by yourself and the devil is hooking you, you need to get hold of the Lord.

Lake's ministry helped my family. Let me tell you. We lived up at a ranch near Diamond Lake, just this side of Newport. Morrie Moser, who married my mother's sister, got diphtheria. My nephew got it also and he died; he was just a baby, three or four years old. They sent a sheriff and a quarantine officer out there and quarantined their home. My dad and I, we stayed together at the ranch, which was

Florence and John Lake

about one-and-a-half miles away, and I started to feel something in my throat too.

I hitched up the team of horses after dark because we didn't have a car, and we were supposed to go to Newport, which had the nearest phone, and call Spokane for help, because we thought we were going to be quarantined too. I got to town and called the Spokane church. I got a hold of somebody and told them we needed prayer. I was praying and testifying to this young fellow. We needed help and we got help. I had victory over this problem I had before I got home. It was either life or death in times like that.

ALICE FRITSCH INTERVIEW

You never tired of hearing him speak. Some of his services would last a long time.

About Florence, his wife: she was simply tremendous. She would sit down in that front row. My brothers would just love to sit by her. They watched her take shorthand of every sermon.

When he would ask her to pray, it was just wonderful. She lived very close to the Lord. She was never down. She would never complain but was always on top.

We kids would go over to the Lake house down on West Indiana. John, although he may not have hardly a penny in his pocket, always seemed to have enough to buy a big old watermelon for all the kids.

You can ask all five of my brothers. Those were the best years of our lives.

Lake had lots of lung power. When he would pray and stomp his foot, he really could fill the whole building with his voice. He was a big, powerful man. He didn't need loudspeakers like they do today, where everyone has a microphone. He would shout, he was sure to be heard. We have lots of good memories. The people in the church were very enthusiastic.

When Lake was down at the Masonic Temple there were a lot of young people down there. They had quite a group, even at that time.

John Lake was great at giving out money to those who needed it, but he could discern right then if it was for real. If it wasn't, he would chop that right off. He would tell them that they were insincere.

I think what touched me the most about John Lake was his generosity. He never kept a thing for himself. Even the humble home they lived in impressed me. His wife handled their home very well. A minister's wife can either make or break a minister. She was a blessing to all of us. She was such a strong testimony of his great work.

Many times during prayer, John Lake would come down in the audience. One Sunday night, we missed because of transportation, John prayed for a blind girl and her eyes were opened.

The church community as a whole was in unity. The press mostly seemed positive in their articles. Lake was mostly well received in Spokane. Our time at Lake's church taught us faithfulness. It really has never left us. I am so glad that I lived in the days when we had such strong ministers of the Word.

IONE EATON INTERVIEW
AUGUST 26, 1990

My parents met in his church when they were young. I remember when I was very small the meetings were deeply impressive to me. He would have afternoon meetings and he invited people of all churches, wherever he went, and on Sunday afternoons many people from other groups would come and fellowship and then go to their own churches on Sunday nights. The building was always just packed every Sunday. People were just standing all around. When they got together something really happened, that wasn't happening in their own organized church groups. And one of the things that impressed me very much among the young people was that the Spirit of the Lord was there and would touch these young people and they would be slain under the power without being touched.

The platform was full of musical instruments. They had two big xylophones, boys and girls playing the instruments. I remember one beautiful tall girl playing the trombone. There was anointing in the music those young people were playing. The young people's services were very special to me, and I do remember Livingstone ministering to the young people. That was before he was married.

I feel the mantle of Brother Lake fell on many people who are scattered all around. In fact, I feel the impact of his ministry in my own heart today very deeply. I have transferred that to my children. This vision that Brother Lake had, had a profound impact in healing and touching people's lives.

When I was sick my mom would call him. Once, my brother broke his arm and he was instantly healed. We were playing tag and he fell over a banister of a porch, and his wrist just snapped. I could hear the pop. He was in severe pain. My dad had a bicycle and he took him on his bicycle to the tabernacle on Lincoln and Sharp on a Wednesday night. They were just starting to let out service, and they took Albert up there and told Brother Lake what had happened. Brother Lake put his hands up and told everyone to stop what they were doing and said, "Agree with me for this one. This little boy has a broken arm." They ministered to him and the pain stopped instantly, and Daddy brought him back home on the bicycle. He was able to sleep that night. We really did rejoice.

He also prayed for my sister, who had a concussion. We called him out to the house. He asked, "Did this girl have a bad fall?" And we said yes. She couldn't stand or walk or anything. She was vomiting and he finally said, "Let's pray." He would say "bless God" a lot. He just started right then in coming against the principalities. He ministered to her, and she was healed instantly. She was able to walk and start to eat. He also cast out all the fears and doubts.

Then my dad, oh you have that in your book about how he ran away as a boy. His mother passed away and his stepmother didn't get along with him very well. They put him in an orphanage and he ran away.

His father went to Brother Lake and asked him to pray that his boy would get in touch with him. My daddy had a vision of Jesus. In it, Jesus opened His arms to him, and then the first thing he wanted to do was write his father. This was told over the radio, I remember hearing it as a little girl. He used to be on about fifteen minutes every day about noon in the thirties, and he told how the Lord sent a runaway boy home.

He was very warm, very impressive. He had a strong spirit, not a strong-willed spirit, just like a father or a grandfather. He used to sit me in his lap and tell me a lot of the missionary stories that happened in Africa.

I can say that no man has ever had a more profound effect on my life than John G. Lake, and I have known many great ministers. He was not dictated to by an organized group.

He encouraged the people to seek the Lord always and in their "closets" and to depend on the Lord for every need. He was very much against doctors. He felt that the Lord created these bodies and He knew more about us than any doctor. He felt that God could take care of those needs.

My grandfather took my mother to the Healing Rooms. She was very sick with inflammatory rheumatism, and she was just a teenage girl. So they took her into the prayer rooms. Brother Lake prayed for her. She had such a miraculous healing that her tonsils shrunk to nothing. It was a total healing of her body.

He very much inspired me during my school years. I had a deep sense of trusting the Lord. I, to this day, don't go to a doctor for anything. The Lord has met with me and my children because of something planted in me. A seed planted in me to trust the Lord. Many things happened in the raising of my own children. I many times fell to my knees in prayer and God came through.

There was a prostitute who was saved, brought to the Lord, and she came to the Tabernacle. I remember her very strongly because she wore a lot of heavy makeup and wore real bright clothes. In those days everybody was more conservative. Some of the older ladies got a hold of her and told her she had to change her ways of dress and not put makeup on. Some of the brethren saw this and went to Brother Lake and told him what was happening. I was there when he did this. Up on the platform he started talking about how the Lord had saved this woman and cleaned her up inside. He talked to these ladies and said, "You old hens, you keep your hands off of her, the Lord has cleaned her up on the inside and He can take care of the outside." He was very emphatic about always letting the Lord do the work.

He would go downtown and minister to people and pray for them right on the street. It didn't bother him when people would stand and look.

Lake encouraged the people to press into the Spirit and to walk close to the Lord. He was responsible for bringing many homes back together with God's help. Many times when husbands and wives were ready to split up he would speak truth into the situation. He had a tremendous counseling ministry.

I had a sore throat, it was worse than strep throat. It was called septic sore throat. He called me up to the platform. He said, "Girlie, come up here." He had me open my mouth. He said this is the worst case of septic sore throat he had ever seen. He laid hands on me and prayed for me. I wasn't healed instantly, but within two days, I was completely healed. My parents didn't let me go out when I was sick, and they didn't take me to the doctor, but they would take me to church.

I remember he would tell new Christians to read the book of John. He felt that it had much in it to encourage the new Christian.

The last time I saw Brother Lake was at a church picnic at Mission Park. The ladies were getting dinner ready. He came up to me and said to the ladies, "This girl looks hungry to me, you fix her a sandwich right now." It kind of embarrassed me. He had me sit down and made those ladies give me a sandwich. It was that night, that he had his stroke.

LETTER MAILED ON NOVEMBER 15, 1989
L. G. LAKE

Personal information about John G. Lake as remembered by his son, Jack (L. G.). Jack is the eldest of five children by John's second wife. Two sisters and Jack are still living.

John liked to take the family to places he had been. One favorite was from Kennewick to Umatilla, Oregon. Before the highway was paved, they would take the ferry across the Columbia River, up the Columbia River highway to Pasco (via Wallula Junction) and then home.

People called him day and night to come pray for them. He drove many miles to their homes.

His wife would send him to the market for groceries but by the time he got home, he had given much to less fortunates he met. He was very generous.

Many times he invited guests for dinner without telling his wife. Many times she had to change the menu because what she had planned to have would not serve the extra guests.

The five children would crawl in bed with their dad on Sunday morning and he would read the "funnies" to them. Then he would listen to them tell of their activities. (Especially if he had been on a preaching stint for a few weeks.)

The family moved from Spokane (where Jack was born) to Portland, then to San Diego, Houston, Texas, and Oakland, California. John lost his voice for a time. At that time his two eldest sons (by his first wife) and he sold advertising for a newspaper.

When John's voice healed, the family moved back to Portland, Oregon. In 1932 they moved back to Spokane. In 1933 he bought the "frame tabernacle" on Lincoln and Sharp.

CONCLUSION
SEPTEMBER 1, 1990

While I never met John G. Lake, his life and ministry have had a profound effect on my life. I have studied many men of God, and have the opportunity not many people get to have. That is, to see where they failed. This opportunity gave me insight as to how to keep on guard in my own life.

The one most outstanding thing in the life of John G. Lake was that he never lost his righteous standard, which so many have.

In faithfulness to his wife, he was above reproach. Financially, there was simply no question as to his honesty, and to God he remained faithful to the end. He was a man of prayer and of the Word.

It has been an inspiration to me to study and write about this pillar of faith, John G. Lake. It is my prayer that it inspires you to excellence as well.

John G. Lake

SECTION ONE:

Chronological Material

he 13th chapter of Acts tells us the story of the ordination and sending forth of the apostle Paul, his ordination to the apostleship. Paul never writes of himself as an apostle until after the 13th chapter of Acts. He had been an evangelist and teacher for thirteen years when the 13th of Acts was written, and the ordination took place that is recorded there. Men who have a real call are not afraid of apprenticeships.

A TRUMPET CALL

1908
Johannesburg, South Africa

There is a growing up in experience in the ministry. When Paul started out in the ministry, he was definitely called of God and was assured of God through Ananias that it would not be an easy service but a terrific one: for God said to Ananias:

> Arise, and go into the street which is called Straight, and inquire in the house of Judas for one called Saul, of Tarsus: for, behold, he prayeth...he is a chosen vessel unto me, to bear my name before the Gentiles, and kings, and the children of Israel: For I will show him how great things he must suffer for my name's sake.[1]

That is what Jesus Christ, the crucified and glorified Son of God, told Ananias to say to the apostle Paul. He was not going to live in a holy ecstasy and wear a beautiful halo and have a heavenly time and ride in a limousine. He was going to have a drastic time, a desperate struggle, a terrific experience. And no man in biblical history ever had more dreadful things to endure than the apostle Paul. He gives a list in his letter to the Corinthians of the things he had endured.

> Of the Jews five times received I forty stripes save one. Thrice was I beaten with rods, once was I stoned, thrice I suffered shipwreck, a night and a day I have been in the deep; in journeyings often, in perils of waters, in perils of

---

[1] Acts 9:11,15-16.

robbers, in perils by mine own countrymen, in perils by the heathen, in perils in the city, in perils in the wilderness, in perils in the sea, in perils among false brethren; in weariness and painfulness, in watchings often, in hunger and thirst, in fastings often, in cold and nakedness.[2]

They stripped him of his clothing, and the executioner lashed him with an awful scourge, until bleeding and lacerated and broken, he fell helpless and unconscious and insensible. Then they doused him with a bucket of salt water to keep the maggots off and threw him into a cell to recover. That was the price of apostleship. That was the price of the call of God and His service. But God said he shall "bear my name before the Gentiles, and kings, and the children of Israel." He qualified as God's messenger.

Beloved, we have lost the character of consecration here manifested. God is trying to restore it in our day. He has not been able to make much progress with the average preacher on that line. "Mrs. So-and-so said so-and-so, and I am just not going to take it." That is the kind of preacher, with another kind of call, not the heaven call, not the God call, not the death call if necessary. That is not the kind the apostle Paul had.

Do you want to know why God poured out His Spirit in South Africa like He did nowhere else in the world? There was a reason. This example will illustrate. We had one hundred and twenty-five men out on the field at one time. We were a very young institution; were not known in the world. South Africa is seven thousand miles from any European country. It is ten thousand miles by way of England to the United States. Our finances got so low under the awful assault we were compelled to endure, that there came a time I could not even mail to these workers at the end of the month a ten-dollar bill. It got so I could not send them two dollars. The situation was desperate. What was I to do? Under these circumstances I did not want to take the responsibility of leaving men and their families on the frontier without real knowledge of what the conditions were.

Some of us at headquarters sold our clothes in some cases, sold certain pieces of furniture out of the house, sold anything we could

---

[2] 2 Corinthians 11:24-27.

sell, to bring those hundred and twenty-five workers off the field for a conference.

One night in the progress of the conference, I was invited by a committee to leave the room for a minute or two. The conference wanted to have a word by themselves. So I stepped out to a restaurant for a cup of coffee and came back. When I came in, I found they had rearranged the chairs in an oval, with a little table at one end, and on the table was the bread and the wine. Old Father Van der Wall, speaking for the company, said, "Brother Lake, during your absence, we have come to a conclusion. We have made our decision. We want you to serve the Lord's Supper. We are going back to our fields. We are going back if we have to walk back. We are going back if we have to starve. We are going back if our wives die. We are going back if our children die. We are going back if we die ourselves. We have but one request. If we die, we want you to come and bury us."

The next year, I buried twelve men and sixteen wives and children. In my judgment, not one of the twelve, if they had had a few things a white man needs to eat, but what might have lived. Friends, when you want to find out why the power of God came down from heaven in South Africa like it never came down before since the times of the apostles, there is your answer.

Jesus Christ put the spirit of martyrdom in the ministry. Jesus instituted His ministry with a pledge unto death. When He was with the disciples on the last night, He took the cup, "when He drank, saying." Beloved, the *saying* was the significant thing. It was Jesus Christ's pledge to the twelve who stood with Him, "This cup is the New Testament in my blood." Then He said, "Drink ye all of it."[3]

Friends, those who were there and drank to that pledge of Jesus Christ entered into the same covenant and purpose that He did. That is what all pledges mean. Men have pledged themselves in the wine cup from time immemorial. Generals have pledged their armies unto death. It has been a custom in the race. Jesus Christ sanctified it to the Church forever, bless God.

---

[3] Matthew 26:26-27, paraphrased.

"My blood in the New Testament. Drink *ye all* of it." Let us become one. Let us become one in our purpose to die for the world. Your blood and mine together. "My blood in the New Testament. It is My demand from you. It is your high privilege."

Dear friends, there is not an authentic history that can tell us whether any one of them died a natural death. We know that at least nine of them were martyrs, possibly all. Peter died on a cross, James was beheaded, for Thomas they did not even wait to make a cross — they nailed him to an olive tree. John was sentenced to be executed at Ephesus by putting him in a caldron of boiling oil. God delivered him and his executioners refused to repeat the operation and he was banished to the Isle of Patmos. John thought so little about it that he never even tells of the incident. He says, "I was in the Isle called Patmos, for the Word of God, and for the testimony of Jesus Christ."[4] That was explanation enough. He had committed himself to Jesus Christ for life or death.

Friends, the group of missionaries that followed me went without food and went without clothes, and once when one of my preachers was sunstruck and had wandered away, I tracked him by the blood marks of his feet. Another time I was hunting for one of my missionaries, a young Englishman, twenty-two years of age. He had come from a line of Church of England preachers for five hundred years. When I arrived at the native village, the old native chief said, "He is not here. He went over the mountains and you know mister, he is a white man and he has not learned to walk barefooted."

That is the kind of consecration that established Pentecost in South Africa. That is the reason we have a hundred thousand native Christians in South Africa. That is the reason we have 1,250 native preachers. That is the reason we have 350 white churches in South Africa. That is the reason that today we are the most rapid growing church in South Africa.

I am not persuading you, dear friends, by holding out a hope that the way is going to be easy. I am calling you in the name of Jesus Christ, you dear ones who expect to be ordained to the Gospel of Jesus

---

[4] Revelation 1:9, paraphrased.

Christ tonight, take the route that Jesus took, the route the apostles took, the route that the early Church took, the victory route, whether by life or death. Historians declare, "The blood of the martyrs was the seed of the Church." Beloved, that is what the difficulty is in our day — we have so little seed. The Church needs more martyr blood.

If I were pledging men and women to the Gospel of the Son of God, as I am endeavoring to do tonight, it would not be to have a nice church and harmonious surroundings and a sweet do-nothing time. I would invite them to be ready to die. That was the spirit of early Methodism. John Wesley established a heroic call. He demanded every preacher to be "ready to pray, ready to preach, ready to die." That is always the spirit of Christianity. When any other spirit comes into the Church, it is not the spirit of Christianity. It is a foreign spirit. It is a sissified substitute.

I lived on cornmeal mush many a period with my family and we did not growl, and I preached to thousands of people, not colored people, but white people. When my missionaries were on the field existing on cornmeal mush, I could not eat pie. My heart was joined to them. That is the reason we never had splits in our work in South Africa. One country where Pentecost never split. The split business began to develop years afterward when pumpkin pie eating Pentecostal missionaries began infesting the country. Men who are ready to die for the Son of God do not split. They do not holler the first time they get the stomachache.

Bud Robinson tells a story of himself. He went to preach in the southern mountains. It was the first time in his life that no one invited him to go home and eat with them. So he slept on the floor and the next night and the next night. After five days and five nights had passed and his stomach began to growl for food terribly, every once in awhile he would stop and say, "Lay down, you brute!" and he went on with his sermon. That is what won. That is what will win every time. That is what we need today. We need men who are willing to get off the highway. When I started to preach the Gospel I walked twenty miles on Sunday morning to my service and walked home twenty miles in the night when I got through. I did it for years for Jesus and souls.

In early Methodism an old local preacher would start Saturday and walk all night and then walk all night Sunday night to get back to his work. It was the common custom. Peter Cartwright preached for sixty dollars per year and baptized ten thousand converts.

Friends, we talk about consecration and we preach about consecration but that is the kind of consecration that my heart is asking for tonight. That is the kind of consecration that will get answers from heaven. That is the kind God will honor. That is the consecration to which I would pledge Pentecost. I would strip Pentecost of its frills and fall de ralls. Jesus Christ, through the Holy Ghost, calls us tonight not to an earthly mansion and a ten thousand dollar motor car, but to put our lives — body and soul and spirit — on the altar of service. All hail! Ye who are ready to die for Christ and this glorious Pentecostal Gospel. We salute you. You are brothers with us and with your Lord.

GUIDANCE

INTERPRETATION OF TONGUES

South Africa, 1908

O, soul, on the highway, from earth unto glory
Surrounded by mysteries, trials, and fears;
Let the life of thy God, in thy life be resplendent;
For Jesus will guide thee; thou need'st never fear.

For if thou wilt trust Me, I'll lead thee and guide thee
Through the quicksands and deserts of life, all the way.
No harm shall befall thee; I only will teach thee
To walk in surrender with Me day by day.

For earth is a school to prepare thee for glory;
The lessons here learned, you will always obey.
When eternity dawns, it will be only the morning
Of life with Me always, as life is today.

Therefore, be not impatient, as lessons thou'rt learning;
Each day will bring gladness and joy to thee here;
But heaven will reveal to thy soul, of the treasure
Which infinitude offers, through ages and years.

For thy God is the God of the earth and heavens;
And thy soul is the soul that He died to save;
And His blood is sufficient, His power eternal;
Therefore rest in thy God, both today and alway.

FORERUNNER OF GOD'S LATTER RAIN

A General Letter to the Christian
Public Pentecost in South Africa
Baptism of the Holy Ghost
with Signs Following
(See Mark 16:14-20)

SPEAKING IN TONGUES, BY THE POWER OF GOD
AS ON THE DAY OF PENTECOST.

MIRACULOUS HEALINGS
THROUGH FAITH IN JESUS.

CONVERSIONS AND SANCTIFICATIONS
THROUGH THE PRECIOUS BLOOD.

"BEHOLD THE BRIDEGROOM COMETH!"

MEETINGS every Monday, Tuesday, Wednesday and Thursday at
3 p.m. and 7:30 p.m. ALSO LORD'S DAY at 11 a.m. and
7:30 p.m. OTHER MEETINGS by announcement.
At the Old Presbyterian Church, corner of
Bree and Von Wieligh Streets.

eloved in Jesus everywhere!

In order that the Christian public may be aware of what God is doing in our midst, we have decided to issue this circular letter to inform our friends everywhere of the marvelous way in which God is working, not alone in Johannesburg, Pretoria, Krugersdorp, and other centers, but in many places throughout the entire land, where the Holy Ghost is being poured out upon the people.

THE FORERUNNER OF "GOD'S LATTER RAIN"
Johannesburg
August, 1908

On May fourteenth, a party of Holy Ghost baptized missionaries arrived from America in Johannesburg and at once commenced to conduct meetings in this city, the principal place of meeting being the old Presbyterian Church at the corner of Bree and Von Wieligh Streets. Right from the commencement of these services, the power of God has been greatly manifested in the salvation of sinners of all classes, many of whom have been sanctified and baptized with the Holy Ghost and have spoken in divers tongues as on the Day of Pentecost. (See Acts 2.) Also, there have been many cases of miraculous healing of all manner of diseases. Preachers and laymen, young men and young women, old men and old women, have alike received from God the baptism of the Holy Ghost and are speaking in tongues and praising God with a new joy and power formerly unknown to them. The universal testimony of those receiving the baptism of the Holy Ghost has been, and is, that God has worked with them, and is working with them, in the salvation and sanctification and healing of others in a degree never before known in their lives. The testimony of one Dutch Christian worker illustrates this point. He says:

> I have been a preacher of the Gospel for years. Up to the
> time that I commenced to attend these meetings I had

never been able to lay my hand definitely upon anyone that I was really sure had been converted and saved under my ministry, but since I have found Jesus as my sanctifier, and since I have received the baptism of the Holy Ghost, and since God has commenced to speak through me in tongues, I have entered into such a nearness with God that now my ministry is all changed. At almost every meeting persons are either saved, sanctified, or baptized with the Holy Ghost.

This work of God that is being made manifest in our midst is only that which is being manifested at the present time throughout the whole world. In every land this same outpouring of the Spirit of God upon all flesh is occurring. We believe it to be the scriptural "latter rain" as promised by the Lord. (See Acts 2:17,21.)

This outpouring of the Spirit of God is manifesting God's preparation of the world for the soon appearing of Jesus Christ in His Second Coming. (See James 5:7-8.)

Almost universally, the first words of the first message that the Lord gives to the newly-baptized soul, either in tongues or their native language, is "Repent, Jesus is coming. The time is at hand. Get ready!"

This outpouring of the Spirit is not confined to any church or sect or people. In Johannesburg, we see persons of every denomination, of every religious creed, alike seeking God for a real and definite work of grace in their souls and all alike at the feet of Jesus receiving from Him the baptism of the Holy Ghost, for "He it is Who baptiseth with the Holy Ghost." (John 1:33 and Acts 10:44-48.)

We find that in the lives of these baptized children of God the signs of a real Gospel ministry follow, as promised by Jesus in Mark 16:14-20.

We are only telling of things that our eyes have witnessed and our ears heard. The most wonderful messages from the Lord, by the Holy Ghost, have been given through many in our midst. It is not uncommon at any public service for the Holy Ghost to use individuals for messages in tongues, the interpretation invariably following, as occurred in the early church of the first century. (See 1 Corinthians 14.)

It is the intent and purpose of this committee, which is composed of only earnest Christian workers and is entirely undenominational in its character, to publish a paper (both in Dutch and English) so that the people of South Africa and the world may have the opportunity of knowing for themselves these wonderful workings of God in these latter days; that they, as well as we, may join in prayer to God that a mighty outpouring of His Spirit upon this land may come and that the tide of sin and iniquity which has so swept and cursed this land shall be turned back and a reign of righteousness be manifestly established and that all people and all nations shall get down low at the feet of Christ our King, that God may bless and prepare each and all for the appearing of our Lord. (John 14:1-3.)

The operations of the Spirit of God are easily identified. (See John 14:12-17,26 and John 16:7-14.)

These Apostolic Faith missionaries who are now in our midst, Brother and Sister Thomas Hezmalhalch, Brother and Sister John G. Lake, Brother Jacob O. Lehman, and Sister Ida F. Sackett, are humble men and women who unquestionably have been sent of God to South Africa at this time with this message. They represent no organization, and their ministry is to the people. There is no board behind them. As in all Holy Ghost work throughout the earth, they trust God and God alone for their support. No charges of any kind are made for religious services, prayers for the sick, or otherwise. No salaries are received, each individual relying solely on God for his and her maintenance, as the apostles did in the early days. (See Luke 9:1-6.)

Marvelous testimonies of miraculous healing are invariably heard at the meetings. These meetings are simply evangelical services where the Spirit of God controls; God in many cases using boys and girls as well as older persons to deliver messages and pray with the sick.

Amongst those who have been baptized with the Holy Ghost are Dutch and English, Jews and Gentiles, black and white, and at a recent meeting a Chinese missionary from Canton, who is ministering amongst the Chinese here, received the baptism of the Holy Ghost and spoke in tongues. That the coming of our Savior Jesus Christ is at hand we who have watched the progress of this work verily believe. In all these messages spoken by the Holy Ghost no times or dates are given, but in every message comes the universal warning: "Be ye also ready, for in such an hour as ye think not the Son of Man cometh."[1]

Our purpose in writing this letter is that the people may know what God is doing. We contract no debts of any character, but obey the command of the Lord: "Owe no man any thing."[2] Consequently, when funds are needed we ask God in prayer to send such funds as are necessary. And we ask every Christian man and woman to join us in prayer to the end that God will provide the means with which to publish a paper in both Dutch and English, which will be known as "God's Latter Rain," in order that the testimonies of those who have been saved, sanctified, and baptized with the Holy Ghost, and others who have been miraculously healed by the Lord, and so forth, may be published, that all may know and become partakers in these latter-day blessings.

This is God's evangelization movement. It is not controlled by man, or the government of man, and is no organization of man's promoting. It is the Spirit of God being poured out upon the people. Instances are known where the Spirit of God has fallen upon families in South Africa, where no preacher or teacher has been — God alone, in answer to prayer, baptizing these children of God with the Holy Ghost, filling and thrilling their souls with the joys and powers of the world to come. (See Hebrews 6:1-6.)

We invite every child of God who is interested in the evangelization of South Africa, white and black, Dutch and English, Chinese or Indian, or any other nationality or color, not alone to join us in prayer, but to obey God as He may direct in this matter of providing funds for the publication of this paper, which will be circulated throughout South Africa free of cost. We shall depend alone on the Lord to provide means to publish this paper.

If you wish to receive copies of "God's Latter Rain," send us your name and address at once, also those of your friends.

---

[1] See Matthew 25:13.

[2] Romans 13:8.

All correspondence, remittances in cheques or money orders, etc., will be directed to "God's Latter Rain," Publication Committee, P. O. Box 1159, Johannesburg.

(Signed)
J. H. L. SCHUMANN.
JOHN G. LAKE.
J. OSBORN.
HY. ULYATE.
J. O. LEHMAN.
THOS. HEZMALHALCH.
ARCHD. H. COOPER.
Requests for Prayer may be sent to Thomas Hezmalhalch,
John G. Lake or J. O. Lehman, P. O. Box 1159, Johannesburg.

The hymn printed below was given to Brother Thomas Hezmalhalch by the inspiration of the Holy Spirit.

JESUS IS COMING

Words by T. Hezmalhalch*

Music by F. A. Graves

Verse 1:

Jesus is coming! Yes, coming for me! Jesus is coming! His glory I'll see;

The clouds are His chariots, The angels His guard; Jesus is coming! How plain are His words.

Chorus:

Coming again, coming again, Jesus is coming, is coming to reign,

The clouds are His chariots, The angels His guard, Jesus is coming,

How precious His Word.

Verse 2:

Jesus is coming! O glory divine! Jesus is coming! The Lord who is mine;

Yes, coming in triumph With shout and with song; Jesus is coming! The time is not long.

Verse 3:

Jesus is coming! He's not far away! Jesus is coming! We'll care not to stay;

The clouds as our chariots, The angels our guard; Jesus is coming! This truth is His word.

Verse 4:

Jesus is coming! The just shall arise! Jesus whose coming, we'll greet in the skies;

The world will not see us, With Jesus we've gone, Singing forever the glad chorus song.

Verse 5:

Jesus is coming! Yes, all then shall know! Jesus whose coming, has conquered our foe;

In vict'ry we'll meet Him; In triumph we'll rise! Jesus has come! We will shout in the skies.

Verse 6:

Jesus is coming! O saints, do rejoice! Jesus is coming! So lift up your voice;

The clouds are His chariots, The angels His guard: Sing of His coming and tell of His word.

Verse 7:

Jesus is coming! Let anthems arise! Jesus is coming! Our God's loving prize;

The world's great Redeemer, The savior of men, Jesus has conquered! He's coming to reign.

*Copyrighted in 1907 by Thos. Hezmalhalch.

THE VISION
INTERPRETATION OF TONGUES

October 10, 1909

> *Jesus thou King! Glorious and eternal!*
> *Mighty and loving! Powerful and grand!*
> *Who through the blackness and darkness infernal*
> *Guideth and holdeth Thy child by the hand.*
>
> *Pierced is Thy soul! Grieved is Thy Spirit!*
> *Bleeding Thy feet are! Wounded Thy hand!*
> *Sorrowing Christ, through the veil now uplifted,*
> *See I Thy beckoning with uplifted hand.*
>
> *Here I Thy voice as to me Thou now speakest!*
> *See I Thy teardrops silently fall!*
> *Know I the anguish Thy sorrowing Spirit*
> *Feels as Thou drinkest this wormwood and gall.*
>
> *What, Lord, the cause of Thy anguish of Spirit?*
> *Why doth this suffering come to Thee now?*
> *Crucified once, on the cross wast Thou lifted?*
> *Have not the cruel thorns pierced Thy brow?*
>
> *Have not the sins of mankind on Thee rested,*
> *Causing Thy soul in anguish to be torn?*
> *Has not the bloodsweat from Thee been wrested?*
> *Have not Thy saints for the crucified mourned?*
>
> *Why is it then that again now I see Thee,*
> *Bruised and bleeding, anguished and lone?*
> *Why is the Spirit of Christ now within me*
> *Witnessing thus of Thy sorrow again?*
>
> *List, to the answer! Let all the world hear it!*
> *Jesus is speaking! Let all hear His voice!*
> *It is because of the sins of My people.*
> *It is because ye will not heed My voice.*
>
> *Do ye not bite and devour one another?*
> *Do ye not slay with your tongues and pen*

Many of My precious daughters and mothers,
Young men and maidens, E'en boys and old men?

Have ye e'er stood in the fire where they're tested?
Have ye e'er felt of the withering blast?
Know ye how long and how hard they've resisted,
Fighting and struggling unto the last?

Why did ye not stretch your hand out to help them?
Why from the soul did not sympathy flow?
Did not My Spirit within Thee say, "Help them
Out of their bondage, or darkness or woe?"

Thus am I crucified! Thus My soul anguished!
This is the cause of My sorrow and woe!
This is the reason that Satan has vanquished
Many who once were as pure as the snow!

O, let thy heart in yearning compassion,
Gentleness, meekness, and tenderness mild,
Give of My grace to the soul swept with passion,
Power to live at My feet as a child.

Then shall the gladness and brightness of heaven
Flood thine own spirit and cause thee to move
Among the crushed and the wounded and broken,
Bringing them sunshine, gladness, and love.

Then shall thy spirit in tune with the heavenlies,
Rapturous joys in the Spirit shall know.
Then shall the power of God rest upon thee.
Then in the fruits of the Spirit thou'lt grow.

Then shall the earth know the glory of heaven.
Then shall dominion over death and over hell
Reign in thine own soul, spread as the leaven,
Causing angels and men My praises to swell.

Then shall the Christ over the earth be victorious!
Then shall the power of My Gospel be known!
My kingdom shall come! Eternal and glorious!
United! The heavens and the earth shall be one!

THE SECRET OF POWER

INTERPRETATION OF TONGUES

LUKE 24:49 AND ACTS 1:8

June 18, 1910

South Africa

He is risen, He is risen! Hear the cry
Ringing through the land and sea and sky.
'Tis the shout of victory, triumph is proclaimed,
Heralds of God announce it, death's disdained.

Shout the tidings! Shout the tidings! Raise the cry.
Christ's victorious, Christ's victorious cannot die,
For the bars of death He sundered, Satan sees that he
*   has blundered,*
As the shouts of angels thundered, "He's alive!"

Catch the shout, ye earth-born mortals, let it roll
Till it echoes o'er the mountains from the center to the poles,
That the Christ of earth and glory death has conquered.
Tell the story, He's the Victor, He's the Victor! So am I.

For this reason that my ransom He has paid,
I've accepted His atonement, on Him laid,
He the Lamb of God that suffered all for me,
Bore my sins, my grief, my sickness on the tree.

I am risen, I am risen from the grave,
Of my sins, my griefs, my sickness, and the waves,
Of the resurrection life, and holy power
Thrill my being with His new life every hour.

Now the lightnings of God's Spirit burn my soul,
Flames of His divine compassion o'er me roll,
Lightning power of God's own Spirit strikes
*   the power of hell.*
God in man, O glory! Glory! All the story tell.

I have proved Him, I have proved Him. It is true,
Christ's dominion yet remaineth, 'tis for you,

Let the fires of holy passion sweep your soul.
Let the Christ who death has conquered take control.
He will use you, He will use you. Zion yet has saviors still,
Christ the Conqueror only waiteth for the action of your will.

Given in tongues by the Holy Ghost to John G. Lake, at two a.m.,
June 18, 1910. Cookhouse C. C., South Africa.

Beloved friends, it is indeed a grief to me today that I am unable to address you in Dutch, knowing that I must consume more time in using an interpreter. A disappointment that came recently was the discovery on looking into my son's schoolwork to find they were not studying, as a specialty, the Dutch language. Upon inquiry, I found they had been advised not to do so. In a country like this where such a great amount of the people use Dutch, I feel this policy in an educational institution is a great mistake.

THE BAPTISM IN THE HOLY GHOST

[This sermon was not dated; however, the booklet that follows was based upon it.]

The baptism of the Holy Ghost is a most difficult subject to discuss with any degree of intelligence, for though we may not care to admit it, the fact remains that the density of ignorance among both the people and the ministry on this subject is appalling. To view this subject with any degree of intelligence we must view it from the standpoint of progressive revelation. Like Christian baptism, the operation of the Holy Ghost must be seen in its various stages of revelation. Otherwise, we shall be unable to distinguish between the operation of the Spirit in the Old Testament dispensations and the baptism of the Holy Ghost in the New Testament.

As we approach even the threshold of this subject it seems as if the Spirit of God comes close to us. A certain awe of God comes over the soul. And it is my earnest wish that no levity, satire, or sarcasm be permitted to enter into this discussion, as such things would be grieving to the tender Spirit of God.

As this morning, when we viewed the evolution of baptism through its various stages of development, so this afternoon we must view the revelation of God to man.

In the beginning of this revelation, after the deluge, it seems as if God was approaching man from a great distance, so far had sin removed man from his original union with God at the time of his creation.

God seems to reveal Himself to man as rapidly as man, by progressive stages of development, is prepared to receive the revelation. Consequently, we see that, as baptism was a further revelation of God's purpose in purifying the heart from sin than was the original ceremony of circumcision. So the baptism of the Holy Ghost is a greater revelation of God than was the manifestations of the Spirit in the Patriarchal or Mosaic dispensations.

Three distinct dispensations of God are clearly seen. Each with an ever-deepening manifestation of God to man. A following dispensation of God never destroys a foregoing one. On the contrary, it conserves its spirit and broadens its scope in a deeper revelation of God. This is plainly seen in looking at the Patriarchal, Mosaic, and Christian dispensations.

In the Patriarchal dispensation we see God appearing to man at long intervals. Abraham furnishes the best example, for to him, God appeared at long intervals of twenty and forty years apart, so with the other Patriarchs.

Under the Mosaic dispensation there is a deeper and clearer manifestation of God. God was ever present in the pillar of cloud and in the pillar of fire. He was present also in the tabernacle where the Shekinah of glory overshadowed the mercy seat. This is a continuous, abiding revelation of God. It was *God with man,* not *to* man as was the Patriarchal dispensation, but *with* man — leading, guiding, directing, forgiving, sanctifying, abiding with man.

But the revelation of God under the Christian dispensation is a much deeper and thicker revelation of God than this. It is *God in man,* for the baptism of the Holy Ghost is the actual incoming of the real Spirit of God to live in man. This, then, brings us to where we can see the purpose of God in revealing Himself to man by progressive stages of revelation of Himself, as man, by progressive stages through repentance and faith, is purified, not alone forgiven for his transgressions, but cleansed from the nature of sin within that causes him to transgress.

This cleansing from inbred sin — the nature of sin, the carnal mind, the old man, the man of sin, etc. — is the actual taking out of our breast the desire for sin. All correspondence with sin in us is severed, and the carnal life is laid a sacrifice on the altar of Christ in glad surrender by us. This inner heart-cleansing that John and the disciples of Jesus demanded before they would baptize a man is the necessary preparation for baptism of the Holy Ghost. A holy God must have a holy dwelling place. O! wondrous salvation, wondrous Christ, wondrous atonement. Man born in sin, shapen in iniquity, forgiven, cleansed, purified outside and inside by the blood of Jesus, and made the habitation (dwelling place) of God.

It was that man, once created in the likeness of God, should again become the dwelling place of God, that the atonement of the blood of Christ was provided.

> Christ hath redeemed us from the curse of the law, being
> made a curse for us: for it is written, Cursed is every one
> that hangeth on a tree: that the blessing of Abraham might
> come on the Gentiles through Jesus Christ; that we might
> receive the promise of the Spirit through faith.

— Galatians 3:13-14

This reveals to us God's purpose in our salvation. We must be prepared by the blood of Jesus Christ to become the habitation of God. "In whom ye also are builded together for an habitation of God through the Spirit" (Ephesians 2:22).

Again, in First Corinthians 6:19 we see Paul in astonishment says, "What? know ye not that your body is the temple of the Holy Ghost?" Let us now see where we are at and we will better understand how to go on.

O, the density of our ignorance on this subject. See, the Holy Ghost is the Spirit of God. His purpose is to dwell in man after man's perfect cleansing from sin through the blood of Jesus. His coming was definite, just as definite as was the advent of Christ. When Jesus was born, His birth was proclaimed by angel voices and chanted by a multitude of the heavenly host praising God. (See Luke 2:9,13-14.) Equally so was the Holy Spirit's advent attested by His bodily form as a dove (Luke 3:22). And by the sound from heaven, as of a rushing mighty wind and by the cloven tongues of fire upon each of them (Acts 2:2-3).

Heavenly dove, tempest roar, and tongues of fire crowning the hundred and twenty were as convincing as the guiding star and midnight shout of angel hosts. The coming of the Holy Ghost upon the hundred and twenty is found in Acts 2. At the Last Supper, when Jesus addressed the disciples He said to them,

> Nevertheless I tell you the truth; it is expedient for you that I go away: for if I go not away, the Comforter will not come unto you; but if I depart, I will send him unto you. And when he is come, he will reprove the world of sin, and of righteousness, and of judgment.

— John 16:7-8

As the disciples were together at Jerusalem after the resurrection, when the two who had walked with Him to Emmaus were conversing with the eleven disciples, Jesus Himself stood in their midst and saith unto them, "Peace be unto you." They were affrighted, believing they had seen a spirit. Jesus addressed them and said unto them, "And, behold, I send the promise of my Father upon you: but tarry ye in the city of Jerusalem, until ye be endued with power from on high." (See Luke 24:36-37,49.) Then in Acts, first chapter, we find that the one hundred and twenty tarried in prayer in the upper room, thus ten days between the crucifixion of Jesus and Pentecost is fifty-three days.

There was a crucifixion day. It was necessary. And now we, the children of God, must be crucified with Christ and freed from sin. Our old man nailed to the cross, we die to sin — a real act, a genuine experience. It's done so we are made partakers in Christ's death, but there was a resurrection day. He arose. He's a living Christ, not a dead one. He lives. He lives. And by our resurrection into our new life we leave the old sin life and the old man buried in baptism (Romans 6) and are made partakers of His new resurrection life. The life of power, the exercise of the power of God is made possible to us.

But Jesus having now elevated us into His own resurrection life by actual spiritual experience, there comes His ascension. It is just as necessary as the crucifixion or resurrection. Jesus ascends to heaven and sits triumphant at the right hand of the Father and, according to His promise, sends upon us the Holy Ghost. This experience is personal as well as dispensational, and it is by the Spirit of God. The Holy Ghost descending upon us, entering into us for the baptism of the Holy Ghost is the Holy God, the Spirit of Jesus, taking possession of our personality, living in us, moving us, controlling us. We become partakers in His glorified life, the life of Christ in glory. So with the hundred and twenty (see Acts 2:2-4).

> And suddenly there came a sound from heaven as of a rushing mighty wind.

(Suppose we heard it now. What would this audience think?)

> And it filled all the house where they were sitting. And there appeared unto them cloven tongues like as of fire, and it sat upon each of them. And they were all filled with the Holy Ghost, and began to speak with other tongues, as the Spirit gave them utterance.

Not as they liked, not when they liked. They spake as the Spirit gave them utterance. It was the Spirit that spoke in other tongues. What Spirit? The Holy Ghost who had come into them, who controlled them, who spoke through them. Listen! Speaking in tongues is the voice of God. Do you hear? God's voice. They spake as the Spirit gave them utterance. Now we have advanced to where we can understand God's manifestations. Not God witnessing to man, not God with man, but God in man. The Holy Ghost in man. They spake as the Spirit gave them utterance.

(Editor's note: At this point the Spirit of God fell on Brother Lake, causing him to speak in tongues in an unknown language. The audience was asked to bow their heads in silent prayer and pray for the interpretation of the words spoken in the tongue. As they prayed the interpretation was given as follows.)

> *Christ is at once the spotless descent of God into man, and the sinless ascent of man into God, and the Holy Spirit is the agent by which it is accomplished.*

Bless God. He is the Christ, the Son of God. His atonement is a real atonement. It cleanses from all sin. Man again becomes the dwelling place of God. Let us now see one of the most miraculous chapters in all the Word of God, Acts, chapter 10. A man, Cornelius, is praying. He is a Gentile centurion. An angel appears. The angel speaks to Cornelius. The angel says, "Send to Joppa for Peter."[1] Peter is a Jew. He don't like Gentiles. Salvation is only supposed by him to be for Jews. God has to teach him something. How does God do it?

Peter goes up on the housetop to pray, and as he prays, he is in a trance. Think of it — a trance. He falls in a trance. Suppose I was to fall on the floor in a trance. Nine-tenths of this audience would be frightened to death. They would instantly declare that my opponent, Brother Du Toit, had hypnotized me. Why? Because of the ignorance among men of how the Spirit of God operates. But listen. Listen! As he lays on the roof in a trance, he sees a vision. A sheet let down from heaven caught by the four corners full of all manner of beasts and crawling things and a voice — what voice? — the Lord's voice, said, "Rise, Peter; kill, and eat."[2]

> But Peter said, Not so, Lord; for I have never eaten any thing that is common or unclean. And the voice spake unto him again the second time, What God hath cleansed, that call not thou common.[3]

That was the Spirit of Jesus, the Holy Ghost, speaking. Peter obeyed. He went with the messengers and see the result: As he spake the Word, the Holy Ghost fell on all of them that heard the Word. And they of the circumcision that believed were astonished, as many as came with Peter, because on the Gentiles also was poured out the gift of the Holy Ghost. How did they know? For they heard them speak with tongues and magnify God.[4] Then answereth Peter:

> Can any man forbid water, that these should not be baptized, which have received the Holy Ghost as well as we?[5]

---

[1] Acts 10:5, paraphrased.

[2] See Acts 10:9-13.

[3] Acts 10:14-15.

[4] See Acts 10:44-46.

[5] Acts 10:47.

And so it all ended in a glorious baptism service in water of all who had already been baptized in the Holy Ghost.

Now let us see the twenty-second chapter of Acts. This again will teach us the manner in which the Spirit of God, the Holy Ghost, operates. Paul is in the hands of a mob. That wasn't dignified was it? He is standing on the stairs and the chief captain gives him the privilege of addressing the mob. He tells them who he is, where he was born, of his education, his religious training, etc. But above all, of his conversion from sin and his becoming a disciple of Jesus Christ.[6]

A party of horsemen is riding to Damascus, officers of the law. Paul holds a commission to arrest all who call on the name of Jesus. Suddenly there shined round them a light from heaven above, like the brightness of the sun, and in Acts the twenty-sixth chapter he says, "When we were all fallen to the earth."[7] Think of it. The whole party fallen to the earth, and while he lay on the road, "And heard a voice saying unto me," and saying in the Hebrew tongue, "Saul, Saul, why persecutest thou me?"

Who is "me?" Who is speaking?

> And I answered, Who art thou, Lord? And he said…, I am Jesus of Nazareth whom thou persecutest. And they that were with me saw indeed the light, and were afraid; but they heard not the voice of him that spake to me. And I said, What shall I do, Lord? And the Lord said unto me, Arise, (get up off the road) and go into Damascus; and there it shall be told thee of all things which are appointed for thee to do. And when I could not see for the glory of that light, being led by the hand of them that were with me, I came into Damascus.[8]

In order to get the force of this scripture we must compare carefully the following chapters, for in each of them a portion of this wonderful incident is related. And only a careful study of all three will give us an understanding of the entire incident and the secret not only of

---

[6] See Acts 21:37-22:16.

[7] Acts 26:14.

[8] Acts 22:7-11.

Paul's conversion, but the secret of his wonderful ministry and of his knowledge of spiritual things. We must find out where he received his knowledge of the Gospel. Did he learn it from others? Was he taught it? How, then, did he get it? He got it by trances, by visions, by revelation from God. It was not communication to his brains. It was revealed to his heart. Compare now Acts 9:1-31 with Acts the twenty-second chapter and Acts the twenty-sixth chapter. Read also Galatians 1:11-12. In fact, read both the first and second chapters of Galatians.

In Acts 22:12, Paul tells of Ananias coming to see him. But how did Ananias know Paul was there? See now Acts 9:10-19:

> And there was a certain disciple at Damascus, named Ananias; and to him said the Lord in a vision, Ananias. And he said, Behold, I am here, Lord. And the Lord said unto him, Arise, and go into the street which is called Straight, and enquire in the house of Judas for one called Saul, of Tarsus.

Now let us see that as we would say it today. The Lord said, "Ananias, go down into Straight Street to the home of Judas. Ask for a man named Saul of Tarsus, for behold he prayeth." And now the Spirit tells him what Paul had seen.

> And hath seen in a vision a man named Ananias coming in, and putting his hand on him, that he might receive his sight.

And Ananias now talks with the Lord. Do you know anything of such communion or talks with God? If not, get the baptism of the Holy Ghost like the early Christians, and you will see as we do the operation of the Lord upon both saint and sinner by the Holy Ghost. Men say to us, "Where do you men get your insight into the Word of God?" We get it just where Paul and Peter got it, from God by the Holy Ghost. (Galatians 1:11-12.)

Beloved, don't read God's Word as I have asked you to do, but read it on your knees. Ask God by His Spirit to open it to your understanding. Read the Word, read it with open hearts. It is a lamp unto our feet, a light unto our path.[9] Ananias went as the Lord directed

---
[9] See Psalm 119:105.

him and found Paul, and Paul was healed of his blindness and was baptized in the Holy Ghost and also baptized in water and spoke in tongues more than ye all. (See 1 Corinthians 1:4-18.)

Now see again Acts 22:14. Ananias is speaking to Paul,

> And he said, The God of our fathers hath chosen thee, that thou shouldest *know* his will, and see that Just One.

Did you notice that? "See that Just One."

> And shouldest hear the voice of his mouth. For thou shalt be his witness unto all men of what thou hast *seen and heard.*[10]

Say, what about the people who say, "Don't tell these things to anyone?"

> And now why tarriest thou? arise, and be baptized, and wash away thy sins, calling on the name of the Lord.[11]

You see, as with Peter at Cornelius' house, all this work of the Spirit, indeed in salvation and baptism, how God through Ananias promised Paul that thou shouldest know His will and see that Just One and hear the voice of His mouth. Now when did that come to pass? Why, three years after when Paul returned to Jerusalem. (See Galatians 1:15-24.)

After three years Paul came to Jerusalem.

> And it came to pass, that, when I was come again to Jerusalem, even while I prayed in the temple, I was in a trance.

> — Acts 22:17

Think of it: The intellectual, wonderful Paul, the master theologian of the ages, the orator of orators, the logician of logicians — in a trance. Bless God for that trance. It was the fulfillment of what Ananias had said to him three years before.

---

[10] Acts 22:15.

[11] Acts 22:16.

> And saw him (Jesus) saying unto me, Make haste, and get thee quickly out of Jerusalem: for they will not receive thy testimony concerning me (Jesus).[12]

Now what is a trance? A trance is the Spirit taking predominance over the mind and body, and for the time being, the control of the individual is by the Spirit. But our ignorance of the operations of God is such that every minister of religion has been known to say it is the devil.

Now let us see where Paul got his commission to preach and instructions about what he was to preach and what was his condition and attitude when Jesus gave him his commission. (See Acts 26:16-18.) He was lying on the road on his way to Damascus. Now if we were to see someone lying on the road talking to an invisible somebody, no doubt in our ignorance we would send for an ambulance or for the police. But this is where the glorified Christ spoke to Paul and gave him definite instructions about what he should preach, and the purpose of his preaching was to be the salvation — not the entertainment — of others.

> But rise, and stand upon thy feet: for I (Jesus) have appeared unto thee for this purpose, to make thee a minister and a witness both of these things which thou hast seen, and of those things in the which I will appear unto thee.
>
> — Acts 26:16

(Jesus promises to appear to Paul again and that was fulfilled while he lay in a trance in the temple three years later.)

Now are the objectives of his preaching:

> To open their eyes, and to turn them from darkness to light, and from the power of Satan unto God, that they may receive forgiveness of sins, and inheritance among them which are sanctified (present experience) by faith that is in me (Jesus). Whereupon, O king Agrippa, I was not disobedient unto the heavenly vision.
>
> — Acts 26:18-19

---

[12] Acts 22:18.

From this we see and are able to understand the operations of God by His Spirit. And now, beloved, is the Holy Ghost in the church today? Verily yes. But you say, "We do not see Him work in this way. Why?" It is because you say, "All these things were for the apostolic days." They were not. Take the Word of God and find for one place where the gifts of the Holy Ghost were withdrawn. You can't. But let me tell you. I have preached in four different countries and over and over in order to demonstrate the ignorance of people and ministers concerning the Word of God have said, "Name the nine gifts of the Holy Ghost." And I never found a minister who could, but one, and today you can imagine how pleased I was to hear Brother Du Toit read them. It shows people are beginning to read and think on these lines.

These nine gifts of the Holy Ghost are found in First Corinthians 12:8-10.

> For to one is given by the Spirit the word of wisdom (that's gift 1); to another the word of knowledge by the same Spirit (that's gift 2); to another faith by the same Spirit, to another the gifts of healing by the same Spirit (gift 3)....to another discerning of spirits (gift 4); to another divers (different) kinds of tongues (languages — not by acquirement, but by the Spirit).

O, I praise God for the discovery of the gifts of the Holy Ghost and especially the gift of healing. May we all learn to know Christ, not alone as our Savior, but as our Sanctifier and Healer too.

Now I will go over these gifts on my fingers. First, wisdom; second, knowledge; third, faith; fourth, healing; fifth, miracles; sixth, prophecy; seventh, discerning of spirits; eighth, divers kinds of tongues; ninth, the interpretation of tongues.

Beloved, we have seen that the Holy Ghost came into the Church at Pentecost and the gifts are in the Holy Ghost. Consequently, if the Holy Ghost is in the Church, the gifts are too. But for lack of faith we do not see them exercised in the ordinary church. Now, we stand for the obtaining of the Holy Ghost through our personal baptism in the Holy Ghost and the enduement of the Holy Ghost power as promised by Jesus, yea, commanded by Him. "Ye shall receive power, after that the Holy Ghost is come upon you" (Acts 1:8).

People ask, "What is tongues?" Tongues is the voice or operation of the Spirit of God. In Acts 2:4 they, the one hundred and twenty, spoke in tongues — the external evidence of the Spirit of God within. When the Holy Ghost came in, He spoke again in Acts 10:44-48. When the Holy Ghost fell on the Gentiles, Peter demanded the right to baptize them in water, saying,

> Can any man forbid water, that these should not be baptized, which have received the Holy Ghost as well as we?

How did they know they had been baptized in the Holy Ghost? See verse forty-six: "For they heard them speak with tongues, and magnify God." Tongues was, then, the evidence of the baptism of the Holy Ghost by which Peter claimed the right to baptize them in water. Again in Acts 19:1-7, Paul at Ephesus met twelve men whom John had baptized unto repentance, but now Paul rebaptized them by Christian baptism. And in verse five we read,

> When they heard this, they were baptized (water baptism) in the name of the Lord Jesus. And when Paul had laid his hands upon them, the Holy Ghost came on them; and they spoke with tongues, and prophesied.[13]

> Tongues are for a sign, not to them that believe, but to them that believe not.
>
> — 1 Corinthians 14:22

---

[13] Acts 19:5-6.

The Apostolic Faith
Mission of South Africa
Central Tabernacle,
73, Kerk Street, Johannesburg

THE BAPTISM IN
THE HOLY GHOST

Reprinted from "The Comforter" of September 1910

Printed and published at
The Apostolic Faith Mission Printing Works,
73, Kerk Street, Johannesburg

ut sanctify the Lord God in your hearts: and be ready always to give an answer to every man that asketh you a reason of the hope that is in you with meekness and fear.

— 1 Peter 3:15

THE BAPTISM IN THE HOLY GHOST

The Rev. S. J. Du Toit, minister of the Dutch Reformed Church, challenged the brethren of the Apostolic Faith Mission to meet him and publicly defend, in open debate, the teaching believed and disseminated by them.

The Rev. S. J. Du Toit is considered one of the ablest and most skillful debaters in Africa.

It was at the Dutch Church, Somerset East, Cape Colony, during 1910, that the Reverend gentleman, according to a Graaff-Reinet paper, "Met his Waterloo," at the hands of two Apostolic Faith Brethren from Johannesburg. To God be the praise.

We give our readers the more important features of Brother Lake's address on the Baptism in the Holy Ghost.

PROGRESSIVE REVELATION OF GOD

This is a subject so profound and so comprehensive, that to intelligently understand it we must view it from the scope of continuous and progressive revelation. Like water baptism of the Christian believer, the operations of the Holy Ghost must be apprehended in its successive stages of revelation, otherwise we shall be unable to distinguish between the operation of the Spirit in the Old Testament and the baptism of the Holy Ghost in the New Testament.

A successive dispensation of God never destroys a preceding one. On the contrary, it conserves its spirit but broadens its scope.

This is obviously seen by comparing the Patriarchal, Mosaic, and Christian dispensations.

In the Patriarchal dispensation we see God appearing to man at long intervals. Abraham furnishes the best example. God appeared to him at intervening periods of time, twenty and forty years apart. The Patriarchal age may therefore be designated the dispensation of God's revelation to man.

There is a perceptible advance under the Mosaic dispensation to a deeper, clearer, and more pronounced manifestation of God. He was ever present in the pillar of cloud and the pillar of fire. Afterwards, His visible presence abode in the Shekinah of glory overshadowing the mercy seat. This was God with man, not to man, as in the Patriarchal dispensation, but God leading, guiding, directing, forgiving, sanctifying, abiding with man. Coming to the Christian dispensation we obtain a clearer and more palpable revelation of God than in the preceding Mosaic dispensation.

THE CLIMAX

Revelation reaches its climax in this, the Christian dispensation. God in man! For the baptism of the Holy Ghost is the actual incoming of that third person of the glorious Trinity to live in man. This, then, brings us to where we can see the purpose of God in revealing Himself to man by progressive stages of revelation.

As the Christian dispensation supersedes and eclipses all other dispensations, so the real Christian is to excel all who have preceded him. He is the culminating point of God's effort for mankind. Man is not only to be forgiven, but through the blood of Jesus is to be cleansed from the nature of sin, from the evil principle which causes him to transgress. This cleansing from "inbred sin" (termed also the "carnal mind," the "old man," the "man of sin") is the actual and experimental taking out of our breast of the desire for sin. All correspondence with sin is severed, and the old self-life is laid in glad and willing surrender on the altar of Christ.

GOD WANTS A CLEAN TEMPLE

This inner heart cleansing that John and the disciples of Jesus demanded before they would baptize a man is the necessary preparation for the baptism of the Holy Ghost. A holy God must have a holy dwelling place. O, wondrous salvation! Wondrous atonement! Wondrous Christ! Man born in sin and shapen in iniquity forgiven, cleansed, purified by the blood of Jesus and made an habitation, a dwelling place of God through the Spirit.

The redemption that Jesus Christ wrought out on Calvary restores to man all the privileges and prerogatives forfeited by the fall.

> Christ hath redeemed us from the curse of the law, being made a curse for us: for it is written, Cursed is every one that hangeth on a tree: That the blessing of Abraham might come on the Gentiles through Jesus Christ; that we might receive the promise of the Spirit through faith.
>
> — Galatians 3:13-14

This reveals to us God's purpose in our salvation. We must be prepared by the blood of Jesus Christ to become the habitation of God, "In whom ye also are builded together for an habitation of God through the Spirit" (Ephesians 2:22). Again in 1 Corinthians 6:19, Paul asks in astonishment: "What? know ye not that your body is the temple of the Holy Ghost which is in you?"

THE CROWNING FACT

The personal coming of the Holy Ghost into human consciousness is the crowning fact of God's manifestation in history! His coming was just as definite and conspicuous as the advent of Christ. Was the Christ's coming proclaimed by angel voices and chanted by "a multitude of the heavenly host praising God?" (See Luke 2:9-13.) Equally, was the Holy Spirit's advent attested by his "bodily shape like a dove" (Luke 3:22), and by the "sound from heaven as of a rushing mighty wind," and by "them cloven tongues like as of fire" (Acts 2:2-3)?

Heavenly dove, tempest roar, and tongues of fire crowning the hundred and twenty were as convincing as the guiding star and midnight shouts of angel hosts.

THE PROMISE GIVEN AND REALIZED

The promise of the Holy Ghost is explicitly given by Jesus in John 16:7, "If I depart, I will send him unto you." The promise was realized on the Day of Pentecost after the disciples had "tarried," according to the command of Jesus, with one accord in prayer and supplication.

THE BELIEVER'S IDENTIFICATION WITH CHRIST IN HIS DEATH AND RESURRECTION

Between the day the Holy Ghost was promised and the event of His coming at Pentecost, there was the great day of our Lord's crucifixion. It behooved Christ to suffer in order to make the gift of the Holy Ghost possible to man. There is also a day of crucifixion to the Christian. He must be crucified with Christ: The "old man" must be nailed to the cross, for in no other way can we be delivered from sin. Dying to sin is a real act, a genuine experience.

Buried with Him in baptism (Romans 6:4), and being made conformable to His death, we become partakers of the resurrection life of Jesus. The new life of power and victory in God becomes ours, and we are elevated through Christ into His own resurrection life, in actual spiritual experience.

Just as necessary as the crucifixion or the resurrection is the ascension. Jesus ascended into heaven. He sits at the right hand of the Father. According to the promise He sends down the Holy Ghost, who is the holy God, the Spirit of Jesus. The Holy Ghost entering into us, taking possession of our personality, living in us, moving us, controlling us, and lifting us into heavenly experiences in Christ Jesus is the baptism in the Holy Ghost, through which we become participators in the ascended life of Christ in glory.

A PERSONAL RECEPTION OF A PERSONAL HOLY GHOST

The outpouring of the Holy Ghost is not only dispensational, but His reception into the heart is to be the personal, conscious experience of every Christian who has "tarried" for the enduement of power from on high. The first Pentecostal experience is given in Acts 2:

> There came a sound from heaven as of a rushing mighty wind.... There appeared unto them cloven tongues like as of fire.... They were all filled with the Holy Ghost, and

began to speak with other tongues, as the Spirit gave them utterance.[1]

Speaking in tongues is the voice of God. It is God speaking through us. (At this point the Holy Ghost spake through Brother Lake in an unknown tongue. (See 1 Corinthians 14:2.) The congregation was asked to engage in silent prayer for the interpretation of the words spoken in tongues. (See 1 Corinthians 14:13.) Immediately, God answered. The interpretation was as follows.)

> *Christ is at once the spotless descent of God into man, and the sinless ascent of man into God, and the Holy Ghost is the agent by whom it is accomplished.*

Bless God! He is the Christ, the Son of God. His atonement is a real atonement. His blood cleanseth from all sin. Man again becomes the dwelling place of God.

WHAT ABOUT MANIFESTATIONS?

Let us now consider some of the wonderful manifestations of God to His people in the New Testament, under the baptism of the Holy Ghost. We will take the 10th chapter of the Acts of the Apostles. Cornelius, a Gentile centurion living in Caesarea, has a vision. An angel appears to him. The angel speaks to him a comforting message from God. This heavenly messenger also gives him the address of Peter the apostle, who was down at Joppa preaching Jesus, healing the sick, and restoring dead Dorcas to the widows who lamented her. Cornelius is commanded to send for Peter: "He shall tell thee what thou oughtest to do."[2]

Two trusted servants and a devout soldier are immediately dispatched to Joppa for Peter. On the morrow, as these messengers drew nigh unto the city, Peter was praying and, in a trance, saw a vision. Through this vision God taught him a very necessary and effective lesson on the brotherhood of man and removed from his heart certain inherent and racial prejudices which Peter, as a Jew, had to the preaching of the Gospel to the Gentiles.

---

[1] Acts 2:2-4.

[2] Acts 10:6.

Think of it, the great Peter in a trance! If I were to fall on the floor in a trance at the present moment, I have no doubt that nine-tenths of this audience would affirm that it was a case of hypnotism — that my opponent, Brother Du Toit, had hypnotized me.

While Peter thought on the vision, he received a message through the Spirit, saying: "Behold, three men seek thee. Arise therefore, and get thee down, and go with them, doubting nothing: for I have sent them."[3]

THE SIGN OF TONGUES

Peter accompanied the three men to Caesarea. He preached the Gospel to the gathering at the house of Cornelius. The whole company was baptized in the Holy Ghost, "And they of the circumcision which believed were astonished, as many as came with Peter, because that on the Gentiles also was poured out the gift of the Holy Ghost" (verse 45). How did they know they were baptized in the Holy Ghost? "For they heard them speak with tongues, and magnify God" (verse 46). This glorious Holy Ghost service ended in a water baptism of those who had already been baptized in the Holy Ghost.

PAUL SPEAKS TO US

In the twenty-second chapter of Acts we read Paul's account of his conversion from Judaism to become a disciple of Jesus Christ. A party of horsemen (Saul and certain officers of the law) is on the way to Damascus. Saul holds a commission to arrest all who call on the name of Jesus. Suddenly, there shone from heaven round about them a light greater than the light of the sun. In Acts 26:14, he says:

> When we were all fallen to the earth (think of it, the whole party fallen to the earth), I heard a voice speaking unto me, and saying in the Hebrew tongue, Saul, Saul, why persecutest thou me?

Who is the speaker?

---

[3] Acts 10:19-20.

I am Jesus whom thou persecutest.[4]

And they that were with me saw indeed the light, and were afraid; but they heard not the voice of him that spake to me.

— Acts 22:9

TRANCES, VISIONS, REVELATIONS

In order to understand the full force of this incident as well as to learn the source of Paul's wonderful ministry and of his profound insight into spiritual things, we must find out where he obtained his knowledge of the Gospel. Was it communicated to him by the other apostles who had been with Jesus during His earthly ministry? No. It was revealed to him in trances and in visions. He received the knowledge of it directly from the ascended and glorified Christ Himself.

But I certify you, brethren, that the gospel which was preached of me is not after man. For I neither received it of man, neither was I taught it, but by the revelation of Jesus Christ.

— Galatians 1:11-12

MORE VISIONS

In Acts 22:12, Paul tells of Ananias coming to see him. How did Ananias know Paul was there? The mystery is explained in Acts 9:10-11.

And there was a certain disciple at Damascus, named Ananias; and to him said the Lord in a vision, Ananais. And he said, Behold, I am here, Lord. And the Lord said unto him, Arise, and go into the street which is called Straight, and enquire in the house of Judas for one called Saul, of Tarsus: for, behold, he prayeth.

---

[4] Acts 26:15.

And now the Lord tells Ananias what Paul had seen.

> And hath seen in a vision a man named Ananias coming
> in, and putting his hand on him, that he might receive
> his sight.

— Acts 9:12

In the next verse Ananias talks with the Lord. Do you know anything of such revelations, of such communion or talks with God? If not, get the baptism of the Holy Spirit like the early Christians had and their knowledge and experiences in God shall be yours. Men say to us, "Where do you get your insight into the Word of God?" We answer, "Where Paul and Peter obtained it, that is, from God through the Holy Ghost."

Ananias went as the Lord directed him and found Paul. Ananias laid hands on him and he received his sight. He was baptized in water and also in the Holy Ghost and spake in tongues "more than ye all." (See 1 Corinthians 14:18.)

Now, see again Acts 22:14. Ananias is speaking to Paul:

> And he said, The God of our fathers hath chosen thee,
> that thou shouldest know his will, and see that Just One,
> and shouldest hear the voice of his mouth.

I want you to notice the phrases, "see that Just One" and "hear the voice of his mouth."

Trance Defined

When did Paul see that Just One? When did he hear the voice of His mouth? Just three years afterwards, when Paul had returned to Jerusalem.

> And it came to pass, that, when I was come again to
> Jerusalem, even while I prayed in the temple, I was in a
> trance; and saw him (Jesus) saying unto me, Make haste,
> and get thee quickly out of Jerusalem: for they will not
> receive thy testimony concerning me.

— Acts 22:17-18

Now what is a trance? In a trance the Spirit predominates over the mind and body, and for the time being, the control of the individual is in the Spirit. Our ignorance of spiritual manifestation is such that even ministers of religion have been known to say that such experiences and conditions are of the devil. Now, let us see when Paul received his commission to preach and his condition and attitude at the time he received it. (See Acts 26:16-18.) Paul received his preaching commission while lying with his face to the ground in the dusty roadway near Damascus, having been shown into that state by the power and glory of the heavenly light shining around him. Now, if we were to see someone lying on the road talking to an invisible "somebody," no doubt in our ignorance we would send for an ambulance or the police. But this is where Paul received his commission and appointment as preacher and apostle to the Gentiles. (See Acts 26:18-19.)

MANIFESTATIONS OF THE SPIRIT

From this we are able to perceive and understand in a measure the operations of God upon those who come under the power of the Holy Ghost. And now, beloved, is the Holy Ghost in the Church today? Verily, yes. But you say, "We don't see Him work in this way in our church!" Why? Because you say, "All these things were for apostolic days." Can you find anywhere in the Scriptures that the gifts of the Holy Ghost were withdrawn from the Church of Christ? There is no biblical authority for such an assertion, but rather we read, "The gifts and calling of God are without repentance" (Romans 11:29).

THE GIFTS

I have preached in four different countries and with one exception, no Christian minister has been able to name me the nine gifts of the Holy Spirit. These gifts are enumerated in First Corinthians 12:8-11. I was very pleased to hear Brother Du Toit read them at the commencement of this service. It shows people are beginning to read and to think along these lines. The gifts of the Holy Ghost are:

(1) Wisdom; (2) Knowledge; (3) Faith; (4) Gifts of healing; (5) Working of miracles; (6) Prophecy; (7) Discerning of spirits;

(8) Divers kinds of tongues (or languages not by acquirement but by the Spirit); (9) Interpretation of tongues. I thank God for these precious gifts of the Spirit, and especially for the gift of healing. May we all learn to know Christ, not alone as our Savior, but as our Sanctifier and Healer too!

GOD RESTORES HIS PEOPLE

Beloved, we have seen that the Holy Ghost came into the Church at Pentecost and that those gifts are there also, but through lack of faith we do not see them exercised.

The Apostolic Faith Mission stands for the obtaining of the Holy Ghost through the personal baptism in Him and "the induement of power," as commanded by Christ, and for which the disciples were commanded to "tarry" before they went forth to preach the Gospel. For, "Ye shall receive power, after that the Holy Ghost is come upon you" (Acts 1:8).

BAPTISM IN THE HOLY GHOST

Speaking in tongues is the external evidence that the Holy Ghost has taken possession of the body of the believer and therefore, of the tongue. It is the voice of God speaking through the sanctified lips of the believer.

In Acts 2:4, the hundred and twenty disciples spoke in tongues. In Acts 10:44-48, when the Holy Ghost fell on the Gentiles, Peter commanded that they should also be baptized in water.

> Can any man forbid water, that these should not be baptized, which have received the Holy Ghost as well as we?[5]

How did they know they were baptized in the Holy Ghost?

> For they heard them speak with tongues, and magnify God.

— Verse 46

---

[5] Acts 10:47.

Speaking in tongues was therefore the evidence of the baptism in the Holy Ghost, by which also Peter claimed the right to baptize them in water. In Acts 19:1-7, Paul found at Ephesus twelve men who had been baptized unto John's baptism. He rebaptized them into Christian baptism, and the name of Jesus Christ. When Paul laid hands on them, the Holy Ghost came upon them, and they spake with tongues and prophesied.

> Tongues are for a sign, not to them that believe, but to them that believe not.
>
> — 1 Corinthians 14:22

In October 1907 the Lord in His goodness baptized me with the Holy Ghost after several months of deep heart searching and repentance unto God at the home of a friend. In company with Brother Thomas Hezmalhalch, was called to my home at Zion City, Ill., to invite me to accompany him to pray for a sister who was an invalid and had been in a wheelchair for a number of years.

DIARY ENTRIES

Editor's note:

In this diary section, we have retained the author's original capitalization.

[This first entry was not dated.]

As we entered the home, I felt a great calm resting upon me. I did not feel to join in the conversation. Brother Tom proceeded to instruct the sister from the Word concerning healing, and I sat in a deep leather chair on the opposite side of the room. My soul was drawing out in a great silent heart cry to God. *O Jesus, I so long for the baptism of the Holy Ghost, but I feel so unworthy, so far from thee. O Christ, if it be possible to baptize such as me, please baptize me. I am so hungry, so tired of trying, so weary of doing things myself. I am sick of sin, sick of self, sick of trying, sick of working, etc. etc.*

Presently, a great quiet came upon me deepening rapidly into a peace such as I had never before known or experienced — a quiet of spirit, soul, and body. My being was soothed in a perfect calm, so deep, so quiet. My mind was perfectly still. I said, "O, Jesus, what is this — the calm of God? Is this the baptism of the Holy Ghost?" Presently, it seemed as if I had passed under a warm tropical rain that was falling not upon me, but through me. The realization of peace was such as I had never known. The rain continued to fall upon me. O, the rest of soul. O, the quiet of God. O, the peace of that hour. The peace — I cannot describe — that passeth all understanding. This condition of peace was so great I feared to breathe. It was as the silence of heaven. The saving rain continued to fall upon me. It soothed my brain. It soothed my body. It soothed my spirit. Would it ever stop? I feared it might. I said, "O God, I did not know there was such a place of rest as this."

Then I became conscious of a change coming over me. Instead of the rain, currents of power were running through me from my head to my feet, seemingly into the floor. These shocks of power came intermittently, possibly ten seconds apart. They increased in voltage until, after a few minutes, my frame shook and vibrated under these mighty shocks of power. Then as I shook and trembled, the shocks of power followed each other with more apparent rapidity and intensity. My forehead became sealed. My brain in the front portion of my head became inactive, and I realized the spirit speaking of His seal in their foreheads. I could have fallen on the floor except for the depth of the chair in which I sat.

Again a change. The shocks of power lessened in intensity and now have taken hold of my lower jaw. It moved up and down and sidewise in a manner new to me. My tongue and throat began to move in a manner I could not control. Presently, I realized I was speaking in another tongue, a language I had never learned. O, the sense of power. The mighty moving of the Spirit in me. The consciousness it was God who had come.

Then Satan came and suggested, "It is not real power. It is only imagination. There are not currents of real power. It is only physic phenomena."

I said, "It's power. I know it, and God in His loving mercy proved it to me." At this point Brother Tom, not yet having observed what the Lord had been doing with and to me, motioned me to come to pray with the sick woman. As I stood up I was trembling so violently I was afraid to put my hands upon her head. Knowing the honeycombed state of the bone in many rheumatic cripples, I was afraid lest the trembling of my body might dislocate the rigid neck. It occurred to me to touch the top of her head with the tips of my fingers only.

Permitting the joints of my fingers to be as thus, no jar to the sick one was [illegible]. As I touched her head I could feel the currents of power shoot through me into her. Brother Tom was still so engaged with the sister, he had not yet observed that Jesus had baptized me. I opened my mouth wide, thus not permitting the moving of my tongue to produce sound. Presently, Brother Tom said, "Let us pray," at the same instant.

Taking one of the sister's hands, at that instant a shock of power shot through me and down through the sister into Brother Tom. He instantly dropped her hand and drew back, apparently not realizing what had happened. He again lifted the hand and started to pray. As he prayed the Spirit deepened on me. I could keep the sounds back no longer and as I prayed the Spirit prayed through.

[This entry is undated, but it seems to follow the previous one.]

...me in another tongue unknown to me. For years I had been used of God in laying hands on the sick. God had given wonderful healing at times, but there was no seeming continuity of healing power. As I prayed the Spirit said, "What shall I give you?"

I said, "O Jesus, my soul has coveted the gift of healing." And I felt that thenceforth, God would use me in that ministry.

Following my baptism in the Holy Ghost came six months of the most terrible fightings, sometimes victory, sometimes defeat, sometimes awful chords and soul storms, with glimpses of God's sunshine. The Spirit talked to me of going up. "All." I did not know what that would mean, but O, brothers and sisters, when we say *all* to Jesus it means much. My home, business position among men, friends, family, even my dear wife could not at this time understand. God said, "Go and preach."

I said, "I will nights, but I must go on with my business." After some months, I found my interest in commercial and worldly affairs was passing away. A man would come into my office. I could not think of his money. I could only think of his soul. O, was he saved? Could I bring him to Jesus? And many times it ended in my telling him of this wonderful Savior and having to pray instead of talking business at all. O beloved, when the Spirit of Jesus, the Holy Ghost, comes, it is Jesus' own passion for souls. You must love them. You can't help it. Jesus died for them. The Holy Ghost is His Spirit. He loves them still. He loves through you. Again, the Lord said, "Follow Me," and like Matthew, I closed my office, arose, and followed Him.

Some months before I was baptized, I sat in a cottage meeting at the home of Brother Fred Bosworth. Brother Tom was preaching. At the close of the meeting, he came to me and said, "Brother, what is your name?"

I said, "John Lake."

He replied, "John Lake, as I was preaching, Jesus told me, John and I are going to preach together."

I laughed, replying lightly, "I wish it were so, but I can't preach. I am not where I ought to be with God."

He said, "Never mind. Jesus is going to fix you up." Some months later as he visited our town again, one day I joined Brother Tom and Brother Fred Bosworth on the sidewalk. As we walked down the street, I stepped between them, taking each by the arm. Brother Bosworth turned to me, saying, "Lake, when are you going to surrender to Jesus?"

I said, "Anytime, Fred."

Tom turned to me saying, "Do you mean it!"

I replied, "I do, Tom." We all three fell on our knees on the sidewalk and right there I surrendered to my Lord. Then I sought God for sanctification and my Baptism in the Holy Ghost.

One day about April 1st, 1908, I went to Indianapolis, Indiana, for a ten-day visit with Brother Tom, who was preaching there. Then I assisted in the services and work. While visiting at the home of a Brother Osborne, as we prayed before retiring, the Spirit of the Lord came upon me and God talked to me concerning Africa.

From my childhood I had been much interested in Africa, especially South Africa, and for years I had felt that one day God would send me to Africa, but never possessing what I regarded as the Divine Equipment necessary for a successful Christian worker, I had banished the thought and stifled the voice within. Then I now had a large family — myself, my wife, and seven children. The way seemed impossible. God gave me at this time a spiritual vision of Africa, especially of the Zion work there, so accurate that when I arrived in Africa four months later, I found it correct in every detail. As my ten-day visit closed, I found myself being drawn strongly to return at once to my business, but God would not give me liberty to do this. And this has always been to me one of the strange workings of God in my life.

My affairs needed my personal attention much. It seemed suicidal to put my complicated business into another's hands to close up. As I said, being overpowered with desire to return to my office and put my affairs in shape, I decided to do so, and then commenced spiritual and physical chastisement so terrific, I felt as though my reason must surely be dethroned. While in this turmoil of soul, one day I met Brother Pearse, now of Australia, a precious, godly man. He said, "Brother Lake, the Lord has been laying it on my heart to invite you to come to my home that we may have an evening of prayer together."

I said, "I will come tonight at 8 p.m." I was there. Brother Pearce, wife, and daughter, and myself made up the praying company. As we knelt to pray, my soul was in such anguish, I felt I must hear from heaven or die. Within a short time after kneeling to pray, I felt myself being overshadowed by the Holy Spirit. Then commenced the most vivid spiritual experience of my life.

The Lord brought to my remembrance from my childhood on every occasion when He had tried to woo me to His way, and I had turned to my own way instead. O the many, many times He had called when I did not heed, times long since forgotten by me. O, how He showed me His love for me. His anxiety to help, but I would not. He showed me the lost world, dying souls, the sick, and suffering, saying, "All this I did for thee. What hast thou done for Me?" until my heart broke in anguish. I cried and told Him I would go all the way with Him, even unto death.

Then the Spirit said, "Will you go?"

I said, "Yes, Lord, anyplace, anywhere. But O, Jesus, the burden must be Yours. The responsibility Yours." Then a series of visions of different cities came before me. First of Zion City, Ill., where the glory of God overshadowed the old Dr. Dowie Tabernacle in Shilvapor as a heavenly light and radiated out over the entire city. O, what a Spirit of Prayer was in me. My soul flowed out in a cry for the lost and perishing world. Then He showed me the downtown district of the city of Indianapolis, Ind., and the same illumination of God's glory, only in a smaller compass. This I understood to be the extent of God's blessing on each place through our ministry. Then Johannesburg, South Africa, and a wonderful illumination of God's glory lighting up the whole land. My soul continued to pour out in a stream of prayer. Then two other places were shown. Again, I heard the voice, "Will you go?"

"Yes, yes!" I cried, "If You will prepare and equip me and go with me." I prayed. "When will I go?"

The Lord said, "Now."

Again I prayed, "Where will I go?" And at once commenced to roll from my mouth in another tongue a single word repeated over and over, perhaps twenty times. I said, "Lord, what is it? What does this word mean?" And at once, the interpretation came, *Indianapolis.* I cried, "Lord, I will go! I'll go at once!" When I arose from my knees it was to find the household in great fear, believing I must have lost my reason. I comforted them, assuring them it was God. On looking at my watch, I was amazed to find I had been on my knees for four hours. The first time in my life such a thing had occurred.

I returned to my own home and told my dear wife. The Spirit so rested upon me that I spoke in tongues or prayed the entire night. In the morning, I packed my suitcase and went to Indianapolis, where I joined Brother Tom in his meetings. As I entered the Hall, he said, "I knew you were coming. Take a seat here by me." The following night as I stood to testify, the Spirit impelled me to say, "Brother Tom thinks he is going to Colorado, but he is not. He is coming to Zion City with me."

Tom laughed, saying, "Not unless the Lord sends me."

I replied, "You will hear from heaven." Some days later while he was praying, the Lord told him to go. O, what a wonderful series of meetings. That was how God poured out His Spirit at one meeting in the upper room of Brother Hammond's Faith home, The Haven. Twenty-five were baptized in the Holy Ghost and spoke in tongues. In perhaps twenty minutes the Spirit of God fell on the meeting like a cloud. Instantly, one after another commenced to speak in tongues. O, what glory. O, what high praises of God. O, what rejoicing. It was estimated that several hundred received the baptism of the Holy Ghost during this series of services lasting, I think in all, about six months.

One day in October, I went out with a young man to saw down a large tree for firewood. I had been praying about guidance for future work for the Lord for some days, believing my mission at Zion City to be fulfilled, when again the Spirit spoke to me and said, "Go to Indianapolis, rent a large hall, prepare for a winter campaign, and in the spring you will go to Africa." I again obeyed without question. On arriving there, I found a little company of saints holding an occasional meeting in a small hall. I told them what the Lord had said and God witnessed to them. It was His message.

We had no money, but we believed God, we prayed, and in a few days had no less than $100 handed in for the Lord's use. We commenced the work in a large hall and from the first, God greatly blessed in saving, healing, and baptizing many in the Holy Ghost. An operation of God occurred at this time. I feel it good to record. For many months Brother Tom and myself had been praying for greater power for the healing of the sick and the casting out of demons. At this time, one morning in coming to breakfast, I found I could not eat, but felt well. At noon it was the same, this continual [illegible] great desire to pray came upon [illegible]. On the evening of the 4th and 5th day, as I knelt to pray, the Spirit of God spoke to me and said, "From hereafter thou shalt cast out demons."

On the following night a young man came to me inquiring, "Do you believe the motto up there?" pointing to a painted motto in large letters on the wall. It was, "In My Name shall they cast out Devils."

I said, "Yes, Brother, I do."

He said, "Are you sure, for I am in earnest?"

I replied, "My Brother, with all the earnestness of my soul."

"Well," he replied, "I have a brother in the asylum. He has been there two years and the doctors cannot give us any hope or, in fact, seem to be at a loss to explain the reasons for his condition." I then inquired under what circumstances his brother had went in. He told me that the brother had been attending a revival meeting and was seeking sanctification and was a religious man who had trained his family in the fear of the Lord. That he had suddenly went insane. They had to put him in the asylum. His family was in great financial distress.

The Spirit of the Lord impressed me it was a case of devil possession, and we arranged the brother should be brought to the meeting on Sunday afternoon. He came in charge of his brother, his sister, and an attendant. He came at once and was persuaded to kneel at the altar. I then called a number of saints whom I knew to be vigorous in faith for healing and casting out of demons. Brother and Sister Flower, their son, Roswell, Miss Alice Reynolds, and others. Then I stepped down, put my hands on his head and rebuked, bound, and cast the devil out. He was instantly delivered and sat up quietly. Three days after, he was discharged from the asylum and went home well, returned to his work in a grain elevator. Four months afterward, his mother, sister, and brother returned to the mission to praise God, saying he was perfectly, permanently delivered. The power to cast out demons continues to abide upon me.

THURSDAY, NOVEMBER 24, 1910

A remarkable case of casting out a devil took place after the evening service. A Mr. Cornelious, possessed of a devil for about one-and-a-half years, said that in a vision, God showed him Brother Gordon Hinds and said he was to come to our tabernacle, and that Brother Hinds and Brother Lake would lay hands on him and cast the devil out. We did. As we prayed, he fell backward on top of the platform, then slipped down into a sitting [position] on the floor with his back against the platform. The devil caused him to cry out and fight with his fists, but in a few minutes he was overpowered by the Holy Ghost and cast out. Throughout the struggle, Brother Lake held his head firmly between his hands [and] at the same time in the name of Jesus commanded the devil to come out, which he did. When the devil was cast out, the glory and praise of Jesus filled his soul. In a few minutes the Holy Ghost [had] such possession of him that he spoke in tongues and praised Jesus.

SUNDAY, NOVEMBER 27, 1910

Brother Heroldt brought a young man who had been ill from sunstroke to the tabernacle from Potschfstroom. He had suffered for six months with violent pains in his head. The dear Lord healed him. Myself and Brother Van der Wall and Brother Heroldt prayed and laid hands on him. The morning service was a glorious one indeed. Bless God. The Holy Ghost so moved on people's hearts that the hymns, announcements, testimonies, and messages were all in one spirit and [we] thought [it was] as though a program had been arranged beforehand.

Evening service, a large audience. Message on, "In My Name Shall They Cast out Devils." Testimonies revealed that during the week, five men had been baptized in the Holy Ghost and spoke in tongues. Also one woman.

MONDAY, NOVEMBER 28, 1910

I was called by Brother Hunt to come to his home at once. A woman was in *violent fits of insanity.* I hastened to the home. As we prayed, the dear Lord cast out the insane devils and when I left, she was laying quiet and preparing to sleep. It was a glorious deliverance. The spirit came upon me, giving me a great and *intense sense of dominion.* Brother & Sister Hunt and Brother Rothchild had been praying with her for hours but had not sufficient dominion to cast the devil out. But being encouraged by my presence, [they] prayed with great power. The Lord united our hearts in a great unity of faith. The woman's name was Farmer.

Monday night, beautiful conversion of a young man at tabernacle. The Spirit came on Brother Scott Moffat. He had a beautiful vision of Jesus holding His hands to him. Brother Moffat is a Wesleyan local preacher.

TUESDAY, NOVEMBER 29, 1910

I visited Mrs. Dockrall's rooms at 56 Mosley Building, Johannesburg, overlooking the market square. The Duke of Connaught with the Duchess and Princes Patrick were visitors in the city. The Duke was laying the cornerstone. Three thousand school children dressed in white occupied the grandstand and sang. About 1 p.m. we started downstairs to the restaurant. Mrs. Dockrall was in front and was down about five or six steps when she was seized with a violent spasm of pain. Her husband took her back to the room. I went down and ate dinner and returned to Dockrall's rooms. As I started upstairs, I was joined by Brother Gordon Hinds.

We found Mrs. Dockrall suffering violently. She was walking about apparently quite insane. We tried to get her to permit us to pray for her, but she refused. Being persuaded she was not responsible for her actions, we took hold of her and prayed. As we prayed, she became prostrated by the Spirit and we laid her on the bed. God answered. The violent suffering ceased, but there remained a considerable pain throughout the afternoon.

At about 6 p.m., as I prayed, the Spirit came upon me intensely. I could feel the Spirit flow down my arm and through my hand into her body. I was praying, and as I prayed, laid my hands on the afflicted part. She became calm. Her pain ceased at once and passed under the power of God. Jesus appeared to her and warned her to be brave and strong, that she was not yet entirely delivered, that her suffering would return. She remained free from pain and slept till 1 a.m., when her suffering returned with great violence.

In the morning, when I came out to breakfast, a telegram from Mr. Dockrall. My home was at 4 Millbourn Road, Bertams, Johannesburg, about two-and-a-half miles from Dockralls. Said Helen had bad night. Come. Signed, Ben Dockrall. I prostrated down, prayed again. The intense suffering ceased. At 10 a.m. a most violent attack came upon her. She begged one to get her morphine, to bring a doctor, etc. I refused and fought the devil with all my power. At the end of one hour, I sent her brother-in-law to call the saints to prayer, for [her]. At about 12 p.m. Mrs. Dockrall suddenly became conscious, turned to me as I knelt at her bedside, and said, "The Spirit of the Lord is upon you," and instantly I realized it was. Again the healing virtue flowed through me. Again the pain ceased. Again Jesus came in a vision to her with a sword in His hand, fighting enemies. She asked the Lord, "Why do You need a sword? Why do You have to fight?" The Lord said, "For you." When the Spirit of God left her, the peace and glory of God remained upon her. I called again at night with Brother Powell and found her recovering.

WEDNESDAY, NOVEMBER 30, 1910

At the tabernacle meeting a widow lady, Mrs. Bovell, came in great distress, knelt at the altar, and cried, "My baby, about two-and-a-half years old, is dying. I want you to pray. Won't you pray?" We all went to prayer. The devil powers were very active. A mighty spirit of rebuke in the Spirit came on me. The baby was at Mrs. Fireslick home, 30 Lilian Road, Findeburg. The Dr. said it was poisoned, having eaten it somehow. We prayed. My spirit seemed to grapple with the Devil. He was overthrown. I felt it and as we arose, I said to her, "Go on home, dear sister. Look up. Your baby is all right." She begged me to come in the morning, and I did, and found that as we prayed at the tabernacle the night before, the child had fallen sound asleep, was healed and well and walking about. Mrs. Bosman, Mrs. Fireslick, and myself knelt and gave thanks to God for His goodness.

THURSDAY, DECEMBER 1, 1910

In the afternoon, I called on Mrs. Dockrall and found her almost entirely well and we praised God. I then went to Kruegersdorg. Mrs. Stuart was very anxious to see and talk with me concerning Mrs. Garninie, a woman at Roundfountain Central Halt *who was given up to die of cancer of the womb.* The Drs. said months ago they could do nothing for her. She went to England for treatment, grew worse, and almost died on the return voyage. I had been to pray with her twice. Mrs. Stuart, Gordan Hinds, and Brother Frisby also had been to pray for her. I felt the burden of her case rested on the Saints at Kruegersdorg. God answered prayer in a great degree for her, so that at different times *two large sections of the cancer passed from the body.* Mrs. Stuart will visit her today and bring me the last section of cancer and I will have [Entry ends here and then picks up].

Brother Oliphant, native overseer, called to report the baptism in water of seventeen native people at Vreyhead Natal on Sunday, November 27, 1910. Also the consecration of five children.

Received letter from Brother Sam Hulley, Cook House, C.C., telling of baptism in Holy Ghost of Brother C. Watson and wife and another young lady. Also of water baptism of four colored people. Also of the baptism in water of his Mrs. Hulley and baptism in the Holy Ghost of a Sister Robinson at Somerset.

FRIDAY, DECEMBER 2, 1910

Came in from Kruegersdorg where I had been all night. Stopped with Brother & Sister Stuart and was greatly blessed by conversing with them. Our fellowship was sweet in God. Attended Court after dinner. James Marisall, charged by our tabernacle as a disturber of the peace, was discharged.

SATURDAY, DECEMBER 3, 1910

Mrs. Stuart wired me to go to Roundfountain Central Halt to see Mrs. Ganie and pray. Found her resting in God but had no assurance of ultimate victory for her healing. Brother Van der Wall went with me and told me of a case of casting out of a devil that occurred at our tabernacle in Johannesburg on Thursday eve last, when I was absent at Kruegersdorg. A man, a train conductor, said that a man appeared to him on the train. His own double. Talked with him at one station. That double collected 7 tickets and brought them to him and another 5 tickets, then together they drank from a pint bottle of whiskey.

The man was *in great agony*. Brother Van der Wall, Sister Welsh, and Mrs. Van der Wall went into the back room, the vestry, and prayed for him. Brother Van der Wall says he prayed several times, commanding the devil to leave the man, when suddenly *he left in a blue flame, visible to all in the room,* and disappeared through the door. Then the people rejoiced and praised God.

While on the train, we met Brother Van Schele who told us of meeting a woman, Mrs. [name does not appear], who was *healed of inflammation of the lungs — double pneumonia.* Very bad. Brother and Sister Van der Wall had gone to pray for her on Sunday and she was greatly relieved. On Tuesday, Brother Van der Wall and myself went to pray for her and God entirely healed her. Brother Van Schele had written a policy on her son-in-law's life and while calling, the old lady told him how Jesus healed her. They were living with their daughter, Mrs. [name does not appear], Royal cottages, Longlaagte deep mine.

SUNDAY, DECEMBER 4, 1910

Today was communion service in the morning at the Tabernacle. The Spirit of God was greatly present. Among the testimonies was one by a young Brother Heroldt of Potschffs, whom the church prayed about two weeks ago. He was run over by a cart and left unconscious, was carried home. His wife would not have a doctor, but trusted God. Telegrams were sent to pray. God heard and answered. The doctors decided he must be operated on to remove the vast quantities of clotted blood, but he refused medical attendance all together. His soul was overflowing with gratitude, and instantly upon giving his testimony, knelt down on the platform and invited the congregation to join him in a prayer of thanksgiving to God.

A little child was prayed for who was ill of rheumatic fever. Mrs. Bovell, whose baby was healed when dying on November 30, was present and praised God for the healing of her child. Evening service at tabernacle: Two native men were present. A delegation from the African Catholic Church, consisting of the Bishop of their church and his chief advisor, who is a grandson of the old Christian Baralong Chief Inoroco of JhaBanchu. They wanted to join our mission and receive the apostolic faith teaching. I spoke briefly on the work of our mission. Brother Van der Wall [spoke] of the native work and the eighteen churches. These native brethren represented and then Brother Scott Moffat, a Wesleyan Methodist local preacher, gave a striking testimony of how on the night of November 28, at the evening service at the tabernacle, the Spirit of God fell on him, prostrating him on the floor for two hours. While there, the Lord showed him a beautiful stairway of wonderful architecture reaching from earth into infinitude and a beautiful figure in white floating down the stairs (not walking). As he approached, he saw it was the Lord.

Mr. Lind, who was an embezzler of a great sum of money from banks in Finland, was converted, confessed his sin, and was forgiven. He used to come to my home, 4 Milbourn Road, every Thursday evening for months for prayer. I only prayed and waited for God to deal with him. Bless God He did. He was gloriously saved, has a fine position of trust, and is a most devout man. His wife was an invalid for many years. No medical aid would avail. Jesus healed her thoroughly as we prayed, about two years ago.

Brother Welsh, a dear Brother from Cape Town raised in a Methodist family, who has been wonderfully baptized in the Holy Ghost, speaks in tongues. The glory of God rests on his soul.

Henrey Dockrall, one of our workers, who was wonderfully saved from a vile life and Baptized in the Holy Ghost. He told of how the dear Lord was using and saving souls in his work at Boksburg North.

Rev. R. H. Van der Wall, a minister of the Dutch Reformed Church, he sinned, was expelled, became a drunkard, but Jesus saved him after we met him. He is now my chief assistant and secretary of the Apostolic Faith Mission executive council. God has wonderfully used him, saved and baptized in the Holy Ghost.

Mrs. R. H. Van der Wall, his wife, a miracle of the healing power of God, who was healed of God when in a state of coma after the doctors had given her up to die. She was prayed for and our Lord in His love healed her, to the amazement of the doctors. Saved and baptized in the Holy Ghost. Glory to God.

Maggie Truter, Mrs. Van der Wall's daughter, who in my own home in June 190[ ]. She was violently ill for a long time. After several weeks' illness, one night the death rattle came into her throat. She kissed her parents and brother good-bye, then as death came upon her she roused and sang very faintly the first verse of "Jesus Lover of my Soul."

> Jesus Lover of my Soul
>
> Let me to thy bosom fly,
>
> While the nearer waters roll,
>
> While the tempest still is high,
>
> Hide me, O my Savior hide,
>
> 'Till the storms of life is past,
>
> Safe into the haven guide,
>
> O, receive my soul at last.

As she sang, her voice died away. The death rattle ceased. Her breathing apparently stopped and so far as human judgment went, she seemed to be dead — have seen many die. As this went on, a strange operation was going on in my spirit. I seemed to see her leave the body and rise upward. She kept getting further away, very slowly. It seemed to me that I was holding her spirit by a grip with my spirit. The Holy Ghost was upon me in power. After a time, I realized she was getting out of my control. I roused myself, prayed with more fervency, and finally with command I said, "You are not going away in the name of Jesus Christ. Come back." My spirit seemed to seize her and forcibly compel her return. Presently, I heard her mother say, "O, see she is trying to breathe." Then in a little while, she was breathing easily. God had heard. The blood availed; Christ was conqueror.

On examination, we found she had been apparently dead 35 minutes. I have never felt free to say she was really dead, as there was no doctor present, but firmly believe if she had not been held by prayer, she would never have breathed again. Her spirit, I believe, had already left the body. Today she is quite well and strong. I visited with her this evening and conversed with her about it. Praise to our Loving Christ. She is saved and baptized in the Holy Ghost.

Mr. Jones, who had been a great drunkard, was present with his wife and sister-in-law. Since his conversion, he has been a dear faithful brother and his gratitude to God has been blessedly marked.

There was a very fine evening audience. It is really wonderful how our audiences have kept up, considering how the devil through Cooper, Bowie, Gillis, etc. have tried to destroy the work.

MONDAY, DECEMBER 5, 1910

Monday at the night meeting a sister was converted. Her brother had been converted the previous Monday night. Spent day among the sick.

TUESDAY, DECEMBER 6, 1910

Meeting at tabernacle in the evening. Terrible rainstorm. Only about 40 were able to be present. I was struck in looking over the audience to note how that most of them were real miracles of salvation and healing and showed how God uses the ministry of healing to get souls saved. Davidson Brown, pianist and soloist. Saved drunkard. Peter Moffat, my brother-in-law (soloist), wonderfully healed. Mrs. Jones, a rheumatic cripple, healed by the Holy Ghost. Mr. Jones saved, drunkard.

Mrs. Jones was a great sufferer. Many years of chronic rheumatism. Medical aid availed naught. Jesus impressed her to pray for her baptism in the Holy Ghost. When she received the Spirit and spoke in tongues to her own astonishment, she found also that God had healed her through and through as she lay under the power of God on the vestry floor. The Lord made it plain to her to pray for the baptism of the Holy Ghost and then she would be healed also. Bless God.

Mrs. Hirak, her sister, recently saved. Miss Wick, my stenographer, saved and baptized in the Holy Ghost before I met her in America when there in 1909. She came to Africa with me and has been a faithful stenographer and a good Christian worker. Many have been saved and baptized in the Holy Ghost under her ministry since she came. God bless her.

Brother A. E. Sharpe, a dear brother saved from drunkenness about three months ago on the market square at an open air meeting. Now baptized in the Holy Ghost and preaching the Gospel of Jesus Christ, especially to the natives at Brakpan.

His son, Brother Sharpe Jr., saved and baptized in the Holy Ghost, a fine young worker.

G. H. Moore, a noble young miner, true to God and a faithful worker in our mission, his testimony was a great blessing.

Wm. May, a young man who was saved and is now organist at Central Tabernacle.

Scott Moffat, a Methodist local preacher who is being led out into the deeper life in God and whom God uses in the Word and Spirit to the salvation of souls. He had a wonderful vision of Jesus recently that has left a profound impression for good on his life.

Brother Welsh, a Methodist brother, recently sanctified and baptized in the Holy Ghost who is filled with the glory and praise of God. His life seems to be covered in the glory of baptism in the Holy Ghost. He recently was given by the Lord a vision of Jesus coming in the clouds with myriads of angels attending.

John Guthrie, a precious brother in the Lord, who is seeking God for a deeper life in the Holy Ghost.

Fred E. Mapstone, a dear young brother, saved and sanctified and baptized in the Holy Ghost.

H. G. Birkigt, a dear brother, now caretaker of Central Tabernacle.

Mrs. Birkigt, his wife, people blessedly saved in whose home many have been helped toward God.

Brother E. E. Brink, a dear brother who related how that he had brought a young man to the tabernacle who was afflicted with a Guinea worm in his foot. Brother Lake prayed for him saying, "Take off your shoe." It was in the foot and was said to encircle the foot 10 times in the flesh. When the worm was active, the torture was terrible. After prayer, he never felt it again. Jesus had killed it. The young man was a friend of Brink's. Through this, Brink himself was aroused and baptized in the Holy Ghost.

M. A. Cullinan, a lady worker in the mission, a devout woman formerly connected with the Salvation Army.

WEDNESDAY, DECEMBER 7, 1910

Called to Park Town North just at time for a meeting. Called Brother Powell to take the service and accompanied the messenger to Park Town North. We were met by Mrs. Gouse. Mr. & Mrs. Boswell accompanied me to a home where we found the woman had been seized with fits of violent vomiting. She had given birth to a child a few days previous. Her condition was very serious. The medical nurse who attended her was greatly astonished to see how [God] answered prayer for the woman, and it gave a blessed opportunity to teach her of Jesus and His power to save from sin and heal from all disease. She pledged me to come and pray for other patients.

I remained at Mrs. Gouse's at Park Town North and in the morning went to pray for a man, Fioushe, sick of [illegible] Phigtis very bad. He had received partial healing when previously prayed for. His heart was very bad and the left lung was very, very bad. His suffering ceased as we prayed, and he was immediately able to breathe down deep into the bottom of his lungs. He was very, very grateful to God.

THURSDAY, DECEMBER 8, 1910

Returned to my home, where I received my American mail. One letter from Brother Studd contained an offering of $120 American Currency (24 Guineas English). Also, two letters written from Africa by E. M. Scurrah to the saints throughout the world. These letters charge me with all vileness of misappropriating funds, of all manner of evil machinations, etc. etc. But none of these things are worthy to be reckoned in comparison with the knowledge of God through Christ Jesus our Lord. Another letter from Brother Garr contained $50. Another $[illegible] from a Brother Eaton of Winnipeg, Canada. At the tabernacle service Thursday night, it was a very sweet service with nothing out of the ordinary. Mrs. Arlow of Whurter, instantly healed of violent internal inflammation.

FRIDAY, DECEMBER 9, 1910

Worked at office. It was too wet at night for meeting at Fiordsburg as arranged.

SATURDAY, DECEMBER 10, 1910

Worked at office. Heavy rains preventing open air meetings at night.

SUNDAY, DECEMBER 11, 1910

Morning service was a baptism service. Ten candidates, eight European and then two native brothers who said they had come from far. I preached on baptism from Matthew 3. Brother Van der Wall gave charge to candidates. Brother Geo. Nlyate performed ceremony. Prayed for several sick at close of service.

MONDAY, DECEMBER 12, 1910

Worked at Miss Wick's office dictating letters till noon and at Mrs. Dockrall's office till night. Got out important letters for overseas mail.

TUESDAY, DECEMBER 13, 1910

Dictated letters during forenoon with Miss Wick. In the afternoon, I went to Mrs. Dockrall's but the Spirit of God fell on us as we talked and we spent most of the afternoon in meditation and prayer. Had a blessed time and God revealed to me His desire for an absolutely abandoned condition of our life to Him, especially for one month with prayer and abstinence and meditation. The Holy Ghost promised to use us mightily. The Spirit of God told her to read the book of Nehemiah, about the manner of working on the walls, chapter 4:16 and 17 was the special message. At night my sister Irene (Mrs. Moffat), who cares for my home, and I went to Jeppestown, to the Jeppe school to pray for Mrs. Robert Bruce. Very sick of bloody flux. God touched her instantly as we prayed and when we ceased praying, all pain had left. We returned at 10:30 p.m. God has been very near this afternoon. Praise His name. It has been a blessed day, notwithstanding I received a letter from Mrs. L. telling me that Mr. M. had charged me with the very vilest possible actions to her at her house. O bless God, beloved Jesus can take the sting out of our hearts.

WEDNESDAY, DECEMBER 14, 1910

Received a splendid representative mailing from ten different points throughout the country giving news of the work, from Ladybrand, from Cape Town, from Blvenfontein, Eastport, etc. And was much blessed in reading reports. Wrote a long letter to Brother McClean of Jamaica, British West Indies. On calling on Miss Wick, I learned that Brother Welsh had been given liberty in tongues in language last night. Also that Brother Scott Moffat had received his baptism in the Holy Ghost at his home last evening, for which I praise God. In the evening I went to Boksburg North, to open the new tent meetings there. There was a very nice audience and God blessed.

THURSDAY, DECEMBER 15, 1910

I have just had a call from Brother Van der Wall who told me that last night at the central tabernacle, Johannesburg, while I was at Boksburg, a woman was instantly healed of a paralyzed arm as Brother Van

(left to right)

Back row: John Lake, Margaret L. Otto, Irene L. Moffat, Fred

Middle row: James Lake, James Jr., Elizabeth Graham Lake

Front row: Clara L. Reibel, Wilford, Bertha L. Scott

All of Lake's brothers and sisters served as missionaries in South Africa and provided funds for the work there. Only Bertha did not go to South Africa, because she stayed home to care for her parents. She always felt cheated for never seeing South Africa.

der Wall, Brother Scott Moffat, and Sister Hunt prayed for her. At the close of the meeting she said her arm was quite well and natural. Praise be to our God. Forever would that all men knew Jesus the Healer. I received today mail from Los Angeles, California, USA, containing copies of letters written by false brethren here. These letters had been sent worldwide denouncing me as all that was wicked and unholy. I also received a most unholy letter from one George Bowie, a man who apparently is or was a Christian worker of some kind, but who seems to be consumed with envy and jealousy. This is the opinion of all the American brethren with whom I am closely associated who assure of their confidence.

FRIDAY, DECEMBER 16, 1910

Spent the day dictating to stenographers. Getting out our mail. Nothing of more than ordinary interest occurred. Find myself suffering much from brain fatigue on account of overwork.

SATURDAY, DECEMBER 17, 1910

Still working on my mail for overseas. Received a beautiful letter from a Brother Hoover, an American missionary stationed at Valpariso, Chile, South America, telling of God's revival there, of his people being baptized in the Holy Ghost, etc. Asking us to pray for his own and his wife's baptism. He says he has a Pentecostal Assembly of 450 people.

SUNDAY, DECEMBER 18, 1910

Had a very sweet morning service. Brother Van der Wall preached. In afternoon, I went to Simmer & Jack Mine Hospital to pray for Brother Jones, sick of double pneumonia. Had no evidence of immediate healing, but assurance that he would recover. Evening service was very blessed. Large, splendid audience. Brother Scott Moffat and Brother Welsh were ordained as evangelists. A brother from Rustenburg was converted. Also prayed for a number of sick and the Lord healed them.

MONDAY, DECEMBER 19, 1910

Dictated overseas mail all day. Did not go to evening meeting on account of weariness. Have been warned by the Holy Ghost of impending troubles coming soon. In conversation with Mrs. Dockrall as we walked on the street she said, "O, I feel as if the devil was working. The air is full of murder and suicide." At the very time or half an hour after, a Mr. Bower shot his wife dead and then shot himself. Both of them was dead in a few minutes. The Holy Ghost continues to forewarn us of difficulty and trouble ahead.

TUESDAY, DECEMBER 20, 1910

Worked at office. Troubled because of lack of sleep from overwork. Had a meeting of our tabernacle ministry at our home in the evening. Had a pleasant social evening. God blessed us all very much.

WEDNESDAY, DECEMBER 21, 1910

A very busy day. Was called in company with Brother Powell to pray for a Mrs. Newbold of 26 Browning Street, Jeppes, who was given up by the doctors. She had Bright's disease. As we prayed, God wonderfully touched her body and she was instantly relieved of all pain and much blessed in her soul. Later I was called to pray for Mr. Gure at 20 Crown Street, Jeppes, suffering from rheumatism all over his body, but especially in his head and left shoulder. I laid my hands on his head and cast the devil out. As I ceased praying, I said, "Where is your pain?" He found it quite gone and praised and glorified God.

THURSDAY, DECEMBER 22, 1910

This is the second anniversary of my darling wife's death. Her maiden name was Jennie Stephens. We were married February 5, 1891, at Millington, Illinois, USA. She was a loving, beautiful wife. Words can never tell all she was to me. God gave us a marvelous unity in the spirit. I worshipped her and she me likewise. O, will I ever forget when I returned from a missionary tour to find her already 12 hours dead. My precious wife. But as I look back over the terrible struggles

(left to right)

Back row: Jennie Stephens Lake, Alexander, Horace Houghten "Joe," Reverend John G. Lake

Center: Otto Brian "Jack"

Front row: Irene, Edna (standing)

(Not yet born were John Lake II and Wallace Stephens Lake.)

Alexander became an author, Horace Houghten became a union organizer of electrical workers, Otto Brian became Rev. Lake's "strong right arm," Edna graduated high school with top honors and married, Irene became one of the San Francisco Public School's first woman principals.

of planting this work in Africa, I now really feel God in His mercy permitted her to escape this awful time of sorrow and trial and fighting by taking her to heaven. Lies, blackmail, suggestion of evil of every kind. They say I am possessed of a devil. That's how people are saved and healed, etc. etc. But Jesus heals the sick and saves the sinful every day and this testimony of God baffles my traducers.[1] They now openly say it is the devil who heals.

At the evening service the dear Lord gave me a strong message from the entire 9th chapter of John, on the healing of the blind man. His cowardly parents, his own testimony, Jesus found him after he was cast out of the synagogue, etc. A note was sent by Ben Dockrall telling me his wife was very ill. We found her suffering greatly with a violent headache and contractions of the spinal chord. As we continued to pray, the Lord instantly touched her. The chord relaxed. Her suffering ceased and she was well and praised God. The Holy Ghost directed me to read for my own comfort Jeremiah, chapter 9, which I take to be a warning to the enemies of God's work, of His wrath upon them. I never knew such terrific malice and envy to exist before as is shown by Mr. Cooper, Mr. Bowie, Gillis, and others.

Brother Tom Hezmalhalch and I have preached together. For several years [we] came together from America, but like Barnabas and Paul, now separate each to go his own way. My heart is grieved and sore on account of his treachery, but feel it due to him to say it was the influence upon him of other false brethren, especially E. M. Scurrah, a stranger who integrated himself into Tom's good will, but who was a bold, vile man. His letters written to America damaging my character and the character of others have been returned to me. I never knew a professing Christian could do and write such things. How Satan has blinded their eyes. They cannot see God or His work for prejudice. How frail we mortals be. What patience God shows toward us all, teaching us to be charitable with one another.

I bear no malice. Jesus won't let me. I only desire to go on my own way unmolested and pray God's blessing on them all.

---

[1] traduce: to attack slanderously. *Webster's Desk Dictionary of the English Language* (NY: Gramercy Books, 1983), p. 946.

FRIDAY, DECEMBER 23, 1910

Received and interviewed workers from different parts of the field. Said good-bye to native ministers going to the Kronstad and other meetings. Helped them as I could with money for fares, etc. God has wonderfully helped me in this matter as my money went down. He sent in two pounds from a friend when it was gone. Sister Dockrall gave me two pounds given by Brother May of Roundfountain Estates, to her for me. So I have been able to put all our workers on the train. In the afternoon, the Council met the brethren of Vrededorfs in Joint Council, at which time certain arrangements were made to induce Brother Thomas Hezmalhalch to bring forward signed charges of misconduct of the war of the mission, etc. And I agreed not to prosecute him in any court on account of the preferment of charges by him. Our thought was to arrive at the truthfulness of these charges and to make the way clear for him to come forward with same through me.

In a letter from Brother Henrey Dockrall from Boksburg dated Monday last says, "The woman who was sick and who asked for prayer the night you were here, was healed when your Helen and Mendelsky laid hands on her." Praise God. Mrs. Rensley of 13 Caywood Street, Port Elizabeth, is visiting us for a time. She suffered with a severe pain in her side for three years and tells me that I prayed for her when I was at Port Elizabeth some months ago and that she was entirely healed. To God be the glory. Tonight at the tabernacle service, Mrs. Jones of Germiston, whose husband was sick of double pneumonia at the Simmer and Jack Mine Hospital and for whom we prayed Sunday last, was present praising God for the marvelous healing of her husband last Sunday. She testified that about an hour after we prayed for him, the Spirit of the Lord came deeply upon him and his disease was gone. God gave her a beautiful vision of her husband's healing to comfort her mind and heart and assure her of his healing. She promised that she would send me a copy of it in writing.

A brother was baptized in the Holy Ghost at the meeting as he sat in his seat. As he walked into the meeting, I burst out in speech to Miss Wick and others saying, "The Lord will baptize that man in the Holy

Ghost tonight." During the service, he was baptized in the Spirit and spoke in tongues.

SATURDAY, DECEMBER 24, 1910

Received Brothers Vanvurean and Van Jonder evangelists. Brother Van Jonder is a new man in our work. He was a prisoner of war in Olylon. A Boer from Africa during the late Boer Wars was baptized in the Holy Ghost and spoke in tongues. On account of the Spirit of God resting upon him, he was thought to be insane and was sent to the hospital. Jesus revealed to him by a vision that in nine years, he would meet people who baptized by triune immersion and that he would then be blessed and anointed of God to preach. Sent a cablegram to my old mother and father at Sault Saint Marie, Michigan, USA, as follows: "Christmas greetings, Lakes, Moffats, everybody fine."

Went to cottage meeting at Van de By Auckland park. Had a sweet time of communion. Returned home at midnight. My heart has been very lonely today. My thought was almost continually with my dear wife in heaven.

O, my darling, what dreary days since you went away. How I praise God for an active mind and body and plenty to do for others that has kept me busy and thereby, kept my soul from being absorbed in the loss of you. My precious wife. You were all in all to me. And though now you have gone to God before me, I bless Him for the 17 years we were permitted to live together here and for our 7 beautiful children that God gave us. Your memory is sweet today. Every book, everything about me speaks to me of you. My own lovely wife. But as a manly man, I can only go on and wait to meet you when my own time comes and I must finish the work He gave me to do, ere I can come to you. Our baby Wallace, who was only 18 months when you went away to heaven, is now a fine boy of three-and-a-half years.

And when you came, you swept the scale with a mighty masters wonderful art. You made the minor keys sob and wail while the low notes rang like a hell in a gale. And every chord in my heart from the deep bass tones to the shrill ones above joined in that glorious harmony. Love, all happiness that human heart could know I found with you. And when you went away, the hours became a winding sheet of woe, and make a ghastly phantom of today. But though the human is lonely, I yet rejoice my darling is with God and sorrow not as those who have no hope, but rejoice that the little while of parting will be over and we shall meet again.

CHRISTMAS
SUNDAY, DECEMBER 25, 1910

What memories sweep my soul today. Overwhelmed at the remembrance of my darling wife's death, I laid down and God permitted my tears to flow freely. As tears always do bring relief, it came. I went to the morning service and was rejoiced to receive a note from Brother Henry Dockrall of Boksburg telling of the baptism in the Holy Ghost of a young brother there. Brother Townsend also told me of the baptism in the Holy Ghost of a brother at Brockpan. Also on Friday, Miss Horack came to tell me that she herself had been baptized in the Spirit on Friday at her own home as she prayed. I had noticed Thursday night she was almost on the point of receiving the blessed Holy Ghost. The brother from Vrededorf who was baptized in the Holy Ghost at the Central Tabernacle Thursday night makes four who were baptized in the Holy Ghost that I know of this week. Bless God.

Mr. Stuart of Kruegersdorg also wrote me of the wonderful healing of Mrs. Wentworth who was insane very bad and also sick from displacement of the womb. Mrs. Dockrall and myself went to Crown Station and prayed for her last Monday. She was very bad. The devil seemed to have taken complete possession of her. As I approached her bed, she grew wild saying, "Don't you pray for me. Don't you pray for me. I don't want prayer. Don't touch me," etc. After a time, Sister Dockrall succeeded in getting her consent to let me put my hands on her head and pray. As I did so, the Spirit of God came upon me and I knew the devil was instantly cast out. In a moment she rose up in bed saying, "It's gone, O, Praise God, it's gone." Her husband and myself retired from the room and Mrs. Dockrall then laid hands on the afflicted parts and Jesus healed her at once. She immediately arose and walked and continued well.

John G. And Jennie S. Lake

MONDAY, DECEMBER 26, 1910

Worked on mail for overseas. In evening went to tabernacle, received a request to come quick to Brother Arlow at 33 Smite Street. Took Mrs. D. Called a cab and went fast. Found him suffering violently, apparently with extreme neuralgia. We prayed. The pain in body and head instantly ceased, but remained in one tooth. We prayed again and I put my finger in his mouth on the bad tooth. God stopped it right there. Then we went to Mr. Edwin Ammus and prayed for Mrs. Ammus' mother. She had a paralyzed arm, the result of an infection of the glands of the throat. We prayed. Her suffering ceased, but no further evidence of healing came. The gland still remained hard and the arm without power. We must go again. Something about her was not clear in the Spirit. I could discern it in the Spirit.

TUESDAY, DECEMBER 27, 1910

Took bundle of letters and papers to Mrs. Dockrall then went to Bramfontern to call on some of our people. Found Mr. Arlow at home. Said he had been well ever since we prayed. Had prayer with the family after which Mrs. Arlow told me the following story of a remarkable healing. She said, "About two years ago, my brother-in-law and his wife and myself brought his sister, a Miss Kotse, an imbecile and unable to speak, to the tabernacle." I prayed for her and instantly she commenced in tongues and from that time on she retained the power of speech.

About two months ago, the same three came to me after an evening service and asked me to pray for the deliverance of their sister confined in the Pretoria Asylum. I said to them, "Let us stand here (we were in the aisle), let us join our hands and hearts and God will deliver her." The next day, her sister went to see her. And the authorities said, "She is suddenly well. We do not understand it, but she is well." Later they signed her discharge but just then, her brother was killed in a dynamite explosion and she had no place to go, so [she] still remained at the institution. I purpose going to see her.

I visited Mrs. Philips. Found her sick in bed. Prayed for her. God touched her. She had formerly been healed of an internal tumor, at the tabernacle. Her husband, who had been a great drunkard, was saved and they have a happy home. Praise God. Henry Dockrall from Boksburg has just called and tells me of the baptism in the Holy Ghost of a Miss Scott this afternoon. Again we praise Him.

WEDNESDAY, DECEMBER 28, 1910

Worked at Miss Wick's office in forenoon. At Mrs. Dockrall's office till 2 p.m. Called on Mrs. Vanderhoff and then took train from Boksburg. Meeting was in Ms. Word's home. The time being wet, four young people came. Gave their hearts to God, then the Lord baptized Mrs. Morgan in the Holy Ghost and she spoke in tongues. Then a man came forward and gave himself to God. We had a blessed time, no preaching, the Spirit just fell on all. Some sang hymns while others prayed and testified. We returned to Johannesburg in a terrific rain.

THURSDAY, DECEMBER 29, 1910

Worked at office. Received overseas mail. I notice Brother George B. Studd of Los Angeles writes a strong endorsement of myself and work in the upper room. I received $96 in offerings from different ones in America today for which I praise God. At tabernacle meeting tonight an air of sadness seemed to weigh upon us. It was in the Spirit. Some were healed. The Lord seems to be laying a burden of intercession on the people. At the close of the meeting, Brother Townsend introduced me to a young colored man who had been baptized in the Holy Ghost on Saturday night in the tabernacle vestry. Praise God.

FRIDAY, DECEMBER 30, 1910

Prepared plans for all-night meeting instead of going to meeting at night. I went for a walk and finally went to a tea room and conversed for a couple of hours with friends.

SATURDAY, DECEMBER 31, 1910

Received workers from different fields coming to the all-night meeting. Brother Saunders of Blomfontien, Henrey Dockrall, Mr. Morgan and wife, Brother Scombie, Brother Schuman of Middleburg,

C.C., Brother Scott Moffat, Brother Welsh, and others. We had a blessed all-night meeting and the dear Lord gave a most blessed time, glorious time. The Holy Ghost gave me a prophetic message outlining the progress of the work during the next year. At midnight, we had communion service closing at five minutes to twelve. Then we remained in prayer, in silence, as the clock struck twelve. The meeting continued till morning.

SUNDAY, JANUARY 1, 1911

Had a beautiful morning service. The Spirit of God was very manifest. The congregation was melted down in tears. Brother Charles Hately praised God for his wonderful healing of a diseased bone in his head, for which there was no medical remedy. Also for the healing of his right hand and forearm paralyzed by an accident. Also for the healing of his leg after a compound fracture, being permanently lame, on crutches. The doctors gave him no hope of a cure. Jesus healed him and his heart overflowed with gratitude. I do not know that I have ever listened to a testimony exhibiting a deeper sense of gratitude.

Evening service was a blessed time and God called sinners to repentance. Four yielded their hearts to God and we all went home praising God for His love and mercy.

MONDAY, JANUARY 2, 1911

Worked on overseas mail. Had a very blessed time indeed. Sent out a great many papers. At the evening service, two drunken men sought God for salvation.

TUESDAY, JANUARY 3, 1911

Prayed for a man at Boysens reserve in delirium tremens. Have never had to listen to such terrible blasphemies. When I suggested I would pray for him, he cursed me in a terrible manner. His wife and cousin tried to quiet him. Finally I went up to him, took his hand forcibly and held him still. At the same time, I commanded him to look into my eyes. He did so. I put my face down within six or eight inches of his, looking attentively into his eyes. His gaze became fixed on my eyes as mine were on his. Then moving my hands, I laid them on his head and in the name of Jesus Christ, commanded the devil to come out of him. I felt it was instantly cast out. He became at once quiet and docile, turned on his face, and wept bitterly, praying God for salvation. It was a blessed experience and I returned home praising God for His mighty power in delivering men from all the power of the devil.

O, soul on the highway from earth into glory,
Surrounded by mysteries and trials so near,
Let the light of thy God in thy life be resplendent.
For Jesus will guide thee, thou needest never fear.

For if thou wilt trust Me, I'll lead thee and guide thee,
Through the quicksands and deserts of life, all the way.
No harm shall befall thee, I only will teach thee,
To walk in surrender with Me day by day.

For earth is a school to prepare thee for glory,
The lessons here learned you will ever obey.
When eternity dawns, twill be only the morning.
Of life with Me, always as life is to day.

Therefore, be not impatient as lessons thou'rt learning,
Each day will bring gladness and joy to thee here.
But heaven will reveal to thy soul of the treasure,
Which infinitude offers through ages and years.

For thy God is the God of the earth and the heavens,
And thy soul is the soul that He died for to save,
And His blood is sufficient, His power is eternal,
Therefore, rest in thy God both today and always.

uring the Confer-
ence I was asked
by the brethren to
deliver a discourse
on the subject of
the Sabbath Day for the guidance of the workers.

THE SABBATH
Johannesburg, South Africa
October 6, 1912

It is not my purpose to deal
with the subject in an argumentative manner, but rather in the form
of a pronouncement of the position of the Church.

The Word of God is sufficiently clear. It has already defined the position for the Christian in the most emphatic way. The second chapter
of Colossians is perhaps as clear a portion of Scripture on this particular issue as any portion of the Word. It seems most difficult for the
Christians to understand and realize, in our entrance into Christ Jesus
by the reception of the Spirit of God who abides within, our Christian experience has been moved into a different place from that in
which we lived before.

I have tried at different times to define the operation of the Spirit of
God in the different dispensations, that we may get a clear basis on
which to rest. I will review this this morning in a word.

THE PATRIARCHAL DISPENSATION

In the Patriarchal dispensation, God seems to have been approaching
man from this standpoint: as if man was far removed from God, and
as if God was endeavoring to reveal Himself to man. Abraham perhaps
furnishes the best example in the Word, and to him God appeared
twice, twenty years apart. There was a lapse of twenty years, in which
Abraham heard nothing from God. Then God spoke to him again.
Now, that is the best revelation from God to man that is given us in
the Patriarchal dispensation and it seems as if the position was, "God
revealing Himself to man."

THE MOSAIC DISPENSATION

The Mosaic dispensation was different. It was a fuller revelation. It
did not destroy any of the revelation of God that the Patriarchs had

known. God was present with the Jewish people in the Pillar of Cloud and the Pillar of Fire, and the Shekinah over the Mercy Seat, an ever-present God.

When the temple was built, the Lord abode in the Holy of Holies. In it, there was no artificial light. The Holy Place was lit by candles, but in the Holy of Holies there was neither window nor door, nor artificial light of any kind. The presence of God illuminated the Holy of Holies, the continuous presence of God with man.

THE CHRISTIAN DISPENSATION

Patriarchal revelation was "God to man," and the Mosaic revelation was "God with man," but the Christian revelation was greater than all. Jesus said in His own words, "He dwelleth with you, and shall be *in* you."[1] And the revelation of God to the Christian is, "Christ within you by the Holy Ghost," not "to" man nor "with" man, but "in" man. Man becoming the embodiment of God.

It will be readily seen, then, that our conception and standard must be in accordance with the revelation that God gave to us, and the Christian cannot base his standard of life upon the Mosaic law in any way. Jesus lifted us up above that standard, as high as the heavens are above the earth.

When the Christian, then, endeavors to go back and live under Christ Jesus and the communion of the control of the law, he has descended from the standard of the Spirit of God abiding within and has placed himself in the same position where the Mosaic people were.

PAUL'S WARNING: Over and over again Paul warns us about this thing, and to the Galatians particularly he gives this wonderful warning that "having begun in the Spirit" they were now going to return to the flesh.[2] And that is the danger with many Christians these days, that having begun in the Holy Ghost, they might return to obedience to commandments.

---

[1] John 14:17.

[2] Galatians 3:3.

THE LORD JESUS RAISED THE STANDARD FOR THE CHRISTIAN DISPENSATION

Then someone says: "What about the commandments?" We can see what Jesus says of them in the Sermon on the Mount. In Matthew 5 Jesus said, "It was said by them of old time, Thou shalt not kill." But Jesus lifted that standard miles above where Moses placed it and said, "But I say unto you, That whosoever is angry with his brother without a cause is in danger of the judgment."[3] That is to say, he is a murderer. (See 1 John 3:15.)

Under the Mosaic law, they had to commit an act in order to be guilty. Under the law of Christ, the presence in the heart of the desire is sufficient to condemn. So in every instance the Lord raised the standard.

The commandment says, "Thou shalt not commit adultery." Jesus says, "That whosoever looketh on a woman to lust after her hath committed adultery with her already in his heart."[4] Jesus took it out of the regime of commandments into the regime of the heart experience and, "as the heavens are higher than the earth, so are my ways higher than your ways, and my thoughts than your thoughts" (Isaiah 55:9).

THE GREAT DEBATE

The greatest debate that has come through these fifty years, between those who contend for the observance of the Sabbath Day (the Seventh) and we who accept the Christian Sabbath, has ever been on that one point. Are we still bound by the law or has Christ made the Christian free from the force of the commandment? And it seems to me that the Word of God makes this clear as daylight, that the Word places our feet emphatically on this ground — that to us, in the Holy Ghost, the law has become a dead thing.

Indeed, it has been spoken of as blotted out (Colossians 2:14), even that which was written on stone (2 Corinthians 3:7-17).

---

[3] Matthew 5:21-22, paraphrased.

[4] Matthew 5:27-28.

The first chapter of Colossians deals with the history of the fact of the indwelling of Christ, and after establishing this fact, Paul goes on to review the subject of our obedience to the law. Commencing with the thirteenth verse of the second chapter, we have the declaration of the expulsion of the law.

> And you, being dead in your sins and the uncircumcision of your flesh, hath he quickened together with him, having forgiven you all trespasses; blotting out the handwriting of ordinances that was against us, which was contrary to us, and took it out of the way, nailing it to his cross; and having spoiled principalities and powers, he made a shew of them openly, triumphing over them in it. Let no man therefore judge you in meat, or in drink, or in respect of an holyday, or of the new moon, or of the sabbath days: which are a shadow of things to come; but the body is of Christ.[5]

Thus far the interpretation is given of the destruction by Christ of the ordinances and laws that were contrary to us, by having established within us by the Holy Ghost of His own indwelling He, having been the Lord of the Sabbath, and we, as sons of God and joint heirs with Jesus Christ, will also enter into that place of dominion, where we too, in Him, become lords also of the Sabbath and every other commandment. Blessed be God!

THE NEW COVENANT

The sixteenth verse: On Thursday last, among the questions that were asked, was this: "Do we advocate the partaking of a meal in connection with the Lord's Supper?" And in this thing once again we see the Christian's failure to separate between the Old and New dispensations. For when Jesus partook officially of the last Passover Supper that was ever given to mankind and by that act forever closed the Jewish dispensation, there was nothing further to do but make the sacrifice on the cross. And the instant after the closing of that Supper the Lord instituted a new ceremony, the one we observe today — the

---

[5] Colossians 2:13-17.

communion of the Lord's Supper. No longer the Passover feast and Passover Lamb, but the Christ of God, who now pledges Himself to shed His own blood for the salvation of the world.

Between these two acts there is as great distance as between East and West. The one was the mark and stamp of that which was old and ready to decay (Hebrews 8:13), and the other was the birth of mankind through the shedding of the blood of Jesus Christ.

And so, beloved, when the Christian undertakes that his life shall be governed by commandments, he is going back again into this old life, into the old realm, forgetting his state with Jesus Christ.

It does not mean we shall turn anarchists and that to us there is no law, but rather that we are now obedient unto the higher law, by the Son of God.

THE SABBATH DAY

On the subject of the Sabbath itself: All the other Commandments are spoken of in the New Testament and reiterated, but the Sabbath Commandment is not; and that no doubt for this reason — that the prophecies all along had pointed to the Son of God, who was Himself the fulfillment of the law. "I came not to destroy the law, but to fulfill it" (Matthew 5:17). For "the law was our schoolmaster to bring us unto Christ." When we got to Christ, beloved, we were beyond the sphere of the law. The law was a schoolmaster to bring us to Christ. Blessed be His name. (Galatians 3:24.)

So with Sabbath, Christ Himself, the Eternal Rest into which the Christian enters, not to abide on the Sabbath Day, but to abide always, every day, and forever; He is our Sabbath alone.

When we live in the Son of God we have come beyond the sphere of commandment, for the law was made for the unlawful and unholy, for murderers of fathers and mothers, for whoremongers, etc. (1 Timothy 1:9-10.) Upon our statute books today there are no doubt a thousand laws that you and I know nothing about, and we care less. Why? They are of no interest to us. We hardly pay any attention to the law of murder, nor can we tell the details because of the fact that being sons of God, we are living in love and are not interested in what the law says of murder. There is no murder in our hearts. Blessed be God! We have passed on.

And so the Christian who has entered into Christ Jesus and is abiding in Him and is a possessor of the Holy Ghost has moved beyond the regime of the law and commandments. They are of no value to him. He lives in obedience to one law and one commandment, the Eleventh. This includes all the rest in one: "That ye love one another, as I have loved you" (John 15:12). Blessed be His name.

AN APT ILLUSTRATION

Henry Drummond, I believe it is, in his *Greatest Thing in the World,* gives an illustration that is so fitting. He says that he visits at a friend's home. He finds that he and his wife have lived together in the most beautiful unity for many years. But a friend of his is still anxious that he shall be a strict observer of the law, and he sits down and writes a code of the rules for the government of this man and wife who have always lived together in unity. He says "Thou shalt not kill her. Thou shalt not bear false witness against her. Thou shalt not steal from her," and so on through the other commandments. He takes it up and laughs. Of what value is such a code to him? Has he not for all the years past been giving to his wife his heart's affection that makes it impossible for such things to enter his soul?

And there is just that much difference between the Christian standard and the standard of the law. May God help us that we shall not take backward steps, but realize our positions as sons of God. We shall live in Him and abide in the Holy Ghost and realize the freedom of sons, not the bondage of servants. Blessed be His name. Nevertheless, to the man outside Christ the commandment still stands. As on our statute books today the law of murder applies to the man who commits murder, but the man in Christ has passed beyond that sphere.

> Let no man therefore judge you in meat, or in drink, or in respect of an holyday, or of the new moon, or of the sabbath days: which are a shadow of things to come; but the body is of Christ.[6]

---

[6] Colossians 2:16-17.

Blessed be His name! Blessed be His name!

Our Highest Christian Privilege

Now, we will never get the force of the second chapter of Colossians, where the Word portrays the exaltation of the Son of God — even to the sitting down at the right hand of the Father in the heavenly places, far above all principality, and power, and might, and dominion, and every name that is named (Ephesians 1:19-23), and the second chapter of Ephesians, portraying our lifting up out of the regime of death and sin into the same exaltation of the Son of God — until we realize our high privileges in Christ Jesus.

Indeed, I have this in my heart, that the low state of Christian experience that is common among men is mostly accounted for by this one fact: that Christians have failed to grasp the exalted place into which Jesus Christ puts us when we have been made sons of God. May God write that deep in our soul, that we may not keep the Seventh Day (which was a shadow of good things to come) but *the body is of Christ*, not the commandments. But by holy Christian privilege one day sacred to God, and that without any commandment at all, but out of the gladness of the Christian heart. Blessed be His name! One day is set aside in commemoration of His resurrection, but with the Christian, and in the life of Christ Jesus, every day is as holy as every other day, and there is no distinction of days whatever, for the life is in Him (in the Son of God), and He is the same every day. Blessed be His name.

The First Day

But, beloved, have we not cause to rejoice that in Christianity there has been established a day of commemoration of His resurrection, and that all together the Christian world unites in exalting the Son of God by keeping that day holy. We may not let down on our reverence for the first day of the week, but may we as Christians exalt the day not by obedience to commandment, but as Jesus Himself did, by making it a day when His life was given forth for the benefit of others, and I know God will bless us.

Now, I hope that forever this question is settled in our hearts. That so far as our church is concerned, God has helped us to come together to recognize the fact that every man has the privilege to be led by the Spirit, not to observe all the law, but led by His Spirit.

THE SABBATH

> The stone which the builders refused is become the head stone of the corner. This is the LORD's doing; it is marvellous in our eyes. This is the day which the LORD hath made; we will rejoice and be glad in it.
>
> — Psalm 118:22-24

When did the rejected stone become the head of the corner? When Jesus rose from the dead on that wonderful resurrection morning. "This is the day the Lord hath made; we will rejoice in it and be glad."[7] This is one reason we worship on the day of His resurrection. It is the Sabbath of the New Covenant.

> A world without a Sabbath would be like a man without a smile, like a summer without flowers, and like a homestead without a garden. It is the joyous day of the week.
>
> — Beecher

---

[7] Psalm 118:24, paraphrased.

DIVINE HEALING
Philadelphia, Pennsylvania
January 30, 1914

f there is something wrong with a man's spirit, he goes directly to God, but the next day he has a pain in his back and he goes down the road to the doctor's. Where do you get your right to do such a thing?

There is a wretched looseness about consecration to God. Christians do not seem to know what consecration to God means. What would you think of Jesus Christ, if you saw Him going down the road and into a doctor's office for some dope? Why, you would feel like apologizing for the Lord, wouldn't you? Well, He has just as much reason to apologize for you. When you become a Christian, consecrated body, soul, and spirit, your privilege of running to the doctor was cut off forevermore.

"Faith cometh by hearing, and hearing by the word of God."[1] This young man who testified says he suffers because of an appetite for cigarettes and he hopes that we will pray so that the next time he wants to smoke he won't. I tell you God says, "Quit your sins and then come to Me, and I will pardon." He don't say, "You come on with your sins, and I will pardon you." He says, "You quit your meanness, you quit fooling with the doctor, and the devil, you quit your secret habits, and come to Me, and I will deliver you." That is the only road to God; that is the way in God.

So a Christian's consecration is not just a consecration of his spirit to God, nor of his soul to God. It's a consecration of body and soul and spirit — the entire man, everything there is of us, and it cuts us forever plumb off from looking for help from the flesh, the world, or the devil.

There are three enemies of man — the world, the flesh, and the devil. Our nature has three departments: spirit and soul and body. What

---
[1] Romans 10:17.

would you think of the Christian who would go to the devil or to some deceitful spirit to find balm for his spirit? Why, you would think he was not a Christian at all, nor would he be. Suppose a man wants peace for his soul (mind), and he appeals to the spirit of the world or the flesh to get it. You would not think he was a Christian at all. Then how will you consider a man who wants healing for his *body* and goes to the world and man to get it?

I am going to preach to you for five minutes out of the fifth of James. He is very explicit in this matter. He is not laying down rules for the people of the world. He is talking straight to the Christians. "Is any among *you* (Christians) afflicted? Let him pray,"[2] not, "Let him go to the devil or the doctor or some human source."

"Is any sick among you? Let him send for the elders of the church," meaning this, if you have prayed and deliverance has not come, unquestionably it is a weakness of your faith. You need help. Then the next thing is, "Let him call for the elders of the church; and let them pray over him, anointing him with oil in the name of the Lord."[3]

When I was preaching at Washington, D.C., recently an old sister said she had anointed her little girl the night before and she had put a whole bottle full of oil all over her. So you see, she was not looking to God to heal; she expected the anointing oil to heal. Satan is a subtle old devil, but the Lord gives us light. He says not the anointing of oil, but "The prayer of *faith* shall save the sick, and the Lord shall raise him up." That is why I never use oil except when requested to do so, because people are looking to the anointing oil instead of to the Lord God. "Let him call for the elders of the church; and let them pray over him, anointing him with oil in the name of the Lord: And the *prayer of faith* shall save the sick,"[4] not the anointing oil. The use of anointing oil is a matter of obedience. It is a symbol of the Spirit of God, and that is all it is.

So we place upon the individual the anointing oil in order that we fulfill the symbol of the Spirit of God as the healer, and that is all.

---

[2] James 5:13.

[3] James 5:14.

[4] James 5:14-15.

"The prayer of faith shall save the sick, and the Lord shall raise him up; and if he have committed sins, they shall be forgiven him."[5] Thus he goes on and makes the teaching broader.

One of the beautiful things about the Gospel of Jesus Christ is that it is progressive in its revelation and application. First, we were asked to pray if we are afflicted. Second, we were asked to call for the elders. Then, the Lord goes down to the real business in a man's heart. "Confess your faults one to another."[6] Get your old tattling, blatting tongue tied up, and confess to the other party that you have been tattling.

If all the Christians had that gag in their mouth, there would not be half as much shouting in the meetings as there is. Now listen, I don't want to pound people on the head, but I want to teach you a lesson. Here is the broad principle of the Gospel, *"Confess your faults."*

When I went to Africa, I had the advantage of getting on absolutely new ground that no one had spoiled with a lot of loose teaching. In this country our people have been slobbered over with teaching that don't amount to anything, and they wobble this way and that way, "like a wave of the sea driven with the wind and tossed." And God says, "Let not that man think that he shall receive any thing of the Lord."[7]

One day when a young man, God brought me in to see my own need when I needed healing from heaven. There was nobody to pray for me and I was not even a Christian in the best sense of being a Christian. I was a member of a Methodist church, but I had seen God heal one dear soul, who was very dear to me. As I sat alone one day, I said, "Lord, I am finished with the doctor and with the devil. I am finished with the world and the flesh, and from today I lean on the arm of God." I committed myself to God and God Almighty right there and then, though there was no sign of healing or anything else, accepted my consecration to Him. That disease that had stuck on my life and

---

[5] James 5:15, paraphrased.

[6] James 5:16.

[7] James 1:6-7.

almost killed me for nearly nine years was gone. It was chronic constipation. I would take three ounces of castor oil at a single dose, three times a week.

The place of strength and the place of victory is the place of consecration to God. It is when a man shuts his teeth and says, "I go with God this way," that victory is going to come. My! This wobbling business makes one think of the old Irish woman who was on a ship in a storm. When the ship rolled one way, she would say, "O good Lord," and when the ship would plunge to the other side, she would say "Good devil." When someone asked her why she did that, she said, "Why, how can I tell into whose arms I will fall?"

May the Lord wake us up in our soul and get us out of this wobbly state and get us where we all commit ourselves once and for all and *forever* to Almighty God, and then live by it and die by it.

People say, like the dear soul last night who sent word to the meeting, "I am very sick, and if I don't get deliverance, I will have to do something." Why sure you can do something. *You can die;* you ought to die instead of insulting and denying the Lord Jesus Christ and turning your back on Him. People say, "I can't die." *Yes you can,* if you are not a coward, *but you cannot sin.* And it is just as much a sin to commit your body to the Lord Jesus Christ and then to run to the doctor as it is to go and commit adultery or any other sin. It is a violation of your consecration to God.

Make a consecration to God and stand by that and live by that and be willing to die by that. Then you will grow up into God, where your faith is active enough to get answers to prayer.

There is no man who lives and has the ministry of healing that could pray for all the sick people. There are so many of them. Why you come to an assembly like this, and every old saint who has a stomachache will come and ask you to pray for them, and there is no time for anything else. God wants us to grow up into Him where we get answers to prayer for ourselves. Then if there is an extreme case and your faith is broken, confess your faults one to another and get the rest of the people to pray for you, and then in the extreme cases send for the elders of the church, *and that is* the mind of God.

In the twelfth chapter of First Corinthians the nine gifts of the Holy Spirit are enumerated.

> To one is given by the Spirit the word of wisdom; to another the word of knowledge by the same Spirit; to another *faith* by the same Spirit; to another the *gifts of healing* by the same Spirit; to another the *working of miracles;* to another *prophecy;* to another discerning of spirits; to another *divers kinds of tongues;* to another the interpretation of tongues.[8]

These are the gifts or enablements that are given by God to certain in the Church. Now here is a thought I want to leave with you. We go over into Ephesians and we see a different order. Not the gifts or enablements are mentioned, but the gifts in this case are individuals. It is *men* to whom God has given definite ministries.

And in the Church of Jesus Christ not only should the gifts exist, but the faith to use them. And they do exist if they are developed, and they are workable when the faith in your heart is made active to use them. But you can have the gifts right out of heaven, and if the faith in your heart is not active, you cannot operate them.

There is only one prayer that is *answered.* It is not prayer that is answered but is the prayer of faith. It is the prayer of faith that shall save the sick. Believing prayer is not much noise. Believing prayer may not be any noise at all. Believing prayer is a committing, an intelligent committing of yourself to God, and your mind is stayed in God and your heart is stayed in God and you are walking in God. You are ready to die rather than go to anyone but God. That is the real believing prayer. That is the continuous prayer. That is prevailing prayer. Blessed be God!

So in Ephesians, the Word of God tells us that there are some apostles, some prophets, some teachers, some evangelists, and some pastors.[9] These are God's gifts, these men — not gifts as they are mentioned in Corinthians, but men are mentioned in Ephesians, and the men with ministries are God's gift to the Church until such time as they shall all come, the entire body of Christ, into the unity of the

---

[8]   1 Corinthians 12:8-10, emphasis Lake's.

[9]   See Ephesians 4:11.

faith, into the likeness of Jesus Christ, into the measure of the stature of the Son of God. "Till we *all* come," not one or two.[10] Blessed be His precious name!

These things will demonstrate to you how far we are behind the Gospel ideal. We are away so far behind. A few years ago many commonly believed that when the baptism of the Holy Ghost was being poured out upon the world, that we were the particular little lot who were to be the bride of Christ and go with Him when He came. But pretty soon it began to dawn on those who looked into the Word that there was not even a tangible body of Christ yet. The body of Christ is the members called of God, united in one spirit and in one hope of their calling. Blessed be God. With one Lord, one faith, and one baptism. That is the body. Then all the other developments, the bride, and all the rest of it are born out of the body. (Ephesians 4:2-6.)

God is getting a body at this present time, and in the body of Christ, the orderly body of Christ, the unified body, He wants to bring it forth today. He hath set His gifts — the word of wisdom, knowledge, faith, gifts of healing, etc. He has set likewise men — apostles, prophets, evangelists, pastors, and teachers.

> For the perfecting of the saints, for the work of the ministry, for the edifying of the body of Christ: till we all come in the unity of the faith, and of the knowledge of the Son of God, unto a perfect man, unto the measure of the stature of the fulness of Christ."[11]

Now healing is not a difficult matter. It does not take a bit more faith to be healed from your sickness than it does to be saved from your sins. The only difference is that in your own consciousness, you knew there was no place to get forgiveness except from God. You had sense enough to know you could not get it from the devil; you had to get it from the Lord.

But your body gets sick and your consciousness, because of your education, permits you to go to the doctor or the sorcerers or the devil, and the one is just as offensive to God as the other. The Christian

---

[10] Ephesians 4:12-13, emphasis Lake's.

[11] Ephesians 4:12-13.

body and soul and spirit is *one*. A real Christian has committed his whole being unto the living God. He consecrates himself to Jesus Christ with all the fullness that Jesus consecrated Himself to the Father at the river Jordan on the day He was baptized. He consecrated Himself unto the uttermost, unto "all righteousness," unto everything that was right, to the will of God forever. Blessed be His name.

Now there are examples in the Word of God that are very striking along this line. You listen to the Word of God. "Cursed be the man that trusteth in man." Talk about your running to the doctor. That is what the Lord thinks about it. "Cursed be the man that trusteth in man, and maketh flesh his arm, and whose heart departeth from the LORD."[12] And the Word of God in the fourteenth of Second Chronicles gives us a most remarkable example of Asa, the King of Israel, who trusted God when the great armies of their enemies came up against them. He went down on his knees before God, and he said,

> LORD, it is nothing with thee to help, whether with many, or with them that have no power: help us, O LORD our God; for we rest on thee, and in thy name we go against this multitude. O LORD, thou art our God; let no man prevail against thee.
>
> — 2 Chronicles 14:11

Their little handful of men conquered the whole mob.

But after awhile, Asa got a disease in his feet and the Word says his disease became exceeding great and in his disease he trusted not the Lord, but the physicians, and Asa died. It is recorded against him as an offense against God that he failed to trust God for the disease in his feet, but instead trusted the physician.[13]

Somebody says, "Well, all right. I will commit myself to the Lord, and then of course, I will not have any more stomachache. I will just be kept, etc." Maybe you will if your faith stands in God strong enough and perhaps you won't if it does not. But there is *one* thing that stands

---

[12] Jeremiah 17:5.

[13] 2 Chronicles 16:12.

— that is your consecration to God. If your faith fails it does not make any difference, you stand consecrated to God just the same. If you do not get answer to prayer, you are consecrated to God just the same, and if God Almighty has got to let the devil thrash you half to death for a week or two months or longer, you take it until the crook is out of your life that the Lord is after and faith has conquered. Then you will learn obedience to God by the things you suffer. That is the only way.

People go around cursing the devil all the time. You go in the ways of the devil, you get crooked in your soul and proud in your heart, and that cuts you off from God and you are left in the hands of the devil. The wisest thing to do with you is just like I did with one of my sons. I said, "Young man, you just take your own way until you bump your head against the wall." When he was hurt almost to death, he was glad to come back to his old dad to be helped out.

We know the Word of God so well, so in our proud hearts we say: "*We* have been baptized in the Holy Ghost," and all that kind of attitude. It is just as offensive to God as it can be, and God has just got to draw back His hands and let you go, like I did my son. And then you will come down with some old disease, and you will lay and fret and fume and cry until you get right with God and open your heart to God, and He will rebuke the devourer, and He will take the thing away. Bless God.

I used to be a member of a church where it was considered just as offensive to take medicine or go to the doctor as it was to go to the devil for health. The Christian who would run to a doctor was on a level with the adulterer or the thief. That is absolutely right. That is according to the Word of God. A whole consecration of your whole being, your body and soul and spirit, is what Jesus demands. It is what Jesus asks, and bless God, that is the only place that is worthwhile.

We go around talking and shouting about the Almighty Christ and what He can do and what He is, etc., and the first time we get a stomachache, away we go to the doctor and get a dose, and the Almighty Christ gets a slap in the face.

Beloved, you listen to me. If there are any people in all the world that ought to be taught of God, who ought to be walking with God, who ought to be consecrated to all the will of God, it is the Christian people, especially those who are baptized in the Holy Ghost. It ought to be absolutely unnecessary for any man at this day to even speak of these things in a public service. We ought to have been so committed from the first day to the Lord Jesus Christ that the committing of ourselves to any man for anything would be highly offensive to our spirits. And if we saw our brother or sister becoming weak and falling into the hands of man, our prayer and love and faith and sympathy ought to get under them as though they were falling into the habit of drinking whiskey again.

It is just as offensive for the Christian to take medicine as for the drunkard to take whiskey. Don't you see, beloved, the great wonderful advantage in the Christian's life of becoming cut clear and free from all dependence on the arm of man? You are cut forever from the world, from the flesh, from the devil. Bless God.

I had a friend in Africa who was greatly distressed because he could not learn to swim. Finally one day he got drunk and walked off the docks into the sea at Cape Town into about five hundred feet of water, and he could swim after that, all right.

Don't you see, beloved, that you will never have faith in God in the world until you launch out into God, until you commit yourself to God and then either live or die? I belong to God and I am done with man, and I am done with leaning on his arm.

I know what these things are. In my home I had seven children. They were born without medicine. One dear brother testified the other night that the Lord had kept disease out of the home. It was not that way in mine. There wasn't a devilish thing came down the road that my family did not get, from pneumonia, small pox, typhoid fever, to a shooting accident, and God let us be tested right up and down the line.

It is one thing to get down on your knees and say I commit my body, my soul, my spirit to God, and it is another thing to stand by your baby until you hear it gasp, and it is another thing to close its eyes in death if necessary, but I am not going back on my Lord. That is the kind of training I got, and that is the cleanness in faith my heart cries out for.

Maybe in another generation we will have a multitude of people who stand in God like giants, and we can have a manifestation of the sons of God and take the world for God and crown the Christ King of kings and Lord of lords.

Now I do not preach to anybody else what I have not been through myself. I tell you the Lord has let me go through the mill. One time I got inflammatory rheumatism and for nine months I suffered. I guess I did. But I shut my teeth and I said, "You devil, you can't put me in bed; I won't go," and I dragged myself home and I would get in bed and feel like crying out in my agony. At the end of nine months God had wrought one thing in my heart, that if I died the devil would not get me to take medicine again. One day I felt in my spirit I needed help. There was nobody there that could pray for me. So I got on a train and went to Chicago to John Alexander Dowie. One day there was a company of people like this, and when I came along it was so packed full I could not even look into the door. After awhile there were some other people who couldn't get in, and finally an old man, an elder, came along and prayed for us out there, and as he did I was healed from the crown of my head to the soles of my feet. Years after he told me that was the only healing he ever had that he knew about.

I often wondered if the virtue came through the old brother or not, but God met my faith. Do you not see, to commit yourself to God means something? I tell you, it is probably going to mean some suffering someday, but that is the way of clearness, the way of truth. That is the way you can look every man in the face and say, "I am not leaning on the arm of flesh; I am going God's way."

We are such a weak, wobbly lot in these latter days. God is just trying to get some backbone in us. We come along and are baptized and about a week after, we can find them doing all sorts of things. The Christians in the old days came down to be baptized, and as they did so a Roman officer took their names and sent them up to Rome. Instantly their citizenship was canceled, their right of protection from Roman government was cut off, their goods were confiscated, they were left as a prey to the avarice of the people, but they got baptized just the same. Bless God.

(left to right) John and Jennie Lake's
two youngest sons with their father.
Wallace Stephens Lake "Ted"
John G. Lake
John G. Lake II

I tell you that is the kind of people that thirty million of them gave their lives to God in the first four centuries and were blotted out of the world in various ways. Thirty million of them! There was some Christian spirit, there was some consecration to God in those days. It was poverty or death or sickness or prison or anything else, but it was God's way of consecration. I tell you God will meet that kind of thing. If they lived, all right, and if they died, all right. They belonged to God, and the world ever since for 1400 years looks back with pride to that list of people who gave themselves to the Lord God. They put the stamp of character on the Christian world. Bless God.

All the heroes, bless God, did not live back there either. You come down to the history of Scotland, to the Convenanters. They wrote a covenant and said, "We will have nae King but Jesus," and you can see the old Scottish man shut his teeth and opening a vein in his arm, signs the covenant. And three hundred thousand of them gave their lives then to make that covenant good and died saying, "We will have nae King, but Jesus."

Now you listen to me. I will guarantee to you that if there are fifty sick people in this room and you commit yourselves to God in that spirit and with that reality, bless God, you won't need anybody to pray for you. You will just get well. Bless God. The devil cannot come around you when that kind of thing is in your soul.

One of my sons was dying with pneumonia once. I prayed for that fellow and I prayed for him, and it was not a bit of good. But one day I was downtown, and I was praying about that boy and the Lord said, "You go home and confess your sins to your wife."

And I said, "I will." I stopped and got one of the old elders to come down to my house. As we rode along we talked together, and I said, "I have some things I want to fix up with my wife before you pray. There has been all kinds of prayer, but He won't hear." So I took my wife in the other room and told her the whole business, all there was, and we went into the other room and prayed for that son and he was healed in a second.

I want to tell you that when Christians are not healed, as a rule you get digging around and get the Holy Ghost to help you, and when they have vomited out all the stuff, they will get the healing.

You listen to me. Healing comes straight down from God. All man is, is a medium through which God can work. God is a Spirit, He needs embodiment. He chooses man as a body. The Church is the body. "Know ye not that ye are the temples of the Holy Ghost?"[14] There is something that gets into your spirit or into your body that is obstructing the free flow of the Spirit of God. Get that thing out, it is between you and God.

I tell you, when you line people up so they will trust God for their bodies as they do for their souls, there will not be one half the backsliding there is now. I was a member of a body of one-hundred-thousand people and I never heard of such a thing as any of them backsliding. They stood for God and they died for God. The character was in them, and they did not know half as much about God as we do by the revelation of the Spirit in these days.

I am twice as anxious this afternoon about this great body of people here, to know whether or not they are going to commit themselves clear in God, than I am about the sick. There may be dozens in this room who are so very sick that they need God. But beloved, listen. Suppose one of them was not healed and the rest were made clear in their consecration to God, you would have a bigger demonstration.

As fast as you get them healed, the Christians without Christ's consecration are down in their faith and becoming sick. After awhile a preacher gets to be a kind of doctor of saints in his little assembly. God does not want it. Get clear; get straight in your consecration to God. Put yourself body and soul and spirit forever in God's hands. Do it today, bless God. Do it today.

How ashamed a Christian ought to be that he is trusting in the arm of flesh or in a medicine bottle somewhere around the house. You go home and gather up the abominable stuff and put it in the alley box and then apologize to the alley box.

You cannot tell me anything about medicine. There never was a bigger humbug practiced on mankind than the practice of medicine. The biggest men in the medical world have declared it over and over again, but the mob do not pay any attention to it.

---

[14] 1 Corinthians 3:16, paraphrased.

Professor Douglas McLaggen, who had the chair of medical jurisprudence, stood up among one thousand students, when asked to lecture on the Science of Medicine, and he said, "I am an honest man, and 'An honest man is the noblest work of God'; from the days of Hypocrates and Galen until man we have been stumbling in the dark, from diagnosis to [illegible]." Sir Ashley Cooper, who was physician to Queen Victoria for twenty-five years, the greatest physician in Great Britain, he said, "The science of medicine is founded upon conjecture and improved by murder." Dr. Magendie of Paris, who has the greatest system of diagnosis in the world, said, "We take up the attention of the patient with our medicine, while nature cuts in and makes a cure." But you cannot tell a third-rate American doctor that.

Yet the Christian world turns their back on the Son of God and goes and puts themselves in the hands of men. No man that ever lived, or ever will live, will ever reduce the subject of medicine to a science. No two doses of medicine will ever produce the same effect in your own person. You can take a dose of medicine today and another tomorrow, and you will have a different effect tomorrow than you had today.

That may be all right for the world. Why the man that is not a Christian has got to have a physician of some kind, but the Christian can't. God cut the privilege off long ago. Bless God. "Is any among you (Christians) sick? Let him call for the elders of the church."[15] That is all the privilege the Word of God gives him. That is the way into God, on the line of divine healing. Bless God.

Bless God, I tell you I am just looking for the day when there will be a great, blessed, true company of men and women in this world who will stand in this through the living God just as clear as crystal, who have cut clear off from the world, the flesh, and the devil. That is the characteristic of the church of Philadelphia all right.

God has let me see healings in every way that human eyes can see them. I have seen them come like the flash of lightning. I have seen the Spirit of God as lightning flash around the room, just like the lightning. God was there in lightning form, and the devils were cast out and the sick healed. I have seen God come as the tender bud

---

[15] James 5:14, paraphrased.

when nobody knew He was there, and people were healed. I have seen people healed in the audiences when cancers would melt away and varicose veins were healed. Nobody prayed for them. They just put themselves in the hands of God. That is all.

There is no man that lives who can define the operations of faith in a man's heart. But there is one thing we are sure of, that when we cut ourselves off from every other help, we never found the Lord Jesus Christ to fail. If there are any failures, it is our failure, not God's. Bless God.

FINIS — THANK GOD.

"**Y**e shall receive power, after that the Holy Ghost is come upon you."[1] We are entitled to it, bless God. We are glad to see some of it and wish, bless God, that we might see a great deal more. And beloved, I have a splendid conviction in my heart that we will.

I want to read some familiar verses, as a basis of thought.

[UNTITLED, BUILDING ON A FIRM FOUNDATION]
Philadelphia, Pennsylvania
March 1, 1914

> When Jesus came into the coasts of Caesarea Philippi, he asked his disciples, saying, Whom do men say that I the Son of man am?
>
> And they said, Some say that thou art John the Baptist: some, Elias; and others, Jeremias, or one of the prophets.
>
> He saith unto them, But whom say ye that I am?
>
> And Simon Peter answered and said, Thou art the Christ, the Son of the living God.
>
> And Jesus answered and said unto him, Blessed art thou, Simon Barjona: for flesh and blood hath not revealed it unto thee, but my Father which is in heaven.
>
> And I say also unto thee, That thou art Peter, and upon this rock I will build my church; and the gates of hell shall not prevail against it.
>
> — Matthew 16:13-18

Those of us who are familiar with this scripture will remember that Peter is very careful to call attention to the fact that Jesus wasn't

---

[1] Acts 1:8.

referring to him as the one upon which the Church was to be built. He speaks in the second chapter of First Peter of how Jesus Christ is the great foundation and is established upon the apostles and prophets, Jesus Christ Himself being the chief cornerstone, etc.

Foundation laying is always a hard process. Over here in the East, with your solid ground, you are not so badly as some cities in the West, Chicago, for example. Chicago is built on a great quicksand bed, which is from seventy to eighty feet deep. After the great Chicago fire, the board of aldermen did a thing that no body of men had ever dared to do till then. They passed an ordinance raising the grade of the city sixteen feet. In sections of the city where the old buildings still stand, you go down a story and a half from the street level to the original street. It was a tremendous undertaking, but it got them everlastingly out of the mud. So sometimes a destructive process is good. The Chicago fire became the great means by which the new and wonderful city came into existence.

I want to talk to you today about foundation building. When I was a young man I was a builder. I looked upon Chicago as the great Mecca of all builders, so I got to Chicago as quick as I could. I looked around among various occupations and I settled on this fact: There were two classes of men always in demand: the man who understood scientific foundation building, and the man who understood scientific roofing. And I said, "I will master these two things."

In those days, they used to build twelve story skyscrapers, sometimes fourteen. Foundation building was not known as it is today. In those days they went to the forests and brought great pilings, seventy, eighty, and ninety feet long. These were driven into the ground until they touched bedrock. At the surface, these were cut off level and railroad iron laid on top. Then they commenced their stone work on top of the railroad iron, and after they got to the street level it would probably be brick.

I lived long enough to see that these great buildings would get out of plumb and it would be necessary for a civil engineer to go over the buildings every three months to see whether they were moving out of plumb one way or another. If they were, great systems of jackscrews were used under the buildings to adjust them. It may surprise some of you to know that some of these great buildings in Chicago would literally stand on a system of jackscrews, which are adjusted every three months by civil engineers. That was too much like hanging a city up in the air, so they said, "We will drive great steel castings down to the rock and we will take out the earth and fill the castings with cement." That system likewise passed away. And now they excavate clear down to the bedrock, four or five stories if necessary. The quicksand and mud is removed. The foundation is laid on the base rock.

For the Church of God and Christian faith to become strong and to be built up in God, it is necessary to get a good foundation. It is a greater problem with most builders to get the old rubbish out of the way than to do the building. If we will look at our own lives, we will observe this: that the things that have been rooted and grounded in our hearts — some tradition of the Fathers, some of it misconception of the meaning of the Word of God; much of our teaching is fragmented — these form the greatest obstacles to the engrafting of the living Word of God. Every one of us who have progressed in God have found that the difficulty was not in believing the Word of God, but the difficulty was to get away from things that were settled in our own being as facts, though untrue. How hardly have we struggled over the matter of, "If it be Thy will," concerning sickness. From our babyhood and all down through the generations, we have been taught that if you are sick, the proper thing to do is to pray, "If it be Thy will," forgetting all the time that the Lord has forever demonstrated and declared His eternal will concerning the subject of sickness by healing all that come to Him.

Well, bless God, some have succeeded in getting over that difficulty and put the subject, "If it be Thy will," behind their back and moved out where they believe the declarations of Jesus Christ. So it was that victory came on that line.

Now dear ones, the thing that the Spirit of God is laying deeply upon my own heart these days is the need of a settled, established state in the Lord Jesus Christ, and the movement of the Spirit worldwide is to bring into unity the children of God who will raise *A Standard of Truth for the World.*

Now listen! This come-together call of the Spirit is not an isolated movement. It don't belong to a little company of people in Philadelphia, nor in any other city. In the last days, months, or the last year, in my correspondence worldwide, I have discovered this quote and the Lord is beginning to move everywhere in this particular line. Only yesterday I received a letter from Los Angeles from one of the prominent leaders. He goes on to outline the processes of development in God through which he has been brought during the last few years and its final result. I had written of what God was doing in our own midst and what God was endeavoring to do in the establishment of the Church, etc. He said, "Brother, your letter is a revelation. We thought that was all confined to ourselves, but I see that this movement, that we supposed was local, is a general movement, and of the Holy Ghost, and it is in your heart just as it has been in ours."

So God is moving in these days on a certain definite line. The man who has a settled, established faith in God has got that faith based on the eternal declarations of the Lord Jesus Christ and is moving in harmony with the revealed plan of God as outlined for this hour in God's Church Plan. The difficulty with most individuals and teachers in times past has been that the revelation of the mind of God, as revealed in the Word, was limited to such a degree that they were compelled to take only a certain few of the great principles of the Gospel, and thus their entire system was based on them. But in these days, as the coming of the Lord approaches and as the added light of the Spirit has been given, God has revealed in a larger way, in a broader manner, the truth. So that in these days it seems to me it is the purpose of God that the Church of the latter day, the Church of Philadelphia (if you like), should be based upon the great broad basis of the eternal truth, as laid down in the New Testament by the Lord Jesus Christ and the apostles, not on any fragmentary principles.

In days past, it was thought necessary to endeavor to bind men's hearts and consciences to certain established truths that the Church was ready to accept. And so these truths were usually embodied in the form of a creed, and they said, "This is all of truth that we accept. This is our faith." So they laid this basis and built a fence around themselves. After awhile, to the amazement of the Church and to her discomfiture, it was discovered that their creeds have been the means that squeezed them in, and instead of being a foundation broad enough for the Word of God, they are strangled inside their unyielding creed and there is no room for expansion. When the dear Lord has wanted to give a revelation of progressive truth, He has been compelled to go outside of the Church fence and raise up a new body. That was because a fence had been built. A certain little enunciation of truth had been collected and the structure established on that instead of on the entire Word of God.

We can see this: The individual who learns truth these days cannot confine it to certain declarations of doctrines. For as the days go by we see the progressive light of God, and if you were to compare your faith now with what you believed ten years ago, you would find there has been a great expansion. Now what is ten years more going to develop? What truths will it be necessary for us ourselves to accept from the Lord in the coming days? Consequently, beloved, there is only one basis upon which the Church of Jesus Christ can rest: That is, upon Jesus Christ and the apostles and the whole body of truth as outlined in the New Testament.

Then, beloved, in that great body of truth there must be the accompanying largeness and Spirit of the Lord Jesus Christ who didn't confine Himself to certain little dogmatic teachings, but He laid the great broad principles upon which the whole great kingdom of heaven rests and upon which a great Christian life can rest eternally.

There never was a teacher like Jesus. He was the one great Mastermind who understood the Spirit of the living God, who understood that all revelation of God was a progressive revelation. And thereby the minds that He must prepare by His own personal teaching were not able to receive all the great body of truth He had to reveal, so He said, "Ye are not able to bear it now."[2] They had to grow up into the place in God where they were able to bear and analyze and utilize the greater truths of the Word of God. Now, beloved, we are in the place, just that place, bless God.

I believe in my heart that God is laying, even in this little company with her one hundred and twenty like the church at Jerusalem, the

---

[2] John 16:12, paraphrased.

foundation of the truth of God that will command the attention of the Christian world.

Yesterday I received an invitation from E. N. Bell, Editor of Word & Witness, Malvern, Arkansas. In April they are having a great convention down there that includes all the Southern states. Among other things he says, "Brother Lake, there are two contending forces; the one which desires a strong organization, the other which don't want any organization, but desires to be a law unto themselves."

As I read the letter I said, "They are both wrong." The man who is an anarchist and is a law unto himself and don't put himself into line with the Word and cooperate with God according to God's plan is just as great a sinner as the other who comes along and wants to organize the Church into a frozen, man-created mass.

Jesus Christ laid down the principles of eternal truth: Every man who accepts the principles, who lives the life, is acceptable to Me.[3] So, beloved, the Church of God these latter days must just return to the blessed basis that the Lord Jesus Christ laid down.

Beloved, the day has long gone past when men's consciences can be bound with certain little doctrines. If we were to take this audience today, of those who are living holy lives, baptized in the Holy Ghost, and note carefully what this brother believes and that brother believes, we would perhaps have twenty different statements before you got through with this little company.

Don't you see, the thing is this: Our hearts are one in the blood of Jesus Christ, our hearts are one in the recognition of a common Spirit of God. Blessed be His name! Every one of us can join hands and hearts on the seven unities demanded and experienced in the Church at Ephesus, "One body, one Spirit, one hope, one Lord, one faith, one baptism, one God and Father of you all, who is above all, through all, and in you all." (See Ephesians 4:4-6.)

So the dear Lord, in these days, is once again moving upon the hearts of men that the body of Jesus Christ shall be brought together in holy oneness, that the power of God may be poured upon her, that the Spirit of the living God may move through her in mighty power and

---

[3] Matthew 5:19, paraphrased.

demonstration, and that through her the last message of this present age may be given to the world — the great kingdom message. Bless God.

It seems to me we are only beginning to understand with what force the kingdom message is going to come and its revolutionary character. A few weeks ago the country was stirred by one man's endeavor to just touch in a small way the first principle of Jesus Christ, that first one, "Blessed are the poor in spirit."[4] I refer to Henry Ford, the manufacturer of the Ford Motor car. He set aside out of his profit, ten million dollars for 1914, to be divided between his twenty-six thousand employees. He established a minimum wage of five dollars per day to be the wage of every man. Then every two weeks, he would receive in a check the proportionate amount of the ten million dollars, in addition to his wages.

We say, "Bless God, that is a good thing." That's a starting point. It indicates that some men are beginning to see the mind of the Lord. It is not by any means a fulfillment [illegible]. Then the selfish man says, "Yes, that will draw to Henry Ford every expert workman in the United States, etc. and his profits thereby will only be increased, not lessened, but it is a start."

Now see, the blessed principles of the Lord Jesus Christ are the principles of unselfishness. That is the one crowning principle that the Lord Jesus Christ wants to lay down in His Church this very day. It makes no difference how it is applied. The Lord Jesus Christ Himself didn't undertake to tell us how to apply that principle. He left it to every man in his own station. But, beloved, the demand upon us is that we live that blessed principle of the Lord Jesus Christ.

My thought is this: Jesus Himself didn't undertake to tell us dogmatically how to apply that principle, but He, on the other hand, laid down the principles and left it to us, His sovereign servants, to apply them just as the Spirit of the Lord illuminated our own hearts and told us to do. That is the great basis upon which the Lord Jesus Christ is founding His Church. It is based on the principles of the Son of God. He don't ask us what we think about this or that petty doctrine, but He lays down the great principles of the kingdom as the essentials:

---

[4] Matthew 5:3.

1. "Blessed are the poor in spirit: for theirs is the kingdom of heaven.

2. "Blessed are they that mourn: for they shall be comforted.

3. "Blessed are the meek: for they shall inherit the earth.

4. "Blessed are they which do hunger and thirst after righteousness: for they shall be filled.

5. "Blessed are the merciful: for they shall obtain mercy.

6. "Blessed are the pure in heart: for they shall see God.

7. "Blessed are the peacemakers: for they shall be called the children of God.

8. "Blessed are they which are persecuted for righteousness' sake: for theirs is the kingdom of heaven."[5]

Beloved, these are the things that God calls us back to today: to the original basis, to the foundation — Jesus Christ Himself the chief cornerstone. We see these blessed principles exemplified all through the New Testament by the apostles themselves, who as the fathers of the Church, were desirous that they should not even become a burden on the Church and endeavored to keep themselves from being a burden. And with their own hands in some instances labored that they might have the privilege of living and preaching the blessed Gospel of the Lord Jesus Christ.

Don't you see, beloved, that every departure from the principles that the Lord Jesus has laid down has weakened the great fabric? Out of that condition has grown our divisions. All our departure from the principles of the Lord has robbed us of that vital faith that was necessary to get answers from God, even for our daily bread. A return to the principles of the Lord Jesus Christ, to the practical life of the Son of God, will bring again upon our souls the blessing of God.

Beloved, that's the entrance into power. That's the final manner of testing the spirit. The spirit must ever be tested by the Word of God, by the principles of Jesus Christ; the law that He laid down by the commandments of Jesus. If the spirit in you won't measure up with the principles that the Lord Jesus Christ laid down, be sure that it is

---

[5] Matthew 5:3-10.

not the Spirit of the Lord Jesus Christ. If the spirit in you exalts itself, etc., just settle it. There is a spirit there that isn't like the Spirit of the Lord Jesus. The way we can see what His Spirit was like is from the principles He laid down and the life He lived.

I feel it this day that the Lord is going to pour a rich and wonderful blessing upon the saints when we come down and return to the blessed principles of the Gospel of Jesus.

If I were to advise you to do anything particular during the coming weeks it would be this: Take the fifth, sixth, and seventh of Matthew and read them and reread them on your knees, until the principles of Jesus Christ enter into your heart. Then, bless God, there will be a good basis laid in your soul for the everlasting blessing of God.

It is as impossible to get the eternal working power of God to appear in a man's life, or the life of the Church, until first the clearing away is done and the rubbish of petty doctrine and littleness is taken out of the way, as it would be to build a Chicago skyscraper without first taking out all the quicksand and mass of rotten stuff. It has got to come out. It has got to be cleared away. When the life goes down on the eternal Rock, Jesus Christ, then the structure will come up and will stand in the power of God.

So this morning I pray God that He will help us this day to take these blessed words of God, the declarations of Jesus Himself as He has outlined them in the fifth, sixth, and seventh of Matthew especially, and get these real basic things settled in our soul.

I have received during the week applications from several persons who want to come up here and receive membership into this body, who desire to receive the right hand of fellowship. You can't keep it from growing, from developing. But O, beloved, is it going to develop in God or is it going to be like every institution has been or is it going to be placed on eternal foundations? And is our life going down into the bottom, to the bedrock, to the foundation stone of Christ Jesus?

Let us pray.

O God, our Father, let our lives be once and forever and for all settled on the eternal Rock, Christ Jesus, Lord God, where our lives shall stand. Blessed be Thy name! And where the Church of Jesus Christ shall stand, Lord God, and the gates of hell shall not prevail against her. Blessed be Thy name! O God, let that deep, true, holy, unselfish working of the Holy Ghost in our lives be so pure and true and real that, my God, there shall not be left a superficial thing in us, Lord, but that our character shall be opened wide, opened to the living God, and wide open to one another. O God, reflecting, showing forth the real life of Jesus Christ. O God, we bless Thee for this day. Lord God, there is an echo of gladness in our soul. There is a shout of praise in our hearts. Lord God, the day has come. Thine appointed hour has come when Thou hast really begun to call together into one body the body members of Jesus Christ whose names are written in heaven. Lord God, we worship at Thy feet, and Lord, we declare our faith in Thee, the Son of God, this very day. Thou art going to bring forth Thy people, Lord God, the Church of Jesus Christ, bless God! Who shall give forth to the world the message of the kingdom. Bless God! Who shall raise up a banner of truth and demonstrate a righteousness that men of God will not have to be ashamed of.

O God, we pray Thee then, that the great virtue of Jesus Christ shall be so inwrought in us that, my God and Father, we shall look with love into the face of every other man. That, O God, our Father, we will have the eyes of Jesus in us and the heart of Jesus in us in such a way that we will not see things that are evil, but O God, we will see the good in the man. We will see the purity, Lord, we will think of the things that are lovely, Lord, and are true, Lord. We will be so pure and clean before God that the light of God and the life of God shall shine in us and flow through us so that mankind will be blessed.

O God, our Father, we rejoice in this day. We rejoice in this hour. Thou art the Son of God, Lord Jesus. We are so glad You have let us live at this time of life. My God, we rejoice in the expectation of Thy soon coming. Bless God! But O Jesus, blessed Jesus, get us ready, get us ready. Lord God, get us ready to give the message that is going to stir the world. Get us ready, Lord, to receive the power of God that is going to demonstrate Christ to mankind, for Jesus' sake.

O God, we pray that upon this Pentecostal Movement worldwide and upon the Church of Christ at large, by whatever name it is known and upon the hidden ones who are known by no name, the power of God shall come. Lord God, once again let the pulsating movement of the

Holy Ghost be felt through the body of Christ. Lord Jesus, draw Thy children together, Lord. Lord Jesus, establish them on the rock. Lord God, build up the body, we pray Thee, Lord. And bless God, we pray that upon our own souls these days there shall be such a passion of the Christ-heart that we will seek the lost, that we will seek the sick, that, my God, religious life, religious service shall forever cease to be a matter of religious entertainment. But O God, make it what Your heart desires, religious service, serving our fellowmen. O God, shedding Your tears with the afflicted, putting Your hands under the weary, lifting them up to God, praying for the stricken ones.

O Christ, let the pure heart and Spirit of Christ throb in every breast for Jesus' sake, that the will of God may come, that the prayer of Jesus Christ may be answered, that we may all be one. Lord God, that Thy kingdom may come and Thy will be done in earth as it is in heaven, Lord, for Jesus' sake. Amen.

hat blessed old simple story is burning in my spirit. Read John 1:6-13.

[UNTITLED, THE HOLY GHOST MADE MANIFEST]
Findlay, Ohio
April 26, 1914

There was a man sent from God, whose name was John. The same came for a witness, to bear witness of the Light, that all men through him might believe. He was not that Light, but was sent to bear witness of that Light. That was the true Light, which lighteth every man that cometh into the world. He was in the world, and the world was made by him, and the world knew him not. He came unto his own, and his own received him not. But as many as received him, to them gave he power to become the sons of God, even to them that believe on his name: Which were born, not of blood, nor of the will of the flesh, nor of the will of man, but of God.

I feel somehow this morning that as a representative body of men and women whose business it is in life to proclaim and exemplify the Gospel of Jesus Christ, the presentation of the Son of God as the Savior of the world is the greatest thing we have before us.

God is looking upon us and expecting us to give that satisfactory demonstration of the Christ-life to other men so that the world may desire Jesus as the Son of God, and that men may look forward and long for the day when the Christ shall come and when He will establish the kingdom of Jesus Christ in the earth. And anything else than this does not seem to me to be worthy of those who have had the special privilege of living in these times when the Spirit is being poured out upon all flesh.

(Tongues and Interpretation)

The days of our childhood in the things of God have gone by and the days of maturity in knowledge of God have now dawned upon us.

And God is demanding from you and me a demonstration of the power of God, the love of God, and the character of Christ that is worthy of the day, the hour, the message, and the time in which we live. This special time when the Spirit of God is being poured upon mankind in preparation for the hour when Jesus shall return and call the saints of God to His own glory, that we may receive from Him during that period of exceptional privilege the instruction, development, capacity, and endument that those receive who are to come again with Him into the establishment of His kingdom and take part and place with our Lord Jesus Christ in the government of this old world — in love, righteousness, purity, holiness, truth, and verity throughout the kingdom age.

Our God, this morning, calls your heart and mine from an ordinary understanding and consciousness of the Gospel of Jesus Christ to a Holy Ghost-quickening consciousness, to that especially illuminated, blessedly glorified, spiritual understanding of the Word of God and the mind of God, that we may be peculiar men and peculiar women, living a peculiar life. Peculiar in love, peculiar in holiness, peculiar in reverence for the living God, knowing the secrets of divine power and government.

And to Thee, O God our Father, we lift our hearts and ask that Thou wilt help us, that we may be worthy of the high calling that God our Father hath bestowed upon us, through the mercy and sacrifice of Jesus Christ. That we may live, O God our Father, according to Thy mind and according to Thy heart, according to Thy way and according to Thy will *in God, in God.*

(Tongues and Interpretation)

Shall it not then be that the voices of all men, and especially the voices of those who realize conscious salvation through the precious blood of Jesus Christ, ring forth in this world God's new message in the peculiar Spirit and power of God, manifesting Christ in man in these days. Giving the message of God, the Savior of mankind, as the Redeemer and Sanctifier of man, as He who doth joy and dwell in the holiness of His children. And [He] cannot look with any degree of toleration upon sin and selfishness, but looks with the eye of pity, sacrifice, and holiness upon man, discovering in the very depth of our nature that which is unlike the living, precious holiness of God. And desires that our nature shall be changed, our hearts shall be lifted up to Him in the joy and praise and gladness of those who know and understand and realize the sanctity of being permitted to be children of God, washed in His precious blood, crowned with His Spirit, looking for His glory.

(Tongues and Interpretation)

So our blessed Lord, this morning, asks those who are discouraged, who are weary, who have lived in the ordinary routine of life, that our hearts shall be lifted up to Him. And that we shall realize that He desires in a peculiar way to stamp it upon our hearts that the Son of God, Jesus Christ our Savior and Redeemer, lay as a dead man in the grave. But that the power of God was sufficient to come and raise Him up out of senselessness into life and quicken Him, strengthen Him, and lift Him up into the place of triumph. Yea, He ascended into the heavenlies and sat down in triumph at the right hand of God.

Let, therefore, our hearts faint not, but with a new hope and a new determination yield ourselves to God that we too may be lifted up indeed, out of the insecurity of the present hour and moment into the life triumphant and heavenly and holy. For our dwelling place is not on earth, but our dwelling is in the heavens.

(Tongues and Interpretation)

For the peculiar work of the Holy Spirit in this present hour is according to our present need. Yea, even that our consciousness may be so quickened and our understanding of God and His ways so enlightened, that our hearts may take on a new hope and our lives ascend into heavenly places in Christ Jesus where all things are beneath our feet and where the powers of earth and the things of life no longer drag us down, but where in the power of the Holy Spirit we move and walk as triumphant men and triumphant women, conquerors of disease, sin, death, and the powers of darkness that drag us down day by day.

The Lord wants us to pray.

(Prayer by Congregation.) [Handwritten note says: Tongues and Interpretation. Wonderful spirit of prayer and intercession through Brother Leonard.]

The Spirit of the Lord, as we prayed, told my soul that the peculiar sin of the present hour among the children of God is a peculiar spiritual lethargy that has been permitted to gradually steal over our souls, robbing us of the quickened consciousness and understanding of the blessed Holy Ghost and of His peculiar presence. That instead of lifting up our hearts and welcoming Him, we have descended into a study of the understanding of His ways and works and methods until a dimness has come over our spirits.

And God wants once again to take us out of the natural things, the exercise of our natural mind and our natural spirit, into the Holy Ghost, into the ascended life, into the life in heavenly places in Christ Jesus where the Spirit of God in enduement and power rests upon our souls. And returning filled with His presence and glory, we may bring into this world the quickened consciousness of the Lord Jesus Christ that the transforming power of the Spirit may be so freely realized that mankind may see and know it is the day of His preparation. That our whole life and being may be so yielded up to the living God that every heart shall be a vessel through which the Spirit of God shall flow to the blessing of the lost world.

That the spirit of criticism of one another, and of all men, shall cease within the Christian heart and the enlightened conscience. That everyone shall realize that he or she has the possession of the degree and measure of the Holy Ghost that God, in His love, has been able to bestow upon the individual in their present state of development. And instead of placing ourselves above another and looking with scorn even upon the sinner, that we shall see even as Jesus sees men and understand others even as the heart of Christ understands. That in love and mercy and sympathy and compassion we shall reach out our arms and embrace our fellows and lead them to the Lamb of God that taketh away the sin of the world.

(Tongues and Interpretation)

When the Christian consciousness and the Christian understanding be illuminated by the presence of the loving God in the measure that God doth desire to give us, the world shall give forth an exaltation of the Lord Jesus Christ so pure and holy and true and blessed that all men shall see and know that there is a living God. And the real Christ and living Savior manifest through the Church, the body of Jesus in the world, through whom the manifestation of the living Christ is being given to all men to the glory of God.

So our blessed God, we lift our hearts up this morning and ask Thee our blessed God that You will take out of our spirit every wretched little bit of hidden selfishness that is hidden within us.

O God, apply the precious blood of Jesus Christ that we may be so purified and so illuminated by the Holy Ghost and the glory of God, that we shall give forth that real reflection of the Lord Jesus Christ in the Holy Ghost, for Jesus' sake.

Lord God, we ask Thee this morning, as we lift our hands to heaven and as we submit our souls to Thee, as we confess our littleness and our meanness and our self-righteousness, that the blessed Christ shall establish within us the Holy Spirit, who Himself shall manifest the truth of the Spirit. For Jesus' sake. For Jesus' sake.

And our God we pray Thee that Thou wilt lift up each one into the presence of God, and that Thou wilt put upon us such a conscious-ness of God, of His love, of His purity, of His holiness, of His power, that, O God, our Christ, our praise to Thee and our worship of God shall be in the beauty of holiness. O God, that we shall worship Thee in spirit and in truth for Jesus' sake. O we ask, our God, that every hidden thing, everything that would not bear the glory-light of God, shall be driven from our nature. That, O God, our Christ, once again we can stand before Jesus even as Nathaniel, an Israelite indeed in whom is no guile.

O God, we ask Thee then that You will sweep from our soul and wash from our nature and cleanse from our heart every unholy thing, every deceitful thing, Lord Jesus, this devilish spiritual pride that is so subtle. O God, sweep them away. Let us stand, O God our Christ, guileless before our God for Jesus' sake.

Blessed be Thy name, O God. We worship Thee and lift our hands and our hearts to heaven and we say this morning, blessed be Thy name. Holy, Holy, Holy is the Lord. Blessed be His name!

Our God, to Thee this morning we offer our praise and worship and adoration and glory and praise and honor unto Thy name forever and ever and ever. Blessed be Thy name. Amen.

(Tongues and Interpretation)

Our God, we pray this morning that the blessing and power of God shall so rest upon us, a yieldedness to the living God and to all the works of the Holy Spirit within us shall be so manifest, our God, that those will be able to lift us up. So that we will be permitted to enter into the exaltation of the Lord Jesus Christ, who has become the Ruler of this universe, King of kings and Lord of lords, with angels and archangels, rejoicing before God because of the triumph of the Son of God, through the spilling of His precious blood for all men and all mankind's acceptance of Him, for Jesus' sake. Amen.

(Song: "Fade, fade, each earthly joy, Jesus is mine.")

esterday I knew what I was to preach about — at least I thought I did — and I was so sure about it that I gave the secretary the subject I was going to preach on, but tonight I do not know. It is all gone.

Somehow or other I feel like telling you of an incident by which God taught me the greatest lesson of obedience to the Spirit that I believe has ever come in my lifetime.

[UNTITLED, THE TRIUNE GOD]
Spokane, Washington
September 27, 1914

I had an adopted daughter. This girl I met at a boarding house when she was about twelve or thirteen years old. Etc. [The story wasn't typed in the original transcript.]

If I were in my own congregation in South Africa, I would expect to see a descent of the Spirit upon the people and appearance of the glory of God, manifest in different ways as the Spirit manifests Himself, as I have many times witnessed.

As the days have gone by since I have ministered at this church, every day has brought an increasing consciousness that God has a great and wondrous purpose that He is endeavoring to work out through this congregation.

One of the things of which my spirit is impressed, is that our consciousness of Christ is not as vivid as it ought to be, and as God desires that it should be.

God's method for man of conceiving Himself was through the manifestation of Himself in Jesus Christ. And the individual who wants to understand the character of God has only to turn his face and heart toward the Lord Jesus Christ, observe His ways, listen to His words, and realize His Spirit to know the heart of God.

Indeed, beloved, I have felt, and I feel today, that the world has never had a proper comprehension of the Lord Jesus Christ. We all realize the common conception of the Christ as it has been presented to us by the Orthodox Church at large. And I want to say with all frankness that while in a large measure that conception of the Church largely is true, yet it is ten thousand miles below the real standard or God's conception of presentation of the Christ as I see it in the Word of God as the Spirit of God has made my own consciousness aware of.

On the other hand, I feel that liberal Christianity hasn't given the Christ His due place, and I believe that God wants to establish a clearness of conscience concerning the Christ in the hearts of men. And this which I desire to say (and I believe not of myself, but by the Spirit of God) is that Jesus Christ was much more than a man. He was the Christ of God, the eternal Spirit.

Somebody says now, "Define the distinction between God and Christ." One of the difficulties that always presents itself to one's heart, and it did to mine from a very early time, was this: It seemed to me Christianity had confused God, and instead of *one* God it had established three Gods. And while in a sense that is true (in the real sense it is true), in the sense it has been presented to the world, mankind has stood facing the fact that there were three Gods. The creed said that they were one, but it has always seemed to be confused in men's hearts how such a thing was possible.

I wish I could refer to other people's experiences rather than my own, but when a man breaks out on a new track he has no guide but his own heart and his own experiences. So I am compelled in teaching some of these things to refer to personal experiences.

One experience I want to speak of because I believe it will give the key that will help many minds to become clear on one of the distinctions, at least, between God the Father and the Son, Jesus Christ, and their union as one.

I have told you in this congregation on another occasion of how a friend of mine arose one Sunday morning in our tabernacle and presented a request for prayer with many tears saying, "I have been a member of this congregation for four years. I have witnessed God heal all kinds of people — the lame, the halt, blind, deaf, dumb, insane, etc. And this morning I am convicted of God that I have never even presented a request for prayer for a cousin of mine, who is in an insane asylum in Wales."

Something about the man's spirit touched my own heart. The Spirit of God was deeply present. I invited the congregation to join in prayer as I knelt on the platform to pray. As my heart went out to God in prayer, something transpired within and to me that I can only describe like this: Presently, my sight and consciousness were awakened to the fact that from this one and that one, from perhaps a hundred divergent streams, faith and power was coming to my spirit and concentrating in me as shafts of light. Indeed, it was the spirit of faith being imparted to my spirit from the hearts of those who knelt throughout the house. An unusual consciousness of God's power and presence swept over me and presently this seemed to take place, and I believe it did take place.

In my consciousness I observed that I was no longer in that tabernacle. The first place I became aware of was passing the city of Kimberly. Then I became conscious that I was at Cape Town, South Africa, one thousand miles from Johannesburg. Presently, I remember of the Cape Verde Lighthouse on the coast of Spain, and I remember distinctly of passing the shores of France. I entered the hills of Wales (I had never been in Wales), but as I went over those hills presently I came to a little village and outstanding was a building that I recognized as the asylum.

I went into that place, walked straight into the room where a woman was strapped to the sides of a cot, and as consciously as I stand here now I put my hands on the woman's head and in the name of the Lord Jesus Christ rebuked the insane spirit that possessed her and cast it out.

Her face became calm, and she smiled up into my face. I recognized in the look of her eyes the awakened consciousness.

All the time I had been kneeling on the platform at Johannesburg, and my heart and my voice had been expressing my desire to God.

You ask me what it was, how do I explain it? And I try to in this way. Perhaps I am right. If so, perhaps it will help us in the question that is before our hearts now.

Throughout the Word of God we read many times this expression, "The Spirit of the Lord caught away Elijah, the Spirit of the Lord caught away Elisha, the Spirit of the Lord caught away Jeremiah," or

Amos or one of the other prophets.[1] Now that doesn't mean that their physical body was transported to another place in all instances, though in some I believe it does. But it does mean that the inner man, the conscious spirit man, was transported for the time being to another place and he saw and performed acts there.

As quickly as a letter could come from Wales, my friend received a letter saying, "A strange thing has happened. Our cousin who has been in the asylum was suddenly and instantly healed on last Lord's day, and she is well."

Beloved, I was there. I could tell you to this hour of the old-fashioned brass that was on the door and the pattern of that old Welsh knocker on the door. There was not a detail of the room that I didn't see, and there was not a detail of the trip from Africa to Wales that I was not as conscious of as I was at a later time when I came via that route on purpose, to prove whether or not it were a fact.

Now beloved, I am going on. "In the beginning was the Word." Capital W-o-r-d.

> And the Word was with God, and the Word was God. The same was in the beginning with God. All things were made by him; and without him was not any thing made that was made. In him was *life;* and the life was the light of men.[2]

And that is the thing that distinguishes Jesus Christ from all other reformers. Varied philosophies have been presented by various minds, but the Christ imparted *life.* "In Him was *life.*" And the individual today who enters into Christ, and whose heart and soul has touched the realm of God-consciousness that God desires we should touch, received from God through that open and quickened consciousness, a ministry of *life* — not a ministry of words, not a ministry of inspiration, but a ministry of *life.* "In Him was *life,* and the *life* was the light of men."

"The light shineth in darkness; and the darkness comprehended it not."[3] If for five minutes God's spiritual illumination could come over

---

[1] See Acts 8:39.

[2] John 1:1-4.

[3] John 1:5.

our souls and our consciousness be awakened and the things of God as they are and our own relationship to our God be realized, there isn't a man or woman in this house that would not fall prostrate on their face before God.

"The light shineth in darkness." It shone then, and it is shining just as brilliantly now.

> The darkness comprehended it not. There was a man sent from God, whose name was John. The same came for a witness, to bear witness of the Light...He was not that Light, but was sent to bear witness of that Light.[4]

Now I will return. Man is the image of God. He was made in His own image. Every function of spirit and soul that we observe within our own souls is but the counterpart of the functions of God.

But someone says, "God has no body. He is Spirit." No, He hasn't a material body, but there is a heavenly materiality as well as an earthly. Spirit itself has a heavenly, or definite, materiality. We cannot define it in the terms of material as we understand it in this world, but consciousness causes us to realize that all things, whether angels or God Himself, have a form of some character of heavenly material.

In my own mind I have tried sometimes to think of what could be the substance of which the person of angels is composed, and my mind has settled on three things as a possibility: Light and fire and spirit.

But be that as it may, the Word declares to us that Christ was "with the Father in the beginning," and that through Him or by Him all things were made that are made, and that "in Him was *life.*"

And this is my thought, be it right or wrong. I give it to you for what it is worth. The individual who knows everything usually knows nothing, and the man who is sure he knows everything is usually an ignoramus.

My person and being was in the attitude of prayer on the platform at Johannesburg, but I was conscious. And the woman was conscious that out from my being something went that carried my consciousness with it, and I consciously performed acts and witnessed scenes

---

[4] John 1:5-8.

that in the natural were impossible. What was it that was transported or projected, for the time being, from my person, but the spiritual entity, the real me, self, or ego in such a degree that it was able to bring back to me all the consciousness that it possessed.

My thought of the Christ is exactly that thing. All through the Word of God we see this. The visible manifestation of God as He appeared to man at different times was in the form of the Christ. I say, "as He appeared to men at various times," for the Word records many appearances of the Christ in the world. Once, He appeared to Abraham as he sat under the tree and conversed with him, ate supper with him as a man in the flesh.[5] The Christ for the time being embodied in flesh. (See Micah 5:2.)

Over and over again throughout the Bible we read of *the* Angel of the Lord, not *an* angel of the Lord, but the spiritual entity of God, the spiritual presence of God, "The Angel of the Lord."

It would be just as proper to speak of the angel of Brother Fogwell, the angel of Brother Mills, the angel of Brother Grier, or anyone else. The spiritual presence that had power to make itself recognized was present. So the Angel of the Lord was the visible, projecting entity of the Spirit of the Lord made visible to the individual.

And my convictions are that the Christ of God, who dwelt in the bosom of the Father from the eternal ages and who has been presented to us usually as one who came to earth to mollify the anger of God against man (this was not finished). And the thought has usually been that the Christ is moving the heart of the Father toward mankind. Why, bless your loving hearts! The Father's heart did not need any moving toward the heart of man. For Jesus Christ, instead of *moving* the heart of the Father was the *movement* of God in behalf of mankind. "He gave his only begotten Son."[6] And the Christ who moved out of God and was present with mankind, in my conviction before God, was the spiritual entity of God Himself.

Then you say, "How can you then explain the Spirit, the Holy Spirit, as separate from the Christ?" And I reply that from your person and

---

[5] Genesis 18.

[6] John 3:16.

mine at this present moment there is a continual radiation of the Spirit of God going on. We feel the conscious presence of the Spirit. We realize the influence of the Spirit. We are conscious of that Spirit passing from our person, not in the form of an entity that carries our consciousness with it or any part of our consciousness, but the simple radiation from within going out.

So God, by the Holy Spirit, is universally present in all the world everywhere.

A way back when the Catholic church divided into the Eastern and Western branches of the church, they separated over this issue: Whether the Holy Spirit proceeded from the Father or whether He proceeded from the Father and the Son. It has just been such foolish questions as that that have interested ecclesiastic minds from times immemorial.

Beloved, no truer word was ever spoken in the world than the pastor of this church spoke this morning, when he said in substance, "The individual who knows himself, knows God." For every function of your being is the counterpart of God and beyond question in a degree that our consciousness has never realized. We are the image of God in truth.

So God the Father, God the Son, and God the Holy Spirit are one God, bless God, just as my person, the entity that proceeds from me, and the influence that radiates from my being is one man — spirit and soul and body. Bless God.

A further word — each one is conscious of our own personality to this extent: At least in our material consciousness, our earth consciousness, we are aware of our environments and the things that take place about us. And through the sensory organs we are brought into harmony with the world about us. All our life and being is on that plane to a great extent, without realizing as we should that the spiritual man and the real man — the God-man, the indestructible, eternal man, the God in us — has a being, a consciousness, and spiritual sensory organs just the same as our material man has.

The soul is the consciousness, the ego, by which either that which takes place in the natural or that which takes place in the spiritual is brought to us and understood by us.

What then can be the greatest awakening that can come to the human heart? Is it not when the clouds are driven back and the soul becomes aware that he is linked to God, that he is a part of God, that he came out of God? How different our lives would be if our spiritual nature was developed on the material so that the things of the Spirit were coming to us as they should, with just as much ease as the things of the natural come to us.

When our fellowship should and could be with the angels of God, with the spirits of just men made perfect, with the things of heaven, what a world this would be! People talk about the heaven they are going to, but I want to tell you that heaven is right here when the consciousness is awakened to comprehend and understand and realize what our environment in the Spirit is.

One day in a time of darkness and distress, as men speak of distress, a time of great strain, but a time that I look back to as the most marvelous of all my life, when for weeks and months I walked in the consciousness of the presence of God, so that when I would lie down and relax my spirit instantly would raise into the realms of God.

One day I was walking through the veldt[7] with my eldest daughter and another young lady, when an awe of the presence of God overshadowed me, and I realized God wanted to manifest Himself to me. So I hurried on to the house and went quickly upstairs and threw myself on the bed, giving myself up to my spiritual reverie. In a moment, in the twinkle of an eye, the heavens seemed to open before me, and there was a choir of angels who sang the most soul-ravishing song that my soul ever listened to. And whether you believe it or not, I declare before God that among that chorus of angels there was one voice that I had known and loved on earth. Those soprano notes were unmistakable. I had heard them on earth, but that voice had a new radius. Heaven is not far away.

Paul said concerning his own personal experience,

> There was a man I knew fourteen years ago. Whether in the body or out of the body I know not. Such an one caught up into the third heaven, and heard things unutterable.[8]

---

[7] veldt: the open country bearing few bushes or shrubs, esp. in S. Africa. *Webster's Desk Dictionary of the English Language* (NY: Gramercy Books, 1983), p. 994.

⁸ 2 Corinthians 12:1-4, paraphrased.

God is not far away. God is right here. Angels are not far away, only our eyes need to be opened to see them.

The incident I am about to relate I have on the testimony of three men whose testimony would be received anywhere on earth on any matter of general knowledge.

A little meeting was going on in a little native tabernacle in South Africa. I was not there, but three other white men were present. One of them was Brother [name was crossed out] from Los Angeles, California. Another gentleman was a businessman from Johannesburg, Mr. [name was crossed out], a Christian gentleman. But the third was a man whose name is Harry [last name was crossed out], a hard-headed businessman, as keen as a razor, a man not given to spiritual life at all as we understand it, but a man who was seeking God. His heart was hungry.

Some hundreds of native children were in prayer. (And if you ever saw a company of native children in prayer you would understand what real prayer is, bless God.) As these children prayed, they said a company of white angel children commenced to file into the church. And they stood in a line all around the wall as they sang: "Suffer the little children and forbid them not, to come unto Me, for of such is the kingdom of heaven." When they had finished the song, they filed out again and one brother said: "I went to the door and stood and looked until they vanished." They seemed to vanish at a distance of one hundred and fifty feet from the church.

You tell me that the kingdom of heaven is a long piece off? Not so. It is right here. It is here tonight. The Spirit of God is as consciously present here in this room tonight as it was on the Day of Pentecost. God is as desirous to pour out His Spirit upon this congregation as He was upon the hundred and twenty of Jerusalem.

I say from the bottom of my heart that I have a conviction that Almighty God wants to pour His Spirit upon this congregation and give this old world a new demonstration of the love and power of God.

We turn our eyes with gladness to the Christ who lived two thousand years ago, but we turn our faces with rejoicing to the Christ that we see living in men's lives today. Right now God's purpose is that the

Christ shall be manifested through every man and every woman, bless God, and that we will realize that in God, in Christ, our union with Him as our elder brother is a fact. Bless God. That He was one manifestation of God to the world, and we are another manifestation of God to the world. Bless God.

INTERPRETATION OF TONGUES

Let the Word of God enter into your hearts with all fullness. Do not be deceived, for God is not only in heaven above, but He is in the earth beneath. The Spirit of God is permeating every body, every spirit, every soul of man that will admit Him.

Let the Word of God enter into your hearts at this time that He may get the glory and the praise therefor. Let the Word of God down in your hearts and your minds.

Be not constrained by the evil spirit to turn away from that just God, but be constrained to enter into the fullness of God. Do not be afraid of the manifestation of the Spirit, whether they be in humility or whether it be for raising up.

FINIS

O God, in this hour we lift our hearts to Thee. We are little children and we desire to know God. Not many of us want to pay the price. But our Lord we feel tonight that there is a new desire in all our hearts and a new yearning that God should have all our life, and that mankind should have all of God in us. Amen.

> Sermon by John G. Lake
> Church of the Truth
> Sunday, 7:30 p.m.
> September 27th, 1914
> Spokane, Washington

THE REAL CHRISTIAN

Church of the Truth Spokane, Washington

October 11, 1914

hen I first commenced to preach the Gospel, at least after I got to the point where I gave up everything else and gave my life exclusively to the Gospel, a number of my friends from the city of Chicago were in the habit of coming out to hear me preach, brokers from the Board of Trade and other business friends who were in my circle. It was sort of a curiosity. One day at the club one inquired from a friend, "Have you heard Lake preach yet?"

He said, "Yes, last night."

And the other said, "How was it?"

"Well," he replied, "it was wonderfully apostolic. He took a text and went everywhere preaching the Word."

When the secretary inquired what the subject of my sermon would be yesterday, I told her it was "The Real Christian." I trust the Lord will let me keep in reasonable touch with the subject. However, I would rather the Lord would have His way than mine.

A Christian is unique. He stands alone. He supersedes all who have gone before. He will not have a successor. He is man at his best and God's best effort for mankind.

When the conception of a Christian has been established within our spirits as the New Testament establishes the ideal Christian, we will understand then how it is that men have been ready to abandon all else in the world in order to attain Christ, in order to attain His character, in order to become the possessor of His Spirit.

I went to South Africa in a most unique time in the nation's history, just after the reconstruction period after the Boer War. On account of the great war the native populace had been frightened practically out of the country. They had gone far back from the war zone, and the war zone covered practically the whole country.

The great mines were depending on the natives for labor, and it became a great issue how it was possible to carry on the work while this condition of fear rested upon the natives. Finally, it was proposed that they should bring one hundred thousand men from China. They were brought on a contract for three years. The British government sent a fleet over there and brought them all out at one time. They were a real living colony. They brought their teachers, preachers, priests, and prophets. Chinese are largely Confucians and Buddhists.

At the same period the East Indian people who live in South Africa (and there are many of them; I think in the Transvaal alone there are two hundred and fifty thousand of them), felt that they were not receiving the attention from the government in the way of education that they ought to, so the British government sent teachers, both religious and secular, to supply them there.

So the Buddha, the Yogi, and many others came there and made their headquarters at Johannesburg. Our ministry was somewhat unique. We were the only ones who held [meetings] and preached on the subject of healing.

After a little time it dawned on me that here was a possibility that had never come into my life before. If I could get these various priests and teachers of the various Eastern religions to come together, we might have an exchange of thought. We would have something accomplished. It would at least give me an opportunity to discuss [illegible]. I was familiar to some extent with the Eastern religions, but I never had any touch with the soul life.

So after some time the matter was arranged. At the same time, we added to our company a Rabbi from Chicago, Dr. Hearst. We had a combination, I presume, representing all the great religions on earth. We were able by wise exchange and guidance and much prayer to finally bring about such a condition of fellowship among these various ones that they spoke out their hearts to each other with a great deal of freedom. Many times we sat from sundown to sunup comparing notes and going over the various teachings, etc.

It had this effect on me, that I left that series with this conclusion: There is lots of light in the world, and men are groping after the light. Some possess it in a larger degree than others, but all possess it in some degree. I said to a man as I walked home on the last morning, "One thing surely has been demonstrated, and that is that in Jesus Christ there is a divine life of which, when a man becomes a real possessor, he has a richer appreciation of his power that no other man possesses." And I have been more of a Christian, of a real Christian, from that day than I ever was before.

I am convinced tonight that there is a profound secret in the life and character, teaching and virtue of Jesus Christ that when a man attains it he is rich indeed beyond measure.

In order to have you appreciate some of the things that I trust the Lord will let me say, I want to relate some incidents. It seems as if I can teach things through incidents that I am not able to teach in any other way.

Among my young friends in South Africa were two young men whom I have regarded as the brightest men I have ever known. One was a Boer. His name was Von Shield, the son of an old-line stock of highly educated Hollanders. The other's name was Kritzmall. He had come from a generation of Church of England preachers. I think his great-grandfather had occupied St. Paul Church in London. I believe he had been baptized there himself.

He has always stood out in my mind as a sort of counterpart of St. Paul, for if I can comprehend the character of Paul, I think he was more largely duplicated in that man than any other I ever knew.

These two men were really the only up-to-date "new thought" men I met in Africa. Von Shield was agent for Christian D. Larson and handled his books in South Africa. He began to attend our meetings and, one day when I was not present, came forward out of the audience and knelt at the altar and sought God for the conscious knowledge of his salvation. And bless God, he received it.

Some days after that when I was present, I was teaching at the afternoon service on the subject of the baptism of the Spirit. And raising up in his seat he said to me, "Lake, do you suppose that if God gave me the baptism of the Holy Spirit it would satisfy the burning yearning that is in my soul for God?"

I said, "My son, I don't know that it would, but I think you would be a long piece on the way."

So without more ado he came forward and knelt, and looking up he said to me, "Lay your hands on my head and pray." And as I did the Spirit of God descended on Von Shield in an unusual manner. He was baptized in the Holy Ghost very wonderfully, indeed. He was a transformed man. I tell you from that hour that man became the living personification of the power of God, and in all my life I have never found a soul through whom such majestic, intense flashes of power would come as through that soul at intervals. He was not a student of the Word of God. Presently, he disappeared. His father came to me saying, "I am troubled about Harry. He took a Bible and went off into the mountains almost three weeks ago, and they tell me he has gone up to such a mountain, a long piece off. I am afraid he is going insane."

I said, "Brother, do not worry yourself. One of these days he will come down in the glory and power of God." I knew what was in that fellow's heart.

One day he returned under such an anointing of the Spirit as I had never before witnessed on any life. Here was a soul who had never read the words of Jesus. He was a full-grown man, but he said to me, "I have never looked into the Bible, unless it was in my childhood. I knew nothing of it."

One day after that he came to me, his face radiant, and said, "Brother Lake, did you know this was in the Bible?" and proceeded to read to me that familiar verse in the sixteenth of Mark: "These signs shall follow them that believe...They shall cast out demons." Among other things it says that the believer shall accomplish is, "he shall cast out devils."[1] Looking up into my face with great earnestness he said, "My! I wish I knew somebody that had a devil." I believe God had planned that situation, for I was reminded that in my mail a couple of days before had come a request for an insane son. The mother said, "As far as I can tell my son has a devil," and her request was that we might come and pray that the devil might be cast out. So I got the letter and handed it to him. He said, "Why this is only a couple of three blocks from where I live." He said, "I am going to find that fellow, and then I am coming back for you."

---

[1] Mark 16:17.

And all the time I said, "Here is a newborn soul just born unto God whose vision enters into the real realm of God-power." I realized that my own spirit had not touched the degree of faith that was in that soul and I said, "I do not want to do a thing, nor say a word that will discourage that soul in the least."

Presently, he came back and said: "Brother Lake, come on." We went and found a boy who had been mad from his birth. He was like a wild animal. He would not wear clothes and would smash himself or anybody else with anything that was given to him. He couldn't even have a dish to eat on. But in the center of the enclosure where he was, they had a large stone hollowed out and they would put his food on that and let him eat it just like an animal.

We tried to catch him, but he was as wild as a lion. He would jump right over my head. Finally his father said, "You will never catch him out here." All this time I realized what the situation meant. I had been somewhat of an athlete in my youth, and I said to V.S. "You get on one side, and if he comes to your side you will take care of him, and if he comes to my side I will take care of him."

Now, beloved, this all sounds strange I know, but I'll never forget that afternoon as long as I live. As I looked across to the young man, Von Shield, I could see the lightning flash of faith, and I knew that if he got his hands on the insane man the devil would come out.

Presently, he landed on my side of the bed, and in an instant Von Shield sprang over the bed, laid his hands on his head, and commanded that devil to come out. In two minutes that man was absolutely transformed and was a sane man. The first moment of sanity he ever knew.

Sometime later the family moved to another section of the country, so I have lost track of him.

One more incident in the man's life will help you to realize this thing. Among the Boer people, especially in the Transvaal, they were a pioneer people. They had moved from Cape Colony and lived among the natives there many years. Finally, they succeeded in establishing their own community and later a republic. They did not have the advantages of good schools. In fact, about the time they passed into the hands of the English, education was becoming a real factor. About the only educated person in a community was the Dutch Predicant. He is a real old aristocrat. The firstborn of houses is the Predicant and everything else likewise. He is the lord of all he surveys and some more. I believe they were people with all authority that the priests of Ireland exercise over the people there.

I wanted to leave you with the conception of a Dutch Predicant and then you can understand how a young fellow, unrecognized as a preacher, is situated when he begins to preach the Gospel of Christ in a different manner than the Predicant.

One day when Von Shield was conducting a service with a couple of hundred people present, the Predicant was there. He arose when he was teaching and told the people that they were being misled, etc., and that these things Von Shield was talking about were only calculated for the days of the apostles.

The young man, naturally, if he had been an ordinary young man, would have been somewhat nonplussed. But presently he said, "I will tell you how we will settle this thing. There is Miss LeRoux, whom we all know. She is stone blind in one eye and has been so for four years. You come here, and I will lay my hands on you and ask the Lord Jesus to make you well." And picking up his Dutch Bible he said, "And when He does, you will read that chapter," designating the chapter she was to read.

God Almighty met the fellow's faith. The woman's eye opened right then and she stood before that congregation and covering the good eye, read with the eye that had been blind, the entire chapter. I know her well; visited at their home a great many times.

Now I will return to the other young man, the most extraordinary incident that I have known in the life of any other human being, unless it was the history of St. Paul when he was on his way to Damascus, when suddenly there shone around about him a light, brighter than the sun, and he says, "When we were *all* fallen to the earth." They were probably on horseback,

> I heard a voice speaking unto me, and saying in the Hebrew tongue, Saul, Saul, why persecutest thou me? it is hard for thee to kick against the pricks. And I said, Who art thou, Lord? And he said, I am Jesus whom thou persecutest.[2]

---

[2]   Acts 26:14-15.

Kratzmall was visiting one night at the home of some friends, a few doors from my home. These young people with whom he was visiting had just recently been baptized in the Spirit themselves, and they were very anxious about this friend and had been praying a great deal about it. This same night he was in the tabernacle and his friends said, "Come down to our home." So he went.

These two men, Kratzmall and Von Shield, were the highest developed men. I believe Kratzmall was the strongest man, physically, I ever met. He was an altogether unusual character. And here was a dealing of the Spirit of God such as I have never known with any other individual.

After a time, I believe it was suggested that they pray. He was going to stay all night. Harry said in speaking of it afterwards, "It was not my custom to kneel. As I sat in my chair I began to realize that a peculiar power was taking hold of me. I said, 'This must be some sort of a psychological condition that I am not familiar with. Anyway, I will have nothing to do with it.'" And he sat up in his chair and shut his teeth and endeavored to resist. The Spirit of God intensified, and he said, "I will not yield."

For two hours and a half he sat there while the perspiration poured off his person, until there were little pools of perspiration oozing from his shoes. But at the end of two and a half hours as this battle was going on, a voice spoke within him and said, "I am Jesus."

And instantly he said, "If You are the Christ, You can do anything You like." The next moment the Spirit of God deepened upon him, and he began to speak in tongues by the power of God.

Kratzmall, after that anointing, became the most remarkable preacher of the Gospel I have ever known anything about. He traveled that country from end to end when he didn't have a cent. I met him once when he had no shoes and his feet were cut and bleeding. But he established congregations of Christian people for three hundred and fifty miles down through the wilderness. Bless God.

Now then I will return. I have told you these incidents in order to demonstrate to you that there is a force in the Christian life that mankind has not gotten hold of in any great degree. But the thing that interests me most, and I endeavor to present to you the facts of a Christian life, is the inquiry that comes to me day by day from souls that I deal with in the healing room, "How can I enter into the consciousness of the presence and power of Christ?"

That is the real issue in all our hearts. We see the thing that was burning in the heart of Nicodemus when he came to Jesus in the nighttime, and said,

> Rabbi, we know that thou art a teacher come from God: for *no man* can do these miracles that thou doest, except God be with him.[3]

But Jesus, disregarding all that, said,

> Except a man be *born again,* he cannot see the kingdom of God.... That which is born of the flesh is flesh; and that which is born of the Spirit is spirit. Marvel not that I said unto thee, Ye must be born again.[4]

The birth again of God, the conscious incoming of the Spirit of God into the life and being and personality, lifts mankind out of the condition of the professing Christian experience into the place of divine consciousness and power.

The baptism of the Holy Spirit was the common experience of New Testament times. The New Testament was written by men who had the baptism of the Holy Spirit. It was written to churches that possessed the baptism of the Holy Ghost. Indeed, in my study of the New Testament the disciples seemed to consider it essential that each individual should himself possess the baptism of the Spirit. When Paul came down to Ephesus the first question he asked them was,

> Have ye received the Holy Ghost since ye believed? And they said unto him, We have not so much as heard whether there be any Holy Ghost. And he said unto them, Unto what then were ye baptized? And they said, Unto John's baptism.[5]

---

[3] John 3:2.

[4] John 3:3,6-7.

[5] Acts 19:2-3.

And then he explained what John's baptism was. He said,

> John verily baptized with the baptism of repentance,
> saying unto the people, that they should believe *on him
> which should come* after him, that is, on Christ Jesus.[6]

Then He laid his hands upon them and they received the Holy Ghost and began to speak with tongues and magnify God and prophesy, etc.

There are only five cases on record in the New Testament of persons receiving the baptism of the Spirit: The church at Jerusalem, one hundred and twenty, in the second of Acts. The church at Samaria under the ministry of Peter and John. That is the case of Simon, the Sorcerer. When he witnessed the manifestation of power that occurred at the hands of the apostles, he offered them money, saying, "Give me also this power, that on whomsoever I lay hands, he may receive the Holy Ghost." But you remember the answer, "Thy money perish with thee, because thou hast thought that the gift of God may be purchased with money."[7]

The next case is in the tenth of Acts, where the Gentile church was baptized in the Holy Spirit, the household of Cornelius, as Peter preached the Word. No altar services there. No laying on of hands. There the Holy Ghost fell on all those who believed.

And I tell you it is my conviction to this hour, that is the real manner in which the Lord desires to pour out the Spirit in these days. We had mighty few altar services or prayer services, but the power fell upon the people as they sat hearing the Word of God. I have witnessed the Lord baptize fifty people in an ordinary service like this on a Sunday evening.

There is a consciousness, that seems to me by the Word of God and by my own personal experience, that must be possessed where any individual can enter into the direct presence of God and receive the baptism of the Spirit. That is the consciousness of *sinlessness*. The consciousness that your sins are gone. You can classify sin in any way you like. There is this much about it, that in our own inner soul we know that sin is offensive to God, because it is offensive to our own spirit.

---

[6] Acts 19:4.

[7] Acts 8:18-20.

So as I said before, the consciousness of sinlessness seems to be God's requirement for those who would seek the baptism of the Spirit. Indeed, I remember in my own experience when my heart began to be stirred along this line, and I definitely began to seek God for the baptism of the Spirit, that as the illumination of the purity and holiness of God began to dawn over my soul, instead of going on boldly, there was an inclination to draw back as I realized the awful extreme between my own heart and the heart of God. And I was compelled to cry out, yea not once, but a thousand times, "Lord God, by the divine process of God cleanse my soul from this condition." And I remember, bless God, how that one night I was present in a friend's home. An ordinary meeting was going on, conducted by a little Quaker woman, but she outlined what seemed to me to be the method of cleansing the soul.

That night as I knelt in Fred Bosworth's home, that consciousness of the cleansing power of Jesus Christ went through my being, and I realized something of what I never realized before. That the battle between my spirit and my soul had ceased and that God reigned, not only my spirit, but in my flesh too. The war that had been in my spirit for years was all gone, and I entered into Beulah land. I really felt that I had crossed the Jordan and everything was new.

I tell you, beloved, that the external evidences of God and the power of His Spirit, no matter how wonderful, are a small matter compared with the consciousness of the Word of God in the human heart; in your heart and mine, bless God.

In the 17th verse of the fourteenth chapter of John there is this one verse. While Jesus was discussing this subject with the disciples, He said, "He is with you," that is, the Comforter. "He is with you, and *shall be in you.*"

There is a definite possession of the Spirit of God by which the individual becomes the conscious possessor of the Spirit of God. Indeed, the Word of God puts it in this forceful manner. "Know ye not that your body is the temple of the Holy Ghost which is in you?"[8] It is God's purpose, as outlined by Jesus Christ and this Word from cover to cover, that man shall be the conscious possessor of the Spirit of the living God, the Holy Ghost.

---

[8] 1 Corinthians 6:19, paraphrased.

That is the *"Real Christian."* That is the thing that has been lacking in the Church throughout the centuries that are past. It was that consciousness of God's presence and God's power in the disciples and the Church of the first centuries that wrote across the pages of history the wonderful, wonderful record of Christianity of the first four hundred years. There were thirty million Christian martyrs, those who were slaughtered in the Christian wars, etc. Thirty million gave up their lives for the Christ. There was a spirit that made it so intense, so powerful, that had such a power of induction that the world got out. Bless God.

But there came a day when the Church traded the communion of the Holy Ghost for the smile of the world, and then the long, long night of the middle centuries followed.

But bless God, I tell you we are living in a day and hour when the Spirit of God has come into the world afresh, when the consciousness of mankind is opening up to God in a manner that they have never opened before. There is an awakening in the world from ocean to ocean, from pole to pole, as there never was before. And I believe, bless God, that God Almighty's outpouring of the Spirit upon all flesh is at hand. And though we are receiving the droppings and our hearts are being warmed under the impulse of the Spirit, the day is not far distant when the flame of God will catch the soul of mankind. And the Church of the latter day will close this era with a place of divine glory excelling that of the early Church.

This is according to the prophecy of the Word. "If the former rain was abundant, shall not the latter rain be more abundant."[9] Bless God.

If the disciples, without the train of Christian history behind them that you and I have, were able to enter into the divine consciousness and power of the Holy Spirit in such a way that they left a stamp upon Christianity, how much more shall men and women who have the advantage of two thousand years of Christian record enter into a diviner consciousness than ever the apostles possessed?

---

[9] Deuteronomy 11:14, paraphrased.

(Tongues and Interpretation)

The eternal God hath ordained that mankind, being united with Him as one heart and as one soul, shall glorify the Lord Jesus Christ in manifesting His life and character, His person and being.

(Tongues and Interpretation)

If then, God's purpose for mankind is to receive the Christ, shall we not yield ourselves body and soul and spirit to the conscious control of the Spirit of God and let Him manifest Himself in us in humbleness and meekness, bowing lowly at the feet of Him whose we are and whom we serve?

Down in the human heart

Crushed by the tempter,

Feelings lie buried that grace can restore.

Touched by a loving heart,

Wakened by kindness,

Chords that were broke will vibrate once more.

Our God, we ask Thee tonight that Thy Almighty power shall be upon each soul. That as we endeavor to yield ourselves to Thee for the conscious cleansing of our nature from sin and its effects, that Thy power shall lift us into that consciousness of oneness with God whereby from Thy soul to our own will flow the divine unction of God. That we, being cleansed from sin, may manifest God to mankind that the hungry world and a dying race and a wandering world may be brought back into oneness with God. Amen.

here has always been a passage in the Declaration of Independence that has rung very deeply in my spirit. It was the thought of the revolutionary Fathers in giving an explanation and reason to the world for undertaking to set up a new government among the families of

THE PLATFORMS OF JESUS

January 24, 1915

nations. They said something like this: out of due respect for mankind they felt it necessary to give a reason for such an act.

As we invite this company of people together in this section of country, I feel that a due word of loving explanation may be helpful.

I have been in this particular manner of ministry for many years. I believe Brother Fogwill and I began in this ministry some sixteen or seventeen years ago, or there about. Of course, we had been Christian ministers before that, but at that period God enlarged our vision of Himself and His purposes.

Personally, I received my ministry in the gospel of healing through John Alexander Dowie, a man whom I have loved with all my soul. And though in his later life he became broken in mind and committed many foolish things so that discredit for a time was brought upon his work, yet I knew him from the beginning until the day of his death. I have gone to his grave since I have returned to this land, and as I have thought over that wonderful life, I have prayed in the silence of the nighttime, "Lord God, endue me with the Spirit of God in the measure that You did that life."

I have always regarded it as a privilege in my life and as a unique thing that after his death I was invited to preach in his pulpit, and I preached there for several months. I remember as I stood on the platform, above my head was a great crown, possibly eight feet in diameter. It was made from boots with iron stirrups on them, thick soles, and all that character of thing that had come from people who had been healed of short limbs. I stood in that place and looked around those walls and saw plaster of Paris casts fastened on the walls — some of which had come off of my own friends who had been healed — iron braces that cripples had worn, cots on which the dying had been brought, one of them Amanda Hicks.

That cot was fastened to one of the walls above the gallery. I thought of that day when she was carried in practically dead and that old man prayed for her and she was healed. And the company of her students who had lovingly escorted her to the station at Berea, Kentucky, said to me, "We carried her as we would if she had been dead, as pall-bearers, and we received her back as from the dead."

Her friends cabled her and telegraphed her from all over the earth, and she gladly told the story, the wonderful story — almost the same character of story that our Brother Zienke told you this morning — of the love of God, of the tenderness of the Christ that mankind has not known, of Jesus the Healer still.

Beloved, there is a deep, passionate yearning in my soul that above all else this congregation may set forth, to the praise of God, such a character of righteousness in God, such a purity of holiness from God, that this people may not only be recognized in this city, but throughout the world, as a people among whom God dwells.

Beginning this work, as I do at this time, I want to say that I do not come as a novice to this time of my life. God has permitted me in the years that are past to assist in the establishment of two great works of God, each of them on a new plane in God. I trust, blessed be His name, that in calling together once again the people of God, that it shall be to establish a work on a new plane. Indeed, a higher one than our souls have ever known, where the radiant purity of the holiness of God shall be shed forth into the whole world. And I believe that is God's purpose.

Jesus Himself stood at Nazareth on an almost similar occasion. He had been raised in one of the country towns. He had disappeared from His community, gone down to the Jordan, and had been baptized of John. The Holy Ghost had come upon Him, and He had returned to His own hometown, to the synagogue where He had worshipped as a boy.

One thing I have always praised God for is that when God put me into public ministry, He made me start in the very town, in the very community, next door to the very home where I had been raised. When a man fights out the battles of life in his own community — in his own hometown, among his own friends and neighbors — and receives love and confidence, I always feel he has received a good preparation for the next step in life. Jesus knew the place for a man to begin to serve God when He had said to the demoniac of Gadara, who was delivered, "Go home to thy friends, and tell them how great things the Lord hath done for thee."[1]

If your wife does not know you are a Christian, nobody else will be likely to, and if your husband does not know you are a Christian, it is a poor testimony. It is the woman that is with you, who eats with you, and sleeps with you, that will know whether you are a child of God or not. It is the man who lives in the same house with you and the people in your community who will know best how much of the life of God radiates from your own soul.

So Jesus once stood in His own hometown of Nazareth and read this wonderful text that I am going to read this morning. It is known, or ought to be, as the platform of Jesus Christ.

> The Spirit of the Lord is upon me, because he hath anointed me to preach the gospel to the poor.[2]

The Poor. (Jesus Christ has an anti-poverty program.) That is the first duty of every child of God and every church of God that ever came into existence. And the church that fails in that duty to mankind has failed in the first principle and has denied the first platform of the platform of the Son of God.

My heart has never gone out in sympathy to a body of Christian people who become a little clique and represent a certain select number of society. My conception of the real Church of God is one where rich and poor, bless God, alike feel at home, where there are no barriers and no boundaries, but where soul flows out to soul and in the larger life, man knows only man and God. Blessed be His precious name.

---

[1] Mark 5:19.

[2] Luke 4:18.

> The Spirit of the Lord is upon me, because he hath anointed me to preach the gospel to the poor.

The ministry of the things of God must ever be without money and without price. My soul could never descend to the place where charges are made for the services of the minister of Christ. Never, bless God!

It is our privilege to make possible a ministry to the people without money and without price, bless God. The magnanimity of the Lord Jesus Christ has stood out as a blessed and wonderful feature in all His ministry. I have sometimes wondered how many people really knew how the Lord existed during His own earth life. The Word of God gives us one little hint in these words: "Joanna the wife of Chuza Herod's steward, and Susanna, and many others, which ministered unto him of their substance."[3] That was how the Son of God was able to minister without money and without price to mankind. We today may have that privilege too. It is ours. I have faith in God. This church will demonstrate Christ's ministry to the poor.

For ten years God has privileged me to preach the Gospel without salary, without collections. I never asked a man for a cent in my life, and I have lived, bless God, and been able to minister every day. God has met me every time, and I believe He will meet every other man and woman who will likewise put their trust in God and go forward.

The second plank in the platform of the Gospel of Jesus of Christ is this: "To heal the brokenhearted."[4]

There are lots of them. I tell you since I have been in Spokane the Lord has let me into the homes of the rich and poor, and it is not in the poor districts that you find all the brokenhearted by any means. "He hath sent me to heal the brokenhearted." That is the ministry of this body. If there is a brokenhearted soul in your locality, you are the one who, in the name of Jesus Christ, has the privilege of ministering in the things of God to that soul — brokenhearted sometimes because of sin, brokenhearted sometimes because of sickness, brokenhearted sometimes because of the conditions around them that they seem unable to control.

---

[3] Luke 8:3.

[4] Luke 4:18.

When I see the living God in His tender mercy touch one and another and make them whole — whether in spirit, in soul, or in body — I rejoice equally in either case, for what God does is always good and worthy of praise. I regard the healing of a man's body to be just as sacred as the healing of his soul. There is no distinction. Jesus made none. He provided a perfect salvation for mankind — all that man needed for spirit, soul, or body.

So this ministry, bless God, will be a healing ministry. This church will be a healing church. This will be a church, bless God, to which you can invite your friends who are ill and bring them here and help them. I trust after a time we will be able to bring the people in great numbers, the sick who are on cots and stretchers and crutches that the Lord Jesus through this church and its ministry may make them well.

It is my purpose that a number of brethren who have had this same burden on their hearts for many years as I have had it may come together in this city as a headquarters, and that from this city we may extend this ministry throughout the land. I have particularly invited my old preaching partner, Brother Cyrus B. Fockler of Milwaukee, my dear, precious brother, Archibald Fairley, of Zion City, a prophet of God and one of the anointed of the Lord, Brother (Rev.) Bert Rice of Chicago, my dear Brother (Rev.) Charles W. Westwood, of Port-land, Oregon, and Reverend Fogwell to assist me in this ministry. Brother Westwood visited with me a few days and is now going on to Chicago to make the necessary arrangements.

This is the outline so far as God has made it clear. This is to be a healing church. Everyone who has been called to this ministry and those who will be called in the future will minister to body and soul and spirit through the Lord Jesus Christ.

The third plank in the platform of Jesus Christ is this: "To preach deliverance to the captives."[5]

How many there are! One day not long ago, I received a telephone call from a lady in one of the missions saying that she had a man there who was a terrible drunk. Every once in awhile he would get delirium tremens. And at that time he seemed to be in a condition of delirium.

---

[5] Luke 4:18.

John G. Lake and Cyrus B. Fockler

Cyrus B. Fockler and John G. Lake

He saw devils. He was haunted by them. The lady said, "We cannot do anything for him. We thought perhaps you could help him." He came up to the church to see me. He sat down to tell me about himself. Right away I could discern that he was a soul who from his very birth had been gifted with spiritual sight. But instead of associating in the spirit with angels, with God, with Christ, according to the condition of his own heart all his spiritual association was with devils, demons, and horrors until he told me that to escape from that condition he had become a drunk in his youth. In order to have relaxation for a time he had paralyzed himself with drink and that was his difficulty.

I said to him, "My son, kneel down. We are going to pray to God." And I prayed that God would bind every last demon and lift his soul into union with God and fill him with the Holy Ghost, so he might associate with the angels of God, become a new man in Christ, and fellowship with the Holy Spirit.

In a few days he returned and said, "O, brother, it is all so new, so different. As I walk along the street there are no more demons, no more devils. But as I came up to the church today an angel, so beautiful, so sweet, so pure, walked by my side. And, brother, there He is now, and He has wounds on His hands and on His feet." But my eyes were dim; I could not see Him. I presume they were like the eyes of the servant of Elisha.[6] They need to be opened. "To preach deliverance to the captives," and more than captives. All kinds of powers, earthly and sensual, bless God. It is the privilege of the real Church to bring deliverance to the captives of sin, of disease, of death, and hell — not only proclaiming the message of deliverance, but exercising the power of God to set them free.

The fourth plank: "Recovering of sight to the blind."[7]

Among the blessed healings of the past few weeks is one dear soul who is not yet completely healed, a blind woman, whose eyes have gradually opened day by day from the first morning of prayer, and who will be present with us in the near future, as Brother Zeinke was this morning, to praise God for her deliverance.

---

[6] 2 Kings 6:15-17.

[7] Luke 4:18.

"Recovering of sight to the blind." But there are many blind hearts, blind minds, blind souls, just as well as blind eyes who do not see the beauty and power of the things of Christ. And to them we bring today the message of our Christ, "Recovering of sight to the blind."

I pray that above every other thing, this church will be a church that will know God so intimately that when men come in contact with any one of us, they will feel that they have met one who is able to reveal the Lord Jesus Christ to them. I believe it will be so.

The fifth plank: "To set at liberty them that are bruised."[8]

There are the bleeding ones, the bruised ones, those who have been hid away, and those whose life has been made a burden. May I tell you this incident?

The last night I preached in my tabernacle in Johannesburg, they brought a young man with whom life had gone so very hard. He had lost hope and gone into despair so, that he tried to blot himself out by committing suicide. He shot himself in the mouth and the bullet came out the back of the head, strangely, without killing him. This left him with a violent pain in the base of the brain that caused him to suffer untold agony, and his neck was rigid.

This night, the greatest part of the congregation was composed of Cornish miners whom I have always regarded as the hardest men I have ever met in South Africa. They live a very hard, terrible life there — dissipated terribly.

This man came up on the platform to be prayed for, and I wanted the sympathy of the people. So I made a plea in some such words as these, "Here is a poor fellow with whom life has gone so hard that he tried to blot himself out and in his endeavor to do so, he shot himself, with the result that he is in the condition you see him in now." Presently, I began to observe that up from the audience there came a wave of warm, loving sympathy. I said, "If you have never prayed in your life, if you have never prayed for yourself, bow your head and pray tonight and ask God to deliver your fellow man."

I put my hands on him and prayed, and the power of God came down upon him and instantly the joints became loose, the neck became

---

[8] Luke 4:18.

pliable, and the pain was gone. Looking up into my face, he said, "Who did that?"

I said, "That was the Lord Jesus Christ."

And dropping on his knees before me he said, "Brother, show me how to find that Christ. I want to know Him."

Down in the audience that night was one of the most cultured gentlemen it has ever been my privilege to know, Lord [name was crossed out] of London. He raised in his seat, and reverently raising his hands, he said, "My Lord and my God." He had not been a Christian, but he saw a new vision of the love of God for man that night.

Way back in the audience, another soul was touched. He was a different type of man. He came from a different environment. He raised up and slapped himself on the hip and shouted, "Bully for Jesus!" It came out of the depth of his soul.

Beloved, it is my conviction that the purity of Jesus Christ and the radiant holiness and the power of God will manifest Christ alike to the cultured and the uncultured, for both hearts are hungry when they see the living Christ.

The sixth plank of the platform: "To preach the acceptable year of the Lord."[9]

Not next year, not in five years, not when you die, but a present salvation, a present healing for spirit and soul and body. All you need, bless God, is to bring your whole being into perfect harmony with the living God, so that the Spirit of God radiates through your spirit, radiates through your mind, and radiates likewise through your body. Blessed be His name.

Among the most precious privileges that is given to the real Church is to be in fact, not in word alone, the body of Christ. The Word of God speaks of "the Church," which is His body. God the Father manifested Himself through that one beautiful, holy, purified body of Jesus Christ in such a manner, such a perfect manner, that when men looked upon Him they did not see the man Jesus, but they saw God. Until He ascended and sent His Spirit to the world, to the Church,

---

[9] Luke 4:19.

to you and to me. What for? That the new body should come forth and the Church, the real Church — united to God, filled with the Holy Ghost, whose names are written in the Lamb's Book of Life — are the body through which God is going to manifest Himself to mankind again.

When God wants to heal a man, the healing does not fall down from heaven, but it does come through the medium of the child of God. Therefore, God has given us the exalted privilege of being co-laborers together with God. And among our high privileges is to radiate, to give forth from the love-passion of our souls, the courage and strength to help other souls to come to God. And the business of the Church is to be a savior, or saviors, for the Word of God says, "There shall be saviors in Zion."[10] That is those, bless God, in such union with God that they are able to lift mankind up to the "Lamb of God, which taketh away the sin of the world."[11]

FINIS

WHAT MUST I DO TO BE SAVED?

Probably the simplest way is to pray, "Father, forgive me all my sins. I take Thy Son, Jesus Christ, to be my personal Savior. I invite You to come and live in my heart."

"Will God hear me?" you may ask. God has commanded all men everywhere to repent. (Acts 17:30.) Certainly He will hear and accept you for you are obeying His own command. Jesus said in John 6:37, "Him that cometh to me I will in no wise cast out." It is God's will that all come to repentance. (2 Peter 3:9.) He is able to save to the uttermost all that come unto God by Him, that is by Jesus Christ. (Hebrews 7:25.) What happens to your sins and iniquities? "And their sins and iniquities will I remember no more" (Hebrews 10:17). What love God is willing to bestow on us! For God so loved the world (you) that He gave His only begotten Son for you and for me. (John 3:16.) Why not bow and repeat from your heart that simple

---

[10] Obadiah 21, paraphrased.

[11] John 1:29.

prayer this very moment. It will revolutionize your life and give you that more abundant life[12] and the peace of God that passeth understanding.[13] God bless you.

> If I were to come as an accredited agent to you from the upper sanctuary, with a letter in invitation to you, with your name and address on it, you would not doubt your warrant to accept it. Well, here is the Bible, your invitation to come to Christ. It does not bear your name and address; but it says, "Whosoever" — that takes you in. It says, "All" — that takes you in. It says, "If any" — that takes you in. What can be surer and freer than that?
>
> — Dr. Chalmers.
>
> The depths of our misery can never fall below the depths of mercy.
>
> — Sibbes.

"Watch ye, stand fast in the faith, quit you like men, be strong" (1 Corinthians 16:13). "Be strong in the Lord" (Ephesians 6:10). "Be strong in the grace that is in Christ Jesus" (2 Timothy 2:1).

> True love never grows heavy. Who would be loved must love. Love warms more than a thousand fires. Love rules without law. Love is master of all arts.
>
> — Italian

God is Love.

---

[12] See John 10:10.

[13] See Philippians 4:7.

he old time Gospel of Jesus Christ comes back to the soul with great freshness and great power. It seems to me in the passage down through the years, faith declined to such a degree that mankind was in danger of losing the vital principles of Christianity.

WATER BAPTISM

Hutton Hall

March 14, 1915

I want to call your attention, in a word or two, to that fact. In the passage of the centuries there have been periods when, through the intensity of spiritual darkness, Christianity was almost lost to the world. I am thinking now of Luther, who was a monk in the Roman church. I presume he was as godly a man as the church possessed, but he did not even know that salvation was to be had through faith in Jesus Christ. Even that primary essential truth of God had been lost. Men had for centuries been endeavoring to obtain salvation for their soul through penance. And Martin Luther, at the moment God spoke to him, was in the act of going up and down the stairway at Rome on his bare knees, doing penance for his sins, thereby trusting that through self-imposed afflictions he might make himself worthy to enter the presence of God. It was while in that act that the Spirit of God spoke to him. Bless God for that Spirit that brings back to the searching heart the truths of God!

The Spirit of God spoke these blessed words that set his soul on fire — that united him with God — and sent him out as one of the greatest ministers of God in the world. "The just shall live by faith."[1] That was a revelation right out of the blue of heaven straight from the heart of God to his soul. "The just shall live by faith!" He sprang to his feet saying, "Then if the just shall live by faith in Jesus Christ, what is the use of tramping up and down the stairway on my bare knees?" And he went out all over Europe with the glad message that "the just shall live by faith."

---

[1] Romans 1:17.

But beloved, have you ever thought of the darkness of the day when men were not even conscious of that truth, "The just shall live by faith"? No wonder the Middle Ages are spoken of as the Dark Ages. But the light dawned, bless God!

The *coming back* to the truths of Christ has always been an illuminating factor in men's lives. Every step back toward Christ is new illumination to the soul. When John Wesley met some Marovian missionaries and they pointed him to the Christ as the Sanctifier from all sin, it was just as much of a revelation to John Wesley as the fact that "the just shall live by faith" was to Martin Luther.

And once again Wesley went out into the world to proclaim a new truth to mankind. New to him, but just as old, bless God, as this dear old Book. But having been lost to the world, it sounded like a new truth, and so the great Methodist body has risen up throughout the whole world. That was the beginning of Methodism.

May I call your attention to this fact: How rapidly decline comes in Christian life. Today, the fundamental truth on which Methodism was founded is no longer taught in her pulpits. The fundamental truth to John Wesley was the sanctifying power to cleanse the soul from sin, from *all* sin. In defining his teachings on the point, John Wesley put it in these words, "Possessing the mind of Christ, and all the mind of Christ." It was about two hundred years between Martin Luther and John Wesley.

Now we move down another couple of hundred years and a woman in Switzerland, Dorothy Trudell, appears, to whom God revealed the fact that Jesus Christ is the same yesterday, today, and forever, and that all the virtue that was in Jesus is in Him still. And His love for mankind is just as deep as ever, that He is just as willing to save a sick body as to save a sick soul. So Dorothy Trudell began to tell the glad tidings. After awhile, they began to gather to her for prayer and the sick were healed. Later labors developed into the first divine healing homes that the world has known in modern times. That was the real origin of the teaching of healing in modern days through faith in Jesus Christ, as we see it today.

John Wesley taught healing as an act of faith in God, and he prayed as readily for the healing of a sick animal as he did for the healing of men's souls, but he did not see it as part of the Atonement.

One of the truths of God I feel the world has lost in these last days is the truth of Christian baptism. I have a feeling that in all the Christian Church there is no ordinance of such profound significance and that contains such profound truth as Christian baptism. But it has been permitted to deteriorate in the hands of the Church and the world so that it means practically nothing anymore. Baptism, once the glorious rallying point in the Christian Church, has ceased to have power over men's souls for the reason that the real purpose has been lost sight of.

In the early days of Christianity, particularly during the awful persecution of Nero, to be a Christian was an offense. When one made himself recognized as a Christian, instantly he lost his rights as a citizen in the Roman empire. His estates were confiscated and he had no protection under Roman law. The result was, he became a prey to the avarice of the people. He became an outcast and a wanderer.

But beloved, notwithstanding such strenuous persecution prevailed, Christians came boldly down to the river, bless God, to be baptized. A Roman officer appeared and took the names. These were sent up to the Imperial Government and immediately their estates were gone, and they became a prey to the avarice of the people, who had a right to take their possessions. No matter what indignities the populace liked to impose upon them, they had no means of redress from the law.

But in the early Christian heart, the question of baptism was so deeply settled that, notwithstanding these things, he rejoiced in the privilege of declaring himself before the world as a child of God. That is the significance that has been lost in the years that are past. Today we bring babies as a matter of sentimentality and have them baptized. But beloved, it was not so in the early Church. It was the men and women who had counted the cost, who were ready to endure all that was necessary to endure. They went to the block and stake and wild animals — not by ones and tens, but by millions — until history records that in the first four hundred years, thirty million gave their lives for God. Beloved, that is what it means when we talk about "the blood of martyrs being the seed of the Church." Bless God!

There was something that entered into a man's soul before he was ready to do that sort of thing. There is a consciousness of God, of His presence, of His power, of His life that has taken possession of that man's nature, that makes everything else in life secondary — even death itself.

So I want to begin to review with you this subject of Christian baptism in order that we may see with distinctness and clearness what that was.

In the years that are past I had, through a strange combination of circumstances, been brought into very active touch with the leaders of the old Cuban rebellion: Garcia, Maclo, and others. I understood the awful oppression that they endured at that time — the tyrannical government of the Spaniards — until my soul was stirred. We who knew determined to do all we could to bring redress to the people that were being oppressed beyond any other people I knew of. You can understand some of the feelings that were in my soul at the time the news came to this country that Maclo had been killed. He was then the active general of the Cuban rebellion. Garcia was an older man who had given up his life to that cause.

You can imagine further what it meant to me when the day finally came that the United States Army went down and became active in their behalf. You will realize with what a joy my soul thrilled when the day came that the Cuban flag was raised, and the Cuban government became a fact.

Christianity had character in it. To be a Christian meant to the early Christians that they were ready to live, and they were ready to die, and they were ready to suffer and to endure all that could be imposed on them, even unto death. That was their consecration. That was the kind of Christians they were. That is the reason that they left such an everlasting stamp of character in the world.

I am beginning today at the very beginning of the subject of baptism in the New Testament, and by the grace of God I expect to occupy three of these services on Sunday morning with this subject. At the close of these addresses we purpose to have a public baptism service somewhere in the city where we can make proper arrangements.

I want to read the third of Matthew this morning.

> In those days came John the Baptist, preaching in the wilderness of Judaea, And saying, Repent ye: for the kingdom of heaven is at hand. For this is he that was spoken of by the prophet Esaias, saying, The voice of one crying in the wilderness, Prepare ye the way of the Lord, make his paths straight. And the same John had his raiment of camel's hair, and a leathern girdle about his loins; and his meat was locusts and wild honey. Then went out to him Jerusalem, and all Judaea, and all the region round about Jordan, and were baptized of him in Jordan, confessing their sins. But when he saw many of the Pharisees and Sadducees come to his baptism, he said unto them, O generation of vipers, who hath warned you to flee from the wrath to come? Bring forth therefore fruits meet for repentance: And think not to say within yourselves, We have Abraham to our father: for I say unto you, that God is able of these stones to raise up children unto Abraham. And now also the axe is laid unto the root of the trees: therefore every tree which bringeth not forth good fruit is hewn down, and cast into the fire. I indeed baptize you with water unto repentance: but he that cometh after me is mightier than I, whose shoes I am not worthy to bear: he shall baptize you with the Holy Ghost, and with fire: whose fan is in his hand, and he will throughly purge his floor, and gather his wheat into the garner; but he will burn up the chaff with unquenchable fire.
>
> — Matthew 3:1-12

During the week, a dear man called on me at the healing rooms and said to me: "You see I am not a sick man. Perhaps I enjoy as good health as any man in this city. That is not the difficulty. Do you know how to show a man how to find God?"

I said, "Yes, Brother, bless God."

He said, "Well, I called on Rev. So-and-so and he said go to Rev. [name does not appear] and I went to him and he sent me to you."

That is what I meant this morning when I spoke of how easy it is for the very fundamental facts of salvation to be lost to men's souls, so that even among ministers of the Gospel they do not understand how to get a soul to God for salvation.

John the Baptist was the last of the prophets and the greatest of them. Jesus said so. "Among them that are born of women there hath not risen a greater than John the Baptist: notwithstanding he that is least in the kingdom of heaven is greater than he."[2]

John was closing up a dispensation that had a profound knowledge of God, but he was the door opener of a new dispensation also, with a better knowledge. In the progressive revelation of God, as one dispensation emerges into another dispensation, nothing that was good in the old was ever destroyed. I wish Christian workers would keep that in mind. Christian workers seem to feel that the essential thing is to break down in the other life all the things that they possess. You leave the soul shattered and broken, and that is about all you succeed in doing. In most cases you wreck their confidence.

Religion among the Jews had become a matter of form. John came with the message of repentance, calling mankind back, calling the Jewish world back to a real knowledge of the real truths of the law of God.

Sinlessness was one of the possibilities that characterized the Jewish dispensation. Formalism was what developed as the years went by, and the real essence was lost. John's call was a call to return to the pure essence of the truth of God and heart worship, instead of a mere formal obedience.

John, in distinction from all the other prophets, was prophesied of. No other prophet was prophesied of, but Isaiah and Malachi both prophesied of John. He was a peculiar messenger, the last prophet of that dispensation. His message to the people was the message of *repentance*. "Repent ye: for the kingdom of heaven is at hand."[3]

The message of repentance is the message that will mark and characterize the message of every real prophet of God as long as the world

---

[2] Matthew 11:11.

[3] Matthew 3:2.

lasts. God's call to mankind is to return to God, to return to the ways of God, and to return to the truths of God. In returning to the ways and truths of God, you will return to the consequent blessings that the Word and truth of God provide.

We are struggling back to God, and that is the peculiar thing that probably characterizes our own ministry. We are endeavoring to get back onto the real lines that God taught. Instead of being occupied with the formalisms and superfluities, our endeavor is to come back under the light of the Spirit of God to the real truths of God. To have them settled in our heart, branded upon our soul, and stamped upon our conscience, that we may walk in truth and power and strength as servants of God.

John's call to "Prepare ye the way of the Lord, make His paths straight," or as Isaiah puts it, Gather up the stones, fill up the valleys, cut down the hills, equalize conditions, is God's call still.[4]

"Prepare ye the way of the Lord, Make His paths straight." You want God to come and bless your own life? Then separate yourself from the superficialities and formalities that have possessed your mind and taken your attention, and come back with directness and simplicity to God and He will bless your soul.

An old brother who was recently healed was a Methodist local preacher. He was seventy-three years old. He said to me with tears, "I have spent almost my little all on the doctors, medicine, etc., during the last four years of my sickness. My wife and I are old. We have gone past the time when I can earn any more money." And he was troubled. He said, "I would give the little all I have left if I could be well."

I said, "Brother, how long have you been preaching the Gospel?"

He said, "Fifty years." Think of that — a half century.

I said, "Brother, haven't you been in the habit of calling on God and getting answers to your prayers?"

He said, "Yes, I have."

I said, "Well Brother, why have you not called on God to take away this evil thing, this sickness that is on your life?"

---

4 Matthew 3:3; Isaiah 62:10, paraphrased.

His old eyes opened with wonder and he said, "I never thought of it." He went home amazed. He and his old wife came back every few days, and they said it was such an awakening that he could look up to God to take away his sickness the same as he could pray about anything else. Yet he had been preaching the Gospel fifty years.

Men are looked upon as strange when they turn their faith to Christ and come back to the Gospel. To him, "Prepare ye the way of the Lord, make His paths straight," was to let his soul awake to Christ's purpose to save and to bless in every department of his life.

Lord God, our Father, there is something within our spirit that we cannot speak, and we ask Thee by the Spirit of God that You will have such control of our spirit that You will be able, Lord God, to give the clear message that we feel within the spirit You want to lay upon this dear people.

Now to return in my thought. When the Cuban War finally came on, I remember listening for the first time in my life to the call to arms. That was a custom that was common in Europe in the old days and was used in the Revolutionary period and revived to some extent during the Spanish War. The fire bells were rung in a peculiar manner. If you ever listen to such a call once, you will always remember it. One day as I walked down the street that sound caught my ears, and I knew that was the beginning of the end of Cuban oppression. I lined up with the rest who were lining up at the enlistment office. I remember as the candidate came in, he solemnly took the oath of allegiance. Then he was handed his card that gave him his uniform and musket, etc.

That is exactly what Christian baptism originally was. It was the Christian's enlistment in the army of the Lord Jesus Christ. It was the supreme act of his whole life. It was the thing for which he had sacrificed everything else. He was ready from that minute to take all the sorrows and all the oppressions and everything else that comes to a good soldier of Jesus Christ. But one thing was settled before the world, before demons and angels, and before Almighty God. He had by that public act declared himself a disciple of Jesus Christ, the Son of God. And then he boldly went out as a servant of the Lord Jesus

Christ, marked and branded and stamped as a disciple of Jesus Christ, just as literally as the man who puts on a United States uniform.

Christianity had character in it, bless God, and it is the desire of my soul to bring the heart of mankind back again to that original standard of Christianity by which the pure, sweet character of Christ shall be so branded and stamped on men's souls, that they are ready to live and die by their principles and their love for the Lord Jesus Christ.

God the Father had commissioned John to baptize. John baptized his candidates in the name of the *Father*. The Christ had not yet been revealed. Paul tells us what John's baptism was. He met the Ephesian elders, and he asked them, "Unto what then were ye baptized?"

They say, "Unto John's baptism."

Then Paul explains. "John verily baptized with the baptism of repentance, saying unto the people, that they should believe on Him which should come after him, that is, on Christ Jesus."[5]

Their baptism pledged them to faith in the Lord God and also pledged them that when the Christ would come they would likewise accept Him. John baptized them in the name of the *Father*. I want to leave this thing in your hearts that you may never have thought of before. He baptized them by a *single immersion*, into the name of the *Father*.

Jesus came. He was the present Christ. He was the one that John had pledged them that they should believe on when He appeared. Jesus instituted a new baptism, though the Word tells us that He baptized not, but His disciples. That is, Jesus did not perform the act of baptism, but His disciples did. His baptism was instituted and is spoken of in the fourth of John. "The Pharisees had heard that Jesus made and baptized more disciples than John."[6]

Now this is the character of the baptism of Jesus I want you to see: It was not the same baptism that John's was. There is a distinction of faith. John's baptism was into the name of the *Father*, and the baptism of Jesus was a baptism into two names, not one — a dual baptism. Christ was the present Savior. Men were baptized as they had been by John and also into the name of the *Son*.

---

[5] Acts 19:3-4.

[6] John 4:1.

Some may question that fact, but I want to say to you, beloved, that I have spent twenty years going into that matter and with perhaps one exception, so far as I know, I have probably spent more time over the issue than any other living man I know of. I had the advantage of the acquaintance of the Reverend Edward Kennedy, whose writings on the subject of baptism are recognized as among the very first in the world. I went to him on one occasion and said, "There is a question I want to settle. I have never been able to find it anywhere. The encyclopedias do not give it with distinctness. Where can I go for the authoritative fact concerning the baptism of Jesus and His disciples and the faith to which they were pledged?" And he referred me to the various writings of the early Fathers. He said, "The only place you will find it in type is in Robin's, but if you go to London, England, to the British Museum...." And so on my way to Africa on one occasion, I went there, because I wanted to see it with my own eyes.

Not to my surprise, because I had recognized the distinctness in the Word of God, but to my joy, I found that what he had told me was absolutely correct, that the early Fathers had distinctly recognized the difference between the baptism of John and of Jesus and declared that the baptism of Jesus was a dual baptism — into the name of the *Father* and into the name of the *Son* — the candidate being immersed in water twice, not once.

The real servants of God, according to the larger light, the presence of the Christ, having accepted Him as the Son of God and Savior of the world by faith, were baptized into the name of the Father, and now into the name of the Son. They accepted Jesus as they accepted the Father. Bless God.

Some of the incidents in the New Testament will come to your mind in a moment now. You remember the case of the Eunuch who came up to Jerusalem to worship. He was a praying man. He was not an Israelite, but would be what we would call a Jewish proselyte, that is, one of another nation who had accepted the Jewish faith. He had been taught concerning God the Father, but he knew nothing of Christ the Son. As he rode along the Spirit of the Lord said to Philip, "Go and join thyself to this chariot," and he did so and found the man reading from Isaiah:

"He was brought as a lamb to the slaughter, and as a sheep before his shearers is dumb, so he opened not his mouth."

The Eunuch asked, "Of whom speaketh the prophet? Of himself or of another?" Then Philip took the Word and showed him Jesus, until the man's soul, being convinced as they traveled along, he said, "Here is much water. What doth hinder me to be baptized."

Philip said, "If thou believest thou mayest."

And he said, "I believe that Jesus Christ is the Son of God," and he was baptized.[7]

Yet, beloved, that is not Christian baptism. This is the process up to Christian baptism. Christian baptism is more than faith in God the Father and more than faith in God the Son. The baptism of Jesus followed that of John and continued until the day of Pentecost. But just before the ascension of Jesus, He gave His disciples the last commission. He said to them: "Go ye therefore, and teach all nations, baptizing them in the name of the Father," as John did, "and of the Son," as the disciples did, and now into a new name, into which no man ever was baptized before — "and of the Holy Ghost."[8]

So for the first time the triune God appears to man, and man is pledged in faith to believe in the triune God and to accept God the Father, to accept God the Son, and to accept God the Holy Spirit, likewise. And that is what gives Christian baptism its force. Christian baptism is a baptism into the name of the Father and into the name of the Son *and* into the name of the Holy Spirit. Bless God!

In the Jewish mind there was never any controversy over God the Father or God the Holy Spirit. With the Jew the controversy was concerning Jesus Christ the Son. Consequently with the Jew, he must always subscribe his faith to Jesus Christ the Son. He had accepted God the Father, he had accepted God the Holy Spirit from time immemorial. He had understood that the Spirit of the Lord came upon the prophets, that the Spirit of the Lord had moved among them in a mighty way, but the introduction of the Son was a new condition and phase of faith to the Jewish mind.

---

[7] See Acts 8:26-38.

[8] Matthew 28:19.

We see therefore the import that was connected with the salvation of the household of Cornelius and their baptism both in water and by the Holy Spirit. Like the Eunuch, Cornelius was a man who loved God, and the Word says he prayed always. The Jewish people said of him: "He loveth our nation, and hath built for us a synagogue." When the angel came to Cornelius, he testified concerning him: "Thy prayers and thine alms are come up for a memorial before God," or had in remembrance before God. The prayers of his faithful heart, and the loving acts he had performed for his fellowmen were had in remembrance before God. But that was not enough.

> Send to Joppa and call for one Simon, whose surname is
> Peter:... he shall tell thee what thou oughtest to do.

When Peter came to Cornelius' house he preached to him of Jesus and the resurrection. Bless God. As their hearts opened to heaven when they received Jesus and the knowledge of His resurrection, the Spirit of God descended upon him and upon his house, and they were all baptized in the Holy Ghost. Bless God![9]

The way to God is as clearly defined in the Word of God as any way can be. There is no mystery about getting to God. The Word of God is so well-defined, so extremely emphatic that we come to God the Father through Jesus Christ the Son by the agency of the Holy Spirit. Bless God. "The Holy Spirit, which proceedeth from the Father and the Son," bless God.[10]

When Jesus ascended after His resurrection into the heavenlies and up to the right hand of God and sat down as immortal at the right hand of God, He received from the Father the gift of the Holy Ghost. And in return, "hath shed forth this, which ye now see and hear."[11]

So, beloved, as I went into this issue from every side with the students of the Word, my own conclusions were as you will find recorded historically in any good encyclopedia. Get an *Encyclopedia Britannica* or any ordinary one and look up the ordinance of baptism. Observe that

---

[9] Acts 10.

[10] John 15:26, paraphrased.

[11] Acts 2:33.

prior to the year 400 the Church baptized her candidates not by one immersion into one name, but by three immersions into three names — God the Father, God the Son, and God the Holy Ghost. Indeed, that continued down until the day of the baptism of Constantine, about the year 400. When Constantine formally accepted Christianity, in writing to a friend he said, "It is not by one immersion we are baptized, but by three immersions into three separate names of the Trinity, and I was so baptized."

It is not at all the form of baptism that is important. Form never interests me. A person who has been immersed by a single immersion, I would hesitate to say, "Be baptized over again." But I tell you what God wants and what His purpose has been from the beginning: If the world and the Church had followed the plain teachings and example of the apostolic church, you can see that faith in Jesus would never have been attacked as it has been. Men have lost the consciousness of the Son of God as the Savior of the world, because these things were confused and were not kept distinct, as the Holy Spirit gave them in the beginning.

What then, should be the attitude of the Church that has determined to return to the teachings and practices of the Lord Jesus Christ? Are we not, beloved, when we receive candidates who have not been baptized, to baptize them in accordance with the plain teachings of the Word of God and the plain teachings of history all down through the line?

This may surprise you. [Name does not appear] was the first teacher to publicly baptize by single immersion, and he denied the deity of Jesus Christ and baptized in the name of the Father. Further, baptism was performed officially in the Church by triune immersion until the eighth century, when Pope Greggory, in these words, changed the form of baptism:

[This quote was missing from the original transcript.]

So baptism was officially changed from triune immersion to single immersion in the Roman church about the eighteenth century, then that was overruled and sprinkling became a fact.

I dislike to discuss the form. It always troubles my soul to be compelled to discuss the form in Christian worship and Christian life. It is not the form, but it is the fact. You may baptize a soul by any form you like, but there is only one thing that is valuable. That is, when a man is baptized, he should be baptized into God the Father and inducted into Jesus Christ the Son and into the Holy Ghost, bless God. Then the fact has taken place in the man's soul.

We can therefore understand how that Paul wrote, as he did in the sixth of Romans, where he called the Christians' attention to this fact: That they have no right to sin; they have no privilege to sin. Christians never had the privilege to sin. Christians cannot have the privilege of sinning. It is foreign to him. It is foreign to his faith. It is foreign to his profession. He is "born again." He is a new man. He received his salvation from God the Father through Jesus Christ the Son. Paul says then that we have been baptized into His death — into death to sin. As Jesus Himself went down to death, so in the name of Jesus, like Him, we are raised up to the new life. Blessed be His name![12]

Do you not see, dear ones, that the subject of the sixth of Romans is not the subject of baptism? It is the subject of "death to sin," and Paul is emphasizing to these Christians that through the fact that they have been baptized into the name of Jesus Christ, they have become dead to sin. Sin no longer has power over them and in consequence, they are new men in Christ Jesus. Blessed be His name!

From the fullness of Thy heart, O God, Thou has bestowed upon Thy children the abundant grace of God. In Thy abundant mercy, Lord, Thou hast made clear and distinct the paths of God. And now, my Father, where the minds of men have become clouded in any manner to the real purposes of God and the real distinctiveness of the Word of God to the human heart, we pray Thee, Lord, that Thou will give us grace, with boldness and strength, to declare the blessed Word of God, that men may see and men may enter the plain ways of God, for Jesus' sake. Amen.

---

[12] Romans 6:1-4.

he relation of the physical man and God's final purpose has been absolutely left out. My convictions are, and they are deeply grounded, that man's interest in the physical man at this present hour is not a maxim, but the natural development that this present hour of necessity brings to the spirit of man.

PHYSICALIZED CHRISTIANITY
Apostolic Temple
November 21, 1915

Historians tell us that prior to the coming of the Lord Jesus Christ and his birth as a man, there was a strange "looking forward" on the part of man for an event, for the coming of someone who would bring a new light, new life, new liberty to the world. The Jews spoke of him as their Messiah. The other nations, according to their philosophers, had one also whom they were looking for and who they are looking for again. For the looking forward to the coming of the Christ by the Christian or for the return of Jesus to this world by the great majority of advanced Christian people has spread very rapidly throughout the whole Christian world during the past few years.

There is a reason why the souls of men catch the gleam, at particular times, of a coming event. The spirit that is anticipating and waiting and longing for and believing in the coming of Jesus of necessity has become sensitized along that line and of necessity will catch the foregleams of the rising sun. I believe it was that internal condition of the spirit of man that the historians and the scribes speak of as an electrical condition of the minds of men which preceded the coming of Jesus to the earth.

I believe at the present moment there is such a condition in the hearts of men throughout the world being repeated. Men are anticipating. They are looking forward to the event that they cannot explain.

About six years ago I made a compilation, or rather made a selection, of quotations from some of the great magazines of the world. Among them I remember a statement of W. T. Stead, who is recognized as one of the greatest editors the world has ever produced. He was editor of the *English Review of Reviews*. He was drowned when the

Titanic went down. In writing on this subject he said... I took the cuttings from his magazine. He had compiled them from various magazines all over the world, experiences that indicated in the minds of men of all classes that men were looking forward to an event soon to occur that they could not understand. However, many felt it. Some even suggested that if there be such a thing it would not be unreasonable to believe that perhaps it might be what is commonly spoken of as the "end of the age" or the "end of the world."

That "end of the world" expression is a misleading term, for there is no end of the world. There is a new age. And every age has its closing events, and the events are peculiar to that age.

Stead went further than some of the rest. He said,

> Christians speak of the return of Jesus Christ, and the establishment of the kingdom of Christ. What events may precede such a thing we know not, but there is nothing unreasonable in believing that perhaps the thing that all feel is produced by the foregleam of the event to take place. Coming events cast their shadows before.

Physicalized Christianity has a reason. It is born because of conditions. It is born because of conditions produced by the Spirit of God, in anticipation of a day when mortal, both the living and those who have fallen to sleep, shall put on immortality. Of necessity, men have begun to recognize a physical change that must be accomplished to make such a condition a possibility. Paul, in the words I read to you from First Corinthians, says,

> Behold, I shew you a mystery; we shall not all sleep, but we shall all be changed, in a moment, in the twinkling of an eye, at the last trump: for the trumpet shall sound, and the dead shall be raised incorruptible, and we shall be changed. For this corruptible must put on incorruption, and this mortal must put on immortality.[1]

In discussing the subject of the resurrection, he says, "This mortal *must* put on immortality." This mortal must put on immortality. Flesh

---

[1] 1 Corinthians 15:51-53.

and blood cannot inherit the kingdom of God. Consequently, a change in the living as well as the dead is an apparent fact.

If I were going to give a reason why the attention of mankind is turning to God today for the bodies of men, I would place it right there, in the fact that the Spirit of God or the rays of the coming age are breaking through into the days of this age, and we are anticipating the age which is to come. The very first gleams of the rising sun of that event must discover that it was not in God's will or purpose for man to live in pain, in sorrow, in sickness, and in poverty. But on the other hand, it is God's purpose and intent of Jesus that mankind should be redeemed from sin, from sickness, and from death, bless God.

No finer phrase was ever coined to express the real thing that the Spirit of God is accomplishing at the present hour than the phrase "physicalized Christianity." The secret of healing, the secret of physical healing is contained in this fact that the spirit of man, in union with the Spirit of God, becomes cognizant of the mind of God concerning itself.

The gleams of immortality that shine into the spirit are transmitted through the soul into the bodies of men, and that is the real issue, the real secret of real healing by the power of God.

I speak of man in the sense that the Scriptures describe him as a triune being — body and soul and spirit. The soul of man has ever been compelled to listen to two voices: The voice of the spirit and the voice of the flesh or natural man.

Those who have studied the subject at all of what is defined in the Scriptures as the fall of man, long ago, very long ago, arrived at this conclusion: That the fall of man was the descent of man from the control of his spirit, or God man, into the control of his flesh, or animal man. And the spirit became to some extent subject to the animal man. Redemption is the restoration of the spirit of man to his normal place of authority, whereby soul and body become subservient to the spirit, not the spirit to the body.

Physicalized Christianity! Bless God for the phrase. It is splendid. It fills a need. It expresses a pregnant thought, the thought that the hour is coming when through the enlightenment of the Spirit of God man has arrived at that place in his growth toward (in) God where he begins to recognize that God has a definite purpose for the body and soul of man as well as for the spirit.

He who works in the greatest calmness, with the holiest and the greatest consciousness of the Father, is he who permits his spirit to dominate his being, not only working with the spirit of man in control of your personality, but more the spirit of man in union with the Spirit of God, whereby the mind of God and the thought of God for this present hour is understood and is being lived up to.

The transmission from the spirit of the thought of God through the soul is a continuous process. The transmission of the power of God from the spirit through the soul and into the body is a continuous process. And the real fact of sickness, the *real* fact of sickness is simply that somehow a portion of our body loses its correspondence with the rest of our being and is not receiving naturally and normally that sufficient measure of the life of God that other portions of the body are receiving.

The intelligent Christian has long since learned that if a portion of his body is not receiving the due measure of life from God that another portion is receiving, it is because there is not being directed to the afflicted portion of the body the due measure of the Spirit that it ought to receive, and that it is the privilege by the Spirit to take the life of God and direct it to any portion of his body that he so chooses. Blessed be God!

The climax of such thought is not simply the mere condition of physical healing. It is more. Of necessity there must come a condition of health, not healing. And I look forward with great joy and great hope and great expectation.

oliness is the character of God. The very substance of His being and essence of His nature is purity. The purpose of God in the salvation of mankind is to produce in man a kindred holiness, a radiant purity like unto that of God Himself. If God were unable to produce in him such a purity, then His purpose in man would be a failure, and

HOLINESS UNTO THE LORD

Spokane, Washington

March 6, 1916

the object of the sacrifice of Jesus Christ would be a miscarriage instead of a triumph.

The triumph of Jesus Christ was attained through His willingness to be led by the Spirit of God. The triumph of the Christian can be attained only in a similar manner. Even though God has baptized a soul with the Holy Spirit, there yet remains, as with Jesus, the present necessity of walking in humility and permitting the Spirit of God to be his absolute guide.

The unveiling of consciousness, of the desire of the flesh, of the sensuality of the nature and the thought of man, the revelation of adverse tendencies, is part of God's purpose and necessary for growth in God. How can the nature of man be changed except that nature is first revealed? So there arises in the heart the desire and prayer for the Spirit of God to eject, crucify, and destroy every tendency of opposition to the Holy Spirit. Think not that thou shalt attain the highest in God until within thine own soul a heavenly longing to be like Him who gave His life for us possesses thine heart.

Think not to come within the court of God with stain upon thy garments. Think not that heaven can smile upon a nature fouled through evil contact. Think not that Christ can dwell in temples seared by flames of hate. No! The heart of man must first be purged by holy fire and washed from every stain by cleansing blood. Know ye [not] that he whose nature is akin to God's must ever feel the purging power of Christ within?

He who would understand the ways of God must trust the Spirit's power to guide and keep. He who would tread the paths where angels tread himself must realize seraphic purity. Such is the nature of God, such the working of the Spirit's power, such the attainment of him who overcomes. In him the joy and power of God shall be. Through him the healing streams of life shall flow. To him heaven's gates are opened wide. In him the kingdom is revealed.

> *Fear not to place thy hand within the nail-pierced palm. Fear not to trust His guidance. The way He trod is marked by bleeding feet and wet with many tears. He leadeth thee aright, and heaven's splendor soon shall open to thy spirit, and thou shalt know that all triumphant souls — those who have overcome indeed — have found their entrance by this path into the realms of light.*

(Given in tongues and interpretation to Rev. John G. Lake, in Spokane, Washington, March 6, 1916.)

(In His name and for God's Glory. L.G.F.)

f I were to choose a subject for the thought in my soul tonight, I would choose "The Calling of the Soul."

THE CALLING OF THE SOUL

Spokane, Washington

March 6, 1916

Someone has given us this little saying that has become prevalent among many people: "My own shall come to me." Jesus framed that thought in different words. He said, "He that hungers and thirsts after righteousness shall be filled." It is the same law. "Blessed are they which do hunger and thirst after righteousness: for they shall be filled."[1]

Righteousness is simply God's rightness — God's rightness in a man's soul, God's rightness in a man's spirit, God's rightness in a man's body. In order that man may be right, or righteous, God imparts to man the power of His Spirit. That Spirit contains such marvelous and transforming grace that when received into the nature of man, the marvelous process of regeneration is set in motion and man becomes thereby a new creature in Christ Jesus.

The deepest call of our nature is the one that will find the speediest answer. People pray; something happens. If they pray again, something still deeper occurs within their nature and they find a new prayer. The desire is obtained.

In my ministry in South Africa, I had a preacher by the name of Van Vuuren. That name means "fire." Van Vuuren had been a butcher in the city of Johannesburg and was given up to die of consumption. His physician said to him, "You have only one year to live." So he gave up his business and went down into the country to develop a farm, that his family might be able to support themselves.

After he left the city, many were baptized in the Holy Spirit and healed, etc., and his friends wrote him a letter and said, "So-and-so, who was sick, has been healed. So-and-so, your niece, has been baptized in the Holy Spirit and is speaking in tongues by the power of God. So-and-so has been blessed of God," etc.

---

[1] Matthew 5:6.

Van Vuuren took the letter and went out into the fields and got down under a thorn tree and spread the letter out before God. Then he began to pray, "God, if You can do these things for the people at Johannesburg, You can do something for me. I have been a Christian for eighteen years, and I have prayed and prayed for certain things which have not come to pass. God, if others can be baptized in the Holy Ghost, surely I can. If others' hearts are made pure by the power of God, the power that made theirs pure can make mine pure also. If others have been healed, then You can heal me."

As he thus gave himself to God and opened his soul to heaven, suddenly the Spirit came upon him, and he became the most transformed creature I ever knew. God moved into the man. For eighteen days, he walked as though overshadowed by the Spirit of God; God talking continuously to his soul, directing him to this one and that one, judges and lawyers, statesmen and physicians, rich and poor. When he would reach them, the Spirit of God would pour forth through his soul such messages of God that, in many cases, they fell down and wept.

This is the point of the story I wanted you to get. He said for eighteen years he had prayed for the real conversion and transformation of his wife, and it had not come to pass. But that morning, after the Lord had baptized him in the Holy Ghost, a new prayer came into his heart. A new depth had been touched in the man's nature, and from that great inner depth flowed out to God a cry that had been going out from his soul for years. But that morning the cry of God touched the soul of his wife, and before he reached the house she had given her heart to God. In three months all his family — his wife, eleven children, and himself — had been baptized in the Holy Spirit.

The desire of which Jesus spoke (for when He spoke of desire, He spoke of this same call of the soul) was not the simple attitude of the outer man. Certainly it included it. Perhaps the desire in the beginning was simply that of the mind, but as the days and years passed and the desirability of obtaining grew in the soul, it became a call of the deepest depth of the man's nature. And that is the character of desire that Jesus spoke of when He said, "Blessed are they that hunger and thirst after righteousness, for they shall be filled."

The spiritual action that takes place within the nature of man, that strong desire for God — His ways, His love, His knowledge, His power — causes everything else, perhaps unconsciously to himself, to become secondary.

Politicians talk about a paramount issue. That is the issue that stands out by itself above all other and is the greatest and largest and of most interest to the nation. It is the paramount issue.

The soul has its paramount issue, and when the desire of your heart is intensified so that it absorbs all your energies, then the time of its fulfillment is not far away. That is the desire that brings the answer. It is creative desire.

A woman testified in my hearing one day to this fact. She had been pronounced hopeless and was going blind. No human remedy could do her any good. Someone opened to her, in a dim way, the possibility of seeing through the power of God. She was not very well-taught, but she said this, "Every day for four years I gave up two and one-half hours absolutely to expressing the desire of my soul for real sight." Not only expressing it in words, but calling the power of God to her that would recreate in her the function of sight in her eyes and make her see. At the end of four and a half years, she said, "My eyes are as well as they ever were."

That is the reward of persistence, of a desire toward God. Your nature may have sent out just as deep a cry to God as my nature has and still is doing. Is the cry to God continuous? Gradually, as the forces of life concentrate themselves in line with that strong desire, the Spirit of God is operating through your heart, is being directed by that desire and concentrated on a particular line, intensifying every day because of the continuous desire of the soul to possess. The effect of that concentration of the Spirit of God on that soul is that by the grace of God there is brought to your soul all the elements necessary to formulate and create and fulfill the desire of your heart. And one morning the soul awakens to discover that it has become the possessor of the desired object.

Jesus started men on the true foundation. Many simply desire health, others temporal blessings. Both are good and proper, but bless God, Jesus started the soul at the proper point, to first desire *righteousness*, the righteousness of God, to become a possessor of the kingdom.

"Seek ye first," said Jesus, "the kingdom of God, and his righteousness; and all *these* things shall be added unto you."[2]

Jesus was bringing forth and establishing in the world a new character, a character that would endure forever, a soul quality that would never fail, a faith that knew no possibility of defeat. In establishing such a character, Jesus saw that the character could only be established in the depth of a man's being, in the very spirit of his being. Then, when once the soul was grounded in the paths of righteousness, all the activities of the nature would be along righteous lines and in harmony with the laws of God.

God has a call in His own Spirit. If we study our own spirit, we will understand the nature of God. The call of the Spirit of God is the call of righteousness, the call of truth, the call of love, the call of power, the call of faith.

I met a young man on one occasion who seemed to me to be the most blessed man, in some ways, of all the men I had ever met. I observed he was surrounded by a circle of friends of men and women, the deepest and truest it had ever been my privilege to know. One day I said to him, "What is the secret of this circle of friends that you possess and the manner in which you seem to bind them to you?" He replied, "Lake, my friendships are the result of the call of the soul. My soul has called for truth and righteousness, for holiness, for grace, for strength, for soundness of mind, for the power of God, and the call has reached this one, and this one, and this one, and brought them to me."

Over in Topeka, Kansas, in the year 1900, one morning a man stepped off the train, walked up the street, and as he walked up a particular street, he stopped in front of a large, fine dwelling and said to himself, "This is the house." A gentleman who happened to be out of sight around the building said, "What about the house?" and this story came out.

He said, "For years, I have been praying God for a certain work of God among Christians known as the baptism of the Holy Ghost. In my research I have visited every body of Christian people in this

---

[2] Matthew 6:33.

country that I knew of that claimed to be possessors of the baptism, but as I visited and examined their experiences and compared it with the Word of God, I became convinced that none of them possess the baptism of the Holy Ghost as it is recorded and demonstrated in the New Testament."

He said one day as he prayed, the Spirit of the Lord said, "Go to Topeka, Kansas." As he prayed, he observed in the Spirit a certain house, and the Lord said, "I will give you that house, and in it the baptism of the Holy Ghost will fall."

So he took the train and came to Topeka, walked down the street, and exclaimed as he passed by, "This is the house."

And the voice around the corner replied, "What about it?" When the man had heard his story, he told him he was the owner of the house, that it had been closed for years. He asked him what he wanted it for, and he replied that he was going to start a Christian school. The owner said, "Have you any money?"

He replied, "No."

He said, "All right, you can have the house without money."

About an hour later, a little Quaker lady came down the street, hesitated, and looked around and said, "This is the house, but there is no one living there." After a struggle with her soul, she went up and rang the doorbell, and the first gentleman answered the bell and asked what she wanted. She said, "I live over in the country at such a place. As I prayed, the Spirit told me to come here to this house."

He said, "Who are you?"

She replied, "Just an unknown Christian woman."

He said, "What have you been praying about?"

She said, "About the baptism of the Holy Ghost."

Beloved, in three weeks, eighteen persons were brought to that house. They formed a little company and began to pray. The company grew to thirty-six. On New Year's night, 1900, the Spirit fell on that company, and the first one was baptized in the Holy Ghost and in a few weeks, practically the whole company had been baptized in the Holy Ghost. And from there it spread over the world.

Yesterday morning a woman came to my healing rooms, a stranger in the city. She said, "I have been praying for healing and asking God to show me where I could be healed. I heard of friends in Chicago who pray for the sick, and I visited them, but when I arrived the Spirit said, 'Not here.'"

She said, "I bought a ticket and was about to take a train back home, but as I sat in the station I was approached by a little lady on crutches and pitying her, I turned to speak a kind word to her. While conversing with her, I saw she was a Christian of a deep nature, rarely found. I told her my story. She said, 'Oh, I know where the Lord wants you to go. The Lord wants you to go to Spokane, Washington.'" (Three thousand miles from Chicago.)

She asked her if she knew anybody in Spokane and the lady replied, "Why yes, I know Mr. Lake. I used to nurse in his home years ago."

I prayed for her and told her the thing to do was to come in for ministry every day until she was well. She said she would. This morning, I received a call on the telephone, and she said, "I am not coming up to the healing rooms."

I said, "Oh, is that the kind of individual you are? The one that comes once and gets nothing."

"No," she said, "I came once and got something and I do not need to come back. I am healed and I am going home."

There is a call of faith in this church that is reaching way out, far out, and in unaccountable ways. Away at the other end the Spirit of God is revealing truth to this soul and that soul, and they are moving into this life and coming into unity with this church.

Is there a note of despair in your heart? Have you not attained the thing your soul covets? Have you desired to be like that sinless, unselfish, sickless one? God will answer the call of your soul. You shall have your heart's desire. But before that call becomes answerable it must be the paramount call of your being. It is when it becomes the paramount issue of the soul that the answer comes. Jesus knew. That is the reason He said, "Blessed are they that hunger and thirst after righteousness, for they shall be filled."

There is not a doubt about it. All the barriers of your nature will go down before the desire of the soul. All the obstacles that ever were will disappear before the desire of your soul. All the diseases that ever existed in your life will disappear before the desire of your soul when that desire becomes the one great purpose and prayer of your heart.

I love to think of one great soul. He was not a great Christian, but he was a great soul. He was the son of a Church of England clergyman and came to South Africa thinking he might get his system back to a normal state of health. He came to the diamond mines at Kimberly and took a pick and shovel and worked with them long enough to understand diamonds. Indeed, he studied diamonds until he knew more about them than any other man in the world. Then he went to studying Africa until one paramount desire grew up in his soul. He said, "I will plant the British flag across the continent." Eventually, this is what he did. He told me that in the beginning his vision extended to the Vaal River, then to the Zambezi, and then across the trackless desert. He also planned a railroad six thousand miles long. John Cecil Rhodes died before he could fully bring to pass the paramount issue of his soul.

"Blessed are they that hunger and thirst after righteousness."

Oh, if I had one gift or one desire that I would bestow on you more than all others, I would bestow upon you the hunger for God.

"Blessed are they that hunger." Hunger is the best thing that ever came into a man's life. Hunger is hard to endure. It is the call of the nature for something that you do not possess. The thing that will satisfy the demands of the nature and the hunger of a man's soul is the call of his nature for the Spirit of life that will generate in him the abundant love of God.

Years ago, I was one of a family of which some member was an invalid in the house for thirty-two consecutive years. During that time, we buried four brothers and four sisters. A call arose in my nature to God for something to stay that tide of sickness and death. Materia Medica had utterly failed. One after another the tombstones were raised. The call arose in my soul for something from God that would stem the tide and turn it backward.

Nothing else but healing could have come to my life, no other thing but the knowledge of it. God had to bring, from the furthest ends of Australia, the man who brought to my soul the message of God and the manifestation of His power that satisfied my heart. And healing by the power of God became a fact to me.

We live that our souls may grow. The development of the soul is the purpose of existence. God Almighty is trying to obtain some decent association for Himself. By His grace He is endeavoring to have us grow up in His knowledge and likeness to that stature where, as sons of God, we will comprehend something of His love, of His nature, of His power, of His purpose, and be big enough to give back to God what a son should give to a great Father — the reverence, the love, the affection that comes from the understanding of the nobleness and greatness of His purpose.

Great Britain produced two marvelous statesmen, a father and his son. They are known in history as the old Pitt and the young Pitt. The young Pitt was as great a statesman as his father. The son grew to that largeness where, catching the vision of his great father, his soul arose to it, and he became his father's equal. As I walked through the House of Commons, I came across the statues of the old and young Pitt. I have forgotten the inscription at the bottom of the elder Pitt's statue, but at the base of the son's statue was these words, "My father, the greatest man I ever knew." Do you see the call of his soul for his father's largeness, for his father's nobility, for his father's strength and influence?

"Blessed are they that hunger." Bless God! What are we hungering for, a little bit of God? Enough to take us through this old world where we will have the dry rot and be stunted and then squeeze into heaven? "Blessed are they that hunger," for the nature and power and love and understanding of God. Why? "They shall be filled." Bless God!

Not long ago I stood before great audiences of the churchmen of the world. They said, "Through all your ministry there is one note. It is the call for power." They said, "Do you not think it would be better if the Church was calling for holiness instead of power?"

And I replied, "She will never obtain the one without the other. There is something larger than holiness. It is the nature of God."

The nature of God has many sides. From every angle that the soul approaches God, it reveals a new and different manifestation of Him: Love, beauty, tenderness, healing, power, might, wisdom, etc.

So the Christian who hungers and hungers, bless God, and lifts his soul to God, brings God down to meet his own cry. The spirit of man and the Spirit of God unite. The nature of God is reproduced in man, as God purposed it should be. There are no sick folk in God. There is no sickness in His nature.

There is an incident in the life of Jesus that is so marvelous. Jesus Christ demanded His right to heal a woman who was so bound by Satan with a spirit of infirmity and was not satisfied until it was accomplished. Devil and church and creed and preacher went down before the call of the Son of God to assert His right to deliver that soul from sin and sickness. "Blessed are they that hunger."

THE SECOND CROWNING

April 16, 1916
Palm Sunday

eading:
Revelation 5.

And I saw in the right hand of him that sat on the throne a book written within and on the backside, sealed with seven seals. And I saw a strong angel proclaiming with a loud voice, who is worthy to open the book, and to loose the seals thereof? And no man in heaven, nor in earth, neither under the earth, was able to open the book, neither to look thereon. And I wept much, because no man was found worthy to open and to read the book, neither to look thereon. And one of the elders saith unto me, Weep not: behold, the Lion of the tribe of Juda, the Root of David, hath prevailed to open the book, and to loose the seven seals thereof. And I beheld, and, lo, in the midst of the throne and of the four beasts, and in the midst of the elders, stood a Lamb as it had been slain, having seven horns and seven eyes, which are the seven Spirits of God sent forth into all the earth. And he came and took the book out of the right hand of him that sat upon the throne. And when he had taken the book, the four beasts and four and twenty elders fell down before the Lamb, having every one of them harps, and golden vials full of odours, which are the prayers of saints. And they sung a new song, saying, Thou art worthy to take the book, and to open the seals thereof: for thou wast slain, and hast redeemed us to God by thy blood out of every kindred, and tongue, and people, and nation; and hast made us unto our God kings and priests: and we shall reign on the earth. And I beheld, and I heard the voice of many angels round about the throne and the beasts and the elders: and the number of them was ten thousand times ten thousand, and thousands of thousands; saying with a loud voice, Worthy is the Lamb that was slain to receive power, and riches, and wisdom, and strength, and honour, and glory, and blessing. And every creature which is in heaven, and on the earth, and under the earth, and such as are in the sea, and all that are in them, heard I

> saying, Blessing, and honour, and glory, and power, be
> unto him that sitteth upon the throne, and unto the Lamb
> for ever and ever. And the four beasts said, Amen. And the
> four and twenty elders fell down and worshipped him that
> liveth for ever and ever.

O God, upon our soul we call the blessing of the Holy Spirit today to quicken every instinct of our being, that by Thy grace we may comprehend the power of Thy Word and the might of Thy Spirit. And we pray that the Spirit of the Lord Jesus Christ may be present in every heart that we may realize, O God, not only the elevation and crowning of our Lord and Savior, but our own elevation and crowning with Him as sons of God.

Somehow, the minds of men the world over have ever been concentrated around the cross of Christ. One of the strangest things to me in all Christian life has been the manner in which the souls of men cling to the cross of Calvary. And I have sometimes felt that that is one of the great reasons why there has been so little progress made in the higher Christian life.

While we revere the cross of Calvary, while the soul of man will ever love to think of Him who gave His life for us, yet I believe the triumph of the Christ began at the cross and ends only when the race, like Himself, has received from God the Father, through Him, the grace, power, and glory of God that makes them sons of God like Himself.

It is a long way between the cross of Calvary and the Throne of God, but that is the way that Jesus traveled, and that is the course for every other soul of man, bless God. I am glad that God is never hurried. He has plenty of time. A few years makes much difference in this life, but God has plenty of time for the elevation of the soul, for the perfect tuition[1] of every heart, until that heart comes into such complete and perfect unison, that the nature of man is absolutely changed into the nature of Christ.

---

[1] tuition: 2. *Brit.* teaching or instruction. *Webster's Desk Dictionary of the English Language* (NY: Gramercy Books, 1983), p. 959.

The triumph of Jesus, as we see it outlined in the scriptures I have just read, has always been one of the splendid inspirations to my own soul. It seems to me, if we had not been permitted to have that foreview of that final triumph of the Son of God, there might have been the conception in the minds of many that after all, the life and death of our Lord Jesus Christ was not the perfect triumph that it ought to have been. It seems, therefore, that no one can have the highest appreciation of the real Christian life and the consciousness that real Christianity brings unless they see the triumph of the Christ.

Yea, more. It is only as we become possessors of that consciousness ourselves, and as the knowledge of His triumph grows in our own souls and takes possession of our heart, that we are able to comprehend what Christianity really is.

If we stop to think that one-half of the great Christian world is still carrying a little crucifix representing a dead Christ, we will realize how the mind of man is yet chained to the cross of Calvary, to a dead Christ, to a tomb not empty, but the tomb that contains the One they love.

Beloved, that is not Christianity. Christianity, bless God, is the ringing triumph that began on the morning of the Resurrection and ends when the race of man has come to the understanding, knowledge, and consciousness of God Himself.

Christianity is not a dreary outlook. Christianity is the ringing, splendid triumph of the mind of God. Christianity is the blessed victory that the individual feels in his own heart of the consciousness of the presence and power of God within the soul, which makes man the master now and gives him the consciousness of mastery over the powers of sickness and death. Yea, bless God, the greater consciousness by which the soul of man comprehends the life eternal, because the forces of darkness and sin and death have been conquered in his own heart through the presence and power of the Lord Jesus Christ in him. Bless God.

I have always wondered how a Christian could be anything less than an optimist. It is a sad thing when you hear Christians with a groan in them. When I meet the groaner I say in my heart, "God, move the man on into the place where he comprehends what Christianity is." The Christian with a groan in him never moved the world except to groans.

In a divine healing meeting some months ago, as I was teaching, I tried to develop the thought that as a man thinketh in his heart, so is he.[2] And I was endeavoring to show the people that the spirit of victory in Christ Jesus in one's heart not only affected the attitude of one's mind, but likewise, his soul. In fact, through the nervous system, man's mental attitudes are transmitted clear through his body.

The attitude of our soul has much to do with not only our mental states and our spiritual life, but likewise our physical health. Indeed, it seems to me that as the spirit of man is tuned with God, all the outgrowth of his life will be in harmony with his spirit. The attitude of his mind will be in accordance, and the condition of his body will be a revelation of the attitude of his mind. That is the reason I have always endeavored in my preaching to bring before the mind of man the consciousness of triumph, the consciousness of victory, the power of mastery. It seems to me there is a great deal of superficial endeavor in the world to pump oneself up to a certain state of consciousness, which is similar to a man taking himself by the bootstraps and trying to lift himself over the fence.

Beloved, the secret of Christianity is the secret of the Christ possessing the heart of man; man being yielded to Him so that His victory, His consciousness, and His power possess your spirit and mind. Then, bless God, we are kings. Not because we say we are kings, but because we know we are kings and because we feel we are kings by the grace of God and His inworking power.

We speak of mastery, not because we are endeavoring to lift our consciousness into the place where we can possibly conceive of mastery, but because the spirit of mastery is born within the heart. The real Christian is a royal fighter. He is the one who loves to enter into the contest with his whole soul and take the situation captive for the Lord Jesus Christ.

They tell a story of an old-time English officer. He was a very important individual, and it would never do for him to speak out his commands so they could be understood. He had a raw Irishman whom he

---

[2] Proverbs 23:7.

was endeavoring to break in. They were engaged in a sham battle. Presently, the officer let a certain kind of roar, and the Irishman broke from the ranks toward the supposed enemy and grabbing a man by the neck, brought him with him. The officer said, "Hold on. What are you doing?"

"Well," he said, "I did not know what you said, but it felt as if you wanted me to go for him, and I did."

When the Lord Jesus Christ is born indeed in the soul of man, when by the grace and power of the Son of God, you and I yield ourselves to God until our nature becomes the possessor of that Spirit that is in Christ, then, bless God, we begin to realize the spirit of mastery that Jesus possessed when he said:

> I am he that liveth, and was dead; and, behold, I am alive for evermore, Amen; and have the keys of hell and of death.[3]

That is the reason I do not spend much time in talking about the devil. The Lord took care of him, bless God! He has the keys of hell and of death, and He has mastered that individual and that condition once and for all. If you and I had as much faith to believe it as we have to believe that the Lord Jesus Christ is our Savior, we would have mighty little trouble with the devil or his power while we walk through this world. It is not worthwhile talking about a man after he is whipped out.

It is a hard thing for the Christian mind to conceive that the power of evil is really a vanquished power. When I think of examples of Christian triumph, my mind very frequently reverts to a minister I have spoken to you about many times. He was a great soul. The consciousness of Christ's dominion seemed to dwell in the man's heart intensely.

I was with him on one occasion when he was called to a dying man down in the slums. It was late at night. It was always interesting to me to watch the sparkle of his eye and to note here and there the splendid flash of his spirit. We were walking through the streets, and I said to him, "Do you know anything about this man's condition?"

---

[3] Revelation 1:18.

"Well," he replied, "the messenger told me the man was in a state of great suffering and likely to die. But he is not going to die."

I said, "Amen."

You see, there was the ring of conscious mastery in his soul that made it possible for such a splendid burst of confidence to come forth from his spirit. I said to myself that night, "There is not going to be much difficulty tonight. The fellow has the victory in his soul in advance." When we finally knelt by the man's side, and he put his hands on him and called on the mighty God to deliver the man, I felt the flash of his spirit, and I knew before I arose from my knees that the man was healed. And he was.

Beloved, you and I have bowed our heads before a vanquished enemy. We have failed, through lack of faith, to comprehend that the Christ is the Master. But he who dares, by the grace of God, to look into the face of the Lord Jesus Christ knows within his own soul the divine mastery that the Christ of God is exercising now.

The power of God through which men are blessed is not an individual matter that belongs to you or to me. It is the conscious presence of the living, risen Son of God dwelling in our heart by the Holy Ghost, which causes you and I to know that the power of God is equal to every emergency and is great enough for the deliverance of every soul from every oppression.

There are times when it seems to me it is not fitting even to pray. There is a life of praise. Once while in conversation with Dr. Myland, the pastor of the Christian and Missionary Alliance Church at Columbus, Ohio, I happened to mention the fact that I had not prayed concerning a certain personal matter. Turning to me he said, "I have not prayed for myself for four years."

That sounded very strange to me at that time. I did not understand. He said, "No, I passed beyond the place of praying, brother, into the place where I was ready to accept what the Lord Jesus Christ has wrought and to receive the power of His Spirit in my life so that the thing that he has wrought for me should become evident through me." And that man had walked for four years in that conscious victory.

And the Spirit of the Lord says within my soul that he who trusteth in the living God shall never be confounded. Yea, according to the

Word of God, "He shall mount up on wings as eagles. He shall run and not be weary, he shall walk and not faint."[4]

Bless God, there is a place of strength, of security, of victory — a life of triumph.

An hour of consternation came to the prophet John as the mighty God unfolded to him that which was to occur in the future. A book appears, a marvelous book, sealed with seven seals. An angel with a trumpet voice proceeds to utter a proclamation, "Who is worthy to open the book, and to loose the seven seals thereof?" And mankind stood dumbfounded. No man in heaven or on earth was able to loose the seals or to open the book. And it seemed to the prophet as if a great disappointment was at hand. He says, "I wept much."

But presently the angel guide said to him, "Weep not: behold, the Lion of the tribe of Juda, the Root of David, hath prevailed to open the book."

John says, "I looked and beheld as it were a Lamb." Blessed be God. The real overcomer does not always evidence His overcoming power with much noise. In this case, His overcoming was in the consciousness that was in His heart. He was as a lamb: gentle, sweet, loving, tender, and true.

But the consciousness of power was *in* the Christ. When others stood dumbfounded, when others stood baffled, the Christ appears. He takes the book, opens the seals, and discusses its contents.[5] Beloved, the triumph of the Christ of God is not the triumph of loud shouting. It is the triumph of what you know in your own soul. The victory of the Christ and the victory of a soul is in the knowledge of the relationship between your soul and the soul of the Christ.

He, into whose heart there comes the Spirit of the living God, has within himself the consciousness of One who has overcome and who is set down at the right hand of God, triumphant over every power of sickness and death and hell. Beloved, the triumph of the Gospel is enough to make any man the wildest kind of an enthusiastic optimist.

It is said of Napoleon Bonaparte that when he was First Counsel of France, he proceeded to proclaim himself Emperor of France. And

---

4   Isaiah 40:31, paraphrased.

5   Revelation 5:7.

one day one of the statesmen came and asked him, "By what authority do you dare to proclaim yourself Emperor of France?"

He replied, "By the divine right of ability to govern." The consciousness of power was in the soul of the man. He knew in his own soul that he was qualified to govern.

The Christian has the consciousness of that character of soul. Within the soul of the real Christian there is born the consciousness of capacity to govern, and the first place to apply it is in his own life. For no man ever successfully governed another life until he was first able to govern himself. "Greater is he that ruleth his own spirit than he that taketh a city."[6] The poise of the father of a household will be revealed in the mind of every child of his family. The attitude of the mother's mind will be evidenced in everyone of the household.

A dear brother came to me recently and said, "I do not know what is the trouble. I have worked so hard, and I am not able to accomplish the thing I am trying to do."

I replied, "My friend, the difficulty is in your own soul. You have not attained the mastery of that condition in your own heart. The same condition of confusion that is in your soul is being evidenced in the soul of others about you. It is transmitted from you to them."

How often have you and I walked into the presence of a man whose calmness gave instant strength? How often in life, when the minds of men were driven to confusion, we have seen a single soul maintain his poise in God and become a balancing power in society? History records that at the death of Lincoln, when the news of his assassination became known in New York, the city was almost on the point of breaking into a mob. Three men lay dead on the streets when James A. Garfield appeared on the verandah of one of the hotels. Raising his hands, he spoke these simple words which brought a calm to the whole mob and the whole city and was transferred all over the nation. "God is our King, and the government at Washington still lives." The storm was over, as when Jesus spoke the marvelous words, "Peace, be still." There flowed over the nation the calm of poise in God.

---

[6] Proverbs 16:32, paraphrased.

It is said at the time of the great Chicago fire that the day following, two hundred men committed suicide in that city. The old *Chicago Tribune* came out with a big red-letter heading: "Any coward can suicide, but it takes a *man* to live under these conditions." And the whole thing stopped. There were no more suicides. That wave of cowardice was broken up. The consciousness of one great soul who had the poise of God within his heart was able, by the grace of God, to transmit it to other lives.

The success of your life as a child of God will be in exact accordance with the consciousness of the Christ and the power of God that is in your heart. The old prophet arrested the great wave of human despair that was sweeping over the nation, on one occasion, with these magnetic words, "Underneath are the everlasting arms."[7] Bless God. The nation was not going to pieces. The world was not going to ruin, for underneath were the everlasting arms in which the souls of men could rest down with confidence, and God brought the victory.

When the souls of men learn to rest in confidence upon the living God, peace will possess this world that will be like unto the kingdom of God — heaven on earth.

Most of our difficulties are the difficulties that we anticipate or fear are coming tomorrow. How many people are worrying about the things of today? But the world is in consternation concerning tomorrow, or the next day, or the next day. Jesus said, "Sufficient unto the day is the evil thereof."[8] Do not worry about tomorrow. Rest down in God. The mighty arms of the living God will be underneath tomorrow, just as they are today.

The Spirit of God says within my heart that the kingdom of Christ, for which every child of God looks, is characterized by the peace of God possessing the soul of men, so that worry and care cease to be because we trust in His arms.

If I could bring to you today one blessing greater than another, it would be the consciousness of trust in God. "Fear not, neither be thou afraid, for the Lord thy God is with thee whithersoever thou goest."[9]

---

[7] Deuteronomy 33:27.

[8] Matthew 6:34.

[9] Joshua 1:9, paraphrased.

A little woman came into the healing rooms recently, weeping so that I could hardly talk to her. She said, "I am the mother of three children. I am afraid I am going to die. The doctor said so-and-so. There is no hope for me. I must leave my husband and children."

I said, "The doctor is a liar." And that woman is sitting in the audience today a well woman. Beloved, she might have been dead. We might have been celebrating another funeral. But confidence in the living God brought the confidence of power over the thing that was crushing the life out of that soul, and it went by the grace of God. No case is too hopeless.

Last evening in the healing rooms, just at six o'clock, I was visited by a woman who I met four or five months ago in the Deaconess Hospital. The dear lady had been given up to die. She had been examined by X-ray, and a large cancer in the stomach was discovered. They told her there was nothing to be done for her. So the dear husband sent for me to speak a kindly word to his supposedly dying wife. I did not understand what I had been sent for and when I got to the dear soul I supposed I had been called to pray the prayer of faith for healing.

I said, "Dear Mother, you do not have to die."

"But," she said, "the doctor says so. The X-ray shows such a sized cancer. I guess, brother, I will have to die."

And I said, "It is a lie. You do not have to die." For two or three months we battled against that condition in the woman's soul. The Spirit of God would come upon her every time we prayed. Her pains would disappear, she would go to sleep, etc., but she was not really healed. That went on week after week and month after month until I was almost worn out before her soul raised to take victory. But last night she walked into the healing rooms. She told me that she weighed only seventy-five pounds when I met her and that now she weighs one hundred twenty pounds. She went to the hospital this week and had the same physician X-ray her. When they saw the picture they said, "There must be some mistake." And they got the original and examined it. They could not understand it.

She said, "Doctor, I found a new Physician, the Great Physician, the Christ of God, and I do not care about your plates. I know the cancer is gone." But the plates showed it was gone. The woman has gone back home a happy woman. But, beloved, the victory only came when the consciousness of the power of the living Christ took possession of that woman's heart. Blessed be God.

Not a dead Jesus, but a living Christ! Not a sepulcher with a dead man in it, but the glorious, risen, present Christ in your heart and mine. The Christ lives, bless God, not only at the right hand of God, but the Christ lives in your soul and mine. The victory that He attained is evidenced not alone by the declaration: "I am he that liveth, and was dead; and, behold, I am alive for evermore," but the victory He attains through you and me now. That was His peculiar victory, but the victory of the Christ that gives the son of God its gladness now is the consciousness that the Christ lives and the Christ reigns and that by the power of God, sin, darkness, death, and hell become obedient to the Christian through the Christ that is in him.

TESTIMONY OF MRS. PETERSON

"I was healed when dying. I was in a state of death forty minutes. My womb and ovaries had been removed in an operation, and at my healing God restored them, and I am a normal woman."

I want to give some of you folks a conception of what a battle for a life means. This soul kept up the fight for her life until her forces weakened and she lapsed into unconsciousness. The last thing she said to Brother Westwood was, "I can fight no more. You have to do it for me or I will die."

And God Almighty healed her through and through, and she stands before the world today a marvel of the power of God, because she refuses to be beaten. This is a miracle, not a healing only. The work of God in her was creative. "To one is given by the Spirit the gift of healing, to another the working of miracles."[10]

The conception of the Lord Jesus Christ that we are battling against in these days is that which the poet has framed in these beautiful words (and I say this with all reverence):

"Gentle Jesus, meek and mild, look upon a little child."

---

[10] 1 Corinthians 12:9-10, paraphrased.

In that child-thought of Jesus there is no conception of the triumphant Son of God who entered into death and took the victory, who established eternal life in the souls of men. Bless God for the Christ who dared to enter into the very jaws of death and to grapple with the enemy that no man had ever dared to tackle and came forth the Victor. He took him captive and broke his power and bound him in chains and declared liberty to a world that was crushed and bound by the consciousness of the power of death.

As the coming of the Christ approaches, that coming which I believe a multitude of Christian hearts are looking for in these days, the flash and flame and consciousness of the Master Son of God takes possession of their hearts and minds, and in the name of Jesus men are raising up everywhere who refuse to be bound by sin and sickness and death.

That is the reason that John saw in his vision of the Revelation a day of triumph, when all that were in the earth and the sea and under the sea, when heaven, earth, and hell united to send forth a shout of triumph that will ring through the eternities, because the Christ of God had become the acknowledged Master, Ruler, Prince, and King of the race.

If the blessed Spirit of God keeps on revealing the mighty power of the living Christ in the souls of men, we will have to have a new hymnbook. We will have to have a new class of poets in the world. It will come too, as sure as you are born. They used to sing dreary old hymns in the little Scotch church when I was a boy, and I remember one particular hymn:

> *Hark! From the tomb a doleful sound.*
>
> *Mine ear, attend the cry.*
>
> *Ye living men come view the ground*
>
> *Where You must shortly lie. Ah.*

Afterward I learned that "ah" was Amen, but I did not know it then.

Oh, bless God for the revelation of the living Christ in the souls of men that lifts the consciousness of men from the place of defeat into the place of power — the exultant, present, mighty power of the living God.

One Sunday afternoon, a tall Englishman walked into my church in Johannesburg, South Africa. He was six feet two-and-a-half inches high and twenty-six inches across the shoulders. He had a top of red hair that made him as conspicuous as a lion. He walked up the aisle and took a seat quite near the front. My old preaching partner was endeavoring to explain the mighty power of the living Christ as best he could, and this man sat listening. Presently he arose, saying: "Old man, if the things you are talking about are all right, I am your candidate."

He said, "I used to be a Christian. I came from Port St. Marys, Isle of Man, and I was a Christian boy. I came to Africa and lived the usual African life, and the result is that for three years I have been unable to do anything, and my physicians say I am incurable. If you mean what you are talking about, tell me what to do."

My old partner said, "John, what shall we do?"

I said, "Call him up. We will pray for him right now." We stepped off the platform, put our hands on William T. Dugan, and instantly, as a flash of lightning blasting a tree or rock, the power of God went through the man's being, and the Lord Jesus Christ made him well.

A few days afterward he came down to my house in the middle of the day and said: "Lake, I want you to show me how to get a clean heart." I took the Word of God and went through it with him to show him the mighty, cleansing, sanctifying power of the living God in a man's heart. Before he left he knelt by a chair and consecrated his life to God. Raising his hands to heaven he said, "Lord God, I receive into my life the sanctifying power of God to dissolve every condition in my nature that is adverse to the living God." And bless God, he received it from heaven, just as he received his healing.

Three months passed. One day he called and said, "Lake, I have had a call from God." I knew it was. There was no mistaking it. The wonder of it was in his soul. He went down into the country where a great epidemic of fever was on. Some weeks afterward, I began to receive word that people were being healed — hundreds of them. Bless God. So one day I concluded I would go down and join in the same work, a couple of hundred miles from where he was. Somehow the news traveled that I was at Potgietersrus, and he came there.

The next afternoon we were called to the home of a man who said his wife was sick with diabetes. We prayed for the wife and several other persons who were present. Then the man stepped out into the kitchen and said, "Would you pray for a woman like this?" When I looked at her, I saw she had clubfeet. The right foot was on an angle of forty-five degrees and the left one at right angles. Dugan replied, "Yes. Pray for anybody." He said to her, "Sit down," and taking the clubfoot in his hands he said, "In the name of Jesus Christ become natural." And I want to tell you, that man is in the glory presence of God today. I am going to stand there some day with him. Before I had a chance to take a second breath that foot commenced to move, and the next instant that foot was straight.

Then he took the other foot up, saying, "In the name of Jesus Christ become natural." Beloved, it was not only the voice of the man or the confidence of his soul, but the mighty divine life of Jesus Christ flashed through him, and it melted that foot into softness and it instantly became normal by the power of God.

Beloved, we have not begun to touch the fringes of the knowledge of the power of God. However, I want to encourage your hearts. I know your soul and my soul is hungering after the living God. I am glad we can say what perhaps has never been said in the Christian world from the days of the apostles to the present time, that since the opening of this work in Spokane about sixteen months ago, ten thousand people have been healed by the power of God.

Is Jesus dead? No, bless God. Is He alive? Is He alive in glory? Is He alive in your heart? Bless God, that is the place to crown the Christ. That is the place in your soul and in my soul.

We are just beginning to grow up. The old prophets were so big in their soul, so gigantic in their spirit life that when a poor soul sinned or the whole nation sinned, the prophet removed his clothes, shaved his head, and put sackcloth on his body and ashes on his head and went down before God. He said, "Lord God, I have sinned. We have sinned." And he poured out his soul before God until the nation returned in repentance and love to the feet of the Holy God. I trust one day we will grow up big enough in God that we can do things like that.

Some three or four years ago, when one of the marvelous anointings of the Holy Ghost was on my life, a man came into my healing room one day to tell me how he was in a dying state and hopeless. As I put my hands on him and prayed, I was conscious of the Spirit of God going through him like a stream of light, and presently, he jumped up vibrating under the power of God until his teeth rattled. When his surprise was over, I said to him, "Brother, how about your pain?" That was the first he had thought about it. He said, "My pain is gone."

I said, "Did you feel the power of God?"

He said, "It went through me like buckshot."

Beloved, one of the sorrows of my soul is this, that though we rejoice in the fact God is healing a multitude of people, even in this city, and now they are coming to this city from all quarters of the land, yet some of them have not been healed at all, and they should have been healed. Some have had to come to the healing rooms twenty times instead of once. But bless God, there is a day coming when the power of God will come upon your soul and mine mightily, so it will be like it was with Christ. They will not have to come back a second time. At the touch of Jesus, the mighty power of God flashed through their life until the disease in them was gone forever. Blessed be His precious name. I do not want to give you an idea that there are not people who are instantly healed. There are lots of them, but not all.

Mr. Greenfield Comes on the Platform

Mr. Greenfield was in the hands of physicians for tuberculosis of the kidneys. He was compelled to leave his work. He was just a poor man, and it meant that he should become dependent on his family instead of being the support of the house. When he came to the healing rooms he talked this over a little. He said, "The doctors say I must die."

I said, "Greenfield, don't you believe it. There is a God in heaven." After I laid my hands on him and prayed, I said, "Greenfield, go back to your work." Bless God, he did, and he does not look much like a man dying of tuberculosis now.

Oh, hallelujah! There is a living Christ. There is a triumphant Son of God. There is a living Spirit of the living God, which will flow through the soul of a man just as it flowed through the soul of Jesus. The trouble is with the soul of man. The trouble I am having is with the soul of this man. And the prayer of my life every day and hour is, "Mighty God, purify the soul of this man like the soul of Jesus was pure, and give my soul the consciousness of faith in God like the soul of Jesus possessed." Then, beloved, you and I can say in deed and in truth, "We are sons of God." Blessed be His name.

All that Jesus was to the world He purposed that the Church of Christ should be. First, He blessed the world through His own physical personality. Second, He established a physical body, composed of many members, joined in one by the Spirit of God.

When He established the second body, the Church, He never intended that it should be of lesser authority or of lesser power than the first. It was His real purpose that the second body, the Church, should exercise and fully accomplish all that the first had done.

Edited by Wilford H. Reidt

MINISTRY OF THE SPIRIT

November 24, 1916

*O*ne of the most difficult things to bring into the spirit of people is that the Spirit of God is a tangible substance, that it is the essence of God's own being.

We are composed of an earthly materiality; our bodies are largely a composition of water and earth. This may sound a little crude, but the actual composition of a human being is about sixteen buckets of water and one bucketful of earth. I am glad that there is one bucketful of good mud in us. Water, you know, is a composition of gases, so you can see how much gas there is in mankind. But we are not all gas.

Now the composition of the personality of God — for God has a personality and a being and a substance, spirit is a substance — that is the thing I am trying to emphasize. All heavenly things are of spiritual substance. The body of the angels is of some substance — not the same character of materiality as our own, for ours is an earthly materiality, but the composition of heavenly things is of a heavenly materiality. In other words, heavenly materiality is spirit. The Word says, "God is a spirit." He is a spirit. Therefore, "They that worship him must worship him *in* spirit."[1]

You see, the spirit of man must contact and know the real Spirit of God — know God. We do not know God with our flesh, with our hands, or with our brains. We know God with our *spirit*. The knowledge of God that our spirit attains may be conveyed and is conveyed to us through the medium of our mind, through the medium of our brains. The effect of God in our body comes through the medium of the spirit of man, through the mind of man, into the body of man.

There is a quickening by the Spirit of God so that a man's body, a man's soul or mind, and a man's spirit all alike become blessed, pervaded, and filled with the presence of God Himself in us. The Word of God is wonderfully clear along these lines. For instance, the Word of God says, "Thou wilt keep him in perfect peace, whose *mind* is

---

[1] John 4:24.

stayed on thee" (Isaiah 26:3). Why? "Because he trusteth in thee." That is the rest that a Christian knows whose mind rests in God in real perfect trust. "Thou wilt keep him in perfect peace, whose mind is stayed on thee."

The Word of God again says that our *flesh* shall rejoice — not our mind — but our very flesh shall rejoice.[2] The presence of God is to be a living presence, not only in the spirit of man, nor in the mind of man alone, but also in the flesh of man, so that God is known in *all* the departments of our life. We know God in our very flesh, we know God in our mind, we know God in our spirit. Bless His precious name.

The medium by which God undertakes to bless the world is through the transmission of Himself. Now the Spirit of God is His own substance, the substance of His being, the very nature and quality of the very presence and being and nature of God. Consequently, when we speak of the Spirit of God being transmitted to man and into man, we are not talking about an *influence*, either spiritual or mental. We are talking about the transmission of the living substance and being of God into your being and into mine — not a mental effect, but a living substance — the living being and actual life transmitted, imparted, coming from God into your being, into my being. Bless God!

That is the secret of the abundant life of which Jesus spoke. Jesus said, "I am come that they might have life, and that they might have it *more abundantly*" (John 10:10). The reason we have the more abundant life is because that, receiving God into our being, all the springs of our being are quickened by His living presence. Consequently, if we are living today and we receive God, we live life in a fuller measure. We live life with a greater energy, because we become the recipients of the energy of the living God in addition to our normal energy, through the reception of His being, His nature, His life into ours.

The wonderful measure that the human being is capable of receiving God is demonstrated by some of the incidents in the Word of God. For instance, the most remarkable in the Scriptures is the transfiguration of Jesus Himself, where with Peter, James, and John the Spirit of God came upon Him so powerfully that it radiated out through His

---

[2] Editor's note: We believe he is referring to Acts 2:26.

being, until His clothes became white and glistening and His face shown as the light.

Now, one must be the recipient of the light, glory, and power of God before he or she can manifest it. Jesus demonstrated these two facts: The marvelous capacity of the nature of man to receive God into his being, and the marvelous capacity of the nature of man to reveal God. In the glory shining through His clothes, in the glistening of the glory of God that made His face glorious and wonderful, He demonstrated man's capacity to reveal God.

The human being is God's marvelous, wonderful instrument, the most marvelous and wonderful of all the creation of God in its capacity to receive and reveal God. Paul received so much of God into his being that when men brought handkerchiefs and he took them in his hands, and the women brought their aprons and handed them to him, that the handkerchiefs and aprons became so impregnated with that living Spirit of God — that living substance of God's being — that when they were carried to one who was sick or possessed of devils, the Word says when they laid the handkerchiefs or aprons on them, the Spirit of the living God passed from the handkerchiefs or aprons into the sick man or into the insane man, and the sick were healed and the devils were cast out.[3]

You see, people have been so in the habit of putting Jesus in a class by Himself that they have failed to recognize that He has made provision for the same living Spirit of God that dwelt in His own life, and of which He Himself was a living manifestation, to inhabit your being and mine just as it inhabited the being of Jesus or Paul.

There is no more marvelous manifestation in the life of Jesus than that manifestation of healing through the apostle Paul.

You remember the incident of the woman who touched the hem of Jesus' garment. Knowing how His whole being, His whole nature radiated that wondrous, blessed life of God of which He was Himself the living manifestation, she said within herself, "If I can but touch His garment I shall be healed." So she succeeded after much effort in touching the hem of His garment, and as she touched the hem of His

---

[3] See Acts 19:11-12.

garment there flowed into her body the quickening life stream, and she felt in her body that she was made whole of the plague. And Jesus, being conscious that from Him something had flowed, said to Peter, "Who touched Me?"

Peter replied, "Why Master, You see the crowd, and do You say, who touched Me?"

"Oh," He said, *"Somebody* touched Me, for I perceive that virtue has gone out of Me."[4] If you will analyze that Greek word you will see it means the life or substance of His being, the quickening, living power of God, the very nature and being of God.

If I transmit to another the virtue of my life, I simply transmit a portion of my life to another — the life power that is in me, blessed be God. The life of God that flows through me is transmitted to another, and so it was with Jesus.

Now then, because of the fact that people brought to Paul handkerchiefs and aprons, and they became impregnated with the Spirit of God, and the people were healed when they touched them, is a demonstration in itself that any material substance can become impregnated with the same living Spirit of God.

In my church in South Africa we published a paper in ten thousand lots. We would have the publishers send them to the tabernacle, and we would lay them out in packages of one or two hundred all around the front of the platform, and at the evening service I would call certain ones of the congregation that I knew to be in contact with the living God to come and kneel around and lay their hands on those packages of papers. And we asked God not alone that the reading matter in the paper might be a blessing to the individual and that the message of Christ come through the words printed on the paper, but we asked God to make the very substance of the paper itself become filled with the Spirit of God, just like the handkerchiefs became filled with the Spirit of God.

And if I were in my tabernacle now, I could show you thousands of letters in my files from all quarters of the world, from people telling me that when they received our paper the Spirit came upon them and they

---

[4] Mark 5:25-34, paraphrased.

were healed, or when they received the paper the joy of God came into their heart, or they received the paper and were saved unto God.

One woman wrote from South America, who said, "I received your paper. When I received it into my hands my body began to vibrate so I could hardly sit on the chair, and I did not understand it. I laid the paper down and after awhile I took the paper up again, and as soon as I had it in my hands I shook again. I laid the paper down and took it in my hands a third time, and presently, the Spirit of God came upon me so powerfully that I was baptized in the Holy Ghost."

Beloved, don't you see that this message and this quality of the Spirit contains the thing that confuses all the philosophers and all practice of philosophy in the world? It shows the clearest distinction which characterizes the real religion of Jesus Christ and makes it distinct from all other religions and all other ministries.

The ministry of the Christian is the ministry of the Spirit. He not only ministers words to another, but he ministers the Spirit of God. It is the Spirit of God that inhabits the words, that speaks to the spirit of another and reveals Christ in and through him.

In the old days when I was in Africa, I would walk into the native meetings when I did not understand the languages and listen to the preacher preach for an hour, and I did not understand a word he said. But my soul was blessed by the presence of the Spirit of God.

As bishop of the church, as I went from place to place holding conferences here and there among white and native people, in many of them people would speak either in English or Dutch. But I was just as much blessed when a Dutchman spoke and I did not understand him, as when an Englishman spoke. Why? Because the thing that blessed my soul was the living Spirit of God. Perhaps I had heard better words than his, perhaps clearer explanation of the Scriptures than he could give, but I was blessed by the presence of God. The thing that the individual was ministering to my soul was the living Spirit of God.

The ministry of the Christian is the ministry of the *Spirit*. If the Christian cannot minister the Spirit of God in the true sense, he is not a Christian. If he has not the Spirit to minister in the real high sense, he has nothing to minister. Other men have intellectuality, but the Christian is supposed to be the possessor of the Spirit. He possesses something that no other man in the whole world possesses, that is, the Spirit of the living God.

LETTERS PRESENTED FOR PRAYER

These letters are to dear people all over the land, and I have this feeling that I would like to revive among us that blessed old practice of believing God for the very substance of the letter, the paper, or handkerchief to become so filled with the Spirit of the Lord God that when it comes into their hands that they would not only feel blessed by the words of the letter, but the blessed Spirit of God would flow into their being out of the substance of the paper itself.

That is Christianity. That is the Gospel of Jesus Christ. That is the thing that goes thousands of miles beyond psychological influence. If you want a clear distinction between psychological religions, as they are called, or mental science, you can see it in a minute. The real Christian ministers the real Spirit of God, the substance of His being. There should never be the necessity for misunderstanding along these lines in the minds of any.

A minister of Jesus Christ is as far removed above the realm of psychological influences as heaven is above the earth. Blessed be God. He ministers God Himself into the very spirits and souls and bodies of men. That is the reason that the Christian throws down the bars of this nature and he invites God to come in and take possession of his being. And the incoming of God into our body, into our soul, into our spirit accomplishes marvelous things in the nature of man.

A man came into my healing rooms one day and said, "I am almost ashamed to call myself a man, because I have simply indulged the animal of my nature so that I am more a beast than a man. You say, 'Why don't you quit such a life?' I have not the strength of my being to do so. Unless something takes place that will deliver me from this condition I do not know what I will do."

I tried to show him what the Gospel of Jesus Christ was. I tried to show him that through living in the animal state, thinking animal thoughts, surrounding himself with beastly suggestion, and contacting the spirit of bestiality everywhere that that element had taken such possession that it predominated in the nature. I said, "My son, if the Gospel means anything, it means there shall be a transference of nature. Instead of this living hell that is present in your being, the living holy God should flow into your life and cast out the devil, dispossess the beast, and reign in your members."

We knelt to pray, and today he came back with tears in his eyes and said, "Mr. Lake, I feel I can shake hands with you now. I am a beast no more. I am a man."

Yesterday a dear woman was present in our afternoon service. She had a tumor that for ten months the physicians believed to be an unborn child. She came with her nurse a few days ago to the healing rooms and told me her symptoms. The thing that fooled the physicians was that there was a movement that they considered similar to life movement, and the result was that during all these months they believed the woman would become a mother, until the normal time had long passed. She was the first one to be prayed for after the Thursday afternoon service.

Today she returned and said, "Mr. Lake, I want you to see me. I have my corsets on, I am perfectly normal. When I went to bed I was not aware that anything had taken place except that the choking had ceased and I felt comfortable. I was not aware of any diminution in my size. But when I awoke this morning I was perfectly normal."

I said, "How did the tumor disappear? Was it in the form of a fluid?"

She said, "No, nothing came from my person."

Now I am going to ask you, where did a great tumor like that go to? What happened to it? (Voice in audience says, "Dematerialized.")

Yes. The living Spirit of God absolutely dematerialized the tumor, and the process was accomplished in one night while the woman slept. That is one of God's methods of surgical operations, isn't it?

Beloved, the Spirit of God took possession of that dear soul's person. That tumor became filled with the Spirit of God, and the effect of the Spirit of God in that tumor was so mighty, so powerful, that the Spirit of God dissolved it.

That is the secret of the ministry of Jesus Christ. That is the secret of the ministry of Christianity. That is the reason that the real Christian who lives in union with the living God and possesses His Spirit has a ministry that no other man in all the world possesses. That is the reason that the real Christian here has a revelation of Jesus Christ and His almightiness and His power to save that no other human in all the world possesses. Why? He is full and experiences in his own soul the dissolving power of the Spirit of God that takes sin out of his life and makes him a free man in Christ Jesus. Blessed be His name forever.

A few weeks ago a dear woman called me over the telephone and said, "I have a young friend who is a drunkard, and the habit has such power over him that he will go to any excess to obtain. Dry state or no dry state he has to have it. He is an intelligent fellow. He wants to be free. We have invited him to my home for prayer, and he is here now. I want you to join me in prayer for him."

I said, "All right, but first you call one of your neighbors to join you in prayer for this man, then when you are ready, call me on the phone and Brother Westwood and Mrs. Perterson and I will join you in prayer." She called me in a little while, and we united our hearts in prayer for the young man, who was on the other side of the city. About twenty minutes afterward he arose from his knees and with tears in his eyes he took the woman by the hand and said, "I am a man of sense. I know when something has taken place with me, and the appetite has disappeared." That is the ministry of the Spirit. The ministry of God to man. Blessed be His name.

Isn't it a marvelous, wonderful thing that God has ordained an arrangement whereby man becomes God's own co-partner and co-laborer in the ministry of the Spirit? "The Church which is His body."[5] Just as Jesus Christ was the human body through which the living Spirit was ministered to mankind, so God has arranged that the living Church — not the dead member, but the living Church, alive with the Spirit of the living God — should minister that quickening life to another and thereby become a co-partner, a co-laborer together with God. Blessed be His name forever.

---

[5] See Colossians 1:24.

Men have mystified and philosophized the Gospel of Jesus, but the Gospel is as simple as can be. Just as God lived and operated through the body of the man, Jesus, so Jesus, the Man on the throne, operated in and through the Christian, also through His body, the Church, in the world. Just as Jesus was the representative of God the Father, so the *Church* is the representative of Christ. And as Jesus yielded Himself unto *all righteousness,* so the Church should yield herself to do all the will of God.

The secret of Christianity is in *being.* It is in being a possessor of the nature of Jesus Christ. In other words, it is being Christ in character, Christ in demonstration, Christ in agency of transmission. When a person gives himself to the Lord and becomes a child of God, a Christian, he is a Christ-man. All that he does and all that he says from that time forth should be the will and the words and the doings of Jesus, just as absolutely and entirely as He spoke and did the will of the Father.

eading: Acts 2

And when the day of Pentecost was fully come, they were all with one accord in one place. And suddenly there came a sound from heaven as of a rushing mighty wind, and it filled all the house where they were sitting. And there appeared unto them cloven tongues like as of fire, and it sat upon each of them. And they were all filled with the Holy Ghost, and began to speak with other tongues, as the Spirit gave them utterance.[1]

CONSCIOUSNESS OF GOD
Masonic Temple
November 26, 1916
3:00 p.m.

On the day of Pentecost, the hundred and twenty who composed the little circle of believers that had met in the upper room after the ascension of Jesus were sitting together in prayer and meditation upon God. Suddenly there came from heaven — not born out of man's emotionalism, but by faith — there came from heaven the sound of a rushing, mighty wind, and it filled the house where they were sitting. And there appeared to them cloven tongues, like as of fire, and it rested upon each of them, and they were all filled with the Holy Ghost, the living Spirit of God. As a result of being thus filled they began to speak with other tongues as the Spirit gave them utterance.

That filling of the Holy Ghost, that coming of the living Spirit of Jesus Christ upon mankind, was the dawning morning of the first Christian day. That was the day-dawn of Christianity. Christianity never existed before. Religion existed, but Christianity never existed before. The Christianity of Christ has its birth then and there, bless God. It had not even manifested itself in the world during Jesus' own lifetime nor during the forty days after His resurrection.

Christianity has a secret, bless God, the secret of divine power, the secret that makes it different from all other known religions. It is the secret of the consciousness that it contains, and the consciousness that Christianity contains is due to the fact that the Spirit of

---
[1] Acts 2:1-4.

the triumphant Son of God, who had entered into death, who had experienced resurrection and thereby power over death, who had ascended in triumph to the right hand of God and sat down a victor, was poured forth upon the world. He poured forth His own living Spirit, containing that consciousness. Consequently, when the Spirit of Christ came upon the disciples on the day of Pentecost, it produced in them, of necessity, that which was in the mind of Christ, the same consciousness of power and victory and dominion and Christlikeness that was common to the nature of Jesus Himself as He sat down in triumph at God's right hand.

When I went to Africa and sat down quietly to study the native peoples and their mind, I was forced to study myself and my people too, and I said, "What is the thing that makes us Anglo-Saxons different from these native people?"

My friend said, "Well, it is our education."

I said, "Education does not do it."

He said, "Yes it does."

I said, "No it don't. I will show you why."

And I took him down to one of the towns and introduced him to an educated native missionary. Some missionaries had sent him over here, and he was educated at Yale, and he was just as much a heathen as he ever was. He was an educated heathen. He was not a Christian.

Another says, "It is our good breeding that makes the difference between the Anglo-Saxon and the African native." It is not our good breeding. It is something else. It is the consciousness that the Anglo-Saxon mind contains that the other man has not. That consciousness is the consciousness of power, a consciousness of mastery, a consciousness of self-control, and all other varied qualities of the sensitive human mind.

How did they get there? They were established in the mind of the Anglo-Saxon through transmission of those who believed. Consciousness is a growth, an evolution, or an impartation. It is all three in most people.

The incoming of the Spirit of God into the disciples was an impartation of the Spirit of Jesus that brought with it the very conditions of the mind of Christ Himself. He was the one who had throttled death and mastered it and rose up in His own consciousness, *King*. Therefore, He could say to His disciples,

> All power is given unto me in heaven and in earth. Go ye therefore, and teach all nations, baptizing them in the name of the Father, and of the Son, and of the Holy Ghost.[2]

In other words, submitting your body, your soul, and your spirit in an act of union with the Father and the Son and the Holy Ghost, with the purpose of establishing in the individual the conscious knowledge of the living Father and the living Son and the living Spirit. Glory be to God.

When I was a little kiddy I was sprinkled like the rest and I suppose I squalled just like the rest did. I was not an angel so far as I know. But when I became a man I put away childish things.

When I became a man, God revealed the real purpose of what real baptism was supposed to bring into a man's consciousness. And I saw that the purpose of Jesus was to produce in the souls and bodies and spirits of man such a consciousness of the living triune God that man became a king, a living king. I saw the dignity, I saw the power, I saw the manifestation of Spirit that Jesus purposed should be evident in the life of the person really baptized into the living God — not just baptized in His *name,* but actually baptized into God — buried in Him, inducted into God, inducted into the nature of God the Father, into the nature of God the Son, into the nature of God the Holy Ghost.

It is almost a sadness to my soul that men should be astonished and surprised at an ordinary tangible evidence of the power of God. A woman came into the healing rooms on Thursday afternoon with a tumor larger than a full-grown, unborn child, and her physicians and nurse had been fooled, believing it to be such, until nature's period had passed. Then they decided it must be something else.

She came to the healing rooms and I interviewed her. She said, "Mr. Lake, I have the opinion of several physicians. They are all different, but each have said, 'It is possible it may be a child,' but now the time has passed, and they do not know what to say."

---

[2] Matthew 28:18-19.

I put my hand upon her for a moment, and I said, "Madam, it is not a child, it is a tumor." She sat down and wept. Her nurse was with her. Her soul was troubled and she did not receive healing.

She came back on Thursday afternoon for prayer and went away like the rest. But she returned on Friday with her corsets on. She said, "I came to show you that I am perfectly normal. When I retired last night at ten o'clock there was no evidence that anything had taken place. Beyond that I felt comfortable and the choking was gone. But when I awoke this morning I was my normal size."

I said, "Did it disappear in the form of a fluid?"

She said, "There was not an outward sign of any character."

Beloved, what happened to it? It dematerialized, did it not? There was nothing else. The tumor dissolved. It was evaporated, taken out of the system, and was gone in a single night.

I called a friend on the telephone to tell him about it. Another friend was present in the room and while he still held the receiver in his hand he turned to his friend and told him about it, and the friend said, "My good God, man, that would be a miracle!"

What is a miracle? It is the tangible evidence of the supreme control of the Spirit of God over every character and form of materiality. The tumor disappeared. It was gone. Why? Because the living Spirit of God entered it and by the power and working of God the woman returned to her normal condition. Blessed be His name.

If these evidences of God's presence and power had no value excepting the mere fact of physical healing, they would not appeal to many thinking minds. Beloved, the power of such an event and of such an act and such a sign is in that it shows you and I that through living, positive, actual contact with the Spirit of God all things are possible. Blessed be His name.

I talked with the husband of the lady, one of the most profane men I have most ever known until Friday morning. He said to me, "Mr. Lake, when I got up on Friday morning and saw my wife I said, 'I will never again take that name upon my lips in vain.'" And he has walked softly, and a new light is shining in his soul and a new presence has made itself evident to that man.

Salvation is the best thing that the mind of God ever evolved. Salvation, *real* salvation, bless God, is that blessed working of God by the Spirit that has for its one object the absolute transformation of a man — body and soul and spirit — into the likeness of Jesus Christ. And there is no man on earth that could imagine Jesus Christ going around with a big tumor stuck on Him anywhere. Why? Bless God, He did not have any tumors in His soul or in His spirit either. Why? Because all His nature was joined in complete and holy union with the living God, and the life and nature and substance of God's being, which is the Holy Ghost, flowed through the spirit and soul and body of Jesus alike.

What marvelous union was accomplished through the consent of His own will, without which Jesus Christ Himself could never have been the spotless Lamb of God! But by saying "Yes" to God, by yielding His nature with His "Yes," He permitted the mighty Spirit of God to possess His life and accomplish the will of God in Him and through Him. Blessed be His precious name!

Men are afraid to say yes to God. When a young man, I sat in a little meeting one night when the Spirit was talking to my heart. I said, "If I am going to be a Christian, I cannot do this, and I cannot do that." Oh, mighty God, it almost makes my soul vomit in these days to think of the average conception a man has of Christianity.

About ninety percent of so-called Christianity is all spelled with four letters, d-o-n'-t. Don't do this and don't do that. The individual restraining himself, putting himself in a harness, walking according to laws and ordinances, etc. Why bless God, religion is all contained in two letters, b-e. Not performing acts, but *being* the thing that God purposed.

I was in a meeting in Los Angeles on one occasion. An old Negro was conducting the services and he had the funniest vocabulary that any Negro ever had. But I want to tell you there were doctors and lawyers and professors listening to marvelous things coming from the old Negro's lips. It was not what he said in words, but it was what he said from his spirit to my heart that showed me he had more of God in his life than any man I had ever met up to that time. It was the God in him that was attracting people.

There was one man who insisted on getting up and talking every little while. Some people have a mania for talking. Every once in awhile he would get up and the old Negro had endured it for a long time. Presently, he got up again, and the old man stuck his finger out and said, "In the name of Jesus Christ sit down." He did not sit down. He fell down, and his friends carried him out.

That is only one manifestation of the living fact of what Christianity is: The divine power of Jesus Christ, by the Holy Ghost, filling a man's soul and body, bless God, flashing through his nature like a holy flame, accomplishing the will of God.

That man may be the temple of the Holy Ghost brings a demand on his consciousness that nothing else in the world can bring. If God has ordained that my spirit and my soul and my body, and yours, may become the living, conscious temple of His Spirit; that He, God, by His Spirit will live in us and manifest Himself through us; what kind of demand does it bring upon us?

We can understand then, what was in the mind of the apostle when he said, "What manner of persons ought ye to be in all holy conversation and godliness?"[3]

Why is it that people are slow to yield themselves to the control and government and guidance of the Spirit of God? Why is it that there is not a divine passion in our hearts that such a blessed control should be made a possibility? Shall you and I today assert our own little humanity and walk according to our own light, or shall we as wise men, as those who seek the divinest in life say yes to God and let God take our being, inhabit our being, and let Him live His life in us, and then He will manifest His life through us?

I have a brother, a splendid fellow, a finely educated man, a professor. I returned from Africa some years ago, and we were visiting together. As we sat visiting, my sister, who was present, said, "John, I have some old neighbors over here. They are old German people and they are having a very hard time. The old man died, and one of the sisters died, this thing happened and that thing happened, and finally the son, who was a shipbuilder, fell one day and was carried

---

[3] 2 Peter 3:11.

to the hospital and they say his leg has to be amputated. Gangrene has set in. The physicians have amputated the toe and a piece of the foot, and now they say the leg has to be amputated. The old mother has been sitting in a wheelchair a rheumatic cripple for two and a half years and cannot move."

My brother and I had been having somewhat of a discussion over this thing. He said, "Jack, don't you think these things are all psychological?"

I said, "Not much."

He said, "I think it is."

He said, "Don't you think it is a demonstration of the power of mind over matter?"

And I said, "No. If that was all it is, you could give just as good a demonstration as I could."

After awhile my sister said, "I have been across the street and made arrangements for you to come and pray for these people."

I said, "All right. Jim, come along."

I said to the old lady, "Mother, how long have you been here?"

And she replied, "I have been here two and a half years." She said, "It is awful hard. Not just hard to sit here all the time, but I suffer night and day, with no moment of relaxation from acute suffering in these two and a half years."

As I listened to her, the flame of God came into my soul and I said, "You rheumatic devil, in the name of Jesus Christ I will blot you out if it is the last thing I ever do in the world." And laying my hands on her, I looked to heaven and called on God to cast that devil out and set her free. I said to her, "Mother, in the name of Jesus Christ get out and walk." And she arose and walked.

We went into the other room where the son was, whose leg was to be amputated. I sat for a few minutes and told him of the power of God. I said, "We have come to you with a message of Jesus Christ, and we have not just come with the message, but with the power of God." And laying my hands on the limb I said, "In the name of the living God they shall never amputate this limb," and it was healed.

I was gone for three to six months and then once again stopped at my sister's home. The young lady called and said, "You must come across and see my mother and brother. They are so well." I called and found the old lady very happy. She said, "Oh Jake, he is not at home. Why he is so well he went down to the saloon and danced all night!"

I waited to see Jake, and I tried to tell him something about the living God that he had felt in his body, and who wanted to take possession of his soul and reveal the nature of Jesus Christ in him.

Five years passed away and I returned again to the United States and was stopping at my sister's home. She said, "Do you remember some people that you prayed for across the road? Here is Jake now coming from his work." We sat on the porch and talked, and I said, "Well, Jake, how is it?"

"Oh," he said, "I do not understand it all, but something has been going on and going on. It is in me. First I could not go to the dance, and next I could not drink beer, and next my tobacco did not taste good, and then a joy came into my heart, then I found it was just Jesus."

Born of God — the nature of man brought into union with God by the Holy Ghost. Blessed be His precious name.

This congregation has perhaps been blessed with the continued manifestation of the presence of God beyond that of any other congregation in the world. This city has been blessed with the manifestation of God's presence perhaps beyond that of any other city in the world. Yet the eyes of many are closed. They have not seen God. Some have seen Brother Lake, some have seen Brother Westwood, but not all have seen God, the living God. Many need the continued process of the Spirit of God in their soul that went on in the heart of Jake, revealing the nature of Christ until all his being said yes to God and he became a Christian in deed and in truth. Blessed be God.

I leave you today with this message of God. Open your soul to Him and let the blessed living Spirit of God have entrance into your nature. Say yes to God. Say yes to God.

John was a prophet. One day as Jesus stood among his friends, John said, "Behold the Lamb of God, which taketh away the sin of the world!"[4] "I indeed baptize you with water unto repentance...he shall baptize you with the Holy Ghost, and with fire."[5]

---

[4]   John 1:29.

[5]   Matthew 3:11.

There is a baptism that belongs to Jesus. It is in His supreme right and control. No other angel or man can bestow it. It comes from Him alone. "He which baptizeth with the Holy Ghost."[6] So the individual who wants the Holy Ghost must come into definite, conscious contact with Jesus Christ Himself. Bless God.

---

[6] John 1:33.

ebrews 2. When I read this chapter there is a thrill that goes down through my soul, and I would to God that the real spiritual truths of it could forever be established in the minds of men.

REALITY
Preliminary
February 11, 1917

I once listened to an eminent divine preaching from the text, "What is man?" and when he got through I had a feeling that man was a kind of whipped cur with his tail between his legs, sneaking out to throw himself into the lake saying, "Here goes nothing." I said, "He has never caught the fire of the thing Jesus is endeavoring to teach through the apostle — that man was the crowning creation of God. That God endowed him with a nature and qualities that by the grace of God can express more of God than any other of God's creations. That God purposed by the Holy Spirit to make the salvation of Jesus Christ so real in the nature of man that 'He that sanctifieth (Jesus Christ) and they that are sanctified' through His grace are both of one nature, of one substance, of one character — one in life, one in the righteousness of His death, and one in the consequent dominion that came because of His resurrection and glory."

> For both he that sanctifieth and they who are sanctified are all of one: for which cause he is not ashamed to call them brethren.
>
> — Hebrews 2:11

Brethren of the Lord Jesus Christ. He the elder brother, we the younger members of the family of the same Father, begotten by the same Spirit, energized by the same divine life of God, qualified through the Holy Ghost to perform the same blessed ministry.

> He took not on him the nature of angels; but he took on him the seed of Abraham.[1]

---

[1] Hebrews 2:16.

I wish I could write these things in your soul and brand them in your conscience.

Sermon

When the purpose of God in the salvation of man first dawned upon my soul, that is, when the greatness of it dawned upon my soul, for experientially, I knew God as Savior from sin. I knew the power of the Christ within my own heart to keep me above the power of temptation and to help me live a godly life. But when I say to you that when I knew the purpose of God and the greatness of His salvation, life became for me a grand new thing.

When by the study of His Word and the revelation of His Spirit it became a fact in my soul that God's purpose was no less in me than it was in the Lord Jesus — and is no less in you and I as younger brethren than it was in Jesus Christ, our elder brother — then bless God, I saw the purpose that God had in mind for the human race. I saw the greatness of Jesus' desire. That desire that was so intense that it caused Him, as King of Glory, to lay down all that glory possessed for Him, and come to earth to be born as a man, to join hands with our humanity, and by His grace lift us in consciousness and life to the same level that He Himself enjoyed.

Christ became a new factor in my soul. Such a vision of His purpose thrilled my being that I could understand then how it was that Jesus, as He approached man and His needs, began at the very bottom, called mankind to Him, and by His loving touch and the power of the Spirit through His Word, destroyed the sickness and sin that bound them and set them free in both body and soul, lifted them into union and communion with Himself and God the Father. Yea, bless God, by the Holy Spirit indwelling the souls of men, Christ purposed to bestow on mankind the very conditions of His own life and being and to give to man through the gifts of the Spirit and the gift of the Spirit, the same blessed ministry to the world that He Himself had enjoyed and exercised.

The old song that we used to sing became new to my heart. Its melody runs through my soul:

> Salvation, O the joyful sound,
>
> In a believer's ear

It soothes our worries, heals our wounds

And drives away our fears.

And lots more, bless God.

I could then understand what was in Charles Wesley's heart when he wrote his famous hymn, "Jesus Lover of My Soul," and penned its climax, that marvelous verse:

Thou, O Christ, art all I want,

More than all in Thee I find;

Raise the fallen, cheer the faint,

Heal the sick and lead the blind.

Just and holy is Thy name;

I am all unrighteousness,

Vile and full of sin I am,

Thou art full of truth and grace.

The same thing was in the spirit of Isaiah when in the beautiful thirty-fifth of Isaiah his exultant soul broke forth in the shout of praise:

He will come and save you. Then the eyes of the blind shall be opened, and the ears of the deaf shall be unstopped. Then shall the lame man leap as an hart, and the tongue of the dumb sing.[2]

I could understand then the thrill that must have moved David when he sang the 103rd Psalm.

"Bless the Lord, O my soul, and forget not all his benefits: who forgiveth all thine iniquities; who healeth all thy diseases."[3]

The vision that has called forth the shouts of praise from the souls of men in all ages is the same vision that stirs your heart and mine today — the vision of the divine reality of the salvation of Jesus Christ by which the greatness of God's purpose in Him is revealed to mankind by the Spirit of the Living One, transformed and lifted and unified with the living Christ through the Holy Ghost so that all the parts and energies and functions of the nature of Jesus Christ are revealed through man unto the salvation of the world. Bless God.

---

[2] Isaiah 35:4-6.

[3] Psalm 103:2-3.

The vision of God's relation to man and man's relation to God is changing the character of Christianity from a groveling something, weeping and wailing its way in tears, to the kingly recognition of union and communion with the living Son of God. Yea, bless God, to the recognition of the real fact that the Word of God so vividly portrayed in the lesson I read. That "in the bringing of many sons into the world," not one son in the world, but in bringing of many sons into the world, "it became him to make the captain of their salvation perfect through suffering."[4] Blessed be God.

I am glad, bless God, that the Scriptures have dignified us with the marvelous title of "sons of God." I am glad there is such a relation as a "son of God" and that by His grace the cleansed soul — cleansed by the precious blood of Jesus Christ, filled and energized by His own Kingly Spirit — that he too by the grace of God has become God's king, God's gentleman in deed and in truth.

The Spirit of the Lord says within my soul that the kingly nature of the Son of God is purposed to be revealed in the nature of every man, that Christ's kingliness may be prevalent in all the world and govern the heart of man, even as it governs the heart of those who know Him and have entered into His glory.

(A young man called up from audience.) I listened to this young man's testimony on Friday night with a thrill in my soul. I want him to tell you what God has done in him and for him.

TESTIMONY

"I do not know whether I can tell it all or not. I am sure there is a good deal I cannot tell.

"When I was a lad of about 14 years old I was forced into the mines to work, and I worked a great deal in the water, which brought on rheumatism. I was crippled up for years in my younger days and gradually grew worse. I could walk around, but you could hardly notice where I was afflicted. It was in the hips and back.

---

[4] See Hebrews 2:10.

"A great many physicians said there was no relief for me. When I came down here to Spokane and was laboring on anything, I could not stoop down. When I would drop my pick or shovel I would have to pick it up with my feet and reach for it with my hands.

"I came to this meeting last fall, and with one prayer by Brother Lake I was healed in thirty minutes of rheumatism, which had been a constant torture to me for years.

"Later on I contracted tuberculosis and was examined by the county physician, Stutz, who advised me that the best thing to do was to go to Edgecliff. Also, other physicians said I was very bad and they did not think I could live more than six or eight months unless I went out there right away.

"I took the same thing for it. I went to the healing rooms for prayer —Brother Peterson also prayed for me and in three weeks I went to Dr. Stutz and he could not find a trace of it. I have gained 11 pounds, and I never felt better in my life."

That is a simple story isn't it? But that story is a revealer of the question that has probably caused more debate in Christian life than almost any other and of which the world has little understanding. That is that the Spirit of God is a living force that takes possession of the nature of man and works in man the will of God, and the will of God is ever to make man like Himself. Blessed be His precious name.

It would be a strange Word indeed and a strange salvation if Jesus was not able to produce from the whole race one man in His own image, in His own likeness, and of His own character. We would think that salvation was weak, would we not?

If the world were nothing but cripples, as it largely is — soul cripples, physical cripples, mental cripples everywhere — then I want to know what kind of a conception the world has received of the divinity of Jesus Christ, of the power of His salvation? Is there no hope, is there no way out of the difficulty, is there no force that can lift the soul of man into union with God so that once again the life of God thrills in his members?

Our purpose, by the grace of God, is to reveal to the world that that is the real truth and purpose and power of the salvation of the Lord Jesus Christ. My soul rejoices every time I see a man set free, for I say within my heart, "There is one more witness to the divine fact that the Christ of God is a living power, taking possession of the nature of man and transforming man's being into His own image."

The mere fact of our brother's deliverance from suffering and inability to help himself and a possible premature death, is a very small matter in itself in comparison with the wonder it reveals to us. The revelation of the power of God at the command of man, to be applied to the destruction of evil — whether spiritual or physical, mental or psychological — shows us Christ's purpose and desire to bring man, by the grace of God, once more into His heavenly estate where he recognizes himself a son of God. Blessed be His name.

Years ago I found myself like my brother, but worse crippled than he. When my legs drew out of shape and my body became distorted by the common curse of rheumatism, my pastor said, "Brother, you are glorifying God."

And my church said, "Brother, be patient and endure it. Let the sweetness of the Lord possess your soul." And I was good enough to believe it for a long time until one day, I discovered that it was not the will of God at all, but the will of the dirty, crooked-legged devil that wanted to make me like himself. And then, bless God, everything was changed and I laid down everything and went to Chicago to the only place where I knew then that a man could get healed. I went to John Alexander Dowie's Divine Healing Home at 12th and Michigan Streets, and an old gray-haired man came and laid his hands on me and the power of God went through my being and made my legs straight, and I went out and walked on the street like a Christian.

Do you know when my legs straightened out it taught me the beginning of one of the deepest lessons that ever came to my life? It taught me that God did not appreciate a man with crooked legs any more than He does a man with a crooked soul. I saw the abundant power of the Gospel of salvation and that it was placed at the disposal of man to remove the unchristlikeness of his life and if there was unchristlikeness in the body, we could get rid of the curse by coming to God and being made whole. For there is just as much unchristlikeness in men's bodies as in men's souls. That which is in the inner life will also be revealed in the outer life. That which is a fact in the mental and psychological will become a fact in the physical also. And, bless God, that which is the divine fact of all facts — that the spirit of man and the Spirit of God are of one substance and one nature, and his mind and body take on the spiritual power imparted until it too becomes Christlike. Blessed be His holy name.

The Spirit of the Lord speaks within my soul and says:

"Within the breast of every man is the divine image of God (living God), in whose image and likeness he was made. That sin is a perversion and sickness an impostor, and the grace and power of God through the Holy Ghost delivers man from all bondage of darkness, and man in all his nature rises into union and communion with God and becomes one with Him in the truest sense — one in the thoughts of God, one in the aspirations of God, one in the Spirit of Jesus Christ as the Savior of man. And man then gives himself a Savior also lifting man by the grace of God to the Lamb of God that taketh away the sin of the world." Blessed be His holy name.

Editor's note: The manuscript does not indicate whether the following is an interpretation of tongues, a song, or a poem.

> *There's a wideness in God's mercy,*
> *Like the wideness of the sea:*
> *There's a kindness in His Justice,*
> *Which is more than liberty.*
>
> *But we make His love too narrow*
> *By false limits of our own,*
> *And we magnify His strictness*
> *With a zeal He will not own.*
>
> *There is welcome for the sinner,*
> *And more graces for the good;*
> *There is mercy with the Savior;*
> *There is healing in His blood.*
>
> *For the love of God is broader*
> *Than the measure of Man's mind;*
> *And the heart of the Eternal*
> *Is most wonderfully kind.*
>
> *If our lives were but more simple,*
> *We should take Him at His word;*

And our lives would be all sunshine
In the sweetness of our Lord.

So the divine realities remain — the reality of God, a living power. The divine assistance, the heavenly nature known to every man who enters by the Spirit through the door, Christ Jesus, into a living experience. The man who doubts is the man on the outside. The man on the inside has no questions to settle that do not comprehend God as that soul that has never been in contact with His life and power does. But Christ invites mankind to enter with Him into the divine knowledge and heavenly union that makes the spirit of man and the Spirit of God to be one in deed and in truth. Bless God!

Man is the divinest reality that God has given in His great creation. Man in the image of God, man renewed by the life of God, filled with the Holy Spirit, revealing and giving forth by the living Spirit, transformed even as himself has been transformed. Blessed be His name.

God has made us in the truest and highest sense co-partners and co-laborers with our Lord and Savior Jesus Christ. He has not withheld one possibility that was manifested in Jesus from any man but on the contrary, invites mankind to come forth in the dignity and power of sons of God and to that Christ, and in Christ, join in the mighty wonder of the salvation of the world over sin and sickness and the power of death and darkness and hell. Bless God.

Salvation, to my heart, is Christ's glorious reality. Under a tree away back in Canada one night, I knelt and poured out my heart to God and asked Him by His grace to take possession of my life and nature and make me a Christian man and let me know the power of His salvation. And Christ was born in my soul. Such a joy of God possessed my heart that the leaves of the trees seemed to dance for months following, and the birds sang a new song and the angels of God witnessed of the glory of heaven in my own heart. Blessed be His name.

Salvation is a progressive condition. The difficulty with church has been that men were induced to confess their sins to Christ and acknowledge Him as a Savior and there they stopped, there they petrified, there they withered, there they died, dry rotted. I believe that in these phrases I have expressed the real thing that has taken place in

85 percent of professing Christians in the world. Oh, bless God, we never saw Christ's intention. That day away back there, when the glory light of God first shone into my soul, was a glorious day, the best I had ever known to that moment.

But, beloved, it would be a sorrowful thing in my life if I was compelled to look back to that day as the best. No, bless God, there were better days than that. There were days when the Lord God took me into His confidence and revealed His nature and revealed His purpose and revealed His love and revealed His ministry. Yea, bless God, there came a day when God once more, in His loving mercy, endowed me with the Spirit of God to be and perform the things that He had planted in my soul and had revealed in His own blessed Word and life.

I invite you to this life of divine reality. I invite you to enter into the Lord Jesus. I invite you to enter into His nature that you may know Him, for no man can say that Jesus is the Lord but by the Holy Ghost. It is through the revelation of the Spirit of Christ in the soul of man that he is privileged to know Jesus as the Lord. Blessed be God. We may know Him as an historic character, we may know Him as the ideal man, we may know Him as the Christ and Savior, but we do not know Him as the living God who imparts His own nature and life and power to us until we know Him as the Scripture says, in the Holy Ghost.[5] Bless God!

He who has lived and felt that religious life was a dream or a myth or an abstract something that was hard to lay your hands on, an intangible condition, has been mistaken. I bless God. In the bosom of the Living One are the divine realities of God, filling and thrilling the soul of Christ Himself, filling and thrilling the soul of every recipient of the life of the Lord Jesus.

And the Spirit of the Lord once more speaks within my heart and says, "The joys of God and the glories of heaven and the understanding of angelic existence and being are only known to him who is privileged in consciousness to enter that life and realm. That God, by His grace, has purposed that man — in his nature and consciousness — shall live in union and communion with our Father God and with the Lord

---

[5] See 1 Corinthians 12:3.

Jesus Christ His Son, the innumerable company of angels and the presence of just men made perfect, and we shall know the power and wonder of the blood of Jesus that speaketh better things than that of Abel."[6]

And the Spirit of the Lord speaks yet again and says, "As Jesus was the Prophet of all prophets, because of the completeness of the union of His nature with God, that man in turn becomes the prophet of prophets as his spirit assimilates with the Spirit of Him, the divine One; that man becomes the lover of all lovers, even as Jesus Christ was the lover of all men, thrilling men with the intensity of His affection in the union of spirit with Himself, binding them by the love of His nature as the bond-slaves of Christ forever."

So the Christian draws to himself the love of men, not because he slavishly desires it, but because of the fact that he obeys Christ's divine law:

> Give, and it shall be given unto you; good measure, pressed down, and shaken together, and running over, shall men give into your bosom.[7]

Blessed be God.

And I want to tell you that this little church is one of the most loved of all churches in all the world. I want to tell you that more hungry hearts are turned in longing toward this little company of people than to any other company of worshippers in the land. Why? They have heard that God is here and the longing of the nature of man to know God causes them to turn their hearts and their faces toward the source of heavenly blessing. Shall we give it to them or will we disappoint them? Shall they receive the blessing of God through our heart, or will they turn away hungry and dissatisfied? Yea, I know your answer for I know the answer of the Spirit, "Give, and it shall be given unto you." Blessed be God.

The greatest giver is the greatest receiver. He who gives most receives most — God's divine law. The reverse of God's law is always

---

[6] See Hebrews 12:22-24.

[7] Luke 6:38.

evidenced in the soul of man as selfishness. Always getting, always getting, always getting, until the nature contracts and the face distorts and the brain diminishes and the life that God gave to be abundant becomes an abomination that men are compelled to endure.

THE MARVEL OF GOD'S TOUCH

Masonic Temple

April 22, 1917

Isaiah 35.

The wilderness and the solitary place shall be glad for them; and the desert shall rejoice, and blossom as the rose. It shall blossom abundantly, and rejoice even with joy and singing: the glory of Lebanon shall be given unto it, the excellency of Carmel and Sharon, they shall see the glory of the Lord, and the excellency of our God.

Strengthen ye the weak hands, and confirm the feeble knees. Say to them that are of a fearful heart, Be strong, fear not: behold, your God will come with vengeance, even God with a recompence; he will come and save you. Then the eyes of the blind shall be opened, and the ears of the deaf shall be unstopped. Then shall the lame man leap as an hart, and the tongue of the dumb sing: for in the wilderness shall waters break out, and streams in the desert. And the parched ground shall become a pool, and the thirsty land springs of water: in the habitation of dragons, where each lay, shall be grass with reeds and rushes. And an highway shall be there, and a way, and it shall be called The way of holiness; the unclean shall not pass over it; but it shall be for those: the wayfaring men, though fools, shall not err therein. No lion shall be there, nor any ravenous beast shall go up thereon, it shall not be found there; but the redeemed shall walk there: and the ransomed of the Lord shall return, and come to Zion with songs and everlasting joy upon their heads: they shall obtain joy and gladness, and sorrow and sighing shall flee away.

MRS. ANNIE E. NORTON'S TESTIMONY

Synopsis by Reverend John G. Lake

One day she was cutting a ham with a saw. (That is a bad business — not to cut ham with a saw, but to cut it with anything.) In the act of cutting the ham she cut her first forefinger to the bone. In a few days the arm had become paralyzed. Then a condition set in that in some respects resembled gangrene. However, it was not gangrene. Physician after physician examined her. Dr. O'Neil of the Paton Building here, a splendid gentleman, had charge of her case.

Dr. O'Neil was so profoundly interested in her case that he called the other physicians of the city to examine her. She was taken to the Old National Bank Building, where 250 of Spokane's physicians examined her. No remedy could be found. The disease had extended up the arm and they believed perhaps they could prolong her life by amputating the arm. So it was done, only to discover that the disease was just as prevalent in other portions of the body as it was in the arm. Amputations therefore were valueless.

Dr. O'Neil, in conjunction with the Medical Association of this city, I believe, offered a thousand dollars to any physician anywhere who would provide a real remedy, but none was found. Her suffering was so terrible that the only easement from pain and the possibility of sleep came through the use of narcotics. In consequence, she became a morphine fiend.

The other day she told me this incident. She was stopping in a public home, conducted by an association of the city, in which one of the features of teaching was that the Bible was written by drunken men and was all foolishness, that wise people took no stock in it, etc. After she reasoned this out for some time, she said in her own soul, "I am not going to attend the meetings of this association any longer. I have had enough." Consequently, one night at nine o'clock, during a drowning rain, the matron pushed her out of the front door and bid her go. She had two suitcases. She carried one of them across the field to where there was a large fir tree, then returned in the rain for the other one. In the meantime the matron, fearing the woman would die of exposure, called up the police station and told them there was an insane woman, and that they ought to come out and take care of her. When the driver of the patrol wagon arrived, he recognized her at once. She was well-known. They brought her downtown and made proper provision for her.

On account of the terrible strain that her husband was subjected to for money and the care of his wife and the loss of his rest continuing for years, he had a paralytic stroke, followed by a second and a third. Finally, the family was reduced to poverty. This is the common story of so many who do not know God. Man's way, when he travels by himself, is a hard way. That is the reason that when the soul of man opens to God and he discovers in Jesus Christ a Deliverer and Savior, his soul rejoices.

Mrs. Norton was taken to Seattle, where the medical fraternity of Seattle, like those of Spokane, examined her. No help was found. Then she was taken to Tacoma and the fraternity there examined her — still no hope. She was taken to Portland and the fraternity there examined her. In all, more than seven hundred physicians examined her and pronounced her hopeless.

But one glad day came to her. From a natural standpoint it was a terrible day. In her sickness and wretchedness and poverty she was dying. Some Christian friends had been to pray with her, I believe four or five times, but without apparent results. Her eyes had turned blind and she could not see the light of the world anymore. The weight of death had settled upon her soul. She was rapidly passing out of the body when two dear women, one a widow with five children, the other the mother of five children, whose husband lived, came to see her.

They were women of care and responsibility, but who longed to take a little time for the Lord's service, and so together they had agreed to visit this sufferer whom they had heard about. They knelt by her side. They were not anxious about the subject of her healing. They were particularly anxious that this soul should not pass into the other life without the consciousness and support of Jesus Christ, a present Savior. So they prayed especially for the light of God and His salvation to dawn in her heart. As they did so, this glorious event took place.

Jesus Himself stood by her side and spoke to her, calling her by name. He said, "If I heal you, will you tell everyone everywhere you can of Christ and His salvation?"

She replied, "Yes, Lord."

He reached forth His hand, touched the tips of her fingers, and the life of God like a heavenly stream instantly flowed through her whole being. Instantly, her pains were gone. Instantly, the mortification and rottenness of her flesh was changed into life and health. Instantly, she arose to praise God, a well woman. This was one year ago, last 23rd of September. From that time to this, our sister has moved around the land telling people, as she will tell us today, of the marvel that God wrought in her.

I wanted to have the privilege of giving this synopsis of her testimony, because I wanted to say some things that I knew might not interest Mrs. Norton as they will others.

Mrs. Norton's case was discussed not only by the local medical fraternity, but by the medical journals of the United States. Also, the *British Medical Journal,* one of the greatest medical publications of the world, published her case in detail, with a photograph showing the decomposed state of her body. Decomposition had become such that the little finger fell off. Her hands were nothing but a mass of rottenness with bones exposed.

Yet they tell us that the days of miracles have passed. They tell us Jesus Christ is the Healer no more. They tell us there is no such thing as a baptism in the Holy Ghost. Who are the doubters, the Medical Fraternity? No sir, the medical association has invited her to come next Thursday and let them hear from her own lips what God has wrought in her. Who opposes her testimony? Who opposes the fact of healing? Not the doctors, but the churches and the preachers. Those who stand to represent the Son of God and proclaim His salvation. What kind of a salvation? A salvation without the power to deliver, a salvation without the power to save a soul from its direst distress and need, a salvation only valuable in the life to come and without the power to deliver a soul from present torment.

Bless God, the testimony of our sister, and those like her, is bringing back to the world again the consciousness of Jesus Christ, a present power, a living Savior — not a dead one — a divine Christ, the living consciousness of the Holy Ghost. Blessed be the name of God.

As I listened to some of the details of our sister's testimony on Thursday afternoon, my soul was thrilled, and I said, "No greater service can be rendered to the people of Spokane and the world than to let them know of the love of the Lord Jesus Christ and the mightiness of His salvation and the reality of His healing power."

Mrs. Norton's Personal Testimony

I am glad to stand before you this afternoon, because every word the brother has said is true. And really, he has not begun to tell you the condition I was in. As the brother has told you, I sawed my finger when cutting a ham bone. I took the saw to saw the ham bone and sawed my finger on the right hand.

They took me to the hospital, but instantly the hand became paralyzed before I could get from the table to the stove, showing the poison there was in that meat. Feeling never came back again.

They took me to the hospital. In eight days blood poison and gangrene set in and I began to have chills and fever. The ninth day I went to Dr. O'Neil. My husband had told me he believed it was blood poison; also my groceryman.

When I came down to the doctor in the afternoon and he saw my hand and I told him how long it had been, he will never be whiter when he is dead. He said, "Are you aware there is gangrene present there now?"

I said, "No."

He said, "It is worse than blood poison. You must go to the hospital tonight."

I was taking care of two babies, one six months old and the other eleven weeks old. I was taking care of them with one hand; thinking as the finger healed the feeling would come back. I told him I could not go to the hospital then. He said, "Well, if you don't go to the hospital you must have a trained nurse."

I said, "All right."

The nurse was supposed to dress my hand every hour and use hot applications, but instead of that she dressed it at ten o'clock and stayed in bed all night. Of course, I was sick all night, and the next morning my fever was very high. My husband called the doctor. His auto broke down, and he knew if he did not go to the bar and report he would lose his job. So he asked this nurse if she would remain until noon. She said, "Yes." He thought she would help take care of the little ones. As soon as he left she wanted me to promise I would keep her by the week instead of going to the hospital, but I told her I could not until the doctor came. So she left.

My fever was 104°. The doctor said, "Babies or no babies, we will have to put them in a home, and you must go to the hospital." So my sister took one and a neighbor took the other, and I went to the hospital.

Dr. O'Neil counseled with other doctors and ordered me put on blood poison treatment, but each morning the finger would raise up blood and lay wide open and clear around this it was black. The doctor would take his lance and cut it off each morning, but the next morning it would be back on the good flesh, black and burning, a burning like fire. They kept on cutting the flesh until they had it cut off back to the hand and scraped the bone. Then they amputated the finger.

About the sixth day the doctor said, "I would let you go home if [sentence incomplete]."

I said, "Doctor, I still feel that intense burning." On the eighth day it broke out as black as black could be, and it would burn out holes. It would commence with a little brown spot. The sister would sit down sometimes and watch them break out. Gradually these spots would get blacker and blacker and in about an hour a hole would be burned clear to the bone. Finally, the hand was a perfect mass of these black holes and the fingernails came off.

Then they thought they could get ahead of the disease by amputating the arm. But it was just a few days later when it spread and began to break out on my breast, and there were sixteen sores at one time. They would not heal. They were just those dry, black holes. It would burn out in these holes, and then it would kind of quit burning, and then start in another place.

It searched up and down my body this way for four years, and the fibers were all eaten out of this left shoulder. After I had been sick about three years, the other arm began to break out. It began first in the elbow as large as and as black as could be. You could not take a saw and saw smoother than this was doing.

Then the hand became affected. It began to appear about six in the evening (showing hand) and you can see how the tendons are eaten out. This is all new flesh now on the back. Fifteen months ago the bone was all bare. The hand became in that condition from six o'clock in the evening until ten o'clock the next morning — the tendons all eaten and the flesh off the hand.

For months I was blind, almost stone blind, and my body in this terrible condition. After the first year they only gave me morphine. Of course, I could not sleep. They gave me every other opiate before they put me on morphine. I did not want to take it, but I went so long they finally began to give me this. They could not give me enough to ease the pain and put me to sleep. They gave me two doses of hyscene and the rest of the time morphine. It seemed to me it did me no good, but the doctor said I could not have stood it without.

This went on for about three and a half years. Then I went to Olympia, through the influence of my sister who wanted me to come there. She did not realize how bad I was. She had two little children, and with my habit of morphine she was afraid to take me into her home. So I went into a little shack, and my boy would come up and stay for two or three days. I really persuaded him to go back where he could make a living for himself. My husband was east of the mountains and did not have any money or means to send me, nor to come to me. I had a little money to get morphine, besides what morphine was sent to me. I did not pray for death for I did not know God. It seemed as if everybody turned me down. Everybody said, "She is only an old morphine fiend," and there was not one, but my sisters that knew the arm was off.

I began to take more morphine. There was one drugstore where I used to get nine dollars of morphine a month, besides from four to six hundred tablets every two weeks, which were furnished me from Spokane. I had two hypodermic needles and when one was out of order I would use the other. I went to Olympia in October and lived alone up until about the first of December, when these saints found me. It was through my little boy. He was down at the restaurant and [sentence incomplete].

He said, "She is awful sick and has one arm off and the doctors want to take the other off." His mother came over and she wanted to know about our circumstance. I told her we had plenty. I still had a good deal of pride. She said, "Do you know you are saved?"

I said, "Yes," but I knew I was not. I knew I was not fit to die but I did not want people to talk to me.

She went to the mission and asked for prayer, and after the morning meeting closed, there was a minister and his wife and this lady and another couple came over and talked and prayed with me. They came about six times in about two weeks.

From the first of December to the twenty-third, the fifth time they prayed for me, I was worse than I had ever been, and it seemed as if there was no hope whatever. The doctor came up that morning. They were not doing anything for me, but just watching the case. He said, "Mrs. Norton, we have got to take off that other arm. You cannot live thirty-six hours." My body was turning black in spots. Mortification had already set in. It was a beautiful sunshiny day, and it was a little room I was in, but it was as dark as the darkest night I ever saw. It seemed as if the light gradually went out. Then it seemed as though there was a heavy weight, similar to a cloud, but it just came down, shutting my life out. My breath was getting shorter. I was sure I was dying. The doctor said by taking off the hand and arm I would live three or four days, but I did not want it.

These people, the mother and her daughter, Ellensburg, came in. They wanted to pray for me. They had already prayed five times. I said, "There is no use of your praying for me. I am worse than I have ever been." Then I acknowledged I was not saved. They wanted to know if they could pray that I would die easy. I said, "Yes." They knelt by the bed and laid hands on me and began to pray. I know they had not prayed over ten minutes until I heard a voice saying, "If I heal your body and forgive your sins will you go anywhere and do anything for Me?"

I knew it was the voice of Jesus. I said, "Yes, Lord, I will, if You will just take this pain away."

Just then, Jesus appeared just as plain as anyone here, first at the foot of the bed, then He stepped around the bed and held out the right arm. He reached out with His right hand and touched the tips of my fingers, and as He did so every bit of pain left my body, and I felt the warm glow go all through my body.

From that minute I have never suffered a minute with that burning sensation. I got right up and walked the floor and praised God for what He had done. I had not eaten a bite for four days, but it seemed I had strength at once. I never was so happy in my life. Then the people started a story about me being insane.

That was about 3:30 p.m. In about an hour's time I settled down, so I dressed myself. I never thought of clothes before. These sisters could not wait until time for meeting to tell the good news, so they telephoned. When they returned, I was eating. They were going to leave me and go to the service, but I said, "I am going with you. Wait until I put on my coat and scarf." I waded the snow and walked two blocks to the mission. I was the first one on the floor that day to tell what the Lord had done for me. He not only healed my body and forgave my sins, but took away the morphine habit. I was buying nine dollars worth a month, and getting from four to six hundred tablets every two weeks besides. I had taken morphine about two p.m. that day, but after I was healed I never touched morphine to take a dose again, and I have had no desire for it whatever. I threw two hundred tablets and two hundred hypo syringes away. I did not throw them away at once, for I had thought of selling them.

The Lord showed me every little thing I had ever done in my life from eleven years old, written off line after line: dancing, playing cards, drinking beer, etc. Then He showed me I must burn these things up. So one morning when three ladies came over, I said, "I do not believe I will go." I just felt so heavy. They insisted on my going, so finally I said, "I have got to burn up these hypo and syringes." So I did, and when I got about halfway across the floor I fell on the floor, and I was under the power of the Spirit for one and a half hours. Jesus came again and showed me heaven, my mansion, crown, and also put the white robe on me, and I wanted to stay. But He said, "No, you will only have to go back for a short time, but you must go and tell the people."

Friends, it will pay you to seek for heaven at any price. If you had only seen what I saw and knew the reality of heaven and hell. I could look down and see my body on the floor, and it seemed as though I could not go back in my body. I was so icy and cold. While lying on the floor I spoke in tongues, and they said I delivered message after message in tongues. No one knows how happy I have been since. There is no day but what I am talking to Jesus.

I have never suffered for anything to eat or wear since I was healed, but I did before.

During my sickness my hair turned perfectly white. After I had been healed a year, this last January, my hair began to turn dark, and I have used nothing on it but soap and water. It began to turn from the ends of the hair up toward my head.

REMARKS
REVEREND JOHN G. LAKE

We have listened to our sister's story from her own lips, and from my private conversations with her I want to say that the story she has told you this afternoon does not convey one-half of the suffering and torture that her private conversations revealed. Everyone understands how difficult it is to convey such things to an audience.

If I had been going to preach this afternoon I would have spoken to you upon the subject of "Christ, the Eternal Healer," for there was never a period when Jesus Christ was not the Healer. Neither will there be a period when Jesus Christ is not the Healer, so long as healing is necessary for the human race.

I anticipate such a period from the Word of God at the end of the kingdom age. We have not yet entered the kingdom age, but the Scriptures portray a kingdom age to come. I anticipate, as I said, a period at the end of the kingdom age, when the Word reveals He, Jesus, "Who hath subjected all things to Himself, will Himself also be subjected unto the Father, that God may be all in all."[1]

---

[1] 1 Corinthians 15:28, paraphrased.

The phase of the Gospel that interests me today, as I know it does you, is that in this day and hour this woman's testimony shows that where souls have touched God and have entered by the way of the cross into a living experience in Jesus Christ, until the baptism of the Holy Spirit comes upon their heart, that to them prayer is answerable, as it ever was; that the dynamic power of God is not lessened, but that His radiant glory still flows from the soul of Jesus, filling spirit and soul and body with His eternal power.

In the midst of the darkness of this world, in the midst of the horrors of war, such a war as the world has never known, in the midst of a period when perhaps there is more human agony than there has been in any similar period in the world's history, our sister's voice and testimony comes like a blaze of light from the throne of God, revealing, bless God, that in the midst of the darkness, he who turns his soul upward may yet experience Christ's heavenly power.

God has laid a burden on my heart which is perhaps somewhat different from that which burdens the soul of most men. I am not half so interested in the hell to come as I am in getting people out of the hell they are in now. To my soul, Jesus Christ is a very present Savior. To my soul, the touch of Jesus has lost none of its holy virtue. To my soul, the salvation of the Son of God is the most pregnant, vital force in the universe of God. The salvation of Jesus is not through the acceptance of a concept or an idea. It is through the acceptance of Himself, and He comes by the living Spirit, a divine dynamic into the nature of man. Bless God.

One thing stands forth in Mrs. Norton's word — that the touch of Jesus imparted to her a life and power and healing virtue and saving grace so mighty, so intense that the curse of hell in which she had lived for four years vanished instantly. Blessed be God.

So the touch of Jesus in the soul of man liberates the nature of man from the bondages of darkness, of sin, doubt, or fear, and lifts the soul of man into the likeness and righteousness of Christ, translating his very spirit into the kingdom of the Lord and Savior Jesus Christ. There is a kingdom of the Lord and Savior Jesus Christ into which the spirit of man has the privilege to enter.

Our sister tells us that her spirit left her body and went with the Lord into the heavenlies; that He showed her the estate of the really redeemed; that He showed her also what those endure who know not God and are yet in darkness. And as she told us these things, one thing came to my soul: a prayer to God that by His grace my soul may grow big enough that when my ministry in this world is accomplished, I may yet have the privilege of proclaiming the salvation of the ever-dying Christ wherever such be needed.

I knew one man who once said in my hearing that he prayed that God Almighty would cause him to grow big enough in God and pure enough in heart that he might go even to the damned and preach Jesus Christ and His resurrection and His salvation. My soul said, "Amen," and it has been saying amen ever since. Blessed be His name.

To my heart Jesus Christ is the Eternal Healer. He was the Healer in the beginning. He was the Healer before there was any flood. He was the Healer after the flood. He was the Healer during His earth life. He is the Healer in this dispensation. He is the Healer forever! Bless God. So long as need of healing exists, Jesus is the Healer. Blessed be His name.

So I have become an enthusiast for the Son of God. His salvation to me is the mightiest conception that ever dawned in the nature of man or God. And I long and pray and rejoice in the expectation of a day to come when the universal race of man and the angels in heaven and creatures of earth will join in one glad song of holy power and glory to the Son of God, saying as the Scriptures indicate, "Honor and might and glory and blessing be unto Him who liveth forever and ever. Amen."[2]

Dear God, we bless Thee for the privilege of being here. We bless Thee for the privilege of listening to the words of our sister. We bless Thee, God, that Christ's salvation reached her soul. We bless Thee, God, that He hath taken captive death and hell through the light of His countenance and the glory power of His being, touching her hand, and the damnation left her, and hell in her was banished, and the Christ came in, and the glory shone forth, and the grace of Jesus was manifested. Blessed be God.

---

[2] See Revelation 5:12-14.

Lord God, we pray Thee that Thou wilt enlarge our hearts, that by Thy grace we may proclaim this uttermost salvation to all men.

And in Thy name, dear Christ, we say once more, that with all the energy of our heart, with all the force of our nature, by all the dynamic power that the Holy Ghost imparts to our soul, we shall proclaim anew the living Christ, the eternal Savior, the abiding Healer. Glory be to God! Amen.

THE TESTIMONY OF A CHRISTIAN DOCTOR

I do not think this service would be complete without a word from Doctor Betten, as a medical man. Doctor Betten, would you please give us a word, as a medical man?

DR. HERMAN B. BETTEN

It was my privilege many months ago to give a message from this platform. I think the burden of my soul then was along the lines of "The Stewardship of Wealth," and the burden has not left me yet. Somehow, I am praying to God for men throughout this country and throughout the world who will present themselves before God to be His stewards.

However, as the brother has asked me to say a word, perhaps it is very far from my mind to say anything today. My soul has been moved so deeply by the testimony.

I have never seen such a clinic as I have seen in Brother Lake's Healing Rooms. I have come up to his healing rooms and talked with them, and (turning to the ministers) you know the joy I have had. And I have put in lots more time with the patients than with the Doctor. That is why I have got such joy in my soul. And I do not know a disease under the sun that has not been healed under my very eyes since I have been here.

I want to say this much. It was my privilege to practice medicine for twelve years in the city of Montesano, and I want also to acknowledge the blessing of God upon my labors during those twelve years, because I was walking in all the light that God gave me. And I believe that God will bless any man or woman that is like Him if he is walking in all the light he has.

However, I thank God that He has given me more light, and now I am duty bound to walk in all the light God has given me. But I have nothing but kindness and love in my heart for the medical profession, because I believe they are doing a great service in the world. There are thousands upon thousands and millions of people who have not the faith to look straight to God for what He has for them in Christ Jesus. And I thank God for what doctors and surgeons are doing in the world. Of course there are good ones and bad ones among us, the same as in all the professions. But I believe the surgeons are doing lots in the world, mostly in the way of prevention. I think that is the most interesting thing in our work. John B. Murphy, who died recently, said that if he had life to live over again he would not be a surgeon. For although it is a blessing, yet it is a confession of helplessness. We cannot do anything for the organ we are cutting out, but to keep it from hurting the body in its faulty condition. The best of surgery is the confession of helplessness. And so Dr. Murphy said, "Had I life to live over again, I would not be a surgeon. I would give my life to the study of preventative medicine."

I have not the time to discuss the whole realm of medicine and surgery.

I have been here for several months. I have been away during the past winter, but before this last winter I spent several months in Spokane, and I have been studying this work. I have spent a great deal of time in the Healing Rooms talking with the people who come there to be prayed for. And if there was any doubt left in my soul as to the readiness of God, through Christ and by the power of the Holy Spirit, of doing the same things that were done during the earth life of the Lord Jesus Christ, I think that doubt vanished during these months.

I feel I must say something in reference to my own experience previous to coming here. I came to the end of my rope once in my practice. It was a case of scarlet fever. The family was a large family and a poor family. They passed through a siege of scarlet fever, not knowing what they had. The last child was twelve years old. She got through with the disease, so far as the disease proper was concerned. But the mother brought her to my office for bleeding at the nose. As any physician would do, I inquired into the history of the case, and on inquiry I found that the whole family had passed through a siege of scarlet fever. The disease in the body of this child had altered the blood. It was thin like water. I attempted to check that hemorrhage of the nose. I used all I knew but without avail. But that condition was only a part of what was going on in the body. That child, even while in my office, was bleeding to death in her own body. I found she had black and blue spots all over her body. I got a sample of the urine. It was like [blank space in manuscript]. There was blood in the stool — blood, blood everywhere. I have never seen a case like it before or since.

They went home without getting any relief. I was curious, so I went out to see her the next day, and if ever I saw a person dying this girl certainly was. And I would gladly give testimony in court anytime that she was dying. She was as white as a sheet and the head was turned back, the eyeballs were staring, and all you could see was the whites of the eyes. Her pulse was a running pulse. It was impossible to count it. The respirations, instead of being fifteen or twenty, were about three or four to the minute. It looked as if she could not last more than an hour or two. The parents were already discussing funeral arrangements.

Finally I said, "There is one thing more we ought to do. I am a physician, but I am working under another, the Great Physician," and I suggested prayer. Bless God for that scene. The father and mother came in, the hired man came in, the children came in. They all knelt in a circle on the floor, and I knelt in the middle of the circle. Then I offered a brief prayer. I did not have the light I have now. I did not know that it is *always* God's will to heal the sick. I did not know that then, but I did the best I knew. I said this in my prayer, "God, they say the age of miracles has ceased. I do not believe it. Jesus Christ, You are at the right hand of the Father Almighty. You are living. I know You are. You are just the same as You always were. You are the same yesterday, today, and forever."

This thought comes to me in that connection. Some of the folks say Jesus Christ did miracles to prove His divinity. I do not say He did not, but I say that Jesus Christ did miracles because He could not help

Himself. He could not help Himself. It was His very *nature* to do so. When He was in the presence of the sick ones He healed them all. He did not do it to establish His divinity, but because it was just like Him to do it. It would not have been like Him if He had not.

Well, if He healed folks in those days it is logical that He does it now, because His nature has not changed. He cannot help manifesting His nature. So if any of you are sick today, just come to Jesus and trust Him to make you whole. It is His *nature* to do it. He cannot help Himself. If you come to Him in faith, believing in prayer, it is impossible for you not to be healed.

So in that simple prayer I said to God — I put in the "if," it was the best I knew then. I said, "If it be for the best interest of all concerned and for the glory of God, raise this child as it were from the dead." That was the best I knew then, because I did not know that it was *always* the will of God to heal the sick. I left without seeing a sign or symptom of the answer.

The next morning, the brother came galloping to my office saying, "Doctor, my sister is well." Some might think it was some sudden mysterious thing that can be explained by saying she had passed the crisis. If it had been a crisis, she would have slowly crept back into health. But from that moment on, she improved rapidly. The next day she was up and walked and did not need any further attention from any human attendant. She did not slowly and painfully make her recovery.

I want to testify that God blesses a man according as he walks in the light God gives him. God blessed me and heard the prayer for it was as far as I could go then.

But after I came to Spokane and listened to the teaching here and also waited on God in prayer, I came to the deep settled conviction that it is *always* God's will to heal the sick — that no imperfection in mind, body, or spirit is in harmony with His will.

I want to explain my position. I feel my brethren are doing good in the world. I will have to admit they are doing a little harm too. I will use an illustration to explain.

Sometimes we want to take a toy or something that is dangerous away from our little one. If I simply walked up and took hold of that thing and tried to pull it away I might have difficulty, but when I hold up before her little eye something that is still brighter and more attractive, I have no difficulty at all. She immediately hands over the thing I wanted her to leave. That is the way I feel about medicine and surgery. It is not that I do not appreciate what my brethren are doing, but then God has given me *something better.* And when I compare, or rather contrast, the flow of the mighty Spirit of God through the body of a man or woman or a child that I am praying for I look up to God and I ask Him, "How is it possible that I ever could have been a dispenser of pills? How is it possible that I ever could have been guilty of carving up people?"

I do not believe I used to sin in the years that I practiced medicine and surgery, but as the new light has dawned upon my soul I have been overcome by contrition as I have seen and felt the power of the mighty Spirit of God sometimes coursing through me, through my own body into the body of the one prayed for. Praise be to His holy name. I certainly have wondered that it had not dawned on me before.

I feel to say, in praise to God, and call attention to the promise that was given to me personally. I believe that all have a similar promise in the Word of God, but there has been a promise given to me personally by the Spirit of God that I shall claim as long as God permits me to walk upon this earth and as long as I shall have the privilege of claiming the promise for any of my fellowmen. I think it will illustrate the difference of the ministry that God has called me to now and the ministry in which I was engaged for so many years.

A lady was out in the waiting room hall. She motioned to me to come and pray for her, and as I placed my hands on her, she said, "O Doctor, God has certainly given you the gift of healing." Now, I do not know whether He has or not, but I know this; that I can by the grace of God pray the prayer of faith, that I can take the promise of God and claim it, whether I have the gift of healing or not. "They shall lay their hands on the sick,"[3] and whether I have the gift of healing or not, I can at least claim that promise. As often as I have claimed that promise the Son of God has honored it.

---

[3] See Mark 16:18.

She had hardly uttered these words when the Spirit came on her, and she began to speak in tongues, and I listened to one of the sweetest messages my soul has ever heard. I cannot give you the message — it is sacred. Much of it was for me personally. But I want to say this, when the sister reached over and put her hands on my shoulder and said, "Doctor, this is for you," I was thinking of the years gone by and how little I was doing for God, and I was bracing my soul for a rebuke. Then these words came: "Your many years of faithful service have not been in vain." I do not know that I ever listened to anything that melted my soul as that did. Then the message went on: "Through the Christ in you, I will do that which the human physician cannot do." The reason I have given up the medical profession is not because I do not think it is a good thing, but because I found something else that is *better.*

I have to admit that I was disgusted with my work in the practice of medicine and surgery. Most of my work was among the acute cases, and I could not help but feel that most of these people would have gotten well anyhow, whether I treated them or not. But every now and then one of the old chronics came along, and I knew I could do nothing for them. There is so little we can do for the chronics and if we cannot do much except in the acute cases, it is not very much.

While I was in college one of the teachers once said, "One-third of the cases you will be called upon to treat are going to get better no matter what you do. Another third of them are going to die no matter what you do. There is another third that maybe you will be able to help a little bit."

But thank God, no man or woman has ever presented themselves to me since I have had the teaching on the subject of healing but what the need of that one was met by God. I have had my battles. Brother Lake and the brethren associated with him know the battles I had in my soul. Nobody ever gets to a place worthwhile in God without battles in the soul. But when I once got hold of the truth that God did not want anything imperfect in me — in my body, spirit, or mind — from that day not one has ever presented himself or herself to me — man, woman or child — that I had any doubt, any question in my mind but what the Son of God, in answer to my faith, would exercise omnipotent power through the Holy Ghost to meet the need of that one. That is a far different experience from what I had as a physician or surgeon.

THE TRUE PERSPECTIVE

The work of the medical profession is man's best effort to bring healing to the world. It is man's invention. It is the best the arm of flesh can do. It is the best man can do to save himself from the works of the devil (sickness and disease). Like all of man's other efforts to bring satisfaction and salvation to the human race it circumvents God's method. God's method of healing is a Person. Jesus said that He was the Way (John 14:6). He is the Way of salvation and healing. He paid for both at Calvary. "For there went virtue (power) out of him, and healed them all" (Luke 6:19). This is God's only way of healing. He works only through His Son.

Like Dr. Betten, there are many Christian doctors who have never seen the true light on divine healing. When they do, they will abandon man's method for God's method. You can no more mix God's way of healing with man's way than you can mix God's way of salvation with man's way of salvation. God's way is so superior there is no comparison. Man's way has its failures and harm. There-is no failure in God. He is true to His Word. If there is any failure it is the people's faith that fails.

When a person receives new light for a deeper walk with God and refuses it, that person comes to a standstill in his Christian experience. He has set a limit on his progress. He has set a limit on his usefulness to God. This is true not only concerning God's way of healing, but in other aspects of the Gospel. A person may take Christ as their Savior and reject the baptism of the Holy Ghost as He was received by the hundred-and-twenty on the Day of Pentecost. God uses people to the limit they will allow Him. People who refuse to go in God will perpetuate their limitation in those they win to Christ. This gives the world the idea that the Church is divided.

Some say all healing comes from God, therefore it makes no difference whether you trust God or the medical profession. This is only a rationalization to justify going to the medical profession. There is

John G. Lake's ministerial staff in Spokane, Washington. When the Better Business Bureau accused him of fraud for saying that he could heal people through the power of God, this group planned the public demonstration that turned the attack into a documentation of divine healing.

only one way of divine healing. They may feel that "the end justifies the means," but this is a false premise. It is false in this case as the teaching and pattern-ministry of Jesus is pushed aside as false and misleading. He never used the medical men of His day in any way, shape, or form.

Some feel it is alright to mix God's way and man's way. They know man's way is not sufficient to meet the need. In mixing the two they are saying that God's way is not sufficient either.

As with the salvation of your soul, it must be Christ and Him alone. He will not share His glory with another. It is the same with divine healing. If you are going to profess Christ is your personal physician then make Him so in fact. He wants first place. There is no room for a second. He will not share His glory with another. God offers you the best way. Why settle for less?

DEMONSTRATION SERVICE
Masonic Temple
May 13, 1917

This ministry purposes not only to teach the things of the Spirit of God, but to teach them in such a way that the common mind, unschooled in the Scriptures and the things of the Spirit, may know, comprehend, and believe.

During the week, I was called into consultation by a group of lawyers — one of them attends our church — concerning an individual whose past state of health and present state of health was a matter of debate in the minds of the judge and lawyers.

This woman had testified that a year or nine months ago, after having been an invalid for fourteen years, she received an entirely instantaneous healing of all her troubles and was a well woman. The evidence figured in a monetary way, and it seemed to be the desire of all parties to get at the real facts.

During the course of our conversation two of the lawyers said, "Mr. Lake, we haven't the least doubt that people who have minor and nervous diseases are healed, but we have a serious question in our minds if people with real diseases are healed." And I ventured the suggestion that if they would send a representative to our three p.m. service at the Masonic Temple, they would find that the majority of people who were healed did not have minor, but major diseases of the worst kind. I am glad that people with nervous diseases get healed also, for it is about the only place they get healed. Nervous diseases are a horror to the medical profession and always have been, and any first-rate physician will confirm my word.

The judge said, "I will send a stenographer to your meeting," and he is here today. Now I am going to call for representatives from the audience this afternoon and give a statement of their case.

Mr. Halford, Mrs. Annie Norton, Mrs. Harriet Petersen, Mrs. H. E. Peterson, Mrs. Carter, Mr. Ben Long, Mrs. Ben Long, Mrs. Carl

Peterson, Mrs. Gilbertson, Mrs. Lamphear. (Mr. Lake: "Have any of you been notified to be here?" Answer: "No.") This is not a pre-arranged service, these witnesses are samples of what God has done to hundreds in this audience.

I believe each one of these individuals were diseased differently from the other. All of these people in times past have given public testimony at one time or another in the services, and our stenographer has the testimonies on record. So it will not be necessary to give them in full. I propose to give a very short statement of their healing and then it can be confirmed from the original record if necessary.

TESTIMONY OF MRS. C. D. PETERSON

Mrs. Peterson's case was a tubercular one — tuberculosis of the spine and kidneys.

Lake: "Mrs. Olson (nurse), how long before her healing was she operated on?"

Mrs. Olson: "About five months."

Five months before her healing, Mrs. Peterson was operated on, and on account of the tubercular condition of the flesh, the wounds refused to heal. Finally, proud flesh[1] grew up in these wounds. The first time I went to her house (I went in a taxi) I could hear her scream when I was within a block and a half of the house.

Her healing began from the time she was first prayed for. Brother Fogwill prayed for her first. Her healing continued without cessation until she was perfectly well.

How many pounds of flesh have you put on since your healing, Mrs. Peterson?

Mrs. Peterson: "About sixty-five pounds" (125-190 pounds).

Medical science admits that the putting on of flesh is the final demonstration of the healing of tubercular people. When they put on flesh that settles the subject of tuberculosis.

---

[1] proud flesh: a new growth of tissue around the edges of a healing wound. [This growth of tissue prevents the wound from healing properly.] *Webster's Desk Dictionary of the English Language* (NY: Gramercy Books, 1983), p. 729.

I might say in a word: We do not examine wounds critically, but after I had been ministering to Mrs. Peterson a short time, the nurse said, "In my examination of the wounds, I find they are full of proud flesh," and she was troubled.

I replied "Never mind. God is bigger than proud flesh," and I went back and prayed again. When we returned the next time the nurse said, "Mr. Lake, the proud flesh has disappeared." Surely!

TESTIMONY OF MRS. BEN LONG

I never could get her testimony without her husband. Mr. Long came on the platform. In order to get before your minds some of the difficulties with which people contend when being healed, let me say: Ben was raised in a Christian family, but he was somewhat of a pugilist. In his boxing bouts he had been violently struck at different times in the region of the stomach, until finally a cancer of the stomach appeared. He was never operated on, but this growth appeared in him, causing the most violent suffering. Physicians believed it to be a cancer.

I asked him what his business was, and he said, "Fighting booze."

Mrs. Long was raised under a different environment. She was a Roman Catholic. She became paralyzed on one side. As Ben returned from work one evening, he met a man who had been an invalid, and when he inquired how it was that he was well, he told him he had been to our healing rooms and was healed. The gentleman advised him to bring his sick wife and also go himself to the healing rooms, so he did. He hired a motor car and brought his wife to the healing rooms.

Mrs. Long came into the healing rooms through the reception room door. We laid our hands on her and prayed. She passed out into the hall and when part way down the hall she discovered, to her amazement, that she was perfectly well. Her paralysis had disappeared. She returned through the waiting room again and came into the healing room to show us that the Lord had healed her. She has been a well woman ever since.

When the brother saw his wife healed, he came himself, and he was healed likewise. Bless God. Healed in body and healed in soul and healed in spirit, to the extent that ever since, or very shortly after their healing, I have been in the habit of calling them on the telephone and sending them to minister to others in the name of the Lord, and they are healed.

I want you to realize that when a soul comes in touch with the Lord Jesus Christ, they are healed not only in their physical being, but healed in the soul as well; and no man ever received the touch of God in his body but what he was enriched in the consciousness of his spirit. So Mr. Long's cancer went with his sin.

TESTIMONY OF MRS. ANNIE NORTON

This is the most medically examined woman I ever knew. She was examined and pronounced incurable by seven hundred physicians. Two hundred and fifty physicians in Spokane examined her at a public clinic in the Old National Bank Building. Dr. O'Neil had charge of the case.

Mrs. Norton was then taken to Seattle, where the physicians of Seattle examined her. Then she was taken to Tacoma and the physicians there examined her, and then she was taken to Portland where the Portland physicians examined her, and later to Olympia, Washington, where the doctors of Olympia examined her. Her case became celebrated in medical history and in the medical journals.

Since her healing, she presented herself to one of the best-known experts of this country, Dr. Blake Baldwin of Seattle, who gave a written statement that there is nothing whatever to show that she was sick, excepting the scars on her body.

Mrs. Norton's case was one of the strangest in medical history. In fact, it has never been diagnosed. Dr. O'Neil told me he would sit by her side and watch brown spots appear on her body. They would burn until in an hour, they would be an inch in diameter and from two to three inches deep. That condition continued for four years. The disease would seem to burn out in one spot, and then another spot would appear a few inches away. And so it went on, searching up and down the body during these terrible years.

Because of her suffering, it was impossible for her to sleep except through the use of narcotics, and consequently she became a morphine fiend. She tells me she received 250 tablets every two weeks from Spokane, besides nine dollars worth a month that she got from one druggist at Olympia.

This hand that you see (raising one hand) became like that in one night. That is, the flesh of the hand absolutely disappeared to the bone and the bones of the hand were entirely exposed, and the little finger fell off at the first joint.

In some respects the disease was like gangrene, but it was not gangrene. In some respects it was like leprosy, but it was not leprosy. The sensation in her body was that of a burning, consuming fire. I have not discussed this phase with the physicians, but my judgment is that a gaseous state of some character was established in her body, and when it broke out in one place on her body, all the gas in the body would come to that spot and burn out. Then another would begin in another place. That is only my own conclusions.

People have an idea that all these healings are performances by Mr. Lake or Mr. Westwood or Mr. LeDoux or Mr. Fogwill or some other official minister or preacher — not at all. This woman was healed when two simple women of her church, one a widow with five children and another married woman with five children, agreed together they would take a little time to give to the service of the Lord. They met her little son at a restaurant and inquiring who he was and so on, he happened to mention that his mother was sick and the doctors had amputated one arm and were about to amputate the other. So they went to see her and found her in the throes of death, blind so she could not see. The physicians had told her that unless she permitted them to amputate the other arm she could not live, and that if they did she would only live a few days.

These women knelt by her side and as they knelt praying, Jesus appeared to her, standing at the foot of the bed. He walked around and spoke to her, saying, "If I heal you will you tell the story of your deliverance wherever you can?" She answered Him that she would. He reached out His loving hand and touched the tips of her fingers and in one instant the Spirit of God flowed through her being and the fire went out and the woman was healed. Blessed be God.

I think her testimony peculiarly valuable in this respect. There has been so much in recent years to sort of professionalize the ministry of spiritual healing, but this healing proves that it does not belong to the professional healer only, but to the child of God.

TESTIMONY OF MRS. GILBERTSON

What would you do if you got your hip out of joint? That is something like, "What would you do if you got a broken arm?"

This sister's disease was something I do not know. She suffered most violently. Her suffering was similar to that of rheumatism, only much more violent. It seemed to be in the glands. Lumps would appear in the glands, as large as golf balls, and when I put my hands on her to pray the lumps would travel down the body through the glands. They moved just as rapidly down the body as my hands did. Finally, there seemed to be such a condition of atrophy that the tendons and muscles relaxed so that the hip came out of the socket and would turn over just like the hip of a jointed doll.

I have seen many people suffer, and suffer intensely, for I have been in this ministry for twenty-five years, but I never knew anyone to suffer more intensely than Mrs. Gilbertson. One morning when I went with Brother Fogwill to see her, her suffering was so terrible I could not bear to witness it, and that has occurred very rarely in my life. Finally, I found I was not getting victory and went out and sat down in the other room, and as I sat quiet in meditation and prayer I felt I should leave her and return to the healing rooms and invite the others to join me in prayer. So I returned to the healing rooms and called Reverend Westwood and Mrs. Peterson and some other folks who were there, and we sat down and joined our hands and our hearts. As we prayed, God Almighty put that hip in its place — no human hands were near her. She lives at 4115 N. Helena Street, four miles from the Healing Room. That's long distance healing by the power of God.

TESTIMONY OF MRS. CARTER

Mrs. Carter is one of my neighbors. She lives at 714 South Sherman. Mrs. Carter had a tumor. For nine months her physicians believed that the woman was pregnant, until after nature's time had passed. She continued to grow larger and larger for thirteen months from the beginning, until it was estimated that the tumor would weigh fifteen pounds. She came to the healing rooms and I ministered to her on three occasions, when there seemed to be no special evidence of healing, beyond that, her body relaxed and became comfortable. But the fourth time she was ministered to, the Spirit of the Lord came upon her so powerfully that the next morning she returned at eleven o'clock perfectly normal in size. The tumor had disappeared, not as tumors usually do, in liquid form, or giving any sign of substance whatever. It simply dematerialized and disappeared and was gone. God Almighty did it, bless His name!

When I stand in the presence of people like Mrs. Carter and realize what God has done in them, it seems to me that if I had been suddenly brought face-to-face with such things in the first time, an awe of God would get hold of my soul as it did twenty-five years ago, when for the first time I saw God heal people.

Twenty-five years ago this ministry was as new to me as it is to you. I went into one of John Alexander Dowie's great meetings in Chicago where a portion of the room was filled with cots on which dying folks lay. My brother, a man who had been an invalid for twenty-two years and the most terrible sufferer I have ever seen, was healed in that room. Dowie came in and sat down to teach for a little while, and as he looked down and saw the intense suffering of my brother, he dropped his Bible and came down to him and said, "Young fellow, I see you are suffering," and he prayed for him. Instantly, the power of God flashed through him. He arose and walked out of the place in his nightgown. Three others, a great deal like him, were on cots. He prayed for each one, and one after another received the healing touch and arose from their cots. When I saw him well, I walked on my tiptoes for about three weeks. The wonder of God's power had been revealed to my Methodist soul.

TESTIMONY OF MRS. H. E. PETERSON

This was a different case altogether. Mrs. Peterson had a catarrhal[2] condition for twenty years, so terrible that in the latter years of her life it would throw her into unconsciousness and she would remain so for four hours at a stretch, absolutely dead to the world. These spells would come about twice a month, sometimes twice a week during the last year.

Mrs. Peterson was healed through and through — not in a moment — her healing was gradual, as many healings are. She became a perfectly well woman and recently gave birth to a beautiful child, and she is a healthy, well, strong woman now. Bless God.

She tells me that the condition of decay was so terrible in the head that sections of bones issued both from the nostrils and the ears.

TESTIMONY OF MRS. LAMPHEAR

Mrs. Lamphear's disease was different from any other I ever knew in some respects. Mrs. Lamphear was an invalid for about thirteen years. Her original sickness was caused by a fall, which caused a prolapse of stomach, bowels, and uterus. Then tuberculosis appeared and later rheumatism. Her physicians had done everything for her they could, and finally they said, "There is only one other thing we can recommend. You go to Soap Lake and take the baths."

So she went. Now the effect of the baths that were given (and the superintendent said they were hotter than they had ever given to any other patient) was such that it caused the disease to leave the other parts of the body and concentrate in the left limb and produced an abnormal growth until the leg grew three inches longer than the other one and the foot about seven-eighths of an inch longer than the other foot. A lump of bone as large as an orange formed on the knee and destroyed the action of the joint.

When her healing took place, all of these conditions were removed. The limb became short at the rate of an inch a week and all the other

---

[2] catarrh: inflammation of a mucous membrane, esp. of the respiratory tract. *Webster's Desk Dictionary of the English Language* (NY: Gramercy Books, 1983), p. 141.

diseases disappeared. The bone on the knee likewise. Mrs. Lamphear was born without the outer rim on the left ear, and no lobe. Look at it now.

Beloved, there is more than healing in God. It is not just the subject of the removal of a disease or some nervous state that has gripped you for awhile. God is a creative power. The Holy Spirit coming into the person of a sick one comes as a living, creative power. It is the creation of life in them that drives out disease. And the incoming of the Spirit of God, the only Creator, does in people just what it has in her, given her an ear that never was there. It has grown gradually from the day God's power came upon her in healing.

TESTIMONY OF MRS. HARRIET PETERSEN

Mrs. Petersen was a tiny little woman when the Lord healed her, but oh my! She has put on seventy-seven pounds since she was healed, a little over a year ago.

I want you to realize the wonder of some of these manifestations of God. Mrs. Petersen was operated on first for fibroid tumors in the uterus and both uterus and ovaries were removed. A few months later she was operated on for gall stones and had a bad recovery. In a short time she passed into the very throes of death, and it was in this state she was finally healed. Brother Westwood knelt in prayer by her bedside and remained all night. Her condition was such that for a period of about forty minutes they were not able to distinguish whether she was alive or not. But the power of God came upon her, and she arose from that condition a well woman. Not only that, but God Almighty gave her back the organs that had been removed. God is a creative power, God in you a creative power. He never intended people to be deficient in body, soul, or spirit. God purposes to come into every life through the Holy Spirit, a divine, living energy, bless God, removing deficiencies, creating strength and life and health and power. Blessed be God.

The old apostle's conception of a well-rounded Christian was, "God hath not given us the spirit of fear; but of power, and of love, and of a sound mind" (2 Timothy 1:7). This is Paul's description of the Spirit of God in man. "He hath not given us the spirit of fear, but of power and of love and of a sound mind," and it takes all three to make a well-rounded Christian. No sin, no mental weakness, no sickness either.

TESTIMONY OF MR. GEORGE HALFORD

Brother Halford was one of the first persons to be healed under my ministry in Spokane, within six months or thereabouts after my coming to Spokane. Mr. Halford was an epileptic. At the time of his healing he had taken fifty-five fits in twelve hours. He was out of one into the other averaging, as you will see, about a fit every twelve minutes.

Of course he was unconscious, and in this condition I found him about nine o'clock in the morning as I went to pray with him and watched the awfulness of his state — the lips all bitten to pieces, blood and foam coming from his mouth — these hellish convulsions tearing him to pieces. Oh, it was the work of the devil.

When I came into the room something from heaven came upon my heart, so intense that I looked up into God's face and said, "God, if You will let me smite this devil I will lend You all the energies of my soul." As I stood by his bedside the Spirit of God came upon me until I could feel God in me like a burning fire. And when I laid my hands on him and commanded the devil to come out of him in the name of Jesus Christ, I knew he came out.

There are oppressions of the devil and there are possessions, and if there is one thing I regard as possessions of the devil, it is epilepsy. It is only where God anoints the soul with the real, pure power of God that epileptics are delivered — none of your psychological influences and mind over matter statements, but God the Holy Spirit to destroy. We have had many epileptics who were not healed because of the fact that there did not come upon our soul that sufficient measure of the Spirit of God to get them delivered.

I wish I could impress it on you that God comes into the personality of a man, a living force, a divine being, bless God. I have been so wearied with psychology in the last few years that it almost makes me puke. Everything in the world is attributed to psychological influences. But I want to tell you that twenty-five years in this ministry has taught me that there is something way up in God a mighty lot higher than psychological influence.

The mind is wonderful, but there are a lot of people in the world who never will be healed by psychological powers because the power of the human mind does not reach the case. It requires the living Spirit of the eternal God to so possess the body and soul and spirit of the servant of God, that God will flame through His nature like a heavenly lightning and destroy the cursed hell that blasts another life, and so bring to pass the will of God.

TESTIMONY OF REVEREND OSBORN

"I have been a Methodist minister for six years. The secretary of our Conference would bear me out in my statement.

"My last sermon in my church was last December. Having been sick in Addy for three months, I came to Spokane. I was removed to the Deaconess Hospital and had five leading physicians of Spokane to take care of me, but they could do nothing. Two weeks ago I was dismissed as a hopeless case. From that time I took God as my physician and have been improving every day and am practically well.

"I thank God for this wonderful light that has come to me. I might say that during my years as a Methodist minister, Bright's disease has troubled me a great deal, and I thank God He has brought me to where I can trust in Him for all the ailments of my body. I thought of the words of the psalmist, 'O taste and see that the Lord is good: blessed is the man that trusteth in him.'[3] And surely I have been blessed since I put my trust in my Christ. I am glad to testify this afternoon that 'Jesus Christ the same yesterday, and to day, and for ever.'[4]

"Brother Fogwill let me into a secret yesterday, and it is a secret I would like to impart to you, for sometimes I have been troubled at night with sleeplessness. Sometimes I would waken at night, and the Lord would put upon my soul a burden of prayer and I would pray for the work.

---

[3] Psalm 34:8.

[4] Hebrews 13:8.

"Yesterday, Brother Fogwill quoted that wonderful scripture that, 'He giveth his beloved sleep.'[5] And last night after retiring it was impossible for me to sleep. I said, "Dear Lord, I am Your beloved, and I want to sleep," and I slept like a child all night. If you have any trouble with sleeplessness, and you are the beloved of God, just make God come through with His promise.

"Some of you will understand my condition better when I tell you it was Bright's disease. In the first analysis they found there was fifteen percent albumin, and the physicians shook their heads and said it was hopeless. And it was hopeless to the physician, but not to Jesus Christ.

"Brother Lake has been speaking about the Holy Spirit. I have prayed since this light came to me that I might have a deeper infilling of the Holy Spirit. And since the Holy Spirit has taken possession of my life, thank God, that power is working in and through me, and I am here to testify to the goodness of God. As I said the other afternoon, I am like the prophet of old. I am here, and I would say, 'Here am I, Lord, send me.' If God calls me to this blessed work, believe me, I am ready to go. My father has been upon the firing line leading souls to Christ a long time.

"As Brother Lake said, I am the son of a Methodist minister, and my father was the son of a Methodist minister, but I say today with all love to the church, He has taken all creeds out of me, and thank God I am trusting in my Savior. I can understand the heart of the old psalmist when he said, 'O taste and see that the Lord is good: blessed is the man that trusteth in him.' He was so full of the living God that he could not express his love for Him. And this afternoon in the language of the beautiful song,

> I cannot tell how precious
>
> The Savior is to me
>
> I only can invite you
>
> To come and taste and see.

'And now since God has healed me, we rejoice together.'"

---

[5] Psalm 127:2.

(Story of man in Africa healed, who was shot through mouth. Did not take it.)

TESTIMONY OF MISS PEARL PAINE

This woman was sent here with diabetes to die, and she was healed and today is a very live, healthy, and happy woman.

TESTIMONY OF MR. ROBERTSON

Thirty years ago, when Robertson was a young boy, he fell and the cartilage was driven in until the bottom of the breast bone and the cartilage were driven in three inches and remained so. This is what I want you to think about for a moment. That remained for thirty years, until the second of April when he came to the healing rooms for the first time, and that bone commenced to come out until it is not quite an inch deep and is coming out every day.

I want you to see what God does. I want you to reason about that for a moment. What does God have to do?

God Almighty is a surgeon. I saw a cartoon once showing how they do things at the St. Luke's hospital, Chicago. They said, "What is the matter with the man's leg?"

And the old doctor said, "Well, I'll be blamed if I know. Cut if off and see."

How many people in this audience have been healed of nervous diseases? (Thirteen hands were raised.)

How many have been healed of other diseases? (Hundreds of hands went up.)

That is my answer. Reporter, take that back to the lawyer and the judge, and the Lord bless you and them too. I bless God that a day has come when lawyers and judges want to know, "Are these things so?" It is a good day. It demonstrates that the mind of man is becoming emancipated, and I prophesy a day to come when divine healing will be recognized worldwide as the highest and surest system of healing practice known to man and will be recognized as both spiritual and scientific. We need to recognize a new science and one day our schools will teach the science of Pneumatology (the science of Spirit).

As I have studied what in my judgment is the deepest need of the world, Christian and unchristian, I believe it to be the necessity for the consciousness of Christ, a living Savior in the soul of man.

The reason we devote a portion of the service once in awhile to a demonstration such as has taken place this afternoon is that the truth is better brought home to the hearts of men through example and by testimony and demonstration than possibly by any words that we could utter.

We are approaching the historical date of Pentecost. Next Lord's day is commonly known as Pentecost Sunday, the anniversary of the original Pentecost, fifty days after the ascension of Jesus when, as the disciples were gathered together with the little Jerusalem church, numbering one hundred and twenty,

> Suddenly there came a sound from heaven as of a rushing mighty wind, and it filled all the house where they were sitting. And there appeared unto them cloven tongues like as of fire, and it sat upon each of them. And they were all filled with the Holy Ghost, and began to speak with other tongues, as the Spirit gave them utterance. [6]

These are the words in which the coming of the Spirit of God to abide as a living, divine life and power in the nature of man are given in the Word of God.

I want you to observe that the outward manifestations marking the coming of the Spirit were as mighty and intense as were those that characterized the birth of Jesus Christ. At the birth of Jesus there was the angel chorus, the shepherd watch, the star of the east, and the wise men who came saying, "We have seen his star in the east, and are come to worship him."[7]

The coming of the Spirit was the return of the Spirit of Jesus Christ, not to abide in the flesh of one man, Jesus, but to live in the flesh of

---

[6] Acts 2:2-4.

[7] Matthew 2:2.

every Christian soul. Even the outward manifestations of the Spirit's coming were as powerful and as convincing as were those that accompanied the birth of the Savior. Tongues of fire, the presence of the Holy Ghost, a rushing, mighty wind, speaking in other tongues as the Spirit gave them utterance are just as mighty manifestations [as] the angel chorus, wise men searchers, the shepherd guard, or the star in the east.

Christianity in her darkness and dimness from the fourth century to this present hour forgot and failed to recognize that Jesus Christ purposed to be the same mighty, divine energy in the nature of man, bless God, that was characteristic of the life of Jesus Christ on earth.

Yea, bless God, the purpose of Jesus Christ indicated in that day, as declared in the Word of God, was to so revolutionize the nature of man, so enrich him with the grace and fullness of the knowledge of Jesus Christ, that in nature and character and power and purity he should be like his Christ. Not like his Christ *a little bit,* but like his Christ within and without, through and through, blessed be God.

I know you feel as you leave this room that your eyes have witnessed and your ears have heard things that possibly the ears of man have rarely heard in fourteen hundred years. I want you to carry away this conviction: The Lord Jesus Christ purposed by the Holy Ghost to be in you.

[UNTITLED: TESTIMONY OF REVEREND OSBORN]

Masonic Temple

May 20, 1917

Hymn: "Oh Touch the Hem of His Garment."

Prayer: Charles J. Westwood

lmighty God, our heavenly Father, we come to the Christ today with thanksgiving, with joy. We bless Thee, O God, for the real consciousness of life. We thank Thee, O God, for the love of the Father. We bless Thee for the knowledge of Jesus Christ, of God as our Savior, as our Healer, as our Cleanser, as our Keeper, as our all and in all. Bless His Holy name!

"Oh God, we thank Thee this afternoon for the conscious presence of real life, that mighty life and power of the Holy Spirit. We thank Thee, O God, that we ever realized that every virtue we possess and every faculty and every thought of holiness, were His alone. We thank Thee for the leading power of the Holy Spirit, 'For as many as are led by the Spirit of God, they are the sons of God.'[1] And oh, we thank Thee this afternoon for the precious gathering of the sons of men. We thank Thee that we are part of the precious body of the Christ of God, that He, the head, is at the right hand of God, our loving Father, interceding for us. We thank Thee for the other Intercessor. He, O God, who is in us, pleading in us and with us for God.

"Oh God, help some precious one to realize in their very innermost being through this service the wooing of the Holy Spirit. Let God fill our hearts with joy and gladness as we come into Thy presence in the might and strength of the Holy Spirit, to demonstrate and praise and give thanksgiving unto Thy name.

"Lord, we bless Thee for what Thou hast been to us through another week. We thank Thee for the Christ, for the strength, for the dominion of the sons of God. And Lord God, we come before Thee as Thou

---

[1] Romans 8:14.

hast invited us to and command Thee that the might and power and love of God shall be felt in this meeting, that we may realize that Jesus Christ in His precious promise is here with us today and the very truth of Thee: 'Lo, I am with you all the time, even unto the end of the age.'[2]

"Precious Christ, You are doing the same things this afternoon. You are blessing everyone that comes to Thee with real salvation; You are blessing everyone that comes to Thee with real healing; You are blessing every one that comes to Thee with every desire of their heart, fulfilled in Jesus Christ. Lord God, we bless Thy name for the reality of the real conscious union with God. We ask Thee that this meeting may be alive with the presence of the Holy One, that the power of God may go through us, fill, and radiate from us that we may realize that Thou art with us as Thou wert with Thy children in Jerusalem. Fill our hearts with joy that we may realize the very consciousness of Thy moving in the camp.

"Lord God, bless those who have asked us to pray for them. Lord God, there are many that we would remember this afternoon. We ask that the very presence of Thy seamless dress may be by every bed of pain, and that they may touch Thee in life's throng and press and be made whole again. Lord, hear and bless us and cause Thy face to shine upon us because of the precious token of Thy love, and we will give Thee the praise. Amen."

Hymn: "Sweetest Note."

Reading: Ephesians 1

Solo: "Unto the Hills I Lift Up Mine Eyes."

Miss Miloradovich.

Reception of Members

TESTIMONY OF REVEREND OSBORN

Mr. Lake: I had promised through the *Chronicle* that Reverend Osborn would be here to tell of his healing by the power of God. When people get in contact with the power of God, we like to have

---

[2] Matthew 28:20, paraphrased.

folks know it. Paul said, "I am not ashamed of the gospel of Christ: for it is the power of God unto salvation to every one that believeth; to the Jew first, and also to the Greek."[3] Brother Osborn is not a Greek. He is a Methodist minister, and the son of a Methodist minister, and I do not know how many, but it goes back to John Wesley.

(Turning to Reverend Osborn)

Brother, I am glad to see you. I am glad we have not had a funeral and buried Brother Osborn and put a lot of flowers on the grave. That is a great joke, that flower business. When they get a man dead, then they cover him with flowers.

John Wesley was the founder of the Methodist church. He was a man of mighty faith. His journal abounds in wonderful answers to prayer. Healings both of the [illegible].

Reverend Osborn: Some have already heard my story of this healing, but it will bear repeating. I made a confession the other afternoon to Brother Lake that during my six years of ministry that each Sunday morning I was obliged to leave my home and go out to the outside appointment. When I started out in the morning, in my rig, if you should have run into me you would have thought it was a moving drugstore instead of a Methodist preacher.

You would have found my smelling salts in my pocket and codeine in each pocket and aspirin once in awhile. My wife is in the building, and she will bear me out in that statement. I was so nervous that I could not preach without aspirin or codeine. I would return home about three P.M. for dinner and would spend the afternoon in bed, until it was time to preach in the evening, and then go to preach like a half dead preacher, with a half dead sermon.

I would like to say that this blessed light that has come to me is one of the most wonderful things that ever happened in my whole experience. I might say, as most M. E. preachers and I will be perfectly frank, that I was very prejudiced, but thank God, He has taken the prejudice out of me.

A dear old saint came to my bedside and she said, "Brother Osborn, did you ever hear of Brother Lake?"

---

[3] Romans 1:16.

I said, "Oh yes, I have heard of Brother Lake, but they can't do anything for me." I was so prejudiced I would not talk about it. I was like most Methodist preachers. I thought he was a fanatic. But now I believe it is the power of God unto salvation — the very power of God.

For three months I laid upon the bed. The doctor said my cause was hopeless. So it was to the doctor. Then I left Addy and came to Spokane and spent one month in the Deaconess Hospital. I had several doctors. Three weeks ago next Tuesday, I left the Deaconess Hospital, you might say, turned away to die. But I could not understand why I had to die when there was so much work to do.

Brother Lake: "No more could the Lord."

Reverend Osborn: That is true, Brother Lake. Before I went to the Deaconess Hospital, just as the taxi pulled up at the door, Brother Fogwill came and said, "Don't go to the Deaconess Hospital, because God knows more in a minute than the doctors know in a lifetime." Friends, I have proven that that is true. Brother Fogwill prayed for me, and that night my kidneys flushed the first time for nearly four months. Yet I [missing pages].

(Turning to Mr. Lake). Brother Lake, I have counted the cost.

I would rather be here this afternoon, well, speaking to you, than as Brother Lake said, a dead Methodist preacher. An Irishman said he would rather be a live Irishman than a dead hero. I would rather be a live witness for Jesus Christ, even if some will consider that I have turned my back on the old church, than be a dead preacher. But, thank God, I have not. My mind goes back to my ministerial education and the life of our beloved Wesley. If there ever was a man who believed in divine healing it was John Wesley. He knew the power of God, and those who know the power of God this afternoon cannot deny the gospel of healing. This is not a new gospel, but is the old gospel that Christians have left to die.

I do not wish to finish without saying a word about my mother. God bless mothers. My mother is one of the saintliest women I know. I have not seen her for six years, but I have heard from her every week, and at the bottom of her letters is always this sentence, "Son, I am praying for you." Some will understand what that means to a young man. During my sickness there was always that thought, that mother was praying for me. Thank God for a godly mother. Thank God for a godly father. Thank God this afternoon that the children will rise up and call the parents blessed, because they have taught them to walk in the nurture and admonition of the Lord.

And now my mother's prayers have a new answer. God has come to me. Jesus Christ is now Savior of both love and body. I am healed and am going to preach this wonderful Gospel wherever I go.

DIVINE HEALING

Magazine Article

November 14, 1917

ivine healing, what is it? It is healing by the Spirit of God, exercised through the spirit of man. Jesus, the Master Healer, not only healed Himself, but empowered His twelve disciples to perform the same ministry. Later, He empowered "seventy others also,"[1] making in all eighty-three men who practiced the ministry of healing during His earth life.

After the resurrection of Jesus, just before His ascension, a great new commission was given to His disciples. He sent them to preach to all men everywhere, commanding them to "preach the gospel to every creature,"[2] and declaring concerning those believers who were to become disciples through their ministry that, "These signs shall follow them that believe; In my name shall *they* (the believer) cast out devils; they shall speak with new tongues...they shall lay hands on the sick, and they shall recover."[3]

A common fallacy in connection with the subject of healing is taught by the churches at large. Namely, first: The days of miracles are past. Second: No one healed but the twelve apostles. These statements exist because of the lack of knowledge on the general subject of healing, as set forth in the Scriptures.

In his first letter to the Corinthians Paul sets forth, in order, the various gifts of the Spirit prevalent in the Church. First, the word of wisdom; second, the word of knowledge; third, faith; fourth, the gifts of healing; fifth, working of miracles; sixth, prophecy; seventh, discerning of spirits: eighth, divers kinds of tongues; ninth, interpretation of tongues.[4]

---

[1] See Luke 10:1.

[2] Mark 16:15.

[3] Mark 16:17-18.

[4] 1 Corinthians 12:8-10.

*John G. Lake being greeted by the Mayor of Spokane,
who called Spokane the healthiest city in the nation
due to Lake's ministry there.*

He commends the church in that "ye come behind in no gift."[5] All these various gifts of the Spirit were exercised among them.

James, in instructing Christians concerning their faith in God, said, "Is any sick among *you?* let him call for the elders of the church; and let them pray over him." Regarding this prayer he said, "The prayer of faith shall save the sick, and the Lord shall raise him up; and if he have committed sins, they shall be forgiven him." He further declares, "The prayer of a righteous man availeth much in its working."[6]

The writings of the Church fathers for four hundred years after Christ emphasized the power of healing as known in the churches of that period. Certain sects of Christians from the days of Jesus until the present have practiced the ministry of healing — namely, the Armenians, the Waldenses of Germany, and the Huguenots. In later years, the followers of Dorothy Truedell of Switzerland; the Buchanites of South Africa. And in our own day, the Christian and Missionary Alliance, with headquarters in New York; the Church of God, and the followers of John Alexander Dowie, who maintain a city in the state of Illinois in which no doctor has ever practiced medicine and where no one employs a physician or takes medicine. They trust God wholly and solely for the healing of their body. And the national vital statistics show that their death rate is beneath the average of cities of the same population in the rest of the country.

Since the establishment of the Spokane Divine Healing Institute in January 1915, Spokane has become the healthiest city in the United States, according to the national record. And Dr. Ruthledge of Washington, D. C., in reviewing this subject said, "Divine healing is no longer a vagary[7] to be smiled at. Through its practice the Divine Healing Institute of Spokane, Reverend John G. Lake, Overseer, has made Spokane the healthiest city in the United States. In this I do not discount all the other splendid agencies of healing, but I call attention to the fact that with the establishing of the Divine Healing Institute of Spokane, the percentage of deaths in the city was lowered to that extent that Spokane became famed as the healthiest city in the United States of America."

---

[5] 1 Corinthians 1:7.

[6] James 5:14-16, paraphrased.

[7] vagary: 2. A whimsical or wild idea. *Webster's Desk Dictionary of the English Language* (NY: Gramercy Books, 1983), p. 989.

We are frequently asked, "What is divine healing?" "Is it Christian Science?" "Is it psychological?" or "Is it spiritual?" We reply: "Divine healing is a portion of the Spirit of God transmitted through the spirit of man. The Spirit of God was imparted by Jesus, through laying His hands upon the sick. Again and again in the Word we read, "He laid his hands on them and healed them."[8] Indeed, the Spirit of God so radiated through and from His personality that His clothing became impregnated by it.

The woman who touched the hem of His garment felt in her body that "She was whole of that plague." Jesus discerned that "virtue is gone out of Me." Having faith to touch His garment, she received the power of the Spirit into her person.[9] So mighty was this power of the Spirit in the apostle Paul that we read in Acts 19 that "from his body were brought unto the sick handkerchiefs or aprons, and the diseases departed from them, and the evil spirits went out of them."[10]

Students have long since discovered a new science. This new science is known as pneumatology, the science of spirit. Pneumatology is a recognition of the laws of the Spirit, a discerning of the modus operandi of the Spirit's working, its effects and powers.

Indeed, scientists have undertaken to demonstrate the psychological and physiological effects of the Spirit of God in man under certain spiritual influences and conditions. In the operation of prayer they declare that the cortex cells of the brain expand, and as they expand they receive and retain the Spirit of God; that through the action of the will, or the desire of the heart, the Spirit is transfused through the whole personality so that the cells of the brain and the cells of the body and the cells of the blood become supercharged by divine Spirit; that this absorption and retention of the Spirit of God in the person of man produces a chemical interaction. Sometimes waves of heat sweep over the individual as hands are laid upon them and the Spirit of God is transmitted to them. Persons will sometimes burst forth in violent perspiration, so great is the chemical interaction taking place within.

---

[8] Mark 6:5 and Luke 4:40.

[9] See Luke 8:43–48.

[10] Acts 19:12.

Most remarkable results are obtained in this ministry. Examples:

Mrs. Daniel Carter, 27 West Courtland Avenue, Spokane, was afflicted with a large tumor. Thirteen physicians examined her, estimating the tumor to weigh fifteen pounds. All agreed that there was no hope of life, except through an operation to remove the mass. She was ministered to through prayer and the laying on of hands at 4:30 in the afternoon. So remarkable and powerful was the Spirit of God in her that by eleven o'clock the following day every trace of the tumor had vanished, and she returned to the healing rooms with her corsets on, normal in size, to show us the wonder that God had accomplished in her.

Mrs. Lamphear, of Gandy Hotel, Sprague Avenue, Spokane, was a sufferer from tuberculosis and prolapses of stomach, bowels, and uterus. She was an invalid eleven years. In addition to this she suffered violently from inflammatory rheumatism. Physicians being unable to heal her, she was advised to go to Soap Lake, wash, and try the hot baths. Baths of normal temperature had no effect upon her. She was then placed in super-heated baths, the result of which was that the poisons seemed to leave the upper portion of the body and concentrate in the left leg, causing an abnormal growth on the limb. The limb became three inches longer than the other, the foot almost an inch longer than the other. A large bone, as large as a medium-sized orange, grew on the inside of her knee, destroying the action of the joint.

Under divine healing ministry the leg shortened at the rate of one inch per week, the bone on the inside of the knee entirely disappeared, and her tuberculosis was healed. All her diseases fled. She was born without the outer rim of one ear, and without the lower lobe. The ear began to grow, and is practically a perfect ear.

We believe that this demonstrates the mightiness of the inward working of a great force and power and should illustrate the wonderful effect produced by the introduction of the Spirit of God in power into the person.

Mrs. Mary Matheny, Johnson, Washington, was under treatment for four years at the Clarkston Cancer Institute, Clarkston, Washington, and was finally discharged as incurable. Her physicians said she had forty cancers in the bladder, the uterus, stomach, breasts, throat, mouth, root of the tongue, and also in the spine. She was brought to the Spokane Divine Healing Institute and in seven weeks returned to her home healed. Her forty cancers had vanished.

During the life of the Institute, from January 1915 to the present time, an average of one hundred persons have received ministration through prayer and the laying on of hands each day — a total of almost a hundred thousand ministrations (treatments) to date.

Every portion of the city and almost every town, village, and hamlet in the state and adjoining states have those who have thus been healed by the power of God.

The financial support of the Institute is provided for by the love offerings of those who have been blessed through the ministry. No fixed charges of any kind are made for any service. A staff of ministers who minister to the sick, etc. through prayer and laying on of hands, are continuously in attendance. Other local churches have difficulty in maintaining one pastor and possibly an assistant. This church has ten and is continuously adding to the staff, so great has become the demand for this ministry.

Almost every known disease has been healed. The lame, the deaf, halt, blind; people with cancers, and [transcription ends].

LAKE'S REPLY TO DR. ELWOOD BULGIN

February 28, 1920

Dr. Elwood Bulgin Spokane, Washington

ear Brother in Christ:

It was my privilege to be present at your meeting at the St. Paul Methodist Church at Spokane last Monday night and listen to your sermon. I was deeply impressed by the masterful manner in which you marshaled your facts and the spirit in which they were presented to your great audience.

Your presentation of the deity of Jesus Christ and the sharpness with which you brought the facts of the denial of the deity of Jesus by the Christian Scientists were striking. The masterful handling of the whole subject commanded my admiration and I believe the admiration of a great majority of your audience.

Men can speak with frankness to each other, particularly when their interests in the Kingdom of Jesus Christ are identical. You have lived, loved, and denied yourself and suffered for the cause of the Kingdom of Christ in the earth. I too, have loved and suffered for my fidelity to the vision of the redemption of Jesus Christ which God revealed to me.

For twenty-five years I have labored, as few men in the world have labored for so long a period, to bring before the world as far as I could the magnificent truths of the redemptive blood and life and power of the Son of God.

Your methods and my methods have been different. You, in your forceful, philosophical manner, have undertaken to destroy faith in Christian Science through opposition, ridicule, and exposure of what you believe to be its fallacies. On the other hand I have undertaken, by specific revelation of the truth of Jesus Christ concerning the healing power of God and its availability for all men today, to show the world that there is no need for any man to leave any stable

Christian body in order to secure the benefits of salvation and healing specifically declared by Jesus Christ Himself to be available to every man.

Jesus, in contrast with the ancient philosophers and reformers of the past and present, first gave Himself in consecration to God — body, soul, and spirit — thereby establishing the pattern of consecration for all Christians forever. His baptism was the dedication and commitment of Himself "unto all righteousness."[1] He undertook to reveal the righteousness of God. Note the nature of this revelation.

Having definitely committed Himself — His body, His soul, His spirit — to God forever, immediately there descended upon Him the witness to His hundredfold consecration. The Holy Ghost came from heaven as a dove and abode upon Him as it ever will upon every man who will meet Almighty God with the same utterances of real consecration to God of spirit and soul and body. This reveals the demand of God upon the Christian's person and conscience and the answer of God from heaven to this fullness of consecration.

Being thus definitely equipped, He proceeded to the wilderness for testing by Satan to see if this consecration of body and soul and spirit would endure.

He overcame all the efforts of Satan to tempt Him in the specific departments of His life: first, the body; second, the soul; third, the spirit. He overcame through reliance on God and His word and came forth in the power of the Spirit. He announced the constructive platform of His life and ministry, containing the following six planks:

The Spirit of the Lord is upon me, because He hath anointed me.

> First — To preach the gospel to the poor.
>
> Second — He hath sent me to heal the brokenhearted.
>
> Third — To preach deliverance to the captives.
>
> Fourth — Recovering of sight to the blind.
>
> Fifth — To set at liberty them that are bruised.
>
> Sixth — To preach the acceptable year of the Lord.[2]

---

[1] See Matthew 3:15.

[2] See Luke 4:18-19.

God's acceptable year had come. No more waiting for the year of Jubilee and all its consequent blessings. God's never-ending Jubilee was at hand in Jesus Christ.

He then went throughout all Galilee teaching in their synagogues and preaching the gospel of the kingdom and healing all manner of sickness and all manner of disease among the people and so established forever the ideal of Christian ministry for the Church of God.

Then He empowered twelve men and "sent them to preach the kingdom of God, and to heal the sick."[3] Profiting by their experience and advancing in faith and knowledge of the power of God, He "called seventy others also."[4] But in sending forth the seventy He reversed the order of instruction. To the seventy He said: "Go into the cities round about. *Heal the sick that are therein,* and say to them, The kingdom of God is come nigh unto you."[5] And they returned rejoicing that even the devils were subject to them "through thy name."[6]

Then came His wonderful entrance into death, His redemption on the cross, His resurrection from the grave, His interviews with His disciples, and His last commission in which, according to Mark, He established in the Church of Christ, to be born through their preaching in all the world, the very same ministry of salvation and healing that He Himself during His earth life had practiced.[7] That ministry contained the message of Jesus to all the world and the anointing with power from on high, just as He had received it at His baptism. Indeed, He commanded them to wait in Jerusalem until "Ye shall be baptized with the Holy Ghost not many days hence."[8]

He declared to them that certain signs should follow, saying: "These signs shall follow them that believe." Everyone, every Christian soul, was thus commissioned by Jesus to heal the sick and sinful from sickness and sin.

---

[3] See Luke 9:1-2.

[4] See Luke 10:1.

[5] Luke 10:8-9, paraphrased.

[6] Luke 10:17.

[7] See Mark 16:15-18.

[8] Acts 1:5.

In my name shall they —

First — Cast out devils.

Second — They shall speak with new tongues.

Third — They shall take up serpents.

Fourth — And if they drink any deadly thing, it shall not hurt them.

Fifth — They shall lay hands on the sick and they shall recover.[9]

The same Holy Spirit of God which flowed through Jesus Christ, the anointing that was upon Him and which flowed through His hands and into the sick, was an impartation of God so real that when the woman touched the hem of His garment she was conscious of the instant effect of the healing in her body through it. "She felt in her body that she was healed of that plague," while Jesus Himself was likewise conscious of an outflow. He said: "Somebody hath touched me, for I perceive that virtue is gone out of me."[10]

Divine healing is the particular phase of ministry in which the modern church does not measure up to the early church. This failure has been due to a lack of knowledge of the real nature and the real process of Christian healing. The above incident reveals the secret of what the power was, how the power operated, and by what law it was transmitted from the disciple to the one who needed the blessing. The power was the Holy Ghost of God, both in Jesus Christ after His baptism in the Holy Ghost, and in the disciples after the baptism of the Holy Ghost came upon them on the Day of Pentecost. It flowed through the hands of Jesus to the sick. It permeated the garments He wore. When the woman touched even the hem of His garment there was sufficient of the power of God there for her need.

The disciples healed the sick by the same method. Indeed the apostle Paul, realizing this law, permitted the people to bring to him handkerchiefs and aprons that they might touch his body, and when they were carried to the sick, the sick were healed through the power of God in the handkerchiefs, and the demons that inhabited their persons went out of them.

---

[9] Mark 16:17-18.

[10] See Luke 8:43-48.

Herein is shown the secret of the early church, that which explains the whole miracle-working power of the apostles and the early church for four hundred years. The same is evident in branches of the modern church. Herein is revealed the secret that has been lost. That secret is the conscious, tangible, living, incoming, abiding, outflowing Spirit of God through the disciple of Christ who has entered into blood-washed relationship and baptism in the Holy Ghost.

This is the secret that the modern church from the days of Reformation onward has failed to reveal. We have, however, retained a form of godliness, "but have denied the power thereof."[11]

When Jesus laid His hands on people the Holy Ghost was imparted to them in healing virtue. When the disciples and early Christians likewise laid their hands on the sick, the Holy Ghost was imparted through them to the needy one. Likewise, the Holy Ghost was imparted to preachers "for the work of the ministry,"[12] including healing. Primitive church history abounds in examples of healing in the same manner. Paul specifically enjoins Timothy to "forget not the gift (power) that is in thee, that came through the laying on of my hands."[13] It was an impartation of the Holy Ghost to Timothy for the work of the Christian ministry.

In the whole range of church history we have retained the form, but have lost its power in a great degree. The pope lays his hands on the head of the cardinals, the cardinal lays his hands on the head of the bishops, the bishop lays his hands on the head of the priest, the priest lays his hands on the head of the communicants when he receives them as members of the church.

In the Protestant church — in all her branches — the laying on of hands in ordination for the ministry is practiced. But in the early church it was not the laying on of hands alone, but through the laying on of hands the impartation of the definite living Spirit of the living God to the individual took place. Through its power in him he was constituted a real priest, a real elder, a real preacher with grace, healing power, and faith anointed of God from on High.

---

[11] See 2 Timothy 3:5.

[12] Ephesians 4:11-12.

[13] 2 Timothy 1:6, paraphrased.

God gave the blood of Jesus to the Christian Church. God gave the power of healing to the Christian Church in the Holy Ghost, and as long as they lived under the anointing of the Holy Ghost and exercised the faith of Jesus in their hearts, the healing power of God manifested and is still manifest where this condition exists. *Christian Science exists because of the failure of the Christian Church to truly present Jesus Christ and His power through the Spirit and minister it to the world.*

Robert G. Ingersoll assailed the Holy Scriptures, laughed at the Christian God, destroyed the faith of men, wrecked their hopes, and left them stranded and abandoned amid the wreckage. Through this means he brought the just condemnation of the world upon himself. The world condemns him to this hour in that he destroyed the faith of men without supplying to their souls something to take its place, as he should have done, and as any man who is honorable and true must do.

You recommended divine healing in one breath and denied its potency in the next. You have attacked Christian Science, the followers of Dowie, and others and arraigned them at the bar and condemned them, without giving to men a tangible way by which the healing of God might be brought to them. Why do you not study and practice Jesus Christ's own way of healing and so make your ministry constructive? What are you going to do with the multitude of dying that the doctors cannot help? Leave them to die? The doctors have got through with them. And in many instances, even though they are still prescribing for them, they are perfectly aware of their inability to heal the sick ones and are candid and willing to say so. Dr. Bulgin, what have you got for these? What have you given to these?

If a man were walking down the street with a very poor set of crutches and a ruffian came along and kicked the crutches from under him and let him fall, every honest soul would rise in condemnation of the ruffian's act and demand reparation.

You come to the dying, kick their hope from under them, and let them fall to the ground and leave them there to die without bringing them the true healing power in the blood and spirit of Jesus. It is not sufficient to say "I believe in divine healing." If they are sick they must be healed.

This must not be construed as a defense of Christian Science. It is not given with that thought, nor in that spirit. It is given rather in the hope that as an influential man in the Christian Church, you may see the weakness of your position and of the position of the Church and by the grace of God call the Church back again to faith in Jesus Christ, the Son of God, for healing for every man from every disease, as Jesus Christ intended it should be and as the Scriptures definitely, positively teach, and make proper scriptural provision for a definite healing ministry.

In the hope of supplying this need of the Church, the Protestant ministers of the city of Los Angeles have agreed in formal resolution to begin the teaching and study and practice of healing. How has this come to pass, and why? They have been whipped into it by the success of Christian Science.

A recent issue of a New York daily paper announces that the pastors of New York have likewise undertaken to teach the people the power of God to heal.

The Protestant Episcopal Church is endeavoring through the ministry of a layman of the Church of England from the old country, a Mr. Hickson, to educate their people in the truth of healing through the atonement of Jesus Christ, the Son of God, by the laying on of hands and the prayer of faith. In a few days the gentleman will appear at All Saints Cathedral, Spokane, for that purpose, and the sick will be invited to be ministered to in the name of the Son of God and healed through His blood purchase.

The Church of England in England and also in Africa, for ten years has been endeavoring to organize societies, not to teach their people Christian Science, psychic therapeutics, or mental healing — all of which belong to the realm of the natural — but to teach and demonstrate the pure power of God from Heaven by the Holy Ghost, purchased by the blood of Jesus Christ, to heal diseases.

Frank N. Riale, a secretary of the Presbyterian Board of Education of New York, with sixty-three universities and colleges under his control and supervision, is the author of a remarkable book, *The Sinless, Sickless,*

Deathless Life, in which he recounts in a chapter entitled, "How the Light and the Fire Fell," the marvelous story of his own conversion. He was a minister of the Gospel and a graduate of Harvard. He found his Lord at the hands of an Indian in Dakota. He tells of the light of God that came to his soul in sanctifying power through the ministry of a Salvation Army officer, Colonel Brengle. He related his marvelous healing, when a diseased and dying wreck, through the reading of a religious tract on healing and his experience in seeing many healed of all manner of diseases by the power of God. You are a Presbyterian, my Brother. You need not go out of your own Church for the truth of God concerning healing.

The question before the Church, now that the break toward healing has come, and it has come, is who is prepared to teach and demonstrate the truth of God concerning healing? Will it be a fact that in the absence of knowledge of God by the ministry of the Church for healing, will the Church in her blindness and ignorance and helplessness be overwhelmed by Christian Science, New Thought, and the thousand-and-one cults which teach psychological healing?

Where is the prophet of God who should come forward to teach and demonstrate the pure spiritual value and power of the Holy Ghost secured for men because Jesus Christ, the Son of God, gave His blood to get it for them? Is it not time that such men as yourself arise in the dignity of Christ, and throw off the shackles of formal religion and by the grace of God enter into the real life of living power through the Son of God in the Holy Ghost and rescue the Church out of her present degradation, reestablishing forever divine healing on its true and scriptural basis — the atonement of Jesus Christ?

Twenty-five years ago, the light concerning healing came to my soul after four brothers and four sisters had died of diseases, when four other members of the family were in a dying state, abandoned by the physicians as hopeless, and after my father had spent a fortune trying to obtain human help. One man of God who had the truth of God in his heart came to the rescue. All four sick ones were healed. I was an ardent Methodist. I loved my church. My parents were members of an old Scotch Presbyterian Kirk. The Presbyterian church had no light on the subject of healing; the Methodist church had no light on the

James Lake Family 1897
Eight of the original sixteen brothers and
sisters died of disease.

subject of healing. I received my light through a man who had been a minister of the Congregational church. He knew God. He knew Christ the Lord. He knew the power of God to save and the power of God to heal.

When I accepted this blessed truth and saw my family healed out of death, what was the attitude of the Church? Just what the attitude of all the leading churches has been. When I declared this truth before our conferences, she undertook to ostracize me; and from that day to this, many of her ministry who have prayed through to God and secured the blessing and power of God upon their soul to heal the sick, have been forced out of her ministry.

Dr. Bulgin, is it not time to quit attacking forms of faith, whether good or bad, and turn your attention and the attention of the Church to the only thing that will deliver her out of her present wretchedness and inability to bless and to bring her back again to Christ — to the foot of the cross, to the blood of Jesus, to the Holy Ghost from on high, to the power of God and the real faith, including healing "once delivered to the saints." Through this healing ministry the church at Spokane reports 100,000 healings by the power of God through five years of continuous daily efforts and the kindred blessed fact that the majority of those healed were saved from sin also.

The dying world is stretching out her hand for help. The Church, on account of her laxness in this matter, opens the doors for the existence of Christian Science and all the thousand-and-one worn-out philosophies that follow in her train. Let the manhood of the Church arise, take the place of the prophet of God, call her back to the ministry of real salvation — a blessed salvation, not alone for men after they are dead or that will give them bliss in heaven when they die, but to a salvation that gives eternal life in Christ, health for the mind, and health for the body and supplies likewise the power of God for the immediate need, for the need of the sick, for the need of the sinful, the wretched, and the dying and the sin-cursed and disease-smitten.

Let the Church return in the glory of God and the power of Christ to the original faith as clearly demonstrated in the New Testament, as perpetuated forever in the Church through the nine gifts of the Holy Spirit. Demonstrating beyond controversy that as long as the Holy

Spirit is in the Church so are the gifts of the Holy Spirit not only present, but exercisable through faith. (See 1 Corinthians, chapter 12.)

For to one is given by the Spirit —

First — The word of wisdom.

Second — The word of knowledge.

Third — Faith by the same spirit.

Fourth — The gifts of healing.

Fifth — The working of miracles.

Sixth — To another prophecy.

Seventh — To another discerning of spirits.

Eighth — To another divers kinds of tongues.

Ninth — To another the interpretation of tongues.[14]

The unchanging order of government, spiritual enduement, and ministry of the gifts of the Spirit are further declared as follows: "And God hath set some in the church, first *apostles,* secondarily *prophets,* thirdly *teachers,* after that *miracles,* then *gifts of healings, helps, governments, diversities of tongues.*"[15]

When the Church exercises these gifts then she may condemn Christian Science, Dowieism, or New Thought. Then she may condemn every other philosophical cult. Then she may condemn Unitarianism and everything else that you preach against. Though she will not need to. Jesus never did. There were just as many strange philosophies in His day as in ours. The constructive righteousness of Christ, the presence of the living Son of God to save and heal, the revelation to the world of His divine power will stop the mouths of every ism and manifest one glorious, triumphant, all-embracing power of God through Jesus Christ, His Son, and its everlasting superiority. Neither will you be compelled as you are to glorify doctors, medicines, surgery, etc., when the greatest physicians on earth have deplored their inability to deliver the world from its curse of sickness. Then you can not only teach the theory of the atonement of our Lord and Savior Jesus Christ, but demonstrate its reality and power to save both soul and body.

---

[14] See 1 Corinthians 12:8-10.

[15] 1 Corinthians 12:28, emphasis Lake's.

All the abstract criticism in the world is powerless to stop the drift from the churches to Christian Science so long as Christian Science heals the sick and the Church does not. Men demand to be shown. When the authority of Jesus to forgive sins was challenged, He met the challenge with the healing of the palsied man, not with negations and criticisms. He said: "Whether is it easier, to say, Thy sins be forgiven thee; or to say, Rise up and walk? But that ye may know.... I say arise and walk."[16] He was too big for abstract criticism. So must the Christian and the Church become.

> "Lake's Book, *Lake's Reply to Bulgin,* is the clearest statement on the truth of divine healing ever written, a remarkable document."

> Dr. Frank N. Riale, Field Secretary,

> Presbyterian Board of Education.

This letter to Dr. Bulgin was printed in the leading daily newspaper in Spokane, Washington, 1920.

---

[16] Luke 5:23-24, paraphrased.

EVOLUTION OF CHRISTIAN CONSCIOUSNESS

Chicago, Illinois

July 15, 1920

Chicago Convention of Pentecostal Assemblies

7th Regiment Armory

I want to talk to you tonight about my Lord. I want you to get acquainted with Him. Some know Him in one way or another. None of us have reached the place where we have it all, but bless God, we are on the way. When I was a boy, I thought the sole aim and object of the Gospel was to keep from going to hell. A good many other folks observe Christianity from that point of view yet. After awhile, evangelists changed the idea somewhat. They began to teach that the object of being a Christian was not to keep from going to hell, but to go to heaven. Then I began reasoning. I said, "One is just as selfish as the other." The one gets saved to keep from going to hell and the other one gets saved to get to heaven. Both are wholly selfish and neither one is the real purpose of Jesus.

Jesus gave one final reason for men being Christians, and strangely very few people have ever discovered, even from the Word of God, what that real purpose is.

But one day Jesus came along by the River Jordan when John was baptizing and asked for the privilege of being baptized. John was startled. He said, "I have need to be baptized of thee, and comest thou to me?" Jesus said, "Suffer it to be so," and then He gave the real reason. In the *King James Version* it says, "For thus it becometh us to fulfill all righteousness,"[1] but in one of the liberal translations it reads: "Unto *all righteousness*."[2]

---

[1] Matthew 3:14-15.

[2] Editor's note: We could not find the translation in which Matthew 3:15 contained that exact wording.

Jesus was going to be baptized as His commitment of His body and His soul and His spirit to God forever, in order that from thenceforth He might *manifest the righteousness of God.*

To manifest the righteousness of God is the real reason for a man's desiring to be a Christian — not to go to heaven when he dies or to keep out of hell, but to *reveal the righteousness of God in this world.* And then heaven and all our rewards will be the natural result of having lived in unity with God and having revealed His righteousness in this world.

God has a wonderful purpose. God's Christian is the most magnificent specimen in all the universe of God. God's ideal for a Christian surpasses everything else in the whole world. Varied churches and varied religious institutions have their peculiar idea of what a Christian is. One of their ideals seems to be that the individual must be able to whoop and hop around and all that sort of thing. But Jesus never did it. He was too big for that. He had outgrown it. We have our ideas of religious meetings. Not one of them is like the meetings Jesus conducted, at least only in a slight way. Then we have our ideas of what constitutes a real message. My! If you will read the Word of Jesus over again, you will discover that few of our messages are like the message of the Lord. His messages were an uncovering of the soul of man, an uncovering of the nature of God so men could discern Him, and when they discerned Him they loved Him. The message of Jesus was constructive, not destructive; positive righteousness, not negative obedience.

Jesus gave a new name to God that nobody had ever given Him before. The prophets were intimate with God, and the Old Testament is one marvelous revelation of intimacy with God. They knew Him as a great Governor, as a great Controller, as the One who guided the affairs of the universe, but Jesus knew Him as "our Father." He introduced into Bible vocabulary a new name to express God to us.

I am going to talk to you along a line that perhaps may seem new. First, I want to place before you God's ideal of a Christian. Then, by His grace, I am going to undertake unfolding, step by step, how men arrive at that stature of Christ.

God's ideal of a Christian is not a man who is ready to go to heaven, nor a man who lives a good life in this world, nor a man who has victory over sin, nor victory over disease. It includes all these things, but it is ten thousand times more than that.

> And he gave some, apostles; and some, prophets; and some, evangelists; and some, pastors and teachers; for the perfecting of the saints, for the work of the ministry, for the edifying of the body of Christ: *till we all come in the unity of the faith,* and of the *knowledge of the Son of God,* unto *a perfect man,* unto *the measure of the stature* of the *fulness of Christ.*
>
> — Ephesians 4:11-13

And that is the *ideal* of my heart and that somehow in God's divine grace, by the wonderful processes of His Spirit, He is going to help me to grow up out of babyhood and infancy into the stature of Jesus Christ. And that is God's ideal for the Christian.

You say, "But brother, I was saved from my sins." Yes, Jesus was. "Don't you know, I was sanctified?" Why surely, Jesus was. Don't you know Jesus was baptized in the Holy Ghost, but He went so far beyond that it reveals these were but the beginnings by which a Son of God was born and came into being. His development was beyond all that and went beyond all our known Christian experiences.

I want to speak now of the growth of the knowledge of God that took place in Jesus Christ. This will sound strange to some of you. But you say, "Jesus Himself was God." Surely He was; He was likewise man. "He took not on him the nature of angels; but he took on him the seed of Abraham" (Hebrews 2:16). "[He] was in all points tempted like as we are, yet without sin."[3]

He came to our level. He demonstrated in the beginning that man could be an overcomer over the powers of darkness through reliance on God and His Word.

His demonstration began first in the order of nature, where He met no mind but His own. He changed the water into wine by the action

---

[3] Hebrews 4:15.

of His own will. He stilled the sea by the word of His command. He walked on the water. Each one of them an ascent over the other. Each one of them revealing that in the soul of Jesus Himself there was an ever-ascending scale in God.

Then the next thing in the life of Jesus was when He began His ministry of healing. When He undertook His ministry of healing, He had another *mind* to meet — the mind of the individual who needed the blessing. "And Jesus went about all Galilee, teaching in their synagogues, and preaching the gospel of the kingdom, and healing all manner of sickness and all manner of disease among the people" (Matthew 4:23).

Then Jesus entered a new realm. If you study the healings that took place under His ministry you will observe that first, it was the healing of disease; next, the healing of the blind; lastly, the healing of the lepers — a gradual, continuous assent. And lastly, the creation of eyes in the man born blind and now there developed in the soul of Jesus a holy dawning of the power of God, even over death, and in His demonstration over the power of death there are three degrees, like the other.[4]

The daughter of Jairus was dead for a *few minutes*. While the father was interceding, the servants came saying, "Thy daughter is dead." Jesus went instantly to her bedside and she arose to life.[5]

The son of the widow of Nain was dead for several hours, and they were carrying him out for burial, when Jesus touched the bier, and he arose.[6]

Lazarus was dead for four days, and the testimony of his sisters was, "By this time he stinketh."[7]

First instance, death in the first degree, dead a few minutes; next, in the second degree, dead a few hours; and in the third degree, dead four days, "by this time he stinketh."

---

[4]   See Matthew 4; 8; 9; and John 9.

[5]   See Matthew 9.

[6]   See Luke 7.

[7]   See John 11.

My, there is a wonderful revelation in connection with the raising of Lazarus that is not given in the story as it appears in the New Testament. I want to quote from the New Testament Apocrypha, from the book of Nicodemus. It will explain a whole lot to you.

Before I give this story I want to call your attention to one other thing, because it concludes the thought I had in mind. There are degrees in the experience of Jesus by which He took one step after another in every single realm until He eventually manifested God's divine perfection. There was the crucifixion, followed by the resurrection, and climaxed by the ascension. Each one of them a degree in the power of God beyond the other.

If Jesus had died on the cross and there had been no resurrection, there never would have been one single soul saved through the blood of Jesus Christ.

If Jesus had died on the cross, gone into the grave, and been resurrected from the grave only, there would still be no such thing as a real salvation in the world.

But because Jesus died on the cross, entered into death, arose from the grave, *and ascended* to the throne of God and finally received from the Father the gift of the Holy Ghost with authority to minister it to men, there is in existence a divine salvation, sufficient to satisfy the nature of every man.

THE STORY OF LAZARUS

In the story that I wanted to bring to you is this marvelous incident. Just prior to the crucifixion of Jesus, Satan appeared in the regions of death and said to Beelzebub, the keeper of the Regions of Death, that he might now prepare to receive Jesus Christ, because he (Satan) had brought to pass such a combination of circumstances that Jesus was to be crucified. Beelzebub replied, "But, Satan, is not this Jesus of Nazareth, who in His divine nature was so strong that He came here and took from our midst Lazarus when he was here, and we could not hold him?"

Satan said, "Yes, He is the one."

Beelzebub said, "But if in His divine nature He was so strong He came and took Lazarus from our hands, and we could not hold him, how can we hold Him Himself?" That was the problem.[8]

Now I am going back. What is the real secret of the resurrection? That Jesus arose from the dead? No! Lots of men had risen from the dead. A way back in the Old Testament they opened a grave to bury a man, and when he touched the bones of Elisha there was enough of the Spirit of God in the old dry bones to give him life, and he arose. But he brought no revelation of God and manifested no particular power of God in the world.

The son of the widow of Nain was truly dead and was raised to life, but he brought no revelation from the dead. Lazarus was dead four days and restored again, but so far as the record goes, Lazarus knew no more after his resurrection than he did before.

At the crucifixion of Jesus Himself many that were dead arose and appeared in the city.[9]

It was not in the mere fact then, that they arose from the dead or that Jesus arose from the dead that gives the secret of the resurrection. I want you to see what it is.

All the way along in the life of Jesus there is a growth in consciousness of God. Step by step Jesus Christ discerned God and His purpose for man and God's purpose for Himself. Step by step Jesus entered into the truth of His vision. Step by step Jesus revealed the power of God in the new light that had dawned upon His soul until finally, after He had manifested His power in these three degrees of death, ending in the resurrection of Lazarus. After he had been dead four days, He began to talk to His disciples about a new problem and a new possibility. He began to open the fact that He Himself was likely to be crucified. In fact, that it was in the prophecies that He should be and in the determined councils of the godhead.

---

[8] The Gospel of Nicodemus Part 2, Chapter 4, from the Apocrypha. The Apocrypha is a collection of writings considered by most Bible scholars to be uninspired and of doubtful authority. Written between 1200 B.C. and 150 A.D., they provide colorful stories and some historical background.

[9] See Matthew 27:52-53.

I want you to distinguish between Christianity and philosophy, for in these days the world is filled with philosophical religions, and everything psychological is used to impress the world that it is religious. And Christians ought to know what it is that makes the distinction between Christianity and philosophy and what makes Jesus distinct from the philosophers, and why it is that Christianity has a power that philosophy has not.

Some of the philosophies were old and gray whiskered and ready to die when Jesus was born. Bavgadghetti was written eight hundred years before Isaiah. Buddha lived hundreds of years before Jesus and taught most of the things Jesus taught. Confucianism was old, Brahmanism was old, most of the ancient philosophies were old when Jesus came to the world. The philosophers wrote their tenets, left them, came to the grave and died, and their revelation ceased. There was nothing remaining but the tenets they had written.

Buddha wrote his tenets, came to the grave; Confucius wrote his tenets, came to the grave; Brahman wrote his tenets, came to the grave; the Zendavestas were written and their authors came to the grave. They all died, and there was no further revelation. The grave ended all.

Not so with the Son of God. Not so the Lord Jesus. Why, Christianity *began* where philosophy left off. The crucifixion of Jesus was but the entrance into the greatest of His divine revelations. Jesus not only rose from the dead, but He determined in His own soul to take captive that power that had been captivating men and subjecting them to death's control. So Jesus entered into the grave. The early church was much more conversant with this phase of the Lord's victory than we are.

The literature of the early church fathers is full of the wonder of what took place in the life and ministry of Jesus after He was in the grave. Peter gives us just two little flashes. He says, "He went and preached unto the spirits in prison; which sometime were disobedient, when once the long-suffering of God waited in the days of Noah, while the ark was a preparing" (1 Peter 3:19-20). Next, He went and preached also unto them that are dead. What for? "That they might be judged according to men in the flesh."[10]

---

[10] 1 Peter 4:6.

He carried His word of testimony and power to the very dead, those that were dead before the flood and those who died between the flood and Himself. There are two classes — the spirits that were in prison from the days of Noah, and He went also and preached to them that are dead that they might be judged according to men in the flesh. Remember that Jesus preached to the dead. The dead of His day had the prophets to listen to and receive and believe their teachings or reject them, just as you and I have. The purpose of His teaching was that they might be judged as men in the flesh.

Next, in the soul of Jesus there grew that wonderful consciousness that having liberated them from death's power there was a step further yet to go. He must take captive the power that was binding their souls. So He entered into death, and His ministry and victory in the regions of death was the result. And one day He came forth from the dead, a living man once more, as He was before He died. (From audience: "Amen! Hallelujah!") (Wonderful demonstration of the Spirit.)

Over and over again, John tells us that He did this and He performed that work and He wrought that marvel and that in order that we might believe, in order that He might reveal to the satisfaction of the souls of those who were trying to believe that there was a foundation and a reason and a substantial ground on which your confidence in Christ could rest.

So He came forth from the dead with the consciousness of God and His power and His ability to command God's power and utilize it, that no other in all the earth or sea or heaven ever had. No philosopher ever had it, or had ever known anything of it. But when *Jesus* came forth from the dead, He came forth speaking a word that had never been spoken in the world before. He said, "All power is given unto me in heaven and in earth."[11] Blessed be the name of God! He had proved it. Faith had become fact; vision was now consciousness.

All the triumph of Jesus in the regions of death had wrought in His soul the wonder of God. No other life ever had it. No other soul ever got the flame of it. No other nature ever felt the burning of it. Bless God.

---

[11] Matthew 28:18.

And He was so anxious to lift His followers into it that, the very first thing He did after His reappearance among them was to *breathe* on them. He said, "Let Me give it to you. Let Me breathe it into your life. Receive ye the Holy Ghost."[12] Let me put it into your hearts, burn it into your soul, establish it into your nature. His victory over death had wrought the marvel.

But beloved, that is not *Christianity.* Christianity is *more than that.* That is not the consciousness of Christianity. The consciousness of Christianity is greater than that. It was holier than that, more powerful than resurrection consciousness. When Jesus came forth from the dead He was able to declare, "All power is given unto me in heaven and in earth. Go *ye* therefore."[13]

Oh, then there were some wonderful days. Forty wonderful days in which Jesus took the disciples, who had been in His own school for three and a half years, through a new course. In these days we would call it postgraduate course. So they went out into the mountains of Galilee, all by themselves, for a postgraduate course with the risen Lord. And He taught them of the all-power of God, and He taught them of power over death and the divine fact that the dominion of the risen Christ is for every soul.

David, describing it, said, "Thou hast led captivity captive." Not only that, but beyond it. "Thou hast received gifts for men."[14]

So one day there came the ascension. He took them out on the Mount of Olivet and as He blessed them, He rose out of their sight to glory. Then there is one of those wonderful divine flashes in the Word of God that just illuminates a whole life.

Peter was preaching on the Day of Pentecost. The power of God had fallen upon the people. The people demanded an explanation. "What is it? What does it mean?" Peter replied: "This is that which was spoken by the prophet Joel."[15] Then he goes on and teaches them concerning Christ, takes them from His crucifixion through His resurrection, His ascension, up to the throne of God. And when He gets

---

[12] John 20:22, paraphrased.

[13] Matthew 28:18-19.

[14] Psalm 68:18.

[15] Acts 2:16.

the people at the throne of God and their minds fixed there, He gave them the final explanation. Jesus, having arrived at the throne of God, an interview between God the Father and Jesus Christ takes place. And God gave to Jesus the gift of the Holy Ghost, and the explanation was "He hath shed forth this, which ye now see and hear."[16]

Say, beloved, the Holy Ghost is born out of the heart of the Father God Himself, ministered through the soul of Jesus Christ, the High Priest of God, into your heart and mine. It is intended to lift our hearts and lift our lives out of Chicago mud, and keep us there forever.

So the real *Christian* ought to be the kingliest man in the whole earth, the princeliest man in the whole earth — as kingly and princely and lovely and holy as the Son of God — as big as Jesus, with the power of Jesus, and the love of Jesus. Bless God.

---

[16] Acts 2:33.

CHRISTIAN CONSCIOUSNESS
Chicago, Illinois
July 16, 1920

*T*here is a wonderful single word that expresses what God is trying to develop in us. That word is *consciousness*. I love it. It is an amazing word. Consciousness means, "that which the soul knows" — not that which you believe or that which you have an existent faith for or that which you hope, but that which the soul has proven, which the soul *knows,* upon which the soul rests — the thing, bless God, which has become concrete in your life.

Consequently God's purpose, and the purpose of real religion, is to create in the nature of man a consciousness of God. And that church which will succeed in creating the highest degree of consciousness of God in the soul of man will live longest in the world. And the only mode of possibility of perpetuating a church in the world forever is to bring into the souls of the people the full measure of the consciousness of God that Jesus Christ enjoys.

It is a good thing not only to be good, but to know *why* you are good. It is not only a good thing to be an American, but to know *why* you are an American. It is a good thing not only to be a Christian, but to know *why* you are a Christian, and to know why Christian consciousness is superior to every other known consciousness.

And I want to declare that Christianity stands superior to every other form of religion under the heavens and in the whole earth, that no other religion under the heavens has the same consciousness of God or the same means of producing a consciousness of God that Christianity possesses.

In 1893 in this city was the great Chicago World's Fair. Among the features of the fair was a Congress on Religions. All the religions of the world were invited to send their representatives and present their peculiar religion for the good of all. Many regarded it as a great calamity that the varied forms of eastern philosophy should thus be introduced into this country. I never felt that way. I have always felt that if Christianity could not demonstrate her superiority over every other religion, then Christianity has not the place and power that Jesus Christ said Christianity had in the world.

But the result of that Congress of Religions was that Christianity was so poorly presented that the Indian philosophers ran away with the whole thing, and in the minds of thousands who listened, it left a belief that their knowledge of God and God's laws and the laws of life were greater than the Christian possessed.

And fellow Christians, there began in my soul a prayer that Almighty God would reveal in my soul what the real secret of real Christianity is, in order that in this world Christians might become kings and priests and demonstrate the superiority of the religion of the Son of God beyond that of every other in the whole earth.

In later years I went to South Africa. It was at a time of peculiar interest in South African history, just following the Boer War. The great industry there is mining. One-fourth of the gold of the world comes from Johannesburg and vicinity. The diamonds of the world come from South Africa, and the United States is the greatest diamond market of the world.

When the Boer War came on, the native people became so frightened over war between white men that after the war was over and settled they could not coax them back to open the mines. The result was that in order to get the industries established again, they had to send to China and get 200,000 Chinese and put them to work to open the shops and mines and all the other industries. These Chinese came in real colonies. Some were Confucians, some were Buddhists, some were Brahmans, some represented this form, and some that form of philosophy. They brought their priests, and their priests ministered unto them.

At the same time, there were in South Africa one and a half million East Indians. These represented all the cults of India. They made complaint that they were not being properly cared for, and the British government sent to India and imported a great company of Buddhist priests and Brahman priests and Yogi priests and all the rest of them, and they came to South Africa to assist their own people.

I had a Jewish friend, Rabbi Hertz, who became famous as a great Rabbi because of his influence for the British during the war. There was also a Roman Catholic priest, Father Bryant, a wonderful man. I listened to Dr. Hertz give a series of lectures on the psalms of David, which I regard as the finest of that character I had ever heard.

One day he said, "Did it ever occur to you what an amazing Congress of Religions we have in this country? It would put the one in Chicago in 1893 in the shade."

I said, "I have thought of it, but do not have sufficient acquaintance among these other men to undertake it, but would gladly give a helping hand." So it was eventually brought to pass.

We gathered once a week. They sat on the floor all night, eastern fashion, a priest with his interpreter, and we gave the individual a whole night if he wanted it or two nights if he wanted it or as long as he wanted to tell out the very secret of his soul, to show the very best he could the very depth of his peculiar religion, and the consciousness of God it produced. It was not the details of his religion we sought, but the soul of it and the consciousness it possessed.

We listened to the Indian Buddhist priest one night and the Chinese Buddhist priest the next night; the Indian Confucian priest one night and the Chinese Confucian priest the next night; the Indian Brahman priest one night and a Chinese Brahman priest the next night; and it went on. Eventually it came to the night that Dr. Hertz, the Jewish Rabbi, was to give the secret of the Jewish religion and tell out the whole of God that the Jewish religion revealed and the consciousness of God that was produced by the Mosaic and the prophetic teachings.

Did you ever stop to think that, in all religious history, the Jewish prophets knew more of God than all the philosophers of earth combined? They superseded all others of the ancients in knowledge of God, His ways and power. They gave to their day and generation such a revelation of God as the world had never known. Stop and think of the wonders of God that the Old Testament revealed. Think of the marvels that it seems would stagger the very soul of modern Christianity.

When the Israelites were traveling over the deserts, God arrested the processes of decay in their very shoes and clothing, and they wore them continually for forty years. Think of the marvel of it, the arrest of the process of decay! And then someone wonders if it is possible to arrest the process of decay in a man's life. Yes, it is, bless God! Jesus Christ arrested the process of death by the power of God, through the introduction of the life and the Spirit of life in Jesus Christ, giving man eternal life.

Think again of the old prophet, who when they had lost the ax in the water and came to him in their distress, takes a stick and holds it in his hands — what for? — until that stick became magnetized by the Spirit and power of God. And when he threw it in the water, the ax arose and came to the stick.[1] Think again of the prophet, when he was called to the dying boy. He said to his servant, "Take this staff," the staff that he carried, "go ahead of me, lay it on the child." What for? Because he carried that staff next to his God-anointed hands until the staff itself became impregnated with the life and power of God. So the servant went ahead, and there was enough of God in that staff to keep the life there and the Spirit there, until he arrived and called the child to life by the power of God.[2]

Later they were burying a man, and in their haste they opened the grave of Elisha, and when the dead man touched his old, God-filled bones, he became alive.[3] There was enough of God in the old bones to quicken him into life again. Bless God.

You say, "Well, how can Christianity demonstrate anything further than that?" When I listened to Dr. Hertz, my heart asked: "Dear God, when I get my turn to reveal what Christianity is, what am I going to say that is going to reveal Christianity as superior to the Jewish dispensations and the consciousness of God that it produced in the souls of the prophet?"

From eight o'clock at night until four-thirty Dr. Hertz pours out his soul in a wondrous stream of God revelation such as my soul had never heard. In the morning, as I started for home, I prayed, "God, in the name of Jesus, when it comes next Thursday night and it is my turn to show forth Jesus Christ, what am I going to say to surmount the revelation of God that he gave?"

---

[1] See 2 Kings 6:5-7.

[2] See 2 Kings 4:18-37.

[3] See 2 Kings 13:21.

I searched Christian literature for it. I had searched the libraries of the world. I could not find it in the writings of the old Christian Fathers. I searched the Word of God for it. I saw flashes of it, but somehow it would not frame in my soul. I decided there was only one way. I gave myself to fasting and prayer and waiting on God. And one day in the quiet, God told me that secret.

And from that day my heart rested in the new vision of Jesus Christ and a new revelation of the real divinity of Christianity came to my heart.

So it came my turn, and I sat down and reviewed for hours with care, step by step, the consciousness that the philosophers and priests had shown as belonging to their respective religions and finally the wonderful consciousness that Dr. Hertz had shown as belonging to the Mosaic dispensation.

Oh, bless God, there is a secret in Jesus Christ. *Christianity is all supernatural,* every bit of it. The philosophies are natural. The Mosaic dispensation and its revelation was supernatural, but its revelation did not have the high degree of overcoming consciousness that belongs to Christianity. Yet you can go around the world, and you will not find one in a hundred thousand that can tell what the real secret of Christianity is which makes it superior to all other religions.

You say, "It is the Holy Ghost." Well, the prophets had the Holy Ghost. There is no more marvelous record given than the Old Testament records. When Moses wanted mechanics and workmen for the new tabernacle, the Lord called a man by name and said:

> I have filled him with the spirit of God, in wisdom, and in understanding, and in knowledge, and in all manner of workmanship, to devise cunning works, to work in gold, and in silver, and in brass, and in cutting of stones, to set them, and in carving of timber, to work all manner of workmanship.[4]

That is the way they learned their trade.

Later they were making preparations for the building of Solomon's temple. That temple is one of the Seven Wonders of the World. Did

---

[4] Exodus 31:3-5.

you ever stop to think of where the plans came from or how they got them? Old David tells us that God gave him the plans of the temple in writing; "while the spirit of God was upon me in writing,"[5] and he wrote the details of it. He put these details down with such accuracy that they prepared the temple in the mountains, and when they came to put it together, there was no sound of a hammer. Every piece fit to piece.

Wonderful movings of God! Wonderful presence of God! Talk about the glory of God. Why, when Moses came down from the mountain, his face shone or radiated with the glory of God so intensely, the people were afraid of him, and he was compelled to wear a veil until the anointing had somewhat left his soul.[6]

But beloved, Christianity is more than that. Paul declares that the glory of Moses' face was superseded. I said a moment ago: Christianity is not a natural religion. It has nothing natural in it. It is *supernatural* from the top to the bottom, from the center to the circumference, within and without. It comes right from heaven, every bit of it. It is the divine outflow of the holy soul of the crucified, risen, glorified Son of God.

Why does God come down from heaven into the hearts of men, into the natures of men, into the bodies of men, into the souls of men, into the spirits of men? God's purpose in man is to transform him into the nature of God. Jesus said, "I said, *Ye are gods*" (John 10:34) [emphasis Lake's].

The philosophers came to the grave and died. They had no further revelation to give. They had left their tenants, and they exist to this day. I have studied the great eastern philosophies. I have searched them from cover to cover. I have read them for years as diligently as I have read my Bible. I have read them to see what their consciousness was. The secret of salvation is *not* in them.

But in my Bible is seen that the Son of God saves men from their sins and changes them by His power in their nature so that they become *like Him*. And that is the purpose of Jesus, to take a man and make a

---

[5] 1 Chronicles 28:19, paraphrased.

[6] See Exodus 34:29-35.

Christ out of him. To take a sinner and wash him pure and white and clean, and then come into his life and anoint him with His Spirit, speak through him, live in him, change the substance of his spirit, change the substance of his body — until his body and his blood and his bones and flesh and his soul and his spirit are the body and blood and bones and soul and spirit of the Son of God. (Ephesians 5:30 and 1 Corinthians 6:17.)

Oh, Jesus was crucified. Jesus was crucified after there grew in the soul of Jesus the divine consciousness that He could go into the grave and through faith in God accept the Word of God and believe that He would raise Him from the dead. Jesus went into the grave with a divine boldness, not simply as a martyr. He was God's *Prince,* God's *King,* God's *Savior.* He went into the grave God's *Conqueror.* He was after something. He went after the power of death and He got it, and He took it captive, and He came forth from the grave proclaiming His victory over death.

No more bowing before the accursed power that had been generated through sin. It was a captive. No more fear of hell! Do you hear it? No more fear of hell after Jesus Christ came out of the grave. He had death and hell by the throat and the key in His hands. He was Conqueror!

When He came forth from the grave, He came forth bringing that wonderful Spirit of heavenly triumph that was begotten in the soul of Jesus because He had not failed. He had gone and done it. No longer a *have,* no longer a *faith,* now a *knowledge* — God's consciousness in His heart. It was done!

Oh yes, bless God, I am coming back to that word with which I started. Do you know the secret of religion is in its consciousness? The secret of Christianity is in the consciousness it produces in your soul. And Christianity produces a higher consciousness than any other religion in the world. No other religion in the world or other revelation of the true God equals it. It is the highest and holiest. It comes breathing and throbbing and burning right out of the heart of the glorified Son of God. It comes breathing and beating and burning and throbbing into your nature and mine, bless God.

So that is the reason I love the religion of the Lord and Savior Jesus Christ. That is the reason the cross of Calvary is a sacred place. That is the reason that the conquest of the Son of God in the regions of death makes a man's heart throb. That is the reason He gathered His disciples together, and as if He could not wait, He said, "Let me breathe it into you. Go forth in its power. All power is given unto Me, both in heaven and in earth. Go ye therefore. These signs shall follow. Cast out devils, speak with new tongues, heal the sick."[7] Amen.

In those early centuries of Christianity, Christianity did not go into the world apologizing. It went to slay the powers of darkness and undo the works of the devil, and it lived in holy triumph.

HEALING CONSCIOUSNESS

I am going into the history of the Old Testament. It is surprising how ignorant people are of the Word of God. God made a covenant of healing with the children of Israel after they crossed the Red Sea, and they lived under that covenant four hundred and fifty years, unbroken. And there never was an Israelite for four hundred and fifty years so far as the record goes, except Asa, who ever took one dose of medicine. One backslider went back on God and called the physicians like the heathen did, but the people trusted God and God alone for four hundred and fifty years or until Solomon got into polygamy. He went down into Egypt and married Egyptian wives, who brought their heathen physicians with them. And eventually the whole nation had fallen from grace and gone back again and were taking pills and medicine and dope, just like some Pentecostal heathen do.

Do you want to get on God's territory? Cut it out. It belongs to the devil and the heathen and the great big unbelieving world.

When you see those holy flashes of heavenly flame once in awhile in a person's life, as we observe in our Sister Etter when someone is healed, it is because her consciousness and Christ's are *one*. She is fused into God. I saw a dying, strangling woman healed in thirty seconds as Mrs. Etter cast out the demon. The flame of God, the fire of His Spirit, ten seconds of connection with the Almighty Christ at the throne of God — that is the secret of it.

---

[7] John 20:22, Matthew 28:18-19, Mark 16:17-18, all paraphrased.

Oh, I would like to get you in touch with the Son of God for five minutes. I would like to see the streams of God's lightning come down for ten minutes! I wonder what would take place.

A few months ago I was absent from the city of Spokane, and when I returned we discovered Mrs. Lake was not at home. It was just time to leave for my afternoon service. Just then someone came in and said, "Your secretary, Mrs. Graham, is in the throes of death, and your wife is with her." So I hurried down to the place. When I got there the wife of one of my ministers met me at the door and said, "You are too late; she has gone." And as I stepped in I met the minister coming out of the room. He said, "She has not breathed for a long time." But as I looked down at that woman and thought of how God Almighty, three years before, had raised her out of death after her womb and ovaries and tubes had been removed in operations, and God Almighty had given them back to her, after which she had married and conceived, my heart flamed. I took that woman up off that pillow and called on God for the lightnings of heaven to blast the power of death and deliver her, and I commanded her to come back and stay, and she came back, after not breathing for twenty-three minutes.

We have not yet learned to keep in touch with the powers of God. Once in awhile our soul rises, and we see the flame of God accomplish this wonder and that. But beloved, Jesus Christ lived in the presence of God every hour of the day and night. Never a word proceeded from the mouth of Jesus Christ but what was God's Word. "The words that I speak unto you, they are spirit, and they are life."[8]

When you and I are lost in the Son of God, and the fires of Jesus burn in our hearts like they did in Him, our words will be the words of life and of spirit, and there will be no death in them. But, beloved, we are on the way.

I have read church history because my heart was searching for the truth of God. I have witnessed with my own eyes the most amazing manifestation of psychological power. I knew an East Indian Yogi who volunteered to be buried for three days, and he came up out of the

---

[8] John 6:63.

grave well and whole. I saw them put a man in a cataleptic state and place a stone fifteen inches square on his body, put his feet on one chair and his head on another, and strike that stone with a twenty-five pound sledge seven times, until it broke in two.

I watched these things, and I said, "These are only on the psychological plane. Beyond that is the spirit plane and the amazing wonder of the Holy Spirit of God, and if God got hold of my spirit for ten minutes He could do something ten thousand times greater than that."

Why, Jesus was the triumphant One. Did you ever stop to think of Jesus at the throne of God? I like to think of the twentieth century Christ — not the Jesus that lived in the world two thousand years ago, not the humiliated Jesus, not Jesus dying on the cross for my sin, but the glorified, exalted Son of God at the throne of God who stands declaring, "I am he that liveth, and was dead; and, behold, I am alive for evermore, Amen; and have the keys of hell and of death."[9] Blessed be God.

And that is the Christ that breathes His power into your soul and mine, and that is the consciousness that is breathed from heaven in the Holy Ghost when it comes to your heart. Amen.

God purposed that the Christian Church should be the embodiment of the living, blessed Son of God — Christ living not in one temple, Jesus, but in multitudes of temples. The bodies of those yielded to God in holy consecration, God's real Church, not in name only but in power. Many members, one in spirit, one divine structure of divine faith and substance — man transformed, transfigured, and transmuted into the nature, the glory, and the substance of Christ.

"That Evil One Toucheth Him Not"

When the Spirit of God radiated from the man Jesus, how close do you suppose it was possible for the evil spirit to come to Him? I believe it was impossible for the evil one to come close to Him. The Spirit of God is as destructive of evil as it is creative of good. I am sure that Satan talked to Jesus from a safe distance.

---

[9] Revelation 1:18.

The real Christian is a *separated* man. He is separated forever unto God in *all* the departments of his life. So his *body* and his *soul* and his *spirit* are forever committed to the Father. From the time he commits himself to God, his body is as absolutely in the hands of God as his spirit or his soul. He can go to no other power for help or healing.

A hundredfold consecration takes the individual forever out of the hands of all but God.

here is one word in the Gospel that is the great inclusive word, comprehending all that God Almighty can accomplish in a human life. That word is *salvation*.

In our modern methods of subdividing the varied exercises and graces of the Spirit and Christian experiences, we are in the habit of speaking of salvation in a very limited sense. Very limited indeed in comparison to the broad sense in which the word is used in the Word of God.

SALVATION: GOD'S BIG WORD
Chicago Pentecostal Convention
July 16, 1920

I like to think of it as Jesus used it, the all-inclusive word. The one great big word of God that comprehends all that God can accomplish in a man's life forever, from the time He finds him as a sinner away from God, until the day that Jesus Christ presents him to the Father, "holy and unblameable and unreprovable"[1] in the sight of God, until that day when, with our Lord and Savior Jesus Christ, we shall be acknowledged at the throne of God as heirs and joint-heirs with Him and given our place and part in the government of God's great kingdom.

There is much in a man's life besides being "good" if he is to fulfill the large place in the world. God's first purpose is to make man good by removing the consciousness of sin from his soul, in order that he may grow up into God and fulfill the great purpose that God has in store for him, becoming a son of God in mind, nature, power, and capacity to bless.

Christianity is different from every other religion in the world. Every other religion in the world, excepting Christianity, has no need of a body or resurrection. Their existence after death is purely in the spirit, a spirit existence, but not so with Christianity. Christianity has necessity

---

[1] Colossians 1:22.

for a resurrection. The reason for the resurrection is that the kingdom of Christ is not to be in heaven entirely. It is to be in this world. And the Lord and Savior Jesus Christ is to rule in *this world*. Consequently, while we live in this world we will need a body like our Lord's, capable of existence here and capable of existence over there.

The Word of God speaks of "the days of heaven upon the earth,"[2] when the conditions now prevalent exclusively in heaven are transferred to earth, and earth and heaven become one. These are "the days of heaven upon the earth." That is the kingdom of our Lord and Savior Jesus Christ.

And I imagine that perhaps there will be railroads in the kingdom and cities in the kingdom, and there will be government in the kingdom. There will be a necessity for men grown up in God to take places of responsibility in the kingdom. If Jesus was to come into this audience tonight and ask for one hundred men who were capable of taking the affairs of Chicago in their hands tomorrow, perhaps not very many would qualify. Perhaps our capacity would be somewhat limited. Would He find us without capacity to successfully operate its affairs? Perhaps we would disappoint our Lord, and we would be very sad indeed.

The purpose of Jesus is not only to save man from their sins, but by the grace of God to begin in the souls of men that marvelous development in the nature and mind and understanding of God our Father, until by the grace of God we are able to take our place and our part in the kingdom of Jesus Christ and bear our share of responsibility.

I lived in South Africa as a missionary for some years and among the craving passions of my soul that developed was a longing, awful longing, to get in contact with men of my own race and type of mind, men who understood the things that were moving my soul and had the proper comprehension of the things I talked about, who could also feed my heart with love and knowledge.

When I returned to America I visited Brother Fockler in Milwaukee, and we talked nearly all night for a week. I just wanted to talk and listen. He could talk about the things my heart was longing to hear.

---

[2] Deuteronomy 11:21.

Then I came to Chicago, and poor Brother Sinclair was nearly worn out, for I was so hungry for fellowship. There was such a passion in my heart to hear his words and assimilate his thoughts and speak out understandingly, such a longing in my soul to hear of the blessing of God and see their point of view. So for almost a year, we traveled from city to city as God led, contacting this soul and that soul until that longing hunger was satisfied, and I felt I could settle down in my own work again.

But you say: "There were lots of people in Africa that were good." Surely, we had many thousand saved native people, and a multitude of them baptized in the Holy Ghost — a wonderful people. But notwithstanding their goodness, they had not been educated in the lines of thought that interested me. They could talk about God, but there were wonderful interests in the world of which they knew nothing, and my heart longed to be able to speak of these things. They were spiritual babies; they were intellectual babies. My heart was longing for companionship on my own plane of life.

Beloved, if God had to exist forever and forever without companionship, the passion in the soul of God would remain unsatisfied. Man came into being because of a necessity in the soul of God. Children are born because of a necessity in the soul of the parents. It is the cry of the real father and the real mother. It is planted there from the heart of God Himself in the souls of man. Every true man and every true woman wants to be a father and a mother and press their own to their bosom and see their own develop to manhood and womanhood and see themselves reproduced and perpetuated in the world.

God is perpetuating Himself in the soul of the Christian. God's heart is being satisfied in you and in me, because by the grace of God He expects us to grow up and out of our little environment and become sons of God and be able to have companionship with our Father. And He will be able to tell us His purpose, He will be able to open His wonderful schemes, and we will be able to take a part and place in the great enterprises of God forever.

Rudyard Kipling, in one of his war ballads, wrote these beautiful lines in trying to reveal this truth:

And oft there cometh the wise Lord God.

Master of every trade,

And He tells them tales of His daily toils,

And of Edens newly made,

And they rise to their feet as He passes by

Gentlemen, unafraid.

The purpose of the Lord and Savior was not only to redeem us out of filth and sin, but that we should grow up into manhood and woman-hood in God and take a place in the world and accomplish the thing that God intended us to accomplish and fellowship with Him on His plane of understanding.

You are just as necessary to God in His plan for the salvation of mankind as God is necessary to you. That is a tremendous statement. I want to repeat it. Christians are just as necessary to Almighty God in order to accomplish His purpose in the world as God is necessary to the Christian. Without God we would not be saved. Without God we could not live. Without God we would never reach a maturity in God. Without man, God would have no medium through which He could express Himself to the world, by which He could minister the Spirit of the living God to the world.

That was the reason God had to send His own Son, Jesus Christ, there being no other competent to take the place of the Son of God. God wondered that there was no man. He "marveled that there was no intercessors so His own right arm brought salvation and His strength upheld Him."[3]

Jesus was the first *body*. He was the human body through which God revealed Himself to the world. After He passed on to glory, He undertook to bring into being again a new body — not a lesser body nor a weaker body, but a body greater than the body of Jesus, a power greater than the power of Jesus. That is the meaning of the words of Jesus: "Greater works than these shall he do; because I go unto my Father."[4]

---

[3] Isaiah 59:16, paraphrased.

[4] John 14:12.

Unless Jesus Christ was the possessor of a divine secret, a secret that others did not understand, such words as these would be words of madness. But because Jesus understood the secret of returning to the Father, understood the secret of the Father's promise, understood what the possession of the Father's promise would mean to Him and to the world, He was able to say those marvelous words: "Greater works than these shall he do; because I go unto my Father."

Men have treated the precious Spirit of God as though it was a method of providing a means of spiritual entertainment for your own soul. Oh, no! God's purpose is far mightier than that. God's purpose is that your spirit be tuned to heaven, your heart capable of hearing and realizing the songs of glory, appreciating companionship of God and feeling flames of His divine love, expressing and revealing it to the hungry world that knows not God.

INTERPRETATION OF TONGUES

> *Out of the treasury of the heart of God there comes to thee*
> *that measure of His presence, that sweetness of His love, that*
> *power of His divinity that exalts thy nature in God and*
> *reveals Jesus Christ in thee. That brings forth the likeness of*
> *Christ in thee so fully that Jesus Christ Himself and man*
> *redeemed by His power stand together, brethren, heirs, and*
> *joint heirs of the wealth of God's nature.*

here are as many degrees in God in the baptism of the Holy Ghost as there are preachers who preach it. Some people are born away down weeping at the feet of the cross. They are still on the earth-plane with Christ. They are still weeping over their sins, still trying to overcome sin and be pure of heart.

THE BAPTISM OF THE HOLY GHOST

Chicago Pentecostal Convention

July 16, 1920

But there are other people who are born away up in the blessed dominion of God, like our Mother Etter. They have resurrection power. All power is given, and it is in our soul.

And beloved, one day there are going to be Christians baptized in the Holy Ghost who are away up in the throne of God, away up in the consciousness that is breathed out of His holy heart. Somebody is going to be born a son of God and be baptized in the Holy Ghost where Jesus is today, in the throne-consciousness of Christ. Where they can say, like Jesus said, where they can feel like Jesus feels: "I am he that liveth, and was dead; and, behold, I am alive for evermore, Amen; and have the keys of hell and of death."[1] Absolute overcoming consciousness!

You dear folks, listen, who are trying to pump up a Pentecost that was worn out years ago. God let it die. God had only one way under heaven to get you to move up into God, and that way is to let you become dissatisfied with the thing you have. And if you have not the consciousness you once had, God Almighty understands the situation. He is trying to get you hungry, so that you will commit your body and your soul and your spirit to God forever, and by the grace of God you will be baptized in the Holy Ghost over again at the throne of God-consciousness, in the power of Jesus Christ, as Jesus is today. *"As he is,* so are we in this world."[2]

---

[1] Revelation 1:18.

[2] 1 John 4:17.

Why, with most of you, when you were baptized in the Holy Ghost, the Lord had to baptize a whole dose of medicine and pills and everything that was in you. Well, God never had to baptize that kind of stuff in the Lord Jesus. Jesus came down to the River Jordan and gave His *body* and His *soul* and His *spirit* to God forever, and He never took a pill or a dose of medicine. He never went to the spirit of the world for assistance or to the devil for help. His *spirit*, His *soul*, and His *body* were God's from that minute, forever.

Beloved, God is calling men and women to a holier consecration, to a higher place in God, and I am one of God's candidates for that holy place in God. I want to get to the throne of God. Oh yes, God baptized me in the Holy Ghost with a wondrous baptism, according to the understanding I possessed ten or fifteen years ago. But I am a candidate today for a new baptism in the Holy Ghost that comes out of the heart of the *glorified* Christ in the lightnings of God, everlasting overcoming on the throne with Jesus.

And that is the experience that is going to make the sons of God in the world. That is the reason they will take the world for Jesus Christ, and the kingdom will be established, and they will put the crown on the Son of God and declare Him "King of kings and Lord of lords" forever. Amen.

By John G. Lake

TONGUES AND INTERPRETATION

Therefore, fear not, for God is able to perform in you even that which He performed in Jesus and raise you likewise in union with Christ Jesus and make you reign in dominion over sin instead of being dominated by the powers of evil and darkness.

Battle Creek, Michigan

September, 1913

Our eyes behold the triumph of Jesus Christ, the glorious and victorious Son of God, who triumphed over death and hell; who arose triumphant, salvation to obtain; that we might behold gladness and joy, and walk triumphant through Jesus Christ, through the blood that washeth whiter than snow.

"In him was life; and the *life* was the light of men."[1] This scripture reveals the difference between Christianity and philosophy. Some are inquiring why it is that there is always that keynote in my addresses.

SCIENCE OF DIVINE HEALING
Chicago, Illinois
July 19, 1920
(INTERPRETATION OF TONGUES BY JOHN SINCLAIR)

God gave me the privilege of intimacy with the philosophic East, where multitudes are ministered to by Buddhist, Confucianist, and Brahman priests. Every cult imaginable has its representatives there. I was amazed to discover that many in the Western world were gradually assimilating the philosophies of the East.

When you take the modern philosophies — Christian Science, New Thought, Unity, Divine Science, etc. — today and examine them, you discover that they are the same old philosophies of India, Egypt, and China from time immemorial. They were constructed before the Redeemer came, so there is no redemption in them. They are an endeavor to redeem one's self through self-effort.

As I said before, the difference between philosophy and religion, particularly the religion of Jesus Christ, is in the words I quoted from the Scriptures. "In him was *life*, and the life was the light of men." Philosophy is light; it is the best light the individual possessed who framed the philosophy. But it is not a *life giver*.

---

[1] John 1:4, emphasis Lake's.

But from the soul of Jesus there breathed a holy life of God that comes into the nature of man, quickens him by its power, and by the grace of God he has the life of Jesus in him, eternal light, eternal life. Bless God.

Many of the ancient philosophies have light. One of the Indian philosophies, it is said by some writers, the Bhagaved Gita, was written eight hundred years before Isaiah. It predicts the coming of Krishna, a son of God, not *the* Son of God. Listen to this philosophic jewel:

> Never the spirit was born.
>
> The spirit shall cease to be never.
>
> Never was time it was not.
>
> End and beginning are dreams.
>
> Birthless and deathless and changeless
>
> Remaineth the spirit forever;
>
> Death hath not changed it at all,
>
> Dead though the house of it seems.

Yet no knowledge of redemption and no knowledge of a redeemer there.

Buddha presented his philosophy five hundred years before Jesus. The philosophies of Egypt tell the story of the flood and were written thousands of years before Jesus Christ. In the writings of each one of them you will find many of the teachings of Jesus. The teachings of Jesus were not unique in that they were all new. They were new in that they contained something that none of the rest possessed. It was the divine *content* in the Word of Jesus Christ that gave His teachings their distinguishing feature from the other philosophies. That content is the *life* of God. "In Him was *life;* and the *life* was the light of men."

The philosophies were man's best endeavor to find an explanation of life. Without knowledge of a Redeemer, they were written before Christ was manifest in the world. Their authors denied the power of sin or nullified its influence as they failed to conceive of a redeeming grace, an in-working of God in man, through the Spirit of Christ, to save from sin's power and change his nature. But there is given unto us "exceeding great and precious promises: that by these ye might be partakers of *the divine nature.*"[2]

---

[2] 2 Peter 1:4.

Beloved, the real Christian and the real Christian Church undertakes to bring to mankind the life of the Lord Jesus, knowing that when the *life* of Jesus comes, the illumination of the soul, the light of civilization and Christianity will follow, but the *life* is first.

As men wandered from God, and as the world neglected God, men naturally fell into their own consciousness and soul states and proceeded in the common way of the world to endeavor to bless the world through *light*. But light never saved a world. Light never will save a world. There must be a divine content from on high that comes to the soul to enrich it and to empower it, to illuminate it and to glorify it, and more, to *deify* it. For God's purpose through Jesus Christ is to deify the nature of man and thus forever make him like unto Christ, not only in his outward appearance and habits of life, but in nature and substance and content, in spirit and soul and body *like the Son of God.*

Jesus never intended Christians to be an imitation. They were to be bone of His bone and blood of His blood and flesh of His flesh and soul of His soul and spirit of His Spirit. And thus, He becomes to us Son of God, Savior and Redeemer forever, and we are made one with Him both in purpose and being.

(TONGUES AND INTERPRETATION)

Our Father God, to Thee we give the praise of our hearts, that by Thy grace we have been privileged to live in a world where not only the light of God was known, but where the life of God has come. We bless Thee that we have the privilege of living in a day when the life of God in a new flood of power and glory from heaven is coming upon a dry and parched and barren world. And we thank Thee that this life of God has been in our hearts the holy water of life, blessing and enriching our nature, filling us with Thy divine grace and power through Jesus Christ the Lord.

Throughout my life, a spirit of investigation predominated. It has never been easy to accept truth readily, until my soul stepped out inch by inch and proved the ground. When approaching this matter of baptism of the Spirit it was with great care, but as a hungry soul. My heart was hungry for God. And one day the Spirit of the Lord came upon me, God flooded my life and baptized me in His Holy Spirit, and then a new and powerful working of God began in my heart which has gone on for fifteen years, until Christ has become in my world a divine reality.

Having formal acknowledgment as a student of science, it is my privilege to attend clinics, which I frequently do. I submitted myself at one time to a series of experiments. It was not sufficient to know that God healed; I had to know *how* God healed. I visited one of the great experimental institutions and submitted myself for a series of experiments.

First, they attached to my head an instrument to record the vibrations of the brain. This instrument had an indicator that would register the vibrations of the mind. So I began by repeating soothing things like the twenty-third Psalm, calculated to soothe the mind and reduce its vibrations to the lowest point. Then I repeated the thirty-seventh Psalm, then the thirty-fifth of Isaiah, then the ninety-first Psalm, then Paul's address before Agrippa. After this, I went into secular literature and recited Tennyson's "Charge of the Light Brigade" and last, Poe's "Raven," with a prayer in my heart that at the psychological moment God would anoint my soul in the Holy Ghost.

My difficulty was that while the reciting went on I could not keep the Spirit from coming upon me, and when I got through with Poe's "Raven," they said, "You are a phenomena. You have a wider mental range than any human being we have ever seen." In reality that was not so. It was because the Spirit of God kept coming upon me in degree, so I could feel the moving of the Spirit within me.

But I prayed in my heart, "Lord God, if You will only let the Spirit of God come like the lightnings of God upon my soul for two seconds, I know something is going to happen that these men never saw before."

So as I closed the last lines suddenly, the Spirit of God struck me in a burst of praise and tongues, and the old indicator on the instrument bounced to its limit, and I haven't the least idea how much further it would have gone if it were a possibility. The professors said, "We have never seen anything like it."

I replied, "Gentlemen, it is the Holy Ghost."

Now in order to get the force of this lesson it is necessary to give you the latest theory of the process of digestion. You will see the assimilating power of your nature, your capacity to assimilate God and take the life of God into your being and keep it in your being. I am not talking about what I believe; I am talking about what I *know*.

For many years God kept me so that sickness and death could not touch me, from the day that I saw in the ninety-first Psalm a man's privilege of entering into God, not only for healing, but *health* and having God and the life of God in every fiber of his being.

Scientists tell us that in a single inch of a man's skin there are one million, five hundred thousand cells, and they have almost doubled that statement now. But be that as it may, the whole structure of a man's being is one wonderful cellular structure. Your blood, your body, your brain, your bone is just one great cellular structure.

According to the latest theory on the process of digestion, the food we eat is reduced to vegetable lymph and is then absorbed into the body cells. But no scientist in the world has ever been able to satisfactorily explain what it is that changes the lymph and makes it *life*. Something happens when it is in the cells that changes it to life. This is transmutation.

I want to tell you what grew up in my soul and how I proved the fact. I could feel sometimes while in the attitude of prayer, just as you have felt hundreds of times, the impulse of the Spirit moving through your brain and your person to the end of your fingers, just little impulses of God's presence in your life. And I said, "If there was an instrument powerful enough, I believe men could see the action of the brain cells and see what takes place."

Here is the secret of digestion: from the spirit-mind of man and through the spirit of man there is imparted to every cell of your body impulses of spirit, waves of life. It is the movement of the Spirit. Spirit impulses passing from the cortex cells of the brain to the very end of your fingers and toes, to every cell of the body. And when they touch that vegetable lymph in the body cells, it is transformed into *life*. That is transmutation.

In the electrical world you can dissolve zinc, and the electrical current absorbs it and transmits it to the other end of the wire. In an experiment in California they dissolved zinc in the battery at the one end and transmitted the zinc to the other end of the wire, deposited, and solidified it at the other end of the wire, a distance of twelve miles. How is it done? There is a process of transmutation. That is what it is called. It is a change from one form to another.

My brother, listen: if that is not true in the spiritual world, there is no such thing as divine *life;* there is no such thing as salvation through the Son of God. For that which is soulish (natural) must be transformed by the Spirit of God in us, until it becomes spiritual — until it is of God. "Ye must be born again" is a truly scientific statement.[3]

Jesus sat with His disciples and ate with them, both bread and fish. He went to the Mount and ascended before them to glory, while their eyes beheld. What happened to the fish and the bread that He had eaten? I tell you there is transmutation. That which is natural becomes spiritual. That which was natural was changed by the power of God into the life of God, into the nature of God, into the substance of God, into the glory of God.

In the second experiment, they attached to my head a powerful x-ray with microscopic attachments in order to see, if possible, what the action of the brain cells were. Then I proceeded, just as in the former experiment. First, I repeated scriptures that were soothing and calculated to reduce the action of the cortex cells to their lowest possible register. Then, I went on into the Scriptures to the better and richer things, until I came to the first of John, and as I began to recite that, and the fires of God began to burn in my heart, presently, once again the Spirit of God came upon me, and the man who was at my back touched me. It was a signal to keep the poise of soul until one after another could look through the instrument. And finally when I let go, the Spirit subsided. They said, "Why man, we cannot understand this, but the cortex cells expanded amazingly."

Oh beloved, when you pray something is happening in you. It is not a myth; it is the action of God. The Almighty God, by the Spirit, comes into the soul, takes possession of the brain, manifests in the cortex cells, and when you will and wish (either consciously or unconsciously) the fire of God, the power of God, that *life* of God, that nature of God, is transmitted from the cortex cells of the brain, throbs

---

[3] John 3:7.

through your nerves, down through your person into every cell of your being, into every cell of your brain and blood and flesh and bone, into the million, five hundred thousand cells in every square inch of your skin, and they are alive with God. That is divine healing.

Men have treated the Gospel of Jesus Christ as though it were a sentiment and foolishness. Men who posed as being wise have scorned the phenomenon taking place in the Christian every day. But beloved, no dear old mother ever knelt before the throne of God and raised her heart to heaven without demonstrating the finest process of divine wireless transmission.

In these days, they are now able to transmit by wireless from six to seven thousand miles and even twelve thousand miles recently. Once again, they have been able to demonstrate that in one-tenth of a second they can transmit the first section of thought twelve thousand miles. Think of it! There is practically no such thing as time; it is practically done instantaneously. This explains instantaneous salvation and instantaneous healing.

Beloved, the very instant your soul moves with your heart cry and your nature yearns after God, it registers in the soul of Jesus Christ, and the answer comes back. So Jesus said, "Whatsoever ye desire, when ye pray, believe, and ye shall have," and "While ye are yet speaking, I will hear."[4]

I said to them, "Gentlemen, I want you to see one more thing. You go down in your hospital and bring the man who has inflammation in the shinbone. Take your instrument and attach it to his leg, leave space enough to get my hand on his leg. You can have it attached on both sides." So when the instrument was all ready I put my hand on that man's shin, and I prayed just like Mother Etter prays, just as you all pray. No strange prayer, but the cry of my heart to God. I said, "God, kill the devilish disease by the power of God. Let the Spirit live in him, let it move in him."

Then I said, "Gentlemen, what is taking place?"

They replied, "Every cell is responding."

---

[4] Mark 11:24 and Isaiah 65:24, paraphrased.

Beloved, all there is to healing, is that the *life* of God comes back into the part that is afflicted and right away the blood flows, the congested cells respond, and the work is done. That is again God's divine science in healing.

My soul long ago grew tired of men treating the whole subject of Christianity as though it were child's play. We have our physical sciences; we have our psychological sciences, the structure of the body and the action of the mind taught in the great schools of the land. But there is something greater. One of these days there is going to be a new chair in our universities. It will be the chair of pneumatology, the science of spirit, by which men will undertake to discover the laws of the spirit of man and the action of God through man. And by the grace of God men shall know that God is alive, and the living Spirit of God is no dream, and its wondrous power in man and through man will be revealed.

In my healing rooms in Spokane, a dear woman came one day whose name is Lamphear. She was the wife of a merchant in the city. She had fallen down a stairs, causing a prolapse of the stomach, bowels, and uterus. She had been an invalid for eleven years. On top of this, she became tubercular unto death. On top of that, the poor woman developed inflammatory rheumatism, until she lived in a hell of torture. The physicians said there was nothing they could do for her, but advised that they take her to Hot Lake, Oregon, and perhaps the baths would do her some good.

So they put her in the hot baths there, and she suffered just as much as ever. Then they tried super-heated baths, and they put her in water hotter than any human being had ever been in before, so the superintendent testified. The result was that instead of having any healing effect, the left leg developed an abnormal growth and it became three inches longer than the other leg, and a bone larger than a big orange grew on the inside of the knee, destroying the action of the knee joint. The foot became an inch longer.

She came away from the institution worse than she went. She got as far as Portland. Her parents were living at the Dalls. She wanted to see her parents before she died, so her husband carried her in his arms to the boat. As he did so, a Pentecostal missionary stepped up and said, "Dear woman, we understand now why God told us to take this boat. He told us last night to take the eight o'clock boat for the Dalls." He called up on the telephone and found that the fare was $1.80 and as that was all the money they had, they went without their breakfast so as to be able to take the boat.

As she lay crying with her suffering (they were timid folks) the man said, "When we get to the Dalls we will pray for you." Eventually, they reached the Dalls and went to a hotel. The two knelt to pray for her, and she says as they prayed and put their hands on her knees, that their hands became illuminated, until they looked like the hands of Jesus, their faces looked like the face of Jesus, and she was afraid. But something happened. The pain went out of her.

Strangely, she retained her tuberculosis and the struggle for breath went on. The leg remained the same length. When she examined herself she was surprised to discover that it was not shorter. She said, "Pray again that the Lord may make it the same length as the other," but the poor missionary was staggered.

He said, "Dear Sister, the pain is gone, you should be satisfied and give praise to God."

So she went on for three and a half years, coughing her lungs out and her leg three inches longer than the other. One day she came to the healing rooms and was ministered to. The healing action of God took place, and she felt wonderfully relieved. She said, "I can breathe clear down into my stomach."

The minister said, "What makes you limp?"

She replied, "There is a big lump on the inside of my knee, and my leg is three inches longer than it should be."

He said, "I'll pray for that."

But she said, "The missionary who prayed for me told me I should be satisfied if the pain was gone."

The minister said, "He had not grown up in God yet." And he put his hands on the lump and prayed and God Almighty dissolved that lump of bone and that leg shortened at the rate of one inch a week. The foot also shortened to its proper length, and she wears shoes like anyone else, the same on both feet.

She was born without the outer ring and lobe on one ear and it also grew and the ear became like the other.

There is a difference between healing and miracle. Healing is the restoration of diseased tissue, but miracle is a creative action of the Spirit of God, creating that which is deficient in a man's life. And the salvation of a soul is a divine miracle of God. Every time Christ speaks the word of life to a man's heart there is a divine, creative miracle of God wrought in him, and he is a new man in Christ Jesus.

One day I sat in Los Angeles, talking to old father Seymour. I told him an incident in the life of Elias Letwaba, one of our native preachers who lived in the native country. I came to his home and his wife said, "He is not home. A little baby is hurt, and he is praying for it." So we went over, and I got down on my knees and crawled into the native hut. I saw he was kneeling in a corner by the child. I said, "Letwaba, it is me. What is the matter with the child?" He told me that the mother had it on her back in a blanket, as natives carry their children, and it fell out. He said, "I think it has hurt its neck."

I examined it and saw that the baby's neck was broken, and I said to Letwaba, "Why, Letwaba, the baby's neck is broken." It would turn like the neck of a doll from side to side. I did not have faith for a broken neck, but poor old Letwaba did not know the difference, and I saw he did not understand, but he discerned the spirit of doubt in my soul, and I said to myself, "I am not going to interfere with his faith. He will just feel the doubt generated by all the old traditional things I ever learned. So I will go out."

And I did. I went and sat in another hut and kept on praying. I lay down at 1 A.M.; at three Letwaba came in. I said, "Well, Letwaba, how about the baby?"

He looked at me so lovingly and sweetly and said, "Why brother, the baby is all well. Jesus do heal the baby."

I said, "The baby is well! Letwaba, take me to the baby at once."

So we went to the baby, and I took the little black thing on my arm, and I came out praying, "Lord take every cursed thing out of my soul that keeps me from believing the Lord Jesus Christ." And Mr. Seymour, to whom I had related the incident, shouted, "Praise God, brother, that is not healing, it is life!"

In my meeting in Spokane is a dear man who came from Texas, Reverend Julias Allen. He told us he was dying of pellagra.[5] He came to Sister Etter's meeting at Dallas. On the train he apparently died, and they laid his body in the station house, covered him with gunnysacks, but discovered in the morning that he was still alive. So they carried him to Mother Etter's meeting and she came down off the platform and prayed for him, rebuking that devil of pellagra, and that man is living and has been preaching the Gospel for seven years at Spokane.

Why there is more science in the mind of God in five minutes than the bloated scholarship of the world ever knew. "In Him is life, and the life was the light of men." The life of God is that which the mind of men and the keenest of them never knew and never understood. "The world through wisdom knew not God."[6] They could not discern the value in His death nor understand the marvels of His life or why the Lord Jesus came and lived and died and entered into Hades and destroyed the power of darkness and death that held the souls of men; or how He liberated them from the chains of darkness, translated them to His own glory, and came forth to speak God's Word and reveal God's power and show God's nature. And by the grace of God man has been privileged to enter into the nature of Jesus, and the fires of God burn in his soul like they burned in the soul of the risen Lord. That explains resurrection faith and resurrection power.

The scientific world has been startled by one of the English scientists, who says he has a formula for transmutation of the grosser metals into gold. The old alchemists claimed to know this secret, but somehow it disappeared from the world. Now it is claimed it can be done again, that they can take lead and silver and iron and transmute (change) them into gold.

Beloved, that is the thing that Jesus Christ has been doing all the time. It is as old as Christianity; it is as old as the Son of God. He has been coming to the hearts of men, taking the old base conditions of the

---

5   pellagra: a disease caused by a deficiency of niacin in the diet, characterized by skin changes, nervous disorders, and diarrhea. *Webster's Desk Dictionary of the English Language* (NY: Gramercy Books, 1983) p. 670.

6   1 Corinthians 1:21.

nature, injecting His life into them, inducting His power into the man, and through the mighty action of the Holy Ghost they have been changed into the pure gold of God. That is divine transmutation.

If there never was another blessing that came to the world through Pentecost but this one of which I am now going to speak, all the price that men paid would be as nothing. Listen! There has been more real divine research by the Holy Ghost into the nature of God and the nature of man in these last fifteen years than there ever was in any similar period in Christian history, and more intelligent discovery of God's action and working in and through man than ever before. That is God's divine laboratory of spiritual knowledge.

And when anyone comes to me with the statement that there is nothing in the baptism of the Holy Ghost but a psychological manifestation, I say, "Brother, sister, come with me and see the gems of God and the beautiful gold that has come out of the dross of dirty lives and then you will know." Saved from sin and healed from disease. That is divine demonstration.

In my Assembly at Spokane is a real little woman who was blind for nine years. She had little teaching along the line of faith of God. She sat one day with her group of six children to discover that her dirty brute of a husband had abandoned her and his children and left her to starve. A debased human being is capable of things that no beast will do, for a beast will care for its own.

You can imagine what that little heart was like. She was crushed, broken, bruised, and bleeding. She gathered her children around her and began to pray. They were sitting on their front porch. Presently, one of them got up and said, "Oh, Mama, there is a man coming up the path and He looks like Jesus! And oh, Mama, there is blood on His hands and blood on His feet!" And the children were frightened and ran around the corner of the house. After awhile the biggest one looked around the corner and said, "Why, Mama, He is laying His hands on your eyes!" And just then her blind eyes opened. That is divine power.

And beloved, if we could have seen the reason we would have seen that there were some Christians, like those at the Brooks' Home, Zion City, or some other place, who were praying the power of God on a hungry world, and Jesus Christ in His search for those who would receive, rushed to her and sent her forth to praise God and teach the Gospel of Jesus.

I would not have missed my life in Africa for anything. It put me up against some of the real problems. I sat upon a mountain in Africa one afternoon and counted eleven hundred native villages within the range of my eyes. I could see the color of the grass on the mountains sixty miles away. I could see the mountains one hundred and fifty miles away, so clear was its rarefied atmosphere.

Then I began to figure, and I said, "Within the range of my eyes there lives ten million native people. They never heard the name of Jesus. In the whole land there are at least one hundred million people, perhaps two hundred million." They are being born at a tremendous rate. Do you know there are more heathen born every day than are Christianized in fifty years? When are we going to catch up by our present method of building schools and teaching them to read? Never! I tell you it will never come that way. It has got to come from heaven by the power of God, by an outpouring of the Holy Ghost. That is divine salvation.

That is the reason that my heart rejoices in the blessed promise that, "In the last days, saith God, I will pour out of my Spirit upon *all* flesh."[7] And every last one of the two hundred million poor black people are going to hear and know of the Lord Jesus Christ. Beloved, I would rather have a place in the kingdom of God of praying that thing into existence and of praying the power of God upon them, than anything else in the world.

Africa is said to be the first settled country in the world, and we believe the world is six thousand years old. Africa has been settled for five thousand years. Two hundred or four hundred million have died every century. Split the difference and say that three hundred million have died every year for five thousand years.

It caused me to pray and meditate. I said, "Has God no interest in these people? And if He has an interest, why is not something done

---

[7] Acts 2:17.

for them? What is the matter with God? Is God unable to help, or does He not care?" My heart was breaking under the burden of it. I said, "God, there must be an explanation somewhere. What is it, Lord? Tell me about it."

Then my heart grew calm, and the Spirit said, "The Church which is His body," and I knew that was God's answer.

I said, "Yes, the Church should have sent missionaries and built schools and done this and that."

But the Spirit kept on saying, "The Church which is His body. The Church which is His body." I sat and listened to that voice repeat that sentence for a half hour.

I said, "My God, my soul begins to see. The Church is the ministering presence of the Son of God in the world. The Church is the generating agency of the power of God in the world. The Church has been negligent in one great trust. She has not prayed the power of God out of heaven."

Then I saw that which has become a conviction in my soul from that day: that there never was a soul born to God in the whole earth at any time until some soul in the world got hold of the living Spirit of God and generated that Spirit in saving grace and creative virtue and ministered it until it took possession of a soul, no difference if it was a million miles away. Thus the life of Christ is begotten in them.

When I try to induce men to forget their little squabbles and little differences and go to praying, it is because my soul feels the burden of it. Mother Etter has been like a marshal for fifty years. The sick have been healed; people have been converted and blessed. But beloved, when I heard of Brother Brook's shutting himself up night and day to pray the power of God on a world, I said, "That is where she gets her fire; that is where it comes from to my soul; that is where it comes from to other souls, through those who pray." That is divine intercession.

Notice how beautifully this armory is lighted. The world lived in darkness for five thousand years, and they had no way of lighting a place like this, except by torches or candles. But there was just as much electricity five thousand years ago as there is today. Somebody found how to handle it, discovered the laws that govern it, learned to apply it to our need. But to this day, there is no man who can tell us what electricity is or what its substance is. We know we can control it this way and guide it that way and make it do this and that, but what it is nobody can tell us. However, down somewhere on the river there is a machine that is called a dynamo, and it draws the electricity out of the air and transmits it over the wires. And these days they are sending it in wireless waves.

Do you know what prayer is? It is not begging God for this and that. The first thing we have to do is to get you beggars to quit begging, until a little faith moves in your soul. *Prayer* is God's divine generator. The spirit of man is God's divine dynamo. When you go to pray, your spirit gets into motion. Not ten thousand revolutions per minute, but possibly one hundred thousand. The voltage of heaven comes to your heart and it flows from your hands, it burns into the souls of men, and God Almighty's Spirit is applied through you to their need.

Over in Indiana some years ago was a farmer who used to be a friend of Brother Fockler and myself. His son had been in South America, had a dreadful case of typhoid fever and no proper nursing, and the result was he developed a great fever sore ten inches in diameter. The whole abdomen became grown up with proud flesh, one layer on top of another layer, until there were five layers. The nurse had to lift up those layers and wash it with an antiseptic to keep the maggots out of it.

When he exposed the body for me to pray for him, I was shocked. I never had seen anything like it before. As I went to pray for him I spread my fingers out wide and put my hand right on that cursed growth of proud flesh. I prayed God in the name of Jesus Christ to blast the curse of hell and burn it up by the power of God. Then I took the train and came back to Chicago. The next day I received a telegram saying, "Lake, the most unusual thing has happened. An hour after you left, the whole print of your hand was burned into that growth a quarter of an inch deep."

You talk about the voltage of heaven and the power of God! Why there is lightning in the soul of Jesus. The lightnings of Jesus heals men by its flash; sin dissolves, disease flees when the power of God approaches.

And yet we are quibbling and wondering if Jesus Christ is big enough for our needs. Let's take the bars down. Let God come into your life. And in the name of Jesus your heart will not be satisfied with an empty Pentecost, but your soul will claim the light of God and the lightnings of Jesus to flood your life. Amen.

"hrist liveth in me."[1] That is the revelation of this age. That is the discovery of the moment. That is the revolutionizing power of God in the earth. It is the factor that is changing the spirit of religion in the world and the character of Christian faith. It is divine revitalization.

CHRIST LIVETH IN ME

Spokane, Washington

August 20, 1920

The world is awakening to that marvelous truth, that Christ is not only in the heavens and in the atmosphere outside; but that Christ is in heaven and in the atmosphere outside, and Christ is *in you.*

The world lived in darkness for thousands of years. There was just as much electricity in the world then as now. It is not that electricity has just come into being. It was always here. But men have discovered how to utilize it and bless themselves with it.

Christ's indwelling the human heart is the mystery of mysteries. Paul gave it to the Gentiles as the supreme mystery of all the revelation of God and the finality of all wonder that he knew. "Christ in you."

"Christ in *you.*"[2]

Christ has a purpose in you. Christ's purpose in *you* is to reveal Himself to you, through you, in you. We repeat over and over that familiar phrase, "The church which is his body,"[3] but if we realized the truth of it and the power of it, this world would be a different place. When the Christian Church realizes that they are the tangible, living, pulsating, flesh and bones and blood and brain of Jesus Christ and that God is manifesting Himself through each one every minute and is endeavoring to accomplish His big will for the world through them, not through some other body, then Christian responsibility will be understood.

---

[1] Galatians 2:20.

[2] Colossians 1:27.

[3] Ephesians 1:22-23.

Jesus Christ operates through you. He does not operate independently of you. He operates through you. Man and God become united. That is the divine secret of a real Christian life. It is the real union, the real conscious union of man and God. There is no substitute for that relationship. You can manufacture all the ordinances on earth, all the symbols there ever were until you become dazed and you lose yourself in the maze of them, and still you must find God.

There is only one reality. That reality is God. The soul of man must contact God, and unless the spirit of man is truly joined to God there is no such thing as real Christian manifestation. All the processes of preparation, by which a soul is prepared by God for such manifestation, are only preliminary processes. The final end is that men may reveal God and that God may not only have a place of residence, but a right of action in the body and spirit of man. Every Spirit-taught man in the world is aware of how gradually his own nature has become subjected to God and His will.

I was visiting with a gentleman this afternoon who had a grouch on me. He said, "I wrote you a twenty-four page letter, and you have not received it. If you had you would not be here." I laughed. That man has been a Christian for thirty or forty years. Always a devout man, and I have spoken often of him to my wife and my friends as one of the most consistent Christian men I ever knew. Yet every once in a while the big human just rises up above the spirit and spoils the beauty and delight and wonder of the life that is revealing God.

God's effort and God's purpose in us is to bring all the conditions of our being into harmony with His will and mind. God's purpose is not to make an automaton. We see a ventriloquist operating a little wooden dummy, and the wooden dummy's lips move and it looks as though it was talking. He is just moving in obedience to another power.

Now God has a higher purpose than making man an automaton. God's highest is to bring out all the qualities of God in your own soul, to bring out all the individuality that is in your life, not to submerge or destroy, but to change it, to energize it, to enlarge it until all your individuality and personality and being are of the nature and substance and quality of God.

You notice among the most devout Christians how continuously their thought is limited to that place where they can be exercised or moved by God. But God's best is more than that. Receive the Spirit, then use the Spirit for God's glory.

While I was in Chicago I met a couple of old friends who invited me to dinner. And while at dinner the lady, who is a very frank woman said, "Mr. Lake, I have known you so long and have had such close fellowship for so many years, I am able to speak perfectly frankly."

I said, "Yes, absolutely."

"Well," she said, "there is something I miss about you. For lack of words I am going to put it in Paul's words, 'I bear in my body the marks of the Lord Jesus.'[4] You do not seem to have the marks of Jesus."

I said, "That depends whether or not it is the marks or mannerisms. If you are expecting that the personality that God gave me is going to be changed so that I am going to be another fellow and not myself, then you will miss it. If that is the kind of marks you are looking for you will not find them. But if you are expecting to observe a man's flesh and blood and bones and spirit and mind indwelt by God, then you will find them — not a machine, not an automaton, or an imitation — but a clear mind and a pure heart, a son of God in nature and essence."

What is all God's effort with the world but to bring out the real man in the image of Christ — the real man with the knowledge of God. That real man, reconstructed until his very substance is the substance of God! And when you stop to reason that to proper conclusion, that it is the only way in which Jesus Christ Himself or God, the Eternal Father, will ever keep from living in loneliness forever.

When one stops to analyze that fact, we see that God is trying to make us in all our nature and being and habits and thought, in all the structure of our life, just as beautiful and just as real and just as clear-minded and just as strong as Jesus Himself. Then we understand what Christ's redemption means. It is the bringing out of Christ in you, until Christ in you is the one manifest — manifest through your eyes just as God was manifest through the eyes of Jesus, manifest through your touch, just as God was manifest through Jesus. It is not a power

---

[4] Galatians 6:17.

or a life separate from yourself but two lives made one, two natures conjoined, two minds operating in one — *Christ in you.*

One day at the Chicago conference, I sat with an old colored lady one afternoon after the meeting, and she told me of her sicknesses and woes — and they were many. After a time, when she had grown somewhat still I said, "Dear Mother, how long have you been a Christian?"

She replied, "Since I was a child." Then I tried to show her that God expected a development of God and His nature and the working and action of God in her in transforming power, through the agency of the Spirit, and that there was a process of remaking and remolding that should change her nature and life and dissolve the rheumatism and Bright's disease and all the other difficulties just as truly as long ago sin had disappeared from her soul.

After the conversation had gone on to the proper point I said, "Dear Sister, anybody can see that Christ dwells in your spirit." Her eyes were lovely, delightful! "Let your mind extend just a little. Let your thought comprehend that just as Jesus dwells in your spirit and also possesses your soul, in just exactly the same way He is possessing your blood and your kidneys and your old rheumatic bones and that the very same thing will happen in your bones when you realize that truth as happened when you were converted at the altar."

She had told me how she had prayed twenty-two days and nights until Christ was revealed in her soul as Savior. She seemed to want to wait twenty-two days and nights for God to manifest Himself in the rheumatic bones, and I was trying to get her away from it.

She said, "Brother, lay your hands on me and pray for me, and I will be healed."

I answered, "No, I want you to get well by realizing that right now that same Christ that dwells in your spirit and your soul is in your bones and in your blood and in your brain." Presently, the old lady hopped to her feet and said, "My God, He is." She made it. Christ had been imprisoned in her soul and spirit. Now He was permitted to manifest Himself in her body.

Brother Tom Hezmalhalch came into a Negro meeting in Los Angeles one day where they were talking about the baptism of the Holy Ghost. He had picked up a paper and read of these peculiar meetings and, among other things, that they spoke in tongues. That was new to him. He said, "If they do and if it is real, that is an advance in the Spirit of God beyond what is common. I am going to get it."

He went, and listened as the old Negro taught. He was trying to develop the thought of conscious cleansing, and he used the beautiful text: "Now ye are clean through the Word I have spoken unto you."[5] That became very real to Tom, and after awhile they were invited to come and kneel at the altar to seek God for the baptism of the Holy Spirit. Tom said to me, "John, I got up and walked toward that old bench with the realization in my soul of the truth of the Word and that the real cleansing and Cleanser was in my heart." "Now are ye clean through the word which I have spoken unto you."

He knelt down and he prayed for a minute or two. His soul rose and his heart believed for the baptism of the Holy Ghost. Then he arose and took one of the front seats. One of the workers said, "Brother, don't stop praying until you are baptized in the Holy Ghost."

He replied, "Jesus told me I was baptized in the Holy Ghost."

Mr. Seymour said, "Just leave him alone. He has got it. You wait and see." A few days passed, and one day Tom said that the Spirit began to surge through him and a song of praise in tongues, angelic voice, broke through his lips.

An old preacher came into my office in Africa and said, "Brother Lake, there is something I want to talk to you about. There used to be a very remarkable manifestation in my life. It was the manifestation of tongues and interpretation. But I have not spoken in tongues for a year. I wish you would pray for me."

I said, "No, go over and lie down and get still and let God move in your life." I was writing a letter. I went on with my writing. Presently, I observed that something wanted to speak in me, and I turned my head just a little to see that the old man was speaking in tongues and I was getting the interpretation of it as I wrote the letter.

Don't you know Christians are stumbling every day over that fact. You are doubting and fearing and wondering if Christ is there. Beloved brother and sister, give Him a chance to reveal Himself. He

---

[5] See John 15:3.

is there. Probably because of your lack of realization your soul is closed, and He is not able to reveal Himself. You know God is never able in many to reveal Himself outside of the spirit or soul. The real secret of the ministry of healing is in permitting the grace of God in your heart to flow out through your hands and your nerves into the other life. That is the real secret.

And one of the greatest works God has to perform is to subject our flesh to God. Many Christians, the deepest Christians, who really know God in their spirits and enjoy communion with God are compelled to wait until there is a process of spiritualization that takes place in their bodies before God can reveal Himself through them. Do not imprison Christ in you. Let Him live, let Him manifest, let Him find vent through you.

There is one great thing that the world is needing more than anything else, and I am convinced of it more every day I live. Mankind has one supreme need and that is the *love of God*. The hearts of men are dying for lack of the love of God. I have a sister in Detroit. She came over to Milwaukee to visit us for two or three days at the convention there. As I watched her moving around, I said, "I would like to take her along and just have her love folks." She would not need to preach. You do not need to preach to folks. It is not the words you say that is going to bless them. They are in need of something greater. It is the thing in your soul. They have got to receive it, then their soul will open and there will be a divine response. Give it to them. It is the love of Christ.

You have seen people who loved someone who would not respond. If there is any hard situation in God's earth, that is it, to really passionately love someone and find no response in them.

I had an English friend and was present at his marriage. Some years later, he and his wife came to visit at our home. He was that cold type of closed Englishman, and she was the warm type. One day as they started out for a walk, I noticed the passionate yearning in her soul. If he would just say something that was tender, something that would gratify the craving of her nature for affection! But he seemed to go along absolutely unconscious of it. After the lady had gone into the house I said, "Hibbs, you are a stiff. How is it possible that you can walk down the street with a woman like your wife and not realize that her heart is craving and crying for you to turn around and say something that shows you love her?"

He said, "Do you think that is the difficulty? I will go and do it now." And everything subsided while he proceeded to do it.

What is it men are seeking? What is it their hearts are asking for when they are seeking God? What is their soul crying for? Mankind is separated from God. It may not be mountains of sin between you and God at all. It may only be that your nature is closed and unresponsive. My, when the real love touch of God is breathed into your soul, what a transformation takes place! There is probably no more delightful thing on earth than to watch a soul crying unto God when the light of God comes in and the life of God fills the nature and that holy affection that we seek from others finds expression in Him.

That is what the Lord is asking from you, and if you want to gratify the heart of Jesus Christ, that is the only way in all the world to do it. You know the invitation is not, "Give me thine head." The invitation is, "My son, give me thine heart." That is an affectionate relationship, a real love union in God, a real love union with God. Think of the fineness of God's purpose! He expects that same marvelous spiritual union that is brought to pass between your soul and His own to be extended, so that you embrace in that union every other soul around you.

Oh, that is what it means when it talks about being baptized in one Spirit, submerged, buried, enveloped, and enveloping in the one Spirit of God.

While I was in Milwaukee recently, I went out one morning with Rev. Fockler to make a call on a sick person. We stepped into one of the most distracted homes I have ever been in. A strange condition had developed in one of the daughters, and the household was distressed. They were the saddest group. They were German people. Fockler speaks German. Presently, he began to talk to the household. I just sat back and watched. Presently, I noticed the faces began to relax and the strain was gone. The girl that was apparently insane came down the stairs, stood outside the door where she could not be seen except by me. He continued to converse with the family, and as their souls softened and their faith lifted her eyes commenced to change.

She was moved upon by the same Spirit until her nature responded too, and in just a little while she stepped into the room. She had tormented that household. Nobody could get near her. She slipped up behind Fockler's chair, stood with her hands at the back of the chair. He understood and disregarded. After awhile she rested one hand on his shoulder. After a little while she put the other hand on the other shoulder. And in fifteen or twenty minutes we left that home and there was just as much distinction between the attitude of these dear souls when we came in and when we went out as between heaven and hell. If hell has a characteristic, it is that of distraction. If heaven has a particular characteristic, it is the presence of God, the calm of God, the power of God, the love of God.

There were days when the church could club men into obedience by preaching hell to them, but that day has long since passed. The world has outgrown it. Men are discovering there is only one way, and that is the Jesus way. Jesus did not come with a club, but with the great loving heart of God. He was "moved with compassion."[6]

This morning I lay in bed and wrote a letter, an imaginary letter to a certain individual. I was getting ready so that when I came down I could dictate the sentences that would carve him right. One of the phrases was, "You great big calf, come out of it and be a man." As I lay there I got to thinking, "If Jesus was writing this letter, I wonder what He would write?" But somehow it would not frame. My soul was not in an attitude to produce such a letter. So I came down this morning and called Edna and commenced to dictate, and I was trying to dictate a letter in the Spirit of Jesus. Presently, I woke up to the fact that I was putting the crimp into it like a lawyer.

After she had it written and laid down for my signature, I commenced to read it over. It was not what I wanted to write at all. The first two paragraphs had a touch of the right spirit, but that was all. So I laid it aside. Then I went in and prayed a little while, and after I had been praying for twenty minutes the telephone rang, and it was that fellow.

---

[6] See Matthew 9:36; 14:14 and Mark 1:41; 6:34.

He wanted me to come down to the Davenport Hotel, and we had three of the best hours without being aware of the time.

We boast of our development in God; we speak glowingly of our spiritual experiences, but it is only once in awhile that we find ourselves in the real love of God. The greater part of the time we are in ourselves rather than in Him. This evidences just one thing, that Christ has not yet secured that perfect control of our life, that subjection of our nature, that absorption of our individuality, so that he is able to impregnate it and maintain it in Himself. We recede, we draw back, we close up. We imprison our Lord.

Beloved, the secret of a religious meeting is that it assists men's hearts to open, they become receptive, and the love of God finds vent in their nature for a little while, and they go away saying, "Didn't we have a good time? Wasn't that a splendid meeting?"

I wonder if there is anything that could not be accomplished through the love of God. Paul says there is not. "Love never faileth."[7] That is one infallible state. Try it on your wife, try it on your children, try it on your neighbors.

Ah, sometimes we need to get things over on the bigger love, the greater heart. It is a good thing to detach your soul. Do not hold people. Do not bind people. Just cut them loose and let God have them. Don't you know that we hold people with such a grip when we pray for them that they miss the blessing. Why, you have such a grip that your humanity is exercising itself and the Spirit is being submerged. Let your soul relax and let the Spirit of God in you find vent. There is no substitute for the love of God. "Christ in You." Oh, you have the capacity to love. All the action of the Spirit of God has its secret there.

I stood on one occasion by a dying woman who was suffering and writhing in awful agony. I had prayed again and again with no results. But this day something just happened inside of me. My soul broke clear down, and I saw that poor soul in a new light and before I knew it I reached out and gathered her in my arms and hugged her up to

---

[7]   See 1 Corinthians 13:8.

my soul, not my bosom. In a minute the real thing had taken place, and I laid her back on the pillow and in five minutes she was well. God was waiting on me, until he could give to my soul the sense of that tenderness that was in the Son of God.

That is the real reason that His name is written in imperishable memory, and the name of Jesus Christ is the most revered name in earth or sea or sky. And I am eager to get that category of folks who can manifest the real love of God all the time.

The life of God, the Spirit of God, the nature of God are sufficient for every need of man.

In the highest sense of the word, he is a *real* Christian whose body, soul, and spirit alike are filled with the life of God.

Healing in any department of the nature whether spirit, soul, or body is but a means to an end. The object of healing is health, abiding health of body, soul, and spirit. The healing of the spirit unites the spirit of man to God forever. The healing of the soul corrects psychic disorder and brings the soul processes into harmony with the mind of God. And healing of the body completes the union of man with God when the Holy Spirit possesses all.

THE BAPTISM OF THE HOLY GHOST

February 23, 1921

Editor's note:

This is sermon one in a three-message series on The Baptism of the Holy Ghost. Sermons two and three were not dated, but in order to keep the series together we have chosen to place them following sermon one in the chronological section.

The baptism of the Holy Ghost is the greatest event in Christian history — greater than the crucifixion, of greater import than the resurrection, greater than the ascension, greater than the glorification. It was the end and finality of crucifixion and resurrection, ascension and glorification.

If Jesus Christ had been crucified and there had been no resurrection, His death would have been without avail, insofar as the salvation of mankind is concerned. Or, if He had risen from the grave in resurrection and failed to reach the throne of God and receive from the Father the gift of the Holy Ghost, the purpose for which He died and for which He arose would have been missed.

It is because there was no failure. It is because Jesus went to the ultimate, to the very throne and heart of God and secured right out of the heavenly treasury of the Eternal Soul, the Almighty Spirit, and poured it forth upon the world in divine baptism, that we are here tonight.

BIRTHDAY OF CHRISTIANITY

The Day of Pentecost was the birthday of Christianity. Christianity never existed until the Holy Ghost came from heaven. The ministry of Jesus in the world was His own divine preparation of the world for His ultimate and final ministry. His ultimate and final ministry was to be *by the Spirit*.

The ministry of Jesus during His earth life was localized by His humanity. Localized again in that His message was only given to Israel. But the descent of the Holy Ghost brought to the souls of men a *universal* ministry of Jesus to every man, right from the heart of God. Heavenly contact with the eternal God in power set their nature all aflame for God and with God, exalted their natures into God, and made the recipient *godlike*. Man became godlike!

HOLY GROUND

There is no subject in all the Word of God that seems to me should be approached with so much holy reverence as the subject of the baptism of the Holy Ghost. Beloved, my heart bleeds every day of my life when I hear the flippancy with which Christians discuss the baptism of the Holy Ghost.

When Moses entered into the presence of God at the burning bush, God said, "Put off thy shoes from off thy feet, for the place whereon thou standest is holy ground."[1] How much more so when the individual comes into the presence of God looking for the baptism of the Holy Ghost and remembers that in order to obtain this gift, Jesus Christ lived in the world, bled on the cross, entered into the darkness of death and hell and the grave, grappled with and strangled that accursed power, came forth again, and finally ascended to heaven in order to secure it for you and me. If there is anything under heaven that ought to command our reverence, our holy reverence, our reverence beyond anything else in the world, it surely is the subject of the baptism of the Holy Ghost.

My! Sometimes my soul is jarred when I hear people flippantly say, "Have you got your baptism?" Supposing that Jesus was on the cross and we were privileged tonight to look into His face at this hour, I wonder what the feeling of our soul would be? Supposing we were to follow tonight behind the weeping company that bore His dead body and laid it in the tomb, what would our feelings be? Supposing we were to meet Him in the garden, as Mary did, in the glory of His resurrection, or supposing that God in His goodness would let us look

---

[1] Exodus 3:5.

into that scene of scenes at the throne of God, when the heavens lifted up their gates, and the Lord of Glory came in. Oh, if we could, beloved, we would have a better comprehension of the baptism of the Holy Ghost.

I love that dear old word "Ghost." The Anglo-Saxon is "Ghest" — a spiritual guest, heavenly visitor, spiritual presence, the Angel One. And the Angel One that comes to you and me comes right out of the heart of the eternal God, breathed through the soul of Jesus Christ! When it came upon a man originally, as it did upon the hundred and twenty at Jerusalem, no one went around saying, "Brother, have you got your baptism?" They were walking with their shoes off, with uncovered heads and uncovered hearts before the eternal God!

I believe that the first essential in a real Holy Ghost church and a real Holy Ghost work is to begin to surround the baptism of the Holy Ghost with that due reverence of God with which an experience so sacred and that cost such an awful price should be surrounded.

A Lesson on Reverence

I sat one day on a kopje in South Africa in company with a lady, Mrs. Dockrall, a beautiful woman of God, baptized in the Holy Ghost. As we sat together on the rocks, meditating and praying, the rest of the company being a little distance away, I observed the Spirit falling upon her powerfully, until she was submerged in the Spirit. Then she began to deliver a message first in tongues, later giving the interpretation in English, and I listened to the most wonderful lecture on the subject of reverence I have ever heard in all my life.

Afterward I said to her, "Tell me what you can about the experience through which you have just passed."

She had never been in Europe, but she said, "I was carried by the Spirit somewhere in Europe. I approached a great cathedral." And she went on to describe its architecture. She said, "As I approached the door, I was greeted by an English priest who led me down the aisle to the altar, and I knelt. A white cloud began to settle down, and presently out of the cloud came the face and form of Jesus Christ. The priest was standing in the rostrum and began to speak, but I could see by the action of the Spirit that the words he spoke were simply words that were being spoken by the Lord." It has always been one of the sorrows of my life that I did not have a stenographer who could have taken that wonderful message on reverence for the works of God.

I have been reading one of the most beautiful books I have ever read. It is written by an English lady, Mrs. Parker, a missionary to India, and describes the life and teaching and mission of one, Sadhu Sundar Singh, an Indian Sadhu. A Sadhu is a *holy man,* who renounces the world absolutely, utterly, never marries, never takes part in any of the affairs of the world, separates himself to religious life, practices meditation on God and the spiritual life. Sundar Singh, when he found the Lord Jesus Christ, conceived the idea of becoming a Christian Sadhu. They walked from place to place. They wore no shoes, they slept on the ground, but their life is utterly abandoned to God.

One of the statements of Mrs. Parker, who wrote of Sundar Singh, was to this effect, "As you approach his presence, an awe comes over the soul. It seems as if you are again in the presence of the original Nazarene." Let us approach the Holy of Holies with a similar awe. Let us be reverential in the presence of the glorified One.

The baptism of the Holy Ghost is peculiar to the Lord Jesus Christ. "I indeed," said John,

> Baptize you with water unto repentance: but...he shall baptize you with the Holy Ghost, and with fire: whose fan is in his hand, and he will thoroughly purge his floor, and gather his wheat into the garner; but he will burn up the chaff with unquenchable fire.[2]

Jesus Christ, the Glorified, must lay His hands on you and on me and bestow upon us all His own nature, the outflow of God, the substance of His soul, the quality of His mind, the very being of God Himself. "Know ye not that your body is the temple of the Holy Ghost which is in you?"[3] A temple of God, a house of God in which God lives!

---

[2] Matthew 3:11-12.

[3] 1 Corinthians 6:19.

A HABITATION OF GOD

Sometimes I have tried to get it clear before my soul that God *lives in me*. I have tried to note the incoming influence and power of that pure, sweet, living Spirit of the Eternal God. I have tried to realize His presence in my spirit, in my soul, in my hands, in my feet, in my person and being — a habitation of God, a habitation of God! God equipping the soul to minister Himself, God, to the world. God equipping the soul of man that he may live forever in harmony of mind with God. God furnishing to the soul of man the *power* of His personality, by which man is made as God. For all the godlike qualities of your heart is due to the fact that God by the Spirit dwells in you. What is it that you look for in another? It is God. You look into the eyes of another to see God. If you fail to see God in the other life, your heart is troubled. You were looking for God.

I am not interested in the form or the figure or the name of an individual. I am interested in seeing God. Is God there? Is God in that man? Is God in that woman? Is it God that speaks? Is it God that moves? Are you seeing God?

YOU MAY HAVE GOD

The baptism of the Holy Ghost was the *incoming* of God in personality in order that the man, through this force, might be moved by God. God lives in him, God speaks through him, God is the impulse of his soul, God has His dwelling place in him.

You may have God. That is the wonder of the baptism of the Holy Ghost. It is not a work of grace; it is God *possessing* you. Oh, your heart may have been as sinful as the heart of man ever was sinful. But Christ comes to your soul. That spirit of darkness that possessed you goes and in its stead, a new Spirit comes in, the Spirit of Christ. You have become a new creature, a saved man, a God-filled man.

A TRANSFORMATION

Sin manifests itself in three ways: in thought, in act, in nature. Salvation is a complete transformation. God takes possession of man, changes his thoughts, in consequence his acts change, his nature is new. A Christian is not a reformed man. A Christian is a man renewed, remade by the Spirit of God. A Christian is a man indwelt by God — the house of God, the tabernacle of the Most High! Man, indwelt by God, becomes the hands and the heart and the feet and the mind of Jesus Christ. God descends into man; man ascends into God! That is the purpose and power of the baptism in the Holy Ghost. A soul is saved. How does Jesus reach them? Through your hands, through your heart, through your faith. When God baptized you in the Holy Ghost, He gives you the biggest gift that heaven or earth ever possessed. He gave you *Himself!* He joins you by the one Spirit to Himself forever.

THE REQUIREMENT

The requirement is a surrendered heart, a surrendered mind, a surrendered life. From the day that a man becomes a child of God, baptized in the Holy Ghost, it was God's intention through Jesus Christ that man should be a revelation of Jesus.

If you were looking to know whether a man was baptized in the Holy Ghost or not, what would you look for? You would look for God in him. You would look for a revelation of the personality of God. God moving in him, God speaking in him, God speaking through him, God using his hands, God using his feet — a mind in harmony with God, a soul in touch with heaven, a spirit united and unified with and in Jesus Christ.

GOD'S GREAT PURPOSE NOT COMPREHENDED

It is not in my heart to discourage any man or to make you disbelieve for one minute in the trueness of your own baptism in the Holy Ghost. I believe that God, by the Spirit, has baptized many in the Holy Ghost. Hundreds and hundreds of people have been baptized in the Holy Ghost during the life of this church in the last six years. But beloved, we have not comprehended the greatness of God's intent — not that we have not received the Spirit, but our lives have not been sufficiently surrendered to God. We must keep on ascending right to the throne, right into the heart of God, right into the soul of the Glorified.

THE HOLY GHOST NOT A GIFT OF POWER BUT OF GOD HIMSELF

The common teaching that my heart these days is endeavoring to combat is that God comes to present the individual with a gift of power, and the individual is then supposed to go out and manifest some certain characteristic of power. No! God comes to present you with *Himself.* "Ye shall receive power, *after* that the *Holy Ghost* is come upon you."[4]

Jesus went to heaven in order that the very treasury of the heart of the eternal God might be unlocked for your benefit and that out of the very soul of the eternal God, the streams of His life and nature would possess you from the crown of your head to the sole of your feet and that there would be just as much of the eternal God in your toenails and in your brain as each are capable of containing. In other words, from the very soles of your feet to the last hair on the top of your head, every cell of your being would be a residence of the Spirit of the living God. Man is made alive by God and with God by the Spirit. And in the truest sense, man is the dwelling place of God, the house of God, the tabernacle of the Most High.

Listen! "The words that I speak unto you I speak not of myself: but the Father that *dwelleth* in me." "...but the Father that dwelleth in me."[5] Where did the eternal Father dwell in Jesus Christ? Why, in every part of His being, within and without in the spirit of Him, in the soul of Him, in the brain of Him, in the body of Him, in the blood of Him, in the bones of Him! Every single, solitary cell of His structure was the dwelling place of God, *of God, of God!*

When you look for God you do not look on the surface. You look within. When you discern a man to see whether God is in him, you look into the spirit of him, into the soul of him, into the depth of him, and there you see God.

---

[4] Acts 1:8, emphasis Lake's.

[5] John 14:10.

How trifling are the controversies that surround the baptism of the Holy Ghost. Men are debating such trifling issues. For instance, does a man speak in tongues or does he not? Do you think for a moment that I am discounting the value of tongues? I am not. But beloved, I will tell you what my heart is straining for. Down there at Jerusalem they not only spoke in tongues, but they spoke the *languages of the nations.*[6]

If it was possible for old Peter and old Paul or for the Jewish nation, then it is possible to every last one. Not to speak in tongues alone, as we ordinarily understand that phrase, but to speak because God dwells in you and speaks to whomsoever He will in whatever language He desires. And if our present experience in tongues is not satisfying, God bless you, go on into languages, as God meant that you should. Dear ones, I feel the need of that, and I feel it away down in my heart to a depth that hurts. I lived in South Africa for a number of years, where it is commonly said that there are a hundred thousand tribes of native people. Every last one of the hundred thousand speaks a different dialect. These tribes number sometimes as low as ten thousand people and sometimes as high as hundreds of thousands, even millions of people.

Supposing we were going to undertake to evangelize Africa rapidly. It would be necessary to have a hundred thousand different missionaries and have them all at one time master one particular language, for there are a hundred thousand of them. No sir! I believe before high heaven that when the Spirit of the eternal God is poured out upon all flesh, that out of the real Christian body will arise a hundred thousand men and women in Africa that will speak in the language of every separate tribe by the power of God.

The unknown tongue of the Spirit was to teach you of God, to be a faith-builder in your soul, to take you out into God's big, practical endeavor to save the world. And that is the reason, dear ones, that I bring this issue to your soul tonight. In the matter of the baptism of the Holy Ghost we are in a state of the merest infancy of understanding, the merest infancy of divine control, the merest infancy in ability to assimilate our environment, including languages.

---

[6] See Acts 2:6-11.

When we go to a school we see classes arranged for every grade. I was talking to a young schoolteacher, who teaches out in the country in a little public school. I said, "How many children have you in your school?"

She replied, "Fifteen."

I asked, "How many grades have you?"

She said, "Eight grades." Fifteen scholars divided into eight grades.

The Christian Church is God's big school. What student in the eighth grade would think of saying to the child learning its A B C's: "You haven't anything. Why don't you have the eighth grade understanding?" Well, in due time he will have it. That is the reason the student does not say it. It is because he knows the child will have it. One day that boy will understand just the same as he does. A weak Christianity always wants to drop to the imperfect and adjust itself to the popular mind. But real Christianity ever seeks to be made perfect in God, both in character and gifts.

MY PERSONAL EXPERIENCE

Dear ones, I want to repeat to you tonight a little of my own personal history on the subject of the baptism of the Spirit, for I know it will clarify your soul.

MY CONVERSION

I knelt under a tree when about sixteen years of age, in repentance and prayer, and God came into my soul. I was saved from my sins and from that day I knew Jesus Christ as a living Savior. There never was a single moment of question about the reality of His incoming into my life as a Savior, for He saved me from my sins. My friend said, "You are baptized in the Holy Ghost."

SANCTIFIED

Sometime later, I think when I was yet under twenty or thereabouts, I met a Christian farmer, Melvin Pratt, who sat down on his plow handles and taught me the subject of sanctification, and God let me enter into that experience. My friends said, "Now surely you are baptized in the Holy Ghost."

Later in my life I came under the ministry of George B. Watson, of the Christian & Missionary Alliance, who taught with more clearness and better distinction between the baptism of the Holy Ghost and sanctification, and I entered into a richer life and a better experience. A beautiful anointing of the Spirit was upon my life.

MINISTRY OF HEALING

Then the ministry of healing was opened to me, and I ministered for ten years in the power of God. Hundreds and hundreds of people were healed by the power of God during this ten years, and I could feel the conscious flow of the Holy Spirit through my soul and my hands.

But at the end of that year, I believe I was the hungriest man for God that ever lived. There was such a hunger for God that as I left my offices in Chicago and walked down the street, my soul would break out, and I would cry, "Oh God!" I have had people stop and look at me in wonder. It was the yearning passion of my soul, asking for God in a greater measure than I then knew. But my friends would say, "Mr. Lake, you have a beautiful baptism in the Holy Ghost." Yes, it was nice as far as it went, but it was not answering the cry of my heart. I was growing up into a large understanding of God and my own soul's need. My soul was demanding a greater entrance into God, His love, presence, and power.

MY BAPTISM IN THE HOLY GHOST

And then one day an old man strolled into my office, sat down, and in the next half hour he revealed more of the knowledge of God to my soul than I had ever known before. And when he passed out I said, "God bless that old gray head. That man knows more of God than any man I ever met. By the grace of God, if that is what the baptism of the Holy Ghost with tongues does, I am going to possess it." Oh, the wonder of God that was then revealed to my heart!

I went into fasting and prayer and waiting on God for nine months. And one day, the glory of God in a new manifestation and a new incoming came to my life. And when the phenomena had passed, and the glory of it remained in my soul, I found that my life began to manifest in the varied range of the gifts of the Spirit, and I spoke in tongues by the power of God, and God flowed through me with a new force. Healings were of a more powerful order. Oh, God lived in me, God manifested in me, God spoke through me. My spirit was deified, and I had a new comprehension of God's will, new discernment of spirit, new revelation of God in me.

For nine months everything that I looked at framed itself into poetic verse. I could not look at the trees without it framing itself into a glory poem of praise. I preached to audiences of thousands night after night and day after day. People came from all over the world to study me. They could not understand. Everything I said was a stream of poetry. It rolled from my soul in that form. My spirit had become a fountain of poetic truth.

Then a new wonder was manifested. My nature became so sensitized that I could lay my hands on any man or woman and tell what organ was diseased and to what extent and all about it. I tested it. I went to hospitals where physicians could not diagnose a case, touched a patient, and instantly I knew the organ that was diseased, its extent and condition and locations. And one day it passed away. A child gets to playing with a toy and his joy is so wonderful he sometimes forgets to eat.

Oh say, don't you remember when you were first baptized in the Holy Ghost and you first spoke in tongues, how you bubbled and babbled? It was so wonderful, so amazing. We just wanted to be babies and go on bubbling and exhilarating. And now we are wondering what is the matter. The effervescence seems to have passed away. My! It is a good thing that it did. God is letting your soul down, beloved, into the bedrock. Right down where your mind is not occupied anymore with the manifestation of God. God is trying to get your mind occupied with Himself. God has come into you, now He is drawing you into Himself.

Will you speak in tongues when you are baptized in the Holy Ghost? Yes, you will, but you will do an awful lot more than that, bless God, an awful lot more than that! You will speak with the soul of Jesus Christ. You will feel with the heart of the Son of God. Your heart will beat with a heavenly desire to bless the world, because it is the pulse of Jesus that is throbbing in your soul. And I do not believe there will be a bit of inclination in your heart to turn around another child of God and say, "You are not in my class. I am baptized with the Holy Ghost." That is as foreign to the Spirit of the Son of God as night is from day. Beloved, if you are baptized in the Holy Ghost, there will be a tenderness in your soul so deep that you will never crush the aspiration of another by a single suggestion, but your soul will throb and beat and pulse in love, and your heart will be under that one to lift it up to God and push it out as far into the glory as your faith can send it.

I want to talk with the utmost frankness and say to you that tongues have been to me the making of my ministry. It is that peculiar communication with God when God reveals to my soul the truth I utter to you day by day in my ministry. But that time of communication with me is mostly in the night. Many a time I climb out of bed, take my pencil and pad and jot down the beautiful things of God, the wonderful things of God, that He talks out in my spirit and reveals to my heart.

Many Christians do not understand the significance of tongues any more than the other man understands the experience of your soul when you are saved from sin. It has taken place in you. It is in your heart, it is in your mind, it is in your being. The man who tries to make you doubt the reality of your touch with God when He saved you out of your sin is foolish. It is established *in* you. The old Methodists could not explain the experience, but they said, "It is better felt than told." They knew it by internal knowledge. So it is in a real baptism of the Holy Ghost. So it is in prophecy. So it is in healing. So it is in tongues. Do not throw away what you have. Go on to perfection.

THE LANGUAGE OF THE SPIRIT

The spirit of man has a voice. Do you get that? The spirit of man has a voice. The action of God in your spirit causes your spirit to speak by its voice. In order to make it intelligent to your understanding, it has to be repeated in the language that your brain knows. Why? Because there is a language common to the spirit of man and it is not English and it is not German and it is not French and it is not Italian or any other of the languages of earth. It is a language of the spirit of man. And, oh, what a joy it was when that pent-up, bursting, struggling spirit of yours found its voice and "spake in tongues."

Many a time I have talked to others in the Spirit, by the Spirit, through the medium of tongues and knew everything that was said to me, but I did not know it with this ear. It was not the sound of their words. It was that undefinable something that made it intelligent. Spirit speaks to spirit, just as mouth speaks to mouth or as man speaks to man. Your spirit speaks to God. God is Spirit. He answers back. Bless God. And I believe with all my heart that is what Paul had in mind when he talked about the "unknown" tongue. The unknown tongues, that medium of internal revelation of God to you. The common language of the spirit of man, by which God communicates with your spirit.

INTERNAL REVELATION MADE INTELLIGENT BY INTERPRETATION

But if you want to make that medium of internal revelation of God intelligent to other folks, then it must be translated into the language that they know. That is the reason the apostle says, "Let him that speaketh in an unknown tongue pray that he may interpret,"[7] that the church may receive edifying. Paul says, *"In the church* I had rather speak five words with my understanding, that by my voice I might teach others also, than ten thousand words in an unknown tongue."[8] Your revelation from God is given to you in tongues, but you give it forth in the language the people understand.

Beloved, settle it. It is one of the divine mediums and methods of communication between your spirit and God's. And as long as you live, when you talk about *tongues,* speak with reverence, for it is God. When you talk about healing, speak with reverence, for it is God. When you talk about prophecy, remember, it is God.

---

[7] 1 Corinthians 14:13.

[8] 1 Corinthians 14:19.

AN ILLUSTRATION

A German woman came to the healing rooms one day and a brother prayed for her. She had been a schoolteacher, but had to give up her profession because of her eyesight. She came back some weeks later, after having been alone for three weeks. She had never been in a religious service in her life where they speak in tongues and had not knowledge of the Scriptures on that line. She came back to me with a volume of written material that God had given her. For when she had been prayed for to receive healing, the Spirit of God came upon her and she was baptized in the Holy Ghost. And now God had commenced to reveal Himself to her, teach her of His Word and of His will, until she filled a volume with written material of her conversations with God. She communed with God in tongues, her spirit speaking to God, but when she came to me I received it in English.

The man that sits alongside of you cannot understand that. He never talked to God. He does not understand anything about getting up in the middle of the night to write down what God has said to him. Well, he needs something else to convince him that there is a God. "Tongues are for a sign, *not* to them that believe, but to them that believe not."[9] But prophecy, the outspeaking for God, is for all. Therefore, Paul does not want them to crush a man who is speaking in tongues, but to keep their hands off and stand back. Leave him alone with God. Let him travel away out in His love and power and come back with messages in his soul, but he must not monopolize the time of hundreds of people in the church with a private communication of God to his soul. But when he has completed his interview with God, he gives forth his knowledge as interpretation or prophecy.

There have been so many controversies over the various gifts of the Spirit, as they appeared one after another. Twenty-five or thirty years ago when we began in the ministry of healing, we had to fight to keep from being submerged by our opposing brethren in Jesus Christ, who thought you were insane because you suggested that the Lord Jesus Christ could still heal. In the state of Michigan I had to go into the

---

[9] 1 Corinthians 14:22, emphasis Lake's.

courts to keep some of my friends out of the insane asylum, because they believed God could heal without taking pills or some other material stuff. (To popularize healing, some have compromised on the use of medicines, but the *real Christian still* trusts God alone.)

It was because they did not understand the eternal and invisible nature of God. They had no idea God could be ministered through a man's hands and soul, fill a sick man's body, take possession of, and make him whole. The world has had to learn this. It is a science far in advance of so-called material or physical science.

Then that marvelous wave of God came over the country from 1900 to 1906 when hundreds of thousands of people were baptized in the Holy Ghost and spoke in tongues. But listen! Old John Alexander Dowie, riding on the wave of that wonderful manifestation of healing power, wanted to build a church and stamp it with healing only, and his church practically did that and died. Other churches branded theirs with holiness only and died. Others with an anointing of the Holy Ghost called "baptism," and they died in power also. Later on, we wanted to build a great structure and stamp it with *tongues*. After awhile the tongues got dry. Somehow the glory and the glow had gone out of them. They became rattly and did not sound right.

What was the matter? Nothing wrong with the experience. God had not departed from the life, but was hidden from our view. We were absorbed in phenomena of God and not in God Himself. Now we must go on.

Now beloved, I can see as my spirit discerns the future and reaches out to touch the heart of mankind and the desire of God that there is coming from heaven a new manifestation of the Holy Ghost in power and that new manifestation will be in sweetness, in love, in tenderness, in the power of the Spirit, beyond anything your heart or mine ever saw. The very lightning of God will flash through men's souls. The sons of God will meet the sons of darkness and prevail. Jesus Christ will destroy antichrist.

A DELUGE OF THE SPIRIT

In 1908, I preached at Pretoria, South Africa, when one night God came over my life in such power, in such streams of liquid glory and power, that it flowed consciously off my hands like streams of electricity. I would point my finger at a man and that stream would strike him. When a man interrupted the meeting, I would point my finger at him and say, "Sit down!" He fell as if struck and lay for three hours. When he became normal they asked him what happened, and he said, "Something struck me that went straight through me. I thought I was shot."

At two o'clock in the morning I ministered to sixty-five sick who were present, and the streams of God that were pouring through my hands were so powerful the people would fall as though they were hit. I was troubled because they fell with such violence. And the Spirit said, "You do not need to put your hands on them. Keep your hands a distance away." And when I held my hands a foot from their heads they would crumple and fall in a heap on the floor. They were healed almost every one.

That was the outward manifestation. That was what the people saw. But beloved, something transpired in my heart that made my soul like the soul of Jesus Christ. Oh, there was such a tenderness, a new-born tenderness of God that was so wonderful that my heart reached out and cried and wept over men in sin. I could gather them in my arms and love them, and Jesus Christ flowed out of me and delivered them. Drunkards were saved and healed as they stood transfixed looking at me.

During that period men would walk down the aisle, and when they came within ten feet of me, I have seen them fall prostrate, one on top of the other. A preacher who had sinned, as he looked at me, fell prostrate, was saved, baptized in the Holy Ghost under my own eyes, as I preached or prayed.

I continued in the ministry of healing until I saw hundreds of thousands healed. At last I became tired. I went on healing people day after day, as though I were a machine. And all the time my heart kept asking, "Oh God, let me know Yourself better. I want You, my heart wants *You*, God." Seeing men saved and healed and baptized in the Holy Ghost did not satisfy my growing soul. It was crying for a greater consciousness of God, the withinness of me was yearning for Christ's own life and love. After awhile my soul reached the place where I said, "If I cannot get God into my soul to satisfy the soul of me, all the rest of this is empty." I had lost interest in it, but I put my hands on the sick and they continued to be healed by the power of God.

I will never forget Spokane, Washington, for during the first six months I was there, God satisfied the cry of my heart, and God came in and my mind opened and my spirit understood afresh, and I was able to tell of God and talk out the heart of me like I never had been able to before. God reached a new depth in my spirit and revealed new possibilities in God. So beloved, you pray through. Pray through for this church, pray through for this work. Oh, God will come! God will come with more tongues than you have ever heard. God will come with more power than your eyes ever beheld. God will come with waves of heavenly love and sweetness, and blessed God, your heart will be satisfied in Him.

Will a man speak in tongues when he is baptized in the Holy Ghost? Yes, he will, and he will heal the sick when he is baptized, and he will glorify God out of the spirit of him with praises more delightful and heavenly than you ever heard. He will have a majestic bearing. He will look like the Lord Jesus Christ, and you will be like Him. Blessed be God.

The greatest manifestation of the Holy Ghost-baptized life ever given to the world was not in the preaching of the apostles; it was not in the wonderful manifestation of God that took place at their hands. It was in the *unselfishness* manifested by the Church. Think of it! Three thousand Holy Ghost-baptized Christians in Jerusalem from the Day of Pentecost onward, who love their neighbor's children as much as their own, who were so anxious for fear their brethren did not have enough to eat that they sold their estates and brought the money and laid it at the apostle's feet. They said, "Distribute it, carry the glow and the fire and the wonder of this divine salvation to the whole world."[10] That showed what God had wrought in their hearts. Oh, I wish we could arrive at that place, where this church was baptized in that degree of unselfishness.

---

[10] See Acts 2:44-45.

That would be a greater manifestation than healing, greater than conversion, greater than baptism in the Holy Ghost, greater than tongues. It would be a manifestation of the *love* of First Corinthians 13 that so many preach about and do not possess. When a man sells his all for God and distributes it for the kingdom's good, it will speak louder of love than the evangelists who harp about love and oppose tongues and the other gifts of the Spirit.

That was the same Holy Ghost that came upon them and caused them to speak in tongues. No more grabbing for themselves. No more bantering for the biggest salary, no more juggling to put themselves and their friends in the most influential positions. All the old characteristics were gone. They were truly loved. Why their heart was like the heart of Jesus, their soul was like the soul of God, they loved as God loved, they loved the world, they loved sinners so, that they gave their all to save them.

Do you want Him? You can have Him. Oh, He will come and fill your soul. Then the Holy Ghost will take possession of your life. He will reveal the wonder of heaven and the glory of God, and the richness and purity of His holiness, and make you sweet and godlike forever.

Thou are not far away, Oh God. Our souls are enveloped in the eternal God. We feel thee round about us. We feel Thy precious, loving arm and the beating of Thy heart and the pulsing of Thy heavenly soul, and we are asking Thee, my God, that the truth of the Eternal shall be breathed into us forever, until all our nature is submerged in God, buried in God, infilled with God, revealing God.

BAPTISM OF THE HOLY GHOST

Sermon 2 of 3

The baptism of the Holy Ghost is a most difficult subject to discuss with any degree of intelligence, for though we may not care to admit it, the fact remains that the density of ignorance among the people and the ministry on this subject is appalling. To view this subject with any degree of intelligence we must view it from the standpoint of progressive revelation. Like Christian baptism, the operation of the Holy Ghost must be seen (comprehended) in its various stages of revelation. Otherwise, we shall be unable to distinguish between the operations of the Spirit in the Old Testament dispensation and the baptism of the Holy Ghost in the New Testament.

As we approach even the threshold of this subject, it seems as if the Spirit of God comes close to us. A certain awe of God comes over the soul. And it is my earnest wish that no levity, satire, or sarcasm be permitted to enter into this discussion. Such things would be grievous to the tender Spirit of God.

In the beginning of this revelation, after the deluge, it seems as if God was approaching man from a great distance, so far had sin removed man from his original union with God at the time of his creation. God seems to reveal Himself to man as rapidly as man, by progressive stages of development, is prepared to receive the revelation. Consequently, we see that the baptism was a further revelation of God's purpose in purifying the heart from sin than was the original ceremony of circumcision. So the baptism of the Holy Ghost is a greater, more perfect revelation of God than was the manifestation of the Spirit in the Patriarchal or Mosaic dispensations.

Three distinct dispensations of God are clearly seen, each with an ever-deepening manifestation of God to man. A preceding dispensation of God never destroys a foregoing, richer revelation of God. This is manifestly seen in looking at the Patriarchal, Mosaic, and Christian dispensations.

In the Patriarchal dispensation we see God appearing to man at long intervals. Abraham furnishes the best example, for to him God appeared at long intervals of twenty and forty years apart, so with the other Patriarchs.

Under the Mosaic dispensation there is a deeper and clearer manifestation of God. God was ever present in the pillar of cloud and the pillar of fire. He was present also in the tabernacle where the Shekinah glory overshadowed the mercy seat. This is a continuous abiding revelation of God. It was God *with man* not *to man* as was the Patriarchal dispensation. God was leading, guiding, directing, forgiving, sanctifying, abiding with man.

But the revelation of God under the Christian dispensation is a much deeper and truer revelation of God than this. It is God *in man*. It is the actual incoming of the Spirit of God to live in man. This brings us to where we can see the purpose of God in revealing Himself to man by progressive stages of revelation.

Man, by progressive stages through repentance and faith, is purified — not alone forgiven for his transgressions, but cleansed from the nature of sin within that causes him to transgress. This cleansing from inbred sin, the nature of sin, the carnal mind, the old man, etc., is the actual taking out of our breast the desire for sin, and all correspondence with sin in us is severed. The carnal life is laid a sacrifice on the altar of Christ in glad surrender by us. This inner heart cleansing that John and the disciples of Christ demanded is the work of the Holy Spirit by the blood and is necessary if maturity in Christ is to be achieved. A holy God must have a holy dwelling place.

Oh wondrous salvation, wondrous Christ, wondrous atonement! Man born in sin, shapen in iniquity, forgiven, cleansed, purified outside and inside by the blood of Jesus and made the habitation (dwelling place) of God. It was that man once created in the likeness of God should again become the dwelling place of God. That is what the atoning blood of Christ provided.

> Christ hath redeemed us from the curse of the law, being made a curse for us: for it is written, Cursed is every one that hangeth on a tree: That the blessing of Abraham

might come on the Gentiles through Jesus Christ; that we might receive the promise of the Spirit through faith.

— Galatians 3:13-14

This reveals to us God's purpose, by the blood of Jesus Christ, for us now to become the habitation of God. "In whom ye also are builded together for an habitation of God through the Spirit" (Ephesians 2:22). Again in First Corinthians 6:19, we see Paul in astonishment saying, "What? know ye not that your body is the temple of the Holy Ghost?" Let us now see where we are at and we will better understand how to go on.

The Holy Ghost is the Spirit of God. His purpose is to dwell in man after man's perfect cleansing from sin through the blood of Jesus Christ. His coming was definite — just as definite as was the advent of Jesus. When Jesus was born, His birth was proclaimed by an angel voice and chanted by a multitude of the heavenly host praising God. (See Luke 2:9,13-14.)

Equally so was the Holy Spirit's advent attested by His bodily form as a dove (Luke 3:22) and by His sound from heaven, as of a rushing mighty wind and by the cloven tongues of fire upon each of them (Acts 2:2-3). Heavenly dove, tempest roar, and tongues of fire crowning the hundred and twenty were as convincing as the guiding star and midnight shout of angel hosts. The coming of the Holy Ghost upon the hundred and twenty is found in Acts 2.

At the Last Supper when Jesus addressed the disciples, He said to them:

> Nevertheless I tell you the truth; it is expedient for you that I go away: for if I go not away, the Comforter will not come unto you; but if I depart, I will send him unto you. And when he is come, he will reprove the world of sin, and of righteousness, and of judgment.

— John 16:7-8

As the disciples were together at Jerusalem after the resurrection when the two who had walked with Him to Emmaus were conversing with the eleven disciples, Jesus Himself stood in their midst. He said unto them, "Peace be unto you."[1] They were affrighted, believing they had seen a spirit. Jesus addresses them and said unto them:

> And, behold, I send the promise of my Father upon you: but tarry ye in the city of Jerusalem, until ye be endued with power from on high.
>
> — Luke 24:49

Then in Acts 1 we find that the one hundred and twenty tarried in prayer in the upper room ten days. Thus, between the crucifixion of Jesus and Pentecost is fifty-three days.

There was a crucifixion day. It was necessary. And now we, the children of God, must be crucified with Christ and freed from sin, our old man nailed to the cross. We die to sin — a real act, a genuine experience; it's done. So we are made partakers of Christ's death. But there was a resurrection day. He arose as a living Christ, not a dead one. He lives. He lives. And by our resurrection with Him into our new life, we leave the old sin life and the old man buried in baptism (Romans 6) and are made partakers of His new resurrection life. The life of power, the exercise of the power of God, is made possible to us by Jesus, having elevated us into His own resurrection life by actual spiritual experience.

Then comes His ascension — just as necessary as the crucifixion or the resurrection. Jesus ascends to heaven and sits triumphant at the right hand of the Father. And according to His promise, He sent upon us the Holy Ghost. This experience is personal and dispensational. The Holy Ghost descends upon us, entering into us. For the baptism of the Holy Ghost is the Holy God, the Spirit of Jesus, taking possession of our personality, living in us, moving us, controlling us. We become partakers of His glorified life, the life of Christ in glory. So it was with the hundred and twenty (see Acts 2:2-4).

> And suddenly there came a sound from heaven as of a rushing mighty wind.

(Suppose we heard it now. What would this audience think?)

---

[1] Luke 24:36.

> And it filled all the house where they were sitting. And there appeared unto them cloven tongues like as of fire, and it sat upon each of them. And they were all filled with the Holy Ghost, and began to speak with other tongues, as the Spirit gave them utterance.

It was the Spirit that spoke in other tongues. What Spirit? The Holy Ghost who had come into them, who controlled them, who spoke through them. Listen! Speaking in tongues is the voice of God. Do you hear God's voice? They spake as the Spirit gave them utterance.

Now we have advanced to where we can understand God's manifestations. Not God witnessing to man, not God with man, but God in man. They spake as the Spirit gave them utterance. (Editor's note: At this point the Spirit of God fell on Brother Lake, causing him to speak in tongues in an unknown language. The audience was asked to bow their heads in silent prayer for the interpretation of the words spoken in the tongues. As they prayed the interpretation was given as follows.)

> *Christ is at once the spotless descent of God into man and the sinless ascent of man into God. And the Holy Spirit is the agent by which it is accomplished.*

He is the Christ, the Son of God. His atonement is a real atonement. It changes from all sin. Man again becomes the dwelling place of God.

Let us now see one of the most miraculous chapters in all the Word of God, Acts 10. A man, Cornelius, is praying. He is a Gentile centurion. An angel appears to him. The angel speaks. The angel says to send to Joppa for Peter. Peter is a Jew, and he is supposed to go into the home of a Gentile. He has not learned that salvation is for the Gentiles. God has to teach him. How does God do it?

Peter goes up on the housetop to pray and as he prays, he is in a trance. Think of it — a trance. He falls in a trance. Suppose I was to fall on the floor in a trance. Nine-tenths of this audience would be frightened to death. They would instantly declare that my opponent had hypnotized me. Why? Because of the ignorance among men of how the Spirit of God operates. But listen. Listen! As he lays on the roof in a trance, he sees a vision — a sheet let down from heaven caught by the four corners, full of all manner of beasts and creeping things. And a voice — what voice? — the Lord's voice, said, "Rise Peter, kill and eat it."

But Peter said, "Not so, Lord. I have never eaten anything common or unclean."

But the voice said, "What I have cleansed that call thou not common." Peter obeyed. He went with the messengers. Now see the result. As he spake the Word, the Holy Ghost fell on all of them that heard the Word. And they of the circumcision which believed were astonished, as many as came with Peter, because that on the Gentiles also was poured out the Holy Ghost.

How did they know? "They heard them speak with tongues and magnify God." Then answereth Peter, "Can any man forbid water that these should not be baptized which have received the Holy Ghost as well as we?" And so it all ended in a glorious baptismal service in water of all who had been baptized in the Holy Ghost.

In Acts 22:12, Paul tells of Ananias coming to see him, but how did Ananias know Peter was there? (See Acts 9:10-19.)

> And there was a certain disciple at Damascus, named Ananias; and to him the Lord said in a vision.... go into the street called Straight, and enquire in the house of Judas for one called Saul, of Tarsus.

Now let us see that as we would see it today. The Lord said, "Ananias, go down into Straight Street to the house of Judas and ask for a man named Saul of Tarsus, for behold he prayest." And now the Lord tells Ananias what Saul had seen (Acts 9:12):

> And hath seen in a vision a man named Ananias coming in, and putting his hands on him, that he might receive his sight.

Here Ananias talks with the Lord. Do you know anything of such communion or talks with God? If not, get the baptism of the Holy Ghost like the early Christians and their knowledge and experiences afterward can be yours, and you will see as we do the operation of the Lord upon both saint and sinner by the Holy Ghost. Men say to us, "Where do you men get your insight into the Word?" We get it just where Paul and Peter got it, from God, by the Holy Ghost. (See Galatians 1:11-12.)

Beloved, read God's Word on your knees. Ask God, by His Spirit, to open it to your understanding. Read the Word with an open heart. It is a lamp unto our feet, a light unto our path.[2]

Ananias went as the Lord directed him and found Paul. And Paul was healed of his blindness and was baptized in the Holy Ghost and was also baptized in water and spoke in tongues "more than ye all" (1 Corinthians 14:18).

Now see again Acts 22:14. Ananias is speaking to Paul, and he said,

> The God of our fathers hath chosen thee, that thou shouldest *know* his will, and see that Just One, and shouldest hear the voice of his mouth. For thou shalt be his witness unto all men of what thou hast *seen* and *heard*.

Say, what about the people who say, "Don't tell these things to anyone"?

> And now why tarriest thou? arise, and be baptised, and wash away thy sins, calling upon the name of the Lord.[3]

You see, as with Peter at Cornelius' house, all this work of the Spirit ended in salvation and baptism.

Now God, through Ananias, promised Paul that he should know "his will and see that Just One, and shouldest hear the voice of his mouth" (Acts 22:14). When did that come to pass? Three years after, when Paul returned to Jerusalem. "Then after three years I went up to Jerusalem" (Galatians 1:18).

> And it came to pass, that, when I was come again to Jerusalem, even while I prayed in the temple, I was in a trance.
>
> — Acts 22:17

Think of it — the intellectual, wonderful Paul, the master theologian of the ages, the orator of orators, the logician of logicians in a trance. Bless God for that trance. It was the fulfillment of what Ananias had said to him three years before.

---

[2] See Psalm 119:105.

[3] Acts 22:14-16.

> And saw him (Jesus) saying unto me, Make haste, and
> get thee quickly out of Jerusalem: for they will not
> receive thy testimony concerning me.[4]

Now what is a trance? A trance is the Spirit taking predominance over the mind and body and for the time being, the control of the individual is by the Spirit, but our ignorance of the operations of God is such that even ministers of religion have been known to say it is the devil.

Let us see where Paul got his commission to preach and instructions about what he was to preach and what his condition and attitude were when Jesus gave him his commission. (See Acts 26:16-18.) He was lying on the road on his way to Damascus. Now if we were to see someone lying on the road talking to an invisible somebody, no doubt in our ignorance we would send for an ambulance or for the police. But this is where the glorified Christ spoke to Paul and gave him definite instructions about what he should preach, and the purpose of his preaching was to be the salvation, not the entertainment, of others.

> But rise, and stand upon thy feet: for I (Jesus) have
> appeared unto thee for this purpose, to make thee a minis-
> ter and a witness both of these things which thou hast seen,
> and of those things in the which I will appear unto thee.
>
> — Acts 26:16

(Jesus promises to appear to Paul again and that was fulfilled while he lay in a trance in the temple three years later.)

Now the object of his preaching was:

> To open their eyes, and to turn them from darkness to
> light, and from the power of Satan unto God, that they
> may receive forgiveness of sins, and inheritance among
> them which are sanctified (present experience) by faith
> that is in me (Jesus). Whereupon, O king Agrippa, I was
> not disobedient unto the heavenly vision.
>
> — Acts 26:18-19

---

[4] Acts 22:18.

From this we see and are able to understand the operations of God by His Spirit. And now, is the Holy Ghost in the church today? Verily yes, but you say, "We do not see Him work in this way." Why is it? Because you say all these things were for the apostolic days. You cannot take the Word of God and find one place where the gifts of the Holy Ghost were withdrawn.

The nine gifts of the Holy Ghost are found in 1 Corinthians 12:8-11:

> For to one is given by the Spirit the word of wisdom; to another the word of knowledge by the same Spirit (gift two; to another faith by the same spirit, to another the gifts of healing by the same Spirit.... To another discerning of spirits (gift three); to another divers (different) kinds of tongues (languages, not an acquirement, but by the Spirit).

Oh praise God for the discovery of the gifts of the Holy Ghost and especially for the gift of healing. May we all learn to know Christ, not alone as our Savior, but as our Sanctifier and Healer too.

Now I will go over these gifts on my fingers. First, wisdom; Second, knowledge; Third, faith; Fourth, healing; Fifth, miracles; Sixth, prophecy; Seventh, discerning of spirits; Eighth, divers kinds of tongues; Ninth, the interpretations of tongues. We have seen that the Holy Ghost came into the Church at Pentecost and the gifts are in the Holy Ghost. Consequently, if the Holy Ghost came in the Church, the gifts are too. Because of the lack of faith, we do not see them exercised in the ordinary church. We stand for the obtaining of the gifts of the Holy Ghost through our personal baptism in the Holy Ghost, and the enduement of the Holy Ghost power as promised by Jesus, yea, commanded by Him. "Ye shall receive power, after that the Holy Ghost is come upon you" (Acts 1:8).

People ask, "What is tongues?" Tongues is the voice (or operation) of the Spirit of God within. When the Holy Ghost came in, He spoke. Again in Acts 10:44 to 48, when the Holy Ghost fell on them, Peter demanded the right to baptize them in water, saying, "Can any man forbid water, that these should not be baptized, which have received the Holy Ghost?" See verse 46, "For they heard them speak with tongues, and magnify God."

Tongues is the evidence of the baptism of the Holy Ghost by which Peter claimed the right to baptize them in water. Again in Acts 19:1-7, Paul at Ephesus met twelve men whom John had baptized unto repentance, but now Paul rebaptized them by Christian baptism. In verse 5, we read that when they heard this they were baptized (water baptism) in the name of the Lord Jesus. And when Paul had laid his hands on them, the Holy Ghost came on them and they spoke with tongues and prophesied. "Tongues are for a sign, not to them that believe, but to them that believe not" (1 Corinthians 14:22).

THE BAPTISM OF THE HOLY GHOST

And Some of the Things It Has Produced in My Life

Sermon 3 of 3

he baptism of the Holy Ghost was of such importance in the mind of the Lord Jesus Christ that He commanded His disciples to tarry in Jerusalem, "until ye be endued with power from on high."[1] And they steadfastly carried out what the Lord had commanded, waiting on God in a continuous prayer meeting in the upper room for ten days until the promise of the Father was fulfilled (Luke 24:49) and that baptism had fallen of which John the Baptist spoke in Matthew 3:11, saying,

> I indeed baptize you with water unto repentance: but he that cometh after me is mightier than I, whose shoes I am not worthy to bear: he shall baptize you with the Holy Ghost, and with fire.

In order to obtain from heaven the Spirit of Jesus (the Holy Ghost), it is first necessary that the individual shall know that his sins are blotted out, that the blood of Jesus Christ has sanctified his heart and cleansed him from the sinful nature, or the Adamic nature — the inherent nature of sin (Ephesians 2:1-3).

Personally, I knew that my sins had been blotted out, but it was only two months prior to my baptism in the Holy Ghost that I learned by the Word of God and experienced in my life the sanctifying power of God subduing the soul and cleansing the nature from sin. This inward life-cleansing was to me the crowning work of God in my life at that period, and I shall never cease to praise God that He revealed to me the depth, by the Holy Ghost, of the power of the blood of Jesus.

---

[1] Luke 24:49.

Many inquire, "What is the reason that when your heart is sanctified and the conscious knowledge of your cleansing has taken place that you are not instantly baptized with the Holy Ghost?" From my own experience and the experiences of others, it is readily seen that, notwithstanding that the heart is cleansed from sin, it is still necessary in many instances for the dear Lord to further spiritualize the personality until the individual has become sufficiently receptive to receive within his person the Holy Ghost. The forces of our personality must be subdued unto God. This we commonly speak of as spiritualizing.

In many instances even though the heart is really pure, yet the individual has not at once received the baptism of the Holy Ghost and in some instances has given up in despair and turned back to his first works, believing that there must still be sin in his heart, thus discrediting what God has already done within him through the blood of Jesus. No, it is not always that the heart is still impure. It is not because you are not thoroughly sanctified. It is only God waiting and working to bring you to the place and to sufficiently spiritualize your personality that you may receive into your being the Holy Ghost.

The baptism of the Holy Ghost is not an influence, nor yet a good feeling, nor sweet sensations, though it may include all of these. The baptism of the Holy Ghost is the incoming into the personality of Him, the Holy Ghost, which is the Spirit of Jesus, taking real possession of your spirit (or inner man), of your soul (the mind and animal life) yea, of your flesh. He possesses the being. The flesh is caused to quake sometimes because of the presence of the Spirit of God in the flesh. Daniel quaked with great quaking when the Spirit of the Lord came upon him (Daniel 10:1-13).

Beloved reader, do you realize that it is the Spirit of Jesus that is seeking admittance into your heart and life? Do you realize that it is the Spirit of Jesus within the spirit, soul, and body of the baptized believer that moves him in ways sometimes strange, but who accomplishes the wondrous work of God within the life that every baptized believer praises God has taken place in him?

While yet a justified man, even without an experience of sanctification, the Lord committed to me in a measure the ministry of healing inasmuch that many were healed, and in some instances, real miracles of healing took place. Yet I did not know God as my Sanctifier. Ten years later, after sanctification had become a fact in my life, a great and wonderful yearning to be baptized in the Holy Ghost and fire came into my heart. After seeking God persistently almost night and day for two months, the Lord baptized me in the Holy Ghost, causing me to speak in tongues and magnify God.

I had looked for and prayed and coveted the real power of God for the ministry of healing and believed God that when I was baptized in the Holy Ghost that His presence in me, through the Spirit, would do for the sick the things my heart desired and which they needed. Instantly upon being baptized in the Spirit I expected to see the sick healed in a greater degree and in larger numbers than I had before known, and for a time I seemed to be disappointed.

How little we know of our own relationship to God! How little I knew of my own relationship to Him. For day by day, for six months following my baptism in the Holy Ghost, the Lord revealed to me many things in my life where repentance, confession, and restitution were necessary, and yet I had repented unto God long ago. Of the deep cleansing, the deep revelations of one's own heart by the Holy Ghost, it was indeed as John the Baptist said,

> Whose fan is in his hand, and he will thoroughly purge his floor, and gather his wheat into the garner; but he will burn up the chaff with unquenchable fire.[2]

First then, I will say the baptism in the Holy Ghost meant to me a heart searching as I have never before known, with no rest, until in every instance the blood was consciously applied and my life set free from the particular thing that God had revealed. As I say, this process continued for six months after my baptism in the Holy Spirit.

Second, a love for mankind such as I had never comprehended took possession of my life. Yea, a soul yearning to see men saved so deep, at times heartrending, until in anguish of soul I was compelled to abandon my business and turn all my attention to bringing men to the feet of Jesus. While this process was going on in my heart, during a

---

[2] Matthew 3:12.

period of months, sometimes persons would come to my office to transact business, and even instances where there were great profits to be had for a few minutes of persistent application to business, the Spirit of love in me so yearned over souls that I could not even see the profits to be had. Under its sway, money lost its value to me, and in many instances I found myself utterly unable to talk business to the individual until first I had poured out the love-passion of my soul and endeavored to show him Jesus as his then present Savior. In not just a few instances these business engagements ended in the individual yielding himself to God.

That love-passion for men's souls has sometimes been overshadowed by the weight of care since then, but only for a moment. Again, when occasion demanded it, that mighty love flame absorbing one's whole being in life would flame forth until, under the anointing of the Holy Ghost, on many occasions sinners would fall in my arms and yield their hearts to God.

Others have sought for evidences of this Pentecostal experience being the real baptism of the Holy Ghost. Some have criticized and said, "Is it not a delusion?" In all the scale of evidences presented to my soul and taken from my experience, this experience of the divine love, the burning love and holy compassion of Jesus Christ filling one's bosom until no sacrifice is too great to win a soul for Christ, demonstrates to me more than any other one thing that this is indeed none other than the Spirit of Jesus. Such love is not human! Such love is only divine! Such love is only Jesus Himself, who gave His life for others.

Again, the development of power. First, after the mighty love came the renewed, energized power for healing of the sick. Oh! What blessed things God has given on this line. What glorious resurrections of the practically dead! Such restorations of the lame and the halt and the blind! Such shouts of joy! Such abundance of peace! Verily, "Himself took our infirmities, and bare our sicknesses"![3]

Then came, as never before, the power to preach the Word of God in demonstration of the Spirit. Oh, the burning, fiery messages. Oh, the tender, tender, loving messages! Oh, the deep revelations of wondrous truth by the Holy Ghost! Preaching once, twice, sometimes

---

[3] Matthew 8:17.

three times a day, practically continuously during these four years and four months. Oh, the thousands God has permitted us to lead to the feet of Jesus and the tens of thousands to whom He has permitted us to preach the Word!

Then came the strong, forceful exercise of dominion over devils, to cast them out. Since that time, many insane and demon possessed, spirits of insanity — all sorts of unclean demons — have been cast out in the mighty name of Jesus through the power of the precious blood. Saints have been led into deeper life in God. Many, many have been baptized in the Holy Ghost and fire. My own ministry. Yea, verily the baptism in the Holy Ghost is to be desired with the whole heart.

Brother, Sister, when we stand before the bar of God and are asked why we have not fulfilled in our life all the mind of Christ and all His desire in the salvation of the world, how will be our excuses if they are weighed against the salvation of imperishable souls? How terrible it will be for us to say we neglected, we put off, we failed to seek for the enduement that cometh from on high — the baptism of the Holy Ghost.

Again, are we close? May we say that it was only after the Lord had baptized us in the Holy Ghost that we really learned how to pray? When He prayed through us, when the soul cries born of the Holy Ghost rolled out of your being and up to the throne of God, the answer came back — His prayers, His heart yearning, His cry. May God put it in every heart, that we may indeed see the answer to our Lord's prayer, "Thy kingdom come. Thy will be done in earth, as it is in heaven."[4]

But someone will say, "How about tongues? We understood that you taught that tongues were the evidence of the baptism in the Holy Ghost." So they are. Tongues are a sign to them that believe not (1 Corinthians 14:22). While I personally praise God for the wonderful and blessed truths of His Word by the Spirit — revelations in doctrine, in prophecy, in poems by the Holy Ghost in tongues with interpretation — that He has given me, yet above all the external evidences, that which God accomplishes in your own lives, demonstrating to your own consciousness the operations of God, no doubt

---

[4] Matthew 6:10.

is the great evidence to the believer himself. For that which is known in consciousness cannot be denied. We stand firmly on scriptural grounds that every individual who is baptized in the Holy Ghost will and does speak in tongues.

Baptism means a degree of the Spirit upon the life sufficient to give the Spirit of God such absolute control of the person that He will be able to speak through him in tongues. Any lesser degree cannot be called the baptism or submersion, and we feel could properly be spoken of as an anointing. The life may be covered with deep anointings of the Holy Ghost, yet not in sufficient degree to be properly called the baptism.

> John G. Lake
>
> 4 Millbourn Road
>
> Bertrama, Johannesburg
>
> Trasvaal, South Africa

eloved, this is our communion service. No other service in the world, perhaps, gives us better or equal opportunity to express the wonderful truth of redemption. Redemption is a marvelous word. It is a revelation. The redemptive life and the redemptive love and the redemptive blood and the redemptive power are some of the phases of redemption. The great redemptive type was the escape of the children of Israel from Egypt, an escape so complete there was nothing left.

COMMUNION SERVICE
Portland, Oregon
October 1, 1921

Redemption is a holy word. When God looked upon the children of Israel and saw their tears and saw their distresses, He purposed their deliverance and came to their rescue and said to Moses, "I have seen their tears, I have heard their cries, I have witnessed their oppressions, I have come down to deliver them."[1] Bless God, there is a time when God comes down for men's deliverance. Bless His name forever. "I have come down to deliver them." The third chapter of Exodus, the seventh verse says, "And the Lord said, I have surely seen the affliction of my people which are in Egypt, and have heard their cry."

Yesterday I was writing to a friend, and I asked the Lord in the Spirit for something for that friend's bitter need when this little verse came to my mind:

> *If I find Him, If I follow,*
>
> *What the guerdon[2] here?*
>
> *Many a sorrow, many a trial, many a tear.*
>
> *If I find him, If I follow,*
>
> *What has he at last?*
>
> *Love victorious, heaven entered, Jordan passed.*

---

[1] Exodus 3:7-8, paraphrased.

[2] guerdon: a reward or recompense. *Webster's Desk Dictionary of the English Language* (NY: Gramercy Books, 1983), p. 401.

"I have come down," said God, "to deliver them." God coming for man's deliverance is a wondrous event. Deliverance was by the Lord. And He has come down to deliver them out of the hands of the Egyptians and to bring them out of the land into a good land and a larger land, into a land that is flowing with milk and honey. Into a place where your enemy passes, God gives victory. And He wants to speak a word of comfort to the struggling heart today. If the enemy possesses, God has promised that He will dispossess him. You and I will possess the inheritance if we put our faith in Him.

That was a national redemption. The nation of Israel was being redeemed from the king of Egypt. The redemption of Jesus is a universal redemption so big, so full, so broad, that it is beyond comprehension in its wonder of love, not only on earth but in heaven too. All things that are in earth and things that are in heaven made one in Him.

In His endeavor again to bring to the consciousness of the people that the redemption of Jesus was a world redemption, both Jew and Gentile, a redemption of all men, redemption from every condition, redemption not only from the pollution and oppression of sin, but redemption into the eternal liberty of Christ Jesus, redemption is wholly by God.

> For God so loved the world, that he gave His only begotten Son, that whosoever believeth on him should not perish, but have everlasting life.[3]

Redemption was the gift of God the eternal Father. Redemption was through the Lord and Savior Jesus Christ. When men come into the realization of oneness with God and the real truth, then they are co-laborers with God. At present there is too much lying back and waiting for God, while God is waiting for the heart that will become an agency to bless and redeem a world. When He wanted to redeem the people of Israel, He had to [blank space in manuscript] redemption. "God looked and there was no man."[4] No sadder statement was ever written. God wondered why there were no intercessors.

---

[3] John 3:16.

[4] See Psalm 53:2-3.

The old intercessors, the prophets, all down the line had an amazing conception of the ministry of an intercessor. The intercessor was not just one that prayed for another who was in distress. He was more. His heart and soul became undivided with his people or nation or those for whom he prayed to the degree that their soul became his soul. That's the secret. God's secret of answered prayer.

As long as your soul is a soul praying for another soul, you will never get very far, nor get very much for that heart. But when your soul melts into that other life and your spirit melts into theirs, you will come to that place where Jesus was when He took upon Himself the sins of the world. And you will come to the place where Moses was when he said, "If you forgive not these people blot my name out of the book."[5] He did not say, "My people are a stiff-necked people." He said, *"We* are a stiff-necked, rebellious people."[6] So God needed a redeemer, and Moses became a redeemer of the children of Israel by the [blank space in manuscript] and commission of God.

It always takes God to redeem. God always has to have a redeemer. God makes his redeemer of a quality of Himself. "Thou shalt be as God."[7] The authority of God was to rest upon Moses. The heart of God was to be in Moses. The voice of God was to speak through Moses. Moses and God became one in a common endeavor to deliver a nation from the power of darkness, blessed be God. Redemption is by God alone. Redemption is ever through a redeemer.

Next, redemption is by blood. You can go up and down the world and seek for the redemption of mankind in any form you want to consider the subject of redemption, and you will find that redemption is by blood. I tell you that when your heart starts out on a mission of redemption for another life, your soul will rise to that place. If you are a success as a redeemer, you will come to that place where you give yourself into the eternal secret of power in God, into power of God, and into ministry of the Spirit.

---

[5] Exodus 32:32, paraphrased.

[6] See Exodus 34:9.

[7] See Exodus 4:16.

Redemption was to be by Jesus alone. Redemption was to be and ever will be by every soul that comes into harmony with Jesus and becomes identified with Jesus' heart and Jesus' life and Jesus' soul. And Jesus Christ is not simply Jesus Christ on the throne of God, but Jesus Christ in you and Jesus Christ in me, blending His soul for the pardon of a dying world. But He is blending it through your heart and pulsing it through your soul, and His compassion is expressed through you. When your heart and my heart melts down into Jesus Christ until the spirit of the Christian becomes one spirit, and the power of God from heaven is mingling with the power of the Spirit of Him who becomes the redeemer. Blessed be His Holy name.

One of the prophets in writing used these beautiful words which I wish I could write in the memory of every soul. "There shall be saviors in Zion,"[8] hearts that are melted into Christ Jesus. Souls that took upon themselves an understanding of His spiritual life and the ministry of His power. Made one with the Lord, proved by God. One day, Jesus Christ is going to have a Church that will be one with Himself. Every one of them will pulse with the living Spirit and victorious life of Jesus Christ, being identified in heart, in mind, and body with the Lord Jesus Christ.

In the progress of my work in Africa this incident took place. There was a family of seven brothers. The father was very wealthy. He had come to Africa in the early days and took possession of a great tract of land. Eventually the old man died and left two thousand pounds in gold besides a large property of vast extent. The youngest son was the black sheep of the family. They had been finely educated and developed for generations. The family could tolerate this black sheep with no leniency whatever. First this disgrace and that disgrace until the family was overwhelmed with the disgrace of it all.

They appealed to their attorney and asked, "What can we do?" They decided to make a contract with him, giving him all his share if he would leave the country, never to return. This was done, and Lew Watson disappeared for years. One of our missionaries was going up into the country one day and met a man with sixty-four zebras. They

---

[8] See Obadiah 1:21.

told him of the power of Jesus and went down and talked with him about his weakness, and Lew Watson was born of God. His heart began to pulse with the Spirit of God. He could only cry and pray for the family he had disgraced.

Finally, he appeared one day in my tabernacle. He related the circumstances of how he left home. He said, "They sacrificed to pay all my money into my hands, and I am worse than the prodigal[9], but I have my Lord. Do you suppose they will receive me, brother?"

I said, "Never, unless God makes it possible."

He said, "How can I go to them unless God baptizes me in the Holy Ghost?"

I replied, "My boy, you have the right idea." And so he knelt down, and I laid my hands upon him and in less than five minutes he was baptized in the Spirit and glory of God. He arose and went to his train. He arrived at the home of his eldest brother. He walked into the beautiful house. His brother recoiled with the shock. Poor Lew! He tried to talk to him, and made the same mistake as many others of us do when we do not let God do the talking for us.

So Lew left the house and down the road a ways he crawled under some prickly pear trees where no person would ever think of following, and he lay there pouring out his heart in mighty sobs and he broke out in the Spirit of Jesus. "When Zion travaileth she will bring forth children."[10] God, we haven't got to travailing enough yet. We have a prayer meeting here every day at one o'clock. Another every Sunday at eleven o'clock. "When Zion travaileth children will be born."

Well, that day when he left the house and went down the road sobbing, he came to where the great prickly pears are so thick you cannot see the light, he crawled away back in there and prayed. When your ears hear that cry of the Spirit they will know it. Away from all psychology, away out of the mental, away down where God is. A young man, the son of Lew Watson's brother, came along the road and heard him praying and knew enough of the words so that he passed on to the house. He said, "Father, I know that something has taken place."

---

9 See Luke 15:11-32.

10 Isaiah 66:8, paraphrased.

The father said, "Boy, you know Uncle Lew and the conditions under which we lived and the sacrifices the entire family made to get him to leave the country, and here he is back on our hands again."

The boy said, "Father, this is not the Uncle Lew we knew. I never heard a prayer like that."

So the Father walked down the road with the son and listened. The tears began to flow down his cheeks, his heart began to sob, he got down on his hands and knees and finally got to Lew and took him in his arms and kissed his tears away. Then he sent and called in the sixty other relatives and every one of them were converted. When that crowd gathered, poor Lew thought that he would have to preach, and he made the flattest kind of a failure. Then he said, "Let us pray." Then God came as he prayed out his heart, and old Tom fell to the floor under the power of God, and it kept on until they were all saved. God just came. More than half of that company were baptized in the Holy Ghost. Just as soon as one confessed Jesus Christ, no matter what time it was, Lew took them to the old farm dam and baptized them.

Men are preaching philosophy. Men are preaching science and preaching this and that. But the heart of mankind is crying out for God. Redemption is by blood. Blessed be God. Brother, when your heart gets to the place where Jesus was, where you are just as ready to give yourself for the one as Jesus was to give Himself, why the flashes of heaven will go out of your heart and ignite the hearts of others. *That is the divine secret.* There is a begetting quality in the soul of a man when Jesus is there that will beget in the heart and beget the Holy Spirit of God in his life.

Redemption is not only by blood, but is followed by power. The blood of Jesus was shed for the purpose that the power of God be made available to man. I have tried to picture a scene in my soul something like this: A lot of people get the redemption of Jesus Christ who do not know much about it. Here is an old Israelite who has killed his lamb and placed the blood on the lintels and doorposts of his house. Across the street from him lives an old Egyptian, who says, "I wonder what he is doing that for? Why has he killed that lamb and put the blood over his door and on the doorposts. I will just do the same and see what happens."[11]

So he goes and kills his lamb and does the same. There was not an Egyptian who had faith enough to do this thing. The sad thing is that sometimes there isn't an Israelite in the land that has the faith either. Old Naaman came down and hunted up the prophet that he might be healed of his leprosy. There were many lepers in Israel but none of them were healed but Naaman, who was an Assyrian. There were many others too. To none of them was Elijah sent.[12]

After they had kept faith with God and marched to the Red Sea, then the flame of God flamed out of the soul of Moses and split the sea and the people marched through. The Egyptians started to follow them, but the lightnings of God flashed out once more, and Pharaoh and his host were no more. I was reading from a history the other day that they had found the bones of every Pharaoh but the one who perished in the Red Sea at the time of Moses. He was left in the midst of the Red Sea. No tomb enshrined him but water.

Redemption is by power. Get under the blood of Jesus Christ and the harmony of His redemption and the power of God will come upon your soul. You cannot keep it off. Our difficulty is that all these things are done in the natural. Men decide in the mental realm that they are going to change their natural life. Some try to bring about a psychological conversion, but I tell you that when God Almighty comes into a man's spirit and God possesses him, he is redeemed in the heart of him and in the soul of him. Jesus Christ possesses the spirit and will manifest Himself in his soul.

Now you can take every blessing of God along the line, that's the heart and the soul of it. People are asking God for healing every day. It's not the healing you want, but the Healer, to come into your soul and take possession of your brains and your interests and your life too, when you are one with Him within and one with Him without. The pulsing life of Him within will make you well. A poor dear soul stood here one night and drew my head down to her ear and said, "Mr. Lake, I have been acting the fool and permitted myself to be led by

---

[11] See Exodus 12.

[12] See 2 Kings 5.

others. Something else has come upon me." I did not ask what was the trouble, for I knew what it was. "I have been away from God."

I said, "Dear one, God will come and help you." As I prayed I felt the lightnings of God strike her. Yesterday she was here again and said, "Brother Lake, that thing is gone. I can breathe perfectly."

Redemption by blood brings power. Lots of people are trying to get the power of God without the cleansing process. God knew and understood and God knew the [blank space in manuscript]. There's a path that no soul knoweth — the way of holiness. The lions whelp nor the fierce lion has not passed over it. I was invited by a group of friends one night to a physician's apartment in the city of Johannesburg. When I arrived, I found that there was a gathering of psychological men. Among them was an English scientist, Turner, who spent a lifetime in India searching for the germ of leprosy and who finally died a leper himself. A wonderful man.

There were great physicians, great psychologists, great hypnotists. They said, "We have been having great meetings and are now going to turn these meetings into a time of demonstration. A great hypnotist put a drunk man in a state of hypnotic trance and nothing we can do will bring him out of it. He is going to die. We have heard of you, that you are a Christian. We do not know that there is such a thing as a man getting into God." Yes, I said in my own soul, when a man gets to the limit, then is the time he needs God. Every quality God has your soul with is beautiful and lovely. If you will just let God come in, He will exercise that quality, but when you leave God out it is [blank space in manuscript].

I knelt by that man and undertook to break that power which held him. But it would not break. My soul went down again and my heart melted, and the sobs of Jesus were in my heart and the first thing I knew, that man was lying there with his eyes open. No devils were cast out. When men's hearts melt down in tears, God comes into their heart and it is then that the lightnings of God flame forth and you speak and act like God. But with most of us it is when our hearts melt before God.

The Israelites went over into the Promised Land and possessed the land of their enemies — God's picture of the eternal triumph. When spirit and soul and body are forever identified with Jesus Christ and life in the victory of God, bless His name, that's what makes a day like this precious. It's that redemption of Jesus that speaks power into this beautiful service. That's why we stand not as men nor stupid individuals, but with clearness and soundness of mind, pureness of heart, and proclaim our faith in the blood of Jesus Christ and its redemptive quality, blessed be God.

That's the reason why we invite you in the [blank space in manuscript] of the present hour, to see the redemption of the blood of Jesus Christ that brought redemption into your being. For the power of God from heaven comes upon the blood to your soul, upon the purified heart, upon the life, upon the spirit that identifies itself with the Lord Jesus. You are identified with Him because of being the possessor of the redemption life.

saiah 35:4-10 "The eyes of the blind shall be opened."[1] Once I was acquainted with a cartoonist who illustrated this very clearly. He pictured three scenes representing the three themes of that chapter. The three themes are:

Salvation

Healing

Holiness

[UNTITLED, THE HIGHWAY OF HOLINESS]
Hillside, Oregon
January 10, 1922

Representing the first theme, a man is kneeling and all around him are the scenes of his life, represented by different animals. The man is kneeling, bowed praying for salvation, and presently the great hand of God is just extended down to pick him up and is in the act of lifting him up. That is *salvation*.

The second theme, healing, is represented by a man standing on crutches. Just above his head was the hand of God. He was reaching to get hold of that hand, and in his effort to do so he forgot his crutches, and they fell this way and that way, and presently the man was walking after the hand. That is faith. That is *healing*.

The third theme is represented by the same individual walking along a highway on which the flowers were blooming and the pleasant waters flowing and down in the distance was the light of eternal glory. And as he went he sang. That is the highway of *holiness*.

"No lion shall be there, nor any ravenous beast shall go up thereon, it shall not be found there; but the redeemed shall walk there."[2]

That is the Christian's state. That is the normal soul state. Christians as a rule are covered with shadows, with fears, and doubts. That is not the realm of God at all. That is the realm of darkness.

---

[1] Isaiah 35:5.

[2] Isaiah 35:9.

Christianity lives in the light. Christianity lives in the glory. Christianity lives in the power of God, in the eternal presence of God. And it is that consciousness of God and union with Him that gives to the soul strength and assurance and confidence and helps the soul to go on its way regardless of conditions and circumstances, so that he is not being governed by this thing or that, but by the faith of God. Instead of conditions controlling him, he is controlling conditions. That is the power of God.

(Kernahan sang "Mother's Prayer.")

Kernahan: "A dwarf never needs to be measured for his clothes, but a growing boy outgrows his clothes."

hen he was come down from the mountain, great multitudes followed him. And, behold, there came a leper and worshipped him, saying, Lord, if thou wilt, thou canst make me clean.

— Matthew 8:1-2

That man knew that Jesus had the power to heal him, but he did not know it was God's will and that Jesus had committed Himself to the healing of

THE WONDERFUL POWER OF THE CHRISTIAN LIFE

January 12, 1922

mankind. If he had known, he would have said, "Lord, heal me."

It is always God's will to heal. Our faith may fail. My faith failed to the extent that unless someone else had gone under my life and prayed for me, I would have died. But God is just as willing to heal me as He could be. It was my faith that broke down. God is willing, just as willing to heal as He is to save. *Healing is a part of salvation.* It is not separate from salvation. Healing was purchased by the blood of Jesus. This Book always connects salvation and healing.

Supposing two men came to the altar. One is sick and lame; the other is a sinner. Suppose they knelt at the altar together. The sinner says, "I want to find the Lord." Everyone in the house will immediately lend the love of their heart and the faith of their soul to help him touch God. But the lame fellow says, "I have a lame leg." Or "My spine is injured. I want healing." Instead of everybody lending their love and faith in the same way to that man, everybody puts up a question mark.

That comes because of the fact that we are instructed on the Word of God concerning the salvation of the soul, but our education concerning sickness and His desire and willingness to heal has been neglected. We have gone to the eighth grade or the tenth grade or the University on the subject of salvation, but on the subject of healing we are in the ABC class.

Jesus put forth his hand, and touched him, saying, I will; be thou clean.

— Verse 3

Did He ever say anything in the world but "I will," or did He ever say, "I cannot heal you because it is not the will of God," or "I cannot heal you because you are being purified by this sickness," or "I cannot heal you because you are glorifying God in this sickness?" There is not such an instance in the Book.

On the other hand, we are told "He healed *all* that came to Him."[1] Never a soul ever applied to God for salvation or healing that Jesus did not save and heal! Did you ever think of what calamity it might have been if a man had come to Jesus once and said, "Lord, save me," and the Lord had said, "No, I cannot save you." Every man forevermore would have a question mark as to whether God would save *him* or not. There would not be universal confidence as there is today.

Suppose Jesus had ever said to a sick man, "No, I cannot heal you." You would have the same doubt about healing. The world would have settled back and said, "Well, it may be God's will to heal that man or that woman, but I do not know whether it is His will to heal *me.*"

Jesus Christ did not leave us in doubt about God's will, but when the Church lost her faith in God she began to teach the people that maybe it was not God's will to heal them. So the Church introduced the phrase, "If it be Thy will" concerning healing. But Jesus "healed all that came to Him." (Matthew 4:23, Luke 9:6, Luke 9:11.)

Notice what it says in Isaiah 35:

> He will come and *save* you. *Then* the *eyes of the blind* shall be opened, and *ears of the deaf* shall be unstopped. Then shall the *lame* man *leap as an hart,* and the tongue of the dumb sing.[2]

Salvation and healing connected! Bless God.

---

[1] See Matthew 8:16; 12:15 and Luke 6:19.

[2] Isaiah 35:4-6, emphasis Lake's.

> That it might be fulfilled which was spoken by Esaias [Isaiah] the prophet, saying, Himself took our infirmities, and *bare our sicknesses.*
>
> — Matthew 8:17 [emphasis Lake's]

And lest we might be unmindful of that great fact that He had "born our sickness and carried our sorrows," Peter emphasizes it by saying

> Who his own self bare our sins in his own body on the tree, that we, being dead to sins, should live unto righteousness: by whose stripes ye were healed.
>
> — 1 Peter 2:24

Not "By whose stripes ye *are* healed," but "By whose stripes ye *were* healed." The only thing that is necessary is to *believe God.* God's mind never need to act for a man's *salvation.* He gave the Lord and Savior Jesus Christ to die for you. God cannot go any farther in expressing His will in His desire to save man. The only thing necessary is to believe God. There is salvation by blood. There is salvation by power that actually comes from God into a man's life. The blood provided the power. Without the blood there would have been no power. Without the sacrifice there would have never been the glory. Salvation by blood, salvation by power.

The Church in general is very clear in her faith on the subject of salvation through the sacrifice of the Lord and Savior Jesus Christ. The Christian world in general, regardless of their personal state of salvation, have a general faith and belief of the Lord and Savior Jesus Christ for the salvation of the world. But they are ever in doubt and very inexperienced in the power of God.

> When he was come down from the mountain, great multitudes followed him. And, behold, there came a leper and worshipped him, saying, Lord, if thou wilt, thou canst make me clean. And Jesus put forth his hand, and touched him, saying, I will; be thou clean. And immediately his leprosy was cleansed. And Jesus saith unto him, See thou tell no man; but go thy way, shew thyself to the priest, and offer the gift that Moses commanded, for a testimony unto them.
>
> — Matthew 8:1-4

Did you ever stop to think that the real things that kill folks, they have no medical remedy for? Take tuberculosis. You cannot kill one tubercular germ. Typhoid fever: Fill the patient with a tank full of medicine and he will go right on for twenty-one days.

In 1913 I was in Chicago in a big meeting, when I received a telegram from the hospital in Detroit, saying, "Your son, Otto, is sick with typhoid fever. If you want to see him, come." I rushed for a train, and when I arrived I found him in a ward. I told the man in charge I would like a private ward for him, so I could get a chance to pray for him. Well, God smote that thing in five minutes. I stayed with him a couple of days until he was up and walking around.

He went along for four or five weeks, and one day to my surprise I got another telegram, telling me he had had a relapse of typhoid. So I went back again. This time there was no sunburst of God like the first time. Everything was as cold as steel, and my, I was so conscious of the power of the devil. I could not pray audibly, but I sat down by his bed and shut my teeth, and I said in my soul, "Now, Mr. Devil, go to it. You kill him if you can." And I sat there five days and nights. He did not get healing the second time instantly. It was healing by process, because of the fact my soul took hold on God; I sat with my teeth shut, and I never left his bedside until it was done.

You may be healed like a sunburst of God today and tomorrow or the next week or the next month when you want healing, you may have to take it on the slow process. The action of God is not always the same because conditions are not always the same.

In the life of Jesus, people were instantly healed. I believe Jesus had such a supreme measure of the Spirit that when He put His hands on a man he was filled and submerged in the Holy Ghost, and the diseases withered out of them and vanished.

But, beloved, you and I use the measure of the Spirit that we possess. And if we haven't got as much of God as Jesus had, then you pray for a man today and you get a certain measure of healing, but he is not entirely well. The only thing to do is to pray for him tomorrow, and let him get some more and keep on until he is well.

That is where people blunder. They will pray for a day or two and then they quit. You pray and keep on day by day, and minister to your sick until they are well. One of the things that has discredited healing is that evangelists will hold meetings and hundreds of sick will come and be prayed for. In a great meeting like that you get a chance to pray once and do not see them again. You pray for ten people and as a rule, you will find that one or two or three are absolutely healed, but the others are only half healed or quarter healed or only received a very little touch of healing. It is just the same with salvation. You bring ten to the altar. One is saved and is clear in his soul. Another may come for a week and another for a month before he is clear in his soul. The difference is not with God. The difference is inside of the man. His consciousness has not opened up to God.

Every law of the Spirit that applies to salvation applies to healing likewise.

> And when Jesus was entered into Capernaum, there came unto him a centurion, beseeching him, And saying, Lord, my servant lieth at home sick of the palsy, grievously tormented. And Jesus saith unto him, I will come and heal him. The centurion answered and said, Lord, I am not worthy that thou shouldest come under my roof: but speak the word only, and my servant shall be healed.
>
> — Matthew 8:5-8

Here is healing at a distance. That centurion understood divine authority, and the same divine authority is vested in the Christian, for Jesus is the pattern Christian.

> For I am a man under authority, having soldiers under me: and I say to this man, Go, and he goeth; and to another, Come and he cometh; and to my servant, Do this, and he doeth it.
>
> — Verse 9

The same divine authority that was vested in Jesus is vested *by Jesus* in every Christian soul. Jesus made provision for the Church of Jesus Christ to go on forever and do the very same things He did and to keep on doing them forever. That is what is the matter with the Church. The Church lost faith in that truth. The result was, they went on believing that He could save them from sin, but the other great range of Christian life was left to the doctors and the devil or anything else. And the Church will never be a real Church, in the real power of the living God again, until she comes back again to the original standard — where Jesus was.

Jesus said, "Behold, I give you authority." What authority? "Over unclean spirits to cast them out, and to heal all manner of sickness and all manner of disease" (Matthew 10:1, paraphrased). Jesus Christ has vested that authority in you. You say, "Well Lord, we understand the authority that is in your Word, but we haven't the *power*. But Jesus said, "Ye shall receive *power*, after that the Holy Ghost is come upon you" (Acts 1:8).

Now the Holy Ghost has come upon every Christian in a measure. It is a question of degree. There are degrees of the measure of the Spirit of God in men's lives. The *baptism of the Holy Ghost* is a greater measure of the Spirit of God, but every man has a degree of the Holy Spirit in his life. *You* have. It is the Spirit in your life that gives you faith in God, that makes you a blessing to other people. It is the Holy Spirit that is *outbreathed* in your soul that touches another soul and moves them for God. Begin right where you are, and let God take you along the Christian life as far as you like.

> When Jesus heard it, he marvelled, and said to them that followed, Verily I say unto you, I have not found so great faith, no, not in Israel.
>
> — Matthew 8:10

Jesus always commended faith when he met it. Jesus did not always meet faith. All the people who came to Jesus did not possess that order of faith. They had faith that *if they got to Jesus* they would be healed. But here is a man who says, "Speak the word only, and my servant shall be healed."

Then you remember the case of the man at the Pool of Bethesda. He did not even ask to be healed. As he lay there Jesus walked up to him and said, "Wilt thou be made whole?"[3] He saw this poor chap who had been lying there for thirty-eight years, and Jesus did not wait for him to ask Him to heal. Jesus said, "Wilt thou be made whole?" And

---

[3] John 5:6.

the poor fellow went on to say that when the water was troubled he had no one to put him in, but while he was waiting another stepped in ahead of him. But Jesus saith unto him, "Rise, take up thy bed, and walk."[4] And he was made whole. Afterward Jesus met him and said, "Behold, thou art made whole: sin no more, lest a worse thing come unto thee" (John 5:14).

Most of sickness is the result of sin. That is the answer always to the individual who sins. For thousands of years men have been sinning and in consequence of their sin, they are diseased in their body. This will give you an idea. Scientists tell us there are tubercular germs in 90 percent of the population. The only difference is that when people keep in a healthy state, the germs do not get a chance to manifest themselves. I am trying to show you the intimacy between sin and sickness. Not necessarily the sin of the individual. It may never have been the sin of the individual.

In the records of the Lake and the Graham family away back, tuberculosis was never known in them until it appeared in my sister. My sister accompanied me to Africa, and she became so ill that when I got to Cape Town we had to wait until her strength returned. God healed her.

Regarding people being healed at a distance, we receive cablegrams from all over the world. Distance is no barrier to God. The United States has just finished the building of the greatest wireless station in the world. They send messages that register almost instantly, ten thousand miles. When the machine is touched here, it registers ten thousand miles away. Well, all right, when your *heart* strikes God in faith it will register wherever that individual is, just that quick. All the discoveries of later years such as telegraph, telephone, wireless, and all that sort of thing are just the common laws that Christians have practice all their lives.

Nobody ever knelt down and prayed but that the instant they touched God their soul registered in Jesus Christ in glory, and the answer came back to the soul. Christians have that experience every day. The wise world has begun to observe that these laws are applicable in the natural realm. I asked Marconi[5] once how he got his first idea for wireless. He replied that he got it from watching an exhibition of telepathy in a cheap theater.

---

[4] John 5:8.

[5] Guglielmo Marconi (1874-1937) was the inventor of wireless radiotelegraphy.

The prayer of the heart reaches God. Jesus replied to the leper, *"I will;* be thou clean." The next was the centurion's servant. The centurion said, "You do not need to come to my house. You *speak the word* only, and my servant shall be healed." And in the soul of Jesus He said, "Be healed." Distance makes no difference. The Spirit of God in you will go as far as your love reaches. *Love* is the medium that conveys the Spirit of God to another soul, anywhere on God's earth.

This is what takes place as you pray. The Spirit of God comes upon you and bathes your soul and a shaft of it reaches out and touches that soul over there. If you had an instrument that was fine enough to photograph spirit, you would discover how this is done.

Is it not a marvelous thing that God has chosen us to be co-laborers with Him, and He takes us into partnership to do all that He is doing? Jesus Christ at the Throne of God desires the blessing of you and me, and out of His holy heart the Spirit comes, and the soul is filled, and we cannot tell how or why.

I have known thousands of people to be healed, who have never seen my face. They send a request for prayer, we pray, and never hear anything more about them sometimes unless a friend or a neighbor or someone comes and tells us about them. Sometimes someone sends in a request for them. They will tell you they do not know what happened. They just got well. But you know why. That is the wonderful power there is in the Christian life, and that is the wonderful cooperation that the Lord Jesus has arranged between His own soul and the soul of the Christian. That is "The Church which is His body."[6]

---

[6] Ephesians 1:22-23.

esus said in Mark 16, "These signs shall follow them that believe."[1] That is your trademark. He meant these words for every last one of you. Jesus said *you* could do it.

I was sitting in the home of De Valeras in Krugersdorp one day, when a man came in looking for me. He had trav-eled over the country, following me from place to place, trying to catch up. He suffered with a sunstroke, which affected his mind. He proved to be a friend of the family I was stopping with. He sat on the opposite side of the room, and after awhile a little child six years old who had been sitting near me went across the room and climbed up on the man's knees. The man had a great cancer on his face. That child put her hands on that cancer, and I saw the thing wither and dis-appear. It was gone in half an hour, and the man was healed in a few days. Then she laid her little hands on top of his head and in a few minutes he said, "Oh, the fire that has been in my brain has gone out." The man's mind was normal.

[UNTITLED: THE POWER OF GOD]
Hillside, Oregon
January 12, 1922

POWER BELONGETH UNTO GOD

The simplest soul can touch God and live in the very presence of God and know His power. Man's intellectuality is not an assistant to knowing God. It is rather a detriment. You have to overcome the treacherous knowledge and pride that has been developed in your own soul before you become childlike enough to believe God like a little child does.

> Except ye be converted, and become as little children, ye shall not enter into the kingdom of heaven.[2]

---

[1] Mark 16:17.

[2] Matthew 18:3.

Go up and down the line, go to our greatest universities, our great hospitals, our great scientific establishments and find a man that really knows God and exercises His power. No sir, you don't.

But on the other hand, you find that these men are ones mostly affected with doubts. They are the prey of questions and doubts. What is the reason? Because of the fact that they have cold, material knowledge. Men have become material in their nature. Their spiritual connection with God has become deteriorated. The element that comes from heaven is not there. The light of heaven has not shined in their soul. The radiation from God's heart is not reaching them.

What is the explanation of a genius? It is the result of a soul that unconsciously goes out into God's great realm and discovers what is there. I had a preacher and friend who was very intelligent. He said one day, "Mr. Lake, while I sat there, something came down and stood there, and it was so visible and clear, I made a drawing of it." It was a baby bed different from anything produced before. So he is getting a patent for it. It came down while I was preaching. What was the secret? Simply, under the inspiration of the Spirit of God his spirit entered that creative realm and produced that thing.

> These signs shall follow them that believe; In my name shall they cast out devils; they shall speak with new tongues; They shall take up serpents; and if they drink any deadly thing, it shall not hurt them; they shall lay hands on the sick, and they shall recover.

— Mark 16:17-18

That was to be the characteristics of Christians forever, no matter where you found them anywhere. Now anybody with reasonable intelligence sees that these are spiritual things. They are not material things. You cannot create them. No man in the natural can cast demons out of another. You cannot manufacture a chemical that will cast a demon out, and yet that is the thing that is going on in the medical world all the time. What do they do with an insane man? They give him bromide. Bromide has no effect on the spirit. It will paralyze the nerves after awhile; that is all.

These things Jesus meant should be purely spiritual. Now the power that was to put these things into operation was to be the power of God. Jesus said, "All power is given unto me.... Go ye therefore [and do these things]... these signs shall follow."[3]

Christianity was not to be just preaching, but *demonstrating*. Go and preach the Gospel — demonstrate it. People have a right to see. Jesus was not a bigot; He did not get mad when people asked questions. When the palsied man came down through the roof, Jesus looked up and said, "Son, be of good cheer; thy sins be forgiven thee." And every old hypocrite got his prejudice up. "Who can forgive sins but God only?" Jesus did not say, "You are a lot of bigots," but turning to them said,

> Why reason ye these things in your hearts? Whether is it easier to say to the sick of the palsy, thy sins be forgiven thee; to say, Arise, and take up they bed and walk? But that ye may know that the Son of man hath power on earth to forgive sins (He saith to the sick of the palsy), I say unto thee, Arise, and take up thy bed, and go thy way into thine house.[4]

And he arose and took up his bed, and I will guarantee the crowd jammed a way through to let him out.

Now when Jesus met the situation in the mind of the disciples, they were asking about power. (Where do you get the connection?) He said, "Ye shall receive *power*," the power to give this manifestation and demonstration, "after that the Holy Ghost is come upon you" (Acts 1:8). "But tarry ye in the city of Jerusalem, until ye be endued with power from on high" (Luke 24:49).

I planned to go to Africa as a boy. Looked forward to it through my young manhood. Eventually, I married and my wife became an invalid, and when she did the door seemed closed. Later on she was healed. My very best friend went to Africa and was insistent that I join him. But I said, "No, I am not ready." I felt in my soul I was not ready. Then a couple of years later the knowledge of God through the

---

[3] Matthew 28:18-19; Mark 16:17.

[4] Matthew 9:2-6, paraphrased.

baptism of the Holy Ghost was brought to me, and God in His love and mercy baptized me.

One day I went out to help a chore boy pull a cross-cut saw to cut down an oak tree and as I did the Spirit of God spoke and said, "Go to Indianapolis. Prepare for a winter campaign. Get a large hall, and in the spring you will go to Africa." And it all came to pass.

It is power. Power is manifest in many ways. There is the power of *faith,* which draws to you what seems impossible. One day after I had gone to Indianapolis, Indiana, and had been preaching for some time, my old preaching partner said, "John, if we are going to Africa in the spring it is time we were praying for the money."

I said, "Tom, I have been praying ever since New Year's, and have not heard from heaven or anybody else."

He said, "Never mind, John, how much will it take?"

I replied, "Two thousand dollars."

He said, "Come on, John, we are going to pray." So we knelt down by Tom's bed and prayed. The answer came to his soul. I heard him saying, "Jesus, You told me You would send that money and it would be here in four days." After awhile he slapped me on the back, saying, "Don't pray anymore, John. Jesus told me He would send the money and it would be here in four days."

Four days later he came back from the post office with a letter containing four, five-hundred-dollar drafts. The letter read, "I was standing in the bank at Monrovia, California, and something said to me, 'Send Tom Hezmalhalch two thousand dollars.' It is yours, Tom, for whatever purpose God has shown you."

We went straight out and bought our tickets. I had a little money. Tom had bought the tickets, but when you are traveling with a wife and seven children there are a lot of other expenses besides tickets. We followed this practice. We never told what our own needs were, but we did tell the Lord. So finally all the little money I had was gone.

When I paid the expressman I had $1.50 left. As the train pulled out of Indianapolis my secretary threw in a $2.00 bill; then I had $3.50. There was a lady in our party traveling with us as far as Detroit. I needed $10 to buy her a ticket to Northern Michigan. As we rode along I said to Mrs. Lake, "Jen, I need $10 to buy Winnie a ticket." So we prayed and came on into Detroit at eight o'clock, and as the train pulled into the station my brother and married sister were there to meet us and among them was a younger brother, Jim. Jim was a student at the University. Jim took me by the arm and we walked to the other end of the station. Then he said, "Jack, I hope you won't be mad about it, but I would like to give you this," and he pulled out a $10 bill. I thanked him and went and bought Winnie her ticket.

I still had the $3.50 left. We took ship at New Brunswick. So I bought some canned beef, canned beans, etc., and still had about $1.50 left. When we finally got on the ship I had $1.25. I gave fifty cents to the table steward and fifty cents to the bedroom steward, and I still had twenty-five cents when we reached England. We were five days in Liverpool, and as we had a through ticket it entitled us to hotel expenses.

So that is the way God got us to Africa.

Now *power* is not only the exercise of dynamic force that casts out demons. Power is the action of the Spirit in you to believe Him and put your confidence in Him and trust Him. That is the secret the Christian has that other men do not know. A nice manly fellow said to me the other day, "I would like to be a Christian, but I don't believe I could stand."

And I replied, "Boy, neither would you unless something happened in your soul that gave you power to stand."

Brethren, we are not living in that relationship to God where we ought to be to command the power of God. There is a power of God to be had. It is for you to command. It may come to your life in the quietest settled state of soul. I am a Quaker in my own makeup, even though I preach loud. Sometimes when the Spirit comes on your soul it will make you a Quaker. I am a Quaker in my spirit, but so far as dependence on the Spirit of God is concerned, God taught my soul that thing of resting in God and letting God work the problem out. You can rave and tear, but that don't help the situation. But if you rest in God and believe Him, it will come to pass. Set your soul toward God and He will bring it to pass.

I told you of Mrs. Frogge, the most developed woman in God I have almost ever known. I asked her one day, "Mrs. Frogge, how long were you praying for the baptism of the Holy Ghost?"

She replied, "Mr. Lake, I never prayed for the baptism. When I knelt down, I said, 'Jesus, what is the reason I am not baptized?' And Jesus would show me this thing and that thing that I must make right." Then eventually there was a final day when she asked, "Why am I not baptized?" And Jesus told her that when she had written five letters to different ones who had wronged her, and whom she held a grudge against, He would baptize her. So she sat down and wrote these letters, carried them out and mailed them, and came back and sat down. As she did so, the Holy Spirit came upon her and she was not able to move and sat there for six hours while the Lord talked to her.

She came to see me, and I saw she had been in contact with God. She said, "Mr. Lake, as I sat at the table in the kitchen, Jesus came and sat on the other side, and I asked Him all the things I wanted to know, and He answered me." I never had any experience like that. I had some questions that were puzzling me, and so I told her about them and asked her to present them to Him the next time He appeared like that and get the answers. About ten days later she came back with the list of questions and answers. When I went over the list, I said, "These answers never came from anywhere else but out of the heart of God." Surely they were God's answers.

That is the intimacy some men possess and that all may possess. I am aware there are differences in our nature. Some are more material in their natural construction than others. I was raised and trained as a financier. My life was spent among that class of people. I ought to have been just as cold-blooded and just as steely hard as could be. That was the difficulty I had to overcome.

I sought God night and day in prayer and tears and fasting for nine months, and I watered my way with my tears every inch, until one day God baptized me, and I do not believe there ever was any man more surprised than I, because I had arrived at the place of despair. Beloved, if you will take these truths of God which I have tried to impart to you and let them be a stepping-stone by which your soul will cultivate that intimacy with God, you will be blessed.

Wonderful flashes of holy power come on occasions to one's soul. One night a gentleman arose in the audience who wanted to give thanks to God. To my amazement, I learned he had been a terrific drunkard. I invited him on the platform, and when he was finishing he said, "Perhaps there are other drunkards who would like to speak." And they began to gather until there were two hundred. God is in the saving business. That is His business. It is a dreadful sadness when men do not know God intimately and well. Men do not know what they are missing. Men have little conception of what He is until you become in intimate touch with God and know Him indeed.

I want to show you the accumulation of spiritual power. Perhaps you have not learned to throw your souls together in believing faith on behalf of the one needing the blessing.

(Told incident of woman in Wales. Did not take it.)

You have wondered about Jesus and His relation to God, and you wonder how Jesus Christ could be the Son of God and be God. Supposing that part of me that was over there in Wales and was able to take in all these things had stayed there. Supposing it had decided to take on itself a body and remain in Wales. What relation would it be to me? It would be born out of my nature. It would be part of myself. I believe God gave me that experience to settle forever in my soul that question of Jesus Christ and His relation to God the Father. And Jesus, though being one with the Father, still maintained His own individuality, and it is no longer a problem to my soul.

I want to tell you that Jesus Christ came out of the soul of God and He came to the world and gave His blood for you and me. And when Jesus gave His blood for you and me, beloved, it was God that did it. To my soul, Jesus is not the Son of God in that He is separate and detached from God. He is God. His blood was the life of the heart of God. It was God's manifestation of His divine affection for the world He had created.

I would rather face any other thing in all God's eternity than to face that Lord who loved me with such a passion that He shed His blood for me and I had been negligent and thoughtless about it. Brethren, we owe Him a duty that we can never know.

That is the reason we love God. God is giving His soul. God is giving everything He can give for our benefit, for our salvation, our healing, to empower us with His Spirit, to bring us into that place where we have a real relationship with Him, where we can become His servants, His sons and co-laborers.

Brethren, if you had to look straight into His eyes, as we are going to have to do one day, what would your answer be? Supposing I should say, "Well, Lord, I was so busy acquiring a little farm over at Hillside that I did not have time to love You. I did not have any time to honor You. I did not have any time to tell anybody else about You?" Well, your farm is gone and you are not there anymore, and here you are at the great day, God's eternal day. How trivial these things would be. We would be ashamed to utter them. Our hearts would smite us so that we would be unable to say them.

Don't you know our attitude toward God is just as childish as that? In the name of Jesus Christ, don't let the trifling things absorb your soul and keep your mind away from God, because the great eternity is out there where we will live forever and ever, and we will want to know all we can of God before we face Him. It is His love and kindness and grace that will be our biggest condemnation. After God has been offering the depth of His nature to us, what a thing it will be to look into the face of our Lord and realize that we have spurned it, instead of realizing the big purpose of God.

That is the reason I want you to give your heart to God, because it is the biggest thing, it is the manliest thing, it is the truest thing a man can do. If there is any honor in a man's soul he will want to do so.

(Sang hymn, "Lord, I'm Coming Home.")

r. Lull gave testimony that he had been delivered from pain due to a spinal trouble he had had since he was eleven or twelve years of age. Was never without suffering more or less, and sometimes unbearable.

[UNTITLED: THE VOICE OF GOD]
Thatcher, Oregon
February 1, 1922

I wonder if you have ever paid attention to the different occasions in reading the Scriptures when the *voice of God* is mentioned. You know the thing that makes the Bible the Bible is the fact that somebody had an interview with God. Somebody heard from heaven before there was any Bible. Then the conversation or the incident or the experience was recorded, and these became the Word of God. Now the Word of God is indestructible because it was a real voice, because it was a real experience, because God really did or said something and the record thereof is true.

If you wanted to prove like you do in mathematics, concerning the Bible and its inspiration, it is very simple. Every child is taught to prove whether his sum is correct or not. And if you have doubts and questions and fears concerning the Bible and its inspiration, we know that if one soul ever heard from heaven another soul may. If ever one soul had one interview with God, another soul may. If any man ever knew his sins forgiven at any period, another man may know his sins forgiven now. If there ever was a man or woman healed by the power of God at any time, then men and women can be healed again. And the only thing necessary is to return again *in soul experience* to that same place of intimacy with God where the original individual met God. Now is that clear?

That is the way you prove the Word of God. That is the reason that Christians love the Word of God. That is the reason that the Word of God becomes the thing that men live by and that men will die by.

I was reading today a little article by W. J. Bryant, in which he quotes the beautiful old hymn:

Faith of our fathers! Living still
In spite of dungeon, fire and sword:
O how our hearts beat high with joy
Whene'er we hear that glorious word:
Faith of our fathers! Holy Faith!
We will be true to thee till death!

The reason men lived for the Word of God and died for the Word of God, the reason they were ready to endure dungeon, fire, and sword was because of the fact that the Word of God became a living reality to them — not just a theory.

No one can estimate the value to my soul that the first healing my eyes beheld was to me. I will never forget it. It did more to establish faith and dismiss doubts and fears than anything else that had ever occurred. I had been converted when comparatively young, and naturally as a man [this sermon is incomplete].

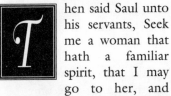

hen said Saul unto his servants, Seek me a woman that hath a familiar spirit, that I may go to her, and enquire of her. And his servants said to him, Behold, there is a woman that hath a familiar spirit at Endor.

SPIRITUALISM

August 26, 1923

And Saul disguised himself, and put on other raiment, and he went, and two men with him, and they came to the woman by night: and he said, I pray thee, divine unto me by the familiar spirit, and bring me him up, whom I shall name unto thee.

And the woman said unto him, Behold, thou knowest what Saul hath done, how he hath cut off those that have familiar spirits, and the wizards, out of the land: wherefore then layest thou a snare for my life, to cause me to die?

And Saul sware to her by the LORD, saying, As the LORD liveth, there shall no punishment happen to thee for this thing.

Then said the woman, Whom shall I bring up unto thee? And he said, Bring me up Samuel.

And when the woman saw Samuel, she cried with a loud voice: and the woman spake to Saul, saying, Why hast thou deceived me? for thou art Saul.

And the king said unto her, Be not afraid: for what sawest thou? And the woman said unto Saul, I saw gods ascending out of the earth.

And he said unto her, What form is he of? And she said, An old man cometh up; and he is covered with a mantle. And Saul perceived that it was Samuel, and he stooped with his face to the ground, and bowed himself.

And Samuel said to Saul, Why hast thou disquieted me, to bring me up? And Saul answered, I am sore distressed; for the Philistines make war against me, and God is departed from me, and answereth me no more, neither by prophets, nor by dreams: therefore I have called thee, that thou mayest make known unto me what I shall do.

Then said Samuel, Wherefore then dost thou ask of me, seeing the Lord is departed from thee, and is become thine enemy?

And the Lord hath done to him, as he spake by me: for the Lord hath rent the kingdom out of thine hand, and given it to thy neighbour, even to David:

Because thou obeyedst not the voice of the Lord, nor executedst his fierce wrath upon Amalek, therefore hath the Lord done this thing unto thee this day.

Moreover the Lord will also deliver Israel with thee into the hand of the Philistines: and to morrow shalt thou and thy sons be with me: the Lord also shall deliver the host of Israel into the hand of the Philistines.

—1 Samuel 28:7-19

The old prophet appeared and proceeded to tell what was going to take place and what was going to happen to Saul and his sons in the battle to come. Now then we read a surprising thing. He had light in the promise of Christ's redemption. Where did he get it? The word was "sheol" or the regions of the dead. They were there without something. What was it? The deliverance of the Son of God.

The prophets prophesied concerning the deliverance the Son of God was to bring after Jesus Christ entered into the regions of death and liberated those who were held by its chains; those who had died in the hope of the promise; those who had died in the fullness of faith; believing that the Redeemer was to come. He came and the actual deliverance from the power of death took place. "He led captivity captive, he ascended up on high"[1] and their place of residence was transferred from that place (sheol) governed by the power of death and the angel of death to wherever the Lord Jesus Christ went. "They

---

[1] Ephesians 4:8, paraphrased.

ascended up on high," and their place of residence was changed. We do not know where those who went with Jesus stopped. You call it Paradise, but so far as Jesus is concerned, it is perfectly plain in the Word that He never stopped until He came to the Throne of God.

You go through the Book and find where anyone was ever called down out of heaven, and you won't find it. Those who have their residence with the Lord Jesus Christ, from the day of His resurrection and onward, would have to be called down, not up.

Now one of the things we have lost out of our Protestant faith from the days of the Reformation onward has been the wonderful truth of the ministry of Jesus in the Spirit to the dead. Do you get it? The ministry of Jesus to the dead. "For this cause was the Gospel preached to them that are dead." Oh, you mean dead in this world, and dead in sins? Not at all, because the rest of the verse explains.

> For this cause was the gospel preached also to them that
> are dead.

Why?

> That they might be judged according to men in the flesh.

—1 Peter 4:6

On the same grounds that men in the flesh were judged. They heard the words of Jesus. They received the words of Jesus or they rejected the words of Jesus, just as men in the flesh do.

"Well, what does it mean?" you ask. "Are you preaching on the subject of a second chance?" No, brother, but I am calling attention to the state of the dead before Jesus came. They died in the *hope* of the promise. Jesus came and the promise was fulfilled. He fulfilled it on the cross of Calvary, and went into the regions of the dead and fulfilled it to them and delivered them and took them out the power of death and transferred them to His kingdom.

> He led captivity captive, and gave gifts unto men.

— Ephesians 4:8

With the above thoughts I have laid a kind of foundation. There is no such thing in the whole New Testament as a reoccurrence of those instances I have just read — no such a suggestion or its possibility in the New Testament. It belonged to a day and an age and a state that ceased to be when Jesus Christ the Lord and Redeemer came.

INTERPRETATION OF TONGUES

[Given by Fred Wilson]

"Oh listen to the Word, the living Word of God that is coming forth. You shall live, you shall live throughout eternity; but deny the living Word and ye shall go down, ye shall go down into the pit. Believe the Word and ye shall live."

A number of years ago when I was a missionary in Africa, I formed the acquaintance of W. T. Stead, who later was one of the victims of the Titanic. I came to London at his invitation and expense for a personal interview. He took me to his office, and after we had become acquainted he introduced this fact: He maintained a spiritualistic bureau associated with his great work known as the Julia Bureau. Julia was a friend who had died, and he believed after she was dead, he could contact the spirit of Julia. So eventually he published a book entitled, *Letters From Julia*. Later he changed the name to *After Death*, and these letters from Julia are published in this book.

Stead presented me with a copy of the book and requested that I should read it carefully. I did so and made notations of the various letters, and when I got a chance to talk to him I said, "Julia, in a very cunning manner indeed, avoids the deity and divinity of the Lord Jesus Christ. Now in order that you may see it, I went over the different letters where reference was made to the Lord Jesus Christ." I said, "You listen, Stead, that cunningness is altogether out of harmony with the other statements in the other letters of the book."

When it came to that subject of the divinity of Jesus, the peculiar cunningness of working was observable, even to the most ordinary mind, by which she carefully, studiously avoided any reference to the divinity or deity of Jesus Christ. I said, "Stead, I am going to put you up against the Word on this matter, 'Every spirit that confesseth not that Jesus Christ is come in the flesh is not of God'" (1 John 4:3). W. T. Stead was a big man and a great soul. He thought that he might convince me if I were at all reasonable.

Finally, a meeting was arranged between Sir Oliver Lodge, Sir Author Conan Doyle, William T. Stead, and myself. I want to say a word concerning these two great men. Both have been knighted by the king as knights of the realm because of their contributions to scientific knowledge.

When a knight is knighted he kneels before the king; the king touches him and says, "Rise, sir knight," etc. What I want you to see is that a man must have contributed something of unusual value to the empire in order to be knighted. He must also be able to maintain his social status as a knight. Both men were great men, great as men speak of worldly greatness; great men intellectually; great men in the secrets of science.

After we had spent a whole night reviewing these varied things (experiences) that we considered vital, I said, "Gentlemen, I want to tell you of one experience that I think goes further than any of these you have told me. My late wife died in South Africa. I buried her on Christmas Eve, 1908 at Johannesburg. The following sixth of May, which was the anniversary of her birthday, as I sat at the table I occupied an hour telling the family incidents of their mother, and trying to fix the memory of their mother in their young minds. The baby was only eighteen months old and the eldest only fourteen years when she died.

"Later I went to the post office and a lady tapped me on the shoulder and said, 'When you are through with your business, come up to the office' and handed me a card with the address. When I was through, I strolled up to the office. I recognized her as one of the members of my audiences. There was a couple of gentlemen in the room, one a Frenchman, Massalie, and another Frenchman.

"As we sat talking I wondered why she had asked me to come up. I observed as I watched her she seemed to be distressed, and one side of her face was purple with erysipelas.[2] I stepped over and asked her if it was because she was sick that she had asked me to come, and she said. 'Certainly.'

"I laid my hands on her and began to pray, and as I prayed I was conscious of the Spirit coming in power, and that purple disappeared as I watched it. The healing was so remarkable that the gentlemen were surprised.

"Massalie said, 'Mr. Lake, what is that?'

"I said, 'Masssalie, that is God.'

"He replied, 'Oh, everything is God. I lived among the East Indians and everything is God.'

"The phrase was offensive to my spirit and I said, 'Well, brother, I do not want to discuss it.'

"He said, 'Well, if it is God, I'll tell you how to prove it.' He said, 'I put over a bad business deal, was very angry and in a high temper one day. Instead of opening the door gently, I opened it with a push. This lady happened to be behind the door. It took her an awful blow on the side of the head. She became unconscious, and in a few days we discovered the skull bone was fractured. Not only that, but the optic nerve had been detached and the eye became blind.'

"He had spent quite a fortune on the woman, but nothing availed. The eye remained blind. He said 'If that is God, you put your hands on her eye and pray sight back into that eye.' The Spirit was resting on my soul. I stepped over and began to pray. Instantly the Spirit came upon her until she was absolutely submerged in the Spirit. She remained in that condition a little while, and this strange thing took place.

"She arose from her chair, her eyes quite shut, and came in my direction. I got up and moved my chair. She walked right around and came to me. She slipped her fingers down, gave me a little chuck just like my late wife would have done, and said, 'Jack, my Jack, God is with you all the time. Go right on. But my baby, my Teddy, I am so lonesome for him, but you pray so hard, you pray so hard.'

---

[2] erysipelas: an acute, infectious bacterial disease characterized by inflammation of the skin. *Webster's Desk Dictionary of the English Language* (NY: Gramercy Books, 1983), p. 304.

"After Mrs. Lake died the little boy fell into a decline, and it required all the energy of my soul to keep that boy alive for months. Eventually he survived.

"After the incident had passed, I asked her to write it." You get people to write things down so you can analyze them.

Listen, it is not dragging spirits up, and it isn't dragging some spirits down. There is nothing about calling spirits down from God in the Word; only about calling them up out of the depths. The apostle Paul says he was "caught up to the third heaven" (2 Corinthians 12:2). The attractive power is where the Lord Christ is. Jesus Christ is the attraction of the blood washed soul. If you are going to travel anywhere you will go His way.

"All right, somewhere in my files I have that incident as she gave it to me. After a while she sat down and the Spirit came upon her. Presently, she said it seemed as if she escaped out of herself and traveled so far and so fast. Presently she said, 'I observed I was being approached by a beautiful lady who was tall (and she gave a general description of her.) She said her name was Jene. "It is sympathy that brings me. I had a visual defect and the Lord healed me. You come with me and I will take you to Jesus, and He will heal you."'

"'She linked her arm in mine and we traveled together. As we went along, I observed the most wonderful landscape. Presently we came to a mountain, and while we stood there, this lady repeated to me the entire 35th chapter of Isaiah.'

> The wilderness and the solitary place shall be glad for them; and the desert shall rejoice, and blossom as the rose.
>
> It shall blossom abundantly, and rejoice even with joy and singing: the glory of Lebanon shall be given unto it, the excellency of Carmel and Sharon, they shall see the glory of the Lord, and the excellency of our God.
>
> Strengthen ye the weak hands, and confirm the feeble knees.
>
> Say to them that are of a fearful heart, Be strong, fear not: behold, your God will come with vengeance, even God with a recompence; he will come and save you.

Then the eyes of the blind shall be opened, and the ears of the deaf shall be unstopped.

Then shall the lame man leap as an hart, and the tongue of the dumb sing: for in the wilderness shall waters break out, and streams in the desert.

And the parched ground shall become a pool, and the thirsty land springs of water: in the habitation of dragons, where each lay, shall be grass with reeds and rushes.

And an highway shall be there, and a way, and it shall be called The way of holiness; the unclean shall not pass over it; but it shall be for those: the wayfaring men, though fools, shall not err therein.

No lion shall be there, nor any ravenous beast shall go up thereon, it shall not be found there; but the redeemed shall walk there:

And the ransomed of the LORD shall return, and come to Zion with songs and everlasting joy upon their heads: they shall obtain joy and gladness, and sorrow and sighing shall flee away.

"This dear woman did not know there was such a chapter in the Bible, until I told her it was the 35th of Isaiah. Then they came to a broad stretch of water and on the opposite side were groups of angels, and Jesus stood in the midst of one of these groups. The lady took her to within a respectful distance and bowed her into the presence of Jesus. She said, 'He looked on me sympathetically and said, "Wherefore didst thou doubt? I am the Lord that healeth thee,"[3] and He stooped down and took the waters of the river and bathed my eyes and bade me see.'

"All this took place as we sat in the office. Presently her eyes opened and she became normal. Her employer asked her what had happened, and if she could see. She looked out across the street to the market square and proceeded to read the signs on the wall. Then he brought a book of ordinary type and she read that. He handed her a Persian Bible he had on his desk. It had very fine type. She opened the book and began to read."

---

[3] See Exodus 15:26.

Well, that was the story I recited to W. T. Stead and the others as we five sat together that night in Stead's office. They said, "Mr. Lake, that is the most wonderful thing we have ever heard. That is the best cause of spiritualism we know of. If you will just give us the privilege of publishing that story."

I said, "Brethren, you have not seen the secret of that. Nobody came up to give that message, and nobody came down." And they opened their eyes.

That dear soul got through. She was a child of God and she started straight for the Lord. And so would you. The day that God sets your spirit free from this old temple, bless God, you will go straight to the Lord Jesus Christ.

Now let me review a moment. *Spiritualism* is trying to drag the dead up to you. *Christianity,* bless God, is making the blood-washed spirit free to go to the Lord. Just as opposite as night and day.

Last Sunday night a lady from upstairs came into this audience for the first time and got under conviction and was saved and gave her heart to God. On Wednesday night she was sanctified by the precious blood of Jesus, and on Friday night she was baptized in the Holy Ghost. Last night I talked to her for a few moments. She said, "Oh, brother, if I could just tell you the delights of my soul during these thirty-six hours. If I could only explain how my spirit has found a freedom in God and how it seems to me my heart would rush to Him!"

Would it not? Where do you think it would go? Who occupies your mind? Who keeps your soul? Where is your treasure? In heaven, bless God! Well, you will go where your treasure is. You will go where the attraction is.

Don't confuse yourself with a lot of Old Testament scriptures concerning the dead. In the Old Testament you read, "The dead know nothing at all."[4] But you never read it in the New Testament. Something happened to the dead when Jesus came. They changed their place of residence, and after that you begin to read, "To be absent from the body, is to be present with the Lord."[5]

---

[4] See Ecclesiastes 9:5.

[5] See 2 Corinthians 5:8.

Now I want to fix this in your mind. The blood washed always go there, and if you ever talk to anyone that is over there, you will go to *them*. They are not going to leave the throne, but they will say, "Brother, come up here." That is the only way you will ever communicate with them.

In these days when this stuff is being proclaimed around the world by men like Lodge, Doyle, and others who have been recognized as leaders of thought, naturally people are ready to listen.

But after a night with them in their office, I said "Dear God, it is absolutely impossible to make an unenlightened, unsaved soul to understand the difference between the Spirit of God and every other spirit. The Spirit of God is the attractive power that animates the Christian heart, and they do not want to listen to anything else."

"My sheep hear my voice."[6]

Years afterward as I considered these things, and discussed them with a brother, he said "Lake, you had a wonderful opportunity. Tell me, what was the effect in your own soul of that night that you spent with these men?"

I said, "Brother, I left there next morning with profound sympathy in my heart. I said as I walked away, 'Dear God, here are the greatest intellects in the world, but concerning the things of God and the light of the Spirit, they are just as blind as though their eyes were sealed.'" And their eyes were sealed concerning the light of God.

Men come in the name of science. Naturally there is a certain reverence for knowledge, but don't you be fooled. Just because somebody comes along with the light of worldly knowledge, no matter how minute and wonderful it may seem, the knowledge he has is worldly; the knowledge you have is heavenly. The knowledge that his soul possesses is material; the knowledge that your soul possesses is divinely spiritual, bless God. It comes from the heart of the Son of God.

So when I came to Portland and Sir Oliver Lodge was announced to speak, I did not take the train a day sooner in order to hear him. I would not take the trouble to go across the street if I could listen to every one of them, because they could not tell me anything that is

---

[6] John 10:27.

vital. The vital things belong to the kingdom of God, to the knowledge of Jesus Christ. The vital things belong to the Holy Ghost.

I would take too long to tell of the thousands that have gone to spiritualism. I mean people honestly deceived. Just one instance. I had a little friend, Jude, and his dear old wife. They were old-fashioned Methodist people. They had one dear daughter who died at sixteen. I was absent most of the time in the city, but our home in the country joined theirs. Some friends said to me one night, "You know our old friend, Jude, whose daughter died, some months past a spiritualistic medium came to South Bend and they began attending. They have gone wild over the thing. We did not know how to help them, and wondered if you cannot help them."

I went over and had a talk with them, and went with them. At the proper time this gentleman was supposed to be giving them a message from their daughter. After they got through, I said, "I would like to talk to her" And I began to talk to this spirit. I said, "Are you Miss Jude? Where were you born? Where did you go to school?"

"The Willow Street School."

Where did you attend church?

"The Willow Creek Methodist Church."

The answers were perfectly correct. Finally I said, "I remember the night at the Willow Creek Methodist Church when a very wonderful thing happened to you. Do you remember what that was?"

She did not know a thing about it. I said, "Your memory don't seem to be good. Don't you remember when a revival meeting was being conducted and you sat with Mrs. Lake and myself, and when the altar service came I invited you to go and give your heart to the Lord, and you did, and the glory of God came into your soul?"

She did not remember anything about that. I said, "That is strange. Don't you remember on certain occasions you used to come to our home and we used to kneel and the glory and presence of God came on your soul?"

She did not remember anything about that. I said, "You are not the spirit of Miss Jude. You are an old liar. In the name of Jesus Christ, you get out of here." And it got out. Beloved, do not be fooled by every voice you hear.

One other thing, Conan Doyle is greatly distressed about President Coolidge, and he thinks the proper thing to do is to immediately confer with the spirit of the late President Harding and be directed about the things of state, or he will make some blunder. This is the advice of one of the greatest scientists of all the world, a man who has been knighted by the king of England because of his knowledge of scientific methods. Strange council, a darkened soul. Bright mind filled with knowledge of this world, but a darkened soul without a knowledge of eternal things. Do you see the distinction?

The instance I told you of has been the practice of men whenever they have had opportunity to go into such matters. One of these days, the first time I hear somebody announcing that they are going to confer with President Harding, I am going to present myself. In case of a public man, his speeches are on record and they have been available to everybody.

Here is an example. In Edinburgh, I attended a seance where the medium was giving a wonderful message, supposedly from the spirit of the late W. E. Gladstone. I put in my pocket several copies of Gladstone's addresses. I had a stenographer take down the message, and I took the old addresses I had in my pocket and this one that had come through the medium and compared them.

I said, "It seems to me that something terrible has happened to W. E. Gladstone if he is the author of this message. The thing is not comparable with the things he uttered in this life. It looks to me as if dying has had an awful bad effect on him." They were very much surprised. Most mediums have gotten wise now. Comparison is a wonderful thing.

There is one source of knowledge — that is God. The sin of Spiritualism is in this fact. God said to His ancient people Israel, "Thou shalt not seek unto them that peep and mutter."[7] This describes the conditions prevalent in any seance. What should they do? "Shall not a people seek unto the Lord their God?" This Word of God does not

---

[7]   Isaiah 8:19, paraphrased.

even give me the privilege of seeking guidance of angels, let alone the spirit of the dead, or the spirit of a living man either. It gives me one privilege. There is one mind that knows all, that is the mind of God, and if I am His child, and if my heart is made pure by the blood of His Son, then I have a right to come into His presence and secure anything my heart may want.

I do not believe the world has ever began to conceive of the treasures of the wisdom of the heart of God. Our conception of the possibility of receiving wisdom and knowledge from God is very limited. Here is an experience from my own life.

In the course of my preaching in Africa, I observed I would begin to quote things from historical records that I had never heard. I could not understand it. After awhile, I became troubled about it and thought I must stop the practice. It was going on the record as a part of my sermon, and I felt if you quoted something historical you ought to be able to lay your hand on the record in order to be convinced. Then I observed there was difficulty when I checked these utterances.

Then I told my stenographer that when these unusual things would come, I would raise my finger and she was to put a special mark on these paragraphs. After awhile, I had quite a collection of them. When I came to the United States I had them with me. I was visiting in the office of Senator Chamberlain, talking with his Secretary, Grant. As I sat talking with Grant, I showed him this list and told him my experience. He was a Holy Ghost baptized man. He said, "That is an easy matter. We have the most phenomenal man in the Congressional Library here. You give him a quotation from any book, and he will tell you where to find it." We sent the list into him one evening and left it with him overnight. The next day when we returned he told us just where we could find each of these quotations.

Beloved, who knows the facts? Some wandering mind somewhere? Some mind of a dead man? No sir, they were in the mind of God and the soul that enters into the mind of God can get them anytime. But, Beloved, it is the blood of Jesus Christ that enters there. "In whom are hid all the treasures of wisdom and knowledge."[8]

---

[8] Colossians 2:3.

Oh God, someday may we become big enough to know God, to appreciate our Christ and our Savior and the wonder of His soul and the Christian privilege of entering there!

he lesson that God seems to have put in my soul tonight is found in 2 Timothy, first chapter. Do you know, we do not read the Scriptures like people read a textbook? Have you ever observed how a scientist reads his textbook? He weighs every single word, and each word has a peculiar meaning. If we read the Word of God like that we would get the real vitality of what it says. I wonder if we have caught the force of this Scripture:

SPIRITUAL DOMINION

December 9, 1924

> Paul, an apostle of Jesus Christ by the will of God, according to the promise of *life* which is *in* Christ Jesus.
>
> — Verse 1 [emphasis Lake's]

There is no life outside of Jesus Christ, no eternal life outside of Jesus Christ by the declaration of Jesus Himself. John said:

> God hath given to us eternal life, and this life is in his Son. He that hath the Son hath life; and he that hath not the Son of God hath not life.
>
> — 1 John 5:11-12.

All the Scriptures are dear to my heart and bring their peculiar ministry and lesson, but the words of Jesus are the supreme words of the Gospel. Jesus said:

> It is the spirit that quickeneth...the words that I speak unto you, they *are* spirit, and they are life.
>
> — John 6:63 [emphasis Lake's]

Do you know the difficulty in our day is that we have run away from *Jesus,* that is, the Church at large has. The world is making a great struggle at the present hour — we are in the midst of it ourselves — to get *back* to Jesus. We have run into false theology, we have run into churchianity[1] and human interpretations and a hundred other follies, but friends, it is a perfectly lovely and refreshing thing to get back to Jesus. Take the words of Jesus and let them become the supreme court of the Gospel to you.

I consider all the Word of God the common court of the Gospel, but the words of Jesus are the supreme court of the Gospel. If there is a question that is not clearly decided according to your vision in the common court of the Gospel, then refer it to the supreme court, which is the words of Jesus, and the words of Jesus will settle anything that is in your mind.

If our questions were settled by the words of Jesus we would be out of all the confusion that the world is in at present. I do not see any other way for the world to come out of their present confusion, unless it is to accept the words of Jesus as final authority, to accept Jesus as the divine finality where all questions are finally adjudicated and stay by the words of Jesus.

Just as an example on that line, I suppose there is not any question in the Scriptures that is more muddled and fuddled and slobbered over than the subject of water baptism, and we have a dozen forms of baptismal practice, emphasizing different phases of baptismal consecration. But, beloved, the Word of Jesus would settle the whole controversy. Jesus' words settle both the *spirit* and the *mode* of baptism forever. All the damnation that the Christian world has been in over that question is because we simply refused to take the words of Jesus and believe and obey them. I am such an enthusiast on the words of Jesus that if I were compelled to choose between the practice of the apostles and the words of Jesus, I would stand by the words of Jesus. It is the only method that has kept my soul from the confusion I see in other lives.

Coming back to our lesson, observe these words:

>According to the promise of life.[2]

There is no promise of life outside of Jesus Christ. Jesus was the most emphatic teacher the world ever saw. He said:

---

[1] This is apparently Lake's own euphemism for religious Christianity.

[2] 2 Timothy 1:1.

Ye must be born again.[3]

And there is no arbitration by which you can get around the matter. There is no possibility of avoiding that truth. You have got to come straight to it and meet it.

According to the promise of life which is in Christ Jesus.[4]

When I call to remembrance the unfeigned faith that is in thee, which dwelt first in thy grandmother Lois, and thy mother Eunice; and I am persuaded that in thee also.[5]

Timothy had two generations behind him of women of faith.

Wherefore I put thee in remembrance that thou stir up the gift of God, which is in thee *by the putting on of my hands*.[6]

Paul had some faith in the value of the putting on of his hands. It was not a mere form. I want to call your attention to the Word of God especially on this line. Paul's own convictions were that through the laying on of hands on this young man, an impartation of God to his life had been given. It was so real that even though Timothy was not aware of it and was not exercising the power of God thus bestowed, yet Paul's conviction was that the power of God was present. Why? Because he had laid his hands on him in the name of the Lord Jesus Christ, and he believed the Spirit of the Lord Jesus Christ had been imparted to him, therefore the gift of God was in him. Therefore, the faith to exercise that gift ought to be present and be believed it was present because of the fact that the faith of God had already dwelt in his mother and grandmother, and he believed in him also.

Beloved, it takes faith to exercise your gift of God. There are just lots of people around everywhere who have gifts of God, and they are lying dormant in their lives, and there is no value for the kingdom of God through them because of the fact that they have no faith in God to put the gift in exercise and get the benefit of it.

---

[3] John 3:7.

[4] 2 Timothy 1:1.

[5] 2 Timothy 1:5.

[6] 2 Timothy 1:6, emphasis Lake's.

Probably Timothy was a timid fellow, and Paul is going to show him why he should be exercising this gift of God which he believed to be in him.

> For God hath not given us the spirit of fear.[7]

I confess I would like to swear sometimes, and I would like to say, "To h—- with preachers who are all the time preaching fear." They preach fear of the devil and fear of demons and fear of this influence and fear of that influence and fear of some other power. If the Holy Ghost has come from heaven into your soul, common sense teaches us that He has made *you* the master thereby of every other power in the world. Otherwise, the Word of God is a blank falsehood, for it declares:

> Greater is he that is in you, than he that is in the world.

> — 1 John 4:4

> Behold, I give unto you power to tread on serpents and scorpions, and over all the power of the enemy: and nothing shall by any means hurt you.

> — Luke 10:19

And if we had faith to believe that the "greater than he" is in us, bless God, we would be stepping out with boldness and majesty. The conscious supremacy of the Son of God would be manifest in our lives and instead of being subservient and bowed down and broken beneath the weight of sin and the powers of darkness around us, *they* would flee from us and keep out of our way. I believe before God there is not a devil comes within a hundred feet of a real God-anointed Christian. That is the kind of vision God put in my soul.

When I went to South Africa years ago, I attended a great missionary conference a short time after I was there. It was a general conference of the Christian missions of the country. On account of our teaching the baptism of the Holy Ghost and the power of God to heal, we were a peculiar feature in the conference. We were bringing a new message and they wanted to hear us and get us sized up and classified.

---

[7] 2 Timothy 1:7.

Among the difficulties they discussed in that conference was the tremendous influence of the native medicine men over the people. They call them witch doctors. They are a powerfully developed, psychic-type of man, and for generations and generations they have studied psychic things until they understand the practice of psychic laws. It is marvelous to see the psychic manifestations they bring to pass. I have seen shocking things take place at the hand of witch doctors, things that nobody would believe unless you beheld them.

On one occasion, two men had become extremely jealous of each other, both native chiefs, and they lived sixty miles from each other. One time as I was in the kraal[8] of one of them, I heard them discussing this difficulty with the other chief, and it was decided by the chief that the next Sunday morning he was going to set the other fellow on fire. I wanted to see this phenomenon, and I got a horse and went across the country to be there on Sunday morning.

The chiefs go out and round up their cattle and herds, look over their flocks, etc. It is a sort of Sunday exercise. I rode along. We had not ridden for more than an hour when I observed this fellow was becoming very hot. Within half an hour he was absolutely purple. I knew somewhat of medicine; I would have said the man was likely to have a paralytic stroke from blood pressure. After awhile he began to complain of terrible pain, and finally he became exhausted, got down and lay on the ground, and passed into a state of terrible exhaustion. I believe the man would have died. I had heard about these sorts of things, but this was taking place under my own eyes. I saw that unless the man got deliverance he would die. When it got to that point, I said to the brethren, "It is time that we prayed." I stepped over and laid my hands on and called on God to destroy that damning psychic power that was destroying the fellow, and God shattered it.

I talked to the Conference about this matter. I said, "It is a strange thing to me that in all the years of missions in this land your hands are tied on account of witch doctors. Why don't you go out and cast the devil out of these fellows and get the people delivered from their power?"

---

8   kraal: a village of South African natives. *Webster's Desk Dictionary of the English Language* (NY: Gramercy Books, 1983), p. 505.

They took a long breath and said, "Cast the devil out? He will cast the devil out of you!" The secret of our work, the reason God gave us one hundred thousand people, the reason we have twelve hundred native preachers in our work in Africa is because of the fact we believed the promise of:

> Greater is he that is in you, than he that is in the world.[9]

We not only went to seek them, but challenged them separately and unitedly and by the power of God delivered the people from their power, and when they were delivered, the people appreciated their deliverance from the slavery in which they had been held through their superstitions, psychological, spirit control, and they are most terrible.

> God hath not given us the sprit of fear; but of power, and of love, and of a sound mind.
>
> — 2 Timothy 1:7

Whenever I got in the presence of one of these fellows and wanted to cast out the devil, I always felt I wanted to get his eye. I search to get his eye. The eyes of a man are the windows of his soul. In teaching a class of children, I asked them what the eyes were for. One little chap said, "Your eyes are for you to look out of." Do you get it? It is not a poetic expression, they are the windows through which you look out. It is wonderful the things you see when you look out. Sometimes you see fear and the spirit of darkness and you see the devil in the other life. Marvelous things that you see with your inner eyes.

The world laughs at our Pentecostal people because they sometimes talk about seeing by the Spirit, and sometimes we talk about seeing psychically. We see all the time naturally, as you and I do now.

God anoints your soul. God anoints your life. God comes to dwell in your person. God comes to make you a *master*. That is the purpose of His indwelling in a Christian. The real child of God was to be a master over every other power of darkness in the world.[10] It was to be subject *to him*. He is to be God's representative in the world.[11] The Holy Ghost in the Christian was to be as powerful as the Holy Ghost was in the Christ. Indeed, Jesus' words go to such an extreme that they declare that:

---

[9] 1 John 4:4.

[10] See Luke 9:1 and 10:19.

[11] See Ephesians 6:11-12 and 2 Corinthians 5:20.

Greater works than these shall he do.

— John 14:12

It indicates that the mighty Holy Ghost from heaven in the lives of the Christian was to be more powerful in you and in me after Jesus got to heaven and ministered Him to our souls than He was in Jesus.

Beloved, who has the faith to believe it? Who has faith to exercise it? We cannot exercise anything beyond what we believe to be possible. Listen:

God hath not given us the spirit of fear.

Fear of the devil is nonsense. Fear of demons is foolish. The Spirit of God anointing the Christian heart makes the soul impregnable to the powers of darkness. How I love to teach men that when the Lord Jesus Christ anoints your soul and baptizes you in the Holy Ghost, that the almightiness of the eternal God the Father, by the Spirit and Jesus Christ combined, has come into your soul.

One of the thirty-six articles of the Church of England says, "The Holy Ghost which proceedeth from the Father and the Son." There is no truer thing in all the world. Do you get it – "which proceedeth from the Father and the Son"? In the fourth and fifth chapters of Revelation you see the distinctive personalities of God the Father and Jesus Christ. God the Father occupies the throne and is holding the seven-sealed book in His hand. And Jesus Christ, the silent Lamb, without an attendant, not an angel to accompany Him, absolutely alone, in lonesomeness as the slain Lamb, presents Himself to the Father, and the Father hands Him the seven-sealed book as He whose right it is to unseal and open the seals.

What I want to bring to you is that the Spirit of God, the divine master, the eternal power of God, the combined life and presence by the Spirit, of the Father and the Son, is given to you — not to leave you a weakling and subject to all kinds of powers of darkness, but to make you a *master*, to give you *dominion* in God over every devilish force that ever was.

God hath not given us the spirit of fear; but of power, and of love, and of a sound mind.[12]

---

[12] 2 Timothy 1:7.

The Spirit of Power is the Holy Ghost, bless God. And not only of power, but of *love* and of a *sound mind* — not craziness and insanity, but a sound mind by which you can look in the face of the devil and laugh.

Once I was called to come to pray for a blacksmith at Johannesburg, South Africa. He was in delirium tremens.[13] When I got to the house they had him locked in a room and the windows barred. The wife said, "Mr. Lake, you are not going into that room?"

I said, "Yes, I would like to."

"But, Brother, you do not understand. My sons are all more powerful than you are and four of them tried to overpower him and could not do it. He nearly killed them."

I said, "Dear sister, I have the secret of power that I believe matches this case."

Greater is he that is in you, than he that is in the world.[14]

"Sister, you just give me the key, and go about your work, and do not be troubled." I unlocked the door, slipped into the room, turned the key again, and put the key in my pocket. The man was reclining in a crouch like a lion ready to spring. I never heard any lips blaspheme as his did. He cursed maybe every expression I ever heard and worse. He threatened me if I came near him, he would tear me limb from limb and throw me out the window. He was as big as two of me. I never saw such an arm in my life.

I began to talk to him. I had the confidence that "greater is he that is in you, than he that is in the world." I engaged him in conversation until the Holy Ghost in me got hold of that devil or a legion as the case might be. I approached the bed step-by-step, sometimes only three inches, and in half an hour I got up close enough where I could reach his hand. He was still reclining in a posture like a lion. I caught his hand and turned his wrists. I was not practicing any athletic tricks,

---

13 delirium tremens: a violent restlessness due to excessive use of alcohol, characterized by trembling. *Webster's Desk Dictionary of the English Language* (NY: Gramercy Books, 1983), p. 239.

14 1 John 4:4.

but I unconsciously turned his wrists over, and as I did it brought my eyes down near his, and all at once I woke up. I could see the devil in that man begin to crawl. He was trying to get away. God Almighty can look out of your eyes, and every devil that was ever in hell could not look in the eyes of Jesus without crawling. The lightnings of God were there.

My spirit awoke, and I could see the devil was in terror and was crawling and trying to get back away from my eyes as far as he could. I looked up to heaven and called on God to cast that devil out and lent Jesus Christ all the force of my nature, all the power of my spirit, all the power of my mind, and all the power of my body. God had me from the crown of my head to the soles of my feet. The lightnings of God went through me, and the next thing I knew he collapsed in a heap and flopped down like a big fish. Then he turned out of the bed on his knees and began to weep and pray, because he had become human again, and the devil was gone.

Dear hearts, don't you see in a moment that the character of education develops a certain confidence in God, and it makes your soul sick when you see Christian men and women sneak around afraid of the devil and teaching people the devil is going to jump on you and take possession of you. Not a bit of it! There never was a devil in the world that ever went through the blood of Jesus, if the individual was in Christ.

In the Jewish Bible, among the listings of the covenants, is one that is known as the Threshold Covenant. That was the covenant by which the Israelites went out of the land of Egypt. When God told them to slay a lamb and put the blood on the doorposts and lintel. And the Jewish Bible adds, they put the blood on the threshold. A lot of people get the blood of Jesus on their head, but it seems to me they do not get it under their feet. The Word of God teaches us to get the blood under your feet and on the right hand and on the left hand and over your head. That is your protection. There was no angel of death in the land of Egypt, or in hell, that could go through that blood unto that family. No sir! He was absolutely barred.

Friends, do you believe it was the blood of the Lamb that was barring the angel of death? Do you believe the red stains on the doors frightened him away? No sir, the blood signified to me that there is one that goes *through* the blood; that is the Holy Ghost. And beloved, the eternal God, by the Spirit, went through the blood to the inside and stayed there and defended the house.

Greater is he that is in you, than he that is in the world.

All these little insignificant devils that come along in this sickness or that sickness or that temptation of sin have no power over you. Dear friends, from heaven there comes to your heart and mine that dominion of Jesus by which the God-anointed soul walks through them, through myriads of demons, and they cannot touch you.

I was in Pretoria, South Africa, visiting with a friend and trying to keep out of the hot sun to meditate and pray; and as I meditated and prayed, I seemed to be lifted up in the Spirit until I was a mile or more above the city and could see the city like you would from an airplane. When I got up there I made a discovery. There were myriads of spirits of darkness and myriads of spirits of light in the most awful conflict I ever saw. Naturally, you think of a weapon when you see a fight. I thought, *If only I had a weapon I would get into that fight.*

Presently, the Spirit of God got hold of me and when these demons came at me from all sides I waded into them and began to knock them down. It continued until I had knocked so many down I had to climb over them to get at the rest.

When the vision lifted I prayed, "Dear Lord, what does it mean?" And the Spirit of the Lord said to me, "This contest that you have seen in the upper air will exist among your own people on the earth in six months. This lesson is to teach you that there is a dominion in Jesus Christ, and 'greater is he that is in you, than he that is in the world.'"

Friends, it is time you and I as the blood-washed in Jesus awoke to our privilege whereby in the name of the Lord we cease to sin and let no unholy condemnation remain upon our life any longer.

I do not know, but maybe I have come through a different school from what others have in the lines of the Spirit, but I am sure of one thing, that if Christianity was to leave me a weakling to be oppressed by the power of darkness I would seek something else because it would not meet the need. It is that which meets the need that gives you divine supremacy in Jesus Christ. Friends, when your heart is surcharged by that faith in God so that "greater is he that is in you, than he that is in the world," you will pray a new prayer.

Moses came to the Red Sea with impassable mountains on the right hand and impassable mountains on the left hand, the army of Pharaoh behind him, and the sea in front of him. If any man had a right to stop and pray surely you might say that man had.

Over and over and over again, when we get to the real ditch we try to jump the thing and put the responsibility back on God. Just watch God make a real man. When Moses got his prayer nicely started, God rebuked him and said,

> Wherefore criest thou unto me? speak unto the children of Israel, that they go forward: But lift *thou* up thy rod, and stretch out *thine* hand over the sea, and *divide* it.
>
> — Exodus 14:15-16 [emphasis Lake's]

I want you Pentecostal Christians to get this. God did not say, "Moses, you stretch forth your hand and *I* will divide the sea." He said, "Stretch forth thine hand over the sea, and *divide* it. You have faith in Me, *you* stretch forth your hand and divide the sea." Jesus said practically the same thing to His disciples:

> When he had called unto him his twelve disciples, he *gave* them power against unclean spirits, to cast them out, and to heal all manner of sickness and all manner of disease.
>
> — Matthew 10:1 [see also Luke 9:1-6]

Beloved, He gives it to you. What is the Holy Ghost? It is the gift of God Himself to you. The Holy Spirit is not simply given that you may be a channel and always a channel. No sir! But instead of that, the most magnificent thing the Word of God portrays is that Christ indwelling in you by the Holy Ghost is to make you a son of God like Jesus Christ, God-anointed from heaven, with the recognized power of God in your spirit to command the will of God.

It may not be that all souls have grown to that place where such a life as that is evident, but surely if the Son of God by the Holy Ghost has been born in our hearts, it is time we began to let Him have some degree of sway in our hearts, and some degree of heavenly dominion of value, and some degree of the lightnings of Jesus Christ breaking forth from our spirits.

That is what the Word of God speaks to my soul tonight. That is why my spirit rejoices in this blessed Word.

> God hath not given us the spirit of fear; but of power, and
> of love, and of a sound mind.

The sanest man is the man that believes God and stands on His promises and knows the secret of His power, receives the Holy Ghost and gives Him sway in his life and goes out in the name of the Lord Jesus to command the will of God and bring it to pass in the world.

At the end of the first three hundred years of the Christian era, there were millions of Christians. Christianity was an aggressive power. Christianity went into the heart of heathendom to undo their superstitions, to break down their psychological forces, to leave the consciousness of Jesus Christ in the heart, to heal the sick, to raise the dead. Oh, God in heaven, bring our hearts back to it. Christianity was a conquering force.

But friends, there was a consecration secret in the life of the early Church. It was this: If they could not conquer, they could die. Dear friends, you will never exercise very much of the dominion of the Son of God in your spirit until your heart is ready to say, "If I cannot get the mastery, I can die." The early Christians died, plenty of them — millions of them. That is the reason people say the blood of the martyrs was the seed of the Church. Bless God, they died for their faith.

Friends, you and I will never know or have the big ministry and the big victory until our souls have arrived at the place where we will die for our faith also. Lord God, help us. These days, if a man gets a stomachache he is afraid he will die. Die if you have to die, but do not disgrace the cause of Christ and weaken in your faith and sell it to man or the devil. When that degree of consecration comes into your heart, when that degree of determination comes into your spirit, you will not have to die.

But I tell you, most of us will do our dying before we enter there. That is the life into which dead men enter. That is the resurrection life. We have to die to get it. You have to die to enter there. We die to our sin, we die to ourselves, we die to the opinions of men, and we die to the old world. We die to fear of spooks and demons and devils and prove the truth of the text, "Greater is he that is in you, than he that is in the world." "In my name they shall cast out devils...."[15] "Resist the devil, and he will flee from you."[16] We live in Jesus Christ. Blessed be His name.

Neither give place to the devil.

— Ephesians 4:27

Put on the whole armour of God, that ye may be able to stand against the wiles of the devil.

— Ephesians 6:11

There hath no temptation taken you but such as is common to man: but God is faithful, who will not suffer you to be tempted above that ye are able; but will with the temptation also make a way to escape, that ye may be able to bear it.

— I Corinthians 10:13

And Jesus said unto them, Because of your unbelief: for verily I say unto you, If ye have faith as a grain of mustard seed, ye shall say unto this mountain, Remove hence to yonder place; and it shall remove; and nothing shall be impossible unto you.

— Matthew 17:20

Behold, I give unto you power to tread on serpents and scorpions, and over all the power of the enemy: and nothing shall by any means hurt you.

— Luke 10:19

---

[15] See Mark 16:17.

[16] James 4:7.

he text tonight is:

Blessed are they which do hunger and thirst after right-eousness: for they shall be filled.

— Matthew 5:6

SPIRITUAL HUNGER
Portland, Oregon
December 11, 1924

Hunger is a mighty good thing. It is the greatest persuader I know of. It is a marvelous mover. Nations have learned that you can do most anything with people until they get hungry. But when they get hungry you want to watch out. There is a certain spirit of desperation that accompanies hunger.

I wish we all had it spiritually. I wish to God we were desperately hungry. Wouldn't it be glorious? Somebody would get filled before this meeting is over. It would be a strange thing if we were all desperately hungry for God for only one or two got filled in a service.

> Blessed are they which do hunger and thirst after right-eousness.

Righteousness is just the rightness of God — the rightness of God in your spirit; the rightness of God in your soul; the rightness of God in your body; the rightness of God in your affairs, in your home, in your business, everywhere.

God is an all-round God. His power operates from every side. The artists put a halo around the head of Jesus to show that there is a radiation of glory in His person. They might just as well put it around His feet or any part of His person. It is the radiant glory of the indwelling God, radiating out through the personality. There is nothing more wonderful than the indwelling of God in the human life. The supremest marvel that God ever performed was when he took possession of those who are hungry.

> Blessed are they which do hunger.

I will guarantee to you that after the crucifixion of Jesus there was a hundred-and-twenty mighty hungry folks at Jerusalem. I do not believe if they had not been mightily hungry they would have gotten so gloriously filled. It was because they were hungry that they were filled.

We are sometimes inclined to think of God as mechanical; as though God set a date for this event or that to occur. But my opinion is that one of the works of the Holy Ghost is that of preparer. He comes and prepares the heart of men in advance by putting a strange hunger for that event that has been promised by God until it comes to pass.

The more I study history and prophecy the more I am convinced that when Jesus was born into the world He was born in answer to a tremendous heart cry on the part of the world. The world needed God desperately. They wanted a manifestation of God tremendously, and Jesus Christ as the Deliver and Savior came in answer to their soul cry.

Many look forward to the second coming of Jesus — His coming again — as though mechanically, on a certain date, when certain events come to pass, Jesus is going to arrive. I do not see it that way. I see on the other hand that there must be a tremendous hunger, an overwhelming hunger, for the Lord's coming in the hearts of men, so that a prayer such as was never prayed in the world before for Christ to come will rise to heaven. And, bless God, when it rises to heaven on the part of sufficient souls, it will take Jesus Christ himself off the throne and bring Him down to earth.

Daniel says that he was convinced by the study of the books of prophecy, especially that of Jeremiah, that the time had come when they ought to be delivered from captivity in Babylon. The seventy years was fulfilled but there was no deliverance. So he diligently set his face to pray it into being (Daniel 9).

Here is what I want you to get. If it was going to come to pass mechanically, by a certain date, there would not have been any necessity for Daniel to get that hunger in his soul, so that he fasted and prayed in sackcloth and ashes that deliverance might come.

No sir, God's purposes come to pass when your heart and mine gets the real God cry, and the real God prayer comes into our spirit and, the real God yearning gets our nature. Something is going to happen then.

No difference what it may be your soul is coveting or desiring, if it becomes in your life the supreme cry — not the secondary matter, or the third, or the fourth, or fifth or tenth, but the *first* thing; the supreme desire of your soul, the paramount issue — all the powers and energies of your spirit, of your soul, and of your body are reaching out and crying to God for the answer. It is going to come, it is going to come, it is going to come.

I lived in a family where for thirty-two years they never were without an invalid in the home. Before I was twenty-four years of age we had buried four brothers and four sisters, and four other members of the family were dying, hopeless and helpless invalids. I set up my own home; married a beautiful woman. Our first son arrived. It was only a short time until I saw that same devilish train of sickness that followed father's family had come into mine. My wife became an invalid, my son was a sickly child.

Out of it all one thing developed in my nature — a cry for deliverance. I did not know any more about the subject of healing than an Indian, notwithstanding I was a Methodist evangelist. But my heart was crying for deliverance; my soul had come to the place where I had vomited up dependence on man. My father spent a fortune on the family, to no avail, as if there was no stoppage to the hell. And let me tell you, there *is no human stoppage* because the thing settled deep in the nature of man; too deep for any material remedy to get at it. It takes the Almighty God and the Holy Spirit and the Lord Jesus Christ to get down into the depth of man's nature and find the real difficulty that is there and destroy it.

My brother, I want to tell you, if you are a sinner tonight and away from God, your heart is longing and your spirit asking and your soul crying for God's deliverance. He will be on hand to deliver. You will not have to cry very long until you see that the mountains are being moved, and the angel of deliverance will be there.

I finally got to that place where my supreme cry was for deliverance. Tears were shed for deliverance for three years before the healing of God came to us. I could hear the groans and cries and sobs and feel the wretchedness of our family's soul. My heart cried, my soul sobbed, my spirit wept tears. I did not know enough to call directly on God for it. Isn't it a strange thing that men do not have sense enough to have faith in God for all their needs; do not know enough to call directly on God for physical difficulties, as well as spiritual ones? But I did not.

But bless God, one thing matured in my heart — a real hunger. And the hunger of a man's soul must be satisfied. It must be satisfied. It is a law of God; that law of God is in the depth of the Spirit. God will answer the heart that cries. God will answer the soul that asks. Christ Jesus comes to us with divine assurance and invites us when we are hungry to *pray,* to *believe,* to take from the Lord that which our soul covets and our heart asks for.

So one day the Lord of heaven came our way and in a little while the cloud of darkness, that midnight of hell, that curse of death, was lifted and the light of God shone into our life and into our home, just the same as it existed in other men's lives and other men's homes. We learned the truth of Jesus and was able to apply the divine power of God. We were healed of the Lord.

Blessed are they which do hunger.

Brethren, begin to pray to get hungry.

At this point I want to tell you a story. I was out on a snow-shoe trip at St. Marie, Michigan, where they used to have four and five feet of snow. I tramped for thirty miles on my snow shoes. I was tired and weary. I arrived home and found my wife had gone away to visit, so I went over to my sister's home. I found they were out also. I went into the house and began to look for something to eat. I was nearly starved. I found a great big sort of cake that looked like corn bread. It was still quite warm and it smelled good. I ate it all.

I thought it was awful funny stuff, and it seemed to have lumps in it. I did not just understand the combination, and I was not much of a cook. About the time I had finished it my sister and her husband came in. She said, "My, you must be awful tired and hungry."

I said, "I was, but I just found a corn cake and ate the whole thing."

She said, "My goodness, John, you did not eat that?"

I said, "What was it, Irene?"

"Why that was a kind of cow bread, we grind up cobs and all." You see it depends on the character and degree of your hunger. Things taste mighty good to a hungry man.

If you wanted to confer a peculiar blessing on men at large, it would not be to give them pie, but to make them hungry, and then everything that came their way, it would taste everlastingly good.

I love to tell this story because it is the story of a hungry man. A short while after, I went to South Africa and God had begun to work very marvelously in the city of Johannesburg. A butcher who lived in the suburbs was advised by his physicians that he had developed such a tubercular state he might not live more than nine months. He wanted to make provision that his family would be cared for after he was gone, so he bought a farm and undertook to develop it, so that when he died his family would have a means of existence.

One day he received a letter from friends at Johannesburg, telling of the coming of what they spoke of as "the American brethren" and of the wonderful things that were taking place. Of how So-and-so, a terrible drunkard, had been converted; of his niece, who had been an invalid in a wheelchair for five years, had been healed of God. How one of his other relatives had been baptized in the Holy Ghost and speaking in tongues; other friends and neighbors had been baptized and healed, of the powerful change that had come in the community, and all the marvels a vigorous work for God produces.

Dan VonVuuren took the letter and crawled under an African thorn tree. He spread the matter out before God and began to discuss it with the Lord. He said, "God in heaven, if You could come to Mr. So-and-so, a drunkard and deliver him from his drunkenness, save his soul and put the joy of God in him; if You could come to this niece of mine, save her soul and heal her body and send her out to be a blessing instead of a weight and burden upon her friends; if You could come to So-and-so, so they were baptized in the Holy Ghost and speak in tongues; Lord, if You can do these things at Johannesburg, You can do something for me too."

And he knelt down, put his face to the ground, and cried to God that God would do something for him. And don't forget it, friends, I have a conviction that that morning Dan VonVuuren was so stirred by the reading of that letter that his desire to be made whole got bigger than anything else in his consciousness. His heart reached for God, and bless God, that morning his prayer went through to heaven and God came down into his life. In ten minutes he took all the breath he wanted. The pain was gone. The tuberculosis disappeared. He was a whole man.

But that was not all. He not only received a great physical healing, but God had literally come in and taken possession of the man's life until he did not understand himself anymore. In telling me he said, "Brother, a new prayer from heaven is in my spirit. I had prayed for my wife's salvation for eighteen years, but I could never pray through. But that morning I prayed through. It was all done when I got to the house. She stood and looked at me for two minutes, until it dawned in her that I was gloriously healed of God. She never asked a question as to how it took place, but fell on her knees, threw her hands up to heaven, and said, 'Pray for me, Dan. For God's sake, pray for me. I must find God today,' and God came to that soul."

He had eleven children, splendid young folks. The mother and he went to praying and inside of a week the whole household of thirteen had been baptized in the Holy Ghost. He went to his brother's farm, told the wonder of what God had done, prayed through and in a little while nineteen families were baptized in the Holy Ghost.

God so filled his life with His glory that one morning God said to him, "Go to Pretoria. I am going to send you to the different members of Parliament." He was admitted into the presence of Premier Louis Botha. Botha told me about it afterward. He said, "Lake, I had known Von Vuuren from the time he was a boy. I had known him as a reckless, rollicking fellow. But that man came into my office and stood ten feet from my desk. I looked up, and before he commenced to speak, I began to shake and rattle on my chair. I knelt down. I had to put my head under the desk and cry to God. Why he looked like God; he talked like God."

He had the majesty of God. He was super-humanly wonderful. Then he went to the office of the Secretary of State, then to the Secretary of the Treasury. Almost the same thing took place in every instance. For eighteen days God kept him going from this one and that one;

lawyers, judges, and officials in the land, until every high official knew there was a God and a Christ and a Savior and a baptism of the Holy Spirit, because Dan Von Vuuren had really hungered after God.

Blessed are they which do hunger.

I was sitting here tonight before the meeting and began reading an old sermon I spoke to a men's club at Spokane, Washington, eight years ago, entitled "The Calling of the Soul." In it I observed I recounted the story of the original people who came to the Parham School in 1900 and whom in answer to the cry of their soul God came and baptized them in the Holy Ghost. All the Apostolic Faith Churches and Missions, Assemblies of God, and other movements are the result.

I knew Brother Parham's wife and his sister-in-law, Lillian Thistleweight. She was the woman that brought the light of God for real sanctification to my heart. It was not her preaching or her words. I sat in Fred Bosworth's home one night before a night of preaching the Gospel. I listened to that woman telling of the Lord and His love and sanctifying grace and power and what real holiness was. It was not arguments or logic; it was herself. It was the divine holiness that came from her soul. It was the living Spirit of God that came out of the woman's life.

I went back in the room, as far away as I could get. I was self-satisfied, doing for the world, well in the world, prosperous with all the accompaniments that go with successful business, but that night my heart got so hungry that I fell on my knees, and those who were present will tell you yet that they had never heard anybody pray as I prayed. Bosworth said long afterward, "Lake, there is one instance that I shall always remember in your life; that was the night you prayed in my home until the rafters shook, until God came down, until the fire struck, until our souls melted, until God came and sanctified our hearts." All the devils in hell and out of hell could not believe there is not a real sanctified experience in Jesus Christ; when God comes in and makes your heart pure and takes self out of your nature and gives you divine triumph over sin and self, blessed be the name of the Lord!

Blessed are they which do hunger.

Beloved, pray to get hungry.

Getting back to Dan Von Vuuren. For several years before I left Africa, he went up and down the land like a burning fire. Everywhere he went sinners were saved and were healed. Men and women were baptized in the Holy Ghost, until he set the districts on fire with the power of God; and he is going still.

Here is a point I want to bring to you. As I talked with Lillian Thistleweight, I observed the one supreme thing in that woman's soul was the consciousness of holiness. She said, "Brother, that is what we prayed for, that is what the baptism brought to us."

Later, Brother Parham was preaching in Texas. A colored man came into his meeting, by the name of Seymour. In a hotel in Chicago he related his experience to Brother Tom and myself. I want you to see the hunger in that colored man's soul. He said he was a waiter in a restaurant and preaching to a church of colored people. He knew God as Savior, as the sanctifier. He knew the power of God to heal. But as he listened to Parham he became convinced of a bigger thing — the baptism of the Holy Ghost. He went on to Los Angeles without receiving it, but he said he was determined to preach all of God he knew to the people.

He said, "Brother, before I met Parham, such a hunger to have more of God was in my heart that I prayed for five hours a day for two and a half years. I got to Los Angeles, and when I got there the hunger was not less but more. I prayed, 'God, what can I do?' And the Spirit said, 'Pray more.'" He said, "I am praying five hours a day now. I increased my hours of prayer to seven, and I prayed on for a year and a half more. I prayed God to give me what Parham preached, the real Holy Ghost and fire with tongues and love and power of God like the apostles had."

There are better things to be had in spiritual life, but they must be sought out with faith and prayer. I want to tell you God Almighty had put the hunger into that Negro's heart, that when the fire of God came it glorified. I do not believe that any other man in modern times had a more wonderful deluge of God in his life than God gave to that dear fellow. Brother Seymour preached to my congregation, to ten thousand people, when the glory and power of God was upon his preaching when men shook and trembled and cried to God. God was in him.

Blessed are they which do hunger for they shall be filled.

I wonder, what we are hungering for? Have we a real divine hunger, something our heart is asking for? If you have, God will answer. God will answer. By every law of the Spirit that men know, the answer is due to come. It will come! Bless God, it will come. It will come in more ways than you ever dreamed of. God is not given to manifesting Himself in tongues and interpretation alone. His life in man is rounded.

When I was a lad, I accompanied my father on a visit to the office of John A. McCall, the great insurance man. We were taken to McCall's office in his private elevator. It was the first time I had ever been in a great office building and ridden in an elevator, and I remember holding my breath until the thing stopped. Then we went into this office, the most beautiful office I had ever beheld. The rugs were so thick I was afraid I would go through the floor when I stepped on them. His desk was a marvel, pure mahogany, and on the top of his desk, inlaid in mother of pearl was his name, written in script. It was so magnificent, that in my boyish attitude, I said, "I'm going to have an office just like this and a desk like that with my name on it when I am a man."

I did not know how much of an asking it was in my nature, and it seemed sometimes my desire had drifted away until I was in my thirtieth year. I was invited to come to Chicago to join an association of men who were establishing a life insurance association. They said, "Lake, we want you to manage this association." We dickered about the matter for three weeks until they came to my terms, and finally the president said, "Step into this office until we show you something. We have a surprise for you." And I stepped into an office just exactly the duplicate of John McCall's office, and there in the center was a desk of pure mahogany and instead of the name of John A. McCall it was

John G. Lake, in mother of pearl. I had never spoken of that soul desire to a person in the world.

Friends, there is a something in the call of the soul that is creative. It brings things to pass. Don't you know that when the supreme desire of your heart is known to God, that all the spiritual energy of your nature and the powers of God given to you begin to concentrate and work along that certain line and form, and there comes by the unconscious creative exercise of faith into being that our soul calls for. That is the creative action of faith, you and God together, evidencing the power of creative desire."

INTERPRETATION OF TONGUES

Mrs. James Wilson — Brother Myreen

*You shall receive the desire of your heart if you come before
Me in prayer and supplication, for I am a God that
answers My children. Go ye forward in the battle for I shall
be with you and fulfill the desire of your heart. Yea, pray
that ye may become hungry.*

*Call and I shall answer, for I am a God that hears. I shall
answer your call. Come before Me. Humble yourselves before
My feet, and I shall answer your call.*

*Be diligent before Me, and pray, yea, be ye in prayer and
supplication, for you are living in the last days, and My
Spirit shall not always strive with men. But ye who humble
yourselves before Me will know I shall be your God, I shall
strengthen you on the right hand and on the left, and ye
shall understand and know that I am your living God.*

As Moses stood at the Red Sea he tried to back out of that relationship God was establishing and tried to throw the responsibility back on God. He was overwhelmed. It was too marvelous. Surely God must not have meant it, but God knew. When he began to recognize himself as an individual and God as another it was offensive to God. He thought he could back up and pray for God to do something for him the same as God did in the old relationship. He could not do it. When he got down to pray, in the mind of God the idea of Moses not backing water and getting out of that close place, that inner relationship, that divine symphony of Moses' soul and God's, it was offensive to him. And God said,

> Wherefore criest thou unto me?

In other words, shut up your praying. Get up out of there.

> Lift thou up thy rod, and stretch out thine hand over the sea, and *divide it*.

> — Exodus 14:15-16

God did not say, "Moses, you stretch forth your hand, and I will divide the sea." But He said,

> Stretch out thine hand over the sea, and divide it.

You and I are one, stretch forth your hand and divide the sea. You have all there is of Me and I have all there is of you. We are one and indivisible. God and man becomes one. The heart of man, the mind of man, the soul of man enters into God, God into him. The divine fires of the eternal Christ, by the Holy Ghost, come from heaven, and the lightnings of Jesus flash through the life, bless God, and the powers of Christ invigorate and manifest and demonstrate through that relationship.

God revealed that to my soul in the days when I first went to Africa, within six weeks after my feet touched the soil, and before God had given me a white church to preach in. I said, "Lord, when You give me a church in which to preach this Gospel, I will preach the highest and holiest thing God's Spirit reveals to my heart. I do not care if anybody else believes it or sees it; I am going to preach the vision the Son of God puts in my soul."

Bless God, He put the high vision of the glorified Christ and the glorified Christian — not a man simply saved from sin, but a man saved from his sins, sanctified by power, infilled with His Spirit, recreated with and in Jesus Christ — one in nature, character, and substance. My heart began to preach it, and my mouth gave the message and my soul sent forth the word, and my spirit called such that wanted to be the character of man to come to the feet of the Son of God and receive His blessing and receive His power. And, beloved, I tell you that in all the modern world there was another hundred and twenty-five preachers who went out of a church to proclaim the power of God with greater power than that first hundred and twenty-five preachers. The thing that was in my soul fired Dan Von Vuuren's soul and kindled the faith of the people. Wherever it spread it set men on fire for God.

Friends, we need a coming up into God. This church, and the church around, needs to come up into God. We have been traveling around in a circle, digging our noses in the ground, and we have had our eyes on the ground, instead of in the clouds, instead of up at the throne. Look up to the glorified One! I want to see His bleeding hands, look to heaven where He is to see them. Do not go back to Calvary to see Him. He is the risen, regnant,[1] glorified Son of God; risen with all power and all authority, with the keys of hell and of death! He is the divine authority, the eternal overcoming, the divine manifestation of God. And you and the regnant, glorified Christ as one, are the divine manifestation of God. Come up to the throne, dear ones. Let the throne life, and the throne love and the throne power and the throne spirit and the Holy Ghost in heaven possess you, and you will be a new man in Christ Jesus! And your tread will be the march of the conqueror and your song the song of victory and your crown the crown of glory and your power the power of God.

Edited by

Wilford H. Reidt

1220 S. Beech

Kennewick, Washington

---

[1] regnant: reigning in one's own right and not as a consort. *Webster's Desk Dictionary of the English Language* (NY: Gramercy Books, 1983), p. 764.

s a basis of a little talk I want to quote Lincoln's Gettysburg address:

DEDICATION

January 1925

Fourscore and seven years ago our fathers brought forth on this continent a new nation, conceived in liberty, and dedicated to the proposition that all men are created equal. Now we are engaged in a great civil war, testing whether that nation, or any nation so conceived and so dedicated, can long endure. We are met on a great battlefield of that war. We have come to dedicate a portion of that field as a final resting place for those who here gave their lives that that nation might live. It is altogether fitting and proper that we should do this. But in a larger sense we cannot dedicate, we cannot hallow this ground. The brave men, living and dead, who struggled here, have consecrated it far above our poor power to add or detract. The world will little note nor long remember, what we say here, but it can never forget what they did here. It is for us, the living, rather to be dedicated here to the unfinished work which they who fought here have thus far so nobly advanced. It is rather for us to be here dedicated to the great task remaining before us, that from these honored dead we take increased devotion to that cause for which they gave the last full measure of devotion; that we here highly resolve that these dead shall not have died in vain, that this nation, under God, shall have a new birth of freedom, and that government of the people, by the people, and for the people, shall not perish from the earth.

This is an introduction to a thought I want to bring to you. I want to call your attention to Daniel's seventy weeks. These weeks are weeks of years, seven years to a week. Daniel's sixty-nine weeks, or 483 weeks, is dated onward from Daniel and ended with the *anointing* of Jesus at the River of Jordan. We speak of that anointing as the "Christing of Jesus," when the Holy Ghost from heaven came upon

Him. He was then presented to Israel as their Messiah. It required the anointing from heaven to give Him His Messiahship.

Beloved, my soul is dedicated to one purpose, and that is the proclamation of the Gospel of the Holy Ghost in our day. If I am left alone in the world as the only voice to declare the full Gospel of the Holy Ghost, I will go on declaring it.

Every great Movement of God in this world, from the beginning until now, has been an operation of the Holy Ghost. And every fresh introduction of the spirit of man into the life of God has brought a new revelation of Christ and His power to save the world.

Every decline that has followed the history of the Christian Church has first had its inception when men began to lay down on the subject of the Holy Ghost. If you want to spell death to an organization that is now alive spiritually, all you have to do is to get them to lay down on the subject of the necessity of the Holy Ghost and the baptism of the Holy Ghost. There will soon be nothing left but a corpse. That is the history of Christianity.

Friends, let us above all else, in the name of Jesus, dedicate ourselves honestly and sincerely to the proclamation of the Gospel of the Holy Ghost, of the power of God through the Holy Ghost, to bring into the spirit of man that revelation of Jesus Christ that is essential and final and able to reveal Him as the Son of God.

If that, then, is the one thing to which our soul is dedicated, we will certainly not be slack in our endeavor to seek God for our personal entrance into the life of the Holy Ghost. We will be ready to pray for the baptism of the Holy Ghost. We will be ready to study the Word of God. We will be ready to covet the Holy Ghost and His revelation beyond all else. Out of it comes churches. Out of it comes preachers. Out of it comes world evangelism. Out of it comes high reforms — everything that has its great incentive in the Holy Ghost.

The greatest thing that Jesus Christ Himself could comprehend as a possibility for mankind was to secure for them the divine right to become the recipient of the Holy Ghost. And in order to do that, He was compelled to die and shed His blood that their hearts, through its power, should be cleansed from sin and prepared to become the habitation of God through the Spirit.

Lift up your heads, and lift up your hands, and lift up your hearts toward heaven, and declare to the world, the flesh, the devil, and every opposing force in the world that you stand with Jesus Christ for the necessity of the baptism of the Holy Ghost, and that your soul is dedicated to God to carry the precious message wheresoever you will, and by the grace of God to minister its eternal power everywhere where God makes it possible! Amen.

here is only one thing I could preach on today, and that is:

THE
BELIEVER

January 11, 1925

Go ye into all the world, and preach the gospel to every creature. He that believeth...

He that *believeth*. He that believeth, bless God. The believer is the big fellow. "He that believeth," Jesus said.

He that believeth and is baptized shall be saved.

— Mark 16:16

Don't you know Jesus Christ was the most drastic teacher this world ever saw? Jesus Christ demanded that every other religion in all the world be abandoned and thrown to the bats, in order that men might receive the Gospel of the Son of God. Do you hear that?

Not only so, Jesus Christ demanded that every other dispensation and revelation of the true God be set aside in favor of the one pure existent demonstration and manifestation of Jesus Christ. That is the reason the Jew is seeking God for salvation through Jesus Christ, though he had the first and the greatest revelation until Jesus came. Christianity is the most drastic thing in its demands on the human conscience that the world has ever known. No other teacher in all the world like the Son of God places such demands on the life.

Listen, dear hearts,

Go ye into all the world.

The Lord began His preparation of the group to whom He said these wonderful words with the closest possible intimacy. My, He called them one at a time out of the course of the world into attachment with Himself; lived with them, ate with them, slept with them, worked with them, taught them, and prayed with them for three years. Bless God, He took them to the bedside of the dying, took them out in the streets among the sick, the lame, the halt and blind, and healed them, and said, "Go out likewise."[1]

He that believeth.

They came into the ranks of Jesus as believers, as believers in Him. Their abandonment of all that had gone before for the divine superiority of Jesus Christ and His revelation was complete. They came to the Lord with open hearts and open minds and open souls to understand and know the way of God and receive the light of heaven into their hearts, and become divinely equipped by His eternal power.

Oh, the believer has a marvelous place. "He that believeth!" Sound it out, dear ones. "He that believeth." Christianity is the most extraordinary democracy that the world ever knew. Jesus Christ laid its groundwork and its strength and its soul and spirit of the life in the believer. "He that believeth." A personal relationship and union with Jesus Christ in heaven, bless God. My, how it sweeps out class distinction, and it wipes away everything and lets the believer stand in the first place of relationship with God.

How struck I was with our Brother Wilson's testimony the other night. He said he had studied Christian Science for five years. He said when he first got the light of Christian Science he thought it was the most beautiful and wonderful thing in the world. After awhile he began to discover it was nice sounding phrases, beautiful words, but lacking in the divine secret, the secret of the eternal power of Jesus Christ through the blood of the Son of God, and he abandoned it.

Oh my, lots of that in the world. Before Jesus Christ came, Christian Science in a hundred forms was old and gray whiskered and outcast and in the dump heap. Buddhism, Confucianism, Zoroastrianism[2] and all the rest of the long line of human philosophy had to go to the dump heap when Jesus Christ the Son of God revealed the Lord from heaven. No place, no contact, "separation" was the word of Jesus. Let them go, dump them for the divine superiority of Jesus Christ by the Holy Ghost in the human heart.

---

[1] See Luke 10:37.

[2] Zoroastrianism: an Iranian religion founded by Zoroaster, postulating a supreme deity. *Webster's Desk Dictionary of the English Language* (NY: Gramercy Books, 1983), p. 1049.

He that believeth.

He that believeth.

Christianity is not based on the mere statement of these words, or mere belief in them. If it was, it would be a philosophy equal to the others, possibly superior in its demands on the conscience, but it would be based on the philosophic demonstration, the same as the other philosophies are. No sir! That is not Christianity. The secret of Christianity is that Jesus Christ based it on an acceptance of *Himself.* Jesus Christ said, "Receive Me, receive Me." "He that receiveth Me." Not he that receiveth My words alone, but he that receiveth Me.

He that receiveth.

He that receiveth Me.

Receive *Him.* That is what constitutes you a believer, when you receive the Lord into your heart. Not when you receive some particular teaching or a partial statement of His Word, but when you receive Him, the Lord, the Christ, the Redeemer into your heart.

He that believeth.

He that believeth Me.

Christianity is the most extraordinary revelation. It so far surpassed everything else in the form of religion in the known earth that there is no comparison whatever.

I have just written a letter to say that I am accepting an invitation to preach at the International New Thought Convention next July, for five days. I am going to preach to them about the Son of God. In conference with them (one or two hundred of them) their national leaders a couple of years ago said, "Lake, we absolutely challenge you to show where the Gospel of Jesus Christ, or the teachings of Jesus are superior to the teachings of the philosophers."

I said, "Dear brethren, it is not in the statements on the demands of the conscience that is in it. That is not the secret of Christianity. The secret of Christianity is that Jesus gave *Himself* to the *believer.* That Jesus Christ comes into the believer's heart. That He comes to dwell within his soul. That He comes to anoint this spirit from heaven. That He comes to take possession of his heart and life; live in him, move in him, act in him, speak in him, pray in him, and all the other activities of the Christian soul."

Did you ever see Buddha come into anybody? Ten thousands have accepted his philosophy, but he never came from heaven to dwell in any man's heart or life. Confucius never came to dwell in any man's heart yet. Zoroaster, in all the marvel of his wondrous teachings, never came from heaven to dwell in the human soul. When he died, he died, and the grave covered him and there was not a thing left but the books that he wrote as a guide for others.

Ah, Christianity began where philosophies left off. I always feel sorry for the individual who only sees Christianity as a human code, or moral law, even though it was given by Jesus Christ Himself. Oh, that is not Christianity. This moral code that Jesus gave must be made a possibility in your soul, in your life, by the Christ who came to dwell in your heart.

He that believeth.

He has entered into an exalted place, into an amazing relationship. Christianity is absolutely distinguished among all the religions of the world in that it provides for the resurrection of the body, and that Jesus Christ himself was made the "firstfruits" of the resurrection.[3] He came forth in a glorified body, in a glorified life, in glorified power, in a glorified being to dwell by the Spirit in the heart of every other man in the world. Bless God.

Think of the royal, regnant,[4] glorified Son of God of heaven, at the eternal throne, coming into my heart, into your heart, believer! To dwell in your life, bless God. Oh say, I wish the blessed Lord would uncover our eyes to the divine majesty of the believer's relationship.

He that believeth.

Why, Jesus had such an exalted concept of the relationship of the believer to the eternal Christ on the throne that He ordained him with Himself. Hear it! He ordained him with Himself. I am telling you that Jesus Christ said that the *believer* had authority from heaven to say to the lame man, "Arise and walk."[5]

---

[3] 1 Corinthians 15:20.

[4] Regnant: Reigning in one's own right and not as a consort. *Webster's Desk Dictionary of the English Language* (NY: Gramercy Books, 1983), p. 764.

[5] See Luke 9:1.

Heaven conferred something on the souls of men when He made it possible for the risen Lord, by the Spirit, to come into your heart and mine. Oh, how the joy bells of heaven ought to be breaking loose in our soul, and the fires of heaven ought to shine forth from us because the Christ came into our hearts. Blessed be His name.

Jesus of Nazareth did His work in the world, shed His tears over mankind, labored in the Spirit for their salvation, died on the cross, and shed His blood. But Jesus my Lord, bless God, came forth out of the tomb — a living, glorified, regnant sovereign of earth and heaven, with all power and authority within His hand. Hallelujah! Jesus of Nazareth was my Lord in the days of His humiliation, but Jesus the Christ at the eternal throne is the divine manifestation of the overcoming of God. The ultimate of all perfection, the final manifestation of all that is God-like. Hallelujah.

If I would not leave another thing in this service in your hearts I would like to leave this one text in your soul, branded in your soul, stamped on your conscience, burned into your heart. That Jesus Christ as is presented in Revelation, the first chapter, which I love to call the Twentieth Century Christ, is not Jesus in tears in Galilee, or on the Mount of Olives weeping over Jerusalem, but the resurrected, glorified, masterful finality of God, who stands out and says,

I am He.

Let the world look, let the universe behold, let the devil see, let the kingdoms of darkness take notice.

> I am he that liveth, and was dead; and, behold, I am alive for evermore, Amen; and have the keys of hell and of death.
>
> — Revelation 1:18

Would it not sound strange if you heard Buddha say that? You do not catch anything like that in his writings. He never gave a revelation like that. It took the Christ to get that.

A famous author of a new religion presented himself to Talleyrand and told him of an amazing religion he had evolved and wanted to know the best means to quickly present it and fix it upon the minds of the people. Talleyrand told him to come back in three days and he would give him an answer. In three days he came back and Talleyrand received him. The gentlemen said, "Have you got my answer?"

He said, "Yes, it is this: You be crucified, lay in the grave for three days, come forth in resurrection, ascend to heaven as the glorified Son of God, and the whole world will receive you."

Beloved, that is what makes Christianity the superior of every other religion. And listen, dear hearts, when Jesus Christ, that glorified Son at the eternal throne, who speaks words that none other in all the universe of God ever spake, when He said,

> I am he that liveth, and was dead; and, behold, I am alive for evermore, Amen; and have the keys of hell and of death.

It is He who by the Spirit deigns to come into the heart of the believer.

Oh, glory to God. If you have not appreciated the baptism of the Holy Ghost look up to heaven and see the glorified One who purposes to come into your life and possess it.

Suppose I could get inside of Mrs. Lake. Can you imagine such a thing? She would be 190 pounds heavier than she is now. She would have a voice like a pirate, and all the other characteristics of me. She would be me. Do you see it?

Oh, listen. There is a divine secret in Christ's salvation. It is Christ in fact in you by the Holy Ghost, dwelling in you, speaking in you, living in you, blazing in you, flashing from you, bless God.

I lay half the night writing a letter to a brother. I have done that three times and each time I have torn them up. I said, "They are not worthy. They have not sufficient of heaven's finality. I am going to wait until God gives the real light that that boy needs. He has never seen Christ at the throne and the glorified, regnant Jesus in heaven that comes into a man's life."

Our eyes become clouded and our soul dimmed with the earthy things that we see around us, and it is only once in a while when our spirit rises above it into the light of heaven that we see the glorified Son of God.

To His feet I call you. To His heart I ask you to join your soul and without that you will never know the abundance of His salvation.

> That if thou shalt confess with thy mouth the Lord Jesus, and shalt believe in thine heart that God hath raised him from the dead, thou shalt be saved. For with the heart man believeth unto righteousness; and with the mouth confession is made unto salvation.

> — Romans 10:9-10

ear Brother Parham: I have been wanting to write to you for a long time, but have been so very unsettled, and when things around me get unsettled I do not write to anybody until they begin to shape again.

103 Roy Street Houston, Texas

March 24, 1927

Brother Charles H. Parham

Baxter Springs, Kansas

It would be difficult for me to explain to you how or why I am in Houston. A something grew up in my soul that I wanted to see and talk with Carothers, and it kept grinding in me so long that eventually I found myself here. Seeley D. Kinne, Carothers, and sometimes others of the preachers here and myself have been in the habit of getting together for little conferences — just to talk over our own soul state, the condition of the work in general, what God's probable next step may be in the Pentecostal work, and other things of that kind. And out of it all there has grown in me a great desire to have a good conference with yourself.

Unfortunately, when you and I get together you have so much petty detail to look after that we never get a chance to sit down and converse about anything that amounts to anything. What I am anxious to talk over with you is your vision of the future of the Pentecostal movement and whether or not any of us have sufficient light from God to know what His purpose is for this hour. Personally, I have never felt that you occupied the place in the movement that God intended you to occupy and that your endeavor to sort of father the movement, in some respects, has been rather an effort to keep from being submerged, rather than to lead the hosts of God.

While at San Diego, I was in the habit of meeting with a few of the brethren in Los Angeles, Dr. Kenyon, Cannon, Wallace, myself, and others. We would get together once in awhile and talk things over. We did not discuss just the interests of the Pentecostal movement only, but whether or not there was anything that a group of sane men could do that would be of real value to the Christian institution. The consensus of opinion was that what the Christian world is suffering for more than anything else is a lack of ideal of Christianity. The world does not know what real Christianity is. Pentecost should have exemplified it. In that it has failed, in my judgment, about 93 percent. However, it has done this much. It has demonstrated that there is such a thing as the baptism of the Holy Ghost. That men may enter into God if they will. That some have in a slight degree. That none have in an outstanding way that would make their life or revelation comparable with the apostles or the leaders of Christianity in the first centuries. We have rather been an order of cheap evangelism, with a rather cheap evangelistic message that is not worthy, in the high sense, of being called Pentecostal.

Next, my own idea was that if I were going to undertake to do for Christianity the thing that seems to me would be the greatest blessing and present to the world the ideal that it needs, I would like to do it through a sort of Bible university that first taught the full-rounded life of Jesus Christ in man.

Second, that sent into the world a group of men to give that ideal to the public.

How my own soul has longed to see yourself above every other man measure up in God to the stature of the need of this hour. And while I take my hat off to you and recognize in you a humble servant of God who has labored hard and while you have been an amazing propagandist of the truth God revealed to you, yet brother, like myself and all the others that I see, there has been an utter failure to measure up to the stature of fatherhood in God, that would mark you as the real father and leader of the Pentecostal forces.

Now, brother, I am not scolding, and I am sure that you know my deep love for the men who bear this Gospel and especially for yourself, so that you will be ready to concede my aim is not only to help you, but to help my own soul and the souls of those about us to rise up in God to be and do and give the real Pentecostal life and vision to the world.

Every little man is doing the best he can on a big job. Gaston, the head of the Assemblies of God, is endeavoring to do his best and is doing a fine work in keeping his institution orderly. True, they have drifted clear away from a true scriptural Pentecostal ideal and every day are becoming more and more a little bigoted denomination. The spirit of denominationalism in the Assemblies of God is probably narrower than even in the old churches from which Pentecostal people have been escaping for the last thirty years. So, as a power to bless mankind and put an ideal before the world such as the scriptures outline and as our soul is longing for, it does not seem to me they are worth discussing or considering.

None of the other divisions of the movement of which I know, except the movement headed by Brother Goss, holds much hope. I see more hope in Goss's division of the movement than in any of the others. There is one thing we will have to concede — and everybody does who is really intimate with their assemblies and with their preachers — and that is that they show more genuine spirituality than any other branch of the movement. The mere fact of their emphasis of Jesus, that the other divisions of the movement regard as extreme, has tended to bless them in that it has brought them into close touch with the Lord's life and Spirit.

The great mass of independent churches in the Pentecostal faith have a local status. They are all trying to do something. One of the things we are all compelled to admit is that so far as real Pentecost from God is concerned, it is rapidly dying out in the world. I believe in this connection that your own overemphasis on the question of false manifestation has done much to break down faith in God for all manifestation.

Now a personal word. For about three years I have been in a very broken state of health. About thirty years of awful strenuosity and life lived at a pace and under a pressure that few men in the world have endured for so long, has had its natural effect in me as I suspect in my soul it is having in you. And I simply had to break off and ease up. So for three years it has been a snail's pace. But, brother, the thing has wrought a marvel in me. With the quiet and semi-rest, even though forced upon me, there has come an expanding vision and a profound conviction that somehow, if this is real Pentecost, there must come out of it eventually the thing that Pentecost produced in the early church and that was the real body of Jesus Christ. Not a church but *the* Church; not an organization, but the real organism that we have always recognized; not an ecclesiasticism, nor a dictatorship, nor a bureaucracy; but a group of Holy Ghost-baptized souls in which dwells and through which is manifest, the life of the Lord.

In the New Testament church we see the Church was a "minister of life unto life," and of "death unto death." The same Holy Ghost, through Peter, flashed out like a sword of glory and smote the disease from the lame man at the Beautiful Gate, was the same sword that flashed out of his spirit and sent Ananias and Sapphira to the graveyard. Maybe God has changed His mind. Perhaps the Church of Jesus Christ is not a church anymore — just a mob. Probably Paul was mistaken when he gave us the church outline in the twelfth of Corinthians.

However, I cannot think so; I am rather inclined to feel, brother, that we have been too small for God's uses and purposes in this matter. And one of the objects of my writing this letter is to ask your soul, as the oldest man in this movement and the one whom God honored in the formulation of its first message and the establishment of the school that was first honored with this latter day outpouring, if you have any message for my soul, or any revelation from God along this line? What does the future hold to you; what is the hope of the future? Or are we to simply witness the dying of Pentecost as other lesser revelations of God have come to the world, fluttered and sputtered for a few years, and then disappeared?

It seems to me that the test as to whether this is real Pentecost or not is in the fact that if it is, through it must be developed the Church of Jesus Christ. Not only as a scattered, one here and one there, unknown to each other, invisible, unrecognized, and unauthoritative body, whose names are written in heaven, but a Holy Ghost-united, authoritative, and God-controlled and God-directed and God-empowered body, through whom God could meet the challenge of Rome and hell and antichrist and every other institution of the devil that the latter days bring forth.

What my soul would give for one real council in God of the now hidden, wearied, discouraged, distracted, heartbroken Pentecostal preachers.

You will be interested to know that Mr. and Mrs. Stanley, who were in your Bible school when the baptism originally fell at Topeka, are members of my congregation here. I recently met another of that group, but have forgotten at this moment who it was.

Now, brother, about Africa. Did you know that Brother Fockler was in Africa this last year and recently went on to Australia? We had word from him recently telling us about his reception at Melbourne, that was very fine. Fockler is a fine evangelist, a man of sane mind, and is one of the growing men in this movement. One of the things, Parham, that is troubling me is that yourself, Fockler, Sinclair, myself, and the hundred others that constituted the original missionaries of this Gospel, are slipping toward the graveyard very rapidly. We are shouting loudly about living until Jesus comes, but one by one our toes are preparing to be grass root extensions. And I have always hoped that before we who saw the first glory and the first sunburst of power passed on, that we would leave behind us something that would at least conserve its history and embody its spirit and continue to bless the world.

The devil has robbed me financially since my breakdown in health, so that now when I am on my feet again and ready to go I am greatly handicapped for lack of resources. You talk of going to Africa. I would like to know definitely if you have plans to that end or are you just "hoping"? I would like to go better than anything else in the world, but unless God would perform a financial miracle it is an impossibility.

Indeed, I am at a loss to know just why I am in Houston. The church at Spokane is crying for my return. By the way, I was there for a week this winter before Christmas. I went from here to pray for an insane woman, who was instantly delivered, and I remained and preached for a week. The church at Portland begs me to come there; the little church at San Diego is moving along. All of them present a better opportunity than Houston. However, in all my life I never saw such distracted, petrified, soul-bound saints as in Houston. The dear little group at Katy are a lovely, godly group. The Richeys are a group of little men with little minds, trying to fill big men's places in life and in the work of God. It is pitiable and laughable to watch the trick monkey stuff. Dad Richey is extremely jealous, insanely so, and this causes him to stoop to such dishonorable little things as no one could believe unless you were on the ground and saw it. It always makes me think of a bantam rooster among a flock of decent-sized chickens. The only thing the bantam can do is strut, and sure dear old Dad is a fine strutter.

Now, Brother, for the finish. What I am interested in is, has God developed in you a sense of fatherhood in this Gospel? Is your little missionary work the fulfillment of your ideal? My soul cannot help but turn to you for an answer. And though in times past your answers have been somewhat childish I cannot help but feel that with increasing years and gray hairs that perhaps God has honored you with the answer to the need of this hour as He once honored you with the answer to the need of thirty years ago.

One thing I observe however, is that the truth of the origin of the Pentecostal movement and its origin in your school at Topeka and the fact that you formulated the first Pentecostal message to the world is growing and is daily becoming a better known fact. So that now, even the prejudices of the Assemblies of God cannot submerge that truth and neither can Florence Crawford of Portland, Oregon, get the world to believe any longer that she was the first white woman baptized in the Holy Ghost after Pentecost came. And the people of Los Angeles cannot use it much further for a Los Angeles advertising stunt.

In my spirit I have been troubled about you. The last time I saw you, you were too fat. You were eating too much and manifestly, you were eating more meat than a man of your years can assimilate without producing blood pressure and heart strain. I am not aware that my advice or council ever did any good — that you have paid any more attention to it than I have to yours. However, I do want to assure you, brother, of my deep heartfelt interest and continued prayer for you. I will never forget the man who brought the glorious message of Pentecost and all that it has meant to both hell and heaven in my life.

Dear Parham, it is said here that you are coming to Houston in June for a campmeeting. I would like to know definitely what your plans are in that respect, as we have been planning a campmeeting to begin around May 1st and continue straight through the whole summer, and I would like to be able to formulate some idea. It was my hope in this campmeeting to be able to secure the real leaders of the movement for at least a couple of weeks at a time. And yet, I do not want to interfere with any personal plans that you may have.

One of these days I trust God Almighty will get me off of the rocks, at least to that extent that I can send you a respectable offering for your paper, which I prize very much.

Your Brother in Christ,

JGL/FL

Dear Brother Parham:

This is a new epistle according to "John." When are you coming around for another race? Am afraid I will lose my speed if you don't come and keep me in practice. We have your little friend Ida in our home, and we think a great deal of her.

Florence M. Lake

r. Chapman said, just before his passing, "I believe the gift of healing is a far greater divine attainment than the gift of the evangelist." No wonder professor A. B. Bruce said in his *Miraculous Elements of the Gospel*, "Cures should be as common as conversion, and that Christ's healing miracles are signs that disease does not belong to the true order of nature and are but a prophecy that the true order must be restored to us."

There is no question but what there is a universal longing for such a faith for the healing and quickening of our mortal

THE TRUTH ABOUT DIVINE HEALING

Editor's note:

The following is a booklet that was taken from a series of articles that appeared in the newspaper "Sacramento Union" Sacramento, California, in July and August of 1927. The articles were expanded and reprinted in this booklet at an unknown date.

bodies as this. Professor Bruce well expressed it in his Union Seminary lectures, which have been a power ever since their utterance.

> What missionary would not be glad to be endowed with power to heal diseases as conferred by Jesus Christ on His disciples when He sent them on their Galilean mission? I know the feeling well. I spent part of my apprenticeship as a preacher and as missionary in a once prosperous but now decaying village in the west of Scotland, filled with an impoverished and exceptionally disease-stricken population. There I daily saw sights which awakened at once intense sympathy and involuntary loathing.

> There were cases of cancer, strange and demoniac-like forms of insanity, children in arms twenty years old, with the face of a full-grown man and a body not larger than an infant's. I returned home oftime sick at heart and unable to take food.

What would I not have given to have had for an hour the charisma of the Galiean evangelists! And how gladly would I have gone that day not to speak the accustomed words about a Father in heaven ever ready to receive His prodigal children, but to put an end to pain, raise the dying, and to restore to soundness shattered reason. Or had I found someday, on visiting the suffering, that they had been healed, according to their report, in answer to the prayer of some saintly friend. I should have been too thankful to have been at all skeptical. I should then have seen how He Himself took our infirmities and bare our sicknesses, and we were to represent God whose supreme purpose is, as Jesus so clearly showed, to forgive all our sins and heal all our diseases.

The place of the gift of healing in the great message of Jesus' full and complete salvation has been voiced in prophetic foregleams all through the Christian centuries as truly as the coming Messiah by the mouth of the prophets before the appearance of Jesus.

During recent years, it has broken forth in many quarters with most unusual power. As far back as 1884 Rev. R. E. Stanton, DD, a leading Presbyterian clergyman who at one time was moderator of the general assembly of the Presbyterian church, wrote in a little volume entitled *Gospel Parallelisms* these remarkable words:

> It is my aim to show that the Atonement of Christ lays the foundation equally for deliverance from sin and deliverance from disease; that complete provision has been made for both; that in the exercise of faith under the conditions prescribed, we have the same reason to believe that the body may be delivered from sickness that we have the soul may be delivered from sin; in short, that both branches of the deliverance stand on the same ground and that it is necessary to include both in any true conception of what the Gospel offers to mankind.

> The atoning sacrifice of Christ covers the physical as well as the spiritual needs of the race.

Colleges Lag in Science Teachings

Seats of learning scored by Dr. John Lake:

Physiology is the science of the body.

Psychology is the science of the soul.

Pneumatology is the science of the spirit.

Ontology is the science of being.

Our schools and universities teach physiology — the laws, direction, and care of the body. In the past thirty years psychology has found recognition so that not only the universities teach this science, but lecturers on psychology are in every city and hamlet. Even business houses now give psychological courses for their employees and salesmen.

Yet the psychic man will die, and the soul is mortal. Psychology is a natural science.

What are the facts of pneumatology? Firstly: That man is triune in his nature and structure — spirit, soul, and body. Secondly: That the spirit and soul are divisible. On this question, the Bible says concerning the Word of God: "Piercing even to the dividing asunder of soul and spirit...."[1]

Psychology — soul science — says that the soul is the seat of the affections, desires, and emotions; the active will, the self. "My soul," said Jesus, "is exceeding sorrowful" (Matthew 26:38). "My soul (self) doth magnify the Lord, and my spirit hath rejoiced in God my Savior."[2]

A type of semi-scholarship, represented by modern material scientists, has despised the Bible. No university in the United States is sufficiently advanced in scholarship to possess a chair of pneumatology.

The apostle Paul at Ephesus was received into the school of Tyrannus, a school of the Grecian philosophies. Psychology was the basis of their philosophy. Tyrannus recognized Paul's knowledge of pneumatology, the higher science, and established a chair of pneumatology. There, Paul taught the Christian philosophy, pneumatology, and psychology as Christian doctrine and experience. This resulted in the establishing of the Christian churches of Ephesus with 100,000 members. It resulted in the appointment of Timothy as the first Christian Bishop of Ephesus.

---

[1] Hebrews 4:12.

[2] Luke 1:46-47.

An outcome of this teaching in the school of Tyrannus was that the Grecian philosophies were discarded for the higher teaching of Christianity. Of this school came Theckla, a Grecian noblewoman, a God-anointed healer, whose ministry of healing is said by students to have set a record.

And still there are those who would deny the right of Christian ministry to women.

The revelation of Jesus Christ as Savior and Healer through the simple teaching of the cross, surpassed in Paul's estimation every other knowledge and led him to declare:

> I determined not to know any thing among you, save Jesus Christ, and him crucified.[3]

> Christ the power of God, and the wisdom of God.[4]

> I am not ashamed of the gospel of Jesus Christ. It is the power of God unto salvation, to the Jew first, and also to the Greek.[5]

Who has authority to pray for the sick? Is this holy ministry only given to the few? Is it a ministry to all Christians or to the clergy only? Jesus said:

> *If* ye shall ask any thing in my name, I will do it.[6]

> Ask, it shall be given you; seek, and ye shall find; knock, and it shall be opened unto you.[7]

> These signs shall follow *them that believe;* In my name shall they (the believers) cast out devils; they shall speak with

---

[3] 1 Corinthians 2:2.

[4] 1 Corinthians 1:24.

[5] Romans 1:16, paraphrased.

[6] John 14:14.

[7] Luke 11:9.

new tongues...they shall lay hands on the sick, and they shall recover.[8]

The apostles were commanded to go into all the world — to *make believers* in every section. The signs were to follow the *believers,* not the apostles only.

This was heaven's characteristic. It was the trademark of the Christ on *His* goods. It was the brand, the stamp burned into the soul of *the believer* with heavenly fire.

Baptism in the Spirit of Jesus was Christ reproducing Himself in *the believer.* To what extent was this reproduction to be a fact? We contend that Jesus taught that *the believer* was empowered by the Spirit's incoming and indwelling so that he was Christ's ambassador on earth.

Then he must perform Christ's most holy ministries to sinful and sick just as Jesus himself would do.

If this is true then the believer is a priest in every respect.

The believer must then perform Christ's priestly ministry.

The believer, then, is expected to heal the sick. Jesus said that a believer should lay his hands on the sick and heal them, they were not to die, they were to recover. They were healed through the believer by the power supplied from heaven by Jesus Christ to the believer.

We desire to ask, should the believer-priest also forgive sins or pronounce absolution to the penitent seeker after God? We believe he should. We are sure that it is the privilege of the modern Church to see this tremendous truth and privilege that was purposed by the Lord to be the glory of Christianity.

Jesus said the believer should cast out devils. He believes he should. He does it. The devil is ejected from further possession.

How did he do it? By the exercise of the bestowed power as Christ's believer-priest he exercises spiritual authority over the devil in the candidate and frees him from control.

---

[8] Mark 16:17-18.

In this, he has performed the Christ-function. The sick likewise are healed through the believer-priest. In this also he performs another Christ-ministry. Then how about sin? Why does not the believer-priest by the same spiritual power and authority destroy the consciousness of sin in the soul and pronounce absolution for sins that are past?

We are asking these questions in order to discover what the believers' ministry as Christ's representative is.

We are not alone in our faith that the believer should perform the full ministry of the Christ.

"I am a priest." — Browning.

"The early Church lost its power when it lost sight of its high priestly office." — Bishop Burnett.

"The church needs to realize in new ways the inherent priesthood of Christian believers." — Lambeth Conference of Anglican Bishops, 1906.

"The authority to pronounce absolution and remission of sins that are past and fulfill the aspirations of the soul for the future, I believe to be spiritual and not ecclesiastical and traditional, and to belong equally to everyone who has received such absolution and remission, and such gifts of the spiritual life." — Lyman Abbot.

"The experience of the Free Church confirms what we should expect from study of the New Testament and modern psychology, that the priesthood of all believers rests on sounder evidence than the priesthood of some believers." — Rev. Dr. Glover of Cambridge.

"With the Quaker it is not that there is no clergy, *but that there is no laity,* for we are all priests unto the Highest." — John H. Graham in the Faith of the Quaker.

"I am ever in the presence not only of a Great Power, or a Great Lawgiver, but a Great Healer." — Lyman Abbot.

Therefore every believer on Jesus Christ is authorized by the Lord to do as He has done, assured of Christ's assistance.

"Greater things than these shall ye do, because I go unto the Father,"[9] said Jesus. The Lord working with them by signs following. "Lo, I am with you alway, even unto the end of the world."[10]

The miracles of Jesus have been the battleground of the centuries. Men have devoted their lives in an endeavor to break down faith in miracles. Yet more believe in miracles today than ever before.

Pseudo-science declares miracles impossible. Yet the biggest men in the scientific world are believers in the supernatural and know that miracles are the discovery and utilization of which the material scientist knows nothing.

The miracle realm is man's natural realm. He is by creation the companion of the miracle-working God. Sin dethroned man from the miracle-working realm, but through grace he is coming into his own.

It has been hard for us to grasp the principles of this life of faith. In the beginning, man's spirit was the dominant force in the world; when he sinned his *mind* became dominant. Sin dethroned the spirit and crowned the intellect. But grace is restoring the spirit to its place of dominion, and when man comes to realize this, he will live in the realm of the supernatural without effort. No longer will faith be a struggle, but a normal living in the realm of God. The spiritual realm places men where communion with God is a normal experience.

Miracles are then his native breath. No one knows to what extent the mind and the spirit can be developed. This is not the power of mind over matter, but the power of the spirit over both mind and matter. If the body is kept in fine fettle there is almost no limitation to man's development.

We have been slow to come to a realization that man is a spirit and that his spirit nature is his basic nature. We have sought to educate him along educational lines, utterly ignoring the spiritual, so man has become a self-centered, self-seeking being.

Man has lost his sense of relationship and responsibility toward God and man. That makes him lawless. We cannot ignore the spiritual side

---

[9] John 14:12, paraphrased.

[10] Matthew 28:20.

of man without magnifying the intellectual and physical; to do this without the restraint of the spirit is to unleash sin and give it dominance over the whole man.

There must be a culture and development of the spiritual nature to a point where it can enjoy fellowship with the Father God. It is above mind as God is above nature.

Man's intellect is ever conscious of supernatural forces that he cannot understand. He senses the spirit realm and longs for its freedom and creative power, but cannot enter until changed from self and sin; the spirit enthroned and in action rather than the intellect — spirit above *both mind and matter.*

GOD DESTROYS SIN — SIN IS DEATH

Does God always heal?

> In him is no darkness at all.[11]

Can darkness come out of light? Can sickness come out of health? Is death born of life?

The issue resolves itself into: Of what is the redemption of Jesus Christ constituted? What existing powers does he promise to destroy?

First, sin. When Christ's redemption is completed sin is gone. "Through sin death entered into the world."[12] Death entered through sin.

Sickness is incipient death — death is process.

"He healed all that were oppressed of the devil" (Acts 10:38). In Luke, chapter thirteen, Jesus demanded His right to heal the woman bowed together with the spirit of infirmity eighteen years as follows: "Ought not this woman whom Satan hath bound these eighteen years be healed,"[13] and overriding traditions of the Jews He healed her then and there.

> The last enemy that shall be destroyed is death.[14]

---

[11] 1 John1:5.

[12] Romans 5:12, paraphrased.

[13] Luke 13:16, paraphrased.

[14] 1 Corinthians 15:26.

> For this purpose the Son of God was manifested, that he
> might destroy the works of the devil.[15]

Sin, sickness, and death are doomed — doomed to death by the decree of Christ Jesus. Sin, sickness, and death are the devil's triumvirate — the triple curse.

Heaven is the absence of this triple curse — heaven is sinlessness, sicklessness, and deathlessness. This is the ultimate of Christ's redemption.

Dr. Frank N. Riale, field secretary for the Presbyterian department of education, is the author of one of the greatest books of the century: *The Antidote for Sin, Sickness, and Death.*

Today, science labors to eliminate sickness and declares, "There is no reason why men should die." Science declares men are so constructed as to be perpetually renewed. Many great scientists declare the elimination of sickness to be their final objective.

Jesus anticipated the world's need. He commanded His power for the use of mankind and invites us to help ourselves to His eternal quality and become, thereby, sons of God.

LOVE OF JESUS HEALED SICK, AFFLICTED

Take the shackles off God.

Jesus did not heal the sick in order to coax them to be Christians. He healed because it was His nature to heal. The multitude surrounded Him. His love gushed forth like an electric billow. "There went virtue out of him, and healed them all."[16]

Some modern evangelists have degraded divine healing by making it a teaser to bring those desirous of healing under the sway of their ministry. Jesus healed both saint and sinner — to the dismay of His apostles, who had not yet grown to the soul stature of Jesus.

They reported to Jesus: "We saw one casting out devils in Thy name, and we forbade him because he followed not us." Jesus replied:

---

[15] 1 John 3:8.

[16] Luke 6:19.

"Forbid him not, for no man can do a miracle in my name and speak lightly of me."[17]

He met a man at the pool of Bethesda, a paralytic. This man did not ask for healing. Jesus went to him and said: "Wilt thou be made whole?"[18] Here Jesus is asking for the privilege of healing the sufferer. He healed him. His love compelled it.

Next day Jesus met the healed man in the temple and said: "Behold, thou art made whole: sin no more, lest a worse thing come unto thee."[19]

Jesus' action is a perpetual rebuke to the priestcraft who endeavor to use the possibility of the individual's healing as a means to force him into the Church.

The outgushing of His love for the world burst all bounds and four times He healed multitudes. But some say: "This was Jesus. No apostle had such an experience."

When Peter went down the street as the evening shadows fell, when his shadow reached across the street, "They brought the sick, that his shadow might overshadow them"[20] The clear inference is that they were healed.

James, writing to the twelve tribes scattered abroad — not the little group of Jews constituting the kingdom of the Jews, but the whole body of the nation of Israel scattered throughout the world, both the ten-tribed kingdom and the two-tribed kingdom — shouts:

"Is any among you sick, let him call for the elders of the church. Let them pray with him," not prepare him for death, but "that any sins, they are forgiven him."[21] He is coming into His own.

Healing was the evidence of God's forgiveness — heaven's testimony that their sins were remembered no more.

---

[17] Mark 9:38-39, paraphrased.

[18] John 5:6.

[19] John 5:14.

[20] Acts 5:15, paraphrased.

[21] James 5:14-15, paraphrased.

Take the shackles off God. Enlarge our theologies to Christ's standard, and the world will love and worship Him forever.

JESUS' HEALINGS NOT INSTANT
Faith Large Factor in Regaining of Health

In one of the letters received from readers this question is asked: "Why are not all persons healed instantly — as Jesus healed?"

The writer of this letter is mistaken in thinking that Jesus always healed instantly. A case in point is the healing of the ten lepers; as they went they were cleansed.[22] The healing virtue was administered. The healing process became evident later.

Again, Jesus laid His hands on a blind man, then inquired, "What do you see?" The man replied, "I see men as trees walking." His sight was still imperfect. Then Jesus laid His hands on him the second time "and he saw clearly."[23]

Healing is by degree, based on two conditions. First, the degree of healing virtue administered. Second, the degree of faith that gives action and power to the virtue administered.

> The word preached did not profit them, not being mixed with faith.[24]

GOD PASSES POWERS TO CURE ON TO ALL FOLLOWERS

Jesus not only healed the sick, but performed a creative miracle on the man born blind (John 9). Being born blind, it is self-evident the eyes were not a finished creation. Otherwise he would have seen.

The narrative reveals that the blind man did not know who Jesus was. Jesus did not make Himself known until after the miracle had been performed. Let us analyze the incident.

---

[22] See Luke 17:14.

[23] See Mark 8:23-25.

[24] Hebrews 4:2.

Jesus discovers the man born blind (verse 1). He then spat on the ground and made clay of the spittle. Why? Because Jesus was a fundamentalist. The story of creation in Genesis says that "God formed man of the dust of the ground."[25] Jesus, in finishing the creation of the eyes, adopted the same method. He stooped down, took up some dust, spat on it, and put it on the blind man. This is not healing. It is a work of creation.

In 1 Corinthians, the twelfth chapter, it is said that in distributing the gifts of the Spirit to the members of the Church, one was given the "gifts of healing;" to another the "working of miracles."[26] Healing is the renewal of the body from diseased conditions. A miracle is in the creative order.

The case of the blind man was an exercise of creative authority, not the restoration of diseased tissue. The man was made whole.

The grouchers made their kick. The Pharisees examined the man and asked, "Who healed you?"

He answered, "I know not."[27]

It is clearly evident to students of divine healing that sometimes the Spirit of God is ministered to the sick person to a degree that he is manifestly super-charged with the Spirit. Just as a person holds a galvanic battery until the system is charged with electric force, yet no real and final healing takes place until something occurs that releases the faith of the individual; a flash of divine power is observed, a veritable explosion has taken place in the sick person, and the disease is destroyed.

This tangibility of the Spirit of God is the scientific secret of healing.

A diseased woman followed Jesus in a crowd. She knew the law of the Spirit and had observed that it flowed from the person of Jesus and healed the sick. She was convinced it must also be present in His clothing. So she reasoned: "If I could but touch the hem of His

---

[25] Genesis 2:7.

[26] See 1 Corinthians 12:9-10.

[27] John 9:10-12. Editor's Note: The biblical account says that the blind man answered that Jesus had healed him, but when asked *where* Jesus was, he answered, "I know not."

garment I would be made whole."[28] She did so. She was healed of a twelve-year sickness that had baffled physicians and left her in poverty.

Jesus was aware that someone had been healed. He turned to ask who it was. Peter said, "See how the multitude is thronging and jostling You."

But Jesus answered, "Someone has touched Me for I perceive that virtue has gone out of Me." Jesus was aware of the outflow.[29]

The woman was aware of the reception. The healing was a fact. Here, faith and the power of God were apparent. It was a veritable chemical reaction. Healing always is.

I believe the reason people do not see the possibilities of divine healing is that they are not aware of its scientific aspects. The grace and love of God in the soul opens the nature to God. The Spirit of God resounds.

When the Pharisees asked the man who had been born blind, "What do you think of Him?" he replied, "He is a prophet."

Later Jesus found him and said to him, "Dost thou believe on the Son of God?"

The man replied, "Who is he, Lord, that I might believe on him."

Jesus answered, "I that speak unto thee am he."[30]

The struggle of the centuries has been to free the soul of man from narrow interpretations. Jesus has sometimes been made to appear as a little bigot, sometimes as an impostor. The world is still waiting to see Him as He is. Jesus the magnificent, Jesus the giant, Jesus the compassionate, Jesus the dynamic — the wonder of the centuries.

Take the shackles off God. Let Him have a chance to bless mankind without ecclesiastical limitations.

As a missionary, I have witnessed the healing of thousands of heathens. Thus was Christ's love and compassion for a lost world revealed. And thus, the writer was assisted into the larger vision of a world-redeemer whose hand and heart are extended to God's big world, and every man — saint and sinner — is invited to behold and love Him.

---

[28] Mark 5:28, paraphrased.

[29] See Mark 5:30-33.

[30] See John 9:17, 35-37.

JESUS USED SCIENCE TO HEAL THE AFFLICTED
Laws of Contact and Transmission Medium
Through Which the Master Wrought Miracles

Mrs. John W. Goudy of Chicago writes, "How can you speak of divine healing as scientific if healing is through the atonement of Jesus Christ? How can the matter of atonement and grace be considered scientific?"

Atonement through the grace of God is scientific in its application. Jesus used many methods of healing the sick. All were scientific. Science is the discovery of how God does things.

Jesus laid His hands upon the sick in obedience to the law of contact and transmission. Contact of His hands with the sick one permitted the Spirit of God in Him to flow into the sick man.

The sick woman who touched His clothes found that the Spirit emanated from His person. She touched the "hem of His garment" and the Spirit flashed into her. She was made whole.[31] This was a scientific process.

Paul, knowing this law, laid his hands upon handkerchiefs and aprons. The Bible says that when they were laid upon the sick they were healed, and the demons went out of those possessed. Materialists have said this was superstition. It is entirely scientific.

The Spirit of God emanating from Paul transformed the handkerchiefs into "storage batteries" of Holy Spirit power. When they were laid upon the sick they surcharged the body, and healing was the result. (Read Acts 19:12.)

This demonstrates, firstly, the Spirit of God is a tangible substance, a heavenly materiality. Secondly, it is capable of being stored in the substance of a handkerchief, as demonstrated in the garments of Jesus, or in the handkerchiefs of Paul. Thirdly, it will transmit power from handkerchiefs to the sick person. Fourthly, its action in the sick man was so powerful the disease departed. The demonized also were relieved. Fifthly, both the sick and insane were healed by this method.

---

[31] See Mark 5:27-29.

While the scientific mind always asks "How and why?" it is not necessary for the soul desiring Christ's blessing to have any knowledge of the scientific process by which healing or salvation is accomplished.

Jesus said, "He that receiveth me."[32] Men receive Jesus Christ into the heart, as one receives a lover. It is an affectionate relationship. Men obey Him because they love Him. They obey Him because they have received Him affectionately. He has become their soul's lover.

His love and power in them redeems them from sin and sickness and eventually, we are promised in His Word, He will redeem us from death also. Redemption from sin, sickness, and death constitutes man's deliverance from bondage to Satan and his kingdom, and establishes the kingdom of heaven.[33]

JESUS HEALED ILL BY WORD, BIBLE SHOWS
Master Exercised Authority Over
Disease by Speaking to Those Afflicted

Yesterday we discussed Jesus healing through the laying on of hands. Today we will examine Jesus healing by the word command, and other methods.

> They brought to him a man sick of the palsy, lying on a bed: and Jesus seeing their faith (the faith of those who brought the man as well as that of the man himself) said... Son, be of good cheer; thy sins be forgiven thee.

The scribes said, "This man (Jesus) blasphemeth." Jesus met this opposition by saying,

> For whether is easier, to say, Thy sins be forgiven thee; or to say, Arise, and walk? But that ye may know that the Son of man hath power on earth to forgive sins, (then saith he to the sick of the palsy,) Arise, take up thy bed, and go unto thine house.

---

[32] See Matthew 10:40 or John 13:20.

[33] See Hosea 13:14.

The man arose and walked. No hands were laid on this man. There was no external ministry of any kind. Jesus He commanded, the man was healed. (Matthew 9:2-7.)

They brought a man dumb, possessed of a devil. When the devil was cast out the dumb spake. The people wondered. This also is His exercise of spiritual authority. (Matthew 9:32-33.) When Jesus commanded, the power of God entered and ejected the demon.

At Capernaum a centurion came saying, "My servant lieth at home sick of the palsy, grievously tormented."

Jesus said, "I will come and heal him."

The centurion answered, "Not so. Speak the word only. It is enough."

And Jesus said, "Go home. It is done." The record shows the servant was healed.[34]

Many have laughed at the idea of man being healed long distances from the one who ministers in Jesus' name. But here is a clear case, and the God-anointed may still command God's power. To the needy distance is no barrier.

I now present mass healing. Four times it is recorded in the Gospels that "He healed multitudes. There went out a virtue from Him and He healed them all." There was no personal touch.[35]

God is not confined to methods. Heaven bows to the soul with faith anywhere, under any conditions. "Whosoever will, let him take of the water of life freely."[36]

Again Jesus said, "If two of you shall agree on earth as touching any thing that they shall ask, it shall be done for them."[37]

"Ask, and ye shall receive," said Jesus.[38]

---

[34] See Matthew 8:6-13.

[35] See Matthew 12:15; 14:14; 15:30; and 19:2.

[36] See Revelation 22:17.

[37] Matthew 18:19.

[38] John 16:24.

The apostle James gave command that elders of the church should pray for the sick and anoint them with oil. Olive oil is the symbol of the healing spirit. This is a command, "Pray for the sick that they may be healed."[39]

Where? Anywhere.

When? Forever. As long as Jesus Christ reigns in heaven. As long as men on earth have faith in Him.

The voice of Jesus still is heard saying, "Whatsoever ye shall ask in my name, that will I do."[40]

"Ask, seek, knock, find Jesus."[41]

"With God all things are possible," and "all things are possible to him that believeth."[42]

Divine healing through prayer is as old as the race of man. The first book of the Bible, Genesis, records the healing of the wives of a heathen king in response to the prayer of Abraham.[43]

The second book of the Bible, Exodus, gives us the terms of a distinctive covenant between the nation of Israel and Jehovah Rophi — "The Lord thy Healer."

In this covenant God not only agreed to heal the people when sick, but not to permit the sicknesses of Egypt to touch them. Its terms are:

> If thou wilt diligently hearken to the voice of the LORD thy God, and wilt do that which is right in his sight, give ear to his commandments and keep his statutes (on this condition, Jehovah agrees), I will not permit any of the diseases of Egypt to come upon thee, for I am the Lord, thy healer.[44]

---

[39] James 5:14-15, paraphrased.

[40] John 14:13.

[41] Matthew 7:7 and Luke 11:9, paraphrased.

[42] Mark 9:23 and Mark 10:27.

[43] See Genesis 20:17.

[44] Exodus 15:26, paraphrased.

Under this covenant the nation, twelve-tribed, lived without doctors or medicine for 450 years, until the nation of Israel had an army of 1,100,000, and Judah an army of 500,000. Figuring on the same basis as the number of Americans in the army during the world war, this would give Israel and Judah a combined population of between 25,000,000 and 30,000,000.

King David of Israel gives the most extraordinary health report that history records. David says, "There was not one feeble one among their tribes."[45]

Such historic data should go far to convince the world of our day that an absolute trust in God is not only a safe policy, but a most scientific guarantee of national health.

In this connection we must examine Israel's national constitution as it was made the basis of national health. Firstly, its basic principles were the ten commandments. Secondly, it contained a law in which Jehovah held perpetual title to the land. Thirdly, a credit and mortgage statute. Fourthly, a distribution of surplus wealth statute. Fifthly, the most extraordinary labor law ever written. Sixthly, an absolutely equitable tax law by which every citizen paid one-tenth of his increase.[46]

This is the only national constitution given direct by Jehovah and is the foundation of all national constitutions.

For keeping this constitution Jehovah guaranteed the nation against wars, pestilences, poverty, destructive droughts, and lastly, "I will take sickness away from the midst of thee."[47]

The broad scope of divine healing in Israel is the basis of all faith in God for healing and was the foundation of the ministry of Jesus Christ, Israel's Redeemer and the world's Savior.

Israel had been kept free of disease for 450 years through divine healing. Outside of Israel there was no divine healing. No other religion in the world possessed healing power. There is not a single instance of this power in the life of India, Egypt, China, or Africa.

---

[45] Psalm 105:37, paraphrased.

[46] See Deuteronomy 5 through Deuteronomy 26.

[47] Deuteronomy 7:15, paraphrased.

The Hebrews alone, from Abraham onward, exhibited the power of healing at this time. Later, knowledge of Israel's God and His power to heal disease spread through the nations of the world.

The prophets of Israel were marvelous men of God. At their word empires rose and fell. Life and death obeyed their will. Earth and sky answered their call. Before their eyes future history marched with events of the present. No men of any other nation equaled them. No bibliotheca of any other nation compared with their Holy Scriptures.

CHRIST, GOD'S GIFT

Christ came as God's gift to Israel and Israel only. To Judah, the remnant of Israel, He came. Despite all that has been imagined and written of miracles in His childhood, there is not a particle of evidence that He performed any miracles until, at Cana of Galilee, He turned water into wine. The Bible states this miracle was the beginning of miracles by Jesus.[48]

Jesus performed no public ministry until He was thirty. The law of Moses forbade it. So we read that when Jesus was about thirty He came to John the Baptist, and was baptized.[49]

His baptism was His dedication of Himself to the Heavenly Father. He dedicated body, soul, and spirit. To John He said, "Into all righteousness."[50]

He was dedicating Himself to God to reveal the righteousness of God. Jesus' dedication was wholly unselfish. But His dedication in itself was not sufficient to qualify Him to reveal God. His humanity must be submerged in the Holy Spirit. As He was baptized in Jordan, this took place.

Now He must be tested. He was led of the Holy Spirit into the wilderness to be tempted by Satan. This was to find if His dedication was a fact or if He would fail under the forty-day test.

---

[48] See John 2:1-11.

[49] See 1 Chronicles 23:3 and Luke 3:21-23.

[50] Matthew 3:15, paraphrased.

Three temptations were applied. Firstly, a psychological temptation to His mind — love of acclaim. Secondly, a spiritual temptation applied to His spirit — that He might by a simple acknowledgment of Satan "secure all the kingdoms of the world." When He conquered, the natural result took place in Himself, "He came forth in the power of the Spirit."

Having overcome, the consciousness of inherent power was radiant in Him. "He returned in the power of the Spirit."[51]

Jesus now makes the next advance. He proclaims His platform. Returning to Nazareth, He boldly declares, "The Spirit of the Lord is upon me. (1) He has anointed me to preach the Gospel to the poor; (2) He hath sent me to heal the brokenhearted; (3) to proclaim liberty to the captive; (4) recovering of sight to the blind; (5) to set at liberty them that are bruised; (6) to preach the acceptable year of the Lord."[52]

No more waiting for the release of the year of Jubilee. Jesus Christ, the Eternal Jubilee, was at hand to save and heal.

Jesus' ministry of healing and the marvelous faith in God He exhibited in miracle working were no accident. Miracles must be His very breath, for 800 years before His birth the prophet Isaiah had proclaimed:

> He will come and save you. Then the eyes of the blind shall be opened, the ears of the deaf shall be unstopped. Then shall the lame man leap as an hart, and the tongue of the dumb sing.[53]

So to be Savior of the world He must be forever the miracle-worker of the ages; the death destroyer; the finality of revelation of the majesty, power, and mercy of Jesus! The very name was a miracle.

The angel announced it.

Jesus' birth was a miracle.

His wisdom was a miracle.

---

[51] See Matthew 4:1-11 and Luke 4:1-13.

[52] Luke 4:18-19, paraphrased.

[53] Isaiah 35:4-6.

His life was a miracle.

His teachings were miraculous.

He lived and walked in the realm of the miraculous. He made miracles common. His death was a miracle.

His resurrection was a miracle.

His appearances after death were miraculous. His ascension was a staggering miracle.

His pouring out of the Spirit on the Day of Pentecost was the outstanding miracle. It was the one event in which His whole Saviorhood climaxed. Out of heaven was given to His followers the Spirit of the Eternal, to do in them all it had done in Him. Sin, sickness, and death were doomed.

He came as a roaring tempest, as tongues of fire crowning the one-hundred-and-twenty as the living eternal Spirit entering into them. He proclaimed His triumphant entry into man through speaking in languages they knew not.

His deity had lifted them into His realm, transfigured, transformed, transmuted.

Jesus bestowed the power to heal upon His disciples:

> Then he called his twelve disciples together, and gave them power and authority over all devils, and to cure diseases. And he sent them to preach the kingdom of God, and to heal the sick.... And they departed, and went through the towns, preaching the gospel, and healing every where.
>
> — Luke 9:1-2, 6

He likewise bestowed power to heal upon the seventy:

> After these things the Lord appointed other seventy also, and sent them two and two before his face into every city and place, whither he himself would come.... Heal the sick that are therein, and say unto them, The kingdom of God is come nigh unto you.
>
> — Luke 10:1, 9

In order to be fully informed on the question of divine healing, let us study this question as part of the fully-rounded development and life of Jesus.

In beginning His revelation of the life of God for, and in, man Jesus chose the order of nature as the realm of His first demonstration. (1) Jesus turned the water into wine.[54] (2) He stilled the waves.[55] (3) He walked on water.[56] These revelations of power over nature each surpassed the other.

Then Jesus astounded His followers by turning to the creative life of God. He fed the multitude by an act of creative power when He created fish and bread to feed five thousand.[57]

This shows the distinction between healings and miracles. Miracles are creative. Healing is a restoration of what has been.

Jesus now advances into a new sphere, the order of sickness. Here He meets the mind of the other that must be conformed to His. (1) Jesus heals Peter's wife's mother. This is first degree healing.[58] (2) Jesus meets the blind man and heals him. This is second degree healing.[59] (3) The lepers are healed. Healing in the third degree.[60]

Again Jesus enters the creative realm and creates eyes in a man born blind. Blindness from birth is evidence of an unfinished condition of the eyes. The creative process was not complete. Jesus stooped, took dust from the road, spat upon it and put it on the man's eyes. In so doing He finished a work of creation — the man saw.[61]

Now Jesus again advances. This time He chooses the order of death. (1) He raised the daughter of Jarius, dead a few minutes. This is the first degree.[62] (2) Jesus meets a funeral procession coming out of the

---

[54] See John 2:1-10.

[55] See Luke 8:24.

[56] See Matthew 14:25.

[57] See Matthew 14:15-21.

[58] See Matthew 8:14-15.

[59] See Mark 8:22-26.

[60] See Luke 17:11-19.

[61] See John 9:1-7.

[62] See Mark 5:22-24; 38-42.

city of Nain. He commands the young man to live, "and he sat up." This man was dead many hours. This is the second degree.[63] (3) His friend Lazarus is dead four days. His body is in a state of decomposition. Jesus commands Lazarus to come forth. He that was dead arose. This was the third degree.[64]

Now Jesus again steps into the creative realm and announces His coming death. He declares of life: "I have power to lay it down, and I have power to take it again."[65]

Through this chain of successive abandonment to God we discover the soul-steps of Jesus. Every step was taken with reliance on the Word of God as the all-sufficient guide.

Jesus took the promises of God in the Scriptures and permitted them to work out in His soul. Therefore, His promises to us are not made on His own speculation, but because of His soul's discovery of the mind of God. But He did not let it rest there. He took each discovered promise and worked it out.

He discovered the promise of supply and fed the multitude. He discovered healing power and made the blind to see, the deaf to hear, the lame to walk. He discovered the promise of "man the master" when anointed of God, and He stilled the waves and turned the water into wine; of life ever-present, and He raised Lazarus and the widow's son; of life everlasting, and He rose Himself from the grave.

He gave His promises as discovered and demonstrated truth and tells us these things shall be ours as we are lifted by the Spirit into the God realm, the Christ-conscious realm.

But it is the one real thing among the myriads of life's illusions and contains in itself man's future hope and his transcendent glory. Herein is the true dominion of man.

Marvelous Experience of Christ's "Death Ministry" Produced in His Soul the Power and Glory of the Resurrection

We have followed Jesus through the continued ascents of His earthly career. Jesus has developed in faith and knowledge and in "favour

---

[63] See Luke 7:11-15.

[64] See John 11:1-44.

[65] John 10:18.

with God and man"[66] at every step. If we were to stop at this point and refuse to follow Him to the throne of the universe we would miss the whole purpose of His life. Divine healing and every other outflow of His holy soul would be beggared and perverted if we failed here.

Christianity is not a mere philosophy. It is more. It is very much more. Christianity is not simply obedience to beautiful commandments. Christianity is not only the acceptance of glorious promises.

Christianity is a divine content. Christianity is a heavenly dynamic. Christianity is the ultimate of all consciousness of God. Christianity is wholly supernatural. Christianity comes down from heaven from the innermost heart of glorified Christ. Christianity is in the innermost and uttermost of man declaring: "I am he that liveth, and was dead; and, behold, I am alive for evermore, Amen; and have the keys of hell and of death."[67] Christianity is the spotless descent of God into man and the sinless ascent of man into God. The Holy Spirit is the agent by whom it is accomplished.

The significance of Jesus' death was not in His sacrifice only, but also in His achievement in the regions of death. He took death captive. He liberated those who, in death, awaited His coming and deliverance. Jesus took them in triumph from the control of the angel of death and transferred them to His own glory.

David prophesied:

> He ascended upon high. He led captivity captive. He gave gifts unto men, even unto the rebellious also, that they might know the mercy of the Lord.[68]

Peter declared:

> He went and preached unto the spirits in prison while once the long-suffering of God waited in the days of Noah while the Ark was preparing.[69]

---

[66] Luke 2:52.

[67] Revelation 1:18.

[68] Psalm 68:18, paraphrased.

[69] 1 Peter 3:19-21, paraphrased.

And lest we fail to comprehend the source of His ministry in death, Peter says again:

> For this cause was the gospel preached also to them that are dead, that they might be judged even as men in the flesh.[70]

The apocryphal book of Nicodemus relates:

> Jesus came to the regions of death, released the captives, and proclaimed liberty.[71]

It was this marvelous experience of Jesus in death ministry that produced in His soul the glory-power of the resurrection. Not only His personal triumph over death but the release of those held in death's chains.

In all the universe there was none with such triumph in His spirit as Jesus possessed when death's bars were broken. When He with power heretofore unknown, commanded His followers, saying, "All power is given unto me in heaven and in earth."[72]

Glorifying in this amazing ascent in consciousness, He instantly found the eleven and breathed in them, saying: "Receive ye the Holy Ghost."[73] This was Jesus' endeavor to lift them into the same soul triumph that He enjoyed.

The ascension was a further advance in triumphant consciousness, climaxed by His presentation of Himself at the throne of God, where, Peter says, "He received from the Father the gift of the Holy Spirit."[74] This was Jesus' divine equipment as world Savior. From then on He was empowered to administer the transcendent glory-power to all who would receive — divine healing, saving power. The empowering of the Christian soul from on high is the pouring forth of the Holy Spirit by Jesus Christ, High Priest of heaven.

---

[70] 1 Peter 4:6, paraphrased.

[71] The Gospel of Nicodemus 6:1, paraphrased. (See also footnote on the apocrypha on page 313).

[72] Matthew 28:18.

[73] John 20:22.

[74] Acts 2:33, paraphrased.

That we may realize the uttermost of ultimate transcendence of the soul of Jesus in glory, hear Him declare anew:

> I am he that liveth, and was dead; and, behold, I am alive for evermore, Amen; and have the keys of hell and of death.

Who would not rejoice to place himself in the hands of such a Savior and physician?

Answering forever the world's questions: "Is He able to heal? Does He ever heal? Does He always heal?" — to all we boldly say: "Yes. He is Jesus, triumphant, eternal, omnipotent."

Jesus called His twelve disciples and commanded upon them power and authority to cast out devils and heal disease (Luke 9). He superseded this by declaring: "If ye shall ask *anything* in My name it shall be done."[75]

The first was a limited power of attorney. The second, unlimited. This unlimited power of attorney was authorized before His crucifixion. It was to become effective when the Holy Ghost came.

On the Day of Pentecost this power of attorney was made fully operative. The Spirit came. First, legally, they had His Word. Then, vitally, He sent His Spirit.

Peter and John instantly grasped the significance of the name. Passing into the temple they met a beggar-cripple. He was forty years old and had been crippled from birth. Peter commanded: "In the name of Jesus Christ of Nazareth, rise up and walk." Heaven's lightning struck the man. He leaped to his feet, whole.

A multitude rushed up. They demanded: "In what name, by what power, have ye done this?"

Peter and John replied: "In the name of Jesus Christ of Nazareth, whom ye slew, whom God raised up." Matchless name! The secret of power was in it. When they used the name power struck. The dynamite of heaven exploded.

Peter and John were hustled to jail. The church prayed for them in "the name." They were released. They went to the church. The entire

---

[75] John 14:14, paraphrased.

church prayed that signs and wonders might be done. How did they pray? In "the name." They used it legally. The vital response was instantaneous. The place was shaken as by an earthquake. Tremendous name![76]

Jesus commanded: "Go ye into all the world."[77] What for? To proclaim the name. To use the name. To baptize believers. How? In the name. Amazing name. In it was concentrated the combined authority resident in the Father, the Son, and the Holy Ghost. Almighty name!

The apostles used the name. It worked. The deacons at Samaria used the name. The fire flashed. Believers everywhere, forever were commanded to use it. The name detonated round the world.

More Bibles are sold today than any other 100 books. Why? The name is in it. It's finality — at the name of Jesus every knee shall bow and every tongue confess![78]

Prayer in this name gets answers. The Moravians prayed — the greatest revival till that time hit the world. Finney prayed — America rocked with the power. Hudson Taylor prayed — China's Inland Mission was born. Evan Roberts prayed seven years — the Welsh revival resulted.

An old Negro, Seymour of Azusa, prayed five hours a day for three and one-half years. He prayed seven hours a day for two and one-half years more. Heaven's fire fell over the world, and the most extensive revival of real religion in this century resulted.

> He said unto them, Go ye into all the world, and preach the gospel to every creature. He that believeth and is baptized shall be saved; but he that believeth not shall be damned. And these signs shall follow them that believe; In my name shall they cast out devils; they shall speak with new tongues; they shall take up serpents; and if they drink any deadly thing, it shall not hurt them; they shall lay hands on the sick, and they shall recover.
>
> — Mark 16:15-18

---

[76] See Acts 3:1-16; 4:1-10, 23-31.

[77] Mark 16:15.

[78] See Philippians 2:10 and Romans 14:11.

And lest healing should be lost to the Church, He perpetuated it forever as one of the nine gifts of the Holy Ghost.

> To one is given by the Spirit the word of wisdom; to another the word of knowledge by the same Spirit; to another faith by the same Spirit; to another the gifts of healing by the same Spirit; to another the working of miracles; to another prophecy; to another discerning of spirits; to another divers kinds of tongues; to another the interpretation of tongues.
>
> — 1 Corinthians 12:8-10

The Church was commanded to practice it.

> Is any among you afflicted? let him pray. Is any merry? let him sing psalms. Is any sick among you? let him call for the elders of the church; and let them pray over him, anointing him with oil in the name of the Lord: and the prayer of faith shall save the sick, and the Lord shall raise him up; and if he hath committed sins, they shall be forgiven him. Confess your faults one to another, and pray one for another, that ye may be healed. The effectual fervent prayer of a righteous man availeth much.
>
> — James 5:13-16

The unchangeableness of God's eternal purpose is thereby demonstrated.

"Jesus Christ the same yesterday, and to day, and for ever" (Hebrews 13:8). "I am the LORD, I change not" (Malachi 3:6).

God always was the Healer. He is the Healer still and will ever remain the Healer. Healing is for you. Jesus healed "all that came to Him." He never turned anyone away. He never said, "It is not God's will to heal you" or that it was better for the individual to remain sick or that they were being perfected in character through the sickness. He healed them all, thereby demonstrating forever God's unchangeable will concerning sickness and healing.

Have you need of healing? Pray to God in the name of Jesus Christ to remove the diseases. Command it to leave, as you would sin. Assert your divine authority and refuse to have it. Jesus purchased your freedom from sickness as He purchased your freedom from sin.

His own self bare our sins in his own body on the tree,
that we, being dead to sins, should live unto righteousness: by whose stripes ye were healed.

— 1 Peter 2:24.

Therefore, mankind has a right to health, as he has a right to deliverance from sin. If you do not have it, it is because you are being
cheated out of your inheritance. It belongs to you. In the name of
Jesus Christ go after it and get it.

If your faith is weak, call for those who believe and to whom the
prayer of faith and the ministry of healing has been committed.

Psalm 91, Isaiah 35, Matthew 8 and 9, Mark 16, Luke 11, John 9,
Acts 3, 4, 8, 9, 10, and 26, 1 Corinthians 12 and 13.

ADDRESS OF WELCOME TO NORTHWEST DISTRICT CONFERENCE OF PENTECOSTAL CHURCH OF GOD

Portland, Oregon

July 15, 1930

 have been asked to give a little address of welcome tonight. I am delighted with this conference. I was delighted with the little group of ministers and saints who were here this morning and the beautiful, blessed presence of God. It indicated to my heart God's love and grace in a very marvelous way.

Just one or two of the things as an echo from the morning meeting: Our Brother Johnson, pastor of the Glad Tidings Assembly, Salem, Oregon, told us about his experience in the old church in which he was pastor for many years. He said they finally got to the place where they scheduled every service, what he was to talk about, the outline for the sermon satisfactory to them, the offerings he was to take, and everything else. He was machined to a finish, until his heart broke under the strain of it. Well, that is very different from our type of service. He told me another thing: That the head of the conference in this district gave an address to the last conference and ridiculed the blood of Jesus Christ as a saving power. He said a blood religion is a religion of savages.

Dear friends, Pentecost brought a testimony from heaven that came in power to the world. That was the blood of Jesus Christ by which men's hearts are cleansed from sin. When this Gospel came to me many years ago, for I was among the very first in this country to be baptized in the Holy Spirit, I was in good standing with a very sound religious institution of our day, very strong and sound in faith

— Dr. Dowie's movement. If you knew him you knew one of the most wonderful men of God who ever lived in this world. It took the world two hundred years to discover Oliver Cromwell. It was Carlyle that discovered him and revealed him to the world. Perhaps two hundred years hence, someone will discover John Alexander Dowie and reveal him to mankind, and when they do it will be a marvelous revelation. He was a man of such amazing faith in God that until within fifteen minutes of his death, they brought the dying to his bedside, and they were healed. It was a very sound institution in their theology and strong in faith.

But friends, when Jesus Christ baptized me in the Holy Ghost, I was invited to preach at his tabernacle, and I preached for nine months there. God kept me preaching on one text for [blank space in manuscript]. It was "Behold the Lamb of God, which taketh away the sin of the world."[1] The Holy Ghost brought a new revelation of the blood of Jesus Christ. That was the particular thing that Jesus Christ said the Holy Ghost would do for mankind. "He will show you Jesus."[2]

Brethren, we welcome you. We welcome you preachers; we welcome you people, because you stand with us for the biggest thing in this world and that is, "Behold the Lamb of God, which taketh away the sin of the world."

We are living in a day under such circumstances as no other people ever lived under. In the early days of Christianity, one of the great Caesars undertook to destroy Christianity and establish the religion of the gods. When he was on his deathbed he exclaimed, as he raised his hand to heaven, "Nazarene, thou has conquered!" Christianity swept over his head and covered the Roman world.

The years 1914 to 1918 was the period of the greatest suffering the world has ever experienced. In these four years statisticians declare that fifty million people died. It was an awful period of physical suffering throughout the world. Statisticians now declare that two hundred million people [blank space in manuscript].

---

[1] John 1:29.

[2] See John 16:13-14.

Following the Great War there came a change, not a physical agony any longer. There came a tremendous mental agony over the world that still endures. Under the power of that mental agony there came revolutions, change of government, breaking down of religious systems, and the world is still staggering.

We have witnessed an absolutely new thing in the world. The Russian nation overtoppling, turning a somersault, and leaving Christianity behind her. An anti-God campaign, not produced by a little society like we have in the United States (we have our society here), but that is insignificant as compared with the nation of Russia. Here we see a nation with one hundred and sixty-five million people controlled by a strong government, with marvelous resources at their back, deliberately undertaking to destroy the knowledge of God.

Missionaries are beginning to minister under circumstances that ministers of the Gospel never had to minister under before.

When I went to South Africa as a missionary, I became known nationally because of one thing God did. They had a native society known as the Ethiopian Movement, which had adopted as their slogan, "Africa for the African." In the course of fifty years they had created eight wars, and it had cost the nation a hundred million dollars. That institution was not organized as a society, but as a church. Their churches were everywhere. They were simply throwing off all white authority and were endeavoring to do like the people of India are doing.

I want you to appreciate what the Holy Ghost can do. This society called a conference fifty miles from Johannesburg. They had three men who were overseers. Their overseers were still godly and still remembered how to pray. Shocked by the dreadful reports that were coming to them, by which they were returning to their original state of heathendom and worse, for when people have once received the light of God and the light of civilization, sin changes in its character. It is not the brutal type of sin, but they adopt the sin of civilization, and they are dreadful. These three men went out to pray, and as they prayed God said to one, "Go to Johannesburg, inquire for a man by the name of Lake, he will help you."

One day they reported at my church and they told me this story. They told me they were overseers of the Ethiopian Movement, and that they had discovered that they did not have power to help their people, that they needed a strong type of man and faith to help them. Other missionaries were clamoring to have opportunity to enter the country, but God gave the whole nation to us.

God baptized these men in the Holy Ghost, and we stepped into two or three thousand church buildings in one day. All they needed was one tremendous thing and that was the Holy Ghost to change their hearts, and unless He did, the organization would prove a damnation to themselves and [blank space in manuscript].

Some months or a year afterward, Premier Bothe called me in and asked me what my nationality was. He said, "We had to know you. Your influence has become so great."

That is the way I got acquainted with the South African government. Friends, the Holy Ghost is not just a nice something that will come and illuminate your soul and then flit away and leave you. He is the agency of the eternal God in this world, and there is no other. When a church or a nation loses her concept of the Holy Ghost, she has lost the concept of everything that is heavenly and valuable and eternal and almighty and powerful to save to the uttermost.

Suppose I was to return to South Africa as I am contemplating somewhat in the future. I am going to find a different condition. In eighteen months, God utterly abolished that Ethiopian Movement, until finally the government said, "Lake, you have got to undertake some educational campaign among these multitudes. Turn your churches into schoolhouses." So we filled the nation with schools where they taught God and the Holy Ghost. It was only a little while until we had one hundred thousand native Christians in the land. I do not know how many there are now. Two years ago they said, "We have 1,250 ordained native preachers."

If I went back to South Africa today I would find the land alive and throbbing among the native people with communistic doctrine. These are the conditions that are everywhere in the world. Soviet Russia has discovered something that we Christians have not yet found.

Russia arrived at the place where they said, "War is bunk; when you are through with the slaughter, the minds of the people are worse than in the beginning." So they propagandized Russia out of the war. They spread their propaganda until the armies and navies of Germany were flooded and there was a rebellion in the navy.

India is seething and alive under Ghandi's endeavor at [blank space in manuscript]. Imagine one hundred and thirty nationalities, which make up the kingdom of India. Their population has increased 130,000,000 since Britain took control of the country.

[Manuscript seems to be incomplete.]

REIGN AS KINGS
Portland, Oregon
January 4, 1931

I want to bring to you a message that came to me today. I have been for years on the verge of this message, but never did I receive it until this morning. In the fifth of Romans and the seventeenth verse, in another translation there is a remarkable rendering.

> For if by the trespasses of the one, death reigned as king, through the one, much more shall they who receive the abundance of grace and the gift of righteousness, reign as kings in the realm of life, through Jesus Christ.

That means that the moment you accept Jesus Christ, God becomes your righteousness. That is the "gift of righteousness." Let me read it again:

> For if by the trespasses of the one, death reigned as king, through the one, much more shall they who receive the abundance of grace and the gift of righteousness, reign as kings in the realm of life through Jesus Christ.

It means every one of us that have been born again come into a kingly, queenly state, and we are accepted by God to reign as kings and queens in the realm of life.

We have reigned as servants in the realm of spiritual death. We have passed out of death, Satan's realm, into the realm of life, into the realm of the supernatural or the spiritual or the heavenlies.

Here are some significant facts. Man was never made a slave. He was never made for slavery. He was made to reign as king under God. If you noticed I showed you this: that that kingly being that was created was created in the image and likeness of God, that he was created on terms of equality with God, that he could stand in the presence of God without any consciousness of inferiority.

I quoted you from the eighth Psalm in which this expression is used:

> What is man, that thou art mindful of him? and the son of man, that thou visitest him? For thou hast made him a little lower than the angels [God][1], and hast crowned him with glory and honour.[2]

What does it mean? It means that God has made us as near like Himself as it is possible for God to make a being. He made you in His image. He made you in His likeness. He made you the same class of being that He is Himself.

He made Adam with an intellect, with such caliber that he was able to name very animal, every vegetable, and every fruit, and give them names that would fit and describe their characteristics. When God could do that with man, then that man belonged to the realm of God.

Adam had such vitality in his body that even after he sinned and became mortal, he lived nearly a thousand years — 930 years before mortality got in its work and put him on his deathbed. Methuselah lived 969 years. Life was so abundant, so tremendous in their minds and spirits that it conquered century after century.

Jesus said: "I am come that they might have life, and that they might have it more abundantly."[3]

More abundantly. Jesus made the declaration: "I am come that they might have life."

The thing that was forfeited in the Garden was regained. God gave him dominion over the works of his hand. God made him His understudy, His king, to rule over everything that had life. Man was master. Man lived in the realm of God. He lived on terms of equality with God. God was a faith God. All God had to do was to believe that the sun was, and the sun was. All God had to do was to believe that the planets would be, and they were. Man belonged to God's class of being — a faith man. And he lived in the creative realm of God. Friends, if you believe what I am preaching, it is going to end your impotence and weakness and you will swing out into a power such as you have never known in your life.

---

[1] The Hebrew word used here is "Elohim," the same word used for the name of God in the first five chapters of the book of Genesis.

[2] Psalm 8:4-5.

[3] John 10:10.

Man lost his place by high treason against God. He lost his dominion in the fall. With the fall went his dominion over spirit and soul. But universal man ever yearned for the return of his dominion.

Brother, do you hear me? Here is one of the most tremendous facts that we have to face: that never a single primitive people that has ever been found that has not yearned for dominion. Not a single primitive people has been found that did not have a golden past where they had dominion, a golden future where dominion was going to be restored. That is the tradition of universal man.

Man has craved dominion. Man has shrunk from bondage. Man has rebelled against it. Man has yearned to gain the mastery again over physical loss, over mind loss, and over the loss of spirit. This long-ago desire to gain the lost dominion is seen in his offerings, in his drinking blood, in his priesthood that he has appointed.

I want to enter this a little bit with you. Darwin foolishly said that the reason man drank blood was because the blood was salty and he craved salt. Friends, human blood was never desirable to any people. Why did they drink it? They drank it in order that they might be like God. They drank it that they might become eternal, immortal.

The desire of immortality of the physical body lies latent in the heart of universal man. And for that reason they drank it, believing if they drank it they would be like God. They took the animal or man and they laid it upon the altar of their god or gods, and when they did they believed that the offering became identified with their god. Then they said, "If we drink that blood of the man or animal, we drink the blood of God, and if we drink enough of it, we will be God."

How far is that removed from the communion table? Do you see the analogy? The communion table is practically unknown as yet to the majority of Christians.

Now the ancients believed this, and the people of Africa, and it caused them to become cannibals. It was not because they loved human blood, but they believed if they could eat the flesh and drink the blood that was given to their god, they would be like God. You will find that all through the legends and poetry of the Old World.

Universal man feels the lost dominion can be regained. They have a conviction that it is going to be regained. And this faith of universal man, reaching Godward, finally challenged God to make it a possibility. He believes that union with God will give him this dominion. He hates defeat. He wants to conquer death. He dreams of immortality. He fears death and disease.

Let me recapitulate. This universal man has believed that somewhere God was going to give him this lost dominion. He believed that that dominion would come through his union with God, if that union could be affected. Can you understand now? It was the universal knowledge and the universal need and the universal cry of man for union with deity that caused the incarnation.

Let me come a step closer. On the ground of what Jesus Christ did, the substitutionary sacrifice, God is able to redeem us from our sins. He is able to impart to us His very nature. He is able to give us eternal life, take us into His own family, so that we can call Him, "Father." Not by adoption only, but by an actual birth of our spirit, so we come into actual relationship and union with God and the age-old cry of universal man has been fulfilled. Do you see? The new birth has brought us into vital union with Jesus Christ.

This thing I am teaching you about our union with God is not known in the great body of Christians. All they have is forgiveness of sin. There is no actual union with God. They do not know that the new birth is a real incarnation. They do not know that they are as much the sons and daughters of God Almighty as Jesus is. The great body of the Christian Church has no dominion, do not know it. They have the most befogged concept of what God has done and what God is to them and what they are to God.

Another step. That incarnation that God has given through the new birth has bestowed upon us the lost authority of the Garden of Eden. And only here and there has a man known it or preached it or dared to assume it.

Let me break in here. J. Hudson Taylor, after his first visit to China, was walking in England and a voice said: "If you will walk with Me, we will evangelize Inland China." He looked and there was no one there. An unseen angel had spoken to him. Then his heart caught the vision and said, "Lord, we will do it." He was founder of the Great Inland China Mission.

Taylor was returning on a sailing vessel and they were going through the Yellow Sea. It was in the section where the seven winds come at eventide, but from a certain hour in the day until evening there is no wind. One afternoon the captain said to Mr. Taylor, "Take this." And he took the glasses and looked. He could see they were nearing land. The captain said, "The worst pirates in all this awful section of the ocean are there. Our vessel is in the clutches of the tide and in three hours will strike the rocks and there is no hope of saving it."

J. Hudson said, "Are you a Christian?"

He said, "I am."

He said, "Are there any other Christians here?"

He said, "Yes, the cook and the carpenter and another man are Christians."

Taylor said, "Call them, and let's go and pray."

He called them and the five or six of them went to their respective places, and they had not been praying but a little while when he heard commands being given on board and men rushing about. He came up and he could see the wind breaking on the sea that had been so glassy. In a few minutes the wind had filled the sails, three hours before nature would have sent it.

In my own experience, I have seen God many times set aside natural law. I told you one day about one miracle. We were putting on a roof on one of our buildings. A storm came up. The boys had unwisely torn off too many shingles for us to cover before the storm reached us. I saw that storm go around us and leave ten or fifteen acres where the rain did not fall for more than one-half hour, and the water flowed down the gutters past our buildings. Those boys worked and sang and shouted. When the last shingle was in place the water fell on it, and we were drenched to the skin. I have seen God perform His prodigies[4] in answer to believing prayer. What God does for one He can do for another.

---

[4]   A less common definition for the word "prodigy" is: something wonderful or marvelous. *Webster's Desk Dictionary of the English Language* (NY: Gramercy Books, 1983), p. 723.

This inferiority complex that makes men seek God and create religions and priesthoods is a relic of the fall and comes because man is conscious that once somewhere he had power, he had dominion, and he galls under it, like a mighty athlete that feels his strength leaving him until, by and by, he becomes helpless as a little child. Oh, the agony of the thing!

Every man has within him the entire history of every man. That cry of agony of the athlete, that cry of agony of the man that once had physical and mental health (strength) is the cry of universal man, crying for the lost authority and dominion that he once enjoyed.

He seeks through rites a new birth, a recreation that does not come. How many lodges and secret societies have a rite, a symbol of the new birth? I cannot mention them, but you look back. You are initiated into such and such an organization; I can name four that have a new birth rite. It is latent in the universal man.

Every religion has some kind of recreation. Why? Every man has a consciousness (I am speaking of men who think) down in them. There is something that cries out against death, against sickness, against sorrow, against defeat, against failure. There is something that rebels against the bondage of fear and that cries for rebirth, a recreation that will give them dominion and mastery over the forces that have held them in bondage.

Our redemption is God's answer to this universal hunger. We saw God's hunger creating man, now you see man's hunger bringing God to recreate him. Can't you understand it, men, that the hunger in the heart of God drove Him, forced Him, until He spoke a world into being for the home of His love project, man. It has driven Him to create universes to hold this world by the law of attraction and make it a safe place for man.

Then when man fell and lost his standing and became a slave and subject to Satan, then this universal cry went up until the very heart of God bled for this broken human. Then He made provision whereby this man that He had created and had sinned and had decreated might come back into fellowship with Him of a higher, holier sort than He had lost at the beginning.

I want to take you through some scriptures. Go with me to Romans 5:17:

> For if by the trespass of one, death reigned as king, through the one, much more shall they who receive the abundance of grace and the gift of righteousness, reign as kings in the realm of life through Jesus Christ.

That by the new birth you have passed out of Satan's dominion and Satan's power and you have come over into God's dominion, and you have come over into the kingdom of the Son of His love.

You will pardon me, but I have this consciousness when I am preaching. There comes up a wave from the congregation of a kind of stultified[5] unbelief. Do you know where it comes from? It comes from all the years you have sat under false teachers. You have been taught that to be humble you have got to say you are a sinner, you are no good, you don't amount to anything. You sing:

> Weak and sickly,
>
> Vile and full of sin I am.

I do not like to preach one thing and Charles Wesley another. If you are born again, you are a son of God. And for you to tear yourself out of your sonship, your relationship, and the righteousness of God and put yourself over in the realm of death and tell God you are dirty and unclean, that His blood has not cleansed you, and His life has not been delivered to you, it is a monstrous thing. It is all right to sing that as an unregenerate, but it is not the experience of the sons and daughters of God.

Here is our position through Jesus Christ: God has become our righteousness. We have become His very sons and daughters. And you sing weakness and you talk weakness and you pray weakness, and you sing unbelief and you pray and talk it and you go out and live it. You are like that good old woman. She said, "I do love that doctrine of falling from grace, and I practice it all the time."

---

[5] stultify: to make appear foolish or ridiculous. *Webster's Desk Dictionary of the English Language* (NY: Gramercy Books, 1983), p. 892.

Another man said, "Brother, I believe in the dual nature. I believe that when I would do good, evil is always present with me, and I thank God that evil is always there." You live it and believe it, and God cannot do anything with you. You magnify failure and you deify failure until to the majority of you the devil is bigger than God. And you are more afraid of the devil than you are of God. You have more reverence for the devil than you have for God. It is absolutely true.

If any saint would dare to say, "I am done with disease and sickness; I will never be sick again," 90 percent of you would say, "Keep your eyes on that person. He will be sick in a week. The devil sure will get them." You believe the devil is bigger than God. Your God is about one-and-a-half inches high, and the devil is one-and-a-half feet high. What you need to do is to change gods and change gods quick. There have been only a few folks that had a good-sized God.

You go over in Genesis and you see the size of God. It is a full-sized photograph. You see Jesus Christ rising from the dead, and you have seen the God-sized photograph of redemption. "We reign as kings in the realm of life."[6] And what is the reaction in you? You say, "That is all right and I wish that was true in my case. I would like to reign as king." And you think this moment how you are whipped, and you think how you have been defeated and how weak you are, and you will be defeated all the next week. You reckon on the strength of the devil and on your own sickness. You say, "If he had what I have he wouldn't talk like that." How can the power of God come through such a mess of unbelief? How can God get near? Ninety percent of those who have received the Spirit have made God a little bit of a side issue — a sort of court of last resort. When you get where the devil can do no more you say, "God, catch me. The devil has finished his work." God is simply a life insurance company that pays the premium at death.

Turn with me to Ephesians 1:7:

> In whom we have redemption through his blood, the forgiveness of sins, according to the riches of his grace.

---

[6] See 2 Timothy 2:12 and Revelation 5:10.

For months and months that scripture has been burning its way into my soul. "In whom we have our redemption through His blood, the forgiveness of our trespasses," and it is "according to the riches of His grace." It is illustrated in Israel coming out of Egypt with the Red Sea before them, with vast desert stretching its burning waste between them and their Promised Land. We do not have any such redemption in our religion. I'll tell you what we need. Have you been in Canada? Do you know when I went to Canada for the first time there was one thing that struck me peculiarly? The signs would read, "John Brown, Ltd." Everywhere I saw that sign, that is a Scotchman's caution.

I was holding meetings in the old St. Andrews Church in Sidney. I asked them one night why they did not put their national symbol on their churches. They wondered what I meant. I said, "Every other business house is 'Ltd.'" Why don't you put it over the church?"

An old Scotchman said, "We don't have to. Everybody knows it." Limited? Sure it is limited. Limit God, limit ourselves, limit His grace, limit the Word. Sure, our God is a little bit of a God. Most of us could carry Him in our vest pocket and it wouldn't bulge the pocket — our God with the "Ltd." on Him.

Brother, sister, that challenge comes to us today to let God loose. There are a few places where they have let God have His way, and how the blessings have come.

In whom we have our redemption.

Have you? If you have your redemption it means that to you, Satan has been defeated. Jesus conquered the devil as a Jew before He died. Then He let the devil conquer Him on the cross and sent Him down to the place of suffering with our burden and guilt upon Him. But after He satisfied the claims of justice, Jesus met the devil in his own throne room and He stripped him of his authority and dominion. And when He arose He said:

> I am he that liveth, and was dead; and, behold, I am alive for evermore, Amen; and have the keys of hell and of death.

— Revelation 1:18

He had gone into the throne room, taken Satan's badge of dominion and authority that Adam had given him in the Garden of Eden. And every man that accepts Jesus Christ was identified with Him when He did it. He did it for you. He did it for me. He died as our substitute and representative. When He put His heel on Satan's neck, He did it for you, and you were in Christ. And to you who believe, Satan is conquered and Satan is defeated. Satan can holler and bellow as much as he wants to, but you withstand him in the faith of Jesus Christ.

I saw a picture this morning. I was reading an article. I saw a company of men walk out, and I saw all the diseases and all the crimes and agonies. I saw cancers and tumors and tuberculosis, and I saw a company of men and women walk down in the midst of it, and I heard them say, "Here comes the sons of God. Here comes the conquerors."

And the sons of God said to disease, "In the name of Jesus, depart," and disease fled. It fled as it did before the Son of God. It obeyed because the Son of God sent them out and gave them His name as authority. I saw the company of men enter into the lost dominion. They put upon them the garments of their authority and dominion and walked out conquerors over death and hell and the grave. They were masters. They were rulers.

Then I saw another picture. I saw David in the old cave of Adullam.[7] I saw men coming down that were broken and in distress and in debt, and men that were in awful physical conditions. And they gathered four hundred strong around David. And out of that crowd David developed and trained the most invincible army that was ever seen.

Then my mind passed over a few years of struggle, and I saw from that company some mighty men come forth. I saw one man come forth and go where there were thousands and thousands of Philistines, men that were shoulders above him, men that wore shields. I saw that man go among those giants and he slew hundreds of them. And I piled them up in hundreds and I had piled eight hundred.

Every one of those mighty men of David were simple men of extraordinary ability.[8] There was no mark to indicate that they were more

---

[7] See 1 Samuel 22:1.

[8] See 2 Samuel 23.

John G. Lake — 1934

*In 1934, the Great Depression brought hard times,
but John G. Lake did not give up his Page touring car
or his optimism. "How can I give hope to others
if I look as if I've lost hope?"*

than common Jews, 5'11", but they knocked down men 6'6" and 6'8". They conquered them because they were blood covenant men.

That is the type of the Church of Jesus Christ. And I said, "Where are God's mighty men today?" Then I saw a picture. David sat there a little way from the spring of Bethlehem, and the Philistines had got control of the water. David said, "Oh, that I had a drink." And those three men came forth. He said, "Where are you going, boys?" They just waved him off, and those three men conquered the whole company of the Philistines, filled their pitchers with water, and set them down at David's feet.

I cried, "My God, my God, where are the mighty men of valor of today? The men that can assail the forces of Satan?" God says they are coming out of you. They are going to arrive. God has in training some men and women that are going to do exploits for Him. Will you not come up and live in your realm?

This is the trouble with most of us. We live up in the faith realm, but we have gone down the back stairs into the reason realm, and a lot of you are hugging your old devilish reason right now. God help you, brother, this afternoon to throw your reason, that has led you into all kinds of doubt and fear, to throw it to the wind and say, "God, here goes. We trust in Your omnipotence to put it over."

his is the first of a series of articles on the general subject of "Adventures in Religion." I want to remind you for a few moments of some of the old mystics who were given glimpses into the unseen that it has not been the privilege of the ordinary man to understand.

ADVENTURES IN RELIGION
Radio Lecture 1
June 24, 1935

The first and foremost was St. Francis of Assisi, whom the world has conceded to be one of the most Christlike characters who has ever lived in the world. At a later period came St. John of the cross, who for ten years seemed to live detached from the world. Today, he is discovered to be one of the most practical men.

At a later period Madam Guyon appeared on the scene, and most every library contains one of her books. The molding of her character was so amazing that it has caused much discussion in the religious world of our day.

We have only, however, to look over the records of our own land to see many others. Such men as Charles G. Finney, founder of Oberlin College and its first president. He was a practicing lawyer. He was seized with a conviction for sin so pungent that he retired to the woods to pray, and the Spirit of the Lord came upon him so powerfully, so divinely, and took such amazing possession of him, that he tells us he was compelled to cry out to God to cease lest he should die. His wonderful ministry in the land is so well-known, his books so frequently found in our libraries, that it is not necessary to discuss him further.

On this list I wish to mention one who is not usually mentioned so lovingly as Finney. He was a Scotch boy, educated in the University of Australia (John Alexander Dowie). In addition to this, the Lord came to him in his own tabernacle one morning as he sat at his desk. Jesus was accompanied by his mother, the Virgin Mary. He advised Dowie concerning his ministry. Jesus laid His hands upon him and from that period his ministry was marked by the supernatural.

It is a matter of public record and one of the most astonishing facts that on one occasion, he invited all persons who were healed under his ministry to attend a meeting at the auditorium in Chicago. Ten thousand people attended the meeting. At the psychological moment they all arose and gave testimony to the fact that they were healed. Those who were not able to attend were asked to send in a card, three and a half inches square, telling of their healing. Five bushel baskets were filled with these cards, representing the testimony of one-hundred-thousand people. At the psychological moment these five bushel baskets of cards were spilled over the stage, to emphasize the extent and power of God's ministry and blessing to the people.

Again, I want to call your attention to another marvelous life, that of Hudson Taylor, founder of the China Inland Mission. To him the Lord came, not only in personal presence, but in prophecy concerning the future. It was Hudson Taylor who prophesied the great revival in Wales ten years before it came to pass, giving almost the very day on which it would begin and its power and extent. All this came to pass just as he had outlined it, while he was in the heart of China.

The Welch revival was one of the most remarkable revivals that was ever produced. It was apparently prayed out of heaven by a single little church whose lights were never extinguished for seven years. This indicates that a portion of that congregation was continually in prayer to God, that God would send a revival. And thus it came, the most astonishing and intensely powerful revival. In small churches which would hold perhaps five hundred people, in one corner fifty people would be singing the praises of God, thirty-five people would be down praying, another group would be praising God and testifying of His power. It was not produced by evangelism, but it was the descent of the Spirit of God on the people. Conviction for sin was so powerful, men knelt in their stores or wherever they were to give themselves to God. Sometimes while men were drinking in the public houses at the bar, they would cry out to God and give their hearts to Him.

Beginning with that revival, there was a movement of God that spread throughout the world. In our own land, we are particularly and wonderfully blessed by a movement that began New Year's Eve, 1900, which was accompanied by the baptism in the Holy Ghost, and multitudes were baptized in the Holy Ghost.

After that revival there arose a phenomenal group of men and women. I am going to mention a few. The first I am going to mention is Aimee Semple McPherson. She was a young girl on a farm in Ontario, Canada. She attended a meeting by a young Irishman, Robert Semple, who was preaching under the anointing of the Holy Ghost. She became convicted of sin, opened her heart to God and found Him, and was baptized in the Holy Ghost. Finally, they were married and went as missionaries to China, where he died of fever. She was left a widow, and soon with a newborn baby. Some friends provided the funds that brought her back to the United States.

Later she formed the acquaintance of a fine young businessman and decided to settle down and forget all her burning call to the Gospel. This she tried to do. Two children were born to them. And then one day God came to Aimee in a meeting at Berlin, Ontario, conducted by Reverend Hall. Her early ministry, for a period of about fifteen years, surpassed everything that we have ever seen in any land since the days of the apostles. (A multitude was healed under her ministry.)

Again, I want to call your attention to another unusual man, Raymond Ritchie, who belonged to Zion, Illinois. His father was mayor of Zion City at one time. This boy was tubercular. They did not seem to understand his difficulty. He had no ambition; he could not work like other boys. He was in a state of lactitude. Eventually he found God. We speak of finding God as the old Methodist Church spoke of being saved, getting religion, meaning one and the same thing. When a man confesses his sin and God comes into his heart and gives him the peace and consciousness of his salvation, he has found God.

Young Ritchie, after his salvation, was so absorbed in prayer, and the family got sort of worried. The father finally told him he had to get to work and help earn his living. But some woman who understood the boy said, "I have a room you can have." Another said she would provide him with food to keep him alive.

The Great War came on, and the epidemic of the flu followed, when men died by the thousands throughout this United States. He became stirred and began to pray for people and they were healed. The Medical Department presently took notice of it, and they sent him to pray for sick soldiers, and they were healed. Very well, he has continued in the ministry from then until now, and some of the most wonderful healing meetings that have ever taken place, he has conducted.

Another man God has marvelously blessed and used is Dr. Price. He belongs to our own locality. Price used to live in Spokane. Dr. Price was baptized in the Spirit. Right away he began to manifest a most amazing ministry of healing. I attended one of his meetings at Vancouver, BC. He had four audiences a day and fifteen thousand people in each and people for a block around who could not get inside. All the churches in Vancouver, I think, united with him in that meeting. It was the most amazing meeting I ever saw. The sick people stood in groups of fifty and he would anoint them with oil according to the fifth chapter of James, and then pray for them. They were so overpowered by the Spirit, they would fall to the floor, and a great number were healed.

ADVENTURES IN RELIGION

Radio Lecture 2

June 25, 1935

No greater book has ever been given to mankind than the Bible. The amazing things recorded there that men experience and that men wrought in the name of Jesus Christ through faith by the power of God stands forever as an incentive to every man who enters and labors where they did. There is a place in God into which the soul enters, a relationship to God that leaves the registry of heaven here in your heart and that makes it possible for the Spirit of God, through you as His agent, to register in the hearts of others.

Henry Fosdick says, "Until the new theology can produce the sinless character of the old theology, it stands challenged." We believe that. We believe that the old-fashioned salvation through the blood of Jesus Christ and the baptism of the Holy Ghost makes possible an experience that no other religious experience in the world has ever been able to produce.

In the year 1900, there came a new wave of heavenly experience to this land and to the world. It began in Topeka, Kansas. It was in a Bible school conducted by Charles Parham. The founding of that school was an amazing thing. He was moved of God to go to Topeka, Kansas. He obeyed the prompting of the Spirit and went to the city. After looking all around for a building suitable for a Bible school and finding none, one day a gentleman told him of a residence on the outskirts of the city. It contained about twenty-two or more rooms, and it was unoccupied. The owner lived in California. He went to see the building and as he stood looking at it the Spirit of the Lord said, "I will give you this building for your Bible school."

And he said to himself, "This is the house."

As he stood there a gentleman came up to him and said, "What about the house?" Parham told him what the Lord had said to him and the man, being the owner of the house, said, "If you want to use this building for a Bible school for God, it is yours," and he handed him the key without any more ado.

The next day he went to the train and met a young woman of his acquaintance. She told him that when she was praying, the Spirit of God told her there was going to be a Bible school here and that she should come. She was the first student. Thirty-five students came, all correspondingly directed by the Spirit of God.

This group began a study of the Word of God to discover what really constituted the baptism of the Holy Ghost. After a month of study, they became convinced that there was one peculiarity that accompanied the baptism of the Holy Ghost — speaking in tongues.

They went to seeking the baptism of the Holy Ghost. Parham was not present at the time. On New Year's night at twelve o'clock, 1900, one of the group, a Miss Osmand, a returned missionary, was baptized in the Holy Ghost and began to speak in tongues. In a few days the entire group, with a couple of exceptions, was baptized in the Spirit. When Parham returned and found that the students in his school had been baptized in the Holy Ghost, he himself went down before the Lord, and God baptized him in the Holy Ghost too.

I want you to keep this story in mind, for it forms the basis of the wonderful experience I want to relate in my next talk.

or a moment I want to call attention to a challenge that has been distributed widely through the ministry of Henry Fosdick, as I mentioned yesterday. Fosdick has said, "Until the new theology can produce the sinless character of the old theology, it (the new theology) stands challenged."

ADVENTURES IN RELIGION

Radio Lecture 3

June 26, 1935

That is our position. We are reminding you, friends, that God is a miracle God. God is a miracle. Jesus Christ is a miracle. His birth was a miracle. His life was a miracle. His death was a miracle. His resurrection from the grave was a miracle. His ascension was a miracle. His reception at the throne of God by the eternal Father was the greatest of all miracles, because that God then gave Him the gift of the Holy Ghost and made Him the administrator of the Spirit forever.

Some things can be better taught by relating experiences than in any other way. I might try to impress you with the beauty and wonder of the baptism of the Holy Ghost, but dear friends, I think the relating of a few experiences will make it clearer to our mind than any other way.

I am reminded of an incident that took place on a railway train. Father Neiswender was stricken with a paralytic stroke. He had not been able to sleep for weeks. When they got him on a train to bring him to Spokane, the motion of the train temporarily soothed him and he fell asleep and dreamed. In his dream an angel came to him and said, "When you get to Spokane, inquire for a man by the name of Lake. He will pray for you and God will heal you."

He was directed to our place, and when we prayed for him he immediately began to use his paralyzed arm and side, but was not completely delivered. The third time I went to pray the Lord showed me a blood clot in the spinal chord as large as a bead. I prayed until the blood clot disappeared. No one could explain an incident like that by any natural law. Consequently, we must classify it in the line of miracles *in our day* — not a thousand years ago.

One more incident of this order: A family by the name of Bashor had a lovely boy who became dissatisfied at home and ran away. He went to a farmer where he was not known, gave another name, and worked for him for a year. In the meantime the family, with the aid of the police, searched everywhere for the boy, but he could not be found. One day the mother came to me brokenhearted and told me the story. We knelt and prayed and asked God that he would cause that boy to get in touch with his parents. Two days later she received a letter from the boy. He told her that on the night we had prayed he went to bed and had an unusual vision. Jesus appeared and talked to him. Jesus said, "I forgive your sins, but I want you to write to your mother and get home to your folks."

The boy was greatly moved, got up and told the farmer the incident, and the result was the farmer hitched up his team and brought the boy in to his home. That boy is now married and has a nice family and still lives in Spokane. The part of that incident that might interest young folks is this. I was preaching at Mica, Washington, where I related this incident. A young lady in the audience listened to the story, and after the meeting she said to me, "I would like to get acquainted with that young man." She did, and he is her husband.

Dear friends, these are some of the things that show us that there is a work of God's Spirit different from what we are ordinarily accustomed to, and these are the things that make religion real to New Testament Christians. Different ones in the Scriptures were guided by dreams. Joseph was guided by dreams. Some were guided by a voice from heaven. Now we are contending and bringing to your attention that there was an experience provided by the Lord Himself that made that intimacy a possibility; that is, the baptism of the Holy Spirit. I wish I might say that with such emphasis that it would penetrate the deep recesses of your spirit.

One more incident: Over in the woods back of Kellogg, Idaho, lived a family by the name of Hunt. I visited in their home just a little while ago. His aged father was given up to die; the son was very anxious about him. The father kept saying, "Son, I ought not to die." The son had been much in prayer about this matter. One day he stood on a log road, and presently he said a man appeared a little distance ahead. And as the gentleman approached, he addressed Mr. Hunt saying, "I am Mr. Lake. I have Healing Rooms in Spokane. If you will bring your father there, the Lord will heal him." He was so impressed, that he got his father and brought him to me for prayer, and the Lord healed him gloriously and he lived many years.

> The value of the ministry of healing is not in the mere fact that people are healed. The value of healing is more largely in the fact that it becomes a demonstration of the living, inner, vital power of God, which should dwell in every life and make us new and mighty men in the hands of God. 1916

When the German army started their famous march on Belgium and France with an army of three million men, they came to the borders only to find that they were met with such a tremendous opposition that for ten full days they were compelled to stay back until they could bring up their heavy artillery. Statesmen of Germany declare that that ten days' delay resulted in their losing the war. France and Belgium were prepared in the meantime to meet the assault.

ADVENTURES IN RELIGION
Radio Lecture 4
June 27, 1935

Jesus Christ, the Son of God, said to His disciples: "Behold, I send you forth as sheep in the midst of wolves,"[1] but He did not send them out without being prepared. They were commissioned and empowered by God, for that is what constitutes the baptism of the Holy Ghost. Jesus Christ gave His disciples a big program before He left them. He told them they were not only to preach the Gospel to the whole world, but that they were to demonstrate its power.

> Go ye into all the world, and preach the gospel to every creature...And these signs shall follow them that believe; In my name shall they cast out devils; they shall speak with new tongues; they shall take up serpents; and if they drink any deadly thing, it shall not hurt them; they shall lay hands on the sick, and they shall recover.

— Mark 16:15,17-18

These signs shall follow them that *believe* — those who accepted their work.

Dear friends, men who were going to put a program like that into effect needed heavy artillery from heaven. That is what Jesus

---
[1] Matthew 10:16.

undertook to give from heaven. So He said they were not to go out right away unprepared. Instead He said:

> Tarry ye in the city of Jerusalem, until ye be endued with power from on high.

— Luke 24:49

That enduement from on high is the equipment of every child of God who follows the biblical pattern. We are trying to impress upon the minds of men that one of the greatest adventures in religion that this world ever has found was when men dared to step across the usual boundaries and dared receive from His hand the baptism of the Holy Ghost, which equips them with the power of God to bring blessings to other lives.

Just for one moment I want to bring you this fact, that the first thing Jesus said would be manifested in the Christian life was: "In my name shall they cast out devils." It was the first thing in the Christian experience, and the exercise of Christian power that Jesus said would follow the Christian's life. They had power to cast out devils.

Jesus first gave that power to the twelve, then He gave it to the seventy, then He gave it to the Church at large on the Day of Pentecost, when the baptism of the Holy Ghost descended upon the hundred and twenty at Jerusalem. Jesus gave the equipment from heaven.

In our day, within the past thirty years, we have seen such a manifestation of God from heaven as no other century in the world's history ever saw, with the exception of the first four centuries of the Christian era. Beginning with 1900, the Spirit of God began to be poured out in power upon the world so that every country in the world has received this amazing power of God. Men who were ordinary businessmen, men who were scholars and teachers, students, and men from every walk in life found this equipment from heaven by the grace of God and stepped out into a great life and ministry for God. This preparation, friends, is not for preachers only, but for the people. Jesus said, "These signs shall follow them that *believe.*"

Friends, there is an adventure for your soul, the most amazing adventure in all the world. It takes a brave soul to step into the light of God and receive the equipment He provides. That is no place for a coward.

A cowardly spirit, a spirit that is always hiding, always apologizing for his faith, will never enter there — that is the gate of God. That is the gate into His Spirit. That is the gate into a life of effectiveness for every one who wants to serve God aright. Friends, you need this equipment to meet the demands of this day.

Sanctification is the cleansing of a man's nature by the indwelling power of the Spirit of Christ, for the purpose of the transformation of the mind and nature of man into the mind and nature of Jesus Christ.

I like John Wesley's definition of sanctification, "Possessing the mind of Christ, and *all* the mind of Christ."

his afternoon I want to talk to you on the subject of *miracles*. From the year 400 until now, the Church has assumed the attitude that the days of miracles are passed — without any scriptural evidence whatever. They have taught that miracles were to demonstrate the divinity of Jesus and, therefore, the divinity of Jesus being demonstrated, there was no longer any need for miracles.

ADVENTURES IN RELIGION
Radio Lecture 5
June 28, 1935

We had a local incident that demonstrates the effect of this teaching, I think. My conviction on the matter is that it has done more damage to the Christian faith than any other teaching that has been promulgated. There is a gentleman who works at the Davenport Hotel in Spokane, O. A. Risdon, who is one of the engineers there. He had a son with a deformed head. The top of the head raised up like the ridge of a roof, the forehead and back of the head also were forced out in similar manner, giving the head the appearance of the hull of a yacht upside down. He was born with what the physicians call a closed head. The boy was always slobbering. The pressure on the brain caused the right side to become paralyzed, and the boy was dumb. He was five years old at this time.

The physicians said there was nothing they could do. Then in desperation, he appealed to his pastor. The pastor told him the days of miracles were past, that the Lord did not heal now, that miracles were given to demonstrate the divinity of Jesus. The father replied, "If Jesus would heal my son I would be convinced that He is divine now. If He is divine He could lift this damnation from our house."

Finally, he came to us seeking help. We began to minister to the child. In a few days we observed that the paralysis began to depart. Instead of walking on one side of his ankles he began to walk on the foot, and that indicated that the pressure was relieved on the brain. In seven weeks the child was perfectly well. The bones of the head softened and came down to normal. The paralysis disappeared and the child began to talk. In three months he was in the public school. He is a young married man now.

Dear friends, if we had continued to believe that the days of miracles were past, that boy would be in the insane asylum. But we believed that Jesus Christ was the same yesterday, today, and forever, and the boy was healed. It is a delight to believe the *words of Jesus*. I have used this rule in my study of the Scriptures. If there is any question on any Scripture I settle it with the words of Jesus. I consider all the Scriptures are a common court of the Gospel, but the *words of Jesus* are the Supreme Court of the Gospel. When I want a Supreme Court decision I appeal to the words of Jesus.

You can read all the words of Jesus in two hours or less in a red-letter New Testament. Make a practice of reading the words of Jesus on any subject that troubles you, and make a compilation of what He says. He ought to be sufficient authority on any question, for the heavenly Father called attention to the fact that He is the Son of God and that we are to hear Him. He said:

> This is my beloved Son, in whom I am well pleased; *hear ye him.*
>
> — Matthew 17:5

esus Christ came on the scene as a Challenger. We have almost come to believe in our day that He was a sentimentalist and an easy type. He was King. He was the Prince of God. He was the Glory of Heaven! He was the representative of the eternal Father! He had a mission. He declared the Father. He stepped among the religions of the earth as the Challenger.

ADVENTURES IN RELIGION
Radio Lecture 6
July 2, 1935

Jesus said there was real sin, that there was real sickness, that there was real death. He was not dodging the issue. He met it foursquare, and He said, "I am bigger than it all. I am the Prince of life." He destroyed sin and obliterated it from the souls of men. He blasted sickness and dissolved it from their system. He raised the dead to life. He challenged the devil, who was the author of death, to destroy Him if he could. He went into the regions of death and conquered and came forth triumphant, so that it became necessary for the Lord to have a new vocabulary. He said after coming forth from the grave,

> All power is given unto me in heaven and in earth. Go ye therefore, and teach all nations, baptizing them in the name of the Father, and of the Son, and of the Holy Ghost.

— Matthew 28:18-19

Sin and sickness and death, the triumvirate of darkness, that Jesus met and overcame were the original forces of evil in the world — the manifestation of the kingdom of darkness. There never will be a heaven; there never could be one, where these exist. Their destruction is necessary. Jesus realized that and He came to do what man could not do for himself. That is one of the reasons why men cannot save themselves. All the good works that man may perform from now to the day of his death will not save him. Sin is of the heart. It is in the nature. Jesus came to reconstruct man's nature and give him, instead of his own evil nature, the nature of God. Sin has made the nature of man vile. Christ came to give him deliverance from this nature and give him a new nature, the divine nature.

Through sin death entered into this world.[1]

Death is not a servant of God, nor a child of God, nor a product of God. *Sin* is the *enemy* of God. The New Testament declared that, "The last enemy that shall be destroyed is death"[2] — not the last servant or friend, but the last enemy. Death is doomed to destruction by the Lord Jesus Christ. Sin and sickness is incipient death.

That is the reason we do not speak of the things of the Lord and His salvation in moderate tones. We are shouting them to mankind. The spirit of a real child of God challenges darkness, challenges sin, challenges sickness. The Lord Jesus came to destroy sickness and wipe it out of the lives of men to make possible the heaven of God in their hearts and lives now. There could be no heaven where disease and sickness are found. Sin and sickness and death must be blotted out. That is the reason, dear friends, that Christianity is always a challenger. Christianity is a thing of strength. Real religion is a source of power. It is the dynamite of God. The Holy Spirit gives the overcoming grace and strength essential to destroy sin, to destroy sickness, to overcome death.

---

[1] See Romans 5:12.

[2] 1 Corinthians 15:26.

I am pleased to greet you today, dear friends, with a real account of one of the marvelous adventures in God. Jesus said,

Heal the sick, cleanse the lepers, raise the dead, cast out devils: freely ye have received, freely give.

— Matthew 10:8

ADVENTURES IN RELIGION
Radio Lecture 7

July 3, 1935

Christianity was not to be stinted in her giving. She was not to be a beggar. She was to be a giver. She had something from heaven to give that the world did not have. She had something to give that would bring deliverance to the world. Jesus was putting His program of deliverance in force through the Church.

The man is a bold man who undertakes to carry out this program of Jesus. The Christian who never has faith enough in God to undertake it, I fear is of the cowardly type. I am afraid modern Christianity stands indicted at the bar of God for cowardliness because of fear to undertake the program of Jesus.

Friends, that is why we urge upon men the necessity of the baptism of the Holy Ghost. It is the only thing that brings the heavenly equipment to the hearts of men, that makes them equal to this program and the possibility of carrying it out.

I want to talk to you today of a bold soul, and in my judgment, a very extraordinary one indeed. I refer to a gentleman who lives in this city, a preacher of the Gospel from the days of his youth, Reverend C. W. Westwood. His home is on Nora Avenue.

A number of years ago, there was born at one of the great hospitals of the city a little child (a girl) from healthy parents, Mr. and Mrs. Young. Mr. Young, for many years had a stall in the Westlake Market. Mrs. Young has been a nurse for many years and also is well-known. When this baby was born it weighed six and a half pounds. Because of some strange difficulty, the child could not assimilate its food.

When she was nine months old she only weighed four-and-a-half pounds. The child looked more like a little dried up alligator than it did like a human being. She finally fell into a state of death and remained in a dying condition. In the meantime, we were called to minister to the child.

Mr. Westwood was assigned to the case. One day when he went to the hospital as usual to minister to the child, they explained that the child was not there. It had died that morning and was in the dead room. He asked if he might see the child, and went into the dead room and took the child down. He sat down on a chair with the baby on his knees. He opened his heart to God, turned the spirit of faith in his heart loose in behalf of the little one. In a little while (and I am saying this with all reverence before God, because I expect to meet this matter when I stand before the great judgment throne) the child revived. He sent for the parents, they took the child from the hospital and put her in the hands of an elderly lady by the name of Mrs. Mason, who nursed her for six weeks. At the end of that period she was as well as any other child. Her name was Agnes Young.

About a year ago I received a telephone call from Agnes Young, asking me if I would perform a marriage ceremony for her and her fiancé. This young couple live at Eugene, Oregon now.

And so I want to leave this testimony, that God is as good as His Word. That faith in Almighty God brings to pass the very same things today that it always did.

ADVENTURES IN RELIGION

Radio Lecture 8

July 5, 1935

The climax of all adventures was the adventure of Jesus, in delivering men from sin and sickness and death. One cannot measure the Man of Galilee with any tapeline or yardstick that comes from human reasoning. Jesus is outside of the realm of reason. In the first place, His history was written by the prophets, ages before He was born. Man can write a better history of Jesus from the Old Testament than they can from the New Testament. In the New Testament we have simply a little fragment about His incarnation and birth, and then thirty years of silence, except for a little glimpse of Him when He was twelve years of age.

All the books that have been written of Jesus have been written almost entirely about His three years of public ministry that began with His baptism in the Jordan and closed with His resurrection. Now men try to write on His pre-existence. Here and there one has caught a glimpse of His ministry, seated at the right hand of the Majesty on High.

I want you to see another fact, that every prophecy that was written before His time was all in the *miracle* realm. His incarnation was a real miracle. He was not born under the natural laws of generation. He was conceived of the Holy Ghost. He was a true incarnation — God uniting Himself with humanity. The scenes surrounding His birth — the angelic visitation, the coming of the wise men were all miracles. The angel's warning to Joseph to flee with the child to Egypt was miraculous. The very silence of those thirty years is considered most miraculous. The divine silences represent the most marvelous elements in the Book we all love. The descent of the Spirit at His baptism was a miracle. From that day until Mount Olivet was a period of miracles.

His life among men was a miracle. The new kind of life that He revealed to the world was a miracle. Jesus' mental processes were miraculous. Our libraries are full of books written by great thinkers like Thomas Edison and others who were incessant thinkers. With

Jesus there is something different. He speaks out from the Spirit that dominated His spiritual faculties. Jesus' spirit ruled His intellect. Gems of divine truth dripped from His lips as honey from the honeycomb. The sermon on the Mount and great portions in Luke and John are as untouched as when they dropped from the lips of Jesus. Men's writings grow old and out of date. God's truth is ever fresh. Yes, Jesus' words and life and contact with men was miraculous; it is still miraculous.

His death on the cross, His three days in the tomb, His dramatic and startling resurrection, were all miracles. His presence among the disciples on different occasions and finally, His ascension in the presence of five hundred witnesses, were miracles. They do not belong to the reason realm — they belong to the miracle realm. Jesus was in the realm of the Spirit, the realm of faith, the realm where God acts, the realm where the real child of God lives. You see, Christians have been translated out of the realm of human thought and reason into the kingdom of the Son of His love, the realm of the Spirit.

It would be uncharitable if we were to criticize the man of reason, who knows nothing about the spiritual realm. Christianity is not the product of human reasoning. Christianity is a divine intervention. Christians are those who have been born from above. They have been recreated. This life of God that comes into their spirit nature dominates the reason so that they have the "mind of Christ,"[1] to think God's thoughts and live in God's realm of miracles.

Friends, when a Christian tries to live by *reason,* he is moving out of God's country into the enemy's land. We belong in the miraculous or supernatural realm.

Christ was a miracle. Every Christian is a miracle. Every answer to prayer is a miracle. Every divine illumination is a miracle. The power of Christianity in the world is a miraculous power. God, help us to realize that ours is a high and holy calling.

---

[1] See 1 Corinthians 2:16.

I want to talk to you concerning some of the purposes of God. Among them is God's amazing purpose to baptize men in the Holy Spirit. I think that even among the deepest Christians in our day, little is understood of the real purpose of God in this wonderful experience.

ADVENTURES IN RELIGION

Radio Lecture 9

July 9, 1935

We say to one another that the baptism of the Holy Spirit is God coming into man; that it is God manifesting Himself in man, and other expressions of this type, but it fails to convey to the mind anything like the great purpose of God in His incoming in us.

The baptism of the Holy Spirit has among its wonderful purposes the dwelling of God in us, the perfecting of His life in us through His Word in our spirit, through His power in our life. Tongues is the peculiar manifestation of God accompanying the coming of God the Holy Spirit into the life. This was the evidence when the Holy Spirit of God descended on the Day of Pentecost at Jerusalem. The Scripture is given in these wonderful words:

> Suddenly there came a sound from heaven as of a rushing mighty wind, and it filled all the house where they were sitting. And there appeared unto them cloven tongues like as of fire, and it sat upon each of them. And they were all filled with the Holy Ghost, and began to speak with other tongues, as the Spirit gave them utterance.

> — Acts 2:2-4

What is the real purpose? What is God doing? Is He giving to the individual certain powers to demonstrate and to convince the world? I do not think that is the real reason. There is a deeper one. God is taking possession of the inner spirit of man. From the day that Adam sinned, the spirit of man was a prisoner. This prison condition continues until God releases the spirit of the individual in the baptism of the Holy Ghost. The spirit remains dumb, unable to express itself to mankind until God, through the Holy Ghost, releases the spirit, and the voice of the spirit is restored.

You understand man is a triune being — spirit, soul, and body — and these departments of our life are very different. God manifests Himself to the spirit of man, and the experience of real salvation is the coming of God into the spirit of man — the infusion of the spirit of man and God.

In the olden days, the Church used to discuss the subject of sanctification but were somewhat hazy in their explanation of what it was. Sanctification is God taking possession of our mental forces, just as He took possession of our spirit when He bestowed on us eternal life. Your mind is brought into harmony with God, even as your spirit was brought into harmony with God. Following the example of Jesus, we dedicate not only our spirit and soul (or mind) to God, but also our body to God. That is the reason we left doctors and medicine behind.

I want to talk to you about speaking in tongues by relating this experience and reciting a poem God gave me when I was a missionary in South Africa and had my residence there. There was a dreadful epidemic of African fever, and within thirty days about one-fourth of the population of some sections of the country, both white and black, died. I was absent from my tabernacle, on the field with a group of missionaries, and we did the best we could to get them healed of God and help bury the dead.

I returned to my tabernacle after about three weeks' absence to discover that the same thing was taking place there. I was greatly distressed. My pianist was gone. My chief soloist was gone, the only daughter of an aged mother. I went to her home to console her and comfort her. As I sat by her table she reminded me that just four weeks before I had been present when the pianist and the soloist were practicing music in that home. My soul was very sorrowful. As I sat meditating I began to pray: "My God, I would like to know what sort of reception such a soul as that gets when they arrive on the other side." Presently, God spoke to my soul and said, "Take your pen and I will tell you about it."

The first thing that came was the name of the poem in tongues. Then the Lord gave me the interpretation. It was called "The Reception."

Then the first verse came in tongues, then I received from the Lord the interpretation, and then the next verses likewise, and so on. In the meantime something transpired in my own spirit. I felt as if I was being elevated into the presence of God, and I could look down on the folks on earth, and it was described in these verses:

THE RECEPTION

List! 'Tis the morning hours in Glory.
A shadow through the mists doth now appear.
A troop of angels sweeping down in greeting.
A welcome home rings out with joyous cheer.

A traveler from the earth is now arriving,
A mighty welcome's ringing in the skies.
The trumpets of a host are now resounding,
A welcome to the life that never dies.

Who is the victor whom the angels welcome?
What mighty deeds of valor have been done?
What is the meaning of these shouts of triumph?
Why welcome this soul as a mighty one?

She is but a woman, frail and slight and tender,
No special mark of dignity she bears.
Only the Christ-light from her face doth glisten,
Only the white robe of a saint she wears.

She is but a soul redeemed by the blood of Jesus.
Hers but a life of sacrifice and care.
Yet with her welcome all the heaven is ringing,
And on her brow a victor's crown she bears.

How come she thus from sin's benighting[1] thralldom,[2]
The grace and purity of heaven to obtain?
Only through Him who gave His life a ransom.
Cleansing the soul from every spot and stain.

---

[1] benighted: overtaken by darkness of night. *Webster's Desk Dictionary of the English Language* (NY: Gramercy Books, 1983), p. 82.

[2] thralldom: slavery. *Webster's Desk Dictionary of the English Language* (NY: Gramercy Books, 1983), p.931.

See! As you gaze upon her face so radiant,
'Tis but the beauty of her Lord you see.
Only the image of His life resplendent,
Only the mirror of His life is she.

See with what signs of joy they bear her onward,
How that the heavens ring with glad acclaim!
What is the shout they raise while soaring upward?
Welcome! Thrice welcome thou in Jesus' name!

Rest in the mansion by the Lord prepared thee
Out of loving deeds which thou hast done.
Furnished through by thoughts and acts which have
     portrayed Me
Unto a lost world as their Christ alone.

Hear how thy lovely harp is ringing.
Touched are its strings with hands by thee unseen,
Note that the music of thine own creating,
Heaven's melodies in hearts where sin has been.

See how the atmosphere with love is laden,
And that with brightness all the landscape gleams.
Know 'tis the gladness and the joy of heaven
Shed now by rescued soul in radiant beams.

Oh, that here on earth we may learn the lesson
That Christ enthroned in our hearts while here,
Fits and prepares the soul for heaven,
Making us like Him both there and here.

Doing the simple and homely duties
Just as our Christ on the earth has done.
Seeking alone that the Christ's own beauty
In every heart should be caused to bloom.

Showing all men that the blood of Jesus
Cleanses all hearts from all sin below,
And that the life of Christ within us
Transforms the soul till as pure as snow.

When we thus come to the dark, cold river,
No night, no darkness, no death is there.
Only great joy that at last the Giver
Grants us anew of His life to share.

Today I want to talk to you concerning one of the remarkable and outstanding incidents in the Word of God. You will find it in the nineteenth chapter of Acts and the eleventh and twelfth verses. It reads:

ADVENTURES IN RELIGION
Radio Lecture 10
July 10, 1935

> And God wrought special miracles by the hands of Paul:
> So that from his body were brought unto the sick handkerchiefs or aprons, and the diseases departed from them, and the evil spirits went out of them.

The people brought their handkerchiefs or aprons to the apostle Paul that they might touch his person. They were then carried to the sick and laid upon them. The demons went out of them and the sick were healed.

An examination of this incident discloses one of the most wonderful facts I know. First, that the Spirit of God is tangible. We think of the air as tangible, of electricity as tangible, and we register the effects of it. And I want to say to you, friends, that the Spirit of God is equally as tangible and can be handled and distributed, can be enclosed in handkerchief or apron and sent as a blessing to the one who needs it.

Get this Scripture and read it for yourself and secure from heaven the blessing it contains, and remember when you are in a struggle and doubts and fears assail you, that God is not far away in the heavens. His Spirit is right here to bless, here to act in your life for a blessing.

Along with this line I want to present this testimony of Mrs. Constance Hoag, who is Dean of Women at the state college, Pullman, Washington. She was visiting her son at Fairfield, Washington. They were going for a motor ride. When she stepped on the running board her son, thinking she was already in the car, started the car. She fell and broke the kneecap and bone protruded through the flesh. They carried her into the house, then called us on the long distance and asked that we pray and send her a handkerchief as soon as possible, by messenger. We sent the handkerchief and in fifteen minutes after she received it the bone had gone back into place. In forty-five minutes the knee was entirely well.

However, her friends began to challenge this healing and she found herself in the midst of a strange debate. A little later almost the same accident happened again. She was thrown to the pavement and the other kneecap was broken and protruded in two sections through the flesh. Once again, we prayed over a handkerchief and sent it to her, and once again the power of God acted, but this time not so quickly as the first time. The second time she said the pain was gone in half an hour, in an hour the bone had gone back in its place, and in an hour and a half the knee was healed and she was well. Friends, the Spirit of God is as tangible today as it was in the days of the apostle Paul.

his morning I was out on the extreme east side of the city. I ran across a strange thing. A man was coming down the street with a pack on his back. The pack was in a cowhide, which was only about half cured. In the sack he had a cow's leg. As I came up to him he said, "Excuse me, sir, but this is my Christian cross."

ADVENTURES IN RELIGION
Radio Lecture 11
July 11, 1935

I said, "Excuse me, but it looks like just the opposite to me." He went down the street and as far as I could hear him he was scolding me.

Then I went to the home of a woman who had been ill a long time. She had lain in bed and was gradually growing worse, and all the time she was accepting this sickness as from God. So I told her this foolish incident, and I said, "Dear woman, if you knew the Word of God, you would never accept a thing like that as the will of God, because Jesus most emphatically declared that sickness was not the will of God but the devil's." She had accepted that rotten, nasty business as God's will and had lain in bed for eight months. It is as offensive to God as the man with his "Christian cross." I want you to know, dear friends, that the Word of God is the foundation upon which our faith is to be built.

Jesus said that He came "to destroy the works of the devil."[1] Acts 10:38 declares:

> How God anointed Jesus of Nazareth with the Holy Ghost and with power: who went about doing good, and healing all that were *oppressed of the devil;* for God was with him [emphasis Lake's].

You do not find "if it be Thy will" in the teaching of Jesus. He never suggested in word or deed that sin, sickness, and death were the will of God. The leper who came to Jesus for healing in the eighth of

---

[1] See 1 John 3:8.

Matthew did say, "Lord, if thou wilt, thou canst make me clean." I suppose he too was accepting the dirty leprosy as the will of God. Jesus instantly said, "I will; be thou clean."[2] The answer of Jesus to the leper is Jesus' answer to you, to every sick man. "If it be thy will" was never suggested in any of Jesus' teaching concerning sickness and disease. Friend, Jesus had declared His will in the most emphatic manner. His will is always to heal, if you but come to Him.

Every student of the primitive Church discerns at once a distinction between the soul of the primitive Christian and the soul of the modern Christian. It lies in the Spirit of Christ dominion.

The Holy Spirit came into the primitive Christian soul to elevate his consciousness in Christ, to make him greater. He smote sin and it disappeared. He cast out devils (demons); a divine flash from his nature overpowered and cast out the demon. He laid his hands on the sick, and the mighty Spirit of Jesus Christ flamed into the body and the disease was annihilated. He was commanded to rebuke the devil, and the devil would flee from him. He was a reigning sovereign, not shrinking in fear, but overcoming by faith.

It is this spirit of *dominion,* when restored to the Church of Christ, that will bring again the glory-triumph to the Church of God throughout the world and lift her into the place where, instead of being the obedient servant of the world, the flesh, and the devil, she will become the divine instrument of God. She will minister Christ's power in salvation, in healing the sick, in the casting out of demons, and in the carrying out of the whole program of Jesus' ministry, as the early Church did. Dr. John G. Lake 1909

---

[2] Matthew 8:2-3.

I want to tell you the story of an unusual family. I am going to call this story, "Following the Trail of Jesus." A number of years ago I felt as if I wanted to do something out of the ordinary to call attention to the subject of divine healing. So I

ADVENTURES IN RELIGION
Radio Lecture 12
August 22, 1935

went to the newspapers and posted $500. Then I announced that if anyone who was sick or diseased would come to the Healing Rooms and be ministered to for thirty days, and if at the end of that time they were not substantially better or healed, they could have the $500.

Over at Monroe, Washington, was a man by the name of Paul Gering, who had got to fooling around with spiritualism. That dear fellow was an open, splendid man. He was a hard-working businessman. After he got to fooling with spiritualism, nobody could live with him. He was more like a raging lion than a human. He went all over the U. S. seeking deliverance from all kinds of folks who were praying for the sick.

He read my announcement and became interested. He sent me a telegram, asking me to come to Monroe and put on a meeting and, of course, pray for him. He met Mrs. Lake and me at our hotel and drove us out to his home on the outskirts of the city. He walked into his home and stopped in the middle of the dining room and fell on his knees, saying, "Mr. Lake, I am waiting for you to pray for me that I may be delivered." We laid hands on him and prayed, and bless God, the power began to go through him. He was completely delivered, the demons were cast out, and he was baptized in the Spirit. From that time on, hundreds of people have been saved and healed and baptized in the Holy Ghost under his ministry. Now he is a great wheat farmer in the Big Bend country.

Last night I spent the evening at his home and conducted a public service for his relatives and neighbors.

Just let me follow the trail of Jesus with you in that family for a few minutes. His sons were unsaved, his daughters were unsaved. One by one after the father's deliverance, the faith of God in his heart laid hold on God for his family. They became converted and baptized in the Spirit until his entire family, including his beloved wife, were saved and baptized in the Holy Ghost.

Mr. Gering had a brother, Joe, a hard fellow and a heavy drinker. He owned a farm down in the country. His wife was distressed, for she saw he was gradually losing his grip on his affairs and squandering his money, and they were getting into financial difficulty. She was a woman of prayer and was praying for him. Finally one day he came to visit Paul Gering. Paul said, "Joe, I am going to Spokane to attend Mr. Lake's meeting. Come, and go with me."

We were conducting meetings in our tabernacle. When they came, we were in the prayer room. The meeting went through without anything unusual occurring, until we were practically ready to dismiss. This man, Joe Gering, was sitting on one of the back seats. A lady turned to me and asked, "Who is that man on the back seat?"

I said, "That is Paul Gering's brother."

She said, "The Lord told me to go and lay hands on him and pray, and he would be saved and baptized in the Holy Ghost."

I said, "Then you had better go and do it, sister."

She went back to him and engaged him in conversation and finally asked if she might pray with him. He said he had no objection to her praying for him. So she laid her hands on him and began to pray. As she did, the Spirit of God from heaven came down on him, and in a few minutes he yielded his heart to the Lord and prayed through until he got a real witness from heaven and began to rejoice in the Lord. After he rejoiced for awhile, she said, "Now you ought to be baptized in the Holy Ghost." He knelt down again and began to pray, and after a few minutes, Joe Gering was baptized in the Holy Ghost. That man's soul was so full of rejoicing that he spent the entire night singing and praying and rejoicing and talking in tongues and sometimes in English. In a few days he was out among the sinful and sick and getting folks saved and healed.

Here is another portion of the story. These men had a sister who lived at Palouse, Washington. She was unfortunately married to a very wicked man. She developed a tumor, and he insisted on her being operated on. She tried to tell him that in their family the Lord always healed them. He would not listen and she was operated on. They brought her to St. Luke's Hospital in Spokane and she was operated on. A dreadful infection developed, and they wired to the family that she was going to die, so the family began to gather here to see her. I knew nothing of these circumstances.

I was riding up Monroe Street when the Spirit of the Lord said, "Go to St. Luke's Hospital and pray for Paul Gering's sister. She is dying." I went immediately and inquired at the office and was directed to her bedside. I laid my hands on her and began to pray, and the Spirit of the Lord came upon the woman, the infection was destroyed, and in ten minutes she was sound asleep and the next day was on the highway to a blessed recovery. These are some of the things that take place when folks get into the line of God.

Their old mother was a godly woman who lived at Palouse. She had been notified that her daughter was likely to die, and when she got the word she went into her closet and interceded with God and prayed for the daughter's deliverance. I believe before God that when God spoke to me it was the answer to that mother's prayer. He sent help through me, and the Lord made her whole.

GERBER GIRL'S HEALING

One day, Mrs. Lake and I were present in a gathering of Christian people, where these Gering people were and some of their neighbors. A family by the name of Gerber had a girl seventeen or eighteen years old. She stood up with her back to us, and I remarked to Mrs. Lake, "Did you ever see such a perfect form; that girl would do for an artist's model." But when she turned around, I was shocked at her appearance. I never saw anyone so cross-eyed. She was a dreadful sight.

Later, I talked to the father, and he told me that surgeons would not undertake to straighten her eyes. They said it was impossible, and if they undertook it she was likely to lose her eyesight. Presently, the young girl came over our way and I said, "Sit down, little woman, I want to talk to you." After talking a few minutes, I stood up and laid my hands on her eyes. The Spirit of God came upon her and in three minute's time those eyes were as straight as they were supposed to be.

She is now married and has a beautiful home and lovely babies. Her eyes and heart are straight.

INTERPRETATION OF TONGUES

Christ is at once the sinless descent of God into man, and the sinless ascent of man into God. And the Holy Spirit is the Agent by which this is accomplished.

Somerset East Cape Colony

South Africa

June 1910 Dr. John G. Lake

[The following note was found among materials. It is a handwritten note by one of John Lake's daughters, Irene.]

May 11, 1976

1. I am John Lake's daughter, Irene, by his first wife, Jennie Stephens Lake, who died in Johannesburg, December 23, 1908. She is buried in Bramfontein Cemetery, plot #19189. She left seven children, only three now living.

2. John Lake's sister, Irene and family, came to Africa for several years to help care for us.

3. I have a Bible given me by John Lake on February 1, 1913. That signified the date he left Africa.

4. My sister, Edna Ferguson, Rt. 1, Box 22, Otis, Oregon 97368, USA, may have photos.

SECTION TWO:

Undated Material

Arranged by Topic

BAPTISM

he following address was delivered by Brother John G. Lake, at the Dutch Reformed Church Hall, Somerset East, Cape Colony, during a tour of the Colony a few years ago.

CHRISTIAN BAPTISM
Somerset East, Cape Colony

To understand this great subject of Christian baptism, we must view it through its various stages of progressive revelation. For like the revelation of God to man, baptism has been continuous and progressive in its meaning and character. In the short time allotted to me to speak I cannot spare the time to read all the scriptures to which I shall refer, but will tell you where they are to be found. When the report of this discussion is published, I urge you not only to read it, but to study it carefully and prayerfully, so that this question may for ever be settled in your minds. For hundreds of years many eminent scholars have tried to connect

INFANT BAPTISM

with the practice of the male-child circumcision in the Old Testament. It cannot be done; there never was any connection, there never will or can be.

But there is a connection between Christian baptism, that is believers' baptism, and the higher or inner circumcision of the heart, the cleansing of the natural man from carnality and sin, which the outward circumcision of the male child's flesh typified.

> Circumcise (purify) yourselves to the Lord, and take away the foreskins of your heart, ye men of Judah and inhabitants of Jerusalem.

— Jeremiah 4:4

Again, "Circumcise therefore the foreskin of your heart, and be no more stiffnecked" (Deuteronomy 10:16). From this Scripture, it will be seen that God demanded not only the circumcision of the body, but the circumcision (the purifying) of the inner heart-life from all sin.

Now we come to the New Testament. John the Baptist was the last of the Jewish prophets. His ministry crowned and closed the dispensation of the Father. When John began his ministry of baptism, Christ had not yet commenced His public ministry. The ministry of John was nearing its close before Jesus commenced His, for John was the forerunner of Jesus Christ. (See Mark 1.)

Was John the Baptist an Innovator?

Did he on his own account introduce baptism? Where did his authority to baptize come from, for he was a Jewish prophet under the Law? The common notion that John was a Christian disciple is an error, for Christ had not yet publicly appeared. Where, then, did his baptism spring from? I propose to show you

The Error of Associating Christian Baptism With Circumcision of the Male Child.

John's baptism had Old Testament precedent and authority behind it. It is ignorance on this point that has caused the farce of infant baptism to obtain credence and support. Turn with me to Exodus 40:12-13, and read. For consecrating persons to the office of priesthood, the Law says:

> And thou shalt bring Aaron and his sons to the door of the tabernacle of the congregation, and wash them with water. And thou shalt put upon Aaron the holy garments, and anoint him, and sanctify him; that he may minister unto me in the priest's office.

The Levites were also separated to the service of the tabernacle, from the Jewish multitude, in a similar manner. (See Numbers 8:6-7.) Note that neither the garments nor the anointing admitted one to the priesthood. This belonged to one by virtue of being a priest. It was the washing that separated him from the Jewish multitude and constituted him a priest.

This separation from the multitude, and at the same time separation from sin, by a real and genuine repentance and a wholehearted turning to God, were the conditions essential to the baptism of John. "John did baptize in the wilderness, and preach the baptism of repentance for the remission (forgiveness and putting away) of sins" (Mark 1:4). In this demand he stood only upon the high plane of circumcision (purifying) of the heart which God demanded.

Now, from whom did he demand repentance? From all who would be baptized though already they, when children, had been circumcised. John himself had been circumcised. (Read Luke 1:59.) Again, in Luke 2:21, we read that Jesus also was circumcised. This brings us to where we can plainly understand the reason

WHY JESUS WAS BAPTIZED

According to the law, a priest must be thirty years of age before he could be consecrated to the priesthood. And in Luke 3:21-23, we read:

> Now when all the people were baptized (Jesus came last, so His baptism was not an example for others), it came to pass, that Jesus also being baptized, and praying, the heaven was opened, and the Holy Ghost descended in a bodily shape like a dove upon him, and a voice came from heaven, which said, Thou art my beloved Son; in thee I am well pleased. And Jesus himself began to be about thirty years of age.

John the Baptist was a priest, the son of a priest, of the Levitical, or priestly, tribe. He was, therefore, a priest according to the Law. He was filled with the Holy Ghost from his birth, which was the anointing and ordination of God. Therefore, by divine as well as human authority and appointment, he was qualified to administer the ordinance of separation to the Son of God. Water baptism was the visible sign of separation from the congregation of Israel to the priesthood according to the law of Moses. (See Exodus 40:12-13.) King by descent from

David, priest through His baptism by John. He was now a royal priest for ever "after the order of Melchisedec" (Hebrews 7:11).

We will now return and further consider the baptism of repentance which John administered to the penitent for the "remission of sins."

John did not baptize all who offered themselves as candidates.

HE REFUSED BAPTISM

to the Pharisees and Sadducees. He demanded from them "fruits meet for repentance,"[1] the undeniable evidence of a change of heart. Children of Abraham according to the flesh, circumcised the eighth day they might be, but without the inner circumcision, without real repentance producing purity of life and character, they were denied the baptism of John.

> But when he saw many of the Pharisees and Sadducees come to his baptism, he said unto them, O generation of vipers, who hath warned you to flee from the wrath to come? Bring forth therefore fruits meet for repentance: And think not to say within yourselves, we have Abraham to our father: for I say unto you, that God is able of these stones to raise up children unto Abraham.

— Matthew 3:7-9

Circumcision was the sign of God's covenant with Abraham.[2] The Pharisees had been circumcised as children, and therefore claimed the advantages and privileges of that covenant. But the covenant with Abraham was conditional: "Walk before me, and be thou perfect."[3] No place there for sin; the heart as well as the flesh must be circumcised. "And I will make a covenant with thee."[4] But the Pharisees (like those who depend upon what they call the covenant of infant baptism) wanted to claim the benefits of the covenant notwithstanding that they were godless and wicked men.

---

[1] Matthew 3:8.

[2] See Genesis 17:10-14.

[3] Genesis 17:1.

[4] Genesis 17:2, paraphrased.

John drove them from him warning them to flee from the "wrath to come." Heart purity was an essential condition to John's baptism.

> And think not to say within yourselves, We have Abraham to our father (like many today who argue, we had Christian parents, and they had us baptized when we were babies): for I say unto you, that God is able of these stones to raise up children unto Abraham. And now also the axe is laid unto the root of the trees (heart-sin, the sinful nature): therefore every tree (the individual) which bringeth not forth good fruit is hewn down, and cast into the fire.

— Matthew 3:9-10

We have shown that the baptism of Jesus was His inauguration to the appointment and office of priest. He demonstrated and enforced His priestly authority when He cleansed the temple by casting out the money-changers and gain-getters. (See John 2:14-17.) When the Pharisees questioned His authority, He answered, "The baptism of John, whence was it?"[5] He refers them to the baptism of John as the official act and seal of His separation and induction to the priestly office, which was the "fulfilling of all righteousness" of which He spake at His baptism. (See Matthew 3:15.) Now we come to

THE EVOLUTION OF BAPTISM

in the New Testament and there learn its deepening significance and its increased demand upon the life and heart and conscience of the baptized.

Into what name did John baptize? Into the name of the Father.

JOHN'S BAPTISM WAS BY SINGLE IMMERSION

into the name of the Father only; for the Son, Jesus, was not yet revealed. The public ministry of Jesus Christ only commenced when John's preaching and baptism were at the climax of power and popularity from that point to decline, to fade, and to pass away to make room for a new development under the preaching and baptism of Jesus. Let us read John 3, verses 26 and 30:

---

[5] Matthew 21:25.

And they came unto John, and said unto him, Rabbi, he that was with thee beyond Jordan, to whom thou bearest witness, behold, the same baptizeth, and all men come to him.

Read on to the 30th verse, for as John said: "He must increase, but I must decrease."

Now we come to the evolution of baptism under the personal ministry of Jesus Christ. Let us read Mark 1, beginning at the 14th verse:

Now after that John was put in prison, Jesus came into Galilee, preaching the gospel of the kingdom of God, and saying, The time is fulfilled, and the kingdom of God is at hand: repent ye, and believe the gospel.

Jesus required repentance towards God and faith in God the Father, even as John taught. In addition, Christ demanded faith in Himself, the Son, as one with the Father and co-existent with Him from all eternity. Those who accepted Him as the Messiah, the Christ, the Son of God were

BAPTIZED BY A DOUBLE IMMERSION

into the name of the Father, as were the disciples of John, and into the name of the then present Son of God. All this only brings us to the practice of baptism as performed during the earthly life and ministry of Jesus Christ.

After the resurrection of Jesus Christ from the dead, He initiates His disciples into the practice and teaching of Christian baptism. This is a

BAPTISM BY TRIUNE IMMERSION

into the name of the Father and of the Son and of the Holy Ghost. In Matthew 28:18-20, we read,

And Jesus came and spake unto them, saying, All power is given unto me in heaven and in earth. Go ye therefore, and teach all nations, baptizing them in the name of the Father, and of the Son, and of the Holy Ghost: Teaching them to observe all things whatsoever I have commanded you: and, lo, I am with you alway, even unto the end of the world. Amen.

Here we have a command to baptize into a new name, the Holy Ghost, into which no man was ever baptized before. Christian baptism requires, therefore, from the candidate for baptism:

1. Faith in God as John the Baptist demanded from his disciples.

2. Faith in God the Son, an indispensable condition to the baptism administered by the disciples of Jesus.

3. Faith in God the Holy Ghost, the new name introduced by Jesus into the terms of the great commission in Matthew 28:19, which we have just quoted.

Like the ministry of John the Baptist, that of Jesus had its baptism. Are these baptisms alike? Again, was John's baptism identical with Christian baptism? It cannot be so for:

1. Christian baptism was administered to those who had already received the baptism of John. This is abundantly clear from what we read in Acts 19:1-6:

> And it came to pass, that, while Apollos was at Corinth, Paul having passed through the upper coasts came to Ephesus: and finding certain disciples, he said unto them, Have ye received the Holy Ghost since ye believed? And they said unto him, We have not so much as heard whether there be any Holy Ghost. And he said unto them, Unto what then were ye baptized? And they said, Unto John's baptism. Then said Paul, John verily baptized with the baptism of repentance, saying unto the people, that they should believe on him which should come after him, that is, on Christ Jesus. When they heard this, they were baptized in the name of the Lord Jesus. And when Paul had laid his hands upon them, the Holy Ghost came on them; and they spake with tongues, and prophesied.

2. Christian baptism was to be administered in the name of the Trinity — The Father, Son, and Holy Ghost — and differed widely in significance from any that had preceded it. In the baptism of John the name of the Trinity was not invoked.

3. The Johnaic baptism discipled the people to John. It was a seal of subjection to him as God's prophet and as a sign of their faith in the after-coming Mightier One, who would baptize with the Holy Ghost and with fire. (See Luke 3:16.)

4. The baptism administered by the disciples of Jesus was the seal of their acceptance of, and subjection to, Him as the promised and now present Savior of man. (See John 3:14-17.)

It is quite obvious, therefore, these three baptisms differed in quality and scope. In central aim, purity, they agreed, and repentance was common to all three. (See Matthew 3:2, Mark 1:14-15, and Acts 2:38.)

But repentance under Christian baptism differs from the other two, being three-fold respecting the Trinity.

I have already proved that between Christian baptism, into the name of the Trinity, and the rite of circumcision, there is an impassable gulf of separation and distinction. When religious teachers endeavor to establish an identity between them, their arguments are unsupported by one honest interpretation of Scripture truth. The whole fabric of such contention is as flimsy as the spider's web, while the earnest investigator is left with a list of specious arguments as groundless as they are unconvincing.

The high character of Christian, or believer's, baptism as instituted by Jesus Christ (Matthew 28:18-20) is best seen and understood in the light of progressive revelation. This is further demonstrated in Romans, the sixth chapter, verses 1-6, which kindly read. We will take the fourth and fifth verses:

> Therefore we are buried with him by baptism into death: that like as Christ was raised from the dead by the glory of the Father, even so we also should walk in newness of life. For if we have been planted together in the likeness of his death (burial in baptism), we shall be also in the likeness of his resurrection.

The "old man" of sin is buried in baptism, and the "new man" after the likeness and character of Jesus Christ is raised up. Lest we should fail to grasp the high and holy demands of God and be satisfied with less than the experimental knowledge of the perfect work of the grace of God within the heart, which God expects us to possess and for which He has made full provision in the redemption wrought by Christ on Calvary, we will further endeavor to emphasize certain important and convincing facts:

1. That John refused to baptize those who had been circumcised under the covenant with Abraham, until they had repented and brought forth the fruits of righteousness. (See Matthew 3:7-8.)

2. That, though their parents had been circumcised when children, John now warns them to "flee from the wrath to come." They were children of wrath, their circumcision and all else notwithstanding, until they had truly repented and turned to God. He further warned them that unless they repented, they would be "cut down and cast into the fire"[6] as worthless and incorrigible.

3. That God demanded circumcision (purification) of the heart, which is a conscious, practical, indwelling heart experience.

4. That John demanded repentance from sin and a turning to God, and that his baptism was the seal of separation to God. This is illustrated both figuratively and literally by the form of baptism which separated Jesus into His priesthood, being also that which separated sinners from their sins. (See Exodus 40:12-13 and Matthew 3:13-17.)

5. That Jesus demanded repentance and faith, and baptized disciples. (See Mark 1:14-15 and John 4:1-2.)

6. That those already baptized by John were re-baptized by Paul. (See Acts 19:1-5.)

7. That Paul declared that death unto sin (separation from sin), resurrection life in God (conversion and sanctification) to be the import, the true significance, and purpose of believer's baptism. (See Romans 6:1-14.) This will bring us to the place where we can see the tremendous importance of baptism as Christ established it. This is not the foolish practice of sprinkling water on a helpless infant's nose.

---

[6] Matthew 3:12, paraphrased.

The Baptism of Infants

is of man's invention, and a wicked parody of the true baptism instituted by Christ. Literally and figuratively it is a screaming farce. On the other hand

Heaven and Earth Bear Witness

to the deep spiritual meaning and significance of true believer's baptism. "There are three that bear record in heaven, the Father, the Word, and the Holy Ghost: and these three are one" (1 John 5:7).

The Father is He that gave His only begotten Son for our redemption[7]; the Word is Jesus Christ, in whom we have redemption through His blood, even the forgiveness of sins[8]; and the Holy Ghost is He that witnessed to our pardon, and to our adoption as sons and daughter of the living God.[9]

Again, there are three that bear witness in the earth, the Spirit and the water and the blood; and these three agree in one. The Spirit witnesses that He convicted us of sin. The water witnesses to our repentance and public renunciation of sin; that we have become disciples of Jesus Christ and that being born of the water and of the Spirit, we have entered the kingdom of heaven. (See John 3:5.) The blood witnesses to the remission of our sins, for the blood of Jesus cleanses from all sin. (See 1 John 1:7-9.)

Oh, is it not sad that this ordinance of God, pregnant with meaning of spiritual worth and significance, should be robbed of all its original sense and purpose and degraded to mean only the outward symbol of a covenant made as with Abraham!

To the early Christians

Obedience to God in Baptism

meant the forfeiture of the rights of citizenship and of the benefits and protection of the law. Secular history records that during the fierce persecution in the reign of Nero, and after the burning of

---

[7] See John 3:16.

[8] See John 1:1,14 and Colossians 1:14.

[9] See Galatians 4:5 and Ephesians 1:5.

Rome, a Roman officer was present at Christian baptisms to take down the name of the candidates, and when this was done, the property of those baptized was confiscated to the State, and they themselves were outlawed to become the defenseless prey of malice, or cupidity,[10] from which the State offered them neither protection nor redress.

They suffered every indignity which the forces of lawlessness and barbaric cruelty could heap upon them. They fought with wild beasts in the public arena. They were butchered to contribute to the enjoyment of a Roman holiday. Paul himself was compelled to take part in a gladiatorial contest, and speaks of fighting wild beasts at Ephesus. (See 1 Corinthians 15:32.) In the eleventh chapter of the epistle to the Hebrews we read:

> They were stoned, they were sawn asunder, were tempted, were slain with the sword: they wandered about in sheepskins and goatskins; being destitute, afflicted, tormented; (of whom the world was not worthy).[11]

May God help us to raise the standard of a true baptism as John did! Let us confess that in continuing the farce of infant baptism, which is one of the errors the Protestant churches have inherited from Roman Catholicism, we have robbed Christian baptism of its dignity and power and deep spiritual significance. Let us nobly acknowledge our error. "The times of this ignorance God winked at (overlooked); but now commandeth all men every where to repent" (Acts 17:30).

Let us

RETURN TO APOSTOLIC PRACTICE

by planting again the standard of baptism as instituted by our blessed Lord and Master. The conditions and blessings attached thereto may be enumerated as follows:

---

[10] cupidity: 2. Eager or inordinate desire, especially for wealth; greed of gain; avarice; covetousness. *Webster's Revised Unabridged Dictionary*, 1913, online @ work.ucsd.edu.

[11] Hebrews 11:37-38.

Repentance towards God's circumcision of heart (heart cleansing); separation unto God; faith in a triune God; baptism of the triune man (spirit, soul, and body) into the name of the triune God (Father, Son, and Holy Ghost), bringing in a triune blessing; death to sin; life in God; and power for service; witnessed to in heaven by the Father, the Word, and the Holy Ghost and in earth by the Spirit and the water and the blood.

The question may well be asked:

WHAT DO YOU DO WITH BABIES?

To ensure an obedient, God-fearing race of children, let the parents themselves become obedient to God. Wayward, disobedient, and wicked children are "a seed of evildoers" (Isaiah 1:4), the product of parents who themselves refuse obedience to the law of their God. "Behold, to obey is better than sacrifice, and to hearken than the fat of rams."[12]

After the birth of the child, the parents in due time appear with their child before God in His house. The pastor receives the child and solemnly dedicates it to the Lord and His service. In this, again, we follow Bible custom and precedent. Let us learn what that means from Luke 2:22:

> And when the days of her purification according to the law of Moses were accomplished, they (Joseph and Mary) brought him (Jesus) to Jerusalem, to present him to the Lord.

Again, in Mark 10:13-16,

> And they brought young children to him (Jesus), that he should touch them (not sprinkle them, but touch them): and his disciples rebuked those that brought them. But when Jesus saw it, he was much displeased, and said unto them, Suffer the little children to come unto me, and forbid them not: for of such is the kingdom of God. Verily I say unto you, Whosoever shall not receive the kingdom of

---

[12] 1 Samuel 15:22.

God as a little child, he shall not enter therein. And he took them up in his arms, put his hands upon them, and blessed them (not sprinkled them).

The parents pledge themselves to bring up their children in the nurture and admonition of the Lord[13]; to teach them the Word of God; and to instruct them in the exercise of faith and prayer until such time as they are converted and so obtain an experience in God of salvation from sin and regeneration of heart through faith in the precious blood of Jesus. Then follows baptism as our Lord commanded, at which time they publicly profess a personal and practical knowledge of the salvation of God; their discipleship to Jesus Christ; and that they have the witness of the Holy Ghost to their adoption.

These conditions being fulfilled, they are then baptized into the name of the Father and of the Son and of the Holy Ghost.

IMMEDIATE OBEDIENCE: A WORD TO YOUNG CONVERTS ABOUT BAPTISM

The late Reverend Charles H. Spurgeon, in "The Sword and the Trowel," alluding to the miracle performed upon Saul when his eyes were opened, says: "One more thing that Saul saw when his eyes were opened was what some do not see, although their eyes are opened in other respects. He received sign forthwith, and 'arose, and was baptized.'[14] He saw the duty of believer's baptism and he attended to it directly. You that believe in Jesus should confess Jesus, and you who have confessed Jesus, should gently bestir the memories of those very retiring young converts, who are afraid to put on Christ in baptism. You know right well that salvation lies in the believing, but still how singularly the two things are put together, 'He that with his heart believeth, and with his mouth maketh confession of Him, shall be saved.'[15] 'He that believeth and is baptized shall be saved.'[16] The two commands are joined together by God; let no man put them asunder. Surely, dear friends, wherever there is genuine faith in Christ there ought to be speedy obedience to the other command."

---

[13] See Ephesians 6:4.

[14] Acts 9:18.

[15] Romans 10:9-10, paraphrased.

[16] Mark 16:16.

Our Faith According to Scripture

We believe in, and preach, the following truths as found in the Scriptures:

First: Repentance and its fruits. Matthew 3:2-3,8; Mark 1:14-15; Luke 15:18-21; 2 Corinthians 7:10-11; Luke 19:8. This embraces the new birth, when one's name is recorded in heaven and one becomes a child of God.

Second: Sanctification, the act of grace which cleanses the child of God from the evil nature, the old man, Romans 6:6; the carnal mind, Romans 8:7; and makes him a partaker of His divine nature, 2 Peter 1:4.

Third: The baptism of the Holy Ghost, the fulfillment of the promise of the Father, the enduement of power for service upon a sanctified life, John 15:3; Luke 24:49; Acts 2:4-5,8; empowering for service with an irresistible message, as Stephen, in Acts 6:10. Also speaking in new tongues, a confirmation to the believer, Mark 16:20, and a sign to the unbeliever, 1 Corinthians 14:22.

Fourth: The full restoration of the gifts to the Church, 1 Corinthians 12:7-10.

Fifth: Divine healing provided for all in the atonement, Isaiah 53:5; Psalm 103:3; Matthew 8:17; John 10:10; 1 John 3:8.

Sixth: The premillennial second coming of Jesus Christ, John 14:3; Acts 1:11; 1 Thessalonians 4:13-18.

Seventh: Baptism by immersion, Matthew 28:19-20; and the Lord's Supper, Matthew 26:26-29; 1 Corinthians 11:23-29.

We are not fighting men nor churches, but seeking to displace dead forms and creeds and wild fanaticism, with living, practical Christianity. "Love, faith, and unity" are our watchwords; and "Victory through the atoning blood" our battle cry. God's promises are true. Hallelujah! Our motto is: "In essentials, unity; in nonessentials, liberty; in all things, charity."

These tracts are distributed free and may be had on application to the Secretary, P. O. Box 1636, Johannesburg.

The cost of production is Four Shillings per 100. Freewill offerings gladly received.

Printed and published at the Apostolic Faith Mission Printing Works, Central Tabernacle, 73, Kerk Street, Johannesburg.

Personal Christian experience is the basis of all religious faith. I am thinking just now of old Jacob, who had been looking after his father-in-law's cattle for fourteen years. He was a shrewd fellow and a real old Jew. He had been practicing a law of suggestion on his father-in-law's cattle, until he practically owned the herd. When they were to separate and Jacob had his things started down the road, I guess his father-in-law thought he had about all there was on the farm. He also started down the road and overtook Jacob, and in the course of conversation Jacob said, "I know by experience that the Lord hath blessed me." No doubt about it. He had the cattle. He was in possession of the herd.[1]

So personal experience is the great basis of all faith and growth in God. It is good and blessed to see what God does with others and for others, but

CHRISTIAN BAPTISM AND KINGDOM CONSECRATION

Sermon Delivered by

John G. Lake
Overseer

Published by

Zion Apostolic Church

Spokane, Washington

Price 25 cents

Personal Experience Is Priceless

the only satisfying thing, and the only thing that satisfies your own nature, is that which God accomplishes within your own heart and that which you yourself are cognizant of, whether it be in salvation, sanctification, consecration, Christian baptism, baptism of the Spirit, or any other Christian experience.

---

[1] See Genesis 31.

THE ORDINANCE OF BAPTISM

It has been a great joy to me in these last few years to realize that God is revealing once again, by the Holy Ghost, the real revelation of the purpose of the ordinances that Jesus Christ established, particularly the ordinance of baptism. This ordinance, in the beginning of the Church's history, was a great and blessed and dignified ordinance of God which caused men and women to come deliberately forward and commit themselves to the Lord as disciples of Jesus, notwithstanding that the mere fact of that deed meant that their names would be taken by a Roman officer. (I speak now of the time of the great and terrible persecution of the Christians after Christ, and which continued until the Third Century.)

A Roman officer would take the names of the Christians who were baptized, and these were forwarded to Rome. Instantly, they ceased to have any further right or protection of law under the Roman government. Their estates were confiscated, and they were counted as enemies of the State. They themselves were left as a prey to the avarice of the populace. It certainly meant something to be baptized, and certainly there was something, an inner something, that these Christians understood was vital and so necessary that it could not be avoided. Otherwise, no such public baptism would have taken place.

BAPTISMAL CONSECRATION

I am looking forward and rejoicing in the return of the old time Christianity and note that when the Holy Ghost began to move afresh in these latter days He brought back the old time spirit of real sacrifice, not only the giving up of that which a man possesses, but the giving up of himself and entire committing of himself, to the Lord his God. And this is the point that I want to speak to you about this afternoon. A real kingdom consecration of all you have and all you are — property and person; body and soul and spirit to Christ and the kingdom.

PRESENTATION

The presentation of ourselves to God was the great original fundamental issue that underlaid the whole subject of baptism in the beginning, when Jesus gave the command that constituted Christian baptism; for there is only one command in the entire Word of God that constitutes Christian baptism and gives instructions as to its mode.

COMMAND

Now you notice what I say, that there is *only one command in the entire Word of God that gives instructions concerning Christian baptism and its mode.* No other command deals with the mode of baptism — just that one command in Matthew 28:19, given by the Lord Himself.

MODE

Coming from the Lord, it is absolutely official and binding, not to be discussed or disputed, but *obeyed.* Indeed, this was His final command ere He was borne upward by the power of God as He stood on the Mount of Olives about to be separated from the disciples. He said to them:

> Go ye therefore, and teach all nations, baptizing them in *(into)* the name of the Father, *and* of the Son, *and* of the Holy Ghost.

MEANING

One of the blessed things I feel the Lord is laying on our hearts today is a return to that ancient practice and mode of baptism instituted by Christ, practiced by the apostles and the Church officially for eight hundred years or until the official introduction of single immersion by the edict of Pope Gregory. Not only in the name *of,* or by the authority of, but there is an inner meaning, a better one. Into the *nature* of, into the *character* of, into the *life* of the Father, *and* of the Son, *and* of the Holy Ghost.

Baptism is not an act of obedience. It is ten-thousand times more. It is an induction into the nature and character and the life of God the Father and God the Son and God the Holy Ghost. In other words, induct them into the life of the Father, induct them into the life of the Son, induct them into the life of the Holy Ghost.

BAPTISM INTO THE FATHER

Therefore, in the life of the individual who has been baptized into the *nature* of the Father of necessity there must come forth the characteristic of the Father-heart, the great Father-quality that loves its offspring; that gives itself for the children; that stands in strength and sacrifice, in dignity and power, to guard the interests of the household. "Into the name of the Father." Into the *nature of the Father.* That wonderful Fatherhood that reaches out and yearns to produce and reproduce itself in mankind. So God the Father is yearning to reproduce Himself in us, in you, in me.

BAPTISM INTO THE SON

The climax of salvation is the reproduction in the human family of the Christ of God, the real Christ of God reproduced in you, in me, as members of the great whole. Just as Jesus Himself was the reproduction of the Father, so the collective Body of Christ, the Church, is the reproduction of Christ in the world.

"Baptizing them into the *nature* of the Son," into the sacrifice of the Son, who gave Himself; the Son who died even that we might live. The Son who yielded Himself unto death in order that the life which He gave forth might be transplanted into the human nature and mind. That is the great purpose of the Gospel — the reproduction of the Christ, the Son of God, in the family, the Body, the saints, the bride of Christ.

Beloved, it is my conviction that the time has come when from the Body of Christ, or Church, from the bride of Christ, who is the chosen of Christ, there shall come forth that which the Scripture portrays, the man-child, or one born out of the bride, just as Jesus was born out of the virgin, filled with power and dignity and purity. Not an individual, but a *company* of the saints of God who are born to rule; to whom God has given by the Spirit ability to govern. Who will be partakers and rulers with the Lord Himself in His kingdom on earth.

BAPTISM INTO THE HOLY GHOST

Once again, there is a phase of baptism that you and I have commonly not recognized. "Baptizing them into the Holy Ghost." As Jesus uttered that command as He stood on the Mount of Olives, He included a name, the *Holy Ghost,* into which no man had been baptized before. We see the Fatherhood of God, we recognize the Sonship of God, the Word speaks to us about the *household* of God, but we fail to recognize the characteristics of the *Spirit* of God.

They are the characteristics of *motherhood.* The Spirit that broods, the Spirit that yearns, the Spirit that endeavors to draw us back to God, the Spirit that reaches forth, that hovers over us, that sustains, that blesses, that comforts, that guides, that controls.

So we see the family of God: The fatherhood of God, the motherhood of God, the sonship of God, the household of God.

So in the life of the real Christian, there should, there *must* be apparent in our character, the characteristics of the triune God. There should be evidence that inborn in the Christian, are the God-qualities of construction, creation, character building, cementing together, and comforting crowned with sacrifice and obedience. It is the mind of God that every one, who by the blood of Jesus is admitted to membership in the Body of Christ, should reproduce in *others* the qualities that God has planted in them. Blessed be His precious name!

FOLLOWING HIS EXAMPLE

Beloved, you and I as sons of God by virtue of our sins having been washed away, after we have yielded ourselves to God, stand before mankind to present ourselves to the Lord, even as Jesus Himself presented Himself to God, a complete consecration *"unto all righteousness."*[2]

THE GREAT BLUNDER

Now may I call your attention to one thing? The question of baptism has usually been presented to the world from the sixth of Romans,

---

[2] Matthew 3:15, paraphrased.

which in itself is not a discussion of baptism at all. The subject of baptism in the sixth of Romans is only used as an illustration of the deeper *death-life* of the Christian. *No mention is made whatever of baptism, either into the Father, or the Spirit. Paul deals only with death of sin, the subject he was emphasizing, which is demonstrated in our one immersion, into the Son, while Jesus commanded an immersion into each separate name of the Trinity.* Paul's teaching all the way through is filled with the subject of the death-life of the Christian.

For years and years, as I have gone into the Word of God and prayed over these questions and heard men teach on the subject of baptism, there was something in my spirit that always revolted against the *cross-death* being taught as the Christian's death. The cross-death is the death of the old man, and our sins are nailed to the cross and are done with.

Therefore, the man who comes to present himself for baptism ought to be considered, and should consider, and reckon himself as finished with sin. It is past and done and gone and now he stands before the world to present himself as one who is finished with sin in all its aspects. He presents himself as a saved man that he may come forth a new man in Christ Jesus, declaring himself forevermore committed unto God the Father, unto God the Son, unto God the Holy Ghost.

THE TYPE

In going into this question of the death-life, my spirit recently has been drawn out to observe that in the Old Testament there is a type and evidence of the real *death-life*. In the sixteenth of Leviticus we have that wonderful picture of the Atonement and *life-death* of the Lord; likewise the Atonement and *life-death* of His people, in the presentation of the two goats to represent the *life-death* and physical *cross-death* of the Lord. The one goat was to be slain; its blood to be sprinkled on behalf of the people; its body to be burned, consumed, and destroyed without the camp.

THE LIFE-DEATH

The one goat, the one I especially want to call your attention to now, is the one that was taken on the towrope by a Levite, three days into the barren sands of the wilderness, until worn and weary of exhaustion and starvation it was left to die. This was the other phase of sacrifice — not the giving of its blood and the burning of its body, but the working out of God in its own being until *in real life it dies.*

JESUS ON THE TOWROPE

We come to the life of the Lord Jesus Christ, who presented Himself at the River Jordan, that *all* the *righteousness of God* might be *fulfilled* in Him, and immediately following, we read that He was *driven,* or led, by the Spirit into the wilderness, to be tempted by the devil.[3] We see that after His baptism, He was under the control of the Spirit of God.

Being under control of the Spirit of God, just like the goat that was led by the Levites, so our Jesus by the Holy Ghost, God's Levite, was led three days, God's time, which is three years (a day for a year) into the wilderness, just as the original goat had been led, until He died out to the claims of this three-fold nature. For three years, not by the death of the cross, but by a *living death,* the yielding of Himself moment by moment, hour by hour, day by day, unto His Father's will, He demonstrated to God and man that He was an overcomer and was the one man who had triumphed over *sin* and over *self.*

THE RESULT

Thus, *He became the author* of eternal salvation,[4] and so our Christ, our Lord, could come and present Himself at the cross as the second goat, for destruction of the body, that His physical life might be poured out, that His blood might be shed for the salvation of man.

NEED OF PROPER TEACHING

Beloved, let me tell you, there has been a superficiality in our dealings with men. We say, "Brother, come and kneel at the altar and die, and yield yourself on the cross," etc. and the individual comes and he finds that when he goes away the operation of death has not taken place in him, as he had desired.

---

[3] See Matthew 4:1-11.

[4] See Hebrews 5:9.

Editor's note: Two pages of text are missing here.

...spirit, in His soul, in His body, to the claims of His own nature — wholly yielded unto God.

TEMPTING THE BODY

Then just as the goat, who yielded himself to the control of the Levite and was taken on the towrope three days into the wilderness to die, so Jesus was led by the Spirit into the wilderness. Mind you, He was *led* by the *Spirit*. He did not get there by accident. It was in the purpose of God that He should be tested and tried in order to demonstrate that His consecration was genuine and in God.

The temptation begins. First Satan presents to Him a temptation peculiar to the demands of the body alone. He had fasted forty days and forty nights, and "was an hungred." God says so. Satan says, "Command that these stones be made bread." But Jesus our Lord remembered that at the Jordan He had committed His *body* and all its claims unto God, and rejected the temptation and put it from Him by the Word of God.[5] God's glory and man's salvation were more to Him than the hunger calls of His *body*. Bless God.

TEMPTING THE SOUL

Once again, Satan seeing that the temptation had failed, makes a claim to the higher realm of his nature — His mind, or soul. He takes Him to a pinnacle of the temple, and says, "Cast thyself down" before these unbelieving Jews so that they, seeing you are able to cast yourself from such a height, will recognize you as their prince, and crown you as king. It is all right, do not be afraid, "He will give His angels charge over you to keep you in all your ways." But our Jesus, remembering that He had committed His self-life, His *soul*, His mind unto God, rejected the temptation; the tempter is turned aside.[6]

No crossless crowning for the Lord. No bloodless glory for the Lord. He had committed Himself to God. God had given Him as a ransom

---

[5] See Matthew 4:2-4.

[6] See Matthew 4:5-7.

for many.[7] He, the Father, gave His only begotten Son, so there was no way for our Lord to go but to go the way the Father had mapped out.[8] Jesus knew no will of His own — only the Father's will.[9] Bless God.

How abundantly this is demonstrated in the Garden of Gethsemane, when the great climax of the great earth-life, or that *death-life,* had arrived. Jesus went into the garden when the sorrows of mankind, the consciousness of sin, came upon Him with such abundant power that from His person there began to flow great drops of blood, falling down unto the ground.[10] Reason, science, everything, demonstrates that when such a thing becomes possible death is very near.

I knew a man who sweat blood. For a time, about three months, blood would ooze out of his pores, and when he would awake his pillow would be dotted with blood because of the tremendous burden of sorrow that he then lived under. That was Judge _____ of _____, during Dr. Dowie's breakdown. His wife told me that for three months she would have to put a napkin over his pillow. Beloved, I tell you there are some hearts, there are some lives, that feel the sorrows of man.

Reason, everything, demonstrates that when such a thing in any measure becomes possible in a human life, that death is apparent. In the case of our Lord it was not a little drop or two, but great drops of blood oozed from His person, so that the Lord Himself, understanding and knowing and being convinced that even His life was passing out, prayed that wonderful prayer in the Garden, "Lord, if it be possible, let this cup pass from me."[11]

Jesus was not a coward. He was not praying for fear of the cross. Instead, He was a hero. He was praying in an agony of fear that He would not reach the cross. God had designed what His end should be, and He by the consent of His own nature, for you and me, had likewise designed that there could only be one end and that was that He should die on the cross. His prayer was heard. Angels came and

---

[7] See Matthew 20:28 and Mark 10:45.

[8] See John 3:16.

[9] See John 5:30.

[10] See Luke 22:44.

[11] Matthew 26:39, paraphrased.

strengthened Him, and then with joy and gladness our Lord went on to the cross and poured out His life's blood.

So we see the temptation to cast Himself from the pinnacle of the temple, making an exhibition of His power and thereby getting the acclaim of mankind, was not God's way nor God's will. He had committed His being, His mind, His soul to God. He could not go that way, and He did not.

TEMPTING THE SPIRIT

Once again, He has committed His spirit unto God. Satan, realizing that the appeal to the animal consciousness of the man had failed, realizing that the appeal to His mind, His soul, His reason had failed, presents a new temptation, a spiritual one. He says "Now Jesus look." And by a supernatural power Jesus is permitted in a glance, in a moment of time, "to see all the kingdoms of the world, and the glory of them." He did not miss any of them. That spiritual vision of the Lord reached forth and saw "all the kingdoms of the earth, and the glory of them." Then Satan said, "Jesus, all these will I give thee, if thou wilt fall down and worship me."[12]

But bless God, Jesus had committed Himself at the river Jordan unto *all* the will of God. He could not worship at the feet of the devil, nor acknowledge him ruler. This *life-death* and His reliance on the Word of God gave victory. He spurned the temptation and the tempter and went God's way, His own choice likewise, to the bloody cross.

Men have magnified the sacrifice of the cross, but have minimized, or have failed to see the magnitude of the victory attained by Jesus in His *life-death* of three years, which left His body, His soul, His spirit so completely surrendered to all the will of God that the cross, the death of the body, was but a fitting climax.

Therefore our Christ, having committed His spirit unto God, rejected the temptation of the devil and started from that hour to demonstrate by His daily life and His daily living, that He was *dead* to *all* the claims of His nature. Thus He could say,

---

[12] See Matthew 4:8-10.

> The words that I speak unto you, they are spirit, and they are life.[13]

> The words that I speak unto you I speak not of myself: but the Father that dwelleth in me, he doeth the works.[14]

> I came down from heaven, not to do mine own will, but the will of him that sent me.[15]

Bless God! There was one life surrendered unto God. The only life in all the race of man that was able to present itself unto God, obedient even unto death; dead to every part of His nature, His *spirit*, His *soul*, His *body*. Blessed be the name of Jesus!

GOD'S DESIGN

Beloved, God has designed for you and me that same blessed, wonderful, triune consecration typified in a triune baptism into the *nature* of the Father *and* into the nature of the Son *and* into the nature of the Holy Ghost.

When these dear ones who are to be baptized go down into the water, let it be with this consciousness that you have committed yourself — your body, your soul, your spirit — unto God. That you voluntarily take the hand of the Spirit of God to be led into the wilderness, or out of the wilderness, on the towrope of the Holy Ghost, whithersoever He leads. Bless God.

HOLY GHOST CONVICTION

I believe in triune immersion. There is no doubt about it. I believe it with all my heart. I believe, as any honest student can see, that the teaching of single immersion is only a partial revelation of the wonderful subject of baptism.

Triune immersion is the Holy Ghost revelation of the subject. It is according to the Word of God and the only form of baptism

---

[13] John 6:63.

[14] John 14:10.

[15] John 6:38.

according to the Word of God. Everywhere I go I find that God is revealing this fact to the saints, the real ones. The superficial may continue to baptize by other modes, but the real kingdom Christian will find satisfaction and gratification and consciousness of full obedience only in fulfilling the *entire command* of the Lord Jesus Christ.

It is the end of all discussion on the subject of baptism. Christians who have been baptized by single immersion are convicted of the truthfulness of triune immersion, because of its greater truth and fuller obedience. But no man having been baptized by triune immersion, could be convicted of single immersion except he be a fool, no more than one having been immersed once, could be convicted of the need of being sprinkled.

I am looking forward to the day when the Church of God will recognize that they have robbed mankind of one of the most glorious privileges of the Christian life, that of a clear, definite committing of all their triune being unto a triune God, that a triune operation may take place in the heart — death to sin, life to God, and power for service. Yea more, that you commit yourself even unto death as Jesus did — your body, your soul, your spirit — that when Satan appears to tempt you, as he will, you will be able to say even as the Lord did and as the Lord showed by His action, that your triune being is committed unto God, and you refuse the offers of Satan because you belong to God. Yea more. *That the all things of every day and the every thing of each day* may be the means by which your life is demonstrated to be in the hands of God and that you are yielded, body and soul and spirit, unto Him.

EMPHASIS

Permit me to emphasize this fact, that the disciples baptized men according to the command of the Lord. When Paul dealt with the death-life of the Christian, in the sixth of Romans, he used the subject of baptism (into Jesus Christ) as an illustration, singling out the one act from a complete triune baptism, the one that best illustrated the subject he was discussing. He said, "You having been baptized into the name of Jesus Christ, have been baptized into His death," into the death of Christ, "that like as He was raised up, so you too shall be raised up to the life of purity, holiness, virtue, and truth."[16] God bless you.

SCHOLASTIC AUTHORITY

Recently I had the great pleasure of visiting with Dr. Kolvoord, the eminent Dutch scholar and authority on technical interpretations of Scripture, a scholar of scholars and teacher of teachers. Dr. Kolvoord has been a Baptist all his life, practicing single immersion. My beloved friend and brother in Christ, Archibald Fairley, in discussing with him the subject of baptism in the great commission of Matthew 28:19-20, asked him to analyze the words "baptizing them" from the Greek, saying to him, "I believe you will find, as I have, that the words mean to immerse *repeatedly,*" for the Greek word used is not the word "bapto," to immerse, but "baptizo," to *immerse repeatedly.*

Dr. Kolvoord examined it in the literal Greek, then in the classical. At the conclusion he said to Brother Fairley, "I am amazed. You are right."

And Brother Fairley said, "Now Brother, you have seen the truth. How about it?"

So we rejoice that the illumination of the Holy Ghost makes clear to the spirit many things that the profoundest minds have failed to see and though the unilluminated still continue to practice baptism by single immersion, some even by sprinkling, again we rejoice that God through the Holy Ghost is establishing worldwide, a real kingdom triune baptism into the name of the Father and of the Son and of the Holy Ghost — three immersions, constituting one baptism. Amen.

A CONVERSATION

Desiring all possible light on this subject by the Spirit of God, I asked for the privilege of a conversation with the God-anointed prophet of the Lord, Brother Archibald Fairley, which was as follows:

---

[16] Romans 6:3-14, paraphrased.

QUESTION

Dr. Lake: Brother, the common understanding of the subject of baptism is single immersion. When Jesus said, "Baptizing them into the name of the Father, and of the Son, and of the Holy Ghost" people fail to see what the Greek really indicates, that it was to be a repetition of immersions. Instead, they simply apply it in a separate manner as though Jesus was speaking to a multitude of people and that each was to be baptized. Won't you let me have your explanation of how the Greek shows that to be a repetition of immersions?

GOD'S ANSWER GIVEN BY THE
HOLY GHOST IN THE SPIRIT OF PROPHECY

Fairley: The Spirit of the Lord gives me this. First of all, the purpose of Christian immersion is that in the act we enter into the death of our Lord Jesus Christ. His threefold nature was a reflex of the God-nature. God the Father, God the Son, and God the Holy Ghost, taking possession of His threefold human nature after it was subjected. This immersion into the name of the Father and of the Son and of the Holy Ghost, was a threefold immersion and typifies the death of the natural spirit, the seat of God-consciousness; that it may become the abode of the Father in Spirit. That in it we reckon our human soul, the seat of self-consciousness, dead; that it may become the seat of Christ-consciousness. And that we, in like manner, judge our body, the seat of animal-consciousness, dead; that it may become the center of Holy Ghost consciousness, the temple of the divine Spirit. Thus, the God-nature was revealed in the God-man, covering His human nature after He made consecration, the consecration of the immersion in the Jordan.

Therefore, Matthew 29:19 means this: Baptizing them *into* the *nature* of the Father *and* of the Son *and* of the Holy Ghost. The act of immersion is that act whereby I reckon my human nature dead, my spirit dead to the working of the human spirit and open to the working of the divine Spirit; and the flesh, my soul, dead to the working of the self-life and open to the working of the Jesus life; and my body really dead, first in faith and finally in fact, to the power of the blood as the factor that determines health and open to the power of the Holy Ghost in the flesh. So I determine the health of my body, not by the evidence of healthy blood, but by the power of the Holy Ghost working in me as He worked in the Christ to raise Him from the dead, and set Him above all principalities and powers on the throne with God.[17]

The great fight in the future, and this side of the glory scene, will be for the possession of the body. Not, I believe that this body will be glorified, but that the flesh will be the scene of conflict. That the sons of the Most High, who are to take the kingdom, the inner kingdom first, must walk by faith and not by sight.[18] Must take their stand in His health, not as they feel it, not the evidence of their five senses, but must believe the record of God's Word. Since they have made a three-fold consecration in the way before mentioned, their *life* is truly hid with Christ in God.[19] In Christ in God, in the victorious Christ, the man on the throne, in the place of *dominion*, where the forces of the enemy are under His feet. This is the victory, even our faith.[20]

The overcomer must begin to walk by faith and not by sight. He must reckon upon the life that now is in his Lord, in his head, and not what his five senses bring to him of life or the emotion of life through the blood.

Dr. Lake: Brother Fairley, what causes the differences of opinion and various interpretations of the same Scripture?

Fairley: Every man who interprets Scripture is biased by his size in God, by his experience in the God-life.

Dr. Lake: In my judgement, that is what causes discussion on the subject of triune immersion. Really, the persons who see only single immersion have not got the size in God, or illumination of the Spirit sufficient to use the depth and power of God's Word to see what God teaches.

Fairley: They believe in the death that occurs in a moment or a day, but not a death that begins now and never ends until the revelation of Christ in the air.

---

[17] See Ephesians 1:19-21.

[18] See 2 Corinthians 5:7.

[19] See Colossians 3:3.

[20] See 1 John 5:4.

The immersion spoken of in Matthew 28:19 is that act that begins by the subjection of my life to God and ends in my being part of the ruling God in the age to come. The best figure to use to cover our relationship with the Christ, is the figure of the bride and bridegroom. The bride has lived her simple, carefree life from babyhood, but from the moment she becomes known to the world by her other name, she professes that she is *one* in nature with her bridegroom, one in everything in him.

Thus, throughout the New Testament the words, "in the name of," the Holy Ghost speaking to those who desire to be the bride class, really means into the name, or rather, into the *nature* of the Christ, of God's Anointed, of the man Jesus, who at the Jordan offered Himself unto *all* the will of God and became the Christ, or God's Anointed. The bride is the wife of God's Anointed. Therefore, she is of the anointed class, the offered-up class, the poured-out class. She enters from the moment of her betrothal, of her offering herself up in a true immersion into the nature of her Lord, sharing His burden, which He now has on the throne for a lost world. The effect of this sharing His burden is that His nature displaces her nature and bit by bit the passion of His love for man possesses her and her life is poured out for the lost world.

John G. Lake (center) and Campaign Workers

HEALING

I want to bring you tonight a message taken from Romans 8:3 — I will read you the first verses:

SIN IN THE FLESH

> There is therefore now no condemnation to them which are in Christ Jesus, who walk not after the flesh, but after the Spirit. For the law of the Spirit of life in Christ Jesus hath made me free from the law of sin and death. For what the law could not do, in that it was weak through the flesh, God sending his own Son in the likeness of sinful flesh, *and for sin,* condemned sin in the flesh.[1]

For a long time I wondered what these two expressions meant — "sin in the flesh" — in the second verse. "For the law of the Spirit of life in Christ Jesus hath made me free from the law of sin and death." And then what it meant about that God condemned sin in the flesh.

In the first place, we know that the physical body does not commit sin. (1 Corinthians 6:18-20.) It may be the instrument or weapon that does the thing, but there is no sin in the physical body itself. Sin lies in the will. If you choose to sin, then you can make your body do it. Now according to law there isn't any sin except it is performed by a physical act. You can think murder as much as you are a mind to — you are not a murderer in the sight of the law because you thought it. If you speak murder, that lays you liable, but the law recognizes nothing that has not been translated into conduct, into an act.

Now there isn't any sin in your physical body, there is nothing wrong with your body. Your body is all right. It is you, the hidden man of the heart, that makes the body do things that are unseemly and are wrong. (Matthew 15:16-20.) Then what does He mean by sin in the flesh? For a long time that bothered me. I think I have found a key to it in the 11th verse of this chapter, because it is all one argument.

> But if the Spirit of him that raised up Jesus from the dead dwell in you, he that raised up Christ from the dead shall also quicken your mortal bodies by his Spirit that dwelleth in you.

---

[1] Romans 8:1-3.

He is not talking about the resurrection. He is talking about giving life, healing life, to our physical bodies. Our physical bodies don't need life unless they are sick, do they? That is the conclusion of the argument of Romans 8:1-11 — that is a progressive single argument. What is He talking about? He is talking about disease and sickness and the sin that is in the flesh is the sin of a broken law in your body.

Now sin is breaking the law, some kind of law, and sin in the body is breaking a law of the body. Disease then is dis-ease, isn't it? Make it two words — dis-ease, broken law, wrecked ease, ease that has been destroyed. Ease is health. Dis-ease is sickness. There are three kinds of sickness — sickness in the body, sickness in the soul, and sickness in the spirit. The basic sickness is spirit sickness. I venture this: If you could be healed in your spirit, every last one of you would be well in your bodies. But the whole problem is cleaning a man up in his spirit. Let me change it to business. If you can become a successful salesman in the spirit, you will put your bodies over.

Do you know the place you are whipped first is not in your mind, not in your body. You say, "Oh, my body is so tired." Your body is tired the moment that the spirit is discouraged. Your body breaks down under it. As long as your spirit is triumphant you are a victor and go right on. A man is defeated only when he is defeated in his spirit. Let a man lose courage — and courage is not a product of the intellect. When he loses courage he is whipped, and the only way to put the man on his feet again is to renew a right spirit within him. That isn't the Holy Spirit; it is to renew the spirit that has been defeated and conquered, whipped.

Healing then is in three planes, isn't it? Spirit healing, soul healing, body healing. Basically, the sick person that is sick in body has been sick in spirit quite a little while likely, and after awhile it has gotten down into the soul, and passed through that into the body.

I cannot tell you, brethren, what this truth I am telling you now has meant to my life. I now can trace every physical change in my body to a spiritual condition. My body responds to my spirit.

Now beloved, I want to give you something that is of infinite value. Just to illustrate it: I was called to a home to see a man of 82 or 83 years of age, day before yesterday. He has been sick now two years.

He had blood poisoning in his teeth and it went through his whole body. And when a man is past 80, it is bad you know. I went into his presence with a well spirit, a conquering spirit. Now I didn't think of this when I went there.

When I went back today I saw the effect. I was there with a triumphant, victorious spirit. His spirit caught the contagion from me. He was whipped. He had sat there in that chair until he was whipped, just defeated. Well, I sat down by his side and began to open the Scriptures, and something in me — this is perfectly scriptural — out from your inner life, that is, your spirit, that is the inner being — shall flow rivers of living water. Out from my spirit went into his spirit healing for his spirit. I didn't see it because he is a Scotchman, very reticent, didn't respond much. But I knew in me that it had gone into him. I knew that.

I talked to him a little while and opened the Word, and then prayed for him and left. This afternoon his beautiful, lovely, motherly wife, a woman along in years, called me up and said, "He wants to see you again. He is going to come down to the hotel to see you, because he don't think it is right to ask you to come away up here." Think of that, will you?

I said, "No, I will go up."

When I went into his presence this afternoon, I carried into his presence — I discovered it in myself immediately after I left the house — that I had carried into his presence health in my own mind, in my spirit. I had carried a dominating, victorious spirit, and that man responded to it. Do you know what happened? Before I left the house I saw the reactions in his physical body. Things had happened in his body. While I sat there and prayed for him his spirit had become adjusted — the spirit in me received its health from the Lord and I communicated something to his spirit and his spirit made contact. Just as you press the button and turn on light, you contact with God's Spirit, and when it did, healing came down into his body. Why he changed his whole outward demeanor, changed everything about him.

I have been defeated, and I am full of defeat and that corroding defeat has come down over me and I have lost out; I have broken connection. Did you ever see a battery in an auto corroded with something, and it had eaten off the wires, and the starter didn't move? What is the matter? Something corroded there. You should have kept that clean.

Corroding cares come and get in around your spirit life, and it just covers you and breaks your connection with the Lord. This is true. The real first healing is the healing of your spirit, getting your spirit adjusted to the Lord. The spirit is the part that contacts the Lord. If the spirit is out of harmony and out of condition, and is sort of broken down, you can't get faith for healing, can you? No, you must become adjusted to the Lord.

I said to a young man a little while ago — he was in a desperate condition, required a first-class miracle to touch his life at all. I sat by his side and I said, "If you will accept Jesus Christ as your Savior and confess Him as your Lord, and you receive eternal life, you are healed."

He said, "What do you mean?"

I said, "Just the moment you are born again, you are healed." I have never been afraid to promise that to any unsaved person. Why I didn't know that for years. Now I can tell you — the simplest thing in the world — the moment they are born again, eternal life comes into their spirit. That spirit then can come into the closest relationship with the Father, the great Healer, and the life of God then pours down into his spirit and soul, into his body, and he is immediately touched and made whole.

You cannot get healing for the body, as far as you are personally concerned — *somebody else's faith may,* but until your spirit is right you cannot get healing for your body. May I call your attention to another thing? Faith is a product of your spirit, not of your intellect. Your intellect does not produce faith. Your knowledge may give you ground for faith, but faith is resident in your spirit.

Joy is something in your spirit. Happiness is something connected with your surroundings. You are happy because of your surroundings. You are joyful because you are in right relation with the Father. Now faith, love, joy, hope — all spring from your spirit being, the hidden man of the heart. All are products of your spiritual life. The reason people do not have rich, beautiful faith is because their spirit is denied the privilege of communion and fellowship with the Father. You understand me? You don't read your Bible; you don't pour over it; you don't live in it; you don't spend any time in fellowship with the Father. Consequently your spirit is depleted and weakened. Faith springs out of it and the faith that grows out of it is a sickly plant.

On the other hand, your spirit life is fruitful and built up and enriched by communion with the Father and by reading His Word. And your spirit becomes strong and vigorous. There issues from it a faith that is triumphant and creative. I venture to say this: The men and women who are weak in faith, that once were mighty in faith, are so because they have stopped feeding on the Word of God and stopped close, intimate fellowship with the Father.

Let me say to you with all frankness, brother, that you cannot lose your faith until you have broken your fellowship. Just as long as your fellowship is rich and your spiritual life is at floodtide, faith is triumphant. I have followed that in my own life. For years I did not understand the law that governs it. I see it now. You see, here is the thing that is mightily important — that the spirit life in man is kept healthy and vigorous, and it is kept healthy and vigorous by three exercises. There are more ways, but three in particular.

One is *feeding on the Word*. Second is a *continual public confession* of what you are and what Jesus is to you. I am not talking of sin: I mean confession of your faith in Christ, of what Christ is to you, of His fullness, His completeness, and His redemption. And the third thing is *communion with Him*. Feeding on the Word, confession, and communion. Three simple things, aren't they? And yet they are the things that produce great spiritual life. You do not have it without them.

There are three planes of healing: spiritual, mental, and physical. Now just for a bit I want to call your attention to another very important fact — the relation of your body to your spiritual life. Paul said, in the 9th chapter of 1 Corinthians, that he kept his body under, lest happily after he preached to others, he himself would be laid aside. Not lost, but laid aside, no longer usable. Why? Because his body had gained the ascendancy over his spiritual life. If you become a glutton, and just live to gratify your appetite by eating and drinking, you will lose out spiritually. But if you will keep your appetite under control and your body under like Paul says he did, your spirit will have a chance to evidence itself.

Now let me state it again. You may be a great spiritual athlete, you may have been a great spiritual athlete, but somewhere you have stopped feeding on the Word. The Word lost its taste and flavor for you. You say, "How can it be?" It is. I know of preacher after preacher that had great power at one time, but they have lost all joy in the Scripture. How do I know? Well, I know by the way they act. When a man loves a woman, he wants her with him, don't he? He doesn't care to go off and spend evenings alone. And when a man loves his Bible you will find the Bible with him, in his arms, somewhere. He has gotten hold of the thing. He is holding it.

When I find a man along in years and his hair is growing gray, and I find he loves his Bible, I know that man is fresh in his spirit life. One of the mightiest men I ever fellowshipped with in my life in prayer — when he and I would be together in prayer, sometimes I would open my eyes and look at him, and he would be on his knees with his Bible and kissing it. Didn't want anyone to see him. Thought my eyes were closed. He was holding it just as a man holds his wife in his arms and kisses and embraces her, kisses and loves her.

Whenever I reach a place where I lose my appetite for the Book, and rather talk with people than read the Bible, or rather read books about the Bible than to read the Bible, then I know I am backslidden in my spirit.

You can trace the downfall of every spiritual giant that I have ever known in my life to these three things. One of the greatest men this country ever produced — I have heard him when the Book was in his hand, when he preached like this, he drove me to my knees. Every time I would hear him I would go out and get alone and pray if I could possibly do it. He just battered me and hammered me and drove me into my hole, so to speak; or else he filled me and thrilled me and lifted me.

I saw him 20 years later, when his name was in the lips of every man, and I heard him preach. I noticed that he quoted a good many Scriptures, but he never picked up his Bible; and I noticed he had a theory and philosophy of redemption instead of the old time simple exposition of the Word. And I saw that man whose name was known in every part of the world, with something like 60 churches back of him, in a building that seated 3500, and the building was not half full. He had the greatest gospel soloist that this country has every produced, but the meeting was dry and dead as any formal service imaginable. They utterly failed.

I said to the singer, who left that field and came with me for a campaign or two, I said, "Charley, what is the matter with him?"

"Well," he says, "I do not know, but he is no more like the man he used to be than anything in the world." There had no sin come into that man's life; his life was just as clean as it had ever been. But here is how it had come: Somehow or other he had broken in his spiritual life with the food of the Spirit, the Bible. And the second thing, he used to have the most marvelous prayer life — he didn't have it anymore. And the third thing, in that whole sermon I didn't hear one personal confession. Because he was preaching in a place where personal confession was taboo, people criticized it. If you said anything about yourself and your own experience, the ministers right off the first thing would say, "He is bragging about his own life, isn't he?"

Brother, you will brag about your own life if you have power with God, and you can't help this bragging; you have something to brag about. You really have. You walk in the fullness of the life and fellowship of your spirit with His Spirit, and you have something to talk about, haven't you? Fresh new experiences are coming into you all the time. You are walking in the realm of miracles. I knew that man when he walked in the creative realm of faith. I knew him when he moved down into the purely intellectual realm.

Healing is basically a spiritual thing. The power that heals the sick comes down from God through your spirit, out through your hands into that man or woman. And if you are having the right kind of spiritual fellowship you will have power with God, and there is no escaping it. But listen, brother, you can't get a powerful current of divine life from a little impoverished wire, can you? And you can't get it when the wire where it connects with you is corroded with world cares. Now we call in the electrician and say to him, "I want you to wire my spirit up with God. I want fresh equipment all the way through." Hallelujah!

You say, "I will tell you what I want. I want to be able to stand about 10,000 volts. I want to be wired up to God so that the fullness of His power can pour down through me, through my soul, and out through my hands and voice to the people."

How does that come to you? Simplest thing in the world. Your spirit interlocks with His Spirit without any foreign substance intervening. One day my Reo car stopped right in traffic. A young lady sat with Mrs. Lake and she said, "Let me try it."

She worked the accelerator and it wouldn't work. She said, "Wait a moment." I jumped out of the car and I raised the hood. She said, "I can tell you where it is." She just opened up the distributor, and she said, "One of those points has got a fleck of dirt on it." She brushed it off with her handkerchief and put in on again. The car started right off. That point of the distributor had some little dust, something under it, some little corroding some way that just broke the current and it was a delicate little thing, it didn't take much.

It doesn't take much to break the connection of your spirit and His. God is a Spirit. You are a spirit. And something breaks the connection and the power no longer flows through. You say you want me to pray for you and I pray for you. There is no power. What is the matter? Something has broken the connection. The power comes down through the one who prays, but it can't get through your spirit and touch you. Or, there may be something in my spirit, and His Spirit wants to communicate with your spirit, but is hindered by something in my spirit. But suppose you and I are both right in our spirits. You will get your healing as sure as God sits on His throne.

"But if the Spirit of him that raised up Jesus from the dead dwell in you, he that raised up Christ from the dead"[2] shall send healing through your spirit into your mortal flesh as sure as God is on His throne.

The second thing that must be done continually is, after you have fed on the Word and your spirit is open to the truth of confession, you can't bottle God up. You can't lock Him up. It has been God's

---

[2]   Romans 8:11.

method throughout all the ages to speak to people through those who are in right relation with Himself, and when you are in right relation with Him, the most normal and natural thing is, that He will use you to communicate Himself to others. And so, you act as the medium through which He is to pour His message, by song or by testimony or by prayer or by some other means, but you are His medium. You are His testifier, you are His spokesman, you are His instrument through which He is going to work. Beautiful, isn't it?

Now you see that keeps you in perfect communion, because you have to continually get new messages all the time from Him, so you live in perfect fellowship with Him, feeding on His Word, and telling out the things He does for you. And no Christian is safe that hasn't a *now* experience with the Lord, because sickness can come on you and you have no power to throw it off. You have your *now* experience in your spirit, and you are continually in contact. The spiritual power is coming down and going back and forth continually. Things are coming down and things are going up — from Him to you and you to Him. Down through your spirit. You have a beautiful picture. Angels ascending and descending. It is the thoughts of God coming down and your thoughts going back. He feeding on you, and you feeding on Him.

Now the relation of your body to your spiritual life is almost an unexplored tableland of possibilities. In Romans 6:12, Paul says, "Let not sin therefore reign as god in your death-doomed body [paraphrased]." Let not sin reign. What is sin? What is sin? It is disease. It is dis-ease. He is not talking about sin, because if there is any sin in you it is not in your body. If there is any sin, it is in your spirit or in your soul, isn't it? It is somewhere active in your thinking processes. But he says, "Let not sin reign as god in that death-doomed body." Sin is a broken physical law in your body; that is sickness.

I have a boil and that boil gains the dominion and runs my body, my mind, and my spirit and all I do is to nurse that miserable, throbbing, aching enemy that is in there raising the devil. That is sin in my flesh, and sin has been condemned in the flesh. God condemned the thing, and now sin has broken out in there.

What is rheumatism? Sin in the flesh. And sin shall not have dominion over you in your body for you are no longer under law, but under grace when your body has become the temple of God. Know ye not your body has become a member of Christ? Shall a member of Christ be made the member of a harlot? That does not necessarily mean a woman who is a harlot as we commonly use the word. It may be money, it may be gluttony, it may be a thousand things; but I have taken my body away from the Lord and the Lord's use, and I have committed it to some other use that should not be. "Let not sin reign in your mortal body as king." Hallelujah. "Neither present your members as weapons of unrighteousness."[3] You turn your body over to be used by doctors to make money out of, and surgeons chop you up for a splendid fee.

A woman said to me recently, "My daughter has determined that she will have an operation."

I said, "What is the matter with her?"

"The doctor doesn't know, but he thinks he ought to explore in there." Did you ever hear of it? And so he is going to cut her open and send in a Livingston in there to explore. Great, isn't it? Then the daughter will go after she is all wrecked and ruined and she can't get any healing, then she will turn to the Lord. Then she will expect to get her healing without asking the Lord's forgiveness for turning her body over to some man for examination and experimentation. "Know ye not that your body is the temple of God?"[4] Shall I take the temple of God, then, and turn it over to idols and to demons?

That body of yours is God's holy house, God's holy dwelling place. Why, it is the most sacred thing on earth. Now the temple that God designed and gave to Israel in the wilderness contained the Holy of Holies, the inner place, didn't it? And in that temple that Solomon was permitted to build for God was the Holy of Holies, for the Shekinah Presence dwelt there. The Shekinah Presence now dwells in your body.

Can you imagine, brethren — here a beautiful church, which cost half a million dollars? Everything is in perfect harmony. Wonderful carpets

---

[3] Romans 6:13, paraphrased.

[4] 1 Corinthians 3:16, paraphrased.

and rugs, wonderful furniture, wonderful decorations, and the most up-to-date lighting scheme; everything is perfectly beautiful and artistic. It is just a dream of architectural beauty. They dedicate it to the Lord and go home. They dedicate it on Saturday. Sunday they are going to hold their first services in it, and when they open the door they make the most awful discovery — a horrible stench rushes out to meet them. What has happened? I will tell you. A sacrilegious man opened the door last night and drove a herd of hogs into the sanctuary, and the hogs have been staying in the beautiful edifice during the night.

That is just what we do with these bodies of ours. We have dedicated them to God; and then we let a flock of unclean thoughts come in; and we let disease come in and settle in our bodies until these precious bodies that belong to God are filled with the children of these unclean things. Tuberculosis is the child of a thought; it is the product of a mental and spiritual condition. That is true, that when we are in right communion and fellowship with the Lord there is not power enough in all hell to put disease upon your little finger.

And we have permitted that flock of that dirty, devilish herd of swine to come into our bodies and fill them with disease.

Now beloved, let us go into the thing a little bit further. Then the real healing of your life begins in your spirit, doesn't it?

> Wherefore he is able also to save [heal] them to the uttermost that come unto God by him, seeing he ever liveth to make intercession for them.
>
> — Hebrews 7:25

Now brethren, if God is able to heal to the uttermost, then there are no healings that are impossible, are there? Absolutely none. It doesn't make any difference how sick you are, there is healing for you if you are in contact with the Healer. I don't care how beautiful your chandeliers are, I don't care how beautiful your fixtures are, if outside there, there is one of the fuses blown out, you won't get any light. And the fuse that lets the light of God into you is your spirit, and if that thing is diseased and weak and sickly you can't get much of a current through it, can you?

A man had a vision. He saw a strange sight. He saw a piece of desert land and sickly flowers and trees growing on it. And he awakened and the picture persisted in following him. The next night he had the same picture come before him again, and it persisted for three nights, and then he said, "Lord, what is this?"

And a voice answered, "Don't you know what it is?"

And he said, "No, Lord, I don't know that I do." He sat looking carefully at it again, and he could see it, oh, so vividly. He said, "Lord, that is me, myself." And he said, "That desert is myself." And he said, "I can see that faith and love and peace and joy that should grow there, are those weak sickly plants."

The Lord said, "What would you do if your garden was like that?"

He said, "I'd hoe it and cultivate it and irrigate it." And the Lord left him to think it over.

Now if your faith is weak and sickly it is because your spiritual connection with the Lord is faulty. Maybe there is a fuse blown. Maybe a switch is out. But there it is. Now there must be a right adjustment of the soul to the body and of soul and body and spirit. Now I am a threefold being, if I want to put it that way. To get the highest results my spirit must be dominant. My soul must be subservient to my spirit. My body must be under control of my soul. Then when my body and soul and spirit are in rapport, when they are in perfect fellowship with each other, they can bring forth real results, can't they?

"Know ye not that your body is the temple of God?" (See 1 Corinthians 6:19-20.) Now when that comes to pass, then there comes two spirits. There are two spirits in your body now; there was one before. It was a renewed spirit, then the great, mighty Holy Spirit came in. Now you have two spirits in your body and one soul.

Now the Holy Spirit wants to dominate your spirit, and He wants, through your spirit, to communicate the unveilings of the Father through the Word to your intellect and bring your intellect and your affections up into perfect harmony with His will. And you yield yourself to Him, and you pour over the Book and take it as your own. You read it, you feed upon it, you eat it — more necessary than your daily food. "Man shall not live by bread alone, but by every word."[5] And

---

[5] Matthew 4:4.

you pour over the Word and you meditate on it, and you get at the heart of the thing, and your spiritual nature grows and develops until it dominates your intellect. But you just read intellectual things, read novels, and cheap stories and your sickly intellect will absolutely dominate your whole life and break your communion with the Lord and leave your spirit life in darkness.

The way to health is back again to where we belong, isn't it? I venture this: It is possible to rebuild your spiritual life, as you can rebuild a broken body. I have told you how many of the great athletes grow strong. One of them I met years ago was given up to die of tuberculosis. Another of the great athletes, one of the great wrestlers, was given over to die of tuberculosis at 18. He became one of the outstanding wrestlers in America. What a man can do in his physical body he can do in his spirit, can be done with his intellect. There is absolutely no reason why our spiritual life should not be up to 100 percent efficiency.

I wish I was keen enough in my spiritual nature, I'd have a blackboard put behind us and I'd have someone come that understood artwork. I would look over the audience, and I'd take each one of them, and I'd say to the artist, "Draw that man's spirit and let me show his spiritual condition," and you would see your spirit up there. If it was a weak, sickly, puny thing, you would see it.

Do you know some folks, if you could see them when they come in the meeting, their spirits are on a stretcher, emaciated, tubercular, no flesh on it, just a skinny, horrible looking living corpse and a great big husky body, but the spirit is a shrinking, feeble, emaciated thing? And you come up and say, "What is the matter with me? I don't seem to have any joy with the Lord." Well, a tubercular spirit will have no special joy. "I know I have spiritual discernment." Imagine! I say, "Brother, you have spiritual tuberculosis. Your spirit is emaciated. I don't know whether it will survive the night."

Another comes to me and says, "What is the matter with me?" I look at him carefully for a moment.

"Do you want me to diagnose it?"

"Yes, sir."

"You have cancer, yes sir, it is on your spirit, it is laying siege to the jugular vein of your spirit, and I don't think it will be but a little while before it will finish your spiritual life. It will kill you outright."

Another man says, "I will tell you what ails me." He said, "I will illustrate it, my little boy used to take his money to buy his lunch at school. Instead of buying lunch, he bought candy and cheap soda water to drink, and he ate pie and cake and ate candy until by and by they found out." The man said, "I found out he would not eat meat, and he wouldn't eat vegetables, and we thought there was something desperately wrong with him, and there was. So we just put a spy on his track and we found out he was buying candy and eating it." Aha.

Now if your spirit has reached the place where it has no appetite for the things of God, you have been playing hooky. You have been feeding on things that you ought not to eat, and you have compelled your poor spirit to feed on trash and cheap scandal and cheap talk and useless talk, wisecracking and everything, and you have never given your spirit any real healthy food for a long time, and the poor thing is dying of hunger.

Do you understand me now? You can't get your healing until you get your spiritual healing. If you get your healing, you will get it through the doctor's faith, don't you see? And you will lose it again. But if you get it through your own spirit being in perfect fellowship with the Lord and somebody praying for you likely, or you praying for yourself, or else nobody praying for you, you will be able to keep it.

The doctor told of an experience he had down in Texas where a whole congregation had come, practically all of them for healing, and he said, "You just sit here and listen to me preach, and I won't pray for you at all." He said the largest percentage of the congregation were perfectly healed in just a little while. They came every day for 30 days. At the end of the 30 days there was only about 7 percent of the whole congregation that was not healed. All they did was get spiritually healed, and when you get spiritually healed, chances are a hundred-to-one you will be healed physically.

And I want to tell you this — I don't want to hurt your feelings, God bless you, but brother, do you know I have discovered this — there are quite a number of folks that come to be prayed for, and they are healed over and over again. The healing you want is not physical but spiritual. You get right and get adjusted so you are feeding on the Word, and so you are giving public testimony, and you will be well or in a condition to get well.

THE POWER OF DIVINE HEALING

My soul used to be able to enjoy as much lightness in the Lord Jesus as anybody, but various processes of life reduced my capacity to enjoy jingle, and God brought me down into the solids of life. No man could live in the environment in which a large portion of my life has been spent, without realizing that unless men can contact the living God in *real power,* power out of the ordinary, power sufficient for tremendous needs and unusual occasions, he could not live. Man could not live!

In South Africa some years ago, in a single night a fever epidemic struck the country for three hundred and fifty miles. As I rode through a section of that country I found men dead in their beds beside their wives, children dead in their beds alongside the living, whole families stricken, dying, and some dead. In one single month one-fourth of the entire population of that district, both white and black, died. We had to organize an army to dig graves and an army of men to make caskets. We could not buy wood enough in that section of the country to make caskets, so we buried them in a blanket, or without a blanket when it was necessary to save the blankets for a better purpose.

I had a man in my company who perhaps some of you know. God had appointed that man to pray as I have never found anybody else anointed to pray. For days he remained under a thorn tree, and when I passed that way in the morning I would hear his voice in prayer, and when I returned in the evening I would hear his voice in prayer. Many times I got a prepared meal and carried it to him and aroused him long enough to get him to eat it. I would say, "Brother, how is it? Are you getting through?"

He would reply, "Not yet." But one day he said, "Mr. Lake, I feel today that if I had just a little help in my faith that my spirit would go through into God." And I went on my knees beside him, joined my heart with his, and voiced my prayer to God.

As we prayed the Spirit of the Lord overshadowed our souls, and presently I found myself not kneeling under the tree, but moving gradually away from the tree some fifty or one hundred feet. My eyes gradually opened, and I witnessed such a scene as I had never witnessed before — a multitude of demons, like a flock of sheep. The Spirit had come upon him also, and he rushed ahead of me, cursing that army of demons, and they were driven back to hell or to the place from whence they came. Beloved, the next morning when we awoke that epidemic of fever was gone. *That is the power of divine healing.* God destroying Satan.

Now when you consider that I have been a man of some scientific training, you can understand what an introduction into a life where everything was made new and of a different order meant. Instead of being on the hard, natural plane of materialistic life and knowledge, suddenly introduced into the Spirit you can realize what a revolution was brought to pass in my soul and how gradually discovery after discovery revealed the wonder of God and the mighty action of God through the souls of men.

There is a little keynote in one of Paul's epistles that gives the real key to successful prayer. In successful prayer there is a divine action, a divine interaction, an interaction just as real as any chemical interaction in any experiment in the world. You bring two opposite chemicals together and you realize a little flash or flame, an explosion. There has been an interaction, your chemicals have undergone a change. They are no longer the same properties they were before.

For instance, oxygen and hydrogen united in water. So it is in the spiritual realm. Paul said in giving us this key: "The word preached did not profit them, not being mixed with faith."[1] There is a quality and content in the soul of man, a necessary quality. That quality is the *power of the Spirit.* And when faith and Spirit come together there is an interaction. There is a movement of God. There is a manifestation of the Spirit. There is a divine explosion! *Faith and God united is divine healing!*

When I was a boy, a neighbor employed a chemist. They were trying to manufacture a new explosive of some kind. A section of the barn

---

[1] Hebrews 4:2.

was being used for the experiments. Johnnie was strictly reminded that he had no business around the barn, but like many Johnnies his curiosity was aroused. One day when they had gone to town he discovered that the door was not thoroughly locked. Just a little picking and prying and it opened, and Johnnie was inside. There were some packages on the bench and some liquid on the floor. Presently, Johnnie bungled: a package fell into a bucket of liquid and that is the last Johnnie remembered. When he came to himself he was some fifty or seventy feet away, and they told me he was carried there by a section of the wall. It just went off. That package and the liquid interacted.

We look at the wonderful powers in nature and marvel. Not long ago, a group of scientists compressed such a quantity of nitrogen in a solid block thirteen inches square that they declared if it would be placed in the heart of the city of Chicago and permitted to explode it would wreck the city. One can imagine somewhat of the terrific energy stored up in that little block of nitrogen thirteen inches square; and when you come to think of the marvel of the nature of God, the dynamic of His being — how staggering His almightiness becomes.

The world's conception of religion is that it is a matter of sentiment. For in the minds of most men religion is just sentiment to them, it is not a thing of power. They do not understand the properties of the soul of God, nor the quality of His life, nor how it is that God moves in the nature of men to change their hearts, to dissolve the sin out of their soul, to cleanse them by His life and power, to heal their bodies, and to reveal His light and life in them.

I believe the very beautiful thing we call *salvation* and the holy statement of Jesus Christ, "Ye must be born again"[2] is itself a scientific fact and declaration of God's divine purpose and intent, based on the law of being. We are inclined to think that God just desires, and our hearts are changed. But I want to tell you, beloved, that there is a process in a man's soul that admits God into his life. Your heart opens because it is touched by the love of God and into the heart, into the nature of man there comes the divine essence of the Living Spirit, and bless God, it has an action in him. *Sin* dissolves from his *nature* and

---

[2] John 3:7.

from the mind of man. The Spirit of God takes possession of the cells of his brain, and his thoughts are changed by its action. There is a new realization of divine holiness. By the grace of God he discovers himself *sanctified* in deed and in truth because Christ in truth dwells there.

Beloved, Jesus Christ had His eye and His soul fixed on that one dynamic power of God — the *Holy Ghost*. And His holy life, His death, His resurrection, His ascension to glory were all necessary in the process of soul development to arrive at the throne of God where He could receive from the Father the gift of the Holy Ghost and have the privilege of ministering to your soul and mine.

So in my heart there has grown a wondrous reverence for the mighty Son of God, who saw beyond the ken[3] of man, who visioned in the distance, who sought in His soul for the key to the mighty powers of the nature of God. Who determined for our relief and for our benefit and salvation to leave the throne of God, come to earth, be born as a man, take upon Him the nature of man (not the nature of angels). He looked to God as men do, overcome by His power. Through reliance on His Word and so believing, so advancing step-by-step in the nature of God and the likeness of God, one day He stood forth the Eternal Sacrifice before the throne of God and received the eternal reward of His fidelity — the Holy Ghost. In life, Jesus the man was in the *likeness* of God. In resurrection, the *nature* of God. In glorification, the *substance* of God and thus became the author of eternal salvation.

The man or the woman who does not understand the Holy Ghost and its magnificence and the wonder of its power, must turn his heart again heavenward and see the price that Jesus paid in order to secure it for you and me. In order to give it to the world that was in sin, sickness, and death — to lift it out of darkness. I love that blessed old hymn, "Ye Must Be Born Again." Can we not sing it?

> A ruler once came to Jesus by night,
>
> To ask Him the way of salvation and light;
>
> The Master made answer in words true and plain;
>
> "Ye must be born again!"

---

[3] ken: range of knowledge or understanding. *Webster's Desk Dictionary of the English Language* (NY: Gramercy Books, 1983), p. 499.

Chorus:

"Ye must be born again!"

"Ye must be born again!"

"I verily, verily say unto thee,

"Ye must be born again!"

Ye children of men, attend to the Word

So solemnly uttered by Jesus the Lord;

And let not this message to you be in vain;

"Ye must be born again!"

O ye who would enter this glorious rest,

And sing with the ransomed the son of the blest;

The life everlasting if ye would obtain,

"Ye must be born again!"

A dear one in heaven thy heart yearns to see,

At the beautiful gate may be waiting for thee;

Then list to the note of his solemn refrain:

"Ye must be born again!"

There is a process of divine *transmutation*. But beloved, by the power of God's Spirit in a man's heart that process is going on every single day of your life. God takes that which is natural, that which is earthly, touches it by His divine power, moves upon it by His heavenly nature, and in the name of Jesus Christ you come forth no longer self and selfish, but now *transformed*, changed by the power of Christ, into the nature of the Son of God, into the likeness of the Lord, into His character and nature and understanding and knowledge. Blessed be the God and Father of our Lord and Saviour Jesus Christ!

"To us is given exceeding great and precious promises, that *by these* we may become partakers of the divine nature." And being a partaker, in consequence, "Escape the corruption that is in the world through lust."[4] Bless God, His divine purpose is not to whitewash the soul, but to change the character, *transmute* the life by the grace of God, make the man a priest and king, a deliverer and a savior in common with the Lord Jesus Christ, his elder brother. If I am a brother of the Lord, then I am bone of His bone and flesh of His flesh and substance of His substance — like my elder brother. The source of life is the same source of life that is in Him. The same purpose that is revealed in Him is His high purpose for you and for me.

Men have little understanding of the quality of faith or what it accomplishes, because of the fact that they are not aware of the process by which that work is done. *Faith* has the quality and power, with the Spirit of God, to do what a match does to powder. It is the touch of God. It is the touch of *faith* through us that ignites the Spirit and produces the divine action that takes place in the soul when sin is rebuked and cast out, when sickness is destroyed and dissolved from the life, the nature set free, and man rejoices as a son of God, saved in spirit, soul, and body.

One day there came to my healing rooms a little boy that we know on the streets as a newsboy, just one of the little ragged chaps. A lady had observed the little fellow on the street in an epileptic fit and afterwards took him by the hand and led him into the healing rooms. We talked to the little chap about the Lord, prayed for him, and told him to return again. The Lord healed him. He was a manly little urchin, and one day he said: "Mr. Lake, I haven't any money to reward you with now, but you are not going to lose any money on me." We smiled and were glad to see the spirit of the little chap, and he went his way. About two weeks later, in the midst of a great meeting he strutted in, marched up, and laid five silver dollars on the table and marched out again.

Then he got up against his first real problem of living his new life in his business. Every boy has a corner. He can sell papers on his own corner and it is up to him to keep all the other boys away. He had given his heart to the Lord. One day he came around with a long face. He said, "It's all off."

---

4 2 Peter 1:4, paraphrased.

"Well, my boy, what's the trouble?"

"They were going to rush my corner, until I could not stand it, and I cleaned up the whole bunch." The little chap was getting his first introduction into the real problem of being a Christian in this old world, under a competitive system, the outgrowth of human selfishness, devised by the devil.

One day, a gentleman came along and wanted to buy a paper. His arm was disabled, and he could not get his purse. He said to the boy, "I have put my purse in the wrong pocket. Put your hand in and get it for me."

The boy said, "What is the matter with your arm?"

He replied, "I have what is called neuritis. My arm is paralyzed."

The little chap said, "Well, if the doctors can't do you any good, I'll tell you where you can get it fixed up. There are some men up in the Rookery Building that pray, and folks get well."

The man said, "How do you know?"

He replied, "I used to take fits and fall on the street, and they would carry me off to the police station. I was like that for four years, but I don't take fits any more. If you want me to, I will take you up there." So he brought him up.

He was the head of a great lumber concern; his name was Rose. He sat down and told me how he was moved by the child's simple words, but he had no more idea of how God could heal a man or save man from sin than one of the Indians. So we began to tell of the Lord Jesus and His power to save and continued to minister to him each day. Three weeks afterward he returned again to the medical clinic, where two hundred and seventy-five physicians had declared four weeks before that they could do nothing for him. They reexamined him and found him perfectly well, healed by the power of God. *That is the power of divine healing.*

I went to the medical association and got a copy of the lecture that was given by Dr. Semple on the seriousness of the disease and the utter impossibility of medicine ever to help him or change his condition. Insofar as they were concerned, he was a cripple. The nerves were dead, atrophied. It would require a miracle, they said, to reproduce the original life and restore power in the tissue of the arm. But the miracle took place because there is a fountain of life, the life of God, available for every man. Bless His name! *That is the power of divine healing.*

When the *life* of Jesus comes in, the death of your soul ends. When the Spirit of God comes in, your *dead* nerves come alive. God, by the Spirit, takes possession of the blood and the brain and the bone. He dwells in the very cellular structure of your whole being. His quickening *life* regenerates you and generates *life* in you and by the Christ of God you come forth, not a dead, senseless lobster, but a *living man*, a *living* Christian.

Let me tell you a story to illustrate this point. They say a man died, and he appeared at the Beautiful Gate and said to Peter: "I am from Philadelphia. I subscribe for the *Ladies' Home Journal*. I have a bed of mint in the backyard, but I never drink intoxicants."

Peter replied, "Go on to heaven and *stay dead.*" He was dead already. Some folks think, you know, that because they are not committing this sin and that sin that they are dutiful, beautiful children of God. But, beloved, there is an awful lot more to Christianity than delivering a man's soul from the power of sin.

Professor Riddell tells this story: "I was walking along the Sea Beach and I encountered a lobster. I said, 'Lobster, did you ever chew tobacco?'

"'Never!'

"'Lobster, did you ever stay out nights?'

"'Never!'

"'Say, Lobster, shake hands. We are both lobsters.'"

Oh, there is a negative thing and that negative thing in religious life is what is killing the real *power* of God. That negative thing, when we are all the time *not doing* this and that and something else. It is a religion of *don't* do this, and *don't* do that. My God! When Christ comes into the soul and into the spirit it is all changed. Instead of deadness, there is *life* in God. Instead of inaction, there is *power* by the Spirit of God. The Christian is a *man*, not a lobster.

> "Down in the human heart,
>
> Crushed by the tempter,

Feelings lie buried

That grace can restore.

Touched by a loving heart,

Wakened by kindness,

Chords that were broken

Will vibrate once more."

Oh, the grace of God is the lovely thing, the grace of God is the powerful thing. The grace of God is the life and Spirit of the Lord and Saviour Jesus Christ. And ministered to the soul, breathed into the heart, transmitted to the life, *man* becomes like Christ because the Christ of God is moving in the heart of him, generating and regenerating, and man comes forth a finished product by the hands of his Lord — saved from sin, healed of disease, kept by the indwelling Christ, who is the power of God.

I am looking to God for some real finished products these days, real men grown up in the Lord Jesus Christ, established in the splendid solidarity of His holy nature and divine character, beautified by His holy glory, enriched by His divine nature — *like the Son of God.*

So, my brother, my sister, I want to bring your heart this afternoon into this blessed confidence, this holy truth, this divine reality. If religious life has been a sort of sentiment, let me tell you beyond it there is the power of God. The moving, dynamic, burning force of *life* in Christ Jesus is waiting to come into your heart, to revitalize your thought, and to change your spirit and indwell the very flesh and bone and blood of you and make you a new man and a new woman in the Lord Jesus. Say, beloved, that is the *power of divine healing.*

On one occasion, I was entertaining myself by examining some typhoid bacteria as they developed in dirty water. A neighbor woman came one morning and was anxious for me to show her one of her hairs under the microscope. I told her I had the microscope set and was waiting for the development of the bacteria and would be obliged if she would come back another day, when my experiment was over. Instead of paying attention to what I said, she returned the next day with the same request. Again I explained to her, but the next morning she was back again, and finally the fourth morning I was annoyed and thought I would just take one of her hairs, let her see it anyway and not disturb the microscope. So I pulled it through under the microscope and let her look. Presently, she jumped up and hurried away and never even said, "Thank you."

When I came home that evening, Mrs. Lake said, "What did you do to Mrs. B.?"

I said, "I really do not know. Why?"

She said, "Well, she has been on the back porch all day, and the servant has been drenching her hair with kerosene." Why, she saw more crawling things than she ever saw before. She saw the bacteria and believed the crawling beasts were attached to her hair. Her hair and head were perfectly clean. The presence of the beasts she saw was explained in another way.

I want to bring home the truth of God. In the minds and lives of many, religion is simply an illusion. There is no divine reality in it. But, beloved, real religion is God's divine reality, for it is the heart of God and the life of Christ. And when it comes into the soul of man it generates the same divine reality and heavenly power in him, and man becomes God's new creature.

In my younger days, when I first touched the ministry of healing and as yet had developed a very small portion of faith in God, a young lady who lived nine miles in the country had a tubercular limb. Her [unfortunately, the manuscript ends here].

eloved, I feel a great personal responsibility in speaking to you on the subject of Divine Healing. This truth was very little known and still less understood prior to the arrival of Brother Tom Hezmalhalch and myself upon these shores, in connection with the introduction and the establishment of the Apostolic Faith Mission in this land.

We had prayerfully considered this subject on our way from America to this country, and had come to the decision that the present was an opportune time to separate this truth

DIVINE HEALING

[These tracts are distributed free, and may be had on application to the Secretary, P. O. Box 1636, Johannesburg. The cost of production is four shillings per 100. Freewill offerings gladly received.]

The following address was delivered by Brother J. G. Lake at the Dutch Church Hall, Somerset East, in October, 1910.

from the dogmas and traditions which bound it, and send it forth on broader lines in harmony with our conception of the truth as it is revealed to us in the Scriptures.

You will therefore appreciate my feelings as I undertake to address you tonight on this subject.

It is affirmed by the thoughtless that we teach new doctrines. It is not so, for

DIVINE HEALING IS NOT NEW

It has come to us through a process of progressive revelation running parallel with man's history and perfected in the vicarious death and suffering of our Lord on Calvary.

In its stages of evolution and development it finds its illustration and parallel in the baptism of the Holy Ghost, which from a revelation from God to man in the patriarchal age advances to that of God dwelling and abiding with man in the Mosaic, and reaching its climax in the baptism of the Holy Ghost in the Christian dispensation — which is God in man, whereby man becomes the habitation of God through the Spirit.

In Exodus 15:26, God reveals Himself to the people of Israel under His covenant name of "Jehovah-Rophi," or "The Lord that healeth thee."

There at the waters of Marah, after they had escaped from the Egyptians, and Egyptian medical practitioners by crossing the Red Sea, God made

AN EVERLASTING COVENANT

with them.

> There he made for them a statute and an ordinance, and there he proved them, and said, if thou wilt diligently hearken to the voice of the Lord thy God, and wilt do that which is right in his sight, and wilt give ear to his commandments, and keep all his statutes, I will put none of these diseases upon thee, which I have brought upon the Egyptians: for I am the Lord that healeth thee.[1]

The covenants of God are as unchangeable and eternal as Himself. The covenant of divine healing stands today steadfast and irrevocable as the day it was made by the eternal, immutable God at the waters of Marah. It is writ large upon the pages of Holy Writ. Saints have rejoiced in it; prophets have confirmed it; David the sweet psalmist of Israel sang in inspired verse of its validity.

> Bless the Lord, O my soul: and all that is within me, bless his holy name. Bless the Lord, O my soul, and forget not all his benefits; who forgiveth all thine iniquities; who healeth all thy diseases.

> — Psalm 103:1-3

---

[1] Exodus 15:25-26.

Jesus Christ, who was God manifest in the flesh, demonstrated the perpetuity of that covenant in Himself, "healing all manner of sickness and all manner of disease among the people" (Matthew 4:23); by communicating the power of healing the sick to all believers (Mark 16:15-17); and through the Holy Ghost, placing the "gifts of healing" as a perpetual manifestation of His power and presence in the Church through all ages (1 Corinthians 12:9).

Jesus Christ, like any great reformer, had a specific mission to fulfill. This was outlined in the inspired words of the prophet Isaiah, chapter 61, verses 1 and 2. In the synagogue at Nazareth, at the beginning of His public ministry, He announced the essential points embraced in that ministry imposed upon Him, and which He said was now being fulfilled. Healing was one of the conspicuous features of that ministry, as we read in Luke 4:18-19

> The Spirit of the Lord is upon me, because he hath anointed me to preach the gospel to the poor; he hath sent me to heal the brokenhearted, to preach deliverance to the captives, and recovering of sight to the blind, to set at liberty them that are bruised, to preach the acceptable year of the Lord.

Like a true reformer and the Son of God, He put His mission into immediate effect and practice. How did He do it? Read Matthew 4:23, and you will see the evolution of the ministry of healing.

> And Jesus went about all Galilee, teaching in their synagogues, and preaching the gospel of the kingdom, and healing all manner of sickness and all manner of disease among the people.

In the ninth chapter of Luke, we read of the first step taken by our Lord suggestive of the broadening, progressive scope of this ministry of healing, by sending forth

TWELVE OTHER MEN WITH POWER TO HEAL

> Then he called his twelve disciples together, and gave them power and authority over all devils, and to cure

diseases. And he sent them to preach the kingdom of God, and to heal the sick.[2]

"And He said unto them, 'take a thousand pounds a year.'" Is that it? (Voices: No!) Then what is it?

> And he said unto them, take nothing for your journey, neither staves, nor scrip, neither bread, neither money; neither have two coats apiece.[3]

Oh, my! That is not much like your modern preachers! Today it means the finest house in town, the highest salary, the smartest carriage and horses! Everybody bows down before this display of so much worldly pomp and temporal greatness! These are some of the reasons why the Church has lost spiritual power and stands impotent in the presence of sickness and suffering. To hide her feebleness and inefficiency, she takes refuge under the discreditable subterfuge, that the gifts of healing have been withdrawn, and the age of miracles is past. No wonder infidelity is eating the heart out of the Church of God! Has Jehovah-Rophi, the eternal covenant God, changed? Or is the modern disciple of a different stamp and pattern to them whom Jesus called in the days of His flesh? Truly, the change is in the disciple, and not in the one unchangeable Lord and Master. I find that the old-time power is to be had today by the old-time men who are willing to walk and work and suffer and die to get this Gospel of Christ to people everywhere.

He endued the twelve with the power. And in the tenth chapter of Luke we read how the Lord took an additional step to the extension of the scope of the ministry of divine healing by sending forth

SEVENTY MORE MEN WITH THE POWER TO HEAL

"After these things the Lord appointed other seventy also"[4]; and in verse 9 we read that Jesus commanded them to "heal the sick that are therein, and say unto them, the kingdom of God is come nigh unto

---

[2] Luke 9:1-2.

[3] Luke 9:3.

[4] Luke 10:1.

you." There were now eighty-three men endued with this power: Christ Himself, the twelve disciples, and the seventy more. At the close of the forty days separating the event of the crucifixion from that of the ascension, our Lord still further extends the range of the ministry of healing by furnishing

EVERY BELIEVER WITH THE POWER TO HEAL

the sick. Every man and woman, in every age, in every land, who has faith in the living, eternal, covenant-keeping God are empowered to lay hands upon the sick, and "they shall recover."[5] The general terms of that great extension of the ministry of healing are found in that great and final commission given in Matthew 28:18-20, "And Jesus came and spake unto them, saying, all power is given unto me in heaven and in earth."

Beloved, has He lost any of that power? Never! He is still the Son of God.

> All power is given unto me in heaven and in earth. Go ye therefore, and teach all nations, baptizing them in the name of the Father, and of the Son, and of the Holy Ghost: teaching them to observe all things whatsoever I have commanded you: and, lo, I am with you alway, even unto the end of the world.

Is He with us still? Yes, bless God. Is He changed? No. "Jesus Christ the same yesterday, and to day, and for ever" (Hebrews 13:8). "I am the Lord, I change not" (Malachi 3:6). "For the gifts and calling of God are without repentance" (Romans 11:29). God has never repented of having placed the gifts of the Holy Ghost in the Church. In the name of Jesus Christ, I challenge any man to show by the Word of God that the gifts and power of God were withdrawn. We have lost the old-time faith, that is where the trouble is! Having forsaken God to lean upon the arms of flesh, and the fountain of living waters for broken cisterns that can hold no water. (Jeremiah 2:13.) Let us honestly acknowledge our sin and return to the Lord our God.

---

[5] Mark 16:18.

Having examined the general terms of that extension of the ministry of healing, let us now consider the peculiar characteristic, the trademark of God's endorsement, which was to be the accompanying circumstance, the continuous sign and symbol of the Gospel of Jesus Christ.

This is given in Mark 16:14-18:

> Afterward he appeared unto the eleven as they sat at meat, and upbraided them with their unbelief and hardness of heart, because they believed not them which had seen him after he was risen. And he said unto them, Go ye into all world, and preach the gospel to every creature. He that believeth and is baptized shall be saved; but he that believeth not shall be damned. And these signs shall follow them that believe; in my name shall they cast out devils; they shall speak with new tongues; they shall take up serpents; and if they drink any deadly thing, it shall not hurt them; they shall lay hands on the sick, and they shall recover.

"And these signs." These are God's own mark and endorsement of the faithful preaching of the Gospel of Jesus Christ. We know the goods by the trademark which they bear. These signs are God's eternal trademark, issued by the Son of God, and sealed in His own blood. The devil has tried to rob us of it by telling the preachers and teachers that these verses are an interpolation, and not found in the Sinaitic manuscript of the New Testament.[6] The Sinaitic manuscript was, however, only written in the fourth century. That these verses are authentic has been proved from the writings of the Church Fathers, which were written prior to the Sinaitic manuscript, and less than two hundred and seventy years after Christ.

This is a matter of history. Lord Hailes[7] is our authority. He tells us that at a dinner at Edinburgh it was decided that a compilation of the New Testament be made from the New Testament references and quotations found in the writings of the Church Fathers, previous to

---

[6] The Sinaitic manuscript, one of the most prominent discovered after 1611, was found amongst trash paper in St. Catherine's monastery at the foot of Mt. Sinai in 1841. It is considered a flawed manuscript.

[7] Lord Hailes was an 18th century Scottish writer.

the year 300. The whole was completed some years ago and found identical with our present edition, except that it lacked seven verses in Hebrews, and these have since been forthcoming. Preachers and teachers of God's Word, don't make any more infidels with such an excuse, but rather confess that the faith to get results is lacking; that the Word is true; that the failure is on the human side.

Have you noticed how frequently church officers and members say: "Oh, I don't believe this or that portion of God's Word!" Why don't they? How could they when the Word of God is continually twisted out of its original sense and meaning by those whose vocation should be to guard it as a sacred deposit? This wresting of the Scriptures is responsible for the unwarranted belief that the gifts of the Holy Ghost have been withdrawn.

Jesus said, "These signs shall follow them that believe" — not the doubter, but them that believe in my name, the name of Jesus.

> They [shall] cast out devils; they shall speak with new tongues; they shall take up serpents; and if they drink any deadly thing, it shall not hurt them; they shall lay hands on the sick, and they shall recover.

Someone asks: "What does it mean to cast out devils?" It means that the man with the Holy Ghost dwelling within him is the master and has dominion over every devilish force and counterfeit. At Johannesburg some said: "Your power is hypnotism." One night, God demonstrated through us the falsity of that accusation. The power that is within the true Christian is the power of the living Christ, and "greater is he that is in you, than he that is in the world" (1 John 4:4).

I can best illustrate this by introducing an incident in my own personal ministry.

THE POWER OF GOD AGAINST HYPNOTISM

In the Johannesburg Tabernacle, at a Sunday evening service about a year ago, God instantly healed a lame girl. She came from Germiston. She had been suffering for three-and-a-half years from what the doctors said was either an extreme case of rheumatism or the first stage of hip disease. She was not able to get up the steps without assistance when she came to the platform to be prayed for. They asked her: "How long have you been sick?"

She said, "For three-and-a-half years."

"Have the doctors treated you?"

"Yes; for two-and-a-half years, and then they gave me up."

"Who has been treating you for the last year?"

"A hypnotist."

Just then, a well-known hypnotist arose in the audience and moved forward and took the front seat. The leader said, "Never mind about the hypnotist, Jesus is going to heal you right now. In two minutes you will be well." They laid hands on her and prayed, and instantly the Lord delivered her, and she walked up and down the platform several times to demonstrate to herself and the audience that she was well.

The leader said, "I stepped back and looked at her, my heart going out in praise to God for His mercy, when suddenly the Spirit of the Lord descended upon me in power, not in any gently influence, but with a mighty intense power, a spirit of revulsion against the spirit in the hypnotist. I stepped on the platform directly in front of him, and said: 'Are you the man who has been hypnotizing this woman?'

"He replied. 'Yes, I am.' He rose to his feet and looked towards me in a challenging attitude.

"I said to him, 'In the name of Jesus Christ, you will never hypnotize anybody again.' And before I realized what I was doing, I reached over the front of the platform, grasped his collar with my left hand, while with my right I slapped him on the back, saying, 'In the name of Jesus Christ the Son of God, you come out of him. Now,' I said, 'go and hypnotize another if you can.'

"He laughed at me and said, 'Do you mean to tell me that I cannot hypnotize anybody?'

"I said, 'Yes, sir, that is the end of the thing. The devil that caused you to hypnotize people is out.'

"He worked all night in an endeavor to hypnotize some subjects, and in the morning at six came to my house saying, 'This is a mighty serious business, mister, this is my bread and butter.' He wanted me to give him back the power to hypnotize. I explained to him that it was not I but Jesus who had cast out the devil. I added, 'Brother, it looks to me as if the Lord wanted you to earn an honest living.'

"He cancelled his engagement at the theatre where he was billed to give exhibitions and last heard of he was working in the mine and earning an honest living."

That demonstrated there is a mighty manifestation of the Spirit of God that has dominion over every other power. It is still true that, "In his name we shall cast out devils."

This afternoon I heard a brother ask, "What about 'They shall take up serpents?'" Let me tell you a story. Brother Fisher, of Los Angeles, California, told me this incident in his own life. He was a Baptist minister at Glendale, a suburb of Los Angeles. He is now associated with Brother George G. Studd in "The Upper Room Mission," 327½ South Spring Street, Los Angeles, California, U. S. A.

BROTHER FISHER AND "THEY SHALL TAKE UP SERPENTS"

"One morning my wife called me up on the telephone and said the water pipe beneath the house was broken. I went home about ten in the morning. I opened the little door in the basement of the house and on putting my hand in to feel for the pipe, I was bitten by a serpent. At once I commenced to swell. The poison worked into my body fast. What was I to do? I said, 'God your Word says, "They shall take up serpents." I trust You for this, You must heal me or I die.'

"That afternoon and evening my sufferings were terrible. By midnight my blood was so congealed I was well nigh insensible. Oh, I shall never forget that sense of death creeping over me, steadily, surely, until three in the morning. I could pray no more. I ceased to struggle, I fell to the floor; and that instant God healed me. The life of God thrilled through my body, and I was healed." It is true, "They shall take up serpents."

Let me give you another illustration of "taking up serpents." It is an event in the life of Brother Tom Hezmalhalch, one of the pastors of the Apostolic Faith Mission in Johannesburg. Brother Tom (as we call him for short) is a man of great faith and simple trust in God. (Brother Tom has since returned to America.)

BROTHER TOM AND "THEY SHALL TAKE UP SERPENTS"

"In Southern California, during one of the harvest seasons, I had an honest young infidel working for me. The young man was engaged in loading, and I was pitching sheaves on the load, when he said, 'Brother Tom, do you believe in the Bible?'

"I said, 'Every word of it.'

"He said, 'Do you believe in Mark 16:18?'

"I said, 'I do.'

"He answered, 'I have never yet met the parson who does.'

"I prayed silently to Jesus, that if He wanted to convince this young man of the truth of His Word, that He send along a snake, and I would take it up. Soon I heard a hissing sound from under the sheaves, I said, 'Jesus sent you along, I want you.' I grabbed the snake some distance from the head, and I lifted it up to my friend on the wagon. He looked at me, and then said, 'Kill it! Kill it!'

"'No.' I said, 'Jesus sent it along, I am going to let it go about its own business.' After awhile he laughed, and said, 'Tom, that was only a common Californian snake.' I judged from his expression he was not satisfied with the test. I prayed again. 'Jesus, why did You send along a common snake? If you want to convince this man, send along a venomous one.'

"Not long after, I heard the hiss of another snake. I cried, 'Hold on there, I want you,' and laying hold of it as I did the former one, I held it up to my friend, saying, 'How about Mark 16:18?' He turned pale and said hastily, 'Drop it! Drop it! Kill it!' I put it quietly down after stroking its head and body with my other hand, and said, 'Go on, Jesus sent you here, I'll not kill you.' When my friend could speak, for he was pale and shocked, he said, 'Tom, did you know what kind of a snake that was?'

"I said, 'No.'

"He replied, 'That was a deadly viper, and if it had bitten you, you would be a dead man.'

"I said, 'It could not bite, Jesus would not permit it.'"

I don't pretend to have that kind of faith, but I am not going to belittle it in the man who has. I am, I trust, man and Christian enough to praise God when I see someone going further than I can.

"IF THEY DRINK ANY DEADLY THING, IT SHALL NOT HURT THEM"

You ask, "What about, 'If they drink any deadly thing, it shall not hurt them?'" History abounds in instances wherein the early Christians were compelled to drink the juice of the deadly hemlock, but through faith in Jesus, one of the deadliest of poisons became as harmless as water. According to your faith be it done unto you.[8] My own sister's son, Fred Moffatt, when a child, entered his father's workshop and ate some Paris green.[9] My sister and brother-in-law sent for me. I quoted the words of our Savior, "And if they drink any deadly thing, it shall not hurt them." Upon this precious promise of God we rested, and Jesus healed the child. His parents now reside at 4 Milbourn Road, Bertrams, Johannesburg, and this their son is a student at the Marist Brothers Schools. (Since returned to America.)

I have outlined the development and progressive revelation of divine healing from the covenant at Marah, and on through succeeding dispensations until it is perfected in the redemption wrought by Christ on Calvary. The blessings of healing in the old as well as the new dispensation, flow from the atonement which Jesus Christ the Son of God made for man's sin and sickness on the Cross of Calvary.

In Matthew 8:16-17, we read,

> He cast out the spirits with his word, and healed all that were sick: that it might be fulfilled which was spoken by Esaias the prophet, saying, Himself took our infirmities, and bare our sicknesses.

---

[8] See Matthew 9:29.

[9] Paris green: an emerald-green, poisonous powder used as a pigment, insecticide, etc. *Webster's Desk Dictionary of the English Language* (NY: Gramercy Books, 1983), p. 660.

In the general epistle of James, the Holy Ghost, through the inspired writer, instructs the Christian what to do when sick.

> Is any sick among you? let him call for the elders of the church; and let them pray over him, anointing him with oil in the name of the Lord: and the prayer of faith shall save the sick, and the Lord shall raise him up; and if he hath committed sins, they shall be forgiven him.

— James 5:14-15

In spite of the clear, convincing testimony of the Scriptures and the ever accumulating cloud of witnesses who testify of healing received through faith in Jesus, many preachers and teachers are still found blindly rejecting the truth to their own final discomfiture and undoing.

GOD HAS A CONTROVERSY
WITH THE CHURCH IN AFRICA

Your own prophet, the Reverend Andrew Murray, was healed of God at Bethshan, London, England, of a throat disease which medical skill had proved itself impotent to heal. Thirty years ago the reverend gentleman wrote a book containing the fundamental teaching on divine healing. Why was it withdrawn from circulation? Why is it not possible to obtain this book at any of the Christian literature depots in Africa?

Why? Because the preachers foresaw that the members of their churches would call upon them for the exercise of that faith which saves the sick! They feared the ordeal which would test their faith in God and the value of their own prayers! Instead of confessing their spiritual poverty and inefficiency and reaching out to touch the springs of life and power in God, they fell back into a state of even greater spiritual apathy and inertness, being satisfied with the cold externals of religious forms and observances, which without the indwelling life-giving power and presence of the Holy Ghost have no saving grace or spiritual virtue.

DIVINE HEALING IS THE SEAL
OF GOD'S ACKNOWLEDGMENT

Divine healing is the seal of God's acknowledgment and the proof to the world that Jesus Christ is the Son of God. John the Baptist was in prison. He was troubled with doubt as to whether Jesus was the Christ. He sent two of His disciples to Jesus to put the question, "Art thou He that should come or look we for another?" His answer was to appeal to the signs of His ministry. These were, and are still, God's answer to doubt or unbelief:

> Go and shew John again these things which ye do hear and see: The blind receive their sight, and the lame walk, and the lepers are cleansed, and the deaf hear, the dead are raised up, and the poor have the gospel preached to them. And blessed is he, whosoever shall not be offended in me.

— Matthew 11:4-6

These are still God's seal and endorsement of the preaching of the true Gospel. The preaching that lacks the signs which Jesus promised lacks the divine attestation, by which God confirms the preaching of His own true Gospel. "Take heed, brethren, lest there be in any of you an evil heart of unbelief, in departing from the living God" (Hebrews 3:12).

And at the end of the age as at the beginning, the command of Jesus Christ to all workers everywhere is:

> Go ye into all the world, and preach the gospel to every creature. He that believeth and is baptized shall be saved; but he that believeth not shall be damned. And these signs shall follow them that believe; In my name shall they cast out devils; they shall speak with new tongues; they shall take up serpents; and if they drink any deadly thing, it shall not hurt them; they shall lay hands on the sick, and they shall recover.

— Mark 16:15-18

The results now, as then, will be, "And they went forth, and preached every where, the Lord working with them, and confirming the word with signs following" (Mark 16:20).

"My Grace Is Sufficient for Thee"

"The other evening I was riding home after a heavy day's work; I felt very wearied, and sore depressed, when swiftly, and suddenly as a lightning flash, that text came to me: 'My grace is sufficient for thee.'[10] I reached home and looked it up in the original, and at last it came to me in this way, 'My grace is sufficient for thee,' and I said, 'I should think it is, Lord,' and burst out laughing. I never fully understood what the holy laughter of Abraham was until then. It seemed to make unbelief so absurd. It was as though some little fish, being very thirsty, was troubled about drinking the river dry, and Father Thames said, 'drink away, little fish, my stream is sufficient for thee.'

"Or, it seemed like a little mouse in the granaries of Egypt, after the seven years of plenty, fearing it might die of famine. Joseph might say: 'Cheer up, little mouse, my granaries are sufficient for thee.' Again, I imagined a man away up yonder, in a lofty mountain, saying to himself, 'I breathe so many cubic feet of air every year, I fear I shall exhaust the oxygen in the atmosphere.' But the earth might say, 'Breathe away, O man, and fill the lungs ever, my atmosphere is sufficient for thee.' Oh, brethren, be great believers! Little faith will bring heaven to your souls." — Spurgeon

> They shall be abundantly satisfied with the fatness of thy house; and thou shalt make them drink of the river of thy pleasures.
>
> — Psalm 36:8
>
> I am come that they might have life, and that they might have it more abundantly.
>
> — John 10:10
>
> But my God shall supply all your need, according to his riches in glory by Christ Jesus.
>
> — Philippians 4:19

Jehovah filleth to the brim the vessels faith presents to Him.

THE PRESENT CIRCUMSTANCE

which presses so hard against you (if surrendered to Christ), is the shaped tool in the Father's hand to chisel you for eternity. Trust Him then. Do not push away the instrument lest you lose its work.

---

[10] 2 Corinthians 12:9.

A NICKEL FOR THE LORD

"Yesterday he wore a rose on the lapel of his coat, but when the plate was passed today he gave a nickel to the Lord. He had several bills in his pocket and sundry change, perhaps a dollar's worth, but he hunted about, and finding this poor little nickel, he laid it on the plate to aid the Church militant in its fight against the world, the flesh, and the devil. His silk hat was beneath the seat, and his gloves and cane were beside it, and the nickel was on the plate; a whole nickel.

"On Saturday afternoon he met a friend, and together they had some refreshments. The cash register stamped thirty-five cents on the slip the boy presented to him. Peeling off a bill he handed it to the lad and gave him a nickel tip when he brought back the change. A nickel for the Lord and a nickel for the waiter!

"And the man had his shoes polished on Saturday afternoon and handed out a dime without a murmur. He had a shave and paid fifteen cents with equal alacrity. He took a box of candies home to his wife and paid forty cents for them, and the box was tied with a dainty bit of ribbon. Yes, and he also gave a nickel to the Lord.

"Who is this Lord?

"Who is He? Why, the man worships Him as Creator of the universe, the One who puts the stars in order, and by whose immutable decree the heavens stand. Yes, he does, and he dropped a nickel in to support the Church militant.

"And what is the Church militant?

"The Church militant is the Church that represents upon the earth the triumphant Church of the great God.

"And the man knew that he was an atom in space, and he knew that the Almighty was without limitations, and knowing this he put his hand in his pocket, and picked out the nickel, and gave it to the Lord.

"And the Lord being gracious, and slow to anger, and knowing our frame, did not slay the man for the meanness of his offering but gives him this day his daily bread.

"The nickel hid beneath a quarter that was given by a poor woman that washes for a living." — Selected

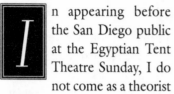

In appearing before the San Diego public at the Egyptian Tent Theatre Sunday, I do not come as a theorist but bring the richness and ripeness of thirty years of strenuous Christian life, such as few in our day have had opportunity to experience. In appealing to God alone and trusting Him only under almost every known circumstance, I have had abundant experience. I relate a few of these for the benefit of your readers.

LETTER TO THE EDITOR

Editor, *The Sun*

In 1911, a scientific party was going into the depths of unexplored Africa. I begged to be permitted to accompany the party for the sake of companionship with white men. When in the depth of tropical African forest the party was stricken with Black Water fever.[1] Four of the seven died in five days, including the doctor and the surgeon. I was the only member of the party not sick. When it became known the surgeon was dead, the three dying men went into the blackness of despair; all were hopeless. I then told them of my faith in Christ as the Healer as well as Savior of men, and begged them to let me minister to them and to trust Him for themselves as best they were able. I spent two days and three nights in fasting and prayer with them. They were healed and we finished the trip without remedy or preventative medicine of any kind.

In 1908, a terrible epidemic of African fever struck the Zuitpansberg district. In one month one-fourth of the entire population, both black and white, died. I was then in Zuitpansberg. In riding from home to home among the isolated Dutch Boers (farmers) I found on the fourth day of the epidemic, women dead in bed by their husbands and vice versa, children two and three in a bed, sometimes two dead; the whole family stricken, no one able to assist another.

I then rode seventy-five miles over the mountains to the nearest telegraph station and reported the situation to Louis Botha, then Premier

---

[1] "Black Water fever" is another name for malaria.

of the Transvaal. He wired me to remain on the job and represent the Government until relieved and that forty ox wagons would leave Pretoria at four a.m. with supplies. An ox wagon has from sixteen to forty-eight oxen attached. When the situation at my missionary headquarters became known, four Europeans volunteered to come and assist me. I buried all four in three weeks and was left alone to do what I could. The Government had reached us with medical assistance and a proper organization set up. In this epidemic I saw thousands healed through prayer only, both white and black. In this service the Transvaal Parliament gave me a vote of thanks.

I not only believe in healing of disease but believe that through faith in God we can be rendered virtually immune from disease and contagion.

In 1912, an epidemic of smallpox ran riot among the isolated Matabele natives; tens of thousands died. We were six hundred miles from civilization. Natives in this district wear no clothes. Imagine trying to lift a big, fat, helpless native from a mat on the hut floor when his naked body is covered with eruptions that would burst under your hands and by the pressure on your body as you carried him about. Do it all day and imagine the state of your clothes by night, when your overalls and jumper would be soaked through with smallpox pus. Then, having no change of clothes you went to the nearest creek and washed them out as best you could and walked about in your birth clothes till they dried, then next day you did it over.

I have lived with and prayed for thousands of African lepers and in all my African experience never contracted disease or carried contagion to my family. It is because of such experiences as the above that I say I do not come to the people of San Diego with untried theories, but out of the strenuous past draw the lessons of faith in God, that makes life to him who has hidden in Christ glorious and gives to the soul of man the divine mastery.

Dr. John Graham Lake

AN ADDRESS TO THE PEOPLE OF THE INLAND EMPIRE

By John G. Lake, Overseer

*I*n the religious life, when one arises with a larger vision of God's purpose for mankind then that usually presented by religious teachers, his declarations are received with question. Men who think desire to be convinced by word, by the Holy Scriptures, and by demonstration, that the teacher's assertions are correct.

It was demanded of the prophets that the signs of a prophet should be seen.

Jesus never intended Christianity to be received and believed on any man's statement, *but provided* that the statement should be accompanied by an exhibition of spiritual power that would convince *the world;* saying to His followers:

> These signs shall follow them that believe; In my name shall they (the believers) cast out devils; they shall speak with new tongues... they shall lay hands on the sick, and they shall recover.[1]

This was Jesus' own test of the truth, also a test of true discipleship.

The people demanded of Jesus: "What sign dost thou show?"[2] They challenged His authority to *forgive sins,* until convinced by His reasoning and the healing of the palsied man, of His authority and power. Jesus was a reasonable man; He was not only willing to discuss the issue with them, but to heal a man in their presence, as He did, saying:

> But that *ye may know* (be convinced) that the Son of man hath power on earth *to forgive sins...* I say to you

---

[1] Mark 16:17-18.

[2] John 2:18, paraphrased.

(addressing the palsied man), Arise, take up your bed, and go to your house; and immediately he rose, took up his bed and went to his house.

— Mark 2:10-12, emphasis Lake's, paraphrased

[This was] a mark or brand by which the world might know an impostor and also recognize the true faith of Christ. Christianity was to be its own witness through its power to deliver from sin and heal from disease all who needed deliverance. (See Mark 16:17-18 and John 5:13-15.)

Paul warns Timothy to *beware* of those who have a form of godliness but no power of God in their lives, saying:

Having a form of godliness, but *denying the power thereof:* from such *turn away.*

— 2 Timothy 3:5, emphasis Lake's

Paul further declares his own preaching was not based on men's wisdom, but was demonstrated by the power of God through *him.* He says

And my speech and my preaching was not with enticing words of man's wisdom, but in demonstration of the Spirit and of power: That your faith should not stand in the wisdom of men, but in the power of God.

— 1 Corinthians 2:4-5

When Peter and John healed the lame man at the beautiful gate of the temple, the people demanded, "By what *power* in *what name* have ye done this?"[3] And Peter replied:

Be it known unto you all, and to all the people of Israel, that by the name of Jesus Christ of Nazareth, whom ye crucified, whom God raised from the dead, even by him doth this man stand here before you whole.

—Acts 4:10

---

[3] Acts 4:7, paraphrased.

Jesus gave a test of the character and quality of the Messenger and the power He exercised. He said, "Ye shall know them by their fruits. Do men gather grapes of thorns, or figs of thistles?"[4]

We contend, by the Word of God, that the world and the Church has been robbed of the presence, power, and blessing of Jesus Christ — a present Healer — because the Church has falsely taught that the days of miracles are past. The days of miracles never passed, only in the soul that lost its faith in God. Where faith is, there ever will be the evidence of God's mighty power to save and heal.

---

[4] Matthew 7:16.

THE MINISTRY OF HEALING AND MIRACLES
Divine Healing Is Scientific

Atonement through the grace of God is scientific in its application. Jesus used many methods of healing the sick. All were scientific. Science is the discovery of how God does things.

Jesus laid His hands upon the sick in obedience to the law of contact and transmission. Contact of His hands with the sick one permitted the Spirit of God in Him to flow into the sick person.

The sick woman who touched His clothes found that the Spirit emanated from His person. She touched the "hem of His garment" and the Spirit flashed into her.[1] She was made whole. This is a scientific process.

Paul, knowing this law, laid his hands upon handkerchiefs and aprons. The Bible says that when they were laid upon the sick they were healed, and the demons went out of those possessed. Materialists have said this was superstition. It is entirely scientific. The Spirit of God emanating from Paul transformed the handkerchiefs into "storage batteries" of Holy Spirit power. When they were laid upon the sick they surcharged the body and healing was the result. (Read Acts 19:12.)

Firstly, this demonstrates that the Spirit of God is a tangible substance, a heavenly materiality. Secondly, it is capable of being stored in the substance of cloth, as demonstrated in the garments of Jesus or the handkerchiefs of Paul. Thirdly, it will transmit power from the handkerchiefs to the sick person. Fourthly, its action in the sick man was so powerful the disease departed. The demonized were also delivered. And fifthly, both the sick and the insane were delivered and healed by this method.

---

[1] See Matthew 9:20-22.

Men received Jesus Christ into their hearts as one receives a lover. It is an affectionate relationship. Men obey Him, because they have received Him affectionately. He has become their soul's lover.

His love and power in them redeems them from sin and sickness and eventually, we are promised in His Word, He will redeem us from death also.[2] Redemption from sin, sickness, and death constitutes man's deliverance from bondage to Satan and his kingdom and establishes the kingdom of heaven.

THE POWER OF THE NAME

Jesus called His twelve disciples and commanded upon them power and authority to cast out devils and heal disease. (See Luke 9.) He superseded this by declaring: "If ye shall ask *any thing* in my name, I will do it" (John 14:14).

The first was a limited "power of attorney." The second was unlimited. This unlimited "power of attorney" was authorized before His crucifixion. It was to become effective when the Holy Ghost came. (See Luke 24:49 and Acts 1:8.)

On the Day of Pentecost, this "power of attorney" was made fully operative. The Spirit came.[3] First, legally; they had His Word. Then, vitally; He sent His Spirit.

Peter and John instantly grasped the significance of His Name. Passing into the temple they met a beggar-cripple. He was 40 years old and had been crippled from birth. Peter commanded: "In the name of Jesus Christ of Nazareth rise up and walk."[4] Heaven's lightning struck the man. He leaped to his feet, whole.

A multitude rushed up. They demanded, "In what name, by what name, by what power have ye done this?" Peter and John replied, "In the name of Jesus Christ of Nazareth, whom ye slew, whom God raised up."[5]

---

[2] See John 8:51-52; Romans 6:4-5 and 8:2; 1 Corinthians 15:26,54; 2 Timothy 1:10; and Revelation 21:4.

[3] See Acts 2:2-4.

[4] Acts 3:6.

[5] Acts 4:7,10, paraphrased.

Matchless name! The secret of power was in it. When they used the name, power struck. The dynamite of heaven exploded.

Peter and John were hustled to jail. The church prayed for them in "the Name." They were released. They went to church. The entire church prayed that signs and wonders might be done. How did they pray? In "the Name." They used it legally. The vital response was instantaneous. The place was shaken as by an earthquake. Tremendous Name![6]

Jesus commanded, "Go ye into all the world."[7] What for? To proclaim that Name. To use that Name. To baptize believers.

How? In the Name (His authority; what He commanded). Amazing Name! In it was concentrated the combined authority resident in the Father, the Son, and the Holy Ghost. Almighty Name!

The apostles used the Name. It worked. The deacons at Samaria used the Name.[8] The fire flashed. Believers everywhere, forever, were commanded to use it. The Name detonated around the world.

More Bibles are sold today than any other 100 books. Why? The Name is in it. Its finality — "At the name of Jesus every knee shall bow and every tongue confess!"[9]

Prayer in this Name gets answers. The Moravians prayed. The greatest revival till that time hit the world.

The grace and love of God in the soul opens the nature to God. When they asked of the blind man, "What do you think of Him?" He replied, "He is a prophet."[10]

Later, Jesus found him and said to him, "Dost thou believe on the Son of God?" The man asked, "Who is He, Lord, that I might believe on Him?" Jesus answered. "I that speak unto thee am He."[11]

---

[6] See Acts 4:3-31.

[7] Mark 16:15.

[8] See Acts 9:31.

[9] Philippians 2:10 and Romans 14:11, paraphrased.

[10] See John 9:17.

[11] John 9:35-37, paraphrased.

The struggle of the centuries has been to free the soul from narrow interpretations. Jesus has sometimes been made to appear as a little bigot; sometimes as an impostor. The world is still waiting to see Him as He is. Jesus the magnificent, Jesus the giant, Jesus the compassionate, Jesus the dynamic — the wonder of the centuries.

Take the shackles off God.

Let Him have a chance to bless mankind without limitations.

As a missionary I have seen the healing of thousands of heathen. Thus was Christ's love and compassion for a lost world revealed. And thus the writer was assisted into the larger vision of a world Redeemer whose hand and heart are extended to God's big world and every man, saint and sinner, is invited to behold and love Him.

In one of the letters received from readers, this question is asked, "Why are not all persons healed instantly — as Jesus healed?"

The writer of this letter is mistaken in thinking that Jesus always healed instantly. A case in point is the healing of the ten lepers; "as they went they were cleansed."[12] The healing virtue was administered. The healing process became evident later.

Again, Jesus laid His hands on a blind man, then inquired, "What do you see?" The man replied, "I see men as trees walking." His sight was still imperfect. Then Jesus laid His hands on him the second time — "and he saw clearly."[13]

Healing is by degree, based on two conditions. First, the degree of healing virtue administered. Second, the degree of faith that gives action and power to the virtue administered.

> The word preached did not profit them, not being mixed
> with faith in them that heard it.
>
> — Hebrews 4:2

The miracles of Jesus have been the battleground of the centuries. Men have devoted their lives in an endeavor to break down faith in miracles. More believe in miracles today than ever before.

---

[12] See Luke 17:12-14.

[13] See Mark 8:23-25.

Pseudo-science declares miracles impossible. Yet the biggest men in the scientific world are believers in the supernatural and know that miracles are the discovery, the utilization of which the material scientist knows nothing.

The miracle realm is man's natural realm. He is by creation, the companion of the miracle-working God. Sin dethroned man from the miracle-working realm, but through grace he is coming into his own.

It has been hard for us to grasp the principles of this life of faith. In the beginning, man's spirit was the dominant force in the world. When he sinned his mind became dominant; sin dethroned the spirit and crowned the intellect. But grace is restoring the spirit to its place of dominion. When man comes to realize this, he will live in the realm of the supernatural without effort. No longer will faith be a struggle, but a normal living in the realm of God. The spiritual realm places man where communion with God is a normal experience. Miracles are then his native breath.

No one knows to what extent the mind and the spirit can be developed. We have been slow to come to a realization that man is a spirit and his spirit nature is his basic nature. We have sought to educate him along educational lines, utterly ignoring the spiritual, so man has become a self-centered, self-seeking being.

Man has lost his sense of relationship and responsibility toward God and man. This makes him lawless. We cannot ignore the spiritual side of man without magnifying the intellectual and the physical. To do this without the restraint of the spirit is to unleash sin and give it dominance over the whole man. There must be a culture and development of the spiritual nature to a point where it can enjoy fellowship with the Father God. It is above mind, as God is above nature.

Man's intellect is ever conscious of supernatural forces that he cannot understand. He senses the spirit realm and longs for its freedom and creative power, but cannot enter until changed from self and sin; the spirit enthroned and in action rather than the intellect — spirit above *both mind and matter.*

The life of God, the Spirit of God, the nature of God, are sufficient for every need of man. In the highest sense of the word, he is *real* Christian whose *body, soul* and *spirit* alike are filled with the life of God.

Healing in any department of the nature, whether spirit, soul, or body is but a means to an end. The object of healing is health, abiding health of body, soul, and spirit. The healing of the spirit unites the spirit of man to God forever. The healing of the soul corrects psychic disorder and brings the soul processes into harmony with the mind of God. And the healing of the body completes the union of man with God when the Holy Spirit possesses all.

John G. Lake

Is it true that today God is abandoning the "virtue that went out of Him and healed them all"[14] for medical science? Would it not be abandoning the perfect for the imperfect?

---

[14] Luke 6:19, paraphrased.

hen he was come down from the mountain, great multitudes followed him. And, behold, there came a leper and worshipped him, saying, Lord, if thou wilt, thou canst make me clean.

— Matthew 8:1-2

"BEHOLD, I GIVE YOU POWER"

That man knew that Jesus had the power to heal him, but he did not know it was God's will and that Jesus had committed Himself to the healing of mankind. If he had known he would have said, "Lord, heal me."

It is always God's will to heal. Our faith may fail. My faith failed to the extent that unless someone else had gone under my life and prayed for me, I would have died. But God was just as willing to heal me as He could be. It was my faith that broke down. God is willing, just as willing to heal as He is to save. *Healing is a part of salvation.* It is not separate from salvation. Healing was purchased by the blood of Jesus. This Book always connects salvation and healing. David said:

> Bless the LORD, O my soul, and forget not all his benefits: who *forgiveth* all thine iniquities; who healeth all thy diseases.
>
> — Psalm 103:2-3

There never has been a man in the world who was converted and was sick at the same time, that might not have been healed if he had believed God for it. But he was not instructed in faith to believe God for healing.

Supposing two men came to the altar. One is sick and lame; the other is a sinner. Suppose they knelt at the altar together. The sinner says, "I want to find the Lord." Everyone in the house will immediately lend the love of their heart and the faith of their soul to help him touch God. But the lame fellow says, "I have a lame leg." or "My spine is injured. I want healing." Instead of everybody lending their love and faith in the same way to the man, everybody puts up a question mark.

That comes because of the fact we are instructed on the Word of God concerning the salvation of the soul, but our education concerning sickness and His desire and willingness to heal had been neglected. We have gone to the eighth or the tenth grade or the University on the subject of salvation, but on the subject of healing we are in the ABC class.

Verse 3:

Jesus put forth his hand, and touched him, saying, I will; be thou clean.

Did he ever say anything in the world but "I will" or did He ever say, "I cannot heal you because it is not the will of God" or "I cannot heal you because you are being purified by this sickness" or "I cannot heal you because you are glorifying God in this sickness?" There is no such instance in the Book.

On the other hand we are told "He healed *all* that came to Him."[1] Never a soul ever applied to God for salvation or healing that Jesus did not save and heal! Did you ever think of what calamity it might have been, if a man had come to Jesus once and said, "Lord, save me," and the Lord had said, "No, I cannot save you"? Every man forevermore would have a question mark as to whether God would save *him* or not. There would not be universal confidence, as there is today.

Suppose Jesus had ever said to a sick man, "No, I cannot heal you." You would have the same doubt about healing. The world would have settled back and said, "Well, it may be God's will to heal that man or that woman, but I do not know whether it is His will to heal *me.*"

Jesus Christ did not leave us in doubt about God's will, but when the Church lost her faith in God, she began to teach the people that maybe it was not God's will to heal them. So the Church introduced the phrase, "if it be Thy will" concerning healing. But Jesus "healed all that came to Him." (See Matthew 4:23, Luke 9:6, and Luke 9:11.)

---

[1] See Matthew 4:24, 8:16, 12:15, and Luke 4:40 and 6:19.

Notice what it says in Isaiah 35,

> He will come and *save* you. Then the eyes of the blind shall be opened, and the ears of the deaf shall be unstopped. Then shall the *lame man leap as an hart*, and the *tongue of the dumb sing*.[2]

Salvation and healing connected!

> That it might be fulfilled which was spoken by Esaias the prophet, saying, Himself took our infirmities, and *bare our sicknesses*.
>
> — Matthew 8:17, emphasis Lake's.

And lest we might be unmindful of that great fact that He had "bare our sicknesses and carried our sorrows," Peter emphasizes it by saying,

> Who his own self bare our sins in his own body on the tree, that we, being dead to sins, should live unto righteousness: by whose stripes ye were healed.
>
> — 1 Peter 2:24

Not "by whose stripes ye *are* healed", but "By whose stripes ye *were* healed." The only thing that is necessary is to *believe God*. God's mind never needs to act for a man's *salvation*. He gave the Lord and Savior Jesus Christ to die for you. God cannot go any farther in expressing His will in His desire to save man. The only thing that is necessary is to believe God. There is salvation by blood. There is salvation by power that actually comes from God into a man's life. The blood provided the power. Without the blood there would have been no power. Without the sacrifice there would have never been any glory. Salvation by blood, salvation by power.

The Church in general is very clear in her faith on the subject of salvation through the sacrifice of the Lord and Savior Jesus Christ. The Christian world in general, regardless of their personal state of salvation, have a general faith and belief in the Lord and Savior Jesus

---

[2] Isaiah 35:4-6, emphasis Lake's.

Christ for the salvation of the world. But they are ever in doubt and very inexperienced on the power of God.

> When he was come down from the mountain, great multitudes followed him. And, behold, there came a leper and worshipped him, saying, Lord, if thou wilt, thou canst make me clean. And Jesus put forth his hand, and touched him, saying, I will; be thou clean. And immediately his leprosy was cleansed. And Jesus saith unto him, See thou tell no man; but go thy way, shew thyself to the priest, and offer the gift that Moses commanded, for a testimony unto them.
>
> — Matthew 8:1-4

Did you ever stop to think that the real things that kill folks they have no medical remedy for? Typhoid fever: Fill the patient with a tank full of medicine and he will go right on for twenty-one days.

In 1913 I was in Chicago in a big meeting, when I received a telegram from the hospital in Detroit, saying, "Your son, Otto, is sick with typhoid fever. If you want to see him, come." I rushed for a train, and when I arrived I found him in a ward. I told the man in charge I would like a private ward for him, so I could get a chance to pray for him. Well, God smote that thing in five minutes. I stayed with him for a couple of days until he was up and walking around. He went along for four or five weeks, and one day to my surprise, I got another telegram telling me he had a relapse of typhoid.

So I went back again. This time there was no sunburst of God like the first time. Every thing was as cold as steel, and my, I was so conscious of the power of the devil. I could not pray audibly, but I sat down by his bed and shut my teeth, and I said in my soul, "Now, Mr. Devil, go to it. You kill him if you can." And I sat there five days and nights. He did not get healing instantly the second time. It was healing by process — because of the fact my soul took hold on God; I sat with my teeth shut, and I never left his bedside until it was done.

You may be healed like a sunburst of God today, and tomorrow, the next week, or the next month when you want healing, you may have to take it on the slow process. The action of God is not always the same, because the conditions are not always the same.

In the life of Jesus, people were instantly healed. I believe Jesus has such a supreme measure of the Spirit that when He put His hands on a man he was filled and submerged in the Holy Ghost, and the diseases withered out and vanished.

But, beloved, you and I use the measure of the Spirit that we possess. (You can as a member of His body possess the Spirit in the same measure as He. God does not expect us to fulfill John 14:12 with less equipment then Jesus had.) And if we haven't got as much of God as Jesus had, then you pray for a man today and you get a certain measure of healing, but he is not entirely well. The only thing to do is to pray for him tomorrow, and let him get some more, and keep on until he is well.

That is where people blunder. They will pray for a day or two and then they quit. You pray and keep on day by day and minister to your sick until they are well. One of the things that has discredited healing is that evangelists will hold meetings, and hundreds of sick will come and be prayed for. In a great meeting like that you get a chance to pray once and do not see them again. You pray for ten people, and as a rule, you will find that one or two or three are absolutely healed, but the other are only half healed or quarter healed or have only a little touch of healing.

It is just the same with salvation. You bring ten to the altar. One is saved and is clear in his soul. Another may come for a week and another for a month, before he is clear in his soul. The difference is not with God. The difference is inside the man. His consciousness has not opened up to God.

Every law of the Spirit that applies to salvation applies to healing likewise.

> And when Jesus was entered into Capernaum, there came unto him a centurion, beseeching him, and saying, Lord, my servant lieth at home sick of the palsy, grievously tormented. And Jesus saith unto him, I will come and heal him. The centurion answered and said, Lord, I am not worthy that thou shouldest come under my roof: but speak the word only, and my servant shall be healed.

— Matthew 8:5-8

Here is healing at a distance. That centurion understood divine authority, and the same divine authority is vested in the Christian, for Jesus is the pattern Christian.

> For I am a man under authority, having soldiers under me: and I say to this man, Go, and he goeth; and to another, Come, and he cometh; and to my servant, Do this, and he doeth it.

— Verse 9

The same divine authority that was vested in Jesus is vested *by Jesus* in every Christian soul. Jesus made provision for the Church of Jesus Christ to go on forever and do the same things as He did and to keep on doing them forever. That is what is the matter with the Church. The Church has lost faith in that truth. The result, they went on believing He could save them from sin, but the other great range of Christian life was left to the doctors and the devil or anything else. And the Church will never be a real Church, in the real power of the living God again, until she comes back again to the original standard, where Jesus was.

Jesus said, "Behold, I give you authority." What authority? "Against unclean spirits, to cast them out, and to heal all manner of sickness and all manner of disease" (Matthew 10:1). Jesus has vested that authority in you. You say, "Well Lord, we understand the authority that is in your Word, but we haven't the *power.*" But Jesus said, "Ye shall receive *power,* after that the Holy Ghost is come upon you" (Acts 1:8).

Now the Holy Ghost is come upon every Christian in a measure. It is a question of degree! There are degrees of the measure of the Spirit of God in men's lives. The *baptism of the Holy Spirit* is a greater measure of the Spirit of God, but every man has a degree of the Holy Spirit in his life. *You* have. It is the Spirit in your life that gives you faith in God, that makes you a blessing to other people. It is the Holy Spirit that is *outbreathed* in your soul that touches another soul and moves them for God. Begin right where you are and let God take you along the Christian life as far as you like.

> When Jesus heard it, he marveled, and said to them that followed, Verily I say unto you, I have not found so great faith, no, not in Israel.

— Matthew 8:10

Jesus always commended faith when He met it. Jesus did not always meet faith. All the people who came to Jesus did not possess that order of faith. They had faith that *if they got to Jesus* they would be healed. But here is a man who says, "Speak the word only, and my servant shall be healed" (Verse 8).

Then you remember the case of the man at the Pool of Bethesda. He did not even ask to be healed. As he lay there, Jesus walked up to him and said, "Wilt thou be made whole?" He saw this poor chap who had been lying there for thirty-eight years, and Jesus did not wait for him to ask Him to heal. Jesus said, "Wilt thou be made whole?" and the poor fellow went on to say that when the water was troubled he had no one to put him in, but while he was waiting another stepped in ahead of him. But Jesus saith unto him, "Arise, take up thy bed and walk."[3] He was made whole. Afterward, Jesus met him and said, "Behold, thou art made whole: sin no more, lest a worse thing come unto thee" (John 5:14).

Most of sickness is the result of sin. That is the answer to the individual who sins. For thousands of years men have been sinning, and in consequence of their sin, they are diseased in their body. This will give you an idea. Scientists tell us there are tubercular germs in 90 percent of the population. The only difference is that when people keep in a healthy state, the germs do not get a chance to manifest themselves. I am trying to show the intimacy between sin and sickness. Not necessarily the sin of the individual. It may never be the sin of the individual.

In records of the Lake and Graham family away back, tuberculosis was never known to them, until it appeared in my sister. My sister accompanied me to Africa, and she became so ill that when I got to Cape Town we had to wait until her strength returned. God healed her.

---

[3] See John 5:2-9.

Regarding people being healed at a distance, we receive telegrams from all over the world. Distance is no barrier to God. The United States has just finished the building of the greatest wireless station in the world. They send messages that register almost instantly, ten thousand miles. When the machine is touched here, it registers ten thousand miles away. Well, all right, when your *heart* strikes God in faith, it will register there wherever that individual is, just that quick. All the discoveries of later years such as telegraph, telephone, wireless, and that sort of thing are just the common laws that Christians have practiced all their lives.

Nobody ever knelt down and prayed, but that the instant they touched God their soul registered in Jesus Christ in glory and the answer came back to the soul. Christians have that experience every day. The wise world has begun to observe that these laws are applicable in the natural realm. I asked Marconi once how he got his first idea for the wireless. He replied that he got it from watching an exhibition of telepathy in a cheap theater.

The prayer of the heart reaches God. Jesus replied to the leper, *"I will; be thou clean."* The next was the centurion's servant. The centurion said, "You do not need to come to my house. You *speak the word only*, and my servant shall be healed." And in the soul of Jesus He said, "Be healed." Distance is no barrier to God. Distance makes no difference. The Spirit of God in you will go as far as your love reaches. *Love* is the medium that conveys the Spirit of God to another soul — anywhere on God's earth.

This is what takes place as you pray. The Spirit of God comes upon you and bathes your soul and a shaft of it reaches out and touches that soul over there. If you had an instrument that was fine enough to photograph spirit, you would discover this is done.

Is it not a marvelous thing that God has chosen us to be co-laborers with Him, and He takes us into partnership to do all that He is doing? Jesus Christ at the throne of God desires the blessing of you and me, and out of His holy heart the Spirit comes, and the soul is filled, and we cannot tell how or why.

I have known thousands of people to be healed who have never seen my face. They send a request for prayer, we pray, and never hear anything more about them sometimes unless a friend or a neighbor or someone comes and tells us about them. Sometimes someone sends in a request for them. They will tell you they do not know what happened. They just got well. But you know why. That is the wonderful power there is in the Christian life, and that is the wonderful cooperation that the Lord Jesus has arranged between His own soul and the soul of the Christian. That is "the church which is his body."[4]

Jesus came to destroy the works of the devil (1 John 3:8.) He healed all that were oppressed of the devil. (Acts 10:38.) He did not use carnal weapons in destroying the work of the devil. He used a spiritual weapon. It is best expressed in Luke 6:19:

> And the whole multitude sought to touch him: for there went virtue (power) out of him, and healed them all.

This is the perfect remedy for all of man's ills. Jesus taught His disciples the use of this weapon. He sent out the twelve. (Luke 9:1-2.) He sent out the seventy. (Luke 10:1-19.) That His training was not fruitless is shown by the book of the Acts of the Apostles. Acting in the name of Jesus, the outflow of power from their lives brought healing to all who came to them. They duplicated His ministry. There is not one record of a failure in the book of Acts. The weapon of their warfare against the work of the devil in forms of sickness and disease was spiritual and not carnal.[5] The same power is available today.

> Behold, I give unto you power to tread on serpents and scorpions, and over all the power of the enemy: and nothing shall by any means hurt you.
>
> — Luke 10:19

God gives the members of the body of His Son power over the devil. He never gives the devil power over them.

One of the marvels of Christianity is the power given the believer. "Resist the devil, and he will flee from you" (James 4:7). The devil

---

[4] See Ephesians 1:22-23.

[5] See 2 Corinthians 10:4.

cannot make a believer do a single thing without the believer's consent or assent. Resist the devil and he flees. Give in and he wins. It is this fact, as simple as it may sound, that constitutes our responsibility for our behavior. So that no person can say, "I sinned in spite of myself," but he or she can only say, "I sinned because of myself."

Cleansed from all sin (root, stem, and branch) so that the devil has no anchor within and having put on the invincible armor of Ephesians 6, the believer is the master in every situation. If the believer stands firm and uses his armor efficiently he is unbeatable by the devil.

Couple all that is said above, with this statement from 1 John 4:4, "Greater is he that is in you, than he that is in the world," why should a believer ever give in to the devil and sin?

I can identify with Jesus as a member of His body when He said, "The prince of this world cometh, and hath nothing in me" (John 14:30). Why let the devil in or put anything in?

"And the God of peace shall bruise (shatter completely) Satan under your feet shortly" (Romans 16:20). In any warfare there comes a time when the enemy is shattered. Stand true and allow God to shatter him under your feet. Stand fast!

ARE THE DAYS OF MIRACLES PAST?

mong the shrewdest and most damaging lies that was ever told was Satan's lie that the days of miracles are past. And the shrewdness of it is in the fact that he got the church, her priests, ministers, and preachers to tell the lie. It has produced more infidels, created more unbelief concerning God than perhaps any other lie. But the days of miracles are never past and never will be past so long as Jesus Christ remains "the same yesterday, today, and forever." (See Hebrews 13:8, 1 Corinthians 12:8-12, Matthew 8:1-17, and Mark 16:17.) Read the following testimonies.

Healing of G.Y. Locke, M.D., Portland, Oregon, August 6, 1921. It gives me the greatest pleasure of my life to testify that I, Dr. Genevieve Y. Locke, Office 708 Dekum Bldg., Res. 535 Yamhill, Phone Auto 527-72, received instant healing from the mighty prayer of Dr. Lake.

About three weeks ago last Wednesday I suffered a broken rib, causing great agony, the shock affecting my heart. I was positive at the time that I had a broken a rib and went soon afterwards to the office of one of the leading chiropractic doctors of the city, had him examine me on the operating table, and to my great surprise he told me there was nothing wrong, there were no broken ribs. So trying to hold up under great suffering in the strength of his theory, I continued to work in my home under difficulties until one Saturday, I was unable to arise from bed at all. Simply exhausted from trying to hold up under the strain all of this time, as no doubt everyone knows the seriousness of a broken bone without proper attention.

I knew that condition was very serious, even critical, yet tried to hide the truth from my friends and loved ones. I was growing weaker and weaker, facing an operation from the medical point of view, believing it to be the only chance. I had the very best physician in Portland called to my bedside. I say the best, because he did not try to hide the seriousness of my case from me but to my surprise, he looked into my eyes and told me the truth with all the heartfelt sympathy that any man or woman can give another. I thanked and blessed him as he left my bedside.

He made a second call, only to say the same as before and to add that I was growing weaker each hour, that my entire body had become affected by the poisonous fluid that had accumulated around the broken rib, and that my heart was leaking until one could hardly feel the circulation.

Two specialists were called to my bedside, only to verify the statements of the first physician. By this time however, my loved ones and friends had begun to realize the seriousness of my condition and were suffering with me, the pain being too great to be suffered silently. My business affairs are always kept in shape so that in case of death there would be nothing to disturb those left behind. I gave myself up into the silence which no one feels until death is hovering near and said "Blessed Savior not my will, but thine be done."

All was well with me as I have always tried to live close to God. Just at that minute at three o'clock in the afternoon, a voice out of somewhere whispered the name Dr. John G. Lake. Instantly I had him called. As soon as he received the message he came immediately to my home. It was four o'clock when he arrived, and I was gasping for breath with the chill of death all over my body. He came to my bedside with his kind, gentle smile that I have since found so characteristic of him and the divine love of God that is within him and knelt at my bedside to pray.

The look of faith in his eyes that reflected to me his own soul gave me the confidence and assurance that even death could be overcome by being close to God in prayer. He spoke only a word or two to me. The bandage around my body which was to support the broken rib seemed to be a hundred pound weight that was crushing me. As he prayed with faith it seemed as though that bandage was slipping, for I began to breathe without the slightest effort and realized the wondrous and marvelous fact that I was receiving instant healing. I could not keep from crying out, "Oh blessed Savior, I am breathing in the breath of life." Dr. Lake knew what had taken place, he smiled and said "You are well and can get out of bed whenever you want to," but advised me to keep a little quiet for a few days.

He left as quietly as he had come. Just as though he had not just proven to myself and friends that he could heal today just as Jesus did. Who could possibly question his relationship to God after such a demonstration of the love of God and the lifting up a soul from the very throes of death?

After he had left the house I sat up in bed to show my friends that I was no longer sick, that God had healed me as sure as there is a God in heaven. I talked and sang, and next morning could scarcely wait to get to the phone to tell Dr. Lake the good news of my perfect healing. I feel so happy and free that I would just love to take the whole world in my arms and tell them the glad tidings that God does and will heal, and it is the only thing that can and will last, God's divine love.

BABY BARNES HEALED FROM DEATH

One of the touching healings is that of the little babe of Mrs. May Barnes of Washougal, Washington. She wrote a pitiful letter of entreaty to us for prayer for her baby, who was born a "blue baby." She said, "Oh Dr. Lake, do not let my baby die! Do not let my baby die! Oh Dr. Lake, you are a father yourself, do not let my baby die." And again "Oh Dr. Lake, pray. Pray. Do not let my baby die."

The child had suffered from weak heart and malnutrition from birth and had three dreadful ruptures, one in each groin and a great naval rupture. She was advised to bring the baby to Dr. Lake. The child was so withered away that it looked like a little wizened up alligator. The power of God came upon the child as prayer was offered, and it began to mend and eat and sleep as other babes. It took on flesh and grew plump and rosy, and when she returned to her home the babe was perfectly well with the exception of one rupture, so one day soon after she returned with the babe the rupture was inflamed and painful, but as hands were laid upon the child in prayer the rupture was instantly healed and though the child has since had a severe attack of whooping cough there has been no return of the rupture or other sickness.

Mr. George Alley was stricken with pneumonia and reported dying. Two of our ministers went to him. When prayer was offered, he was so blessed and healed that he soon fell asleep. Not knowing that the man had already received healing, Dr. Wallace and his wife went to the house and found that the family were asleep, so they did not trouble to awaken the people but knelt down in the dark on the front porch and prayed. When they had ceased to pray Dr. Wallace told his wife that he had heard from God and that the man was well, and he was.

On Friday night last, fifty-two testimonies of recent miracles of healing were given. These testimonies included healings through absent prayer in Norway, Great Britain, Africa, and Canada, besides many who were healed at the healing rooms.

Since our last circular was issued we have had two great public meetings, one at the Auditorium. The Oregonian reported an attendance of more than three thousand persons, three-hundred and sixty-three persons testified by rising, to being healed by the power of God, and special testimonies were presented which were: Dr. Wood, instantly healed of paralytic stroke as Dr. Lake laid hands on her in prayer. Mrs. Mary Matheny, healed of forty cancers. F. J. Kelly healed of multiple sclerosis. Grover Risdon, healed of malformed head and was dumb and paralyzed, believed to be the greatest miracle of healing in the world. Mrs. Ione Stanton, healed from death of glandular tuberculosis. Mr. Roy Ferguson, whose testimony appears in this pamphlet, was healed out of a plaster cast; and many others.

Another great public meeting was held at Oaks Park Rink. A New York medical specialist who was present, pronounced it the most remarkable religious meeting he had ever attended, if not the most wonderful ever held in the world. He pronounced Dr. Lake's address given on this occasion of surpassing power and convincing force and the miracles of healing genuine beyond all question. He visited Dr. Locke and personally examined her and pronounced her absolutely healed.

AFFIDAVIT

Head Bookkeeper for the Industrial Insurance Commission, Healed out of a Plaster of Paris Cast of Tuberculosis of the Spine

I, Roy Ferguson, herewith certify, praise God, I am well and perfectly healed and realize the solemnity of this oath. I was twenty-nine years of age the seventh of last January, resident of Salem, Oregon, 775 S.

13th St. While head bookkeeper for the Industrial Insurance Commission, I was stricken with a severe sickness, diagnosed as tuberculosis of the bone. The doctors amputated my left leg close to the thigh to try to check the spread of the disease throughout my entire body.

It was a useless effort. The disease next appeared in my spine, until four vertebra were affected and in a process of dissolution. I was then placed in a plaster of Paris cast, my suffering was terrible. I came to Dr. Lake's Divine Healing Institute, 129 4th St., Portland, Oregon, and in answer to prayer was instantly healed. My years of agony are over. I am now perfectly well, have put on flesh rapidly, and am praising God continually for His saving and healing power and am praying God's blessing upon Dr. Lake and his people continuously.

Signed — Roy Ferguson

The Healing Rooms are open at 10 a.m. to 10 p.m. for personal and private ministry through prayer and the laying on of hands. Divine Healing Teaching Meeting every day of the week at 3 p.m. At the close of this service, all who desire are ministered to for any need of body, soul, or spirit. If you are a doubter, come and see, and tell us what it is worth to you. If you are an unbeliever, bring your sick friends or come with your own difficulty, be blessed of God, and test what it is worth to you. If you are a professed Christian with little faith in God, come and be vitalized by the Spirit and tell us what it is worth to you. If you are the ordinary man or woman of the world and have paid no attention to religious things and have a question mark in your mind, come and see for yourself and decide how much it is worth to you and if real Christianity that gets results and demonstrates them is worth the price.

he blind receive their sight, and the lame walk, the lepers are cleansed, and the deaf hear, the dead are raised up, and the poor have the gospel preached to them.[1]

PNEUMATOLOGY

SOMEBODY HAS LIED

Who is it? The preachers of many of the regular churches, theologians, professors in almost every university and college, and the man who has not investigated have all said that the days of miracles are past. We contend that the days of miracles are here now, they always have been here, and always will be here to him who hath faith in God. We contend that God answers prayer today as readily as God ever did, and further, that the same faith that has received an answer once will bring an answer from God again. That the same power of the Spirit of God that moved upon the waters and that performed wonders both in nature and in man, both in the spiritual and the physical, is still available. It is here in Portland. It is at work every day. If you do not believe it, come to our Healing Rooms and observe for yourself.

THE BLIND RECEIVE THEIR SIGHT

Mr. Adam Streit of St. Johns, Portland, was blind for several years in both eyes. He was ministered to on three different occasions through prayer and laying on of hands by the ministry of The Church at Portland. He is now perfectly healed and gave public testimony to his healing in The Church at Portland, at 129 Fourth Street, a few days ago.

THE LAME WALK

A most conspicuous case. Mr. Roy Ferguson, head bookkeeper for the State Industrial Insurance Commission at Salem, the state capital, was

---

[1] Matthew 11:5.

stricken with tuberculosis of the bone. The disease affecting the spine, he was encased in a plaster of Paris cast and confined to his bed for more than a year. One leg was amputated just below the hip in the hope of checking the progress of the disease, but without avail.

He was abandoned to die by his physicians and brought to Portland specialists who said nothing could be done. He was brought to the Healing Rooms, was prayed for, and God instantly healed him. He is well. He was saved from his sins and baptized in the Holy Ghost and is now ministering this power of God to others and is one of the representatives of our work in Salem, Oregon.

THE DEAF HEAR

Mrs. Mary Evans of Corvallis, Oregon, was deaf for twenty years. She heard of the healing of Mr. Roy Ferguson through friends and came to Portland to visit the Healing Rooms and called Dr. Lake on the phone to come to the Multonomah Hotel parlors where, in the presence of a group of friends and others from the city who were present, she was ministered to and was instantly healed and conversed freely with her friends and Dr. Lake. She reported by long distance phone today that her healing was perfect and she will come to Portland in the near future to give public testimony and praise to God in The Church at Portland.

LEPERS ARE CLEANSED

Mrs. I____ S____ of Council Crest, Portland, a beautiful, cultured, high-class woman, became diseased so that a score of physicians and institutions assured her there was no possibility of recovery through medical assistance. The disease progressed until she was a skeleton, her throat became so badly affected from the disease that her power of speech was almost entirely ruined, and her mind became affected. She was brought to the Healing Rooms, ministered to, and as prayer was offered and hands laid upon her, the power of God came mightily upon her and the disease was destroyed.

There began from that moment a gradual reconstruction of her entire person. She is now in perfect health and soundness of mind, the bloom of wholesome, healthy womanhood in her face, the joy of God in her soul, the peace of God in her heart, and the victory of God in her life. She was baptized in the Holy Spirit and has begun, in turn, to minister the same blessed Spirit to other lives.

THE DEAD ARE RAISED UP

Mrs. W. E. Stoughton, Portland, Oregon, was sick of double pneumonia, hemorrhaging over a pint of blood at one time. We knelt by her bedside while she was in the very throes of death and even as we prayed her heart ceased to beat, her respiration stopped, and she lapsed into apparent death. We continued to pray — nine long minutes passed before evidence of returning life were manifest. We continued in faith and prayer but in less than twenty minutes another lapse came, this time eleven-and-a-half minutes of seeming death, and yet again thirteen minutes, and then came the final struggle when for nineteen minutes no evidence of life was apparent.

We believe that the spirit and body were kept united through the persistent and unwavering faith of those who prayed. At two-thirty in the morning, the glory of God burst from her soul and flooded her with the joy and the presence of God. She was perfectly healed and arose from her bed glorifying God — a well woman.

Her little daughter, Beaulah, was healed of cancer of the mouth after surgeons had said the child's life could only be saved through an operation to remove a portion of the roof of the mouth, which would have destroyed her speech. She was healed through faith in Jesus Christ, not only the cancer disappeared, but she was also healed of leakage of the heart through prayer at the Church at Portland.

I, Harley Day, 189 Mill Street, Portland, 18 years and nine months old, being first duly sworn and realizing fully the solemnity of this my oath, do testify: I was born dumb and was thereby unable to speak, also my nasal passages were malformed so that it was impossible for me to breath through my nose. I underwent six surgical operations on my throat, but was not benefited and gave up in despair.

Lately, friends advised me to go to Dr. John G. Lake, divine healer, which I did. Dr. Lake prayed for me at the close of the evening service, laying his hands on my throat. As he prayed, a stream of healing power poured from his hands and diffused itself through my entire person. Instantly something in my throat relaxed and a sense of freedom came upon me. In his prayer Dr. Lake prayed that the dumb demon be cast out. I felt at once that it was done, and in a few minutes I began to speak and each day am able to speak with greater clearness.

On another occasion, as prayer was offered and hands laid upon me in faith, my nasal passages opened and I have been able to breathe through my nose naturally ever since. I have become a sincere Christian and am now a member of Dr. Lake's church and praise my Lord for His saving grace and healing power.

Signed — Harley Day

The Poor Have the Gospel Preached to Them

Day by day we go among the poor and the lame and the halt and the blind, sin-stricken and disease smitten, ministering God's blessed love and power, fulfilling once more the declaration of Jesus, the mark and stamp of real Christianity, "The poor have the gospel preached to them."

These Signs Shall Follow Them That Believe

These signs shall follow them that believe; In my name shall they cast out devils; they shall speak with new tongues; they shall take up serpents; and if they drink any deadly thing, it shall not hurt them; they shall lay hands on the sick, and they shall recover.

— Mark 16:17-18

To the Citizens of Portland,

Dr. John G. Lake, overseer of The Church at Portland, undertakes to make Portland the healthiest city in the United States.

IS IT WORTH THE PRICE?

Our fellow citizen, O. G. Blake of Number 10, 9th St. Portland, Oregon, was abandoned to die by his physicians of diabetic gangrene. The entire foot and lower limb were in a state of mortification. The stench of the rotting foot would almost drive one from the room. With tears, his physicians bade him good-bye and left him to die. Materia Medica had no remedy.[1] The medical expert said: "I am stumped, there is nothing I can do for you further." Amputations were useless, as the diabetic state permeated his whole person.

He called Reverend John G. Lake of The Church at Portland, a businessman's church in the Gordon Building, 283 Stark Street, conducted by preachers who are businessmen. One of the ministering staff was sent to minister to this dying man. He is perfectly healed. What science could not do, God accomplished.

His big toe rotted off. He has it in a bottle of alcohol. You can see it. New flesh and bone grew on. He is walking around the city and has taken his place again as one of the heads of the Yeoman Society of the state of Oregon.

Fellow citizens, what is it worth to you? What is it worth to his home? What is it worth to his wife? What is it worth to Portland? What is it worth to Oregon? What is it worth to the United States? What is it worth to the world? What is it worth to the kingdom of heaven?

AFFIDAVITS

I, Mrs. D. C. Tappan of 874 Pardee St., Portland, Oregon, being first duly sworn, under oath, depose and say that I am 63 years of age, of a sound mind, and that I make the following statement fully realizing the sacredness of my oath: That two years ago a cancer formed on the

---

[1] Materia Medica: The material or substance used in the composition of remedies; a general term for all substances used as curative agents in medicine. *Webster's Revised Unabridged Dictionary,* 1913, online @ work.ucsd.edu.

end of my spine, and it grew and spread in the form of a horseshoe until it became three inches in diameter, causing me great pain constantly. Many physicians of Portland and Seattle treated me from time to time, but the cancer steadily grew worse and discharged more and more.

When all our funds were exhausted in this way and complete hopelessness and despair settled down over my family and I was facing a miserable death, a friend sent word to us that Dr. Lake was praying for the sick and was having wonderful cures through prayer. A new hope was born in our hearts, and we immediately sought him that his associates, Dr. Lake being absent from the city, would pray for us. His secretary, Reverend Harriet Graham, knelt with me and most earnestly prayed God to deliver me from this cancer. Immediately all the terrible pain left my body and has never returned.

During the intervening three months, the cancer continued to dry up and now there is nothing left but the scar to remind me of those awful days. No one can ever know how the sun shines on us after the hand of God has touched the body and scattered all our clouds.

My daughter was also a great sufferer from violent headaches. It was she who brought me to the healers, and without especially being prayed for, when the healing came to me, she was also touched by its power and she, too, was immediately healed.

Signed — Mrs. D. C. Tappan.

Subscribed and sworn to before me, a Notary Public for the State of Oregon, this 11th day of October, 1920. My commission expires Jan. 29, 1924 D. N. McInturff, Notary Public

Witnesses:

H. H. Marble.

Mrs. Margaret Higgins

What is it worth to you to know that God answers prayer today? How much is it worth to you to know that even after the best physicians in the land have despaired, that God will heal all who come to Him? How much is it worth to you to know that when the church tells you that the days of miracles are past, that they lie?

We, Mr. and Mrs. Marble of 1004 E. 32nd St., being first duly sworn under oath, depose and say that we both are of mature age and of sound mind and make the following statement fully realizing the sacredness of such an oath: Our daughter, Edith May Marble, seventeen years of age, contracted flu eight months ago, which caused pleurisy and developed into tuberculosis. She went down to death, and by September fifteenth she was in the very throes of death. We had six doctors, but she steadily grew worse. She was operated on and seemed some better for a few days, but again sank rapidly.

Mr. Wright, of Reverend Lake's Healing Rooms, was called and prayer offered. A week later, she vomited quantities of digitalis which had accumulated in her system during her sickness, which was given her in course of treatment. She began to recover and the wound healed. She is now up and walking around, praising God, eating well, taking on flesh rapidly. We desire the public to know of this miracle of God's power and give thanks for these godly people who brought the light of divine healing to us.

Signed — Mr. and Mrs. H. H. Marble

Subscribed and sworn to before me, a Notary Public for the State of Oregon, this 11th day of October, 1920. My Commission expires Jan. 29, 1924. D. N. McInturff, Notary Public.

What is it worth to you to know that God is healing tuberculosis? What is it worth to you to know that God will save your dear ones from the grave? What is it worth to you to know that all sickness, sin, and disease do not come from God, but that they belong to the evil one?

Mr. Frank Roles of the Pacific Agency, Inc. in the Swetland Bldg., one of the leading real estate brokers of the Pacific Coast, was stricken with a violent attack of neuritis until his cries of agony resounded through the house. He says: "My suffering was so intense that I could not keep from crying out."

Mr. E. S. Anderson of Royal Court, an ordained deacon of the Church of Portland, of which John G. Lake is overseer, with his wife, was called to his bedside. Moved by his terrible suffering, they fell upon their knees and laid their hands upon him. The power of God came upon him. He was instantly healed and in fifteen minutes was out of pain. He slept like a child and next day returned to his office.

Citizen, what is this fact worth to you? What is it worth to know that God is not far away? What is it worth to you to know that "Jesus Christ the same yesterday, and to day, and for ever."[2]

Harold Rooney, grandson of Mrs. Josephine Raymond of 2914 Fairmont St., Vancouver, Washington, seven years old, was an epileptic, subject to fits from infancy. He became dumb. His mind became affected. The physicians said, "There is not a thing can be done for him." He was brought to Reverend Lake's Healing Rooms, 283 Stark St. Prayer was offered. The epileptic demon was cast out. The fits ceased. His speech returned. His mind became normal, and he put on flesh rapidly and is now a rosy, healthy, happy boy, attending school.

Fellow citizen, what is this cure by the power of God worth to you? It has saved the expense of an inmate for life in a state institution. It has restored to society a life that will add wealth to the nation, citizenship to the state, a home and family to the city of Portland — a man with faith in God, and a Christian to the kingdom of heaven.

Dr. D. N. McInturff, a man with a successful law practice, a supreme court lawyer of note, seeing these things, gave up his practice of law and became pastor of the Church of Portland. He himself ministers to the sick and they are healed. Last week among the numerous healings under his ministry there were three cases of blindness. What is it worth to hear the shout of joy when blind eyes open by the power of God sufficient to heal blindness?

Reverend Harriett Graham, a professional nurse, hospital matron, herself a miracle of healing by the Lord, is also one of Dr. Lake's associates, and under her wonderful ministry people are healed every day.

Dr. Herman Wallace, noted divine businessman, author, and economist is on our staff. He is a thinker of thinkers and a man of exceptional spiritual power. Realizing the wonderful possibilities of Dr. Lake's undertaking for Portland and the world, he has become one of the ministering staff.

---

[2] Hebrews 13:8.

Reverend William C. Wright operated a stock ranch in the state of Wyoming. He was discharged from the United States Army at the close of the war and was pronounced incurable. More than a hundred X-ray pictures were taken of his person by the government experts in their effort to determine the nature of the disease. He was operated upon many times without success. His case is a matter of government record.

He says: "When suffering the agonies of the damned, I was ministered to by Reverend Lake, Reverend Harriet Graham, and others. The Lord healed me. He filled me with His Spirit, and I now minister to the sick throughout the city that are confined to their homes and are unable to be brought to the Healing Rooms."

Mr. Blake, whose healing appears at the head of this pamphlet, was one of his patients. He will call at your home anywhere if you so desire. What is this life worth to the United States? What is it worth to Portland? What is it worth to see hundreds of healed and saved people gather together in the Church at Portland, giving thanks to God? What is it worth to Portland to foster and sustain this work and thereby become the healthiest city on earth?

Lake and healing home workers in
Spokane, Washington, 1915-1920
Lake is in the front row, fifth from right.

On June 15 we were waited upon at our Healing Rooms by a committee of the Better Business Bureau of the city of Spokane, whose duty in part it is to investigate the truthfulness of all public announcements appearing in the city papers. For some time previous to this, we had been publishing some of the wonderful testimonies of healing by the power of God that had taken place in the daily course of our ministry at the Divine Healing Institute.

Among the testimonies that had appeared was the wonderful testimony of Mrs. John A. Graham, nee[1] Peterson, whose healing astonished the medical world. The testimony of Reverend Joseph Osborne, left to die of Bright's disease at the Deaconess hospital, analysis showing 15 percent albumen; Reverend Charles B. LeDoux,

LAKE AND DIVINE HEALING INVESTIGATED AND GOD ON DIVINE HEALING

By

Dr. John G. Lake
Divine Healing Institute
615 Broadway,
San Diego, California

Meetings Daily 2:30 and 7:30

Price 25 cents

Lake and Divine Healing Investigated How God Healed in Spokane, Washington

---

[1] nee: born (used to introduce the maiden name of a married woman). *Webster's Desk Dictionary of the English Language* (NY: Gramercy Books, 1983), p. 605.

healed when in very death from pneumonia; Mrs. Mary Mero, Mrs. Leana Lakey, Grover Risdon, Baby Agnes Young, Mrs. Mary Matheny, of Portland, Oregon, who was healed of forty cancers, and others.

These testimonies were so astounding that complaints reached the Better Business Bureau to the effect that the testimonies must certainly be untrue. The Better Business Bureau promptly undertook an investigation and the call at our Healing Rooms was for that purpose.

In the presence of the committee, as they waited, we called eighteen persons whose testimonies had appeared in the public print, who in turn, gave testimony as to their own condition and the wonder of their healing by the power of God in the name of the Lord Jesus Christ under this ministry. After eighteen had been examined we presented them with names of many healed persons in the city, desiring them to go personally to these persons and investigate for themselves whether these things were so.

Realizing the amount of labor necessary for a proper investigation, I suggested to the committee that on Sunday, June 23, at three o'clock in the afternoon at our public service, we would present one-hundred cases of healed persons for their investigation and invited them to form a committee composed of physicians, lawyers, judges, educators, and businessmen, who should render a verdict.

In the days lapsing between the interview at the Healing Rooms and Sunday, June 23, the committee continued their investigation, interviewing persons whose names we had furnished them. On Friday, June 21, before our great Sunday meeting, we received a letter from the committee, assuring us that they had no desire in any way to interfere with the good which we were doing and gently let themselves down so that their appearance at the Sunday meeting would not be necessary. Two members of the committee saw us privately and said that the committee was astounded. They said, "We soon found out, upon investigation, you did not tell half of it."

One of the committee was visiting at Davenport, Washington, where the firm had a branch store. As he looked around the store he found printed announcements advertising a meeting which we were about to conduct at Davenport. He made inquiry from the manager as to why these announcements were being made through their store, and the manager replied as follows:

"The whole countryside around Davenport is aflame with surprise at the marvelous healing of a girl in this community, well-known to me, and, I believe, well-known to yourself, Miss Louise Reinboldt, daughter of Mr. Jake Reinboldt.

"About three-and-a-half years ago, Miss Reinboldt and her sister were operated on for what the doctors thought was appendicitis. The one girl died as the result of the operation. Louise came out of it unable to speak. She was taken to throat specialists, who pronounced her case absolutely incurable. Recently she was taken to Spokane to Mr. Lake's Healing Rooms and ministered to for twenty-six days. On the twenty-sixth day she startled her mother and family and, in fact, the whole countryside, by calling her mother on the long distance telephone and announcing to her in plain words the fact that she was healed."

While preparing for her daily visit to the Healing Rooms she suddenly discovered herself whistling, and said to herself, "If I can whistle I can speak also," and so discovered the paralyzed condition of her throat was truly healed.

Other members of the committee reported similar remarkable healings, and not being desirous of becoming a public laughingstock, they hastily wrote as above quoted.

Mr. Lake, however, announced that there would be no change in the program, but that the meeting as announced would take place, and if the Better Business Bureau would not take their place he would appeal to the public for a verdict. The meeting took place at the Masonic Temple before a large audience estimated by the police to number thousands, hundreds being compelled to stand throughout the entire service and hundreds were refused admittance.

After a brief statement by Dr. Lake on the reasons for the meeting and of the desire to glorify God by permitting the city and the world to know that Jesus Christ has never changed, that prayer was answerable today as it ever was, and the days of miracles had not passed, but were forever possible through the exercise of faith in God, the following testimonies were given:

Reverend R. Armstrong, a Methodist minister, of N2819 Columbus Avenue, healed of a sarcoma growing out of the left shoulder three times as large as a man's head, was healed in answer to prayer.

Reverend Thomas B. O'Reilly of 430 Rookery Building, testified to being healed of fits so violent that when stricken with them it required seven policemen to overpower and confine him in the hospital. Of his instantaneous healing and perfect restoration to health through the prayer of faith.

Baby Agnes Young, N169 Post Street, healed of extreme malnutrition. Patient at the Deaconess hospital for nine months, from the time of birth until her healing. She weighed six-and-a-half pounds at birth and at the age of nine months, only four-and-a-half pounds. One evening, when one of the ministers from Reverend Lake's Healing Rooms called to minister to her, she was found in the dead room. The nurse, believing her to be dead, had removed her to the dead room. He took the child in his arms, praying the prayer of faith; God heard and answered. He removed her from the hospital and placed her in the hands of a Christian woman for nursing. In six weeks she was perfectly well and strong. The father and mother arose to corroborate the testimony. They are both members of Dr. Lake's church.

Mrs. Chittenden, pastor of the Church of the Truth at Coeur d'Alene, Idaho, testified to her healing of cancers of the breast; one breast having been removed in an operation and the other breast becoming likewise affected with cancer. She was healed of the Lord in answer to prayer.

Mrs. Everetts, 1911 Boone Avenue, testified to her healing of varicose veins. She had suffered from them for thirty-eight years. The veins were enlarged until they were the size of goose eggs in spots. Under the right knee there was a sack of blood so large that the knee was made stiff. She had exhausted every medical method. After being ministered to at the Healing Rooms for a short period, she was entirely well and the veins are perfectly clear.

Mrs. Constance Hoag, Puyallup, Washington, broke her kneecap. A section of the bone protruded through the flesh. She wrote requesting that the ministers of the Healing Rooms lay their hands upon a handkerchief in faith and prayer and send it to her, in accordance with

Acts 19:12. This was done. She applied the handkerchief to the knee and in fifteen minutes the pain had gone, and in an hour the bone had returned to place and was perfectly healed.

Mrs. Walker, Granby Court, was an invalid at the Deaconess hospital from internal cancer; after an exploratory operation was pronounced incurable by the doctors. She also had a severe case of neuritis. Her suffering was unspeakable. She testified to her healing and of her restoration to perfect health, the cancer having passed from her body in seven sections. Since then, many have been healed through her prayer and faith.

Mrs. John A. Graham, E369 Hartson, a nurse and hospital matron, was operated on for fibroid tumors. The generative organs were removed and at a later date, she was operated on a second time for gallstones. The operation not being a success, she was eventually left to die, and when in the throes of death and unconscious, she was healed by the power of God in answer to prayer of one of the ministers called from the Healing Rooms. The organs that had been removed in the operation regrew in the body, and she became a normal woman and a mother. (Wonderful applause.)

Mr. Asa Hill, a farmer from Palouse, Washington, testified that he had been a rheumatic cripple for fifteen years and was instantly healed at a meeting conducted by Mr. Lake, through prayer with the laying on of hands. The meeting was held at a theater at Moscow, Idaho.

Mrs. Wolverton was injured in a Great Northern railroad wreck and was awarded large damages by the court. (See court record.) Physicians testified her injuries to be such that motherhood was impossible. After her marriage, the physician's testimony was confirmed. She was healed in answer to prayer and gave birth to a son and since has given birth to twins.

Miss Jennie Walsh, S116 Fiske Street, had a disease of the gall bladder, which became filled with pus. Her physicians insisted on an immediate operation to save her life. Mr. Lake laid hands upon her in prayer at eleven o'clock p.m. Ten minutes afterward her pain ceased, the pus emptied from the bladder naturally, and she was entirely healed.

Mrs. Lamphear, 115½ Sprague Avenue, was an invalid for eleven years, suffering from prolapse of the stomach, bowels, and uterus, also from tuberculosis and rheumatism. Her husband carried her from place to place in his arms. After eleven years of terrible suffering, upon the advice of her physicians, who were unable to assist her, she was sent to Soap Lake, Oregon, for bath treatments. Ordinary baths had no effect on her, and the superintendent testified that they had finally placed her in super-heated baths, hotter than they had ever put any human being in before.

Through this treatment an abnormal growth was started in the left leg and foot. Her leg became three inches longer than the other and her foot one inch too long. A bone as large as an orange grew on the knee. She received an instant healing of rheumatism. The leg shortened at the rate of an inch a week, the foot also shortened to its normal length, and the bone growth on the knee totally disappeared. Her tuberculosis was healed and she is praising God for His goodness. She was born without the outer lobe on her ear, it also grew on.

Mrs. Ben Eastman, nee Koch, 1115 First Avenue, was pronounced incurable from tubercular glands by seventy-three physicians. She was operated on twenty-six times and remained in the same dying condition. Later she was taken to the Osteopathic Institute in Los Angeles, California, and was a patient there for three-and-a-half years. Her father testified that his daughter's illness cost him three houses in the city of Davenport, a valuable wheat ranch of one-hundred and sixty acres, one-hundred-forty-seven carloads of wood, and all the money he had. She is now healed of the Lord and since then has become the happy wife of Mr. Ben Eastman.

Mrs. Carter, of S714 Sherman Street, wife of Policeman Carter, was examined by seven physicians who pronounced her to be suffering from a fibroid tumor, estimated to weigh fifteen pounds. She was ministered to at the Healing Rooms at four-thirty in the afternoon and at eleven o'clock the next day, returned to the Healing Rooms perfectly healed and wearing her corsets. The enormous tumor dematerialized. (See her wonderful testimony in our pamphlet, "The Story of S714 Sherman Street.")

Mrs. O. D. Stutsman, Hansen Apartments, testified to having been an invalid for thirteen years. On one occasion, she lay in the Sacred Heart Hospital with a twenty-pound weight attached to her foot for thirty-two days, while suffering from inflammatory rheumatism. Her suffering was so intense that she begged her husband to take her home, preferring to remain a cripple rather than endure such suffering. The Reverend Lake was called to minister to her at her home; as prayer was offered, the power of the Spirit of God surged through her. Five minutes after his hands were laid upon her she arose from her bed, perfectly healed.

Mr. John Dewitt of Granby Court, testified on behalf of Frederick Barnard, thirty-two years of age, who was injured in his babyhood from a fall from a baby cab, causing curvature of the spine. As he grew to boyhood and manhood he was never able to take part in the sports common to boyhood and manhood. When the great war came on he would stand around the recruiting office, longing and covetously watching the men who enlisted for the war. One day he expressed to Mr. Dewitt the sorrow of his soul that he was not able to enlist also. Mr. Dewitt told him of Mr. Lake's Healing Rooms and invited him to come and be ministered to. The curvature of his spine straightened and his height increased one inch. He applied for enlistment in the Canadian army and was accepted by the army physician as first class and sent abroad.

GOD IN SURGERY

Mrs. O. Gilbertson, N4115 Helena Street, testified that through disease her hip came out of joint and her limb would turn like the leg of a doll, showing that it was entirely out of the socket. Her home is about five miles distant from the Healing Rooms. Reverend Lake and his co-workers engaged in prayer for her at the Healing Rooms, and as prayer was offered the power of God came upon her, resetting the joint.

The following remarks were made by the Reverend Lake as the testimony was given: "Do you hear it, you folks who worship a dead Christ? You doctors hear it? You preachers who lie to the people and say the days of miracles are past, do you hear it? You doubters hear it? God set the woman's hip. Because faith in God applied the blessed power of God to her life and limb."

Now comes one of the most remarkable cases in history. The Risdon family stood holding their six-year-old son on their shoulders. This boy was born with a closed head. In consequence, as he increased in years, the skull was forced upward like the roof of a house, the forehead and the back of the head also being forced out in similar manner, giving the head the appearance of the hull of a yacht upside down. The pressure on the brain caused the right side to become paralyzed and the child was dumb.

Physicians said that nothing could be done for him until he was twelve years old, and then the entire top of the head would have to be removed, the sides of the skull expanded and the entire head covered with a silver plate. Under divine healing ministration, in answer to prayer the bones softened, the head expanded, the skull was reduced to its normal size, the paralysis disappeared, and the dumbness was gone. He speaks like other children and now attends the public school.

Remarks by Reverend Lake: "I want you to see that in the Spirit of God there is a science far beyond physical or psychological science and the man or woman who enters into the Spirit relation with God and exercises His power, is most scientific; that the power of God in this instance was sufficient to soften the bones of the head, expand the skull, and bring the head down to normal when the child was four-and-a-half years old. Something that no medicine could do and no surgical operation could accomplish without endangering the life of the child."

CASTING OUT OF DEMONS AND HEALING OF THE INSANE

Mrs. Lena Lakey, W116 Riverside Avenue, testified of having suffered with violent insanity. She was a cook at a lumber camp. She told of the men at the camp endeavoring to overpower her and tie her in the bed; of her tearing the bed to pieces and braking her arms free; of how she struck one man with the side of the bed, rendering him unconscious. Another was in the hospital three weeks recovering from injuries. She escaped into the woods in a drenching rain. Eventually falling exhausted in a copse of trees, where she lay unconscious for six hours until a searching party found her.

She was brought to Spokane in an auto by six men and was tied with ropes. Before taking her to the court to be committed to the insane asylum, they decided to take her to the Healing Rooms. Reverend Lake laid his hands on her in prayer and the demons were cast out and she was instantly healed. An abscess in her side, from which she had suffered for fifteen years, totally disappeared in twenty-four hours, and a rheumatic bone deposit between the joints of the fingers and toes, so extensive that it forced the joint apart, was gone in forty-eight hours. She was made every whit whole.

Mrs. Holder gave testimony of healing by the power of God in answer to prayer, having been healed from insanity while an inmate of the Medical Lake Insane Asylum, in answer to the prayers of Mr. Lake and his assistants.

OTHER INCURABLES

Mr. and Mrs. Harry Lotz stood holding their baby in their arms. The baby developed pus in the kidney and was pronounced incurable by several physicians. The child was brought to the Healing Rooms. Reverend Lake laid his hands upon the child in prayer and it was instantly healed.

Mr. Allen, pastor of the Pentecostal mission, was dying of pellagra[2]. He was carried unconscious from the train. The men thought him to be dead and put him in the baggage room. He was instantly healed through the laying on of hands and prayer. His case is a matter of record by the government pellagra investigation commission.

Mrs. Ben Long, 1971 Atlantic Street, testified to being instantly healed of paralysis of the left side. She was brought to the Healing Rooms and ministered to by Dr. Lake, and when ten feet from the Healing Room door she found that she had been made whole. Discovering that she was well, she returned to the waiting room and showed herself to Mr. Lake and offered praise to God for her healing.

---

[2] pellagra: a disease caused by a deficiency of niacin in the diet characterized by skin changes, nervous disorders, and diarrhea. *Webster's Desk Dictionary of the English Language* (NY: Gramercy Books, 1983), p. 670.

Mrs. John Dewitt, Granby Court, gave testimony to having been healed of neuritis after years of suffering. Later she was healed when in a state of apparent death following two strokes. A group of friends were present and witnessed her instant healing as Reverend Lake prayed.

Mrs. Mary Mero, lady in waiting at the Healing Rooms, who resides at W717 Nora Avenue, broke her ankle when a child. In endeavoring to favor the broken ankle, the other ankle became diseased and for fifty years she had suffered violently. She was instantly healed after she was ministered to at the healing rooms. She was also healed of ulcers of the stomach after twenty years of suffering.

Mrs. Miles Pearson, E2815 Illinois Avenue, suffered a broken ankle a year ago. It was not properly set and remained inflamed and swollen as though the leg would burst. She was healed in answer to prayer two weeks ago.

Mrs. Thomas Olsen, Rowan Street, healed when dying of internal cancer. For ten days she had neither touched food or drink. A group of Christian friends gathered about her and prayed. As prayer was offered, Jesus appeared to her, standing in front of her, reaching out His hands appealingly. She endeavored to rise from her wheelchair and grasp the hands of her Lord and as she did so thrills of divine life flashed through her body and she was healed. Two days later she vomited the entire cancer, body and roots.

Mrs. Richards, Sandpoint, Idaho, testified that she had been healed when dying of paralysis on one side and tumors. After prayer the tumors loosened and passed from the body.

Mrs. Allen of Waverly, rising in audience with a friend who corroborated her testimony, was dying from internal cancers. She was brought to Spokane by Mr. Ramey, a hardware merchant of Waverly. She was perfectly healed and is now earning her living as a saleslady.

Mrs. Kellum, Portland, Oregon, testified to having been blind nine years. As prayer was offered a vision of Jesus laying His hands upon her eyes appeared to her, and she was instantly healed.

Addressing the audience, Mr. Lake said: "All persons who have been healed by the power of God and who desire to add their testimony to these who have already been given, stand." Two hundred and sixty-seven persons arose. While they stood Mr. Lake said: "Gentlemen of the committee and audience, you see these witnesses, you have heard the testimonies. Gentlemen of the committee and audience, has this been a fair presentation?"

(Shouts of "Yes, Yes," from all parts of the house.)

"Did God heal these people?"

(Cries of "Yes, Yes!")

"Is divine healing a fact?"

(Replies from audience, "It surely is.")

"Gentlemen of the committee and audience, are you entirely satisfied?"

(Replies from the audience, "Indeed we are.")

The services then closed with the following prayer of consecration, spoken clause by clause by the Reverend Lake and repeated by the audience.

MY GOD AND FATHER

In Jesus' name I come to Thee, take me as I am. Make me what I ought to be, in spirit, in soul, in body. Give me power to do right, if I have wronged any. To repent, to confess, to restore. No matter what it cost, wash me in the blood of Jesus, that I may now become Thy child and manifest Thee, in a perfect spirit, a holy mind, a sickless body. — Amen

Healing by God, through faith and prayer was practiced by the patriarchs.

Abraham prayed unto God: and God healed Abimelech, and his wife, and his maidservants; and they bare children.

— Genesis 20:17

THE WORD OF GOD ON DIVINE HEALING

2. *God made a covenant of healing with the children of Israel.* A covenant is an indissoluble agreement and can never be annulled. The laws of South Carolina recognized marriage as a covenant, not a legal contract. Therefore in that state there is no divorce. A covenant cannot be annulled, as the unchangeable God is one of the parties.

God tested the nation at the waters of Marah and made a *covenant* with them, known as the Covenant of Jehovah-Rophi. (The Lord, thy healer.)

a. "If thou wilt diligently hearken to the voice of the LORD thy God,

b. and wilt do that which is right in his sight,

c. and wilt give ear to his commandments,

d. and keep all his statutes,

I will put none of these diseases upon thee, which I have brought upon the Egyptians. For *I am the* LORD *that healeth thee.*"

— Exodus 15:26, emphasis Lake's

3. *David rejoiced in the knowledge of this covenant.*

Bless the LORD, O my soul: and all that is within me, bless his holy name. Bless the LORD, O my soul, and forget not all his benefits: who forgiveth all thine iniquities; who *healeth all thy diseases.*

— Psalm 103:1-3, emphasis Lake's

4. *Isaiah proclaimed it.*

> Then the eyes of the blind shall be opened, and the ears of the deaf shall be unstopped. Then shall the lame man leap as an hart, and the tongue of the dumb sing.

— Isaiah 35:5-6

5. *Jesus made healing one of the planks of His platform.*

   a.   *"The* Spirit of the Lord is upon me, because he hath anointed me to preach the gospel to the poor;

   b.   he hath sent me to *heal* the brokenhearted,

   c.   to preach deliverance to the captives,

   d.   *and recovering of sight to the blind,*

   e.   to set at liberty them that are bruised,

   f.   to preach the acceptable year of the Lord.

   — Luke 4:18-19, emphasis Lake's

6. *Jesus ministered healing to the sick.*

> And Jesus went about all Galilee, teaching in their synagogues, and preaching the gospel of the kingdom, *and healing all manner of sickness and all manner of disease among the people.*

— Matthew 4:23, emphasis Lake's

7. *Healing is in the atonement of Christ.*

   (See Matthew 8:1-7 and Matthew 8:17.)

   a.   Healing of the leper. Matthew 8:1-4.

   b.   Healing of the centurion's servant. Matthew 8:5-13.

   c.   Healing of Peter's wife's mother. Matthew 8:14-15.

   d.   Healing of the multitude. Matthew 8:16.

   e.   *His reason given* for these healings, verse 17:

> That it might be fulfilled which was spoken by Esaias the prophet, saying, *Himself took our infirmities, and bare our sicknesses* (Emphasis Lake's).

8. *Jesus bestowed the power to heal upon His twelve disciples.*

> Then he called his twelve disciples together, and *gave them*
> *power and authority over all devils,* and to *cure diseases.* And
> he sent them to preach the kingdom of God, and to *heal*
> *the sick...* And they departed, and went through the towns,
> preaching the gospel, and *healing everywhere.*
>
> — Luke 9:1-2,6, emphasis Lake's

9. *He likewise bestowed power to heal upon the seventy.*

> And after these things the Lord appointed other seventy
> also, and sent them two and two before his face into every
> city and place, whither he himself would come...*heal the*
> *sick* that are therein, and say unto them, The kingdom of
> God is come nigh unto you.
>
> — Luke 10:1,9, emphasis Lake's

10. *After Jesus' resurrection He extended the power to heal to all who*
    would believe.

> He said unto them, Go ye into all the world, and preach
> the gospel to every creature. He that believeth and is bap-
> tized shall be saved; but he that believeth not shall be
> damned. And these signs shall follow *them that believe;* In
> my name shall they *cast out devils;* they shall speak with
> new tongues; they shall take up serpents; and if they drink
> any deadly thing, it shall not hurt them; they shall lay
> *hands on the sick, and they shall recover.*
>
> — Mark 16:15-18, emphasis Lake's

11. *And lest healing should be lost to the Church, he perpetuated it*
    forever as one of the nine gifts of the Holy Ghost.

> For to one is given by the Spirit the word of wisdom; to
> another the word of knowledge by the same Spirit; to another
> faith by the same Spirit; to another the *gifts of healing* by the
> same Spirit; to another the *working of miracles;* to another

prophecy; to another discerning of spirits; to another divers kinds of tongues; to another the interpretation of tongues.

— 1 Corinthians 12:8-10, emphasis Lake's

12. *The Church was commanded to practice it.*

Is any among you afflicted? let him pray. Is any merry? let him sing psalms. Is any sick among you? let him *call for the elders of the church; and let them pray over him,* anointing him with oil in the name of the Lord: and the prayer of faith *shall save the sick,* and the Lord shall raise him up; and if he have committed sins, they shall be forgiven him. Confess your faults one to another, and pray one for another, that ye may be *healed.* The effectual fervent prayer of a righteous man availeth much.

— James 5:13-16, emphasis Lake's

13. *The unchangeableness of God's eternal purpose is thereby demonstrated.*

Jesus Christ the same yesterday, and to day, and for ever.

— Hebrews 13:8

I am the LORD, I change not.

— Malachi 3:6

God always was the healer. He is the healer still, and will ever remain the healer. Healing is for *you.* Jesus healed, "All that came to him."[3] He never turned anyone away. He never said, "It is not God's will to heal you," or that it was better for the individual to remain sick or that they were being perfected in character through the sickness. He healed them *all,* thereby demonstrating *forever* God's unchangeable will concerning sickness and healing.

Have you need of healing? Pray to God in the name of Jesus Christ to remove the disease. Command it to leave, as you would sin. Assert your divine authority and refuse to have it. Jesus purchased your freedom from sickness as He purchased your freedom from sin.

---

[3] See Matthew 4:24, 8:16, 12:15, 14:14, 15:30, 19:2, Mark 1:34, 6:13, Luke 4:40, 6:19, 9:11.

His own self *bare* our sins in his own body on the tree, that we, being dead to sins, should live unto righteousness: *by whose stripes ye were healed.*

— 1 Peter 2:24, emphasis Lake's

Therefore, mankind has a right to health as he has a right to deliverance from sin. If you do not have it, it is because you are being cheated out of your inheritance. It belongs to you. In the name of Jesus Christ go after it and get it.

If your faith is weak, call for those who believe and to whom the prayer of faith and the ministry of healing has been committed.

See also Psalm 91, Isaiah 35, Matthew 8 and 9, Mark 16, Luke 11, John 9, Acts 3,4,8,9,10, and 26, and 2 Corinthians 12 and 13

John G. Lake, Overseer

he Southern Association of Evangelists, who recently met at Hot Springs, Arkansas, in a convention, wrote as follows:

Reverend John G. Lake

Spokane, Washington

Dear Sir:

We are submitting the following questions to about twenty-five of the leading professors, preachers, and evangelists for reply and recognizing your extensive experience in the ministry of healing, trust that you will favor us with an early reply.

The questions are as follows:

First: Is God able to heal?

Second: Does God ever heal?

Third: Does God always heal?

IS GOD ABLE TO HEAL? DOES GOD EVER HEAL? DOES GOD ALWAYS HEAL? DOES GOD USE MEANS IN HEALING?

by

John G. Lake

Overseer

The Church at Spokane

Price 50 cents

Is God Able to Heal?

Fourth: Does God use means in healing?

These questions were suggested to us through their having been used in a discussion of healing by Philip Mauro of Washington, D.C.

THE REPLY

The first question, "Is God able to heal?" coming as an inquiry from the Church of Christ in her varied branches, as represented by your association, which includes ministers and evangelists of almost every known sect, is a confession of how far the modern Church has drifted in her faith from that of the primitive Church of the first four centuries.

That this apostasy is true, may be readily seen by a study of the New Testament, together with the writings of the Christian fathers of the first centuries. That Jesus Christ was the accepted and recognized healer, and the *only* healer (healing through His followers) in the Church for the first four hundred years of the Christian era, is the testimony of every first-rate student.

That Jesus Himself healed *all* who came to Him, that the apostles also after His resurrection and after the outpouring of the Holy Spirit upon the Church on the day of Pentecost, continued to do the same, is a New Testament fact.[1] It is also well known that the Church Fathers testified to the vast extent of the miracle-working power of Christ through His followers until the days of Constantine. The early Christians accepted Jesus as a Savior of spirit, soul, *and body.* His consecration of Himself to God as the pattern consecration for all Christians for all times, is declared by many of the Christian writers.

With the establishment of Christianity as the state religion under Constantine, a flood of heathendom poured into the Church, and the vitality of the faith in Christ as Savior and healer disappeared. Hordes of unbelievers came into the Church with a very slight knowledge of Christ, bringing with them many heathen customs and practices, some of which quickly predominated in the Church. Among these was trust in *man* rather than *Christ* as healer of the body.

That isolated saints of God and groups of Christians have trusted God exclusively, and proved Him the healer, is found in the experience of the Church in every century. Among those in modern times were the Huguenots of France, who excelled in their faith in God. Many of

---

[1] Jesus healed all, see Matthew 4:24, 8:16, 12:15, 14:14, 15:30, 19:2, Mark 1:34, 6:13, Luke 4:40, 6:19, 9:11. The apostles continued to heal, see Acts 3:1-8, 5:16, 8:7, and 28:8.

them were consciously baptized in the Holy Ghost, and history records that many of them spoke in tongues by the power of the Holy Spirit. The sick were healed through their faith in Jesus Christ and the laying on of hands. Many prophesied in the Spirit. In these things the Huguenots were a reproduction of the original New Testament Church.

The Waldenses knew Christ as their healer and recorded many instances of wonderful healings.

With the coming of Protestantism, and the establishment of the great churches of the present day, little knowledge of Christ as the healer existed. Protestantism was established on one great principle, the revelation of Martin Luther, his watchword and slogan, "The just shall live by faith."[2] Not by works of penance, but through faith in the living, risen, glorified Son of God.

Isolated cases of healing are recorded by Luther, John Knox, Calvin, Zewengle, and others of the reformers.

With the birth of Methodism, under John Wesley, a fresh impetus was given to the teaching of healing through faith in Jesus. Wesley records in his journal many instances of wonderful healings of the sick, of casting out of demons, and remarkable answers to prayer. Healing was recognized by Wesley as a possibility of faith. He apparently, however, failed to see that the healing of the body is definitely, certainly included in the atonement of the Lord and Savior Jesus Christ and is part and parcel of the common salvation.

The modern teaching of healing received a new impetus through Dorothy Trudell, a factory worker in one of the German provinces. Under her ministry many were healed, so that eventually the German government was compelled to recognize her healing institution at Mannendorf, and license it.

During the present century, a great number of men have definitely taught and practiced the ministry of healing. Among the writers on the subject of healing, who are well-known in the Christian Church, are A. J. Gordon, Dr. A. B. Simpson of the Christian and Missionary Alliance, and Reverend Andrew Murray of South Africa.

---

[2] Romans 1:17, Galatians 3:11, and Hebrews 10:38.

The Reverend Andrew Murray's experience in healing was as follows: He was pronounced incurable of a throat disease, known as "preacher's throat," by many London specialists. In despair, he visited the Bethsan Divine Healing Mission in London, conducted by Dr. Bagster. He knelt at the altar, was prayed for by the elders, and was healed. He returned to South Africa and wrote and published a book on divine healing,[3] which was extensively circulated in the Dutch Reform Church of South Africa, of which he was the recognized leading pastor.

The effect of the book was to call the people's attention to the fact that Jesus was the healer still. Great celebrations took place in the various churches of South Africa when Andrew Murray returned, a living example of Christ's power and willingness to heal.

In a short time, persons who had read of his ministry of healing made request to their pastors to be prayed for, that they might be healed. In some instances the pastors confessed that they had no faith and could not honestly pray with them for healing. Others made one excuse or another. Eventually, the people began to inquire what was the trouble with their pastors. Andrew Murray, the chief pastor, had been healed. He had written a book on healing. Members of the Church throughout the land were praying through to God and finding Him their healer still. But the preachers in general were confessing lack of faith.

So the circulation of the book became an embarrassment to them. Instead of humbly confessing their need to God and calling upon Him for that measure of His Spirit's presence and power that would make prayer for the sick answerable, they decided to demand the withdrawal of Andrew Murray's book from circulation in the Church, and this was done. Although the truth of the teaching of divine healing, and the personal experience in healing of the Reverend Andrew Murray and hundreds of others through his ministry and the ministry of believers in the Church remained unchallenged, the Reverend Murray was requested not to practice the teaching of divine healing in the Dutch Reform Church of South Africa.

---

[3] This book was simply entitled, *Divine Healing*. It is still available today.

This experience illustrates with clearness the difficulties surrounding the introduction of a more vital faith in the living God in the modern Church. Every church has had, in a greater or less degree, a somewhat similar experience. The usual custom in the modern Church is that when a preacher breaks out in a living faith and begins to get extraordinary answers to prayer, he is advised by the worldly-wise, and if persistent, is eventually made to feel that he is regarded strange. If he still persists, he is ostracized and actually dismissed by some churches and conferences.

Experiences like the above are entirely due to failure of the modern Church to recognize the varied ministries of the Spirit, as set forth in the New Testament. The Word, in the twelfth of 1 Corinthians says concerning the order of ministers in the Church that:

> God hath set some in the church, first apostles, secondarily prophets, thirdly teachers, after that miracles, then gifts of healings, helps, governments, diversities of tongues.[4]

Thus, a ministry for every man called of God is provided. No one conflicting with the other. All recognized as equally necessary to the well-rounded body of Christ.

The modern Church must come to a realization of other ministries in the Church besides preaching. In the modern Church, the preacher is the soul and center and circumference of his church. The primitive Church was a structure of faith composed of men and women, each qualifying in his or her particular ministry. One was a healer, another a worker of miracles, another a teacher of the ways and will and Word of God, another an evangelist, another a pastor, another an overseer.

It should be an easy matter for any modern Church to adapt itself to the gifts of the Spirit and so remove forever the difficulty that befell the Dutch Reform Church in South Africa, and has befallen our own churches. Instead of discouraging a ministry of the Spirit through the practice of varied persons, these ministries and powers may be conserved and utilized for the upbuilding of the kingdom.

---

[4] 1 Corinthians 12:28.

Our neglect in this matter has forced into existence such institutions as Christian Science and one-thousand and one new thought societies and varied philosophies which endeavor to supply that which in the primitive Church was supplied through the Lord Jesus Christ and the ministry of spiritual gifts by His followers in the Church.

Nevertheless, the knowledge of Jesus, the healer now and forever, has spread among the masses of the people until in almost every city there are organized groups of Christian people who trust in God wholly and solely and proclaim Jesus their only healer.

A new day is dawning, and a knowledge of the reality and power of the redemption of Jesus Christ is recognized on every hand. A little over five years ago, we established in Spokane, Divine Healing Rooms with a competent staff of ministers. They believe in the Lord as the present, perfect healer and minister the Spirit of God to the sick through prayer and the laying on of hands. The records show that we minister to about two-hundred persons per day; that of these two-hundred, one-hundred and seventy-six are non-church members. The knowledge of and faith in Jesus Christ as the healer, has gripped the world outside of the present church societies, and the numbers of those who thus believe are increasing with such rapidity that in a short time they will become a majority in many communities.

These healings have been of the most extraordinary character, as shown by the fact that great numbers of them have been declared incurable by physicians and surgeons, proving the fallacy of the oft repeated foolish statement that "the days of miracles are past." It demonstrates that the day of miracles never passes where faith is present to believe God for the thing declared in His Word.

A boy of twelve years, suffering from tuberculosis of the spine so extreme that he was compelled to wear a steel jacket both day and night, was brought to the Healing Rooms a few days ago for prayer. In less than ten days his condition was so improved that he discarded the jacket entirely; his shoulders had straightened; and his vertebrae remained fixed. The boy, James Early, returned to his home at Rosalia, Washington, praising God that he had proven that in our own city in March, 1919, Jesus Christ is still the healer.

ANOTHER INCIDENT

We ministered to Grover Risdon of 914 Rockwell Avenue, Spokane, and God performed one of the most remarkable miracles of healing that is known to history. When Baby Grover was born, he was found to have a closed head; the opening in the top of the head that permits the skull to expand was closed. The brain grew, forcing the skull *upward three inches,* like the ridge of a house roof. The forehead was forced upward in the same manner and the back of the head likewise.

The pressure on the brain caused paralysis of the right side and leg, also the foot. The *child was dumb.* Medical science could give no relief or offer a cure. Surgical science said, "Wait until he is ten years old, then we will cut the skull into eight sections and put a plate over the head to cover the brain." Surgeons frankly said, "We fear such an operation may destroy his life, but it is his only chance."

Then the parents, in distress, turned to the church and pastors, but they told them, "God does not hear prayer for healing now; that was to prove to the people in Jesus' day that He was divine."

The father said, "If He healed my stricken son it would prove to *me* that He is *divine now.*"

Then hope came. The mother suffered with prolapse of the uterus. She came to the Healing Rooms and was healed. *Faith grew.*

Her daughter, Alice, was partially blind and could only see by the use of the most powerful glasses. She was stricken with appendicitis. When suffering tortures, holy hands were laid upon her in Jesus' name, and she was healed.

Then Grover was brought to the Healing Rooms. As we ministered to him the second time the paralysis was destroyed. He could walk like other children. Then the head began to come down and expand normally, and in a short time he could speak like other six-year-old children.

God's work is perfect. He is wholly well. And the boy, his parents, his family, the neighborhood, the city of Spokane, and the world is better because Jesus Christ was honored as Savior and healer still.

Thousands healed by God's power in the city of Spokane and the surrounding country join with them, proclaiming that they too, have proved the Lord Jesus Christ — "The same yesterday, and to day, and for ever"[5] — Savior and healer.

This letter is respectfully submitted as an answer to your question, "Is God able to heal?" For Jesus said, "If ye believe me not believe the works for the works' sake."[6] He also said, "Whether is it easier to say, thy sins be forgiven thee; or take up thy bed and walk?"[7]

DOES GOD EVER HEAL?

The New Testament records forty-one cases of healing by Jesus Himself. In nine of these instances not only were the individuals healed, but multitudes, and in three instances it especially says "great multitudes."[8]

With the growth of His life's work the demand for extension was imperative, and in Luke 9, we read:

> He called his twelve disciples together, and *gave them power* and authority over all *devils,* and to cure *diseases.* And he sent them to preach the kingdom of God, and to *heal the sick.*[9]

When they in turn were overwhelmed with work we read, in Luke 10, that Jesus appointed seventy others also, and sent them into the cities round about, saying, "Heal the sick that are therein, and say unto them, the kingdom of God is come nigh unto you."[10]

If there was any foundation whatever for the foolish belief that only Jesus and the apostles healed, the appointment of these seventy should settle it. When the seventy returned from their first evangelistic tour, they rejoiced, saying, "Master, even the demons were subject to us in thy name."[11]

---

[5] Hebrews 13:8.

[6] John 10:37-38, paraphrased.

[7] Mark 2:9, paraphrased.

[8] See Matthew 12:15, 15:30, and 19:2.

[9] Luke 9:1-2.

[10] Luke 10:9.

[11] Luke 10:17, paraphrased.

In addition to the seventy, we read that the disciples complained to Jesus, saying, "We saw one casting out devils in thy name; and we forbad him, because he followeth not with us." And Jesus replied, "Forbid him not, for no man can do a miracle in My name and speak light of Me. He that is not against us is for us."[12]

This, then, makes a New Testament record of eighty-four persons who healed during the lifetime of Jesus. Jesus, the twelve apostles, seventy others, and the man who "followed not us."

Paul and Barnabas were not apostles during the lifetime of Jesus, but we read in the Acts of their healing many. Paul himself was healed through the ministry of Ananias, an aged disciple who was sent to him through a vision from the Lord.[13]

Philip was one of the evangelists who preached at Samaria, and under his ministry there were remarkable "signs and wonders."[14]

Under the ministry of the apostle Paul the sick were not only healed and the dead raised, but handkerchiefs were brought to the apostle that they might contact his person. When laid upon the sick, the disease disappeared and the "demons" departed from them.[15]

The book of James gives final and positive instructions of what to do in case of sickness. Commanding that, if sick, one shall send for the elders of the Church. Concerning their prayer of faith the Word says,

> The prayer of faith shall save the sick, and the Lord *shall raise him up;* and if he have committed sins, they shall be forgiven him.[16]

Forty years after Jesus, Clement, Paul's contemporary, said, "Men received gifts of healing." Irensaus, a hundred and ten years after Christ, says, "Men healed the sick by laying their hands upon them."

---

[12] Mark 9:38-40 and Luke 9:49-50, paraphrased.

[13] See Acts 9.

[14] See Acts 8:13.

[15] See Acts 19:12.

[16] James 5:15.

Justin Martyr (110-163 AD) writes concerning the operation of God in the Church in his day, "For one receives the spirit of understanding, another of council, another of strength, another of healing, another of teaching, and another of the fear of God." And again he says, "For many demoniacs throughout the whole world and your city, *many of our Christian men* exorcising them in the name of Jesus Christ, who was crucified by Pontius Pilot, have healed and do heal."

Two hundred years after Christ, Origen says, "Men had marvelous power of curing by invoking the divine name. They expel evil spirits and perform many cures and foresee certain events, according to the will of the Logos."

St. Ambrose, Bishop of Milan (340-397 AD) tells of one Severne, a butcher by business, who became blind and was healed of the Lord.

It is recorded of St. Macarius of Alexandria (375-390 AD), "A man withered in all his limbs and especially in his feet was anointed in the name of the Lord, and when commanded in the name of the Lord Jesus Christ... 'arise, and stand on thy feet, and return to thy house,' immediately arising and leaping he blessed God." Again, "There was brought to him from Thessalonica a noble and wealthy virgin, who for many years had been suffering from paralysis. With his own hands he anointed her, pouring out prayer for her to the Lord...and so sent her back cured to her own city."

St. Augustine (426 AD) declares, "But the miracles that persons ascribed unto their idols are in no way comparable to the wonders wrought by our martyrs."

In 698 AD, a man named Bethwegan, paralyzed on one side, prayed at the tomb of Cuthbert: "In the midst of his prayer he fell, as it were, into a stupor...felt a large hand touch his head where the pain lay. ...He was delivered from the weakness, restored to health down to his feet. He rose up in perfect health, returning thanks to God for his recovery." It is said that the very garments that St. Cuthbert had worn during life, remained so impregnated by the divine Spirit of God, that like the handkerchiefs taken from Paul's body to the sick, the virtue from his garments cured many, as may be seen in the book of his life and miracles.

Mediaeval history records miracles of healing having taken place at the following shrines:

That of St. Thomas at Canterbury, Our Lady at Walsingham, St. Edward the Confessor at Westminster, St. William at York, St. Cuthbert at Durham, St. Thomas at Hereford, St. Osmund at Salisbury, St. Erkenwald at London, St. Hugh at Lincoln, St. Wulfstan at Worcester, Little St. William at Norwich, St. Werburgh at Chester, St. Frideswide at Oxford.

In this connection, may we say that in the canonization of saints it was necessary to establish before a court the fact that in at least two instances there had been actual miracles performed. In this connection we quote, "The evidence was sifted to the utmost and every disqualifying feature was made the most of." So the Benedict XIV had a right to say that, "The degree of proof required is the same as that required for a criminal case."

These mediaeval miracles, therefore, deserve respectful treatment and the cumulative evidence of so much concurrent testimony by distinguished and upright men makes it impossible to think that they were all deluded and mistaken.

Among those canonized, and others in whose lives there was positive evidence of the healing power of Christ in well-established cases, are (according to Bede): St. John of Beverly (721 AD), St. Bernard (1091-1153 AD), St. Francis of Assisi (1182-1226 AD), St. Thomas of Hereford (1282-1303 AD), St. Catherine of Siena (1347-1380 AD), Martin Luther (1483-1546 AD), St. Francis of Xavier (1506-1552 AD), St. Phillip Neri (1515-1595 AD), Pascal's niece (1646 AD), George Fox (1624-1691 AD), John Wesley (1703-1791 AD), Prince Hohenlohe (1794-1847 AD), Father Matthew (1790-1856 AD), Dorothea Trudel (1813-1862 AD), Pastor Blumhart (1805-1880 AD), Father John of Cronstadt (1829-1908 AD).

Concerning the reliability of the present existence of the miracle-working power of God, permit me to quote Richard Holt Hutton, justly estimated as one of the broad-minded writers and who was regarded as a profound materialist. "But whatever miracles be, history shows a great amount of evidence...that such events have happened in all ages. ...Enthusiasm and fraud cannot be asked to account for as much evidence on this subject as exists."

It is a matter of common knowledge that ten thousand persons were healed under the ministry of Dorothea Trudel of Mannendorf.

The records of the Russian courts show that such a multitude of persons where healed under the ministry of Father John of Cranstadt, who died in 1908, that the Church of Russia, fearing his growing and powerful influence decided to have him imprisoned. Because of the great numbers who were healed under his ministry and who became his faithful adherents, and because of his extreme age, they decided that it was wiser to let him live out his natural life than to undertake his control by the Church.

During the life of John Alexander Dowie, before his mentality was affected through overwork, he established a city in the state of Illinois, forty miles north of Chicago, on the lakeshore, known as Zion City. This city was established in 1901. In twelve months it had a population of four thousand. In three years the population was estimated to be ten thousand. The city council passed by-laws banishing forever doctors, drugs, medicines, and use of swine's flesh. None of these are used by his followers if they wish to remain in good standing.

Their vital statistics reveal that their death rate is lower than that of other cities of the same population. Insurance companies were afraid to insure the Zion people because of the well-known fact that they would not employ physicians or take medicines. But at present, insurance companies are seeking their business. They are now recognized to be among the healthiest people in the United States.

On an occasion at the Chicago Auditorium, persons from all parts of the world who had been healed through their ministry, were invited to send testimonies on a card two-and-a-half by four-and-a-half inches. It required five bushel baskets to hold these cards. They numbered sixty thousand. Ten thousand persons in the audience rose to their feet testifying to their own personal healing by the power of God, making a grand total of seventy thousand testimonies.

In South Africa, divine healing now holds such sway among both black and white, that army officers estimated that in the recent war, twenty out of every hundred refused medical aid and trusted God only. This necessitated in the army the establishment of the Divine Healing Corps, who ministered healing by the Spirit of God.

By the most careful estimates The Church at Spokane reports one-hundred thousand healings in the past five years. Spokane has become celebrated as the greatest divine healing center in the world.

The hotels of the city testify to the continuous supply of patients coming from all parts of the world to receive ministry, and among the healed are a goodly number of physicians who, like others, have found the Lord Jesus Christ the true and Great Physician.

Among prominent physicians who have not only been healed of God, but who have adopted the ministry of healing through faith in the Lord Jesus Christ are: Phineas D. Yoakum of Los Angeles, head of the Pisga Institution, whose blessed ministry of healing is recognized by Christians everywhere. Dr. William T. Gentry of Chicago, who was not only prominent in his profession as a physician, but as the author of Materia Medica in twenty volumes, to be found in every first-class medical library. His publisher sold over one hundred thousand copies of this work. Dr. A. B. Simpson, the founder and head of the Missionary and Christian Alliance, which is said to maintain a thousand foreign missionaries in different parts of the world, is another former doctor under whose ministry miracles of healing have continuously occurred.

To this I add my personal testimony, after twenty-five years in the ministry of healing, that hundreds of thousands of sick have been healed of the Lord during this period, through churches and missionary societies founded on the pattern of the primitive Church, finding God's divine equipment of power from on high.

With this weight of testimony before us it seems childish to continue debating the ability or willingness of God to heal the sick. Let us rather with open minds and heart, receive the Lord Christ as Savior and healer, trusting Him with our bodies as we trust Him with our souls and so permit His hundredfold salvation for every need of the spirit, soul, and body to be exemplified and our consecration as the children of God stand unchallenged.

DOES GOD ALWAYS HEAL?

In considering the subject of divine healing and its applicability to present-day needs, the question, "Does God always heal?" is uppermost. The Church at large has taught that healing is dependent on the exercise of the will of God and that the proper attitude for the Christian to assume is, "If it be thy will." Continuously, we hear men say, "No doubt God can heal; He has powers, and He can heal if He will."

We believe that this attitude of mind and this character of reasoning is due to ignorance of the plain Word and will of God, as revealed through Jesus the Christ. We contend that God is always the healer. We contend further that it is not necessary for God to will and that He does not will the healing or non-healing of any individual. In His desire to bless mankind, He willed once and for all and forever that man should be blessed and healed. He gave Jesus Christ as a gift to the world, that this blessing might be demonstrated and His willingness and desire to heal forever made clear.

Christians readily admit that Jesus is the entire expression of the law, the life, and the will of God. As such, He demonstrated forever by His words and acts, what the mind of God toward the world is. He healed all who came to Him, never refusing a single individual, but ever bestowed the desired blessing. In healing *all* and never refusing one, He demonstrated forever the willingness of God to heal all, both saint and sinner.

It is absurd to think that only the good were healed by Jesus. He "healed all that came."[17] Their *coming* was sufficient to secure the blessing. He healed because it was the nature of God to heal, not because it was a caprice of the mind of God or not because the mind of God was changed toward the individual through some especial supplication. Whosoever was ready and willing to receive healing received it from the Lord. His grief, in one instance, is expressed in the Gospel narrative in that, "He could there (at Nazareth) do no mighty works because of their unbelief, save that he healed a few sick folk."[18]

---

[17] See Matthew 4:24, 8:16, 12:15, 14:14, 15:30, 19:2, Mark 1:34, 6:13, Luke 4:40, 6:19, 9:11.

[18] Mark 6:5, paraphrased.

Men have assumed that it is necessary to persuade God to heal them. This we deny with all emphasis. God has manifested through Christ, His desire to bless mankind.

> He *gave* his only begotten Son, that whosoever believeth in him should not perish, but have everlasting life. For God sent not his Son into the world to condemn the world; but that the world through him might be saved.[19]

> I am come that they might have life, and that they might have it more abundantly.[20]

His method of saving the world and what constituted His salvation, is shown in Matthew 4:23:

> Jesus went about all Galilee, teaching in their synagogues (revealing the will of God), and preaching the gospel of the kingdom, and healing all manner of sickness and all manner of disease among the people.

The facts of God's will, of His purpose to establish the kingdom of Christ, and of His deliverance from sickness — a kindred blessing for spirit and soul and body are here provided, the common salvation.

The redemption of Jesus does not rest on His crucifixion alone. It rests equally in a combined victory of crucifixion, resurrection, and ascension. Each step was an elevation in divine consciousness to one end, the bestowal of the Holy Spirit upon the world. Through His crucifixion, He fulfilled the type and fact of the Jewish sacrifice.[21] Through His resurrection, He manifested and demonstrated His power over death and that death itself was made a captive.[22] Through His ascension to the throne of God and through receiving from the Father, the gift of the Holy Ghost, He was now equipped to bestow universal salvation upon whosoever would receive.[23]

---

[19] John 3:16-17.

[20] John 10:10.

[21] See Hebrews 9:26 and 10:12.

[22] See Romans 6:9, 2 Timothy 1:10, and Revelation 1:18.

[23] See John 14:12-17, Acts 1:4-8 and 2:38.

The method by which men receive the healing power is parallel to the method by which we light our homes through the use of electricity. A dynamo is set up. Through its motion it attracts to itself from the atmosphere, the quality known as electricity. Having attracted electricity, it is then distributed through the wires wherever man wills, and our homes are lighted thereby. The dynamo did not make the electricity. It has been in the atmosphere from time immemorial. It was the discovery of the ability to control the electricity that made the lighting of our homes a possibility. Without it, we would still be living by the light of a tallow candle or a kerosene lamp.

In the spiritual world, the spirit of man is the dynamo. It is set in motion by prayer, the desire of the heart. Prayer is a veritable Holy Spirit-controlling dynamo, attracting to itself the Spirit of God. The Spirit of God being received into the spirit of man through prayer, is distributed by the action of the will wherever desired. The Spirit of God flowed through the hands of Jesus to the ones who were sick and healed them. It flowed from His soul, wirelessly, to the suffering ones and healed them also.

The Holy Spirit is thus shown to be the universal presence of God — God omnipresent. The Spirit of God is given to man for his blessing and is to be utilized by him to fulfill the will of God.

The will of God to *save* a man is undisputed by intelligent Christians. The will of *God* to *heal* every man is equally God's purpose. God has not only made provision that through the Spirit of God received into our lives, our souls may be blessed and our bodies healed, but further, we in turn are expected and commanded by Jesus to distribute the Spirit's power to others, that they likewise may be blessed and healed. "In my name," said Jesus, "they shall lay hands on the sick, and they shall recover."[24] This refers not to a special priest or a particular individual endowed with peculiar powers, but to the *believer*, the everyday man who accepts the Gospel of Jesus Christ and who becomes a declared disciple of the Son of God. (Read Mark 16:14-20.)

The Spirit of God is ours to embrace. It is ours to apply to the need of either soul or body. It is the redeeming quality of the nature of God

---

[24] Mark 16:17-18.

that Jesus Christ regarded as essential to the world's blessing. His life on earth, His death on the cross, His resurrection from the dead, and His ascension to glory were all necessary to secure its benefits and bestow them upon the world. It was Christ's means of supplying a universal salvation for whosoever will.

On the Day of Pentecost, when the floodtide of the Holy Spirit broke over the church at Jerusalem and its glory-power radiated through their souls and rested upon them as tongues of fire and they were filled with the Holy Ghost and began to speak with other tongues as the *Spirit* gave them utterance, the people demanded an explanation of the phenomena.[25]

Peter replied,

> This Jesus hath God raised up, whereof we all are witnesses (resurrection). Therefore being by the right hand of God exalted (ascension), and having received of the Father the promise of the Holy Ghost (fulfillment of the promise of the Father), he hath shed forth this, which ye now see and hear.
>
> — Acts 2:32-33

Through His crucifixion and through His victory over the grave, Jesus secured from the Father the privilege of shedding the Holy Spirit abroad over the world. This was the crowning climax of the redemptive power of God ministered through Jesus Christ to the world. And from that day to this, every soul is entitled to embrace to himself this blessed Spirit of God which Jesus regarded so valuable to mankind, so necessary for their healing and salvation, that He gave His life to obtain it.

Consequently, it is not a question, "Does God always heal?" That is childish. It is rather a question, "Are we willing to embrace His healing?" If so, it is for us to receive. More than this, it is for all the world to receive, for every man to receive who will put his nature in contact with God through opening his heart to the Lord.

---

[25] See Acts 2:1-12.

Jesus, knowing the world's need of healing, provided definitely for physicians (disciples, ministers, priests, healers) who would minister, not pills and potions, but the *power of God*. The gift of healing is one of the nine gifts of the Spirit provided for and perpetuated forever in the Church. (See 1 Corinthians 12:8-11.)

It is an evidence of ignorance of God's Word to continue to discuss the question, "Does God always heal?" as though God healed sometimes, and sometimes He did not. Enlightenment by the Spirit of God, through the Word, reveals that God always was the healer, is the healer today, will be the healer forever. The Word says, "Jesus Christ the same yesterday, and to day, and for ever."[26] Consequently there is healing from every disease for every man who will in faith, embrace the Spirit of God promised by the Father and ministered through Jesus Christ to the souls and bodies of all who desire the blessing.

Peter, in his exposition of this fact says, "By whose stripes ye *were* healed."[27] The use of "were" in this text indicates that the healing was accomplished in the mind of God when Jesus Christ gave Himself as the eternal sacrifice and has never had to be done over again for the healing of any individual. He *willed* it once, it is done forever. He made the provision and invites the world to embrace it. It is yours to have, yours to enjoy, and yours to impart to others.

Does God Use Means in Healing?

By the term "means," is understood the varied remedies, medicines, and potions commonly used by the world at large and prescribed for the sick — in short, Materia Medica.

This should be an extremely easy question for anyone to decide. The world has always had her system of healing. They were the thousand and one systems of healing evolved in all the centuries. They were mankind's endeavor to alleviate suffering. They existed in the days of Jesus, just as they exist today.

---

[26] Hebrews 13:8.

[27] 1 Peter 2:24.

Systems of so-called healing are without number. The ancient Egyptians used them and were apparently as proficient in the practice of the same as our modern physicians. Indeed, their knowledge of chemistry seems to have superseded ours, as they were able to produce an embalming substance that preserved the human body and kept it from dissolution, for almost every museum of note has its samples of Egyptian mummies.

It is the unintelligent who suppose that the ancient physicians were any less skillful in the healing of the sick through their means, remedies, and systems than the modern physician.

Of the supposed curative value of our modern medical practice, there is an abundance of testimony from the varied heads of the medical profession that should be sufficient to convince any candid thinker of their valuelessness.

The public commonly believe that medicine is a great science and that its practice is entirely scientific. Whereas, so great a man as Professor Douglas McGlaggen, who occupied the chair of medical jurisprudence in the University of Edinburgh, Scotland, declared, "There is no such thing as the science of medicine. From the days of Hippocrates and Galen until now we have been stumbling in the dark, from diagnosis to diagnosis, from treatment to treatment, and have not found the first stone on which to found medicine as a science."

Mr. James Mason Good of London, England, who was so eminent in his profession that for twenty-five years he had in his care the royal house of Britain, declared his convictions before the British Medical Association in these words, "The science of medicines is founded upon conjecture and improved by murder. Our medicines have destroyed more lives than all the wars, pestilences, and famines combined."

The famous Professor Chauss of Germany, states with emphasis, "The common use of medicines for the curing of disease is unquestionably highly detrimental and destructive and in my judgment, is an agent for the creation of disease rather than its cure, in that through its use there is continuously set up in the human system, abnormal conditions more detrimental to human life than the disease from which the patient is suffering."

Our own Dr. Holmes of Boston, formerly president of the Massachusetts Medical Association, said in an address before the Massachusetts Medical Association, "It is my conviction, after practicing medicine for thirty-five years, that if the whole Materia Medica were cast into the bottom of the sea it would be all the better for mankind and all the worse for the fishes."

From these quotations from the heads of the medical profession in various countries, we perceive the power of the Word of God, which declares, "In vain shall they use many medicines. There is no healing for thee there."[28]

Dr. John B. Murphy, the greatest surgeon our country has ever produced, has spoken his mind concerning surgery as follows, "Surgery is a confession of helplessness. Being unable to assist the diseased organ, we remove it. If I had my life to live over again, I would endeavor to discover preventative medicine, in the hope of saving the organ instead of destroying it."

Just prior to his death he wrote an article entitled, "The Slaughter of the Innocents," condemning cutting out of tonsils and adenoids, demonstrating that the presence of inflammation and pus and the consequent enlargement was due to a secretion in the system that found lodgment in the tonsils and that the removal of the tonsils in no way remedied the difficulty, the poison being generated in the system. He purposed to give his knowledge to the public for their protection from useless operations that he regarded as criminal.

GOD'S WAY IN CONTRAST TO MAN'S WAY

What then, did Jesus have in mind as better than the world's systems of healing, which He never used or countenanced? God's remedy is a person, not a thing. The remedy that Jesus ministered to the sick was a spiritual one. It was the Holy Spirit of God. The tangible, living quality and nature of the living God, ministered through the soul and hands of Jesus Christ to the sick one.

---

[28] Jeremiah 46:11, paraphrased.

So conscious was the woman who was healed of the issue of blood that she had received the remedy, and of its effect and power in her upon only touching the hem of His garment, that she "felt in her body that she was made whole of that plague." Jesus likewise was aware of the transmission of the healing power, for He said, "Someone hath touched me, for I perceive that virtue has gone out of me."[29]

This same virtue was ministered through the hands of the apostles and of the seventy. It was also ministered by the early Christians when they received from God, through the Holy Ghost, the ability to minister the Spirit of God to others. Of the twelve apostles it is said,

> He...gave them power and authority over all devils, and to cure diseases. And he sent them to preach the kingdom of God, and to heal the sick.
>
> — Luke 9:1-2

Of the seventy it is written

> He sent them two by two into every city and place whither he himself would come, and said unto them, *heal the sick that are therein,* and say to them, the kingdom of God is come nigh unto you.[30]

So vital was this living Spirit of God and its healing virtue in the lives of the early Christians, that it is recorded of Paul that they brought handkerchiefs and aprons to him, that they might touch his body, and when these were laid upon the sick they were healed and the demons went out of them. (See Acts 19.) In this instance even inanimate objects, handkerchiefs and aprons, were receptacles for the Spirit of God, imparted to them from the Holy Spirit-filled person of the apostle Paul.

This was not an experience for the early Christian alone, but is the common experience of men and women everywhere who have dared to disbelieve the devil's lie, so carefully fostered and proclaimed by the church at large, that the days of miracles are past.

---

[29] See Luke 8:43-48.

[30] Luke 10:1,9, paraphrased.

Every advanced Christian who has gone out into God, who has felt the thrill of His Spirit, who has dared to believe that the Son of God lives by the Spirit in his life today, just as He lived in the lives of the early Christians, has found the same pregnant power of God in himself. Upon laying his hands in faith upon others who are sick, he has seen with his own eyes the healing of the sick take place and realized the transmission of divine virtue. Today, millions of men and women trust God only, for the healing of their body from every character and form of disease.

What, then, is this means of healing that Jesus gave as a divine gift to Christianity forever? It is the living *Holy* Spirit of God, ministered by Jesus Christ to the Christian soul, transmitted by the Christian because of his faith in the word of Jesus, through his soul and his hands to the one who is sick. This reveals the law of contact in the mind of Jesus when He gave the commandment: "They shall lay hands on the sick, and they *shall* recover" (Mark 16:18).

With praise to God we record to His glory, that through twenty-five years in this ministry we have seen hundreds of thousands of persons in many parts of the world, healed by the power of God. Throughout these twenty-five years, in different lands, we have established churches and societies composed of Christian men and women who know no remedy but the one divine remedy, the Lord Jesus Christ. They have faith in His redemption and in the presence and power of the Spirit of Christ to destroy sin and sickness in the lives of men forever.

In our own city, for five years, no day has passed in which we have not seen the healing of many. For five years we have ministered, with our associate pastors, in The Church at Spokane alone, to an average of two hundred sick per day, who come from all quarters of the land and even from foreign countries, to receive the healing power of God. These healings have included almost every known form of disease.

The majority of these healings have been of persons pronounced hopeless by their physicians. Many of them had spent their all, some tens of thousands of dollars, for doctors, medicines, and operations. They found the Lord Jesus Christ and the ministry of healing by the power of God just as efficacious today as it ever was, thereby demonstrating the truth of the Word of God.

CONSECRATION PRAYER

My God and Father,

In Jesus' name I come to Thee. Take me as I am. Make me what I ought to be in spirit, in soul, in body. Give me power to do right. If I have wronged any, to repent, to confess, to restore — no matter what it costs. Wash me in the blood of Jesus, that I may now become Thy child and manifest Thee in a perfect spirit, a holy mind, and a sickless body, to the glory of God. — Amen

"PEACE BE TO THIS HOUSE" — AND WHY

he Lord appointed other seventy also, and sent them two and two before his face into every city and place, whither he himself would come... And into whatsoever house ye enter, first say, Peace be to this house.

— Luke 10:1,5

The Seventies of the Church at Portland, 129 Fourth St., (third floor) are going to every home in Portland with this message because our Lord Himself would come to every home:

First — To save from sin.

Second — To heal from all sickness.

Third — To lead you into the way of holiness. To save you and yours body, soul, and spirit, both in this life and the one to come.

Preachers everywhere say that the Lord will save you from sin, or at least from the consequences of it, but when it comes to the ailments of the body or, in fact, anything at all that is tangible or subject to demonstrable proof of any kind, they hold aloof, if indeed, they do not openly deny it. Sometime, somewhere, somehow in some indeterminate place or state at a future time, when and where nobody in creation can tell, God is ready to do something — nobody knows what or how; but as to any real vital ministry to present-day necessities there is almost none of it.

If Christianity is not a real, vital ministry to real, vital needs of today it is not worth considering. But it is. And because we know that it is and that it is even more than we have claimed or can claim for it, we are vitally concerned to have all men everywhere made acquainted with it.

We speak not only from the Word of God but from experimental knowledge. We have put it to the test — not once, nor a hundred times, but scores of thousands. It is of daily occurrence. Just a list of the names of those who have received healing and other helps through the prayers of the members of this church would fill a good sized book. Here are a few of the cases.

What the Lord Is Doing Among Us Every Day

From the recent testimonies given in Dr. Lake's Thursday 3:00 p.m. Divine Healing Meetings.

Mrs. Musselwhite, Goodenough Building: I was almost blind. My physicians said they could not help me; I would be blind. Dr. Lake ministered to me through prayer and laying on of hands, and the Lord restored my sight and healed the disease, and I can see to read now. Praise God.

Joseph Maplethorpe, foreman of Portland Woolen Mills, St. Johns, Oregon: I was stricken with very death. Sixteen doctors had given up my case. I was in the agonies of hell. Mine was not just a healing of disease. I was veritably raised from the dead. As prayer was offered, Jesus appeared to me and put His arms about me, saved my soul and healed my body.

Miss Nelson, professional nurse: The aperture to my stomach began to close. My doctors did their best, but could not heal me. I was in a sanitarium for months. Then I came here through the influence of friends, and the blessed Lord healed me entirely. I am sound and well and working every day.

Mrs. Copeland: I have just been healed of a terrible inward goiter that was strangling me to death. I desire to render praise to God for my healing and to thank Dr. Lake and all the dear people of this church who prayed so earnestly for my healing.

Mrs. Ida laVeres, 1610 Chautaqua Street: I suffered with appendicitis. My doctor ordered my room arranged for an operation and sent the ambulance for me. My nurse advised me to send for Dr. Lake, as she had herself been healed through prayer. He prayed, the Lord healed me. The ambulance came to the door, but I was healed and am in perfect health. And best of all, I found my Lord and Savior Jesus Christ, to me, both Savior and healer evermore.

Mrs. Herndon: I was born with a crooked back, almost a hunch back. I developed a tumor of the bladder when I was forty-six years old. I was instantly healed of this tumor when Dr. Lake prayed. My back snapped five times as hands were laid on me in prayer, and in one minute I was straight as I am today. How I love to praise God for it all.

These are only a few representative cases. We cite them to show, not what hairsplitting doctrinal questions we might raise, but what is actually being accomplished in this day and generation in the city of Portland, and we can multiply them a thousand times.

We believe in a Gospel that can be demonstrated, and we prove it.

The Poor Have the Gospel Preached to Them

This is what we are doing daily; going about among the poor and the lame and the halt and the blind, sin-stricken and disease-smitten, ministering God's love and power, fulfilling once more the declaration of Jesus, concerning the mark and stamp of real Christianity, "The poor have the gospel preached to them."[1]

These Signs Shall Follow Them That Believe

> In my name shall they cast out devils; they shall speak with new tongues; they shall take up serpents; and if they drink any deadly thing, it shall not hurt them; they shall lay hands on the sick, and they shall recover.

— Mark 16:17-18

---

[1] Matthew 11:5.

n the *Spokane Daily Chronicle* of January 17th, there appeared a condensed report of a sermon by the

LETTER TO THE EDITOR

Reverend F. E. Beattey of the Lidgerwood Presbyterian Church. The article is head-lined "Healing by Faith Can't Be Expected."

The article presents so much absurdity that it is difficult to imagine that it was actually delivered to an intelligent congregation.

The reverend gentleman stated that Jesus said to His disciples, "As my Father hath sent me, even so send I you."[1]

"Jesus' work may be summed up under three general heads, preaching, teaching, and healing," he says. "The church, therefore, is to preach the truths of eternal salvation and eternal punishment. Teach the Word of God that men may know the Scriptures, which will make them wise unto salvation, and also make known the fact that the sick are not to be neglected."

He states the fact of Jesus' ministry as teaching and preaching and healing. He quotes the words of Jesus, "As the Father hath sent me, even so send I you." Nobody with sense could imagine that the disciples were sent to do anything else than what Jesus had done, in the manner He had done it. Is the disciple going to accomplish by another method different from the method of Jesus, the thing Jesus sent him to do? If the sick are to be healed, then we must discover how Jesus healed and how the disciples healed. In Luke 9:1-6, we distinctly read that "He called unto him his twelve disciples and *gave them* power and authority over all devils, and to cure diseases, and sent them to preach the kingdom of God and heal the sick" (paraphrased).

He did not present them with a medicine kit. He sent them with the conscious power of God upon their lives, with spiritual dominion over sickness and demon powers. The Scriptures abound with healings through the ministry of the apostles. There is no question in any intelligent mind as to what the method was.

---

[1] John 20:21.

In connection with the revival in the city of Samaria, it is distinctly recorded in Acts 8:6-7,

> The people with one accord gave heed unto those things which Philip spake, hearing and seeing the miracles which he did. For unclean spirits, crying with loud voice, came out of many that were possessed with them: and many taken with palsies, and that were lame, were healed.

These healings took place, not at the hands of the original twelve, to whom the power had first been given, but now at the hands of a new disciple, Philip.

The reverend gentleman says further, "I believe in the power of prayer, and I believe that some have been healed through prayer. Paul the greatest apostle of the early church besought God for help because of an infirmity, but he was not healed or given relief." We would like to inquire what this statement is based upon. If we can read the Scriptures correctly, certainly Paul was healed. He had prayed three times. He was not healed the first time, nor the second time, but he prayed the third time and declares that the Lord said to him, "Paul, my grace is sufficient for you."[2]

Surely the grace of God is sufficient for every man. It was sufficient for Paul's need too. The assertions that he was not healed is one of the centuries-old theological jokes. Does our reverend friend expect a 1916 audience to believe that Paul was not healed when he prayed?

Again, there is not the least evidence in the Scriptures that he needed any healing. What his "thorn in the flesh" was is a pure conjecture. One thing we know, Paul was not only healed himself when blind, through the laying on of the hands of Ananias, but that he himself healed others.[3]

On his way to Rome when his ship was wrecked, he healed the father of the governor of the island, and many others.[4] The assertion that he was not healed himself is almost as stale an argument as the reference to Luke as the beloved physician.[5] Jesus was a beloved physician too.

---

[2] 2 Corinthians 12:9, paraphrased.

[3] Paul healed, Acts 9:17-18. Paul heals, Acts 14:9-11 and Acts 28:8.

[4] See Acts 28:8.

[5] See Colossians 4:14.

So were each of the apostles. So is any man who brings healing to the sick. There is not the least evidence in the Scriptures that Luke ever owned a medicine kit in his life, and if he did, he most certainly left it behind him when he accepted the ministry and power of the Lord Jesus Christ.

Our land is filled with men who have been physicians and who have abandoned the practice for the better way and method of the Lord Jesus Christ. Dr. Finnis B. Yoakum, of Los Angeles, California, one of the leading physicians of his city, abandoned the practice of medicine and adopted the ministry of healing through the prayer of faith and the laying on of hands, as the superior method. Dr. W. D. Gentry, of Chicago, a writer on diagnosis, whose treatise on the subject are found in every first-class library, abandoned his practice of medicine and for years has ministered in the name of Jesus, through the prayer of faith and laying on of hands as Jesus commanded. Likewise Dr. A. B. Simpson of New York, a leading osteopath, abandoned his practice of medicine, and many others.

Each one of these are "beloved physicians," but they do not give pills. They have graduated into the higher way.

What a strange thing it is when Christian ministers are found endeavoring to dodge the real issue of healing, instead of building up faith in God. In many cases, they are among the first to endeavor to break it down and try and explain away by some cunning method the real plain facts of the Scriptures. How much more honorable it would be if ministers would acknowledge, as they should, that Christ has not changed, that faith is the same quality it ever was, but that they do not possess it and so are not able to secure answers to prayer for the sick.

Reverend Andrew Murray, the head of the Dutch Reform Church of South Africa, whose books are throughout all Christendom and who is generally recognized as one of the saints of this age, was dying of an incurable throat disease. The physicians of Africa gave him no hope. He came to London, England, but received no hope from the medical men there. He went to Bagster's Bethsan Divine Healing Home and was perfectly healed.

He returned to South Africa and wrote a book on the subject of healing, and it was placed on sale by the church. After a little while, the ministers of the Dutch Reform Church discussed it in conferences. They said, "If we leave this book in circulation the people will read it. Then the next thing we know they will ask us to pray the prayer of faith that saves the sick, and we have not the faith to do it, and our jobs will be in danger." So it was decided to withdraw the book from circulation.

Why not give the people the light of the scriptures? Let them know that Jesus is the healer still, that He empowers men today through the Holy Spirit, to heal the sick, just as He ever did. That the Spirit of God is not obtained through the Church, but that it comes upon the soul of man, straight from God Himself when necessary hundredfold consecration is made.

John G. Lake

I am going to read a familiar portion of the Word of God. It is the Lord's Prayer as recorded in the eleventh chapter of Luke.

I purpose this afternoon to speak on this subject, "Have Christians a right to pray, 'If it be Thy will' concerning sickness?" Personally, I do not believe they have, and I am going to give you my reasons.

HAVE CHRISTIANS A RIGHT TO PRAY "IF IT BE THY WILL" CONCERNING HEALING?

> And it came to pass, that, as he was praying in a certain place, when he ceased, one of his disciples said unto him, Lord, teach us to pray, as John also taught his disciples. And he said unto them, When ye pray, say, Our Father which art in heaven, Hallowed be thy name. Thy kingdom come. Thy will be done, as in heaven, so in earth. Give us day by day our daily bread. And forgive us our sins; for we also forgive every one that is indebted to us. And lead us not into temptation; but deliver us from evil.

— Luke 11:1-4

Beloved, if there is one thing in the world I wish I could do for the people of Spokane, it would be to teach them to pray. Not teach them to say prayers, but teach them to pray. There is a mighty lot of difference between saying prayers and praying.

> The prayer of *faith* shall save the sick, and the Lord shall raise him up; and if he have committed sins, they shall be forgiven him.[1]

---

[1] James 5:15, emphasis Lake's.

The prayer of faith has power in it. The prayer of faith has trust in it. The prayer of faith has healing in it for soul and body. The disciples wanted to know how to pray real prayers, and Jesus said unto them, "When ye pray say, Our Father which art in heaven...thy will be done."

Everybody stops there, and they resign their intelligence at that point to the unknown God. When you approach people and say to them, "You have missed the spirit of the prayer," they look at you in amazement. But, beloved, it is a fact. I want to show it to you this afternoon as it is written in the Word of God. It does not say, "If it be thy will" and stop there. There is a comma there, not a period. The prayer is this, "Thy will be done on earth as it is done in heaven." That is mighty different, is it not? Not "Thy will be done."

"Let the calamity come. Let my children be stricken with fever or my son go to the insane asylum or my daughter go to the home of the feebleminded." That is not what Jesus was teaching the people to pray. Jesus was teaching the people to pray, "Thy will be done on earth as it is in heaven." Let the might of God be known. Let the power of God descend. Let God avert the calamity that is coming. Let it turn aside through faith in God. "Thy will be done on earth (here) as it is in heaven."

How is the will of God done in heaven? For a little time I want to direct your thought with mine, heavenward. We step over there and we look all about the city. We note its beauty and its grandeur. We see the Lamb of God. We do not observe a single drunken man on the golden streets, not a single man on crutches, not a woman smelling of sin.

A man came in the other day and was telling me what an ardent Christian he is. But after he left, I said, "Lift the windows and let the balance of the man out." Men ought to smell like they pray. We defile ourselves with many things.

A dear man came to me the other day in great distress. He said his eyes were going blind. The physician told him he had only a year of sight, perhaps less. As I endeavored to comfort him and turn his face toward God, I reverently put my hands on his eyes and asked God for Christ's sake to heal him, and as I did so the Spirit of God kept speaking to my soul and saying "Amaurosis." I said, "What is amaurosis?"

As soon as I could get to the dictionary, I looked up the word to see what it is. It is a disease of the eyes, caused by the use of nicotine. That was what was the matter with the man. The Spirit of the Lord was trying to tell me, but I was too dull. I did not understand. I do not know what the man's name is, but the other day God sent him back to my office. As we sat together I related the incident to him and said, "My brother, when you quit poisoning yourself, the probability is that you may not need any healing from God."

We defile ourselves in various ways. We go on defiling ourselves and some people are able to stand the defilement a long time and throw it off. Others are not able to. It poisons their system and destroys their faculties. One man may drink whiskey and live to be an old man. Another may go to wreck in a few months or years. Some systems will throw off much, others will not.

Now, when we get to the beautiful city, we did not find any of these conditions, and so we say, "Angel, what is the reason you do not have any sin up here?"

"Why, the reason we do not have any sin here is because *the will of God is being done.*"

I have been used to looking for the sick and if I see a man with a lame leg or a woman with a blind eye, I will see that a way down the street. I have mingled with the sick all my life. So I look around up there, and I do not see anybody on crutches or anybody that is lame, no cancers or consumption, or any sickness at all. So I say to my guide, "Angel, tell me what the reason is that you do not have any sickness up here."

The angel replies, *"The will of God is being done here."* No sin where the will of God is being done. No sickness where the will of God is being done.

Then I return to the earth, and I can pray that prayer with a new understanding. "Thy will be done in me on earth as Thy will is done in heaven." Just as the will of God is done there, so let the will of God be done here. Let the will of God be done in me. "Thy will be done, as in heaven, so in earth."

But someone says, "Brother, do you not remember in the eighth of Matthew how a leper came to Jesus one day and said to Him, 'Lord, *if thou wilt,* thou canst make me clean'? The leper said, when he prayed, 'If it be thy will,' why should I not say that too." Well, he was ignorant of what the will of Christ was concerning sickness. Perhaps he had been up on the mountainside and had heard Jesus preach that wonderful sermon on the mount. For it was at its close that he came to Jesus and said, "If thou wilt, thou canst make me clean."[2]

He knew Christ's ability to heal but did not understand his willingness. Jesus' reply settled the question for the leper and it should settle the question for every other man forever. Jesus said, *"I will;* be thou clean."[3] If He ever had said anything else to any other man, there might be some reason for us to interject "If it be thy will," in our prayers when we ask God for something He has declared His will on. *If* always doubts. The prayer of faith has no ifs in it.

Suppose a drunken man kneels down at this platform and says, "I want to find God. I want to be a Christian." Every man and woman in this house who knows God would say, "yes," right away. "Tell him to pray, to have faith in God, and God will deliver him." Why do you do it? Simply because there is no question in your mind concerning God's will in saving a sinner from his sins. You know He is ready to do it when a sinner is ready to confess his sin. But you take another step over, and here is another poor fellow by his side with a lame leg, and he comes limping along and kneels down, or tries to, and right away a lot of folks say, "I wish he would send for a doctor," or also pray, "If it be thy will, make him well," forgetting "who forgiveth all thine iniquities; who healeth all thy diseases."[4]

Instead of Christians taking the responsibility, they try to put the responsibility on God. Everything there is in the redemption of Jesus Christ is available for man when man will present his claim in faith and take it. There is no question in the mind of God concerning the salvation of a sinner. No more is there concerning the healing of the sick

---

[2] Matthew 8:2.

[3] Matthew 8:3.

[4] Psalm 103:3.

one. It is in the atonement of Jesus Christ, bless God. His atonement was unto the *uttermost* — to the last need of man. The responsibility rests purely, solely, and entirely on man. Jesus put it there.

Jesus said, *"When* ye pray, believe that ye receive, and *ye shall have."*[5] No questions or ifs in the words of Jesus. If He ever spoke with emphasis on any question, it was on the subject of God's will and the result of faith in prayer. Indeed, He did not even speak to them in ordinary words, but in the custom of the East, He said, "Verily, verily."[6] Amen, amen — the same as if I would stand in an American court and say, "I swear I will tell the truth, the whole truth, and nothing but the truth, so help me God." So the easterner raised his hand and said, "Amen, amen," or "Verily, verily — with the solemnity of an oath I say unto you." So Jesus said, "When ye pray, believe that ye receive, and ye shall have."

James, in expounding the subject, says concerning those that doubt, "Let not that man think that he shall receive any thing of the Lord."[7] Why? Well, he says, "A man that doubteth is like a wave of the sea, driven with the wind and tossed."[8] There is no continuity in his prayer. There is no continuity in his faith. There is no continuity in his character. There is no concentration in God for the thing that he wants. He is like the waves of the sea, scattered and shattered, driven here and there by the wind because there is *if* in it. "Let not that man think he shall receive anything of the Lord."

Now that leper did not know what the mind of Jesus was concerning sickness. Perhaps he had seen others healed of ordinary diseases, but leprosy was a terrible thing. It was incurable and contagious. The poor man was compelled as he went down the road to cry out, "Unclean! Unclean!" in order that people might run away from him.

In my work in South Africa I saw dozens of them, hundreds of them, thousands of them. I have seen them with their fingers off of the first joint, at the second joint, with their thumbs off, or nose off, their

---

[5] Mark 11:24, paraphrased.

[6] This phrase is used throughout the book of John.

[7] James 1:7.

[8] James 1:6, paraphrased.

teeth gone, the toes off, the body scaling off, and I have seen God heal them in every stage. On one occasion in our work, a company of healed lepers gathered on Christmas Eve and partook of the Lord's Supper. Some had no fingers on their hands, and they had to take the cup between their wrists, but the Lord had been there and healed them.

That was not under my ministry, but under the ministry of a poor, black fellow, who for five or six years did not even wear pants. He wore a goat skin apron. But he came to Christ. He touched the living One. He received the power of God, and he manifests a greater measure of the real healing gift than I believe any man ever has in modern times. And if I were over there, I would kneel down and ask that black man to put his hands on my head and ask God to let the same power of God come into my life that he has in his.

You have no more right to pray "If it be Thy will" concerning your sickness than the leper had. Not as much, because for two thousand years the Word of God has been declared and the Bible has been an open book. We ought to be intelligent beyond any other people in the world concerning the mind of God.

"But Brother," someone says, "you have surely forgotten that when Jesus was in the garden He prayed, 'Lord, if it be possible, let this cup pass from me. Nevertheless, not as I will, but as thou wilt.'"[9] No, I have not forgotten. You are not the Savior of the world, beloved. That was Jesus' prayer. No other man could ever pray that prayer but the Lord Jesus. But I want to show you, beloved, what caused Jesus to pray that prayer, because a lot of folks have never understood it.

Jesus had gone into the garden to pray. The burden of His life was upon Him. He was about to depart. He has a message for the world. He had been compelled to commit it to a few men — ignorant men. I believe that He wondered, "Will they be able to present the vision? Will they see it as I have seen it? Will they be able to let the people have it as I have given it to them?" No doubt these were some of the inquiries, besides many more.

---

[9] Matthew 26:39, paraphrased.

Do you know what the spirit of intercession is? Do you know what it means when a man comes along, as Moses did, and takes upon himself the burden of the sin of the people and then goes down in tears and repentance unto God until the people are brought back in humility and repentance to His feet? When in anxiety for his race and people, Moses said, "Lord, if you forgive not this people, blot my name out of thy book."[10] He did not want any heaven where his people were not.

Think of it! Moses took upon himself that responsibility, and he said to God, "If you forgive not this people, blot my name out of thy book." God heard Moses' prayer, bless God!

Paul, on one occasion, wrote practically the same words. "I would be accursed for my brethren, my kinsmen according to the flesh."[11] He felt the burden of his people. So Jesus in the garden felt the burden of the world, the accumulated sorrows of mankind, their burdens of sin, their burdens of sickness. And as He knelt to pray, His heart breaking under it, the great drops of sweat came out on His brow like blood falling to the ground. But the critics have said, "It was not blood."

Judge V. V. Barnes, in his great trial before Judge Landis, actually sweat blood until his handkerchief would be red with the blood that oozed through his pores. His wife said that for three months she was compelled to put napkins over his pillow. That is one of the biggest men God has ever let live in the world. His soul was big, and he saw the possibility of the hour for a great people and desired as far as he could to make that burden easy for them. He did not want the estate to go into the hands of a receiver. The interests of one hundred thousand people was in his hands, the accumulated properties of families who had no other resource. He was so large that the burden of his heart bore down on him so that he sweat blood, and did so for three months. But people of these days say, "It looked like blood," and are so teaching their Sunday school scholars. The Lord have mercy on them! The blood came out and fell down to the ground.

---

[10] Exodus 32:32, paraphrased.

[11] Romans 9:3, paraphrased.

Jesus thought He was going to die right there in the garden, but He was too big to die there. He wanted to go to the cross. He wanted to see this thing finished on behalf of the race of man, and so He prayed, "Lord, if it be possible, let this cup pass from me. Nevertheless, not as I will, but as thou wilt."[12] What was the cup? What is the cup of suffering that was breaking Him down, that was draining the life blood out right then and that would be His death instead of the cross? But He towered above that and prayed, "Lord, if it be possible, let this cup pass from me. Nevertheless, not as I will, but as thou wilt." Instantly, the angels came and ministered to Him and in the new strength He received, He went to the cross and to His death as the Savior of mankind.

Beloved, I want to tell you that if there was a little sweating of blood and that kind of prayer, there would be less sickness and sin than there is. God is calling for a people who will take upon them that kind of burden and let the power of God work through them.

People look in amazement in these days when God answers prayer for a soul. A week ago last night, my dear wife and I went down to pray for a soul on the Fort Wright line, a Mrs. McFarland. She is going to be here one of these days to give her testimony. Ten years ago a tree fell on her and broke her back. She became paralyzed, and for ten years she has been in a wheelchair, her limbs swollen, and her feet a great senseless lump that hang down useless. She says many preachers have visited her in these years, and they have told her to be reconciled to the will of God, to sit still and suffer longer.

She said, "Oh, I would not mind not walking. If the pain would just stop for a little while, it would be so good." We lovingly laid our hands upon her and prayed. You say, "Did you pray, 'If it be Thy will'?" No! You bet I did not, but I laid my hands on that dear soul and prayed, "You devil that has been tormenting this woman for ten years and causing the tears to flow, I rebuke you in the name of the Son of God. And by the authority of the Son of God I cast you out."

Something happened. Life began to flow into her being, and the pain left. In a little while, she discovered that power was coming back into

---

[12] Matthew 26:39, paraphrased.

her body. She called me up the other day and said, "Oh, such a wonderful thing has taken place. This morning in bed I could get up on my hands and knees." Poor soul, she called in her neighbors and relatives because she could get on her hands and knees in bed.

Do you know you have painted Jesus Christ as a man without a soul? You have painted God to the world as a tyrant. On the other hand, He is reaching out His hands in love to stricken mankind desiring to lift them up. But He has put the responsibility of the whole matter on you and me. That question of the *will of God* was everlastingly settled long ago — eternally settled — no question about the will of God.

The redemption of Jesus Christ was an uttermost redemption, to the last need of the human heart, bless God, for body, for soul, for spirit. He is a Christ and Savior even to the uttermost. Blessed be His name. Who shall dare to raise a limit to the accomplishment of faith through Jesus Christ? I am glad the tendency is to take down the barriers and let all the faith of your heart go out to God for every man and for every condition of life, to let the love of God flow out of your soul to every hungry soul.

Instead of praying, "Lord, if it be thy will," when you kneel beside your sick friend, Jesus Christ has commanded you and every *believer* to lay *your* hands on the sick. This is not my ministry, nor my brethren's only. It is the ministry of every believer. And if your ministers do not believe it, God have mercy on them; and if your churches do not believe it, God have mercy on them.

In these days, the churches are screaming and crying because Christian Science is swallowing up the world, and that it is false, etc. Why do the people go to Christian Science? Because they cannot get any truth where they are. Let the day come when the voices of men ring out and tell the people the truth about the Son of God, who is a redeemer even unto the uttermost for body and soul and spirit. He redeems back to God. Beloved, believe it and receive the blessing that will come into your own life. Amen.

here are four modes of healing, and more than that. But four principle modes

MODES OF HEALING

taught in the Word of God. The first is the *direct prayer of faith* of those, who just like the leper, come to Jesus and say, "Lord, if thou wilt, thou canst make *me* clean." Jesus answered the leper, *"I will; be thou clean."*[1] And His *I will* has rung down through the ages, for He healed *all that came to Him.*[2] He never turned one of them away. And in healing all that came to Him, He demonstrated forever what the will of God concerning sickness was.

"But, brother" you say, "are all the people healed that you pray for?" *No*, they are not, and it is my sorrow, for I believe that if I was in the place before God where Old Peter was and Paul was, bless God, all the people would be healed. And it is the purpose of my soul to let God take my soul into that place of real communion and consciousness of the power of God, through Jesus Christ, where all the people, and not some of the people, are healed.

However, beloved, I want to say God made me too much of a man to try to dodge the issue and throw the responsibility off on God. My! How the Church has worked at this acrobatic trick of throwing the responsibility over on God.

> These signs shall follow them that believe...they shall lay hands on the sick, and they shall recover.[3]

Now here is a sick man, and here comes the minister. As he gets close to him he sees he is pretty bad. He is in trouble. He says to himself, "If I pray for him and he is not healed, the people will think I have not much faith in God." So he does the acrobatic trick and says, "It may not be the will of God that you should be healed." Do you see it?

---

[1] Matthew 8:2-3, Mark 1:40-41, and Luke 5:12-13.

[2] See Matthew 4:24, 8:16, 12:15, 14:14, 15:30, 19:2, Mark 1:34, 6:13, Luke 4:40, 6:19, 9:11.

[3] Mark 16:17-18.

How many did Jesus heal? *All* that came to Him, and in healing them all He gave to mankind forever the finality concerning the will of God about healing the sick.

There is no further to go in demonstration than Jesus went on the subject of the will of God. If He had ever turned one poor fellow away and said, "No, it is not God's will to heal you," then there could be a question mark set up, but having healed them all, He left the will of God concerning sickness forever settled and indelibly stamped forever on the human mind.

I am glad we know that kind of a Christ. An awful lot of people have been sent down the broad way through that old lie about the will of God and sickness.

"Well, brother," you say, "how are you going to get the people to heaven, if they are all healed? Why, they will live forever." Well, bless God, I am going one step further. However, we have not reached the place of faith yet where it is applicable in our lives. We are still discussing healing for the body.

Jesus said,

> Your fathers ate manna in the wilderness and are dead, but he that eateth of the bread that I shall give him shall *never die*. Believest thou this?[4]

> And they turned away and walked no more with Him. They said, "This is a hard saying, who can receive it?"[5]

The faith of the Church has never reached up to the place where we could dare to claim it, but beloved, I praise God that an ever-increasing number of men and women are raising up every day, who will enjoy stepping over the boundary into that hundredfold consecration, where they will consecrate once and forever their *body*, and their *soul* and their *spirit* to God. Blessed be His name.

The consecration of our body to God is just as sacred as the consecration of our soul. No man can understand what the Christian life

---

[4] John 6:49-50 and John 11:26, paraphrased.

[5] John 6:66, paraphrased.

ought to be, what Jesus intended it to be, until they see the consecration that He made of Himself to the will of God. It is a pattern consecration for every other Christian. He was the first Christian, blessed be God. He consecrated His spirit to God, His soul to God, His body to God. Each were equally precious in the sight of God. Think of it!

Suppose that just once in His lifetime, when in trouble concerning the things of the Spirit, He had gone to the devil for help. Would He have been the spotless Lamb of God? Never! He would have been blemished. Suppose that in His mental distress, He had turned to the world for help and accepted the spirit of the world as His comforter. He would have been blemished in His soul life. He would not have been the spotless Lamb of God. Suppose one morning you would see the Lord Jesus sneaking around the back door into a drugstore, to get ten cents worth of pills for His body. Can you imagine such a thing? It is too horrible to imagine. If He had He would never have been the spotless Lamb of God. He would have been blemished in His faith for His body before His Father.

But because the Christ demonstrated His power to trust God for His spirit, for His soul, and for His body, He became the author of eternal salvation, and was able to present Himself to God a spotless conqueror and unblemished sacrifice.

And the hundredfold Christian, who received through the Holy Ghost the power of God and the dominion of the spirit, will present himself to God in the same manner, body and soul and spirit unto God, a reasonable sacrifice and service. Blessed be His precious name.

> Know ye not that your bodies are the temples of the Holy Ghost, which dwelleth in you?[6]

Shall I take this temple that I endeavor, by the grace of God, to lend to God for the purpose that He may dwell in my life by the Spirit, and fill it up with cocaine or digitalis or some of the other thousand and one damnable things that destroy human life and produce abnormal conditions in the system? Never, if I am a hundredfold child of God!

---

[6] 1 Corinthians 6:19, paraphrased.

Here again is the ministerial acrobat with the gifts of the Holy Ghost.

> To one is given by the Spirit the word of wisdom; to another the word of knowledge by the same Spirit; to another faith by the same Spirit; to another the gifts of healing by the same Spirit; to another the working of miracles; to another prophecy; to another discerning of spirits; to another divers kinds of tongues; to another the interpretation of tongues.[7]

Paul says correctly, that not all have these various gifts. That is perfectly correct. But beloved, the subject of gifts has nothing whatever to do with the principle of faith in God. The gifts are entirely extraordinary. The normal life of a real Christian with faith in God commands the power of God for his own need through *faith*. Have you ever noticed that the anointing of oil and the prayer of faith saves the sick have nothing to do with the *gift* of healing?[8] It is an entirely different operation of healing. The elder or the priest comes in the name of Jesus. He anoints the man with oil, and prays the prayer of faith. The prayer that expresses my faith in God that He will raise this man up. That is the *prayer of faith*. It is not the *gift of healing* at all. Simply the prayer of faith.

How far is it applicable? Jesus said,

> If two of you shall agree on earth as touching any thing concerning my kingdom, it shall be done for them of my Father which is in heaven.[9]

The first healing I ever knew was the healing of a Roman Catholic girl who had formerly worked for my wife. Seven members in her family died of consumption between the ages of eighteen and twenty-one. She was the last of the family. At the age of twenty the disease appeared in her likewise. She was engaged to be married to a splendid fellow, but day by day she withered away, just as the others had done.

---

[7] 1 Corinthians 12:8-10.

[8] See James 5:15.

[9] Matthew 18:19, paraphrased.

In those days I knew nothing about healing through God. A friend came to her and said, "Mary, let us observe a venue." That is nine days of prayer. These two women, without any help from anyone, and who knew little or nothing of the Word of God, believing in the Christ as their Savior, began to pray throughout the nine days that God by His mighty power would raise the woman up. Her friend said, "When the Lord heals you, get up and come to my house." So on the ninth morning, when the time was complete and Mary did not appear at the friend's house, she got troubled and started down to see about it and on the road, met her coming. God had met the faith of two poor, simple women who had no teaching whatever on the subject of healing.

Among all the classes of people who come to our healing rooms, we find that Roman Catholics receive healing more readily than any other particular class of church people. You ask me why. They are educated to have faith in God. They are not educated to doubt Him. A great deal of modern preaching is an education in doubt concerning God. If you cannot explain the thing and you cannot demonstrate it, over you go, turn a somersault, tell them it means something else.

A friend of mine in the city, who is a ministerial brother, used to be my pastor in the Methodist church when I was a young man. He was assistant pastor. Now he is one of the great ecclesiastical lights. I remember a sermon of his. He was explaining the fall of the walls of Jericho. Paul says: "By faith the walls of Jericho fell down, after they were compassed about seven days."[10] By *faith*, by the united faith of the people who dared to believe God, the very walls crumbled and came down. Their instructions were to compass the city seven days and on the seventh day to compass it seven times, and when the final march was completed, the priests, with their trumpets and their rams' horns, were to sound a blast of triumph to God, and the people were to give the shout of faith. When they had sounded, the walls came down, *by faith*.

My friend very wisely said, "Every structure has a key note, and if you just find and sound the key note of the structure, down it will come.

---

[10] Hebrews 11:30.

The wise priests sounded the key note and down the walls of Jericho came." That was his vision. Paul had a different one. He said, "By faith the walls of Jericho fell down after they were compassed about seven days."

Faith is not always characterized by beautiful phrases, nor sweet prayers. I had a minister in my work in South Africa, a very strong, vigorous man. He had a military training, he was an officer in the army during the Boer war. His name was W. I had a another minister, who was a nice, sweet, gentle, tender man. He had none of the strong qualities that W possessed, but he loved God and had faith in Him.

One evening a Church of England minister sent in a call about his wife, who was dying of a cancer. The doctors could do nothing more, and now they wanted to trust God. That is where a lot of people get. God Almighty have mercy on you. That is what we call "Last Resorters." We have an expression among ourselves, "Is he a last resorter?"

I reasoned that it would never do to send Brother W down to that house, because he was such a strenuous man. He was likely to shock them. I said, "I will send Brother J, because he is one of those nice polished men." So he went down and prayed for quite a long time. The rector knelt reverently at the foot of the bed and prayed with him, but there was no evidence of a real healing. After awhile the telephone rang, and Brother J was on the line. He said, "Brother Lake, I wish you would send W down here. I cannot get the victory, and I need help."

I said, "Surely, brother." So I told Brother W to go down and help him. He said, "All right I will go," and away he started. When he arrived, he said, "What is the trouble, Brother J?"

He said, "I do not know."

W said, "Let us pray again." As he prayed he said, "You damned cancer, get to hell out of here, in the name of Jesus Christ." The Spirit of God flamed in him and the power of God fell on the woman. The cancer withered and the woman was healed. After awhile the telephone rang again. Brother J said, "It is all right, brother, she is healed, but the rector has not recovered from the effect of Brother W's prayer yet."

Bless God! There is something better than polished phrases. It is the faith of God that permits a soul to break through the darkness and the doubt that the devil and the world and the unbelieving church has heaped upon the souls of men.

It takes the power of God and the faith of God to break the bands that bind men's souls and get them through into the daylight of God. That is where healing, real healing is found. I wish I could take a whole lot of you sick folks and get you broke through into the presence of God. You would not have to come to the Healing Rooms day after day if you did.

I have a conviction that there are a mighty few Christian ministers who can tell you what divine healing is. In the world at large I know there is a great deal of confusion. There is natural healing, medical healing, psychic healing, and there is divine healing. I am quoting my brother Beatty now. We recognize them all, but I want to tell you, beloved, the real Christian, the hundredfold Christian, the man who gives himself to God and receives the power of God, is not fooling around with medical healing, nor psychic healing either. They are all good enough in their place, but God has given a better way and a higher way. There is as much difference between spiritual and psychic healing as there is between natural or medical, and psychic healing. It is a higher plane and the higher life by a higher power, the power of God through the Holy Spirit.

Jesus demonstrated that to us so beautifully. He was walking down the road. A poor woman with an issue of blood twelve years, said within herself, "If I can but touch His garments, I will be healed."[11] You say that was faith. She could have had faith in a bread pill, because the doctors tell you if you have not faith in them, their drugs will do no good. You see, the virtue is not located in the remedy. It is in what you think of the doctor and your confidence in him. Every good doctor knows that fact.

It was not her faith in the sense we usually talk about faith. It was the virtue that was in Him. "If I could but touch the hem of His garment, I would be whole." How did she know it? Because she saw that those upon whom He laid His hands received virtue and were made whole. The virtue that was in Him, flowed out and healed them. So she stole

---

[11] Matthew 9:21, paraphrased.

up in the crowd and touched the hem of His garment, and bless God, His very clothing was filled with the virtue of God and it flowed from the garment to the woman, and she felt in her body that she was made whole, and Jesus felt it too. Peter said, "Master, don't you see the multitude that is thronging you, and say, 'Somebody touched me.'?"

"Yes, but I perceive that virtue hath gone out of me."[12] Hers was a different touch. It was the touch that received the life of the Christ into her own being.

Divine healing is life. The life of God. Healing is transmitted into your being, whether it comes from heaven upon your own soul, or is transmitted through a man of faith. It does not make any difference. It is the touch of the living Christ.

But you say, "Jesus was Jesus. Other men did not have that virtue." Do you remember old Paul in the nineteenth of Acts, when they brought handkerchiefs and aprons that they might touch his body?[13] Then they were taken to the sick, and the sick were healed. Here is dear old Paul. A mother comes to him. "Oh Paul, I have a sick boy at my house. He is dying of epilepsy, or typhoid fever, or cancer. Paul, here is my apron. Take it so that the Spirit of God will flow into it from your being." Then she takes the apron home with her and puts it on the boy, and the power of God that was in the apron flows out of it into the boy, and the boy is healed. That is divine healing.

So it is with every man who is really baptized in the Holy Ghost. Last Wednesday night, as our service was about to commence, I laid my Bible on the table. A man came in and took up the Bible and dropped it as though it was hot.

Then a woman sitting by reached out and took it up and the power of God came upon her and she commenced to shake. They said, "Isn't that strange!" Not at all. That is the Bible over which Brother West-wood and Brother Fogwill and I kneel in the Healing Rooms and ask God to open its blessed pages, that we may understand the Spirit of the Word of God and receive the power of God that makes these people well. I believe the very paper becomes saturated with the power of God.

---

[12] See Luke 8:43-46.

[13] See Acts 19:12.

Both animate and inanimate objects can become filled with the Spirit of God. Even the bones of those who have trusted in the living God have retained their virtue. The old prophet had been in his grave many a day, when one day in their haste to bury a man, they opened the same grave in which the prophet's bones lay. But when the dead man touched the bones of that Holy Ghost filled man, he became a living man and rose up well.[14]

Oh, the most vital thing in all the universe is the Holy Spirit. It is more real than electricity, more powerful than gravity. It is more subtle than the ether in the air. It contains more energy than any natural power. It is the vitality of the living God, the fire of His soul, the very substance of His being. Bless God! Open your nature to God. Receive the Christ into your heart. Confess your sins and acknowledge the Lord Jesus Christ as your Savior. Receive Him as your Savior and healer *now*, and God will bless you.

Reverend Andrew Murray is a patriarch of the Dutch Reform Church of South Africa. He is about ninety-four years old. One of the most blessed saints and ministers of God that perhaps the world has ever known. Years ago, he was dying of an incurable disease of the throat. The physicians of Africa could do nothing for him. He went to Britain and was treated there by the very best physicians, but was given up to die.

One day he wandered down the street and came to Bagsters Divine Healing Mission. He knelt at the altar. Hands were laid upon him and his throat was healed through and through. He was raised up by the power of God and returned to Africa for thirty-five years more of wonderful ministry for God. His books are known and loved throughout Christendom. He wrote a book on the subject of healing. It was the property of the Dutch Reform Church and was issued by their publishing house.

Then the trouble began. People came to the preachers, saying, "This is Reverend Andrew Murray's book, and he is the head of this church. Now we want you to pray for us."

[The manuscript ends here.]

---

[14] See 2 Kings 13:21.

A boy who was healed under Lake's ministry.

THE HOLY SPIRIT

DISCERNMENT
1 Corinthians 12:8-12

My first great interest in Africa was stimulated when a child, through reading of Livingstone's travels and explorations and of Stanley finding Livingstone in the heart of Africa and still more by reading of Stanley's trip across the continent and down the Congo.[1]

As the years of my boyhood passed, I became conscious of a certain operation of my spirit, which I shall endeavor to describe.

In my sleep, and sometimes during my waking hours, it seemed to me as if I was present in Africa instead of America. At such times I would note the geography of the country, the peculiarities of the landscape, the characteristics of the various tribes of native people. I became deeply sympathetic with the efforts of the Boers as I watched them endeavoring to establish their republics.

As I reached manhood these excursions in the spirit became more intelligent to me. On one occasion while in the attitude of prayer, I approached South Africa from the Indian Ocean and traveled through Zululand over into the mountains of Basutoland. I noted the distinctions of the tribal characteristics as I passed through these states. I also travelled through the Orange Free State and the Transvaal from Basutoland to Johannesburg.

This excursion, projection of spirit-consciousness, or whatever it may be termed, occurred during hours of communion with God in prayer.

---

[1] In 1866, explorer David Livingstone went to Africa to search for the source of the Nile River, then he disappeared. Five years later, reporter Henry Morton Stanley set out to find him and on November 10, 1871, he did. Source: "The Scoop of the Century: Was getting the story worth the cost?" *National Geographic's World Magazine* [available online] @ nationalgeographic.com.

While meditating and praying while on the sea on my way to Africa, I would become suddenly conscious of the political conditions of South Africa. I would feel the struggles of the various political elements in their contest for supremacy. Then again, I would realize the condition of the country financially and still again see the religious aspects of the nation. I saw the predominating thought that bound the Boer people as a nation to the Dutch church and the struggles of the civilized native people to attain a religious independence.

While in the spirit I comprehended not only present fact, but my consciousness would project itself into the future so that I saw the train of national events that were yet to take place. And I also saw the West Coast of Africa, when they had become great commercial seaports with lines of railways extending up into the Transvaal.

Much of this vision I have seen fulfilled at this writing. Namely, the uniting of the South African states into a national union (Natal, Orange Free State, Cape Colony, and the Transvaal); the great religious upheaval; the settlement of political and financial problems, etc. I saw the conquest of German Southwest Africa by the British, including some of the battle scenes of the present war there. (World War 1).

No one could realize, unless they had been associated with me in the work in Africa, how thorough this knowledge of the conditions in Africa was made to me. This was not the result of reading, for I had read practically nothing of Africa since my childhood.

In traveling through the country after my arrival, there was nothing new. I had seen it all in advance and could recollect times and circumstances when in my visions of Africa I had visited one city or another.

This knowledge of affairs was of inestimable value to me when I was actually on the ground. Businessmen and statesmen alike frequently expressed surprise at the intimate knowledge I possessed of conditions in the land, little realizing how this knowledge had come to me.

This spiritual consciousness of conditions, or great gift of knowledge, continued with me throughout my first years as president of the Apostolic Church of South Africa.

It was my custom to dictate my letters in the morning before going to my office or out among the sick for the duties of the day. At such times, if I wanted to write a letter for instance, to Cape

Town, Peitermaritzburg, Pretoria, or some other place, I would bow my head in quiet before God for a few moments. While in this attitude, there would be born in my consciousness the conditions of the assembly or district, or town, as the case might be. I could see the difficulties the brethren were having there, if any, and hundreds of times have written, revealing to them an inside knowledge of the conditions among them that they were sure no one knew about.

In the conduct of our native work, this feature was so marked that after a time, an adage grew up among the natives, "You cannot fool Brother Lake, God shows him." Many, many times when the natives would come and present perhaps only one side of the matter, I would be able to tell them the whole truth concerning the difficulty.

On one occasion, a man came from Robertson and made charges against a brother who was one of the elders in the work there. When he got through I said to him, "Brother, let us bow our heads in prayer." Instantly, I seemed to be in Robertson. I observed the assembly, saw the various brethren there, noted their piety and devotion to God, and I saw that the condition was almost the reverse as it had been presented. The man, himself, was the troublemaker.

On another occasion, a woman came to me several times requesting prayer for her deliverance from drunkenness. I urged upon her the necessity for repentance unto God, confession of her sins, etc. She assured me many times that she has done all of this.

One day she came while I was resting on the cot. My wife brought her into the room. She knelt weeping by the cot. As usual, she asked me to pray for deliverance. I said to her, "What about the two hundred and fifty pounds sterling worth of jewelry that you stole from such and such a home?" She threw up her hands with an exclamation of despair, supposing that I would deliver her to the police or tell the party from whom she had stolen it. I calmed her by assurance that as a minister of Christ no one should know from me concerning the matter. I regarded the knowledge as sacred before God, because God had revealed it to me in order to assist her out of her difficulty. She was delivered from her drunkenness and remained a sober woman, working earnestly in the vineyard of the Lord.

Some days afterward, a woman came to me, saying, "I have heard that So-and-so (naming the lady of whom I have spoken) has been converted, and I know she must have confessed to you that she stole jewelry from my home." I explained to her that even if such a confession had been made, as a minister of Jesus Christ I could not reveal it and would not reveal it.

As we conversed I told her I believed God had sent her in order that we might discuss together the forgiveness of God. I showed her that God expected us to forgive, even as we are forgiven. Indeed, that we are commanded to forgive.[2] The Spirit gave me such a consciousness of the forgiveness of God that as I presented it to her, it seemed to flow in liquid love from my soul. She broke down and wept, asking me to pray for her that God would deliver her from her own sins and establish in her the knowledge and consciousness of His presence and life. She left saying, "Tell So-and-so that as far as the jewelry is concerned, I shall never mention it again. There will be no prosecution, and by the grace of God I forgive her."

My wife possessed the spirit of discernment in a more marked degree than I did, especially concerning difficulties in people's lives — particularly regarding those seeking healing. She had the power to reveal the reason they were not blessed of God.

It was my custom in receiving the sick in my office, to let them stand in a line, and I would pray for them, laying hands on each as they passed me. Some would not receive healing and their suffering would continue. Some would receive healing in part, and some were instantly healed. I would pass those who received no healing into the adjoining room, and when I had finished praying for the multitude, I would bring my wife into the room where these unhealed ones were. She would go close to one and would say, in substance, "Your difficulty is that at such and such a time you committed such and such a sin, which has not been repented of and confessed." To another perhaps it would be, "God wants you to make restitution for such and such an act that you committed at such and such a time." To another,

---

[2] See Matthew 6:14-15.

"The pride of your heart and the love of the world have not been laid on the altar of Christ."

Upon hearing the inner things of their heart revealed, many would bow at once and confess their sins to God. We would pray for them again and the Lord would heal them. Some would go away unrepentant. Some would go through the motions of repentance, but it was not of the heart, and they would not be healed. Thus we are taught to value highly the gifts of God, of which Paul speaks in 1 Corinthians 12:10, "to another the discerning of spirits."

The Spirit of God is like the bread that the disciples held in their hands. When they broke it and distributed it to the multitudes, there was more remaining than when they began.[3] The Spirit of God is *creative, generative, and constructive,* and the more you give the more you receive. Jesus laid down a perpetual law when He said, *"Give,* and it shall be given unto you."[4]

Dr. John G. Lake

---

[3]   See John 6:11-13.

[4]   Luke 6:38.

My Baptism in the Holy Spirit and How the Lord Sent Me to South Africa

*O*ut of the darkness of night have called thee,
Into the glorious light of the day,
Into the knowledge of God's own salvation,
Entered through Jesus the Truth, Light, and Way.

He who hath planted within thine own bosom
Conscious salvation through Jesus the Lord,
Now waits to see the result of the ransom
Fulfilled in thee through the Spirit and Word.

Yield then, thy being, like Him, thine own Master,
His way for thee is the way of the cross;
Perfected He, e'en through sorrow and suffering,
Obedient even, even to death.

Here as with Him is the secret of victory,
That, having died, from the grave He arose,
In the new life of power divine and majesty,
Triumphing over death, hell, and all foes.

Ascending upward above all the heavens,
Into the realms of glory divine,
Reigning as Conqueror, sending His Spirit,
Abiding ever in your heart and mine.

By

Dr. John G. Lake
Divine Healing Institute
Portland, Oregon
U.S.A.

Price 25 Cents

The Call of God

> *Thus in our nature the Spirit of conquest*
> *Presses us forward in God's holy war,*
> *Advancing, compelling, delivering, destroying*
> *All power of darkness wherever they are.*
>
> *Through death to the victory, through trial to conquest.*
> *Through suffering to glory, dominion and power;*
> *Thus Calvary ever becomes then door opened*
> *To Jesus, to heaven, to discipleship now.*

MY BAPTISM IN THE HOLY SPIRIT

Eight years had passed after God revealed Jesus the Healer to me. I had been practicing the ministry of healing. During that eight years every answer to prayer, every miraculous touch of God, every response of my own soul to the Spirit, had created within me a more intense longing for an intimacy and consciousness of God, like I felt the disciples of Jesus and the primitive church had possessed.

Shortly after my entrance into the ministry of healing, while attending a service where the necessity for the baptism of the Spirit was being presented, as I knelt in prayer and reconsecration to God, an anointing of the Spirit came upon me. Waves of holy glory passed through my being, and I was lifted into a new consciousness of God's presence and power.

I ministered for a number of years in the power of this anointing. Answers to prayers were frequent and miracles of healing occurred from time to time. I felt myself on the borderland of a great spiritual realm and consciousness, but was unable to enter in fully, so that my nature was not gratified and satisfied with the attainment. Friends said: "You have the baptism of the Spirit. If you did not have it you could not enjoy such a fruitful ministry as you do," and other statements of this character. Yet the longing in my soul was to me the evidence that there was a better experience than my soul knew.

Finally, I was led to set aside certain hours of the day that I dedicated to God as times of meditation and prayer. Thus a number of months passed, until one morning as I knelt praying the Spirit of the Lord spoke within my spirit, and said, "Be patient until the autumn." My heart rejoiced in this encouragement. I continued my practice of meditation and prayer. It became easy to detach my soul from the course of life, so that while my hands and mind were engaged in the common affairs of every day, my spirit maintained its attitude of communion with God. Thus, silent prayer became habitual practice. Indeed, it had been to a great extent all my life.

In the autumn I was brought into contact with a minister of the Gospel who was preaching a clear message of God and the baptism of the Holy Spirit. In my study of the man and his teaching I was struck with the fact that his interpretation of the Word of God was exceedingly true to what my soul understood as the real spirit of the Word.

Through his teaching I was led into a deeper and clearer consciousness of God's power to keep the heart of man free from the consciousness of sin. Instead of the usual struggle against evil in my inner life, such a consciousness of God's cleansing power in my inner nature became evident that a joyous, victorious note came into my soul.

At this time, in addition to my work as a minister of the Gospel I was engaged as manager of agents for a life insurance company. During the period of which I now speak, I preached practically every night. After our services I was in the habit of joining a circle of friends, who like myself, were determined to pray through into God to where we could receive the baptism of the Holy Spirit, as we believed the early disciples had received it.

It was my belief that not only should my spirit ascend into a new consciousness of God's presence, but that the evident and conscious power of God should come upon my life. In my consecration to God, again and again I said, "God, if You will baptize me in the Holy Spirit and give me the power of God, nothing shall be permitted to stand between me and a hundredfold obedience."

I continued to meet with these friends almost every night for months. A blessed woman of God who was visiting in our city and was being entertained at my home, observing the anguish of my spirit, said to me one day, "Come aside and let us pray." As we knelt she said, "As we pray, if God reveals any cause of hindrance to you why you do not receive the baptism of the Spirit you will tell me, and if He reveals any cause to me, I will tell you." We prayed, and no hindrance was revealed to either of us. Then she said, "We will obey the

Word of God and the practice of the early church." And laying her hands on my head she prayed God that I might receive the baptism of the Holy Spirit.

A deep calm settled upon me. In the afternoon a brother minister called and invited me to accompany him to visit a lady who was sick. Arriving at the home, we found a lady in a wheelchair. All her joints were set with inflammatory rheumatism. She had been in this condition for ten years.

While my friend was conversing with her, preparing her to be prayed with that she might be healed, I sat in a deep chair on the opposite side of the large room. My soul was crying out to God in a yearning too deep for words, when suddenly it seemed to me I had passed under a shower of warm tropical rain, which was not falling upon me, but falling through me. My spirit and soul and body, under this influence, were soothed into such a deep, still calm as I had never known. My brain, which had always been so active, became perfectly still. An awe of the presence of God settled over me. I knew it was God.

Some moments passed; I do not know how many. The Spirit said, "I have heard your prayers, I have seen your tears. You are now to be baptized in the Holy Spirit." The seeming rain ceased, but oh, it had left such a calm, such a quiet of God upon me as my words cannot tell. Then currents of power began to rush through my being from the crown of my head to the soles of my feet. These shocks of power increased in rapidity and voltage. As these currents of power would pass through me, they seemed to come upon my head, rush through my body and through my feet into the floor. This power was so great that my body began to vibrate intensely so that I believe if I had not been sitting in such a deep, low chair I might have fallen upon the floor.

An overwhelming consciousness of God's presence possessed me. A new rush of power, taking hold of my very flesh, seemed to come from my feet and move upward. My throat and tongue began to move in a strange manner, and I found that I was unable to speak English. And presently, I began to speak in another language, one that I had never learned, by the power of the Spirit.

For years I had been a profound student of psychic phenomena and had observed among different bodies of Christian people various manifestations. Sometimes they would be of the Spirit of God, but other times they were purely psychic. I prayed, "Father, You know that I have witnessed many phases of psychic phenomena. Is this the power of God that is coursing through my being, or is it some character of psychic manifestation that the world is not familiar with? Is it real power or do I just think it is power? Father, I want to know."

God answered that heart cry in the following manner: At that instant I observed my friend was motioning me to come and join him in prayer for the woman who was sick. In his absorption he had not observed that anything had taken place in me. I arose to go to him, but found my body was trembling so violently that I had great difficulty in walking across the room, and especially in controlling the trembling of my hands and arms. I was familiar with sick people, having ministered to them for so many years. I knew it would not be wise to thus lay my hands upon the sick woman, as I was likely to jar her.

It occurred to me that all that was necessary was to touch the tips of my fingers on the top of the patient's head, and then the vibrations would not jar her. This I did. At once, the currents of holy power passed through my being, and I knew that it likewise passed through the one who was sick. She did not speak, but apparently was amazed at the effect in her body. My friend, who had been talking to her, in his great earnestness had been kneeling as he talked to her. He arose, saying, "Let us pray that the Lord will now heal you."

As he did so he took her by the hand. At the instant their hands touched, a flash of dynamic power went through my person and through the sick woman, and as my friend held her hand the shock of power passed through her hand into him. The rush of power into his person was so great that it caused him to fall on the floor. He looked up at me with joy and surprise and springing to his feet said, "Praise the Lord, John, Jesus has baptized you in the Holy Ghost!"

Then he took the crippled hand, that had been set for so many years. The clenched hands opened and the joints began to work — first the fingers, then the hand and wrist, then the elbow, shoulder, etc.

These were the outward manifestations, but oh! who could describe the thrills of joy inexpressible that were passing through my spirit? Who could comprehend the peace and presence of God that filled my soul? The sanctifying power of the Spirit in my very flesh, subduing all my nature unto what I understood was the nature of Christ. The revelation of His will, the unspeakable tenderness that possessed me, a love for mankind such as I never had known were all born within.

Even at this late date, ten years afterward, the awe of that hour rests upon my soul. My experience has truly been, as Jesus said: "He shall be within you a *well* of water, springing up into everlasting life."[1] That never-ceasing fountain has flowed through my spirit, soul, and body day and night, bringing salvation and healing and the baptism of the Spirit in the power of God to multitudes.

How the Lord Sent Me to South Africa

Shortly after my baptism in the Holy Spirit, a working of the Spirit commenced in me, that seemed to have for its purpose the revelation of the nature of Jesus Christ to me and in me. Through this tuition and remolding of the Spirit, a great tenderness for mankind was awakened in my soul. I saw mankind through new eyes. They seemed to me as wandering sheep, having strayed far, in the midst of confusion, groping and wandering hither and thither. They had no definite aim and did not seem to understand what the difficulty was or how to return to God.

The desire to proclaim the message of Christ and to demonstrate His power to save and bless grew in my soul until my life was swayed by this overwhelming passion.

However, my heart was divided. I could not follow successfully the ordinary pursuits of life and business. When a man came into my office, though I knew that twenty or thirty minutes of concentration on the business in hand would possibly net me thousands of dollars, I could not discuss business with him. By a new power of discernment I could see his soul and understand his inner life and motives. I recognized him as one of the wandering sheep and longed with an overwhelming desire to help him get to God for salvation and find himself.

---

[1] John 4:14, paraphrased.

This division in my soul between business interests and the desire to help men to God became so intense that in many instances what should have been a successful business interview and the closing of a great business transaction, ended in a prayer meeting, by my inviting the individual to kneel with me while I poured out my heart to God on his behalf.

I determined to discuss the matter with the president of my company. I frankly told him the condition of soul I found myself in, and its cause. He kindly replied, "You have worked hard, Lake. You need a change. Take a vacation for three months and if you want to preach, preach. But at the end of three months $50,000 a year will look like a lot of money to you, and you will have little desire to sacrifice it for dreams of religious possibilities."

I thanked him, accepted an invitation to join a brother in evangelistic work, and left the office, never to return.

During the three months I preached every day to large congregations and saw a multitude of people saved from their sins and healed of their diseases and hundreds of them baptized in the Holy Ghost. At the end of the three months, I said to God, "I am through forever with everything in life but the proclamation and demonstration of the Gospel of Jesus Christ."

I disposed of my estate and distributed my funds in a manner I believed to be for the best interest of the kingdom of God and made myself wholly dependent upon God for the support of myself and family and abandoned myself to the preaching of Jesus.

While ministering in a city in Northern Illinois, the chore boy at the hotel where we were stopping was inquiring for someone to assist him in sawing down a large tree. I volunteered to assist him, and while in the act of sawing the tree down, the Spirit of the Lord spoke within my spirit clear and distinct: "Go to Indianapolis. Prepare for a winter campaign. Get a large hall. In the spring you will go to Africa."

I returned to the hotel and told my wife of the incident. She said, "I knew several days ago that your work here was done, for as I prayed the Spirit said to me, 'Your husband is going on.'"

I went to Indianapolis. The Lord directed in a marvelous way so that in a few days I had secured a large hall and was conducting services, as He had directed. About this time the following incident took place, which has had so much to do with the success of my ministry ever since.

One morning when I came down to breakfast I found my appetite had disappeared. I could not eat. I went about my work as usual. At dinnertime I had no desire to eat, and no more in the evening. The next day was similar, and the third day likewise. But toward the evening of the third day, an overwhelming desire to pray took possession of me. I only wanted to be alone to pray.

For days following, this condition remained upon me. I could neither eat nor sleep. I could only pray. Prayer flowed from my soul like a stream. I could not cease praying. As I rode on the street car I prayed. As soon as it was possible to get a place of seclusion I would kneel to pour out my heart to God for hours. Whatever I was doing, that stream of prayer continued flowing from my soul.

On the night of the sixth day of this fast that the Lord had laid on me, while in the act of washing my hands, the Spirit said to me once again, "Go and pray." I turned around and knelt by my bedside. As I knelt praying, the Spirit said, "How long have you been praying for the power to cast out demons?"

And I replied, "Lord, a long time."

And the Spirit said, "From henceforth thou shalt cast out demons." I arose and praised God.

The following night at the close of the service, a gentleman came to me, and pointing to a large red letter motto on the wall, which read, "In my name shall they cast out devils,"[2] he said, "Do you believe that?"

I replied, "I do."

He said, "Do not answer hastily, for I have gone all around the land seeking for a minister who would tell me that he believed that. Many have said they did, but when I questioned them I found they wanted to qualify the statement."

I said, "Brother, so far as I know my soul, I believe it with all my heart."

---

[2] Mark 16:17.

Then he said, "I will tell you why I asked. Two and a half years ago my brother, who was manager of a large elevator, was attending a religious service. He was seeking the grace of sanctification, and suddenly became violently insane. He was committed to the asylum, and is there today. Somehow in the openness of his nature, he apparently became possessed of an evil spirit. Physicians who have examined him declare that every function of his body and brain are apparently normal, and they cannot account for his insanity. If you say that you believe in the casting out of demons by the power of God, I will bring him here on Sunday from the asylum, and I will expect you to cast the devil out."

I replied, "Brother, bring him on."

Then we knelt and prayed that the officers of the institution would be inclined by the Spirit of God to permit the man to be brought.

On Sunday in the midst of the service, the man came. He was in the charge of his brother and an attendant from the institution. His old mother was also one of the company. They came in during the preaching service. I stopped preaching, and said to the attendant, "Bring him here; let him kneel at the altar." Then I looked over the audience and selected half a dozen persons whom I knew to be people of faith in God and invited them to come and kneel in a semicircle about the man and join me in prayer for his deliverance.

When they had knelt and were praying I stepped from the platform, laid my hands on his head, and in the name of Jesus Christ, the Son of God, commanded the devil that possessed him to come out of him. The Spirit of God went through my being like a flash of lightning. I knew in my soul that that evil spirit was cast out and was not surprised when in a moment the man raised his head and spoke intelligently to me. In a few minutes he arose from the altar and took a seat in the front row beside his mother and brother. He listened to my address in perfect quiet. When the congregation arose to sing, he acted embarrassed because no one had offered him a hymn book. So I stepped down and handed him mine, and he sang the hymn with the rest of the congregation. After the service was dismissed he remained and talked with me in a perfectly normal manner.

He returned to the asylum. The brother and attendant told of what had taken place. The physicians examined him and advised that he remain for some days until they were satisfied as to whether he was healed or not. On Wednesday he was discharged. On Thursday he returned to his home and took up his former position as manager at a grain elevator, a healed man.

Thus, God verified His word to me, and from that day to this the power of God has remained upon my soul, and I have seen hundreds of insane people delivered and healed.

One day during the following February my preaching partner said to me, "John, how much will it cost to take our party to Johannesburg, South Africa?"

I replied, "Two thousand dollars."

He said, "If we are going to Africa in the spring it is time you and I were praying for the money."

I said, "I have been praying for the money ever since New Year's. I have not heard from the Lord, or from anyone else concerning it."

He said, "Never mind. Let's pray again."

We went to his room and knelt in prayer. He led in audible prayer, while I joined my soul in faith and prayer with him. Presently, he slapped me on the back, saying, "Don't pray any more, John. Jesus told me just now that He would send us that two thousand dollars, and it would be here in four days."

A few days later he returned from the post office and threw out upon the table four five-hundred dollar drafts, saying, "John, there is the answer. Jesus has sent it. We are going to Africa."

We purchased tickets for the entire party, from Indianapolis, Indiana, to Johannesburg, South Africa. The gift of money had been sent to Brother H. He read me a clause of the letter. As nearly as I can remember it said, "While I was standing in the bank at Monrovia, California, the Lord said to me, 'Send Brother H. two thousand dollars.' Enclosed find the drafts. The money is yours for whatever purpose the Lord has directed you to use it." I never knew who the writer of the letter was, as he desired no one else to know.

We left Indianapolis on the first day of April, 1898, my wife and myself and seven children and four others. We had our tickets to Africa, but I had no money for personal expenses enroute, except $1.50. As the train pulled out of the station a young man ran alongside of the train and threw a two-dollar bill through the window, making $3.50. A young lady who had been one of our workers, accompanied us as far as Detroit, Michigan. She needed $10 to purchase her ticket to destination. As we rode along I said to my wife, "When we reach Detroit I will need $10 for W.'s railway ticket, and I have no money." So we bowed our head and prayed.

I had never taken any of my family or friends into my confidence concerning my affairs. They were not aware of whether I had money or not. However, when we reached Detroit a party of friends were waiting to say good-bye. As I stepped off at the station my brother took me by the arm and walked across the station with me. He said to me, "I trust you will not feel offended, but all day long I have felt that I would like to give you this," and he slipped a $10 bill in my vest pocket. I thanked him, turned about, purchased the young lady's ticket, and rejoined the party.

Out of my $3.50 we purchased some canned beans and other edibles, which we used on the train enroute to St. Johns, New Brunswick, where we took ship for Liverpool. On leaving the ship I gave half of this to our waiter as a tip. We remained a week in Liverpool at the expense of the transportation company, waiting for the second ship.

One day Mrs. Lake said to me, "What about our laundry for the party?"

I replied, "Send it to the laundry. I have no money, but perhaps the Lord will meet us before we need to get it." Being very busy, I forgot about it entirely. On the last night of our stay in Liverpool, just after I had retired about midnight, my wife said, "How about the laundry?"

I replied, "I am sorry, but I forgot it."

She said, "Just like a man. But now I will tell you about it. I knew you did not have any money, neither did I. I prayed about it and after praying I felt that I should go down to the laundry and inquire what the amount of the bill was. I found it was $1.65. I was returning to the hotel. I passed a gentleman on the street, and presently he said to me, 'Pardon me, but I feel I should give you this,' and he handed me a number of coins. I returned to the laundry, counted it out to the laundryman, and found it was just the amount of the bill."

We rejoiced in this little evidence of God's presence with us. That next morning we left by train for London and that evening boarded our ship for South Africa.

When I got on the ship I had an English shilling. I purchased a shilling's worth of fruit for the children when our ship stopped at Maderia, one of the Canary islands, and the last penny was gone.

Through my knowledge of the immigration laws of South Africa, I knew that before we would be permitted to land, I must show the immigration inspector that I was the possessor of at least $125. We prayed earnestly over this matter and about the time we reached the equator a rest came into my soul concerning it. I could pray no more. When I say I felt that we were "prayed up" on that question, Christians who get answers from God will know what I mean.

About eight or ten days later we arrived in Cape Town Harbor, and our ship anchored. The immigration inspector came on board, and the passengers lined up at the purser's office to present their money and receive their tickets to land. My wife said, "What are you going to do?"

I said, "I am going to line up with the rest. We have obeyed God thus far. It is now up to the Lord. If they send us back we cannot help it."

As I stood in the line awaiting my turn, a fellow passenger touched me on the shoulder and indicated to me to step out of the line and come over to the ship's rail to speak with him. He asked some questions, and then drew from his pocket a traveler's check book and handed me two money orders aggregating forty-two pounds sterling — $200.

I stepped back into the line, presented my orders to the inspector, and received our tickets to land.

Johannesburg is one thousand miles inland from Cape Town. Throughout the voyage and on the train, we earnestly prayed about the subject of a home. We were faith missionaries. We had neither a board, nor friends behind us to furnish money. We were dependent on God. Many times during the trip to Johannesburg we bowed our heads and reminded God that when we arrived there we would need a home. God blessed and wondrously answered our prayer.

Upon our arrival at Johannesburg Brother H. stepped off the train first. I followed. I observed a little woman bustling up, whom I instantly recognized as an American. She said to Brother H., "You are an American missionary party?"

He replied, "Yes."

She said, "How many are there in your family?"

He replied, "Four."

"No," she said, "You are not the family. Is there any other?"

He said, "Yes, Mr. Lake." Addressing me she said, "How many are in your family?"

I answered, "My wife, myself and seven children only."

"Oh," she said, "you are the family!"

I said, "What is it, madam?"

As I recall her answer it was, "The Lord sent me here to meet you, and I want to give you a home."

I replied, "We are faith missionaries. We are dependent on God. I have no money to pay rent."

She said, "Never mind the rent. The Lord wants you to have a home."

That same afternoon we were living in a furnished cottage in the suburbs, the property of our beloved benefactor, Mrs. C. L. Goodenough, of Johannesburg, who remains to this day our beloved friend and fellow worker in the Lord. She is now a resident of Florida and has visited us in the West.

LIFE IN CHRIST

e are gods.

— John 10:34

As he is, so are we.

— 1 John 4:17

DIVINE LIFE

Definitions:

1. In one sense the term,
    divine life, is equivalent to the terms, *eternal life, everlasting life,* and to *live forever.* Only those who believe that Jesus is the Son of God (John 3:36) and receive Him (1 John 5:12) have everlasting life. However, the term as being used by some really refers to the development of the spiritual life of a person, being made like Him.

2. "Ye are gods" (small "g") (John 10:34). This was spoken by Jesus to those who were about to stone Him. It therefore applies to unbelievers as well as to believers. To believers it has a great significance. In general, it signifies God's estimate of the race He created.

3. "As he is, so are we" (1 John 4:17). This applies only to the believers. In what sense are we as He is? What is the scope of this passage?

What is man?

> And the Lord God formed man of the dust of the ground, and breathed into his nostrils the breath of life; and man became a living soul.
>
> — Genesis 2:7

> Saith the LORD, which stretcheth forth the heavens, and layeth the foundation of the earth, and formeth the *spirit* of man within him.
>
> — Zechariah 12:1

Of what substance was the spirit of man formed? It was formed of the same substance of which angels are made. It is a spirit and it is a heavenly substance (Hebrews 1:14). So man is spirit, soul, and body. (See 1 Thessalonians 5:23.)

Since man is spirit, soul, and body does each have its own will and mind?

Does the spirit of man have its own will and mind?

Does the soul of man have its own will and mind?

Does the physical body of man have its own will and mind?

Plainly, the answer is *no*. Man is a unit with his spirit, soul, and body under the control of a single will and mind.

Was man's spirit involved in the fall?

The whole man rebelled as a unit. It is shown in 2 Corinthians 7:1,

> Let us cleanse ourselves from all filthiness of the flesh and spirit, perfecting holiness in the fear of God.

It is further shown in Proverbs 16:32,

> He that is slow to anger is better than the mighty; and he that ruleth his spirit than he that taketh a city.

The spirit and soul, the inner man, is the real you. Proverbs 16:32 speaks of self-control. Salvation, in the vastness of its scope, involves the whole man as a unit.

Jesus answered them, "Is it not written in your law, I said, Ye are gods?" (John 10:34.) He was quoting from Psalm 82:6. Why is such a statement made in the Word of God? For one thing, it shows God's true estimate of the race He created and still loves. For another thing, God created man a little lower than Himself but far above the animals. "Thou hast made him a little lower than the angels" (Psalm 8:5). The word "angels" is translated from the Hebrew word *Elohiym,* which is one of the prevalent names of God in the Old Testament. That is why the Creator [manuscript ends here].

THE BOOK OF HEBREWS

THE BELIEVER IN THE BOOK OF HEBREWS

A. So Great Salvation:

1. Salvation so great — because

   a. Announced by an incomparable preacher (Hebrews 2:3).

   b. Attested by many infallible proofs (Hebrews 2:4).

   c. Accomplished by an infinite price (Hebrews 2:9).

   d. Accompanied by many inestimable privileges (Hebrews 2:11-15).

2. Do not neglect (Hebrews 2:1-5). Escape is impossible.

3. Produces correct attitudes:

   a. To equals in the assembly (1 Thessalonians 5:11,13).

      (1) Comfort and edify one another, and be at peace with all.

   b. To elders in the assembly (1 Thessalonians 5:12,13).

      (1) Know who they are and esteem them highly.

   c. To erring saints in the assembly (1 Thessalonians 5:14).

4. Four portraits of the man of God:

   a. A man fleeing (Joseph — Illustration). 1 Timothy 6:11; 2 Timothy 2:22; Genesis 39:12.

   b. A man following (Elisha — Illustration). 1 Timothy 6:11; 2 Kings 2:6.

   c. A man fighting (Paul — Illustration). 1 Timothy 6:12; 2 Timothy 4:7.

   d. A man furnished (Timothy — Illustration). 2 Timothy 3:16-17; Ephesians 6:13-18.

5. Produces contentment. "Godliness with contentment is great gain" (1 Timothy 6:6).

   a. Contentment is:

(1) An evidence of conversion — Be content with your wages (Luke 3:14).

      (2) The exclusion of covetousness — Be content (Hebrews 13:5).

      (3) An expression of confidence — Having food and raiment therewith to be content (Hebrews 13:5-6).

      (4) An exhibition of comradeship — Be content and go with thy servants (2 Kings 6:2-3).

      (5) The essence of consecration — I have learned in whatsoever state I am, therewith to be content (Philippians 4:11-13).

B. The Believer's Inheritance:

1. Heirs of salvation — served by God's angelic messengers (Hebrews 1:14).

2. Heirs of promise — with the sure and steadfast hope of an entry into heaven (Hebrews 6:17).

3. Heirs of righteousness — by faith in the unchanging Word of God (Hebrews 11:7).

4. Heirs of the world — through the righteousness of faith (Romans 4:13).

5. Heirs of the Kingdom — by the election of God, as poor yet rich in faith (James 2:5).

6. Heirs according to the hope of eternal life — by the grace of God that justifies us (Titus 3:7).

7. Heirs of God and joint-heirs with Jesus Christ — because we are children of God (Romans 8:17).

There are certain attributes in which man cannot be equal with God. I will mention four of them.

1. God is infinite and has no beginning. Man is finite and has a beginning.

2. God is omniscient (all-knowing); man is not.

3. God is omnipresent (power to be present in all places at the same time); man is not.

4. God is omnipotent (all powerful); man is not.

These are all true of Jesus because He was with the Father from eternity (1 John 1:1-2). "I came down from heaven, not to do my own will, but the will of him that sent me" (John 6:38). Also Jesus spoke these words, "Before Abraham was, I am" (John 8:58). The Son of God was with the Father before the world was. "And now, O Father, glorify thou me with thine own self with the glory which I had with thee before the world was" (John 17:5).

Now let us look at Philippians 2:5-8:

> Let this mind be in you, which was also in Christ Jesus: Who, being in the form of God, thought it not robbery to be equal with God: but made himself of no reputation, and took upon him the form of a servant, and was made in the likeness of men: and being found in fashion as a man, he humbled himself, and became obedient unto death, even the death of the cross.

From eternity He was on equality with God. But He did something when He came down from heaven and was incarnate. ("And the Word was made flesh" John 1:14.) "But made himself of no reputation, and took upon him the form of a servant, and was made in the likeness of men" (Philippians 2:7). The words, "no reputation," come from the Greek words that mean He "emptied Himself," that is, He laid aside all His divine prerogatives and became obedient even to the death of the cross. So He could say, "I came down from heaven, not to do mine own will, but the will of him that sent me" (John 6:38). "Now is my soul troubled; and what shall I say? Father, save me from this hour: but for this cause came I unto this hour" (John 12:27). He came into the world to give His life a ransom for all who will believe.

We must have the same mind as the Lord and consider it not robbery to be equal with our Father. But what does that equality involve?

1. We cannot be equal with God as He had no beginning — we have a beginning.

2. We cannot be equal with God as He is omniscient (all-knowing) — we are not all knowing.

3. We cannot be equal with God as He is omnipresent (present in all places at the same time) — we are not.

4. We cannot be equal with God as He is omnipotent (all-powerful) — we are not.

In what way then are we equal with Him? In what way can it be said, "As he is, so are we" (1 John 4:17)? How can people see Jesus in you — Christ in you? What is the actual manifestation that proves He is in you? The vastness of the subject precludes that it will be impossible to cover it all in this short dissertation.

Equality does not refer to our physical bodies for we have not been resurrected. One day that will be true, for our bodies will be made like unto His glorious body (Philippians 3:21).

It is equality in:

1. Love: "As he is, so are we" in love.

    a. "Herein is our love made perfect, that we may have boldness in the day of judgment: because as he is, so are we in this world" (1 John 4:17).

    b. "Be ye therefore perfect, even as your Father which is in heaven is perfect" (Matthew 5:48). You will notice the context of this passage is love.

2. The fruit of the Spirit (Galatians 5:22-23).

    a. We have a new heart.

    And will give them an heart of flesh: that they may walk in my statutes, and keep mine ordinances, and do them: and they shall be my people, and I will be their God.

    — Ezekiel 11:19-20

    Forasmuch as ye are manifestly declared to be the epistle of Christ ministered by us, written not with ink, but with the Spirit of the living God; not in tables of stone, but in fleshly tables of the heart.

    — 2 Corinthians 3:3

b. Because God has given us a new heart we speak and act out of the abundance of our hearts, and we bring forth that which is good (Luke 6:45). That is why they shall know us by our fruits (Matthew 7:17,20). It is the manifestation of the fruit of the Spirit in the life of the believer.

3. Righteousness:

    a. Jesus is our righteousness (1 Corinthians 1:30).

    b. We are the righteousness of God in Christ (2 Corinthians 5:21).

    c. "As he is, so are we" in righteousness.

4. Blessed are the poor in spirit (Matthew 5:3).

    a. We hold our possessions, whether much or little, as a trust from God to be administered as He directs. It is being good stewards.

    b. "As he is, so are we" in being poor in spirit. It means humility of mind.

5. Blessed are the merciful (Matthew 5:7).

    a. Mercy is an ingredient of love.

    b. "Be ye therefore merciful, as your Father also is merciful" (Luke 6:36).

    c. "As he is, so are we" in mercy.

6. Blessed are the meek (Matthew 5:5).

    a. Jesus said, "I am meek and lowly in heart..." (Matthew 11:29).

    b. Meekness is said to be strength under control. It is using power and authority to serve as He used it. We exalt Jesus, not ourselves.

    c. "As he is, so are we" in meekness.

7. Blessed are the pure in heart (Matthew 5:8).

    a. The blood of Jesus Christ cleanses from all sin, leaving neither root, stem, nor branch (1 John 1:7,9).

b. "Follow righteousness, faith, charity, peace, with them that call on the Lord out of a pure heart" (2 Timothy 2:22).

c. "As he is, so are we" in purity of heart.

8. Blessed are the peacemakers (Matthew 5:9).

a. "And the fruit of righteousness is sown in peace of them that make peace" (James 3:18).

b. "As he is, so are we" in making and distributing peace.

9. Blessed are they that are persecuted (Matthew 5:10).

a. "Ye are partakers of Christ's sufferings" (1 Peter 4:13). It is a privilege to endure hardness for our Captain (2 Timothy 2:3).

b. "As he is, so are we" in suffering for righteousness' sake.

10. "He that is joined unto the Lord is one spirit" (1 Corinthians 6:17).

a We are one in objectives.

b. We are one in intent.

c. We are one in purpose.

d. We are one in our outlook on life.

e. We are one as we look at sinners. We see them as blind, staggering "in darkness, searching for they know not what, and as being beaten down by a heartless devil. We see how the devil has maimed, diseased, blinded, crippled, and caused them to be deaf and dumb, etc., yet Jesus came and destroyed all these works of the devil by delivering them" (Matthew 15:30).

f. "As he is, so are we" in all of the above aspects.

It should be obvious by now that we are like Jesus in character. The things that characterize the Son of God should be manifested in and through us.

It is also equality in:

1. Power over all the power of the enemy:

a. "Behold, I give unto you power to tread on serpents and scorpions, and over all the power of the enemy" (Luke 10:19).

We are provided with an armor with an invincible shield of faith that quenches all the fiery darts (missiles) of the devil (Ephesians 6:14-18). Jesus declared in Matthew 28:18, "All power is given unto me in heaven and in earth." As members of His body we share in the power of the head.

2. We share in His triumph:

   a. The believer is never the victim of a circumstance but always the victor. Jesus "always causeth us to triumph" (2 Corinthians 2:14).

   Persecutions, afflictions, which came unto me at Antioch, at Iconium, at Lystra; which persecutions I endured: but out of them all the Lord delivered me.

   — 2 Timothy 3:11

   b. He is the triumphant Christ (Revelation 1:18). "As he is, so are we" in triumph.

3. In the demonstration of the Spirit and power in our preaching and teaching (1 Corinthians 2:4).

   a. "He that believeth on me, the works that I do shall he do also; and greater works than these shall he do; because I go unto my Father" (John 14:12).

   b. "As he is, so are we" in seeing mankind delivered from the power of the devil, whether the difficulty lies in the spirit, soul, or body of the person.

   c. "As he is, so are we" by the use of His name in destroying the work of the devil. "For this purpose the Son of God was manifested, that he might destroy the works of the devil" (1 John 3:8). "Peace be unto you: as my Father hath sent me, even so send I you" (John 20:21).

Now you may think of other aspects in which "as he is, so are we" and you can incorporate them into your study. Identification with Christ is a reality and a great study. The purpose of this paper is to reveal that there are aspects in which we cannot claim equality with the Supreme Being. Jesus said, "For without me ye can do nothing" (John 15:5).

That is why God is the big "G" and we the little "g." We are totally dependent on Him. We cannot operate apart from Him.

A UNIQUE RELATIONSHIP

There is a unique relationship between the believer and the Lord Jesus Christ, "Ye in me, and I in you" (John 14:20). "Abide in me, and I in you" (John 15:4). This relationship is so unique that it cannot be pictured by any single illustration or analogy. Many are used to depict various aspects of it. Let us consider some of them.

1. John 10, The Shepherd and the sheep.

    a. This illustrates the care of the Shepherd for the sheep. He will give His life for the sheep. (John 10:15).

    b. It also illustrates the total dependence of the sheep upon the Shepherd. The Holy Spirit is to guide us into all truth (John 16:13). Without His guidance we would not be able to find our way. That is why God is the big "G" and we are the little "g."

    "Ye are gods."

    c. This analogy does not depict all the uniqueness of the union of the Savior and the believer. Sheep do not make good soldiers.

2. Hebrews 2:10 and 2 Timothy 2:3, The army, the Captain, and the soldier(s).

    a. This analogy depicts discipline. It shows total submission to the Supreme Commander.

    b. We do not go to war on our own (1 Corinthians 9:7).

    c. We are supplied with a complete set of armor that includes a shield of faith that quenches all the fiery darts (missiles) of the devil. It also includes the sword of the Spirit, the Word of God, for stabbing the devil.[1] In any warfare the enemy is sooner or later shattered. "And the God of peace shall bruise (shatter completely) Satan under your feet shortly" (Romans 16:20). You see, our armor is invincible.

---

[1] See Ephesians 6:11-18.

d. "The steps of a good man are ordered by the Lord" (Psalm 37:23). Our Captain gives us orders and we obey. We are totally dependent on Him. That is why God is the big "G" and we are the little "g."

e. "The weapons of our warfare are not carnal" (2 Corinthians 10:4).

For we wrestle not against flesh and blood, but against principalities, against powers, against the rulers of the darkness of this world, against spiritual wickedness in high places.

— Ephesians 6:12

Besides our shield of faith and our sword of the Spirit, other weapons are prayers, intercessory prayer, fasting and prayer, breaking the power of the enemy over a person by bringing divine healing, etc.

3. John 15, The Vine and the branches.

a. This illustration shows the interdependence of the Vine and the branch. The Vine cannot bear fruit without the branch and the branch cannot bear fruit without the Vine. In this case the divine life of the Vine, Jesus Christ, is constantly and ever flowing in and through the branch.

b. Jesus is the Vine and in Him and from Him flows perpetual divine life. Take the branch out of the Vine and it withers and dies, but the Vine remains and never dies.

c. That is why God is the big "G" and we are the little "g". "Ye are gods."

4. Colossians 1:18, the Head and the body.

a. This analogy depicts the total submission of each as a member of a living organism. No part of the body can function without the head.

b. It also depicts the interdependence of the various parts of the body.

5. Romans 11:16-27, grafted in.

a. This illustration shows that as the root is holy, so are the branches. We are dependent on Him for our holiness.

"Be ye holy; for I am holy" (1 Peter 1:16). The Root bears the branch. Cut the branch out of the tree and it withers and dies. The Root remains, for in Him is eternal, divine life.

b. From Christ flows an endless stream of life through the branches. That endless stream of divine life supplies all the needs of every branch.

c. That is why God is the big "G" and we the little "g." "Ye are gods."

DIVINE LIFE

What is the purpose of God toward the believer? First, it is to bring about a development in the life of the believer so he may be a good soldier of Jesus Christ. After he becomes a disciplined soldier he is ready for service. What kind of service? "Go ye into all the world, and preach the gospel to every creature" (Mark 16:15). All soldiers are actively involved in reaching the lost. Some are on the front lines and others in the work of training new recruits and equipping them for the work of the ministry (Ephesians 4:11-13). "And he gave some, apostles; and some, prophets; and some, evangelists; and some, pastors and teachers" (Ephesians 4:11). What is the purpose of these ministries? "For the perfecting (equipping) of the saints" (Ephesians 4:12) for two reasons:

1. "For the work of the ministry" (Ephesians 4:12).

    a. It is for the purpose of reaching the lost. Even those engaged in these ministries are also responsible for the lost souls they come in contact with in the course of their lives.

2. "For the edifying (building up) of the body of Christ" (Ephesians 4:12).

    a. This work is to continue "till we all come in the unity of the faith, and of the knowledge of the Son of God, unto a perfect man, unto the measure of the stature of the fullness of Christ" (Ephesians 4:13).

That ye may be blameless and harmless, the sons of God, without rebuke, in the midst of a crooked and perverse nation, among whom ye shine as lights in the world.

— Philippians 2:15

No matter the degree of our spiritual development, God needs us here to shine as lights.

b. Jesus asked us to "Pray ye therefore the Lord of the harvest, that he will send forth labourers into his harvest" (Matthew 9:38). Nowhere in His teachings did Jesus indicate that a person should develop in divine life or spirituality that God would take them through death regardless of age. It is a violation of the promises of God concerning longevity. In my study of longevity in the lesson entitled "Life Here — How Long," I discovered that only two things should cause a person's life to end early. One is martyrdom and the other would be the catching away of the saints at the rapture. (1 Thessalonians 4:14-17.) The only apostles to die early were those who suffered martyrdom. (Acts 7:59-60 and Acts 12:1-2.)

There were two extremes in particular that showed up in the writings of the early proponents of "divine life." The one we have just dealt with. The other extremism was the avoidance of physical death. Some believed you could develop so far in "divine life" that you would not have to die. God would just take you up. There isn't any record of such ever happening since our New Covenant was established, and there is no indication that it would be so.

But we all, with open face beholding as in a glass the glory of the Lord, are changed (metamorphosed) into the same image from glory to glory, even as by the Spirit of the Lord.

— 2 Corinthians 3:18

"In His image" is the height of spiritual development. "The disciple is not above his master: but every one that is perfect shall be as his master" (Luke 6:40).

This lesson is not a treatise on spiritual development. There are lessons that give instructions on identification with the Lord Jesus Christ. This is written so we may avoid teaching that a person can be so spiritual or so full of divine life that God will take him through death at an early age or that one does not need to die physically.

"But he that is joined unto the Lord is one spirit" (1 Corinthians 6:17). "For we are members of his body, of his flesh, and of his bones" (Ephesians 5:30). Jesus is in me and I am in Him. I am a member of His body, which is a living organism, pulsating with His life. Into and through me is flowing the life-stream of Jesus. The Spirit is given to me without measure even as with Him, "For God giveth not the Spirit by measure unto him" (John 3:34). Of us Jesus had this to say, "He that believeth on me, as the scripture hath said, out of his belly shall flow rivers of living water. But this spake he of the Spirit..." (John 7:38-39). Rivers of living water are flowing from us — that flow is immeasurable. It is without measure. God does not expect us to do the work Jesus laid out for us with less equipment than Jesus Himself had. In Him we have the authority and power to duplicate His ministry.

When Jesus was on this earth He ministered through His physical body. Now that He has ascended to the right hand of the Father He needs another body to minister through. That body is you and I collectively and individually. "We are labourers together with God" (1 Corinthians 3:9). He "hath given to us the ministry of reconciliation" (2 Corinthians 5:18). This is "the high calling of God in Christ Jesus" (Philippians 3:14). We are kings and priests unto God (Revelation 1:6).

"As he is, so are we in this world" (1 John 4:17). Let us be sure that we live and act as He did at all times. It is not hard with Him dwelling in us and we in Him. It ought to be easier for us to live a Christian life with God in us than it was to live a sinful life with the devil in control of our lives. "Greater is he that is in you, than he that is in the world" (1 John 4:4).

"As he is, so are we in this world." He is my victory — I will operate at all times from the standpoint of victory. He is my wisdom — I will operate at all times from the standpoint of His wisdom. He is my righteousness — I will operate at all times from the standpoint of righteousness. In Him I died unto sin — I will operate at all times from the standpoint that I am dead to sin and alive unto Him. In Him I have dominion over the devil and evil — I will at all times operate from the standpoint of dominion. We sit in heavenly places in Christ Jesus (Ephesians 2:6) — I will act from the standpoint at all times. He gives me power over the enemy — I will operate from the standpoint of power at all times.

"As he is, so are we."

"For ye are dead, and your life is hid with Christ in God" (Colossians 3:3). Unto what are we dead? "But God forbid that I should glory, save in the cross of our Lord Jesus Christ, by whom the world is crucified unto me, and I unto the world" (Galatians 6:14). Crucifixion is not an end in itself but a means to an end, and that end is death. By the cross the world is dead unto me and by the cross I am dead to the world. The word "world" here, refers to the kingdom of darkness.

> Know ye not that the friendship of the world is enmity with God? whosoever therefore will be a friend of the world (the kingdom of darkness) is the enemy of God.
>
> — James 4:4

There is no compromise, no friendship, and no affinity between the kingdom of God and the kingdom of darkness. I operate from the standpoint that there can be no friendship with the kingdom of darkness whatever. I also operate from the standpoint that my life is "hid with Christ in God" which is the place of joy.

"As he is, so are we."

"For the joy of the Lord is your strength" (Nehemiah 8:10). "Your joy no man taketh from you" (John 16:22). God "will joy over thee with singing" (Zephaniah 3:17). I operate from the standpoint of the joy of the Lord. "I will bless the Lord at all times: his praise shall continually be in my mouth" (Psalm 34:1).

"As he is, so are we."

"And hath made us kings and priests unto God and his Father" (Revelation 1:6). We are royalty. (See 1 Peter 2:9.) In Jesus, I operate from the standpoint I am a reigning sovereign over my entire person, keeping all of my person in subjection to the great Sovereign of the universe whom I love with all my heart.

The triumph of the Gospel is enough to make any man the wildest kind of an enthusiastic optimist.

od has been seek-
ing a habitation a
long time. God
found a habitation
in Jesus Christ,
and He became the dwelling
place of God. Christ's purpose
for the world was that men like
Himself should become the
dwelling place of God. It was

THE HABITATION OF GOD

not purposed that Jesus Christ was to be a particular or special
dwelling place of God. It was rather purposed that mankind should be
just as much a holy and desirable dwelling place of God as Jesus
Himself was. The purpose of the Gospel of God was that through
Jesus Christ His Son many sons should be begotten of God, should
be begotten of Christ.

Christ's undertaking was to save mankind from their sins and transform them into sons of God like Himself. That is the purpose and
work of our Lord and Savior Jesus Christ.

In the fifteenth of 1 Corinthians we read of the consummation of His
purpose, that is, the finality, the conclusion of that purpose, when
Jesus Himself having subjected all things unto Himself, is Himself
also subjected unto the Father that God may be all in all.[1] There will
not be a dissenting voice nor a rebellious heart. The will of God has
been received, and as a result of the will of God having been received
there is no longer a necessity for a Savior. Jesus Christ in His capacity
of Savior of the world has been completed. His mission is completed.

We are so liable to feel in this great struggle we see about us, and the
struggle we recognize in our nature, that there cannot possibly be a
time of ultimate and final victory of the Lord Jesus Christ in the souls
of men. I want to encourage you, beloved. The Word of God portrays
a time and conception of the purpose of Jesus Christ when the world,
being redeemed unto Christ, no longer needs the redeeming merit of
the Savior. So Jesus, having subjected all things unto Himself, is
Himself also subjected unto the Father, that God may be all in all.

---

[1] See 1 Corinthians 15:28.

God is not all in all and never will be all in all, until the will of God rules in the heart of every man, in the soul of every man; until the redemption of Jesus Christ in its great and ultimate purpose becomes a reality, a finality.

PAUL SEES CHRIST'S PURPOSE

I have always regarded the first and second chapters of Ephesians as two of the most remarkable in the entire Word of God. Perhaps no soul ever envisioned the real purpose of God and portrayed it in words with more clearness than did Paul in these two chapters.

In the first chapter he begins by showing us that Jesus fulfilled the purpose of the Father. That as a reward for His consecration to the will of God — His death, resurrection, ascension, and glorification — the power of God ruled in His nature and in very truth He was the Son of God, to whom was committed all power. Principalities and powers, Paul says, being subject unto Him.[2]

Then, in the second chapter he begins to make this truth applicable to our own heart, and he undertakes to show us that just as Jesus Christ was dead and in the grave so mankind, possessed and dominated by the powers of sin and selfishness, have become "dead in sin," that is, senseless to the Spirit of God.[3] And as Jesus was raised from the dead, so He has purposed to lift the veil or cloud, the obsession or possession of sin, and cleanse the nature of man and unify him with God.

When he reaches this climax he puts it in this terse form: "For to make in himself of twain one new man, so making peace."[4] He shows that the ultimate and final peace that comes to the soul of man comes as the result of a divine union having taken place between Jesus Christ and the Christian soul, and there is no longer any worry or discussion over commandments or ordinances. The soul has risen above them. It has risen out of the region of commandments and laws, into a government of love. The soul joined to Christ in His divine affection, the spirit of man entering into Christ, the Spirit of Christ entering into

---

[2]   See Ephesians 1:21.

[3]   See Ephesians 2:5.

[4]   Ephesians 2:15.

man causes such a transformation that the man becomes a new creature. All his impulses have changed, the ruling of his human nature ceases, and finally he is a son of God.

That is the wonder of the cleansing power and cross of Christ in the nature of man. The wonder is that Jesus purposed to make your heart and mine just as sweet and lovely and pure and holy as His own. That is the reason that He can accept the Christian as His bride. Who could imagine the Christ accepting Christians polluted, defined, of a lower state of purity or holiness than Himself?

INTERPRETATION OF TONGUES

The Spirit of the Lord says that thus is the wonder of the redemptive power of Jesus Christ revealed to man and in man. Such is the transforming grace that through Him, through His merit, through His love, through His Spirit the soul of man cleansed, purified, beautified, glorified becomes like the soul of Jesus Himself, and man and Christ meet as equals in purity. Blessed be His name.

If you have felt, dear brother or sister, that you have been a sinner above all that dwelt in Jerusalem, as some did, be assured that the cleansing power of Jesus Christ is equal to your need, and the thoroughness and almightiness of His Spirit's working in you can make you a king and prince, lovely and beautiful, pure of heart and life like unto Himself.

The triumph of the teacher is always in bringing his student to his own understanding and even more than that, endeavoring to inspire within the student the possibility of going beyond himself in his search of knowledge and truth. Could we expect of Jesus a lesser purpose than that which we recognize in teachers everywhere? If Jesus is a redeemer, unto what is He to redeem us? What is the ideal, what is the standard to which Christ purposes to bring us? Is the standard less than that which He holds Himself? If so, it would be unworthy of the Son of God. He would not be giving to us the best of His soul.

Verily, the Word of God stands clear in one respect, that "the blood of Jesus Christ his Son cleanseth us from all sin."[5] Bless God. We

---

[5]   1 John 1:7.

become clean in our nature, thoroughly infilled by His grace, every atom and fiber of the spirit and the soul and the body of man made sweet and holy, like unto Jesus Himself. Bless God.

THE PURPOSE OF CLEANSING

Now this marvelous cleansing by the Spirit and power of Jesus Christ is for a definite purpose; it is a definite preparation. When we make an elaborate preparation of any kind, it is that something may follow. So this preparation in holiness and righteousness and truth in the nature of man by Jesus Christ, the Word declares, is that there may be a fitting climax; the climax is *that man may become the dwelling of God.*

God demands a holy temple in which His holiness and through which His holiness may be revealed. Consequently, it becomes a matter of necessity to the Lord Jesus Christ that if He is to reveal Himself in a hundredfold measure through the Church to the world, He must have the ability to cleanse the Church and present her, as the Word portrays, "not having spot, or wrinkle, or any such thing."[6] Blessed be the Lord. She must be pure as Jesus is pure, beautiful within, beautiful without. The scars and wrinkles must disappear. So Christ will receive the really Christ-cleansed Church as His own virgin, the Bride. Blessed be the Lord.

THE WONDER OF HIS GRACE

The wonder of the grace of God is revealed in that, though we have sinned, though we have become polluted, though in our soul-life we have practiced adultery with the spirit of the world until the nature of the world has entered into our nature and soiled it and made it unlike the nature of Jesus Christ — the wonder of His grace is revealed in that He receives us, cleanses us, purifies us, saves us and being thus redeemed and cleansed by the Spirit of Christ, we stand sweet and lovely and holy in His presence, prepared to be His bride. One in which He can live, with whom He can fellowship, into whose nature He purposes now to come and abide.

---

[6] Ephesians 5:27.

THE APOSTLES' CLEANSING AND BAPTISM

If you will study with care the life of the apostles you will observe that there was a process that took place in their lives so thorough and complete that Jesus said unto them, just prior to His departure, "Now ye are clean through the word which I have spoken unto you."[7]

They had arrived in soul cleansing at the place where, by the grace of God, they were prepared for the next experience and higher purpose of Jesus, which was that they might now receive the Holy Ghost. That is, that the Spirit of Jesus Christ might come from heaven to abide in them, and thus in very truth cause them to become the dwelling place of God.

The purpose of Christ was that not only the twelve and the hundred and twenty upon whom the Holy Ghost came at Jerusalem and the church at Samaria and the household of Cornelius should be cleansed and receive the Holy Spirit, but that every son of God should receive a like experience. (The church at Samaria was different from the church at Jerusalem, in that it was composed of the wandering heathen tribes, and it was different from the household of Cornelius, which were intelligent Romans. But they all in common with all the race became the habitation of God through the Spirit.)

In common with these, the Ephesian elders in Acts 19 who were advanced in righteousness and holiness and entrusted with the care of others as shepherds of the flock likewise received the Spirit of the Lord.

In all these instances then, we see the purpose of God is not only to cleanse a man, but being cleansed to empower him, infill him, indwell him by His own blessed almighty Spirit. The Spirit of Christ present in a holy temple has appeared to reveal Himself through that person, just as He did through the Lord Jesus Christ.

If we study the manner by which the Spirit of God revealed Himself through Jesus, then we will have the pattern or example of how the Spirit of God reveals Himself through all believers all the time.

---

[7] John 15:3.

The Spirit of God spoke through Him the word of love, the word that brought conviction, the word of power. Through His nature there flowed a subtle something that no religionist but Himself and His followers possessed — the living Spirit of the living God, the anointing of the Holy Ghost, bless God, the one characteristic that makes Christianity a distinctive religion forever. It can never be identified with any other. So long as Christianity is dependent on the presence of the Holy Ghost it will remain distinctively the one religion — that of divine power and saving grace.

PRAYER

God, our heavenly Father, our hearts are asking that since the wondrous provision has been made, that we may seek with all the earnestness that should characterize men and women, for this blessed almightiness, that the cleansing grace and power be revealed in our own life. May this not be just a beautiful vision tonight, but oh Lord, may we receive Thee in this moment into our hearts as our Lord, our Savior, our Redeemer, that the Word of Christ may be accomplished in us and that in very truth we may look into the face of Jesus, knowing that our souls are cleansed. Amen.

When I was a young man, I stood in an aisle of the Methodist Church and was introduced to a young lady. As I touched her hand, the marvelous moving of our natures was revealed. Presently something from her soul, that subtle something that Christians know and recognize as spirit, her spirit, passed to me, went through my person until presently I realized that my soul had rent itself in affection for that woman, and we never had looked into each others eyes in an intimate way before. From me went that subtle something to her. The result was that we were just as much soul mates and lovers in the next ten minutes as we were in the next seventeen years and had raised a family.

She was a woman of fine sensitive qualities, and she told me later that she had been in the habit of searching a young man's spirit to know if he was pure; but she said, "In your case, the strange thing was that my spirit made no such search. I just knew it." I want to tell you in that matter she was not wrong for when I was a boy, though I was surrounded by as vile a set of men as ever lived, I determined in my soul that one day I would look into a woman's soul and tell her that I was pure.

If you held the hand of Jesus tonight, do you suppose your spirit would be capable of searching His soul to know whether He was pure? No, instinctively something in that purer spirit would cause you to know that it was your Lord.

Then I want to ask you on the other hand, suppose the Spirit of Jesus searched our own, what would He discern? That is the question, that is the big question that men are compelled continually to ask of themselves. What would the Spirit of Jesus discern in you? What would the Spirit of Jesus discern in me? Would the Spirit of Jesus be drawn to us, or would we repel Him because of unholiness?

The Word of God lays blessed and splendid emphasis in the fact, we need the cleansing power of Jesus to make our spirit pure and sweet and lovely like His own. Then having cleansed us and sanctified us to Himself, then He Himself by the Spirit, the Holy Spirit, comes in to dwell in our nature and take up His eternal abiding and residence in us. This we welcome, bless God, the *habitation of God* through the Spirit.

I sat one day on the platform of a great tabernacle in the presence of ten thousand persons who had collected to hear me preach. I had received a promise from God the night before for that occasion. The Spirit of the Lord had given, in His own words, an outline of the history of man's nature from the creation to the redemption and empowering by the Spirit of God. But the anointing from heaven that would make possible the presentation of such an ideal and make it acceptable to the hearts of thousands who listened, had not yet come.

Presently, from the soul of an old gentleman next to me as I sat praying, I was conscious of the Spirit falling about me until my nature was overcome by it. It was difficult to maintain my seat, waiting for the preliminaries to be finished so that I could get a chance to deliver the message.

That man became the agency of divine transmission of the Spirit of God to me, just the same as Jesus Christ was the agency of divine transmission through which the Spirit of God was imparted to the people of His day.

Such is the marvel of the nature of man united to the Lord Jesus Christ, when all the abundant fullness — the *abundant fullness* — of His holy nature may come to you and me when our temple has been prepared to receive Him.

Beloved, if you have been getting along with an ounce of healing, bless your soul, if you have been getting along with a limited measure of blessing in your daily life, let me encourage you that the fountain will not be exhausted when your spirit is filled with the overflow.

The Spirit of God is like the bread that the disciples held in their hands; when it became filled with the Spirit of God it multiplied in their hands. When they broke off some there was more remaining than when they began.[8] The Spirit of God is creative, generative, constructive, and the more you give the more you receive. There must be a great opening in the nature of man in order that he may be a large receiver, and the strangeness of it is that it depends upon whether you are large givers. Nothing like it in the world. It is a violation of every law of man, but it is the common law of the Spirit. Why? Because the Spirit, unlike other things, is creative. It grows, it magnifies in your soul, it multiplies as you distribute it to another.

So Jesus laid down a perpetual law: "Give, and it shall be given unto you; good measure, pressed down, and shaken together, and running over, so shall men give into your bosom."[9]

In my experience of twenty-five years of healing ministry, I have known very few instances of a person being healed when they approached you with such words as these: "If I am healed, I will give the church so much." Or "I will make a large donation." You see, the reason is that the Spirit is not received at that place. We are just entering into a knowledge of the law of Jesus Christ: "Give and it shall be given unto you." God tried through the Mosaic Law to demonstrate to mankind that the way of blessing was the way of giving. See old Isaac when he approached God, coming with his lamb or dove in his hand, or whatever the sacrifice was that he was about to offer on his behalf.

---

[8] See Matthew 14:19-21.

[9] Luke 6:38.

THE CHRISTIAN'S OFFERING

But beloved, Christianity has a deeper revelation of the same truth. We come, not with a dove nor a lamb nor a he-goat nor a heifer. No, we come with our *life,* we come with our nature, we come with our all offering it to the Lord — not bargaining with Him, not endeavoring by a shrewd bargain to obtain the blessing. That is the reason many a soul loses its blessing. Quit it.

Very rarely have I known people to miss the blessing of God when they came openly saying, "I desire to receive; I want to give." Their spirit, their nature has come into harmony with God's law, "Give and it shall be given unto you." Don't you know that is the secret of all affection between man and man, between the sexes. Men are not always seeking for someone to love them, they are seeking for someone that they can love. When two souls are seeking for the one they can love, there is a union, and the world very gradually is learning that there are real marriages. There is a union of spirit so indissoluble that nothing on earth or in heaven will ever sunder them.

Christ is seeking for the soul that will receive His love, and the Christian, the real one, is seeking for the Christ who will receive his love. Bless God. Both are practicing the unalterable law of God, "Give, and it shall be given unto you."

Frequently, we observe that sympathy becomes the door through which affection enters lives. I once talked with a nurse, and I asked her what the hardest thing in a nurse's life was. She said, "If you remain a woman and do not become steeled in your nature and hardened in your affections you will find it most difficult to keep from permitting your affections to follow your sympathy." And over and over, as a law of life, a woman will nurse a man and before she is through she will love him. Why? Because sympathy for him has opened the door of her nature and unconsciously has flowed out in affection to him.

There is one thing that is dearer to God than anything else and the only thing that is worthwhile. It is the same thing that is dearer to every man. That thing is the affection of your heart. You can see your son rise to a place of eminence and respect in the world, and yet he will disappoint your soul. Why? Because the soul of the real father is seeking something besides that. He is seeking the affection of the son, and if he fails to receive it all the rest is barren.

Christ is seeking the affection of mankind, the union of their spirit with His, for without their affection there can never be that deep union of the spirit between God and man that makes possible a richness of life made glorious by His indwelling. That is why the love of God is held forth in the Word as the one supreme attraction to draw the soul of man in returned affection.

And you can give to your Lord your money and your property and your brain and all the other things that are usually considered to be very excellent, but if you withhold your affections from Him and give them to another, the Word says you are an adulterer.

PRAYER

Our Father, teach us to love Thee, teach us, dear Lord, its value, teach us its power, teach us our spirit's need. My God, in the richness of Thy beautiful Spirit all the impoverished nature's need is supplied. In turn, if we can add to Thy joy by giving to Thee the affection of our heart, Great God, who could withhold? Amen.

So long as religion exists you will never be able to separate real religion from the emotions of the soul. The emotions will be an open door which the Spirit uses to gain access to your life. When you reduce religious life to a science and take from it the warmth of Christ's affection, you have robbed of its charm and its almighty power.

GOD IN MAN'S MIND

When we become the habitation of God, God lives in the mind, God lives in the brain, what will be the result? What will we do and what will we say or think? What will be the tenderness of our emotions, of our soul, and what will be the depth of our feeling? What will be the growth of our capacity to love?

GOD IN MAN'S SPIRIT

When God lives in a man's spirit, the spirit of man reaches out into the boundless, touching the almightiness of God, discerning His nature, appropriating His power, securing His almightiness.

GOD IN A MAN'S BODY

God living in a man's flesh, giving off a vibration of God-life, God-power; God indwelling his blood, God indwelling his hands, God indwelling his bones and marrow — a *habitation of God*.

A real Christian woman will keep her heart clean and calm, a real Christian man will take a bath as often as he needs it and a lot of other things. Otherwise, he has a poor conception of the Son of God, who inhabits man. He will be beautiful within, beautiful without. You cannot retain the dirt and filth and rottenness and Jesus Christ at the same time. But if there begins a mighty war in your nature, the Spirit of God striving with devils and God overcomes, then you will understand the power and redemption of Christ.

I was present in a meeting in Los Angeles one time, when the Spirit fell on a man, he fell prostrate on the floor, and a group of friends gathered around. He would fight like a mad dog until he would actually swear. In the next two or three minutes that spirit would be overpowered by the Spirit of God, and he would be a saint and cry for help. Again that evil spirit would come into evidence.

The brethren said, "Mr. Lake, why don't you cast the devil out?" I replied, "God wants someone else at that job." So we sat until four in the morning. At two minutes 'til four, the evil spirit departed and the glory of God broke forth, and the worship of the man, when he recognized his Lord, was wonderfully sacred. The man arose, transformed by the indwelling of the living God.

Beloved, I want to say that if any unholiness exists in the nature, it is not by the consent of the Spirit of God. If unholiness exists in your life it is because your soul is giving consent to it, and you are retaining it. Let it go. Get it out, and let God have His way in your life.

PRAYER

God my Father, as we kneel tonight, some may feel and do feel the Spirit of God upon to overpower and cast out every unholy thing. Lord God we are glad that Christ made this divine provision for our deliverance. We would be Thine. We would be Thine alone. We would be Thine forever and forever. It is not that we may come to heaven when we die. We put away that littleness and that selfishness from our minds; and it is not, Lord God, that we may escape from punishment, for God we put away that devilish littleness.

We would be Thine because it is worthy of a son of God to be like his Lord. We would be Thine because we have desired to join our hands and hearts in the biggest miracle the world ever knew — the *redemption of the race to God forever.*

Father God, with such a vision we look to Thee, asking that by Thy grace Thee cleanse our hearts and make us indeed the dwelling place of God. Amen

The triumph of the Gospel is enough to make any man the wildest kind of an enthusiastic optimist.

Man in God and God in man — one mind, one purpose, one power, one glory.

The unifying of the nature of man and God is the crowning achievement of Jesus.

> Edited by
> W. H. Reidt
> 1220 S. Beech
> Kennewick, Washington 99336

very student of the primitive church discerns at once a distinction between the soul of the primitive Christian and the soul of the modern Christian. It lies in the spirit of *Christ dominion*.

CHRIST DOMINION

The Holy Spirit came into the primitive Christian soul to elevate his consciousness in Christ, to make him a master. He smote sin and it disappeared. He cast out devils (demons); a divine flash from his nature overpowered and cast out the demon. He laid his hands on the sick, and the mighty Spirit of Jesus Christ flamed into the body and the disease was annihilated. He was commanded to rebuke the devil, and the devil would flee from him. He was a reigning sovereign, not shrinking in fear, but overcoming by faith.

It is this spirit of *dominion* when restored to the Church of Christ, that will bring again the glory-triumph to the Church of God throughout the world, and lift her into the place, where, instead of being the obedient servant of the world and the flesh and the devil, she will become the divine instrument of salvation in healing the sick, in the casting out of devils (demons), and in the carrying out of the whole program of Jesus' ministry, as the early Church did.

his sermon was delivered in London, England, by Reverend John G. Lake at a conference of Church of England ministry presided over by Ingram, Bishop of London, who said, "It contains the spirit of primitive Christianity and reveals the distinction between the Christian soul of the first and twentieth century, the Spirit of Christ dominion, by which primitive Christianity attained its spiritual supremacy...It is one of the greatest sermons I have every heard and I recommend its careful study by every priest."

TRIUNE SALVATION

"Mr. Lake had been invited to address us and has traveled 7000 miles to be here. A committee of the Church of England was sent to South Africa to investigate Mr. Lake, his work, his power, his teaching, and his ministry. His presence here is the result of their satisfactory report."

Sermon delivered at London, England, and Washington, D.C., by Reverend John G. Lake.

Text:

> I pray God your whole spirit and soul and body be preserved blameless [without defilement, corruption] unto the coming of our Lord Jesus Christ. Faithful is he that calleth you, who also will do it.[1]

In the beginning of all things, even before the creation of man at all, there was a condition in which all things that then existed were obedient to God. Angels were obedient to the Lord. But there came a time when angels themselves rebelled against the government of God. In Isaiah, Satan is spoken of as "Lucifer, son of the morning."[2] Again the Word says, in substance, concerning him, "Wast thou not pure and holy until pride was found in thine heart?"[3]

---

[1] 1 Thessalonians 5:23-24.

[2] Isaiah 14:12.

[3] See Isaiah 14:13-15, paraphrased.

Pride was the condition which, in the angel who was pure and holy, generated the desire to be separated from God and to rebel against Him.

It was the same pride, or desire to substitute his will for the will of God, which caused Adam to sin. From Adam, humanity has derived the same instinctive desire to insist on their way instead of God's way. Through the continued exercise of the human will and the world's way, the race has drifted into misty conceptions of the real will and the real way of God. This is particularly true in regard to the nature and substance of God.

It seems difficult to think of Him as a Being and a Substance. God is Spirit, but Spirit is a materiality. And God Himself is a materiality, a heavenly, not an earthly materiality. The forms of angels are a substance, otherwise they would not be discernible. It is not an earthly substance or material, but a heavenly one.

As we think of the substance of which heavenly beings are composed and of which God Himself must necessarily be a composition, the mind settles on light and fire and spirit as a possibility.

Then the Word tells us that God breathed into Adam the breath of life, and man became a living soul.[4] There came a time when God made man. The Word tells us, "He made man's body of the substance of the earth."[5] He made man, the Word says, "in his own image, in the image of God created he him"[6]; not just in the form that God was, but God breathed into him His own self, His own being — that heavenly materiality of which God consists. He injected or breathed Himself into the man, and the man then became a composition of that heavenly substance or materiality and earth or the substance of the earth.

Adam was the created son of God. He was just like God. He was just as pure as God was pure. God fellowshipped with him. The Word of God tells us that God came down into the garden in the cool of the day and walked with Adam and talked with Adam. There was perfect

---

[4] See Genesis 2:7.

[5] Genesis 2:7, paraphrased.

[6] Genesis 1:27.

fellowship between God and Adam. He was a sinless man. He could look right into the face of God, and his eyes and his spirit did not draw back. The purity of God did not startle him. He was just as pure as God was pure. That was the original man.

Man being composed of God — of heaven — of a heavenly materiality and his body of the earth, being a sovereign like God, being equal with God in sinlessness. God treating him on an equality and giving him dominion over the earth. Man was a reigning sovereign on the earth.

Everything, all conditions, spiritual and physical were subject to that God-man. The way of sin was this: that man chose to follow the inclinations of his earth-being, animal consciousness, or body instead of his God-man, God-being, or spirit. The result was that because of the suggestion of Satan there developed calls of the earth for the earthly. After awhile he partook of things earthly and became earthly himself. Therefore the fall of man was his fall into himself. He fell into his own earthly self, out of his heavenly estate, and the separation was absolute and complete.

God had said, "In the day that thou sinnest, thou shalt die."[7] That is, in the day thou sinnest, partaking of that which is earthy, the conditions of the earth being that of decay, the death process begins. So death reigneth from the time that sin came.

Sickness is incipient death. Death is the result of sin. There is no sickness in God. There never was, there never will be, there never can be. There was no sickness in man — in the God-man — until such time as he became the earth-man, until by the operation of will he sank into himself and became of the earth, earthy. Therefore, sin is the parent of sickness in that broad sense. Sickness is the result of sin. There could have been no sickness if there had been no sin.

Man, having fallen into that condition and being separated from God, needed a Redeemer. Redemption was a necessity because the Word says, "Ye must be born again."[8] God had to provide a means of getting man back into the original condition in which he had once

---

[7] Genesis 2:17, paraphrased.

[8] John 3:7.

been. One man cannot save another because one man is of the earth, earthy even as another is, and man in the natural cannot save another. One cannot elevate another into a spiritual condition or put that one in a spiritual condition which is not in himself.

Thus it became necessary for God, in order to redeem the race, to provide a means of reuniting God and man. So Jesus was born, even as Adam had been made. He was begotten of God. He was born of God, but He partook of the tendencies of the natural life and received His natural, physical body through His mother, Mary. The Word of God speaks of the first Adam and the last Adam.[9] They were both Adams. They both came to produce a race. The first Adam had fallen and sinned. Therefore, the race that was produced through him was a race of sinful people with the same tendencies in their natures which were in his.

The last Adam, Jesus, had no sin. He had exactly the same privileges that the first Adam had. He could have sinned if He so chose. Jesus was a man in this world just as every man is. "He took not on him the nature of angels; but he took on him the seed of Abraham."[10] He did not take upon Him a heavenly condition. He took upon Himself the natural condition of the human family — fallen human nature.

But Jesus Christ triumphed over that condition of fallen human nature and did not sin, though the Word of God emphasizes that "[He] was in all points tempted like as we are, yet without sin" (Hebrews 4:15). The Word also says, "Having been tempted, he is able to succour (or to save, or deliver) them that are tempted, having himself been tempted even as we are tempted" (Hebrews 2:18, paraphrased). This is what makes Him a sympathetic Savior and Christ.

The purpose of Jesus in the world was to show us the Father. So Jesus came and committed Himself publicly at His baptism at the Jordan before all the world in these words, "unto all righteousness,"[11] to do the will of God. He willed *not* to obey His own natural human will, but to do the will of the Father and to be wholly and solely and entirely obedient to the will of God. He declared, "I came... not to do mine own will, but the will of him that sent me."[12]

---

[9] See 1 Corinthians 15:45.

[10] Hebrews 2:16.

[11] Matthew 3:15, paraphrased.

[12] John 6:38.

When a Christian is born of God and becomes a real Christian, he is made a Christ-man. If the world wants to see Jesus, it must look upon the Christian who is the Christ-man, just as we who want to look upon the Father and understand Him look upon the man Jesus, who was the embodiment of the Father. Everything that Jesus did was the will and the Word of the Father. So everything the Christian does, if he is a real one, should be the will and Word of Jesus Christ. The Christian commits himself as entirely to the will of Jesus and becomes a Christ-man as Jesus committed Himself to the will of the Father and became a God-man.

A low standard of Christianity is responsible for all the shame and sin and wickedness in the world. Many Christians think it is all right if they pattern after Jesus in a sort-of way. They imitate Him and they do the things which He did; that is, they outwardly do them. They perform kind acts and they do other things which Jesus did. But the secret of Christianity is not in doing, the secret is in being. Real Christianity is in being a possessor of the nature of Jesus Christ. In other words, it is being Christ in character, Christ in demonstration, Christ in agency of transmission. When one gives himself to the Lord and becomes a child of God — a Christian — he is a Christ-man. All that he does and all that he says from that time on should be the will and the words and the doings of Jesus, just as absolutely, just as entirely as He spoke and did the will of the Father.

Jesus gave us the secret of how to live this kind of life. Jesus showed us that the only way to live this life was to commit oneself, as He did, to the will of God and not walk in his own ways at all, but walk in God's ways. So the one who is going to be a Christ-man in the best sense and let the world see Jesus in him, must walk in all the ways of Jesus and follow Him. He must be a Christ-man, a Christian, or Christ-one.

Therefore, the things which possess the heart and which are unlike God fasten themselves because the inner being is not subject to the will of God. One of the reasons for this low standard of Christian living is the failure to recognize the trinity of our own being. Man is triune — body and soul and spirit — just the same as God is triune, being Father and Son and Holy Ghost.

Salvation begins at the time when the spirit is surrendered to God, where the name is written in the Book of Life, and we receive the conscious knowledge of sins being forgiven. Then God witnesses to the spirit that our sins are blotted out. The Word, in the eighth of Romans, says, "His Spirit itself beareth witness with our spirit, that we are the children of God."[13] That is, the testimony of the Spirit of God to our spirit is that we are the children of God when we surrender our spirits to God.

People wonder why, after having given their hearts to God and after having received a witness of the Spirit, they are troubled with evil desires and tempted in evil ways. The nature has three departments, and therefore, the surrender of the spirit to God is not all that He demands. God demands also the mind and the body.

The mind is the soul life; and it continues being of the earth, earthy, and doing earthy things until God does something, until we seek God for a new mind. It is similar to the change which occurs in the spirit, and the mind that formerly thought evil and that had wicked conceptions becomes as the mind of Christ.

The Church at large recognizes the salvation of the spirit. But they have not recognized the salvation of the mind from the power of sin, and that is why many Church people will say there is no such thing as sanctification.

There are Christian bodies that believe in the power of God to sanctify this mind, even as the spirit is saved. John Wesley, in defining sanctification, says that it is "Possessing the mind of Christ, and all the mind of Christ." An individual with all the mind of Christ cannot have a thought that is not a Christ-thought, no more than a spirit fully surrendered to God could have evil within it.

In later years, as the revelation by the Spirit of God has gone on, man has begun to see that there is a deeper degree of salvation than these two. He is a triune being. As he needed salvation for the mind and spirit, so he has a body which needs to be transformed by God. The whole question of physical healing, the redemption of the body, the possible translation, the resurrection, are included there.

---

[13] See Romans 8:16.

Christ is a Savior of the whole man — of spirit, of soul, of body. When Jesus at the Jordan committed Himself unto all righteousness to His Father, He committed His body just as He committed His mind and just as He committed His spirit. Christians have not been taught to commit their bodies to God, and therefore they feel justified in committing them to someone else, or something else, rather than to God.

Therefore, it is clear that in a whole salvation it is just as offensive to God to commit the body to the control of man as it would be to commit the spirit to man for salvation. Salvation for the spirit can only come through Jesus, through the blood of Christ, through receiving His Spirit. Salvation from natural thoughts and ways and the operation of the natural mind can only come through the natural mind being transformed into the mind of Christ. Salvation for the body is found in the same manner, by committing the body now and forever to God.

No one would think of sending to any other power than God for a remedy for the spirit. There is no spirit that one could go to, unless it is the spirit of the world or the spirit of the devil; and one goes not to either of these for the healing of the spirit or mind.

The real Christian is a separated man. He is separated forever unto God in all the departments of his life, and so his body and his soul and his spirit are forever committed to God. Therefore, from the day that he commits himself to God, he can go to no other power for help or healing, except to God. This is what gives such tremendous force to such Scriptures as this: "Cursed be the man that trusteth in man, and maketh flesh his arm, and whose heart departeth from the Lord" (Jeremiah 17:5). Second Chronicles 16, relates that Asa, the king of Israel, who in the thirty and ninth year of his reign became diseased in his feet, and in his disease he trusted not the Lord but the physicians, and he died. Asa had been trusting God for many years by taking his little, insignificant army and delivering the great armies into his hand. But when he became diseased in his feet, he trusted not the Lord but the physicians, and that was the offense of Asa against God.[14]

---

[14] See 2 Chronicles 16:12-13.

The impression I wish to leave is this: that an hundredfold consecration to God takes the individual forever out of the hands of all but God. This absolute consecration to God, this triune salvation, is the real secret of the successful Christian life.

When one trusts any department of his being to man he is weak in that respect and that part of his being is not committed to God. When we trust our minds (soul) and our bodies to man, two parts are out of the hands of God and there remains only our spirits in tune with heaven. It ought not to be so. The committing of the whole being to the will of God is the mind of God. Blessed be His name

Such a commitment of the being to God puts one in the place where, just as God supplies health to the spirit and health to the soul, he trusts God to supply health to his body. Divine healing is the removal, by the power of God, of the disease that has come upon the body. But divine health is to live day by day and hour by hour in touch with God, so that the life of God flows into the body just as the life of God flows into the mind or flows into the spirit.

The Christian, the child of God, the Christ-man, who thus commits himself to God ought not to be a subject for healing. He is a subject of continuous, abiding health. And the secret of life in communion with God, the Spirit of God, is received into the being, into the soul, into the spirit.

The salvation of Jesus was a redemption of the whole man from all the power of sin, every whit — sin in the spirit, sin in the soul, sin in the body. If salvation or redemption is from the power of sin and every sin in our being, then the effect that sin produces in us must disappear and leave when the source is healed. Thus, instead of remaining sick, the Christian who commits his body to God becomes at once — through faith — the recipient of the life of God in his body.

Jesus gave us an example of how perfectly the Spirit of God radiates not only from the spirit or from the mind, but from the body also. The transfiguration was a demonstration of the Spirit of God from within the man radiating out through his person until the illumination radiated through his clothes, and his clothes became white and glistening, and his face shone as the light. It was the radiation of God through his flesh.

In a few instances, God permitted me to see Christians thus illuminated in a measure. I am acquainted with a brother in Chicago, whose face is illuminated all the time; there is a radiation from it. His countenance is never seen in a condition of depression or as if the pores of his flesh are closed. There is an unmistakable something that marks him as one through whom the Spirit of God radiates.

God radiated through the purified personality of Jesus so that even His very clothes became white and glistening. Christians are Christ-men and stand in the stead of Jesus. The Word of God says to the Christian and to the Church: "Ye are His body."[15] The accumulated company of those who know Jesus, who really have the God-life within, are the body of Christ in the world and through that body of Christ all the ministry of Jesus is operative.

The nine gifts of the Holy Ghost are the divine equipment of God by which the Church, His body, is forever to continue to do the works of Jesus. "To one is given the word of wisdom, to another the word of knowledge, to another faith, to another the gifts of healing, to another working of miracles, to another prophecy, to another the interpretation of tongues."[16] All these gifts Jesus exercised during His earthly ministry. The people who exercise these gifts create another practical Christ — the Church which is His body, Christ being the head.

When this truth is seen, Christianity will be on a new-old basis. The illumination of God, the consciousness of our position in the world, the consciousness of our responsibility as the representatives of Christ, places upon us as Christ-men and Christ-women the burden of Christ for a lost world. Of necessity, this lifts the heart and spirit into a new contact with God and the consciousness that if a son of God, if a Christ-man to the world, then one must be worthy of his Christ. The only way to be worthy is to be in the will of Jesus.

Men have mystified the Gospel; they have philosophized the Gospel. The Gospel of Jesus is as simple as can be. As God lived in the body and operated through the man Jesus so the man on the throne, Jesus, operates through His body, the Church, in the world. Even as Jesus

---

[15] See Ephesians 1:22-23 and Ephesians 5:29-30.

[16] 1 Corinthians 12:8-10, paraphrased.

Himself was the representative of God the Father, so also the Church is the representative of Christ. As Jesus yielded Himself unto all righteousness, so the Church should yield herself to do the will of Christ.

"These signs shall follow them that believe"[17] — not the preacher or the elder or the priest, but the believer. The believer shall speak in new tongues, the believer shall lay hands on the sick and they shall recover. The believer is the body of Christ in the world. The Word says, "There shall be saviors in Zion."[18] As Jesus took us and lifted us up to the Father, and as He takes the Church and lifts it to the Father and gave Himself to sanctify and cleanse it, so the Christian takes the world and lifts it up to the Christ, to the Lamb of God that taketh away the sin of the world.[19]

The wonderful simplicity of the Gospel of Jesus is itself a marvel. The wonder is that men have not understood always the whole process of salvation. How was it that men mystified it? Why is it that we have not lived a better life? Because our eyes were dim and we did not see and we did not realize that God left us here in this world to demonstrate Him, even as the Father left Jesus in the world to demonstrate the Father.

The man with Christ in him, the Holy Ghost, is greater than any other power in the world. All other natural and evil powers are less than God; even Satan himself is a lesser power. Man with God in him is greater than Satan. That is the reason that God says to the believer, he shall cast out devils.[20] "Greater is he that is in you, than he that is in the world."[21] The Christian, therefore, is a ruler; he is in the place of dominion, the place of authority, even as Jesus was.

Jesus, knowing that all power had been given unto Him, took a basin and a towel and washed His disciples' feet. His power did not exalt Him. It made Him the humblest of all men. So the more a Christian possesses, the more of a servant he will be. God is the great servant of

---

[17] Mark 16:17.

[18] Obadiah 1:21, paraphrased.

[19] See Ephesians 5:25-26 and John 1:29.

[20] See Mark 16:17.

[21] 1 John 4:4.

the world. The One who continually gives to men the necessity of the hour. Through His guidance and direction of the laws of the world, He provides for all the needs of mankind. He is the Great Servant of the world, the greatest of all servants.

Yea, Jesus, knowing that all power had been committed to Him, and as God gave the power to Jesus, so Jesus commits through the Holy Ghost, by His own Spirit, all power to man.

I tell you, beloved, it is not necessary for people to be dominated by evil, nor by evil spirits. Instead of being dominated, Christians should exercise dominion and control other forces. Even Satan has no power over them, only as they permit him to have. Jesus taught us to close the mind, to close the heart, to close the being against all that is evil; to live with an openness to God only, so that the sunlight of God shines in. The glory radiance of God shines in, but everything that is dark is shut out.

Jesus said: "Take heed therefore *how* ye hear,"[22] not *what* you hear. One cannot help what he hears, but he can take heed how he hears. When it is something offensive to the Spirit and the knowledge of God, shut the doors of the nature against it and it will not touch you. The Christian lives as God in the world, dominating sin, evil, sickness, bless God. I would to God, He would help us to so present Jesus in the true light, that this church and the Church that is in the world, the Christian Body, would be lifted up until they would realize their privilege in Christ Jesus. Bless God, it is coming.

By the God within we cast out or expel from the being that which is not God-like. If you find within your heart a thought of sin or selfishness, by the exercise of the Spirit of God within you, you cast that thing out as unworthy of a child of God and you put it away from you.

Beloved, so should we do with our bodies. So must we do when sickness or the suggestion of sickness is present with us. Cast it out as evil; it is not of God. Dominate it! Put it away! It is not honoring to Jesus Christ that sickness should possess us. We do not want disease. We want to be gods. Jesus said, "I said ye are gods."[23] It is with the attitude of gods in the world that Jesus wants the Christian to live. Blessed be His name!

---

[22] Luke 8:18.

[23] John 10:34.

Evil is real. The devil is real. He was a real angel. Pride changed his nature. God is real. The operation of God within the heart changes the nature until we are new men in Christ Jesus, new creatures in Christ Jesus. The power of God, the Holy Ghost, is the Spirit of dominion. It makes one a god. It makes one not subject to the forces of the world or the flesh or the devil. These are under the Christian's feet. John said, "Beloved, now are we the sons of God."[24]

Beloved, God wants us to come, to stay, and to live in that abiding place which is the Christian's estate. This is the heavenly place in Christ Jesus. This is the secret place of the most high. Bless God!

The Word of God gives us this key. It says, "That wicked one toucheth him not."[25] When the Spirit of God radiated from the man, Jesus, I wonder how close it was possible for the evil spirit to come to Him? Do you not see that the Spirit of God is as destructive of evil as it is creative of good? It was impossible for the evil one to come near Him, and I feel sure Satan talked to Jesus from a safe distance.

It is the same with the Christian. It is not only in his spirit that he needs to be rid of sin, nor only in his soul that he is to be pure, it is God in the body that the individual needs for a well body. It is just God that he needs.

The complaint of the devil concerning Job was, "Hast not thou made an hedge about him?"[26] He was not able to get through that hedge to touch the man. Don't you know that the radiation of the Spirit of God around the Lord Jesus was His safeguard? The artists paint a halo around the head of Jesus. They might just as well put it around His hands, feet, body, because the radiation of the Spirit of God is from all the being.

Now the Spirit of God radiates from the Christian's person because of the indwelling Holy Ghost and makes him impregnable to any touch or contact of evil forces. He is the subjective force himself. The Spirit of God radiates from him as long as his faith in God is active. "Resist the devil, and he will flee from you."[27] "For this purpose the Son of

---

[24] 1 John 3:2.

[25] 1 John 5:18.

[26] Job 1:10.

[27] James 4:7.

God was manifested, that he might destroy the works of the devil."[28] "Whatsoever is born of God overcometh the world...even our faith. Who is he that overcometh the world, but he that believeth that Jesus is the Son of God?"[29] The reason people become sick is the same reason that they become sinful. They surrender to the suggestion of the thing that is evil and it takes possession of the heart.

Sickness is just the same. There is no difference. The suggestion of oppression is presented, and becoming frightened, the disease secures a foothold. "In my name they (the believers) shall cast out devils."[30] The believer says, "In the name of Jesus Christ I refuse to have this thing."

For 15 years God has let me move among all manner of contagious diseases, and I have never taken one of them. The devil could not make me take them. I have prayed with smallpox patients when the pustules would burst under the touch of my hands. I have gone home to my wife and babies and never carried contagion to them. I was in the "secret place of the most High."[31] Indeed, contact with diphtheria, smallpox, leprosy, and even bubonic plague and the whole range of diseases was part of my daily work in connection with the work of the Apostolic Church of South Africa.

"Behold, I give you power over all the power of the enemy, and nothing shall in anywise hurt you."[32] So the prayer of the apostle comes to us with a fresh understanding. "I pray God your whole spirit and soul and body be preserved blameless (without corruption, defilement) unto the coming of our Lord Jesus Christ. Faithful is he that calleth you, who also will do it."[33]

---

[28] 1 John 3:8.

[29] 1 John 5:4-5.

[30] See Mark 16:17.

[31] Psalm 91:1.

[32] Luke 10:19, paraphrased.

[33] 1 Thessalonians 5:23-24.

CONSECRATION PRAYER

My God and Father, in Jesus' name I come to Thee. Take me as I am. Make me what I ought to be in spirit, in soul, in body. Give me power to do right if I have wronged any, to repent, to confess, to restore. No matter what it costs, wash me in the blood of Jesus that I may now become Thy child and manifest Thee in a perfect spirit, a holy mind, a sickless body. — Amen.

THE RESURRECTION

Sermon #1

he resurrection of Jesus Christ is the greatest event in the human history, without any doubt. I believe that every sane man, every man who is accustomed to think through on the great problems of life, wants to believe that Jesus rose from the dead. I cannot believe that any man who is accustomed to weigh evidence can be happy as a skeptic.

The resurrection of Jesus Christ furnishes a solution to the human problem. By the "human problem," I mean man's being here. We may say what we will, the fact that man *is* is tremendous. His ultimate end, the reason for his being, reaches up and grips our minds and holds us in deadly embrace. And if Jesus is not the Son of God, there is no solution to the human problem. It is an enigma.

If Jesus rose from the dead the human problem is solved. We understand it. It solves the sin problem and that is the paramount problem. The universal man is conscious of the guilt of sin. I know by the altars that are built that cover the earth, by its universal priesthood. Thirty million priests in India. Why? Because India, with the rest of mankind, is conscious of guilt. Man's consciousness of guilt has made him formulate religions.

These are weighty matters I am bringing you tonight, gentlemen. These are the great basic problems of life. This is the solution of the sin problem. No religion among the religions of the world has ever offered a solution for the sin problem. Jesus Christ alone has brought the solution.

There is another problem that Jesus answers. Universal man has craved union with God. He has not only wanted to get rid of the sin problem and the sin burden and the sin guilt, but he wanted to be able to partake of the life and nature of God.

Man became a blood drinker. We call them cannibals. He became a blood drinker because he believed that if he would drink the blood of the victim who lay on his altar, he would partake of the God-nature and never die. You can see the Lord's table behind that, can't you?

The outreaching of man after God are among the saddest of all the facts of human life. Man is God-hungry. Jesus is the solution of that problem. Through Jesus Christ we become partakers of the divine nature.[1]

If Jesus arose from the dead, then redemption is a fact. If Jesus arose from the dead, man can go to heaven. At first that may not seem much to you. But you know, men, whether you have thought it through or not, the universal man believes in the life beyond the grave. Human religion has never had an adequate conception or hope.

What do I mean by human religion? The religions of India: Hinduism, Brahamanism, Buddhism. All are human religions. Christian Science is a human religion purely based upon philosophy. The very first step is to destroy the personal God, the conviction and concept of a personal God. I want to say with all candor that I believe that the men and women who have written against Christian Science, New Thought, and Unity have made the greatest mistake that was ever made in the world of apologetics. They have ridiculed it, but they have missed the crux of the matter.

Christian Science is built upon atheism. The communism of Russia has been atheistic. Christian Science as a religion is atheistic. The very first step is the destruction of the personal God. God is a person. They destroy that utterly and when they destroy that, aren't they atheists? If some man would write a book proving that Christian Science is atheism, it would destroy Christian Science in a great measure.

I am going to carry you through some facts that I want you to study with me tonight. If you are going to have a bonafide resurrection, it is necessary that you have an absolute death. You cannot have a genuine resurrection without a genuine death. I remember that Mr. Anderson, who was a disciple of Mr. Ingersol, wrote a book. I found it one day on the desk in one of my student's rooms. In it, Mr. Anderson made this assertion: that Jesus did not die, that He was in a state of coma. I want to refute it.

---

[1] See 2 Peter 1:4.

Turn to the nineteenth chapter of John. First, the Jewish Sanhedrin accepted the verdict of the Roman government that Jesus was dead. The Roman government pronounced Jesus dead. The Jewish Sanhedrin that had caused the death of Jesus accepted the verdict of the Roman government. But I want to give you something else.

John 19:31, Jesus is on the cross.

> The Jews therefore, because it was the preparation, that the bodies should not remain upon the cross on the sabbath day, (for that sabbath day was an high day,) besought Pilate that their legs might be broken, and that they might be taken away.

It was customary when they wanted death to come quickly to a crucified man that they would break his legs. That jar upon the nervous system would act upon the heart so that they would die suddenly.

> Then came the soldiers, and brake the legs of the first, and of the other which was crucified with him. But when they came to Jesus, and saw that he was dead already, they brake not his legs: But one of the soldiers with a spear pierced his side, and forthwith came there out blood and water.[2]

Let us get the picture clearly. Jesus is hanging on that cross. He has been there on the cross since three in the afternoon. It is now almost sunset. The Roman soldiers come, and the two men who were crucified with Jesus are not dead. They are hanging there moaning, and the soldiers break their legs. Death comes mercifully. One of the soldiers comes to Jesus, and His head is hanging forward. The body is cold and stiffened, and the soldier stands there and looks up at Him and then takes his spear and pierces the left side — not the right side that all the artists paint. Then he lifts on it.

That spearhead that is four to six inches wide, sharp as a razor, penetrates the side of Jesus; it goes up into the body, pierces the sack that holds the heart, and the miracle happens. Water flows out, and from that wide wound, four to six inches across, rolls great clots of coagulated blood. What happened? Jesus died of a ruptured heart. That last

---

[2] John 19:32-34.

cry was the death agony cry. His heart had ruptured, and when it ruptured the blood came pouring in from every part of the body to the heart and filled it; and as the body began to grow cold, this blood gathered there separated. The red corpuscles came to the top. The white serum settled to the bottom, and then when that soldier pierced that body and reached the heart sack, the water poured out first, and that is what John saw, then the blood.

Jesus was dead. His heart had been ruptured. The prophecy of the 22nd Psalm had been fulfilled. It was written a thousand years before Jesus died, and it is the most graphic picture ever written. I want you to note now, that Jesus was dead.

Read the last part of this chapter beginning with verse 38.

> And after this Joseph of Arimathea, being a disciple of Jesus, but secretly for fear of the Jews, besought Pilate that he might take away the body of Jesus: and Pilate gave him leave. He came therefore, and took the body of Jesus. And there came also Nicodemus, which at the first came to Jesus by night, and brought a mixture of myrrh and aloes, about an hundred pound weight. Then took they the body of Jesus, and wound it in linen clothes with the spices, as the manner of the Jews is to bury.[3]

What was the custom of the Jews? The wealthy Jews followed the processes that they had learned in Egypt. And all of the wealthier Jews had slaves that had learned the art of embalming the human body. It was not the total process.

So they took the body of Jesus from the cross. Joseph of Arimathaea was wealthy. Nicodemus was wealthy. And they washed the precious body. Then they took the linen cloth and they tore it up into strips one and a half to two inches wide, and they took this sticky substance, a hundred pounds weight, and they smeared that cloth as you would a salve. Then they took a toe and wrapped it. Then the foot, then the leg, then the fingers and hands and arms. Then the body was wrapped round and round until they used one hundred pounds of that sticky substance. And they used linen cloth enough to use one hundred

---

[3] John 19:38-40.

pounds. Jesus weighed likely two hundred pounds before His crucifixion. He must have been a perfect man — six feet, broad of shoulders, deep chest. He was God's crown of creation, the Master man, and He stood a king and peer among men.

If He weighed two hundred pounds, He must have shrunk twenty pounds at the crucifixion. He would be one hundred and eighty pounds plus one hundred pounds. Jesus body would weigh two hundred and eighty to three hundred pounds. The body was hermetically sealed. Across the chest it must have been three inches thick, perhaps more. One hundred pounds smeared like that over the body would be over one inch thick.

The entire body was covered except the face. That was left for loving hands to embalm, and the women came down to finish the embalming. If Jesus had not died of a ruptured heart and had not died of the spear thrust, after the body had been covered by the substance as I have indicated — hermetically sealed, so no air could get to it — He would not have lived four hours.

I want you to know that Jesus was dead. Rome pronounced Him dead. The Sanhedrin pronounced Him dead. The spear had found a ruptured heart. Blood and water had flowed out of it. He is now hermetically sealed and put in a tomb and that tomb is as dry as it is around Los Angeles in the summertime. And that body put in that place, it would only take a little while until the grave clothes would harden. You know that cloth would shrink more or less and tighten on the body.

Jesus is dead, in Joseph's tomb, and His body is hermetically sealed, and just that little place around the face is uncovered.

Turn with me now to the twentieth chapter of John. Do you know anything about the value of narrative evidence before a jury or judge? Suppose a man has been killed down here on the street in a brawl and the trial has come. Here is the value of narrative evidence. The trial goes on, and finally a little newsboy goes on the witness stand. He is fearless in the presence of the judge. He knew the judge. He knew the lawyers. He had sold them papers. He stands there unabashed in the presence of the judge, and presently the prosecuting attorney says, "Tell us what you saw." And in the vernacular of the street he begins to tell. He says, "I saw that guy over there and the man that was killed quarreling. Mickey and I were shooting craps, and we heard the scrap and we saw that fellow there, judge. I saw him pull out a knife and stab and then run."

What do they do with that kind of evidence? That is narrative evidence. The boy describes it exactly as he saw it. The judge sits and listens, the jury sits and listens, and the court draws out of the child the whole picture. You cannot bring any kind of rebuttal. That boy's story has been the evidence. The boy saw it. That settles it; he saw it.

Here is a narrative evidence. Here is the type of evidence that has been overlooked by people trying to prove the deity of Jesus.

> The first day of the week cometh Mary Magdalene early, when it was yet dark, unto the sepulchre, and seeth the stone taken away from the sepulchre. Then she runneth, and cometh to Simon Peter, and to the other disciple, whom Jesus loved, and saith unto them, They have taken away the Lord out of the sepulchre, and we know not where they have laid him. Peter therefore went forth, and that other disciple, and came to the sepulchre. So they ran both together: and the other disciple did outrun Peter and came first to the sepulchre. And he stooping down, and looking in, saw the linen clothes lying; yet went he not in. Then cometh Simon Peter following him, and went into the sepulchre, and seeth the linen clothes lie, and the napkin, that was about his head, not lying with the linen clothes, but wrapped together in a place by itself. Then went in also that other disciple, which came first to the sepulchre, and he saw, and believed.

— John 20:1-8

Now what was it John saw that made him believe in the resurrection? "For as yet they knew not the scripture, that he must rise again from the dead."[4] Not one of the disciples believed that Jesus was going to rise from the dead. And after He arose from the dead they doubted it, and Jesus upbraided them for their unbelief.

---

[4] John 20:9.

Now what was it that made John believe? Let us go back and look at the story. Mary and the other women came down to finish the embalming of Jesus. Three days had gone by and before the face lost its beauty to them, they were going to cover it like the rest of the body. A napkin had been lying on the face. But when Mary arrived she found someone had been there and opened the sepulchre. She did not stop to look in. Filled with anger and indignation, for to the Jew the dead is sacred, she starts back to the city to tell Peter and John.

Down through the city she runs, bursts into the room where they were and says, "They have taken away the body of the Lord, and I do not know where they have laid Him." Then Peter, who had gone through hell for three days and three nights because he had denied Jesus in the face of the Sanhedrin said, "John, let's go." Peter is large and heavy of body and they run, and John outruns him, and he comes to the sepulchre hewn out, and a big stone had been rolled against it and sealed, but the stone is away now. And John drops on his knees and looks in. John has in him that refinement that you can feel through his writings.

But when Peter comes, he is a coarser type. He ducks his head and goes into the sepulchre. Then John reverently follows him. John *saw* something that made him believe. When God revealed this thing to me, he revealed it to a skeptic. I had been preaching for years, but in my secret heart I had questions about the resurrection of Jesus.

Come now, we will step inside the sepulchre. If John, when he went in, had seen that someone had come and ripped down that thing, he would not have believed. If John had seen that some wild animal had torn those grave clothes to shreds, would he have believed? No! Well, had John gone in and had seen the grave clothes intact and that Jesus had come out of the cocoon without destroying the rest of it, what would John have done? What would you have done? You would have believed.

I want to tell you what I did when I saw that empty cocoon, and I saw that the broad shoulders of Jesus had come out of the aperture for His face, that had hardened like a board. I slipped off my chair on to my knees, and I said what Thomas said, "My Lord and my God!"[5] I knew Jesus had risen from the dead. I submit this to you. This is perfectly in harmony with Jewish custom of burying. It is within reason.

Josephus tells us there were more than a million visitors in Jerusalem. It was one of the cycle years when the Jews came from all over the world to make their sacrifices. Outside the city booths were built. Jews who were commercial travelers had come to their old home in Jerusalem. There was one thing that filled the very air — the story of Jesus. Thousands, ten thousands, had gone out and had seen the dead body of Jesus hanging on the cross. He was crucified early in the morning and the city was shaken to the foundation. Everybody was talking about it.

And when Peter and John came down over the hillside to the cemetery where Jesus was buried, what do you think they did? What do you think impulsive, warmhearted Peter did? Did he keep it quiet? Peter, rushing down to the first man he met, what do you suppose he said? What do you suppose John said? I know what you would say; I know what I would say. "He is risen." You would not have to say, "Jesus is risen."

In an hour's time, the whole city of Jerusalem was stirred to its foundations. It stirred under the impulse of the new miracle. What did they do? Do you suppose they stood and talked, or do you think they made a rush for the sepulchre? You can see them going. If it had been in Portland, a hundred thousand people would have visited it that day. A hundred thousand Jews visited that hillside and smote their breast and tore their hair, and they went back to tell it. All that day the empty cocoon preached and told the story that Jesus had risen from the dead. It went on day after day and week after week until forty-nine days, less three. For forty-seven days the clothes on the hillside preached, and countless thousands of men were stirred and shaken to the foundation.

And then, after the forty days John says, "I saw Him!"

Peter says, "I saw Him." And five hundred men followed Him to Olivet and saw Him ascend. What do you suppose the five hundred men told the multitude of visitors? There was no other subject talked about. That goes without arguing.

---

[5] John 20:28.

Then fifty days later another staggering thing happened. Early in the morning they heard the rushing, mighty wind, like a thousand airplanes over the town.[6] God had planned the drama.

One hundred and twenty men and women in that great square filled with people, and they heard those men and women speaking in tongues and glorifying God, telling of the resurrection of Jesus. Every man and woman hears in his own language. Every man hears the first message of Jesus in his own tongue and from the lips of Galilean fishermen. Some laugh, but others were serious.[7] It was the climax that for fifty days had rocked Jerusalem and staggered the Jewish nation.

Peter stands forth. In the presence of whom? The Sanhedrin, the Senate, and the elders of Israel. Who is Peter? He is a humble fisherman. He is an untutored man. He has the same reverence for the high priest that the Roman Catholics have for the Pope. The Sanhedrin was sacred to him. He bowed before it. He feared it. The High Priest was sacred to him.

Yet, Peter stands out in the presence of the Sanhedrin, and he indicts first the Roman Governor as having murdered the Son of God. Second, he indicts the Sanhedirn, then the Senate and priesthood as murderers of the Son of God. His indictment is the most severe, the most amazing ever uttered.

Peter speaks only about twenty-five or thirty minutes, not longer than that, and what happens? Three thousand Jews broke with Judaism and accepted Jesus Christ of Nazareth as the Son of God and were baptized.

Where did he preach that sermon? Within the very shadow of that cross, within ten or twelve minutes of where Jesus hung stark naked one day crowned with thorns as an outcast. And three thousand Jews broke with Judaism. And every Jew who accepted Jesus Christ indicted the Sanhedrin, the Senate, and the Roman government with the murder of Jesus.

That was the most dramatic thing that ever happened in history. There is nothing like it. If that thing was not true, all Ananias or Caiaphas had to do was to stop it — raise his hand and say, "Gentlemen,

---

[6] See Acts 2:2.

[7] See Acts 2:5-13.

we know where the body of Jesus is. It has never raised." But Caiaphas never raised his voice. Caiaphas knew Jesus had risen from the dead. The Sanhedrin could have wiped out the whole thing in one day, but they dared not move until finally, two thousand more Jews accepted Christ Jesus. In the next two or three days five thousand and a large company of the priesthood swung into line.

They had Peter and John arrested because they healed a man. I want to read to you from Acts 4:6:

> And Annas the high priest, and Caiaphas, and John, and Alexander, and as many as were of the kindred of the high priest.

This was the same crowd that crucified Jesus.

> Then Peter, filled with the Holy Ghost, said unto them, Ye rulers of the people, and elders of Israel, if we this day be examined of the good deed done to the impotent man, by what means he is made whole; be it known unto you all, and to all the people of Israel, that by the name of Jesus Christ of Nazareth, whom ye crucified, whom God raised from the dead, even by him doth this man stand here before you whole. This is the stone which was set at nought of you builders, which is become the head of the corner.[8]

"If we have been arrested and locked up for healing a tramp, a beggar, an outcast, for a good deed, be it known unto you and to all the people of Israel, that in the name of Jesus Christ of Nazareth, whom *ye* crucified, whom God raised from the dead, even in him doth this man stand here before you whole."

That is the most masculine piece of frenzy ever used in the world.

> Neither is there salvation in any other: for there is none other name under heaven given among men, whereby we must be saved.[9]

---

[8] Acts 4:8-11.

[9] Acts 4:12.

And when they heard it, they could say nothing against it; and they sent them out, and said:

> That indeed a notable miracle hath been done by them is manifest to all that dwell in Jerusalem; and we cannot deny it. But that it spread no further among the people, let us straitly threaten them, that they speak henceforth to no man in *this name.*[10]

You can preach anything you want to, but don't preach in *the name.* The name has dynamite in it. The name will raise the dead, heal the sick, cast out devils. The name: It is Jesus again on earth.

What are you going to do with that kind of evidence? Did Jesus rise from the dead? Before Jesus died He said something that would forever brand Him as an impostor. He said, after I am gone I am going to give you legal right to the use of my name, and "Whatsoever you shall ask the Father in my name, I will do it."[11]

No other human being ever dared to talk like that. When a man was dead, he was dead. But here was a man that was going to do bigger things after He died than when He was alive, and He was going to give us the legal right to use His name. "Just whisper My name, and whatsoever you say, it will be done." That was the most staggering thing that was ever said. That brands Jesus as the very Son of God or as an impostor.

What happened? Did His name have power after He was dead? Jesus is the Son of God. I think I have made my case, haven't I?

I believe, gentlemen, that this thing is only a little fragment out of the body of truth. I believe that if it were given to the world that 90 percent of our skepticism would cease to be.

I want to make a few deductions. What are the implications if Jesus Christ rose from the dead? What then? Here are three things. We know He is the Son of God. We know that "He died for our sins

---

[10] Acts 4:16-17.

[11] John 14:13-14 and John 16:23, paraphrased.

according to the Scriptures, and rose again for our justification."[12] We know that every man who accepts Jesus Christ, God redeems that man, and we know that Romans 3:26 is true:

> That he might be just, and the justifier of him which believeth in Jesus.

God automatically, when you confess Jesus and accept Him as your Lord, becomes your righteousness. And the moment that God becomes your righteousness, that moment your standing is like the standing of the Son of God.

For years I hunted for this thing I have given you tonight. That ounce of unfitness and unworthiness (or as they call it in psychology, that inferiority complex) swamped me. But when I saw that God became my righteousness I said, "I want you to know, Satan, that you have lost your case." I know what I am now.

> For he hath made him to be sin for us, who knew no sin; that we might be made the righteousness of God in him.
>
> — 2 Corinthians 5:21

You, by the new birth, have become the righteousness of God, and God has become your righteousness. God could not make it any stronger than that.

I say to you reverently, friends, that if you have accepted Jesus Christ and are born again, you are standing in the presence of the great eternal Father God as Jesus is. You have just as much right to step into the presence of God Almighty's presence as Jesus has.

Don't you see what that means? It means that Satan cannot stand before you any more than he can stand before Jesus. Not only that, Jesus gave you the legal right to use His name. And the first thing He tells you to do is to cast out demons. The first thing He told the twelve to do was to cast out demons.[13] When He sent the seventy out, He told them to cast out demons.[14] When He gave the Great Commission He said, "They that believe shall cast out demons."[15] This is the first thing. Why?

---

[12] Romans 4:25 and 1 Corinthians 15:3-4, paraphrased.

[13] See Matthew 10:8.

[14] See Luke 10:17.

[15] Mark 16:17, paraphrased.

The devil is the opposer, and as long as the devil reigns over the sinner, the sinner cannot do anything. It is your business to break his power. Can't you see sickness is called *sin in the flesh*, and God *"has condemned sin in the flesh,* that the righteous requirement of the law might be fulfilled in us, who walk not after the flesh, but after the Spirit."[16]

Your sickness has been condemned, indicted, and found guilty before the high court of God. And it has no more right in your body than I have a right to be in some other man's house or store that is locked up. And if I am found there, I will be arrested. And that disease has no right in your body, and you have no right to leave it there, to sympathize with it or to harbor it or to console it. You are consoling the enemy of God that is under indictment and condemnation. It is a serious thing I am bringing, gentlemen. Jesus Christ has absolutely redeemed you, for He rose from the dead, and disease has no right in your body and no power to stay there if you take sides with Jesus. You have a right to your healing, to redemption, to victory. You have a right to prayer. You have a right to your Father's fellowship.

---

[16] Romans 8:3-4, paraphrased.

THE RESURRECTION
Sermon #2

hrough Jesus Christ, Christianity stepped into the arena of the world religions as a challenger. The Son of God, just as the ancient athlete did, threw down His gauntlet on the ground and challenged the religions of the world to take it up. Heaven's challenge still stands. Sophisticated religions, uncertainties, philosophic illusions and delusions have claimed the world's interest, but Heaven's challenge stands just as vigorously today as it ever did. So long as the blessed Word of God lives in the world, so long shall that challenge endure.

Other religions were old, long-whiskered, and gray haired when Jesus Christ entered the arena. Christianity was a babe among the ancient religions. Zoroaster[1] had lived, taught his "purification by fire," and worshipped the human soul — the fire god. Zoroaster could conceive only one possibility of purifying the human soul, a process of fire cleansing. There could be no other. That was the conclusion of the ancient world.

Buddha followed about 500 BC, but with no better hope than Zoroaster. His ideal was oblivion, personality lost, individuality gone, merged into the great whole, without distinctive consciousness, vacuity.[2]

Mohammed came at a later period, about 550 years after Jesus Christ. His heaven was a harem, the possibility of everlasting sensuality. Then, in modern days Mormonism followed with its "spiritual marriages" and dream of eternal polygamy, all abominable to the Spirit of the Son of God and as unlike Christianity as anything could be.

Into the muck and the mess and the darkness came the Son of God with the glory of holiness, divine righteousness, heavenly purity, angelic estate, never ceasing consciousness, perpetuated individually, life forevermore, resurrection from the dead, man's enjoyment of God eternally, yourself a son of God, like the Son of God, Himself; in His likeness immortalized.

---

[1] Zoroaster was a 6th century Persian religious teacher.

[2] vacuity: absence of ideas or intelligence. *Webster's Desk Dictionary of the English Language* (NY: Gramercy Books, 1983), p.989.

Heaven stood aghast, earth stood aghast, and hell stood aghast when Jesus Christ stepped into the arena. Could He accomplish the thing He talked about? Was there power in heaven or on earth to revolutionize the nature of man, change the darkness, take away sin, and obliterate the night from his soul? Could the darkened soul be lightened from on high? Could the spirit of man, begotten in iniquity, be changed into loveliness, heavenliness, and holiness? Could the personality of man be preserved? Were Christians going to die just like others die? Did He truly possess eternal life? Could He impart it to others? Was Jesus Christ a boaster or a Savior?

Christianity did not come to the world to apologize for its existence or to beg a place to live. It came as heaven's champion. It has the champion soul. "It shall bruise thy head, and thou shalt bruise his heel" (Genesis 3:15). That champion-consciousness is in the soul of the Christian. Being born of God, he is champion of the Son of God and a demonstrator of His salvation. He is the champion of God. He cannot be anything else. "As he is, so are we in this world."[3]

In our day, we have almost come to the place where the world is being taught to believe that the message of Christianity is morality — be decent, don't act like a pig, keep the beast under control. That is about the message of modern Christianity. Jesus Christ never wasted His time establishing mere morality. Jesus Christ, the Son of God, declared *immortality* to be the goal of Christianity, its attainment, the purpose of God for you and me. "I will raise him up at the last day,"[4] said Jesus. "I will give him eternal life."[5] "The dead in Christ shall rise first."[6]

No religion in the world except Christianity ever suggested resurrection as its declared intent. Who in the world except Christianity ever suggested resurrection as its declared intent? Who in the world was ever bold enough to suggest a resurrection? What dying creature could? It was only the Son of God Himself, out of heaven, with the knowledge of immortality and eternal life that would dare to suggest such a climax for mankind. If there were no other evidence of Jesus

---

[3] 1 John 4:17.

[4] John 6:40,44,54.

[5] John 10:28, paraphrased.

[6] 1 Thessalonians 4:16.

Christ's eternality but that, it would be sufficient. "Who only hath immortality."[7] "In him was *life;* and the *life* was the light of men."[8] "He that liveth and believeth in me shall never die."[9] "Destroy this temple, and in three days I will raise it up."[10] Marvelous Redeemer!

Christianity stands today absolutely unique. No other religion on earth has our hope, or our consciousness, or our power. I fear sometimes that we moderns somehow have lost the spirit of original Christianity. We have lost the smash of it. We have lost the charge of it. We have lost the overcoming of it. We are begging the devil for a place in the world, apologizing for our faith in God, trying to conform our religion to the mind of the world.

Salvation is the transforming power of God. Jesus Christ looked upon the world which was saturated with sin, shapen in iniquity, and said that the task was not too great for Him. The biggest contract in this universe was undertaken back in the eternal ages when one time, in the council of the Godhead, Jesus Christ, the responsible Creator, became the responsible Saviour and settled the sin question by offering Himself as the Saviour of the world. He wrought our redemption. "He that...believeth on him that sent me, hath everlasting life" (John 5:24).

His dying on the cross was the first incident in connection with our redemption but it was not the conclusive incident. If Jesus had died on the cross and the process of salvation had ceased then, there would not be a redeemed sinner today.

David was sitting on the mountainside one afternoon watching his sheep, and his spirit traveled out into the regions of God. He began to observe, as a seer does, the things that were taking place; and he broke out shouting,

> Thou hast ascended on high, thou hast led captivity captive: thou hast received gifts for men; yea, for the rebellious also, that the Lord God might dwell among them.
>
> — Psalm 68:18

---

[7] 1 Timothy 6:16.

[8] John 1:4.

[9] John 11:26, paraphrased.

[10] John 2:19.

Lift up your heads, O ye gates; and be ye lifted up, ye everlasting doors; the King of Glory is coming in.

— Psalm 24:7 FFV [11]

That is the Christ of God; that is His salvation!

This was a battle of worlds. It was not a battle of earthly religions. It was the battle of every power of light and darkness in heaven and earth. Jesus Christ, the champion of righteousness and salvation, had to make good or, like the philosophers, pass into oblivion at the grave. Instead of being the life-giver, He would have been just the propounder of another philosophy.

The resurrection morning came. Jesus, discussing His life had said, "I have power to lay it down, and I have power to take it again" (John 10:18). He took it at His will. He commanded life! He lived, and death became a captive. Jesus Christ, the Son of God, was victor — none like Him in all the universe. He came out of the battle with the "keys of hell and of death"(Revelation 1:18). No other soul in heaven or earth ever had such an experience. None other had ever challenged death. No other had ever taken death and hell captive. Jesus Christ stood unique in earth, in hell, in heaven.

When Jesus came forth in the resurrection, something breathed and throbbed and pulsed in Him that had never breathed or throbbed or pulsed before. It was the new *eternal* life. He used a new vocabulary — the ordinary language was not big enough. He said, "All power is given unto me in heaven and in earth."[12] Who else in the universe had ever experienced such a thing? None but the Son of God. *"All power"* language exists in Christian vocabulary only. Christianity came from the heart of the Glorified. Christianity is the heavenly triumph. Christianity is 100 percent supernatural — God possessing man.

Just as God breathed the breath of life into Adam, so Jesus Christ breathed upon His disciples. If He could breath this consciousness of

---

[11] "FFV" is the Ferrar Fenton Version of the Bible, entitled *The Holy Bible in Modern English*. It is a direct translation from Hebrew, Chaldee, and Greek published in 1903 by Destiny Publishers in Merrimac, Massachusetts.

[12] Matthew 28:18.

triumph into them, they would become triumphant also. If they could take the deathless life of Christ, they would become deathless likewise. "He breathed on them, and saith unto them, Receive ye the Holy Ghost" (John 20:22). In Peter's Pentecostal sermon he gives a revelation that no other writer gives us. Peter's broken heart was penetrative. He saw into the glory. He saw Jesus ascending to the throne of God. He saw the Almighty God receive Him at the throne. He observed what took place. He said,

> Having received of the Father the promise of the Holy Ghost, he hath shed forth this, which ye now see and hear.[13]

He saw Him get the eternal saving marvel for universal distribution to all mankind.

Right then Jesus became the world's Savior, the Savior of all mankind. He now possessed the saving grace, the Holy Spirit. God had fulfilled His promise. It completed His Saviorhood. It made Him heaven's High Priest. He had qualified as High Priest of things eternal. It was His right now to pour out the Holy Spirit on every hungry heart that was ready to receive. They were baptized in the Holy Spirit. So may you be.

A TWO-PART RESURRECTION

God offers a two-part resurrection to every sinner. When a person accepts Jesus as his Savior, he will experience a spiritual resurrection.

> And you hath he quickened, who were dead in trespasses and sins... Even when we were dead in sins...and hath raised us up together, and made us sit together in heavenly places in Christ Jesus.
>
> — Ephesians 2:1,5,6

It is Christ in you (Colossians 1:27). We are partakers of the divine nature (2 Peter 1:4).

---

[13] Acts 2:33.

Consider the result of being born into the family of God. It means a new Father, a new Savior, a new Captain, a new armor, a new Physician, a new Comforter, a new Guide, a new Teacher, a new Truth.

It brings within, a new heart, a new mind, a new grace, a new hope, a new peace, a new joy, a new calmness, a new outlook on life, and a new purpose for living and being.

It is reflected in a new gentleness, a new kindness, a new cheerfulness, and a new love.

This new life brings with it a new power, a new protection, a new message, a new responsibility, a new rest, and a new shout of victory. We are a new creation in Christ Jesus (2 Corinthians 5:17). Even the physical body is quickened by the Spirit that dwelleth in us, that we may have good health (Romans 8:11).

The second part is the resurrection of the physical body. This is the mark of the prize of the high calling of God (Philippians 3:14). Paul realized that he needed to attain unto the resurrection (Philippians 3:11). It is the redemption of our bodies (Romans 8:23). It will be a permanent condition.

What will the resurrected body be like? In Luke 24:39, Jesus had His disciples handle Him and see, for a spirit hath not flesh and bones. That will be the composition of the resurrected body.

When will the resurrection take place?

> At the last trump: for the trumpet shall sound, and the dead shall be raised incorruptible, and we shall be changed. For this corruptible (the dead) must put on incorruption, and this mortal (those alive) must put on immortality.
>
> — 1 Corinthians 15:52-53

How long does it take to raise the dead and change the living? In the twinkling of an eye (1 Corinthians 15:52).

God has a plan for your life. It can only be realized on one condition. That condition is the (your) personal acceptance of Jesus as your Savior. Today is the day of salvation.[14] God loves you and wants to bless you and give you rest and peace.

---

[14] See 2 Corinthians 6:2.

THE COMMANDMENTS AND THE PROMISES OF JESUS

Published by

Zion Apostolic Church

John G. Lake, Overseer

Spokane, Washington

Price 25 cents

THE COMMANDMENTS OF JESUS
The Only Real Basis for a Kingdom Consecration
Rev. John G. Lake

ow far the world and the Church are away from the standard of Jesus Christ can best be understood by a study of the commandments of Jesus.

The commandments of Jesus are binding and constitute His standard for the Christian conscience. The degree of our Christ-likeness can be ascertained by the practical application of these commandments to our life. As a test of the spirit, they are the only infallible rule. If the spirit in us honors, teaches, and causes us to live in absolute harmony with the principles and commandments and teachings of Jesus Christ, then it is the Spirit of God.

The eight Beatitudes are the basis for the real Christian's consecration. When they are embodied in us in actual fact, we are citizens-elect of the kingdom of heaven. In the millennial age, when Jesus establishes on this earth His universal kingdom, consisting of "A parliament of man, the federation of the world,"[1] and governs the same as King, the eight Beatitudes or principles, together with the Sermon on the Mount, (Matthew 5, 6, and 7) and the commandments of Jesus, will be the constitution and the laws of the kingdom.

He who obtains a place in the kingdom of heaven does so through being born again. From his new birth, his life should be governed by the principles and commandments of Jesus. The tremendous selfishness of the world and the average Christian life is best understood by the application of the unselfish principles and commands of Jesus. Observation demonstrates that the really great in God who bless

---

[1] We were unable to locate a source for this quote.

mankind are those who live in absolute accordance with the teachings of Jesus. With what force then the words of Jesus come to us, as spoken at the close of His Sermon on the Mount:

> Therefore whosoever heareth these sayings of mine, and doeth them, I will liken him unto a wise man, which built his house upon a rock: And the rain descended, and the floods came, and the winds blew, and beat upon that house; and it fell not: for it was founded upon a rock. And every one that heareth these sayings of mine, and doeth them not, shall be likened unto a foolish man, which built his house upon the sand: And the rain descended, and the floods came, and the winds blew, and beat upon that house; and it fell: and great was the fall of it. And it came to pass, when Jesus had ended these sayings, the people were astonished at his doctrine: For he taught them as one having authority.

— Matthew 7:24-29

PREFACE TO THE SECOND EDITION

The commandments of Jesus are the authoritative declaration of the Son of God and are forever binding on the Christian soul. They supersede the Ten Commandments of the Law of Moses, as is seen clearly in the fact that Jesus declared, "It is written in your law, 'Thou shalt not kill,' but *I say unto you* that he that hateth without a cause is a murderer."[2]

What is the value of the former commandment when superseded by one making a superior demand upon the conscience?

> Again the Law says, "Thou shall not commit adultery." But *I say unto you* he that looketh on a woman to lust after her, has committed adultery already with her in his heart.[3]

And so the original commandment was made null and void by the holier commandment.

---

[2] Matthew 5:21-22, paraphrased.

[3] Matthew 5:27-28, paraphrased.

The commandments of Jesus embody the entire teaching and practice of real Christianity. How a Christian can live without a copy of the commandments of Jesus is a surprise. That they have never been compiled and published except by ourselves is one of the greatest surprises. They should be in the hands of every person, saint and sinner, who is interested in knowing what real Christianity is and what *Jesus* really taught.

John G. Lake.

THE SEVENTY COMMANDMENTS OF JESUS

Editor's note: In the following scriptures, all italicized words are Lake's emphasis.

> He that hath my commandments, and keepeth them, he it is that loveth me: and he that loveth me shall be loved of my Father, and I will love him, and will manifest myself to him.

— John 14:21

> Blessed are they that do his commandments, that they may have right to the tree of life, and may enter in through the gates into the city.

— Revelation 22:14

> Seek ye first the kingdom of God, and his righteousness.

— Matthew 6:33

> Thou shat love the Lord thy God will all thy heart, and with all thy soul, and with all thy mind.

— Matthew 22:37

> A new commandment I give unto you, That ye *love one another;* as I have loved you, that ye also love one another.

— John 13:34

What therefore God hath joined together, let not man put asunder.

— Matthew 19:6 (See also Matthew 5:32.)

Thou shalt love thy neighbour as thyself.

— Matthew 22:39

Love your *enemies.*

— Luke 6:27

Bless them that *curse* you.

— Luke 6:28

Do good to them which *hate* you.

— Luke 6:27

Therefore all things whatsoever ye would that men should do to you, do ye even so to them.

— Matthew 7:12

Be ye therefore *merciful,* as your Father also is merciful.

— Luke 6:36

Judge not, and ye shall not be judged.

— Luke 6:37

Condemn not, and ye shall not be condemned.

— Luke 6:37

Resist not evil: but whosoever shall smite thee on thy right cheek, turn to him the other also.

— Matthew 5:39

If any man will sue thee at the law, and take away thy coat, let him have thy cloak also.

— Matthew 5:40 (See also 1 Corinthians 6:7.)

Agree with thine adversary quickly, whiles thou art in the way with him.

— Matthew 5:25

If thy brother shall trespass against thee, go and tell him his fault between thee and him alone.

— Matthew 18:15

Leave there thy gift before the altar, and go thy way; first be reconciled to thy brother, and then come and offer thy gift.

— Matthew 5:24

First cast out the beam out of thine own eye; and then shalt thou see clearly to cast out the mote out of thy brother's eye.

— Matthew 7:5

If thy right eye offend thee, pluck it out.

— Matthew 5:29

Be not ye called Rabbi: for one is your Master, even Christ; and all ye are brethren.

— Matthew 23:8

Neither be ye called masters: for one is your Master, even Christ.

— Matthew 23:10

Call no man your father upon the earth: for one is your Father, which is in Heaven.

— Matthew 23:9

Enter ye in at the strait gate.

— Matthew 7:13 (See also Luke 13:24-30.)

If any man will come after me, let him deny himself, and take up his cross daily, and follow me.

— Luke 9:23 (See also Luke 14:27.)

What is that to thee? *follow thou me.*

— John 21:22

Repent: for the kingdom of heaven is at hand.

— Matthew 4:17

Follow me, and I will make you fishers of men.

— Matthew 4:19

Tarry ye in the city of Jerusalem, until ye be endued with power from on high.

— Luke 24:49 (See also Acts 1:8, 2:38-39.)

Take my yoke upon you, and learn of me.

— Matthew 11:29

Search the Scriptures.

— John 5:39

What I tell you in darkness, that speak ye in light: and what ye hear in the ear, that preach ye upon the housetops.

— Matthew 10:27

Go home to thy friends, and tell them how great things the Lord hath done for thee.

— Mark 5:19

Go ye therefore, and teach all nations, baptizing them in the name of the Father, and of the Son, and of the Holy Ghost: teaching them to observe *all things* whatsoever *I have commanded you:* and, lo, I am with you alway, even unto the end of the world (age).

— Matthew 28:19-20

As ye go, preach, saying, The kingdom of heaven is at hand. *Heal* the sick, *cleanse* the lepers, *raise* the dead, *cast out* devils: freely ye have received, *freely give.* Provide neither gold, nor silver.

— Matthew 10:7-9

In the same house remain, eating and drinking such things as they give: for the labourer is worth of his hire. Go not from house to house.

— Luke 10:7

He that believeth and is baptized shall be saved.... And these signs *shall follow* them that believe; In my name shall they cast out devils (demons); they shall speak with new tongues.... they shall lay hands on the sick, and they shall recover.

— Mark 16:16-18 (See also Luke 10:1-12.)

Master, we saw one casting out devils in thy name...and we forbad him, because he followeth not us. But Jesus said, *Forbid him not.*

— Mark 9:38-39 (See Numbers 11:27-29; Luke 9:50.)

Pray ye therefore the Lord of the harvest, that he will send forth labourers into his harvest.

— Matthew 9:38

Go your ways: behold, I send you forth as lambs among wolves.

— Luke 10:3

Be ye therefore wise as serpents, and harmless as doves.

— Matthew 10:16

When men shall revile you, and persecute you, and shall say all manner of evil against you falsely, for my sake. *Rejoice,* and be exceeding glad.

— Matthew 5:11-12

Murmur not among yourselves.

— John 6:43

In your patience possess ye your souls.

— Luke 21:19

Fear not them which kill the body, but are not able to kill the soul: but rather fear him which is able to destroy both soul and body in hell.

— Matthew 10:28

When they deliver you up, take no thought how or what ye shall speak: for it shall be given you in that same hour what ye shall speak. For it is not ye that speak, but the Spirit of your Father which speaketh in you.

— Matthew 10:19-20

Take heed *what* ye hear.

— Mark 4:24 (See also 1 John 4:1.)

Beware of *false* prophets.

— Matthew 7:15

Give not that which is holy unto the dogs, neither cast ye your pearls before swine.

— Matthew 7:6

Beware ye of the leaven of the Pharisees, which is hypocrisy.

— Luke 12:1 (See also Matthew 16:6; Mark 8:15.)

I say unto you, Swear not at all.

— Matthew 5:34

When ye fast, be not, as the hypocrites, of a sad countenance: for they disfigure their faces, that they may appear unto men to fast. Verily I say unto you, They have their reward. But thou, when thou fastest, anoint thine head, and wash thy face; that thou appear not unto men to fast, but unto thy Father which is in secret: and thy Father, which seeth in secret, shall reward thee openly.

— Matthew 6:16-18

When thou prayest, thou shalt not be as the hypocrites are: for they love to pray standing in the synagogues and in the corners of the streets, that they may be seen of men. Verily I say unto you, They have their reward. But thou, when thou prayest, enter into thy closet, and when thou hast shut thy door, pray to thy Father which is in secret; and thy Father which seeth in secret shall reward thee openly.

— Matthew 6:5-6

After this manner therefore pray ye: Our Father which art in heaven, Hallowed be thy name. Thy kingdom come. Thy will be done in earth, as it is in heaven. Give us this day our daily bread. And forgive us our debts, as we forgive our debtors. And lead us not into temptation, but deliver us from evil: For thine is the kingdom, and the power, and the glory, for ever. Amen.

— Matthew 6:9-13

When ye pray, use not vain repetitions.

— Matthew 6:7

Pray for them which despitefully use you, and persecute you.

— Matthew 5:44

When ye stand praying, *forgive,* if ye have ought against any.

— Mark 11:25

What things soever ye desire, when ye pray, *believe* that ye receive them, and ye shall have them.

— Mark 11:24

Ask, and it shall be given you; seek, and ye shall find; knock, and it shall be opened unto you.

— Matthew 7:7 (See also Matthew 18:19-20; Mark 11:23-24; Luke 18:2-14; John 15:7.)

Freely ye have received, freely give.

— Matthew 10:8

Love ye your enemies, and *do good,* and *lend,* hoping for nothing again; and your reward shall be great, and ye shall be the children of the Highest.

— Luke 6:35

Take heed that ye do not your alms before men, to be seen of them: otherwise ye have no reward of your Father which is in heaven.

— Matthew 6:1

Give to *every man* that *asketh* of thee.

— Luke 6:30 (See also Deuteronomy 15:9-10.)

Of him that taketh away thy goods ask them not again.

— Luke 6:30

From him that would borrow of thee turn not thou away.

— Matthew 5:42

Give, and it shall be given unto you; good measure, pressed down, and shaken together, and running over.

— Luke 6:38

Be not therefore *anxious,* saying what shall we eat, or what shall we drink, or wherewithal shall we be clothed?

— Matthew 6:31 RV[4]

Lay not up for yourselves treasures upon earth.

— Matthew 6:19

Lay up for yourselves treasures in heaven.... For where your treasure is, there will your heart be also.

— Matthew 6:20-21

Let your light so shine before men, that they may see your good works, and glorify your Father which is in heaven.

— Matthew 5:16

Be ye therefore perfect, even as your Father which is in heaven is perfect.

— Matthew 5:48 (See also Matthew 19:21; Luke 6:36-40.)

---

[4] This wording does not match the *Revised Standard Version* of the Bible or the *New Revised Standard Version.* We were unable to determine if there is another translation noted as RV. This could simply be a paraphrase.

Sweet are the promises, kind is the word,
Dearer far than any message man ever heard;
Pure was the mind of Christ, sinless I see;
He the great example is, and pattern for me.

THE PROMISES OF JESUS

Rev. A. C. Grier

Editor's note: Although the following was not written or preached by Dr. Lake himself, it was included in the booklet "The Commandments and The Promises of Jesus," which was published by Dr. Lake. He considered both the commandments and promises of Jesus of equal importance, so we have included this portion of the booklet as well.

The commandments of Jesus are the most drastic proposed by any teacher of mankind. They reach absolutely to the heart of conduct. And, viewed apart from the subtle secret of Jesus, they are too heavy to be borne by any man.

By the side of these austere commands of Jesus are the tenderest promises that have ever fallen on human ears. They are so extraordinary that the world could not believe them. They seemed to apply to some other (and now impossible) set of conditions — conditions that could only prevail in another world than this. It is true, from the same point of view, that His commandments were absolutely impossible. But in the light of the secret of Jesus the promises are absolutely rational and the commandments are our "reasonable service."[5]

Both commandments and promises arise from the subtle fact which Jesus discovered, that the soul that becomes alive with the consciousness of God is endued with a power that transcends all earthly power. And in this consciousness would the commands be kept because of the power of the promises. Jesus made these promises, not on His own speculation, but because of His soul's discovery of the mind of God. But He did not rest there, He took each discovered promise and worked it out. He discovered the promise of supply and He fed the

---

[5] Romans 12:1.

multitudes[6]; of meat they knew not of and fasted forty days[7]; of healing power, and He made the blind to see, the deaf hear, the lame walk[8]; of man, the Master, and He stilled the waves[9] and turned water into wine[10]; of life ever-present and He raised Lazarus[11] and the widow's son[12]; of the life everlasting and He Himself rose from the grave.[13]

He gives us these promises, then, as discovered and demonstrated truth, and He promises that all these things shall be ours as we enter into the God-realms, the Christ-conscious realm. The mine is so rich that men have called it a dream. But it is the one real thing among the myriad of life's illusions and contains in itself man's future hope and his transcendent glory. Herein lies the true dominion of man. Let us enter into its power and glory.

> *Sweet is the tender love Jesus hath shown,*
> *Sweeter far than any love that mortals have known:*
> *Kind to the erring one, faithful is He;*
> *He the great example is, and pattern for me.*
> *List to His loving words, "Come unto me,"*
> *Weary, heavy laden, there is sweet rest for thee;*
> *Trust in His promises, faithful and sure;*
> *Lean upon the Savior, and thy soul is secure.*

THE PROMISES OF JESUS

Verily, verily, I say unto you, Hereafter ye shall see heaven open, and the angels of God ascending and descending upon the Son of Man.[14]

---

[6] See Matthew 14:15-21 and Matthew 15:32-38.

[7] See John 4:32 and Matthew 4:2.

[8] See Matthew 11:5; 15:30; 21:14 and Luke 7:21.

[9] See Mark 4:39.

[10] See John 2:1-11.

[11] See John 11:1-44.

[12] See Luke 7:12-15.

[13] See Matthew 28:1-8.

[14] John 1:51.

Whosoever drinketh of this water shall thirst again: but whosoever drinketh of the water that I shall give him shall never thirst; but the water that I shall give him shall become in him a well of water springing up unto everlasting life.[15]

He that believeth on me, as the scripture hath said, out of his belly shall flow rivers of living water.[16]

Blessed are the poor in spirit: for theirs is the kingdom of heaven. Blessed are they that mourn: for they shall be comforted. Blessed are the meek: for they shall inherit the earth. Blessed are they which do hunger and thirst after righteousness: for they shall be filled. Blessed are the merciful: for they shall obtain mercy. Blessed are the pure in heart: for they shall see God. Blessed are the peacemakers: for they shall be called the children of God. Blessed are they that have been persecuted for righteousness' sake: for theirs is the kingdom of heaven. Blessed are ye, when men shall revile you, and persecute you, and shall say all manner of evil against you falsely, for my sake. Rejoice, and be exceeding glad: for great is your reward in heaven: for so persecuted they the prophets which were before you.[17]

Seek ye first the kingdom of God, and His righteousness; and all these things shall be added unto you.

— Matthew 6:33

Think not that I am come to destroy the law, or the prophets: I am not come to destroy, but to fulfil. For verily I say unto you, Till heaven and earth pass, one jot or one tittle shall in no wise pass from the law, till all be fulfilled.[18]

---

[15] John 4:13-14.

[16] John 7:38.

[17] Matthew 5:3-12.

[18] Matthew 5:17-18.

But love ye your enemies, and do good, and lend, hoping for nothing again; and your reward shall be great, and ye shall be the children of the Highest: for he is kind unto the unthankful and to the evil. Be ye therefore merciful, as your Father also is merciful.[19]

Fear not, little flock; for it is your Father's good pleasure to give you the kingdom.[20]

Take therefore no thought for the morrow: for the morrow shall take thought for the things of itself. Sufficient unto the day is the evil thereof.[21]

Whatsoever ye shall bind on earth shall be bound in heaven: and whatsoever ye shall loose on earth shall be loosed in heaven. Again I say unto you, That if two of you shall agree on earth as touching any thing that they shall ask, it shall be done for them of my Father which is in heaven. For where two or three are gathered together in my name, there am I in the midst of them.[22]

Verily I say unto you, If ye have faith as a grain of mustard seed, ye shall say unto this mountain, Remove hence to yonder place; and it shall remove; and nothing shall be impossible unto you.[23]

If ye had faith as a grain of mustard seed, ye would say unto this sycamine tree, Be thou plucked up by the root, and be thou planted in the sea; and it should obey you.[24]

All things are possible to him that believeth.[25]

---

[19] Luke 6:35-36.

[20] Luke 12:32.

[21] Matthew 6:34.

[22] Matthew 18:18-20.

[23] Matthew 17:20.

[24] Luke 17:6.

[25] Mark 9:23.

Have faith in God. For verily I say unto you, That whoso-ever shall say unto this mountain, Be thou removed, and be thou cast into the sea; and shall not doubt in his heart, but shall believe that those things which he saith shall come to pass; he shall have whatsoever he saith. Therefore I say unto you, What things soever ye desire, when ye pray, believe that ye receive them, and ye shall have them.[26]

He that believeth on me, the works that I do shall he do also; and greater works than these shall he do; because I go unto my Father. And whatsoever ye shall ask in my name, that will I do, that the Father may be glorified in the Son. If ye shall ask any thing in my name, I will do it. If ye love me, keep my commandments.[27]

Again I say unto you, That if two of you shall agree on earth as touching any thing that they shall ask, it shall be done for them of my Father which is in heaven. For where two or three are gathered together in my name, there am I in the midst of them.

— Matthew 18:19-20

I am the vine, ye are the branches. He that abideth in me, and I in him, the same bringeth forth much fruit: for without me ye can do nothing...If ye abide in me, and my words abide in you, ye shall ask what ye will, and it shall be done unto you.[28]

Verily, verily, I say unto you, Whatsoever ye shall ask of the Father in my name, he will give it you. Hitherto have ye asked nothing in my name: ask, and ye shall receive, that your joy may be made full.[29]

---

[26] Mark 11:22-24.

[27] John 14:12-15.

[28] John 15:5,7.

[29] John 16:23-24.

My doctrine is not mine, but his that sent me. If any man will do his will, he shall know of the doctrine, whether it be of God, or whether I speak of myself.[30]

Ye shall know the truth, and the truth shall make you free.[31]

If a man keep my saying, he shall never see death.[32]

I am the resurrection, and the life: he that believeth in me, though he were dead, yet shall he live: and whosoever liveth and believeth in me shall never die.[33]

Behold, I give unto you power to tread upon serpents and scorpions, and over all the power of the enemy: and nothing shall by any means hurt you. Notwithstanding in this rejoice not, that the spirits are subject unto you; but rather rejoice, because your names are written in heaven.[34]

And these signs shall follow them that believe; in my name shall they cast out devils; they shall speak with new tongues; they shall take up serpents; and if they drink any deadly thing, it shall not hurt them; they shall lay hands on the sick, and they shall recover.[35]

For there is nothing covered, that shall not be revealed; neither hid, that shall not be known.[36]

And I, if I be lifted up from the earth, will draw all men unto me.[37]

---

[30] John 7:16-17.

[31] John 8:32.

[32] John 8:51.

[33] John 11:25-26.

[34] Luke 10:19-20.

[35] Mark 16:17-18.

[36] Luke 12:2.

[37] John 12:32.

My sheep hear my voice, and I know them, and they follow me: And I give unto them eternal life; and they shall never perish, neither shall any man pluck them out of my hand. My Father, which gave them me, is greater than all; and no man is able to pluck them out of my Father's hand. I and my Father are one.[38]

Let not your heart be troubled: ye believe in God, believe also in me. In my Father's house are many mansions: if it were not so, I would have told you. I go to prepare a place for you. And if I go and prepare a place for you, I will come again, and receive you unto myself; that where I am, there ye may be also. And whither I go ye know, and the way ye know.[39]

Come unto me, all ye that labour and are heavy laden, and I will give you rest. Take my yoke upon you, and learn of me; for I am meek and lowly in heart: and ye shall find rest unto your souls. For my yoke is easy, and my burden is light.[40]

There shall not an hair of your head perish.

— Luke 21:18

There is no man that hath left house, or brethren, or sisters, or father, or mother, or wife, or children, or lands, for my sake, and the gospel's, but he shall receive an hundredfold now in this time, houses, and brethren, and sisters, and mothers, and children, and lands, with persecutions, and in the world to come eternal life. But many that are first shall be last; and the last first.[41]

For he that hath, to him shall be given: and he that hath not, from him shall be taken even that which he hath.[42]

---

[38] John 10:27-30.

[39] John 14:1-4.

[40] Matthew 11:28-30.

[41] Mark 10:29-31.

[42] Mark 4:25.

Whosoever shall exalt himself shall be abased; and he that shall humble himself shall be exalted.

— Matthew 23:12

These things have I spoken unto you, being yet present with you. But the Comforter, which is the Holy Ghost, whom the Father will send in my name, he shall teach you all things, and bring all things to your remembrance, whatsoever I have said unto you. Peace I leave with you, my peace I give unto you: not as the world giveth, give I unto you. Let not your heart be troubled, neither let it be afraid. Ye have heard how I said unto you, I go away, and come again unto you. If ye loved me, ye would rejoice, because I said, I go unto the Father: for my Father is greater than I.[43]

I have yet many things to say unto you, but ye cannot bear them now. Howbeit when he, the Spirit of truth, is come, he shall guide you into all truth: for he shall not speak from himself; but whatsoever he shall hear, that shall he speak: and he will shew you things to come.[44]

I will see you again, and your heart shall rejoice, and your joy no man taketh from you. And in that day ye shall ask me nothing.[45]

And I will pray the Father, and he shall give you another Comforter, that he may abide with you for ever; even the Spirit of truth; whom the world cannot receive, because it seeth him not, neither knoweth him: but ye know him; for he dwelleth with you, and shall be in you. I will not leave you comfortless: I come to you.[46]

---

[43] John 14:25-28.

[44] John 16:12-13.

[45] John 16:22-23.

[46] John 14:16-18

And I say unto you, Ask, and it shall be given you; seek, and ye shall find; knock, and it shall be opened unto you. For every one that asketh receiveth; and he that seeketh findeth; and to him that knocketh it shall be opened.[47]

Yea rather, blessed are they that hear the word of God, and keep it.[48]

Whosoever shall do the will of my Father which is in heaven, the same is my brother, and sister, and mother.

— Matthew 12:50

According to your faith be it unto you.[49]

But when they deliver you up, take no thought how or what ye shall speak: for it shall be given you in that same hour what ye shall speak.[50]

Are not two sparrows sold for a farthing? and one of them shall not fall on the ground without your Father. But the very hairs of your head are all numbered. Fear ye not therefore, ye are of more value than many sparrows. Whosoever therefore shall confess me before men, him will I also confess before my Father which is in heaven. But whosoever shall deny me before men, him will I also deny before my Father which is in heaven.[51]

He that findeth his life shall lose it: and he that loseth his life for my sake shall find it.[52]

---

[47] Luke 11:9-10.

[48] Luke 11:28.

[49] Matthew 9:29.

[50] Matthew 10:19.

[51] Matthew 10:29-33.

[52] Matthew 10:39.

Whose soever sins ye remit, they are remitted unto them; and whose soever sins ye retain, they are retained.

— John 20:23

For whosoever shall give you a cup of water to drink in my name, because ye belong to Christ, verily I say unto you, he shall not lose his reward.[53]

Give, and it shall be given unto you; good measure, pressed down, and shaken together, and running over, shall men give into your bosom. For with the same measure that ye mete withal it shall be measured to you again.

— Luke 6:38

I am the bread of life: he that cometh to me shall never hunger; and he that believeth on me shall never thirst.[54]

If any man thirst, let him come unto me, and drink. He that believeth on me, as the scripture hath said, out of his belly shall flow rivers of living water.

— John 7:37-38

This is the will of him that sent me, that every one which seeth the Son, and believeth on him, may have everlasting life: and I will raise him up at the last day.[55]

All that the Father giveth me shall come to me; and him that cometh to me I will in no wise cast out.

— John 6:37

Every man therefore that hath heard, and hath learned of the Father, cometh unto me.[56]

---

[53] Mark 9:41.

[54] John 6:35.

[55] John 6:40.

[56] John 6:45.

He that hath my commandments, and keepeth them, he it is that loveth me: and he that loveth me shall be loved of my Father, and I will love him, and will manifest myself to him.

— John 14:21

Every plant, which my heavenly Father hath not planted, shall be rooted up.[57]

If a man love me, he will keep my words: and my Father will love him, and we will come unto him, and make our abode with him.

— John 14:23

These things I have spoken unto you, that in me ye may have peace. In the world ye shall have tribulation: but be of good cheer; I have overcome the world.[58]

And, lo, I am with you alway, even unto the end of the world.[59]

Ye shall be hated of all men for my name's sake: but he that endureth to the end shall be saved.

— Matthew 10:22

Behold, I send the promise of my Father upon you: but tarry ye in the city of Jerusalem, until ye be endued with power from on high.

— Luke 24:49

---

[57] Matthew 15:13.

[58] John 16:33.

[59] Matthew 28:20.

hey "searched the scriptures daily, whether those things were so" (Acts 17:11).

A group is searching the Word to see if a certain teacher or preacher is correct. Mr. A. finds the teaching contains an unscriptural item and suggests it be rejected. Mr. B. speaks up and says, "You are attacking the teacher. I reject what you say because I love the teacher."

"AGAPE" — GOD'S LOVE VERSUS INORDINATE AFFECTION

Which of the two is manifesting God's love? Mr. A. is. What is Mr. B. manifesting? Inordinate affection. He loves the man more than he loves the truth.

When a person becomes so emotionally involved with a person they will reject truth to defend that person, he or she is manifesting inordinate affection.

(Inordinate means "exceeding reasonable limits; not regulated." Inordinate affection is unregulated love. It is outside God's love.)

This is often true of people who were converted under a certain preacher. They will defend him, right or wrong. That is manifesting inordinate affection.

Further, if a teacher or preacher requests another to back him right or wrong, he is asking for inordinate affection. Agape "God's love" would say, "Search to see if I'm right. If I am wrong reject the wrong and cling to the good. Don't be afraid to say I was wrong to the group if I'm not there. What I taught is a matter of public record. There is a difference between correcting something I taught and attacking me personally."

Again, if in a public teaching session, a listener points out a scripture that will change or modify what is being taught and the teacher refuses to consider it, then the teacher is guilty of inordinate affection. He loves himself and what he believes more that he loves the truth.

Beware of "inordinate affection" (Colossians 3:5). Love God so much you will stand for the truth at all times. Love Him and His Word so much you will be willing to be corrected even in public. Paul corrected Peter openly. (See Galatians 2:11.)

ne of the outreachings of the natural, universal man is to be in union with God. Christianity brings us into union with God.

INCARNATION

Here is a point in this great truth that is utterly ignored: the ministry of Jesus at the right hand of the Majesty on High. Some of you are critical Bible students, and if you have been critically studying the book of Romans you know the great argument closes with the redemption argument. You have probably said, like me, "It is not all there."

Now, the book of Romans from the third through the eighth chapters is the great redemption program. It covers exactly three days and three nights. The nailing of Jesus on the cross through His resurrection from the grave. I said, "Lord, where is the rest of it?"

Like a flash of lightning, I saw it was in Hebrews. The center around which Hebrews revolves is Jesus' ministry at the right hand of the Father. We see Jesus taking the blood and carrying it into the Holy of Holies and pouring it out on the mercy seat. Only in the book of Hebrews is He called the great High Priest. That is His great ministry. He sat down. A man sat down. He had to be incarnate so a man could sit down at the right hand. He is sitting there as a mediator between God and man. He has a new ministry. He is there as the intercessor. He is there as the Lord. He is there as the head of the Church.[1]

A man. He simply had to become man for that reason. I want you to understand that He is perfectly man. He is perfectly God, seated there at the right hand of the Majesty on High. And that man can be touched with the feeling of our infirmity.[2] He is our representative at the throne of the highest authority in the universe. He is there as our substitute and representative.

My little girl said to me one day: "Papa, I don't like this number work."

I said, "Why don't you like mathematics?"

---

[1] See Hebrews 8:1; 4:14; 10:12; 8:6; 9:15; 12:24; and 7:25.

[2] See Hebrews 4:15.

She said, "Papa, what is the use of it?"

I said, "Dear, you are going to use it all the time."

She said, "I never use it."

I said, "Suppose you had eight apples and I told you to give three to your chum. If you did not know anything about mathematics how could you tell how many three are?" By and by she said, "Papa, it is some good, isn't it?" And she had courage to go on.

You have the theory of redemption, but you don't know how to put it into practice. Every time I go over these great teachings I get one step nearer the goal. So I am going over them again and again, not only for your sake, but for mine too. My privileges and place in Christ becomes more real. The tremendous possibilities of the divine life are almost within grasp. Sometimes when the Word is unfolding itself to me it seems to me if I would close my eyes I could plunge into it.

Christ is at once the spotless descent of God into man, and the sinless ascent of man into God. He was God coming down into man, and He did no violence to His Godhead when He united to man, but He is God. Being glorified as He took on man, He did no injury to man, but He magnified man by taking man on. It is God incarnate. It is God living on earth.

Turn to John 14:8-9.

> Philip saith unto Him, Lord, show us the Father, and it sufficeth us. Jesus saith unto him, Have I been so long time with you, and yet hast thou not known me, Philip? he that hath seen me hath seen the Father; how sayest thou then, Shew us the Father?

Of course I can understand that Philip's eyes were not open yet. But after the Day of Pentecost, then his eyes were open.

I want you to hear what Jesus said about Himself. God was in Christ, wasn't He? An incarnation. God is in you, an incarnation — if you are born again. You are incarnate. God is in you. God was in Christ, reconciling the world unto Himself. God is in you. He has committed unto us the word of reconciliation. (See 2 Corinthians 5:19.) As God was in Christ, so God is in you. (See John 14:23 and 17:23, 1 John 4:15-16.) God is in you in two ways. Jesus is in you by imparting His nature. (See 2 Peter 1:4.) Second, in the person of the Holy Spirit. (See John 14:16-17.) He is imparted to you, so you are an incarnation.

The first time I saw it I stood before a mirror, and I said, "Is it possible that inside of that suit of clothes there dwells a man in whom God dwells?" God has not only come in, in the person of the Holy Spirit, but He has imparted to me His own nature, so that God's nature has come in and dispossessed me of another nature and imparted to me His own nature. (See 2 Peter 1:4.) And after He did that, then He said, "I will live in you" (2 Corinthians 6:16, paraphrased). And He has come in. Oh, the miracle of the thing! The life of God is in me, the Spirit is in me. We are members of the Body of Christ. (See 1 Corinthians 6:17 and Ephesians 5:30.) That is an incarnation.

If you could hear this every morning and then about noontime and then at evening time and again before you went to bed, after a while it would seep into you.

A young man said to me: "There is one lesson, identification, that thrilled me through and through. I laid your manuscript down and went about my daily business, but my mind kept coming back to it." He said, "I am going to read it over with all those scriptures every day." And I wanted him to tell me why. He said, "I am going to do it for this reason. It is not mine yet, it is not a part of me."

He said, "I remember when I took up Latin. I studied it for two years before Latin became mine so I could translate English into Latin and Latin into English." He said, "Now I know about this incarnation. I know about this indwelling of God. I know my legal rights, but it is not mine yet in a practical way so I can use it. The devil has me at a disadvantage still, but I will stand before the devil just as Jesus stood before the devil yet."

That young man has the same life as Jesus had. He has the same Holy Spirit as Jesus had. Friends, you are a son of God. You are a partaker of the divine nature. That is incarnation. Plus that, you have the Holy Spirit dwelling in you. You have the nature of God in you. You are His child. You have the name of Jesus.

After a little bit this truth will get hold of us, and after a little while it will master us. He says this is yours. All He wants of you is to go and act normal.

Do you know what miracles are? Miracles that Jesus performed was God coming down out of His realm, the faith realm, down into the human realm, the reason realm, and doing things that were normal up there, but abnormal down here.

When this thing I am telling you, when the new birth fact becomes a reality to me, having received the nature of God and when I reach the place quietly that "Greater is he that is in you (me), than he that is in the world,"[3] I will get this eternal life of God clear and this indwelling presence of God and the name of Jesus, it puts me on a par with God. He says, "All things are possible to God" (Matthew 19:26 and Luke 1:37, paraphased). "All things are possible to the believer" (Mark 9:23 and Matthew 17:20, paraphrased). The believer has the right to the use of the name of Jesus.

If I could teach that to little children they would get it off the bat. Reason runs contrary to fact. Faith does not come out of reason. Both come out of your spirit. That is the reason that faith and reason do not work together. They are jealous of each other. Reason is always jealous of faith. Reason is butting in on it all the time.

When you and I learn the three centers of our being — the spirit center, the soul center, and the body center — we will have gone a long way.

You have eternal life, haven't you? You have become a new creation. (See 2 Corinthians 5:17.) You are His son, you are God's child. You are a life child. You are not just an adopted child; you are a blood child. You are a life child. You could be adopted. That would be legal. But you are His real honest to goodness child. (See Ephesians 5:30.)

You know you have His nature. You *know* that is a fact. You do not have to believe that you are born again. You do not have to believe that the Bible is true and that you are born again. You *know* that. You do not have to believe that you have eternal life. That is a *fact*. You *know* that. You do not have to believe that the Holy Spirit has come in. He *is* there.

This is the process of elimination. You do not have to believe you are a child. You do not have to believe you have received eternal life. You

---

[3] 1 John 4:4.

do not have to believe you are an incarnation. You *have* the Holy Spirit. Then all things are possible to them that believe. You are a believer because you are a son.[4] You are a child.[5] You have received eternal life.[6] You have the Holy Spirit and the name of Jesus.[7] That means you are in the thing. To be a full-fledged believer, then all these things are possible to you. You do not have to try to believe it.

You are in the family of God. You have a right to the use of the name of Jesus just like a pass belongs to you when you work for the railroad. You are part of a definite system. You are in the family of God. You have a right to the name of Jesus. That is the pass. It carries you up into the Holy of Holies.

Now another thing, beloved, you do not have to try to believe the Word, do you? That would be an awful thing for me to have to try to believe my own Father. How would I feel if I were to write to my little boy and say, "Son, I am going to send you $5.00." And then he would go to his mother and say, "I want you to help me believe that papa will send me $5.00. I want you to stand with me in faith that I will believe that papa will send me the $5.00."

Do you know I would get a telegram from her if he would talk like that? She would say, "John, you better pray for that boy. Something has gone wrong with his head." There must be something wrong with us when we try to believe what He says. Let's stop all that baby business. In the name of Jesus Christ, don't ever magnify the devil by letting him know you do not believe that book. Don't you ever lower the standard. Don't you weaken it. It is God's book. Of course you believe it. His people for ages and ages have believed it, and it has never failed.

This is what we have done. We have sung unbelief. We have talked unbelief until we have robbed ourselves of our strength and Him of His glory. Are you an incarnation? If you are you are in the family and He is yours and you are in Christ.

---

4   See Romans 8:14; Galatians 4:6; and Philippians 2:15.

5   See Romans 8:16 and Galatians 3:26.

6   See John 10:28; Romans 6:23; 1 John 2:25 and 5:11-13.

7   See John 20:22; Acts 2:4 and 2:33, and Mark 16:17; John 14:14 and 16:24.

Now let us take the next step up. Now you walk in the realm of faith. "We walk by faith, not by sight."[8] Sight means reason. You walk by faith, not by reason. You are a faith walker. That puts you absolutely in the class with the Lord.

Now Jesus was a faith worker. The Father was a faith worker before Him. Our heavenly Father has done everything He has done by faith. When He wanted the earth He said, "Let there be."

> Through faith we understand that the worlds were framed by the word of God, so that things which are seen were not made of things which do appear.
>
> — Hebrews 11:3

All He had to say was, "Let it be." He said: "I want you to come into being." And Orion and Pleiades come into being. He said to the place where the North Star was, "Let it be," and it was.

You are following in the footsteps of a God that says to the things that are not and they become, and who says to the things that are and they stop being.

Sometimes I tell the story of a woman who had a cancer in her mouth. Dr. Dowie put his finger on it and began to feel of it and by and by faith said something to that cancer, and then Dr. Dowie took the cancer out of her mouth and put it in a bottle.

What was that? Could reason do that? Oh, no, no, reason would say, "You have to have that cut out." Faith says, "It is dead, and after it is dead I will pull it out." Dowie acted in Jesus' stead. I am to walk in Jesus' footsteps, and Jesus is my example in faith.

I had a sister, Maggie Otto, who had cancer of the breast. She had been operated on five times at Detroit, Michigan, by Dr. Carstens, and finally turned away to die with five cancers. We took her on a stretcher to Dr. Dowie. He was conducting a healing meeting. She was writhing in pain on a cot. The old doctor laid his Bible down, stepped down and prayed for her, and she was utterly healed.

---

[8]   2 Corinthians 5:7.

A few days afterward I got to examining the breast and discovered the cancer was black as your boot. One morning I put my finger in and touched the cancer, and I saw it was detached from the body. I had the other case of Ethel Post in my mind. I began to twist that thing and it came out, roots and all. Some roots were an eighth of an inch in diameter, some were a sixteenth of an inch, some were as fine as thread, some were as fine as a silken hair. We put that cancer in alcohol and it was in Dr. Carsten's hospital for years.

That puts a man in God's class. Can you see what the incarnation means? It is not something to reason and talk about. It is life. I do not want you to try to believe that. You *are* that. I want you to go over it in your mind until you can say it. Just like my little daughter did with her mathematics.

In my school work I said to the teachers, "We must teach geometry." There was a debate on. They said, "What has geometry to do with the Holy Spirit and teaching the Word?" But I made my case. They said, "I do not believe God brought me here to teach geometry, but to teach the Bible."

I looked over and said to one woman, "Will you teach geometry? I do not want you to teach geometry like you did in school, but I want you to teach it as a spiritual duty, a part of your daily life." I could see her eyes open. She began to teach geometry, and the other teachers had to fight to keep the interest in their classes up to hers. Geometry was in everything. It became a living part of their lives. She learned how to teach it as God would teach it.

Friends, you have the theory of this thing. Now in the name of the Lord Jesus Christ you have seen the reality of it. You go out and let this reality govern your life.

A fellow in California and his boy were working in the garden about two years ago. They had to dig up a stone and in digging out the stone they discovered a packet of gold nuggets, something like six or eight thousand dollars worth. The father said, "Let's not say anything. Maybe this was buried here." They dug around a little more and the boy found about two thousand more, and they found they had a gold field, a limited one.

There is none of you folks here but have a gold field. First, you have the nature and life of God. Second, you have the great, mighty Holy Spirit. Third, you are the son of God. Do you need any more capital to begin to do business?

What are you? A child of God. You are in the family. You do not have to try to do that. You have the nature of God. You do not have to try to have that. You have the use of the name of Jesus. You have the authority in heaven and earth in the name of Jesus and in the commission. (See Mark 16:17-18 and Luke 10:19.)

You do not have to try to exercise authority. "Whatsoever is bound on earth is bound in heaven."[9] You do not have to believe anything when you use the name. "In my name you shall do it..."[10] You have the use of the name of Jesus.

You have a lot. You have all the authority there is in heaven. All you have to do is to go and practice it. You have the Holy Spirit in you. You do not have to believe anything. *He is in you.* He is speaking to you, "Let me have charge of things now."

The meaning of the word "incarnate" as a verb: To embody in flesh; cause to a living form. 2. to give or endow with shape or form; actualize; as a doctrine incarnated in institutions. 3. to embody in a living being; as, the warrior incarnates the spirit of battle.

Incarnate, adjective: 1. Invest with flesh. 2. Hence embodied in flesh; personified in such cases as a fiend incarnate, the adjective is nearly synonymous with arrant, unmitigated. 3. Flesh-colored; roseate.

Incarnation, noun: 1. The act of becoming incarnate; especially the assumption of the human nature by Jesus Christ as the second person of the trinity. 2. That which is personified by, or embodied in or as in human form; personification; embodiment of a quality, idea, principle, etc., specifically an avatar. 3. The process of healing in a wound.

Some additional scriptures: John 15:5, Galatians 2:20, 2 Corinthians 13:5, 2 Corinthians 3:16-18, 2 Corinthians 6:16, Ephesians 4:6.

---

[9] Matthew 18:18 and 16:19, paraphrased.

[10] Mark 16:17, paraphrased.

Until Christ be formed in you anew

— Galatians 4:19

Filled with all the fulness of God.

— Ephesians 3:19

The triumph of the Gospel is enough to make any man the wildest kind of an enthusiastic optimist. The unifying of the nature of man and God is the crowning achievement of Jesus Christ. The reason for the cross was thus revealed. Man in God and God in man, one and indissoluble — one mind, one purpose, one effort, one power, and one glory.

want to read a series of portions of scriptures this morning, with this one general

CHRISTIAN COMMUNION

thought in view — the presence of Christ. Some of you may have read a little booklet by an old monk, whose name was Brother Lawrence. It is called "Practicing the Presence of God."[1]

One of the things the Christian world does not get hold of with a strong grip is the conscious presence of Christ with us *now*. Somehow there is an inclination in the Christian spirit to feel that Jesus, when He left the earth, returned to glory and in consequence is not present with us now.

I want to show you how wonderfully the Scriptures emphasize the fact of His presence with us now. When He was talking to the eleven just prior to His ascension (See Matthew 28), after delivering to them the great commission, He said:

> Go ye therefore, and teach all nations, baptizing them in the name of the Father, and of the Son, and of the Holy Ghost.[2]

He ended the statement with these words:

> And, lo, I am with alway, even unto the end of the world.[3]

It would naturally seem as if a separation had been contemplated because of His return to glory, but no such separation is contemplated on the part of Christ. Christ promises His omnipotent presence with us always. Christ omnipresent everywhere — present in the soul, present in the world, present always unto the end of the age.

As Paul was going down the road to Damascus, when the presence of God's glory shown around him he fell prostrate on the earth and

---

[1] This book was written in the 1600s, but is still published today.

[2] Matthew 28:19.

[3] Matthew 28:20.

heard a voice speaking to him. When he demanded to know who it was, the voice replied, "I am Jesus." Jesus was present with him as a Savior to deliver him from his difficulties and his sins.[4]

At a later time in Paul's career, he returned to Jerusalem and was in danger of his life. While he prayed in the temple, he was overshadowed by the Spirit, and says,

> I was in a trance; and saw Him saying unto me, Make haste, and get thee quickly out of Jerusalem: for they will not receive thy testimony concerning me.[5]

Paul endeavors to argue with the Lord about it. That conversation has always been a blessing to my soul. It is so real. I have always been so glad that Paul answered back to the Lord, and the details of the conversation have been recorded.

Paul said,

> Lord, they know that I imprisoned and beat in every synagogue them that believed on thee: And when the blood of thy martyr Stephen was shed, I also was standing by, and consenting unto his death, and kept the raiment of them that slew him.[6]

> But the Lord replied, "Depart: for I will send thee far hence unto the Gentiles."[7]

Jesus is just as close to the Christian soul as He was to Paul. There is a beautiful verse that expresses that so sweetly, "Closer is He than breathing, and nearer than hands and feet."[8]

Christ is the living presence not only with us, but to the real Christian he is in us a perpetual joy, power, and glory in our life. When a soul reaches to the heights of God it will only be because of the guiding and counseling and indwelling and infilling of the Christ.

---

[4] See Acts 9:3-5.

[5] Acts 22:17-18.

[6] Acts 22:19-20.

[7] Acts 22:21.

[8] This is a line from the poem, "The Higher Pantheism," by Alfred Lord Tennyson.

INTERPRETATION OF TONGUES

Blessed Jesus, Lord and God, He who dwells within.
Blessed Jesus, He who came to free our hearts from sin.
Give us now Thy presence in us
Sweetly verified by Thy Holy Word.
Give us now Thy presence
That we too may call thee Lord.
Precious Jesus, Lord of Heaven,
Blessed Jesus, come and dwell.
Blessed Christ of all the Heaven,
Dearer to our heart —
Christ of God come in and dwell,
That within us we may be
Perfectly conscious of that indwelling,
And ever from sin set free.

Many of us no doubt have been struck with the beautiful war story that has been going the rounds of the magazines for some months, called "The Comrade." It is the sense of comradeship that makes the Lord Jesus not only a Savior in the ordinary sense, but a Savior and companion in all our ways and walks of life, filling the place in our soul that only a comrade can fill.

On one of my exploring expeditions while in Africa, I met a man in Portugueso, East Africa, who told me he had lived for eleven years with only natives as his associates. One evening as we came along, passing through the veldt,[9] I observed this little cabin which indicated the presence of a European. So I started over, expecting to discover a man with some white blood in him at least. But I was overjoyed to find he was an intelligent English gentleman.

He had come to Africa in the early days with his wife and children. His sons had been killed in a native uprising. His wife had died of fever and only he was left. I said, "Why didn't you return to England?"

He replied, "I did not have any desire to return. Many of my friends I used to know had died or gone to Australia, or with a new set of people. I concluded I would just settle down and spend the rest of my days here."

---

[9] See note on page 153.

We sat all night and talked about the ordinary things that were going on in the world about us. It was the first time he had any outside news in several years. We sat fellowshipping during the night.

Before I went away in the morning I asked him what it was he missed more than anything else since he had been out there. He replied, "Mr. Lake, I guess one word will cover it, 'comradeship.'" The lack of that real soul comradeship which makes life so dear to every man.

That is the place that Jesus purposes to occupy in the Christian life. That place of real comradeship, whereby through His grace and love He supplies to us that thing that we need so much to make this life the joyous, victorious life He purposed it to be. His presence with us, His guiding counsel, His transforming grace, His soul-absorbing presence which in the ultimate, commands all the intensity of our nature. Paul expresses it so wonderfully in the words, "Christ is all, and in all."[10]

Paul gives us a still different vision of the presence and power of Christ with us in the fourth of Ephesians. This time it is as a transformer.

> Till we all come in the unity of the faith, and of the knowledge of the Son of God, unto a perfect man, unto the measure of the stature of the fulness of Christ.[11]

This shows the ultimate purpose of Christ as Savior, of Christ as a Companion, of Christ as the Indweller. Christ's presence with us is not just as an outward companion, but an indwelling, divine force, revolutionizing our nature and making us like Him. Indeed, the final and ultimate purpose of the Christ is that the Christian shall be reproduced in His own likeness, within and without.

Paul again expresses the same thing in the first of Colossians, the 22nd verse, where he says,

> To present you holy and unblameable and unreprovable in his sight.

That transformation is to be an inner transformation. It is a transformation of our life, or our nature, into His nature, into His likeness.

---

[10] Colossians 3:11.

[11] Ephesians 4:13.

How the mechanical fades away in view of the living fact that Christ purposes to accomplish in us through the Spirit. How wonderful the patience and marvelous the power that takes possession of the soul of man and accomplishes the will of God, in His absolute transformation into the real, beautiful holiness of the character of Jesus.

Our heart staggers when we think of such a calling, when we think of such a nature, when we contemplate such a character. That is God's purpose for you and me.

In emphasizing this truth the apostle again puts it into a different form. He says,

> Until Christ be formed in you.[12]

Or, until by the transforming operation of the Spirit of God we are remade, or transformed. Until our nature is transformed by the operation of the Spirit of God in our soul, then we are remade or transformed. Until our nature is transformed into the nature of our Lord and Savior Jesus Christ.

His was the perfect character. Consequently, every other character that can be conjoined with Him in real heirship must be like God's Son. Jesus never can present that which is faulty or evil or weak to the Father. The transforming grace of God must take away, and does take away, sin from the soul of man. It gives him His strength instead of human weakness. It supplies the grace that makes him like the Lord Jesus Christ.

That is the mission of the Lord Jesus Christ. That is the marvel He has undertaken to accomplish, to transform the soul of man into the likeness and character of Himself, and then present mankind to the Father, "Holy and unblameable and unreproveable in His sight."

When Jesus stood before the disciples, just prior to His going out into the Garden, He delivered to them that wonderful address of the fourteenth, fifteenth, and sixteenth of John. He climaxed it with that marvelous high priestly prayer of the seventeenth chapter. He endeavored to bring them to understand His nature and power. Knowing that all power had been given unto Him, He took a towel and a basin and

---

[12] Galatians 4:19.

proceeded to wash the disciples' feet. When He had finished He said, "Know ye not what I have done unto you?" In explanation He said, "If I then your Lord and Master, have washed your feet, ye also ought to wash one another's feet."[13] In assuming the attitude of a servant He had taught mankind what their relation as brother should be.

When we examine the human heart and endeavor to discover what it is that retards our progress, I believe we find that pride in the human soul perhaps is the greatest difficulty we have to overcome. Jesus taught us a wonderful humility, taking the place of a slave. So we are enjoined to thus treat and love one another.

His presence with us, His presence in us, must produce in our hearts the same conditions that were in His own. It must bring into our life the same humility that was in Him. It is one of the secrets of entrance into the grace of God.

INTERPRETATION OF TONGUES

When the precious Christ enters into the unregenerated heart He becomes the very center of their being. He becomes the very acme of their ambition. That they might be like Him. He, through true humility of His soul, left the things of His glorious Father's Kingdom to come into this world of woe and sin; by which He was enabled to live the life of perfection in this earth and become the real Redeemer and Sympathizer of mankind.

In the story of the comrade, the substance of it is practically that the comrade is ever-present. In the course of the conversation with the comrade it is observed that there are wounds in His hands, and He replies, "Yes, they are old wounds, but they have been giving Me a good deal of trouble of late."

That is the vital sense of real comradeship that makes the Spirit of Jesus one with us, so that we realize and He realizes when the conditions of our nature and mind affect Him.

---

[13] See John 13:4-14.

For two days I have been under a tremendous burden, one of these spirit burdens that come at times, when you cannot define them. I could not tell whence it came. But every little while I felt I wanted to sit down and cry. Presently, during the day a friend came and unloaded the burden of her soul to me, and then I realized that I had been under the burden for that soul for two days. I had not known the trouble existed.

That is the character of comradeship, which is between the real Christian and the Christ. The Christian feels the burdens of the Christ, and the Christ feels the burdens of the Christian and being united as one spirit, the interest of the Christ are the interest of the Christian, and the interests of the Christian are the interests of the Christ. That relationship is of the truest, deepest order. It is the relationship of spirit with spirit.

When a young man, before I had entered into this life, indeed from my boyhood, there were times when my spirit would become over-shadowed with the burden of another life, sometimes with the sorrows of another. I had one of these experiences when perhaps not more than ten or eleven years of age.

On a particular Sunday, I arose with one of these burdens on my spirit, and I walked out into the fields. There was a high hill on my father's farm. The sun had not yet gotten over this hill. When I got to the top I looked down over the beautiful field. There was a lake, and I was thinking how beautiful it was and all the surroundings. In the midst of it tears commenced to run and I sat down on a stone and cried. After awhile I got up and wondered why I was crying. Several days later, we received a letter telling that dear old Grandfather had died. And then the old Grandmother had said, "Well, I do not want to live anymore," and she died also. Around them were a group of sorrowing friends, and somehow my spirit contacted that sorrow.

One of the truest things in all my life, in my relationship with the Lord Jesus Christ, has been to feel that He was capable of knowing my sorrows, and yours. And that in the truest sense He thereby became our Comrade.

In Isaiah there is a verse that wonderfully expresses that fact.

In all their affliction he was afflicted, and the angel of his
presence saved them: in his love and in his pity he
redeemed them; and he bare them, and carried them all
the days of old.

— Isaiah 63:9

There is a union between the Christ and the Christian that is so deep,
so pure, so sweet, so real that the very conditions of the human spirit
are transmitted to His, and the conditions of the Christ's Spirit are
transmitted to ours. It is because of the continuous inflow of the
Spirit of Christ in our heart that we appreciate or realize His power
and triumph. It lifts man above his surroundings and causes him to
triumph anywhere and everywhere.

The Christian life is designed by God to be a life of splendid, holy
triumph. That triumph is produced in us through the continuous
inflow and abiding presence of the Spirit of the triumphant Christ. He
brings into our nature the triumph that He enjoys. Indeed the mature
Christian, having entered into that consciousness of overcoming
through the Spirit of Christ, is privileged to transmit that same overcoming power and spirit to other lives, in and through the power of
the Spirit of God.

That is why the Christian who is joined with the Christ lives, moves,
and has his being in the same life, in the same Spirit that the Christ is
and has and is therefore the reproduction of the Lord Jesus Christ.

THE STRONG MAN'S WAY TO GOD

usicians talk of an ultimate note. That is a note you will not find on any keyboards. It is a peculiar note. A man sits down to tune a piano, or any fine instrument. He has no guide to the proper key, and yet he has a guide. That guide is that note that he has in his soul. And the nearer he can bring his instrument into harmony with that note in his soul, the nearer perfection he has attained.

There is an ultimate note in the heart of the Christian. It is the note of conscious victory through Jesus Christ. The nearer our life is tuned to that note of conscious victory, the greater the victory that will be evidenced in our life.

In my ministry in South Africa there was a young lady, one of the most beautiful souls I have ever known. She was baptized in the Spirit when perhaps only seventeen or eighteen years old. One of the remarkable developments in her after her baptism in the Spirit was that the Spirit of God would come powerfully upon her on occasions, and at such times she would sit down at the piano and translate the music her soul heard. Other times the Spirit would come upon her so powerfully that she would be caused to sing the heavenly music in some angelic language.

God gave her the gift of interpretation, so that quite frequently when the Spirit would come upon her, she would re-sing the song in English, or Dutch as the case might be. Her father and mother were both musicians. They soon learned that when the Spirit thus came upon her, they could record the music. The father would stand at one side and take the words of the song as she sang them, while the mother stood at the other side and recorded the music as she played the music on the instrument. In this way, a great deal of the music was preserved.

Some years later, Clara Butts, the great prima donna, came to Africa. She was singing at the Wanderers Hall in Johannesburg. One evening after the concert, while being entertained at the hotel, I was introduced to her. She said to me, "Mr. Lake, I have been very anxious to meet you, for I have heard that among your people is a remarkable woman who receives music in the Spirit, apparently of a different realm than ours."

I said, "Yes, that is a fact." She inquired if it would be possible to meet her, and so a meeting was arranged.

One evening, we went to her hotel and as we sat down, Clara Butts said to the young lady, "I wish you would sit down and play some of the music I have heard about." She did not understand that such music only came at such times as the Spirit came powerfully upon the woman. However, the young lady sat down at the piano. I said to the company, "Let us bow our heads in prayer." As we did and waited, presently the Spirit of God descended upon her, and then there poured through her soul some of that wondrous, beautiful, heavenly music. I waited to note the affect on the company. When the song was finished, I looked especially at Clara Butts, who was weeping silently. She arose to her feet and, coming forward to the piano, she reached out her hands, saying, "Young lady, that music belongs to a world that my soul knows little about. I pray every day of my life God may permit me to enter. In that realm is the ultimate which my soul sometimes hears, but which I have never been able to touch myself."

Beloved, in the Christian life, in the heart of God, there is an ultimate note. That note which is so fine and sweet and true and pure and good that it causes all our nature to resound to it and rejoices the soul with a joy unspeakable.

All down through the ages some have touched God and heard that ultimate note. I believe that as David sat on the mountainside as a boy, caring for his father's sheep, God by the Spirit taught him the power and blessing of that ultimate note. I believe at times his soul ascended into God, so that many of the psalms of David are the real soul note of that blessed expression of heavenly music and heaven consciousness which came into the soul of the shepherd boy.

Mary, the Mother of Jesus, understood that note. I remember when I was a young man in a Methodist Bible class, which I taught, we were discussing the subject of the Magnificat. That glorified expression which burst from the soul of Mary as she met Elizabeth, when the Spirit came upon her and revealed to her friend that she was to be the mother of Jesus. In our worldly wisdom we decided, of course, that the Jewish women of necessity must have been educated to compose that character of poetry spontaneously.

Many a day afterward as I saw the Spirit of God descend upon a soul, and the soul break forth into a song of God, the song of the angels, in a note so high and sweet and pure and clear as no human voice ever had produced perhaps without it. I understood the marvel that was taking place in the soul of Mary when she broke forth into the heavenly expression of that holy song.

> My soul doth magnify the Lord, and my spirit hath rejoiced in God my Saviour. For he hath regarded the low estate of his handmaiden: for, behold, from henceforth all generations shall call me blessed. For he that is mighty hath done to me great things; and holy is his name. And his mercy is on them that fear him from generation to generation. He hath shewed strength with his arm; he hath scattered the proud in the imagination of their hearts. He hath put down the mighty from their seats, and exalted them of low degree. He hath filled the hungry with good things; and the rich he hath sent empty away. He hath holpen his servant Israel, in remembrance of his mercy.[1]

It was the Spirit of the Lord. Her spirit had ascended, bless God, into the heavenlies. Her spirit had touched heaven's note. Her spirit was receiving and reproducing the song of joy that she heard, possibly of the angels, or perhaps intuitively from the heart of God.

There is a Christianity that has that high note in it, bless God. Indeed Christianity in itself, real Christianity, is in that high note of God, that thing of heaven that is not of earth and is not natural. Bless God, it is more than natural. It is the note of heaven. It comes to the earth. It fills the soul of man. Man's soul rises into heaven to touch God and in touching God receives that glorified expression and experience into his own soul, and it is reproduced in his own life and nature.

---

[1] Luke 1:46-54.

Beloved, there is a victory in God, the victory that characterizes the common walk of a highborn Christian. It is the strong man's salvation. It is the salvation that comes from God because of the fact that the spirit of man touches the Spirit of God and receives that experience that we commonly speak of as the blessing of salvation from God.

But Beloved, the soul that receives from God into their spirit that heavenly touch *knows*, bless God, he does not have to be told by man, he knows by the Spirit of God that he has become the possessor of the consciousness of union with the Spirit of God which has enlightened his heart, filled his soul with holy joy, and caused his very being to radiate with God's glory and presence.

The hunger of my soul for many a long day has been that I might be able to so present that high, true note of God that the souls of men would rise up in God to that place of power, purity, and strength where the presence and character and works of Christ are evidenced in and through them. There can be no distinction between the exercise of the real power of God as seen in Jesus and its reproduction in a Christian soul. There is a purity, the purity of heaven, so high, so holy, so pure, so sweet that it makes the life of the possessor radiant with the glory and praise of God.

During one of the periods of extreme necessity in our great work in South Africa, our finances became cut off for various reasons. I was anxious that there should be no letting down of the work we were then doing and was trusting that it would not be necessary to withdraw our men, who had labored and suffered to get the work established on the frontier.

However, not being able to supply funds to those on the front, I deemed it the only wise thing to do to get them all together in a general conference and decide what was to be our future action. By great sacrifice, a sacrifice too great for me to tell you of this afternoon, we succeeded in bringing in our missionaries from the front for a council. I told them the existing conditions, and we sat down in the nighttime to decide what would be our future policy.

After a time, I was invited by a committee to leave the room for a minute or two. While I was in the vestry, the brethren in the body of the tabernacle continued their conference and went on discussing the general question. When I returned, they said to me, "Brother Lake, we have arrived at a decision." Old father Van der Wall spoke for the company. He said, "We have reached this conclusion. There is to be no withdrawal of any man from any position. We feel that the time has come when your soul ought to be relieved of responsibility for us. We feel we have weighted your life long enough, but now, by the grace of God, we return to our stations to carry on our work. We live or die depending on God. If our wives die, they die. If our families die, they die. If we survive, we survive; but we are going back to our stations. This work will never be withdrawn. We have one request. Come and serve the communion of the Lord's Supper to us once more while we stand together."

As I took the cup they arose and stood in a large circle. I took the bread and passed it. It went from hand to hand around the circle. When it came time to pass the wine, I took the cup in my hand, and with the usual statement that Jesus gave in the committal of Himself to God, "My blood in the New Testament."[2] I passed it on and the next one, looking up to God, he said too, "My blood in the New Testament." And so it passed from hand to hand clear around the circle.

Within a few months I was compelled to bury twelve out of that company. Every one of them might have lived if we could have supplied the ordinary essential things they ought to have received. But beloved, we had made our pledge to God. We had declared by the love of God in our souls and because of what Christ had done for us, that we would be true to Him, and that in the name of Christ, His Gospel should be spread abroad as far as it was in our power to do.

Men have said that the cross of Christ was not a heroic thing, but I want to tell you that the cross of Jesus Christ has put more heroism in the souls of men than any other event in human history. Men have lived and rejoiced and died, believing in the living God, in the Christ of God whose blood cleansed their hearts from sin and who realized the real high spirit of His holy sacrifice, bless God. They manifested to mankind that same measure of sacrifice and endured all that human beings could endure, and when endurance was no longer possible

---

[2] See Matthew 26:28 and Mark 14:24.

they passed on to be with God, leaving the world blessed through the evidence of a consecration deep and true and pure and good, like the Son of God Himself.

We see the note that was in the soul of Paul, and which characterized his message, when he made the splendid declaration which I read from Romans 1:16:

> I am not ashamed of the gospel of Christ: for it is the power of God unto salvation to every one that believeth; to the Jew first, and also to the Greek.

You see the note that touched the souls of men, the note that rang down through the centuries, and which rings in your heart and mine today. Christianity *never was designed by God to make a lot of weaklings.* It was designed to bring forth a race of men who were bold and strong and pure and good, blessed be God. The greatest and the strongest and the noblest is always the humblest.

The beautiful thing in the Gospel is that it eliminates from the life of man that which is of himself and is natural and fleshly and earthly, bless God. It brings forth the beauteous things within the soul of man, the unselfishness, the life of purity, the peace, the strength, and the power of the Son of God. How beautiful it is to have the privilege of looking into the face of one whose nature has been thus refined by the Spirit of the living God within. How beautiful it is when we look into the soul of one whom we realize God has purged by the blood of Christ until the very characteristics of the life and attitudes of the mind of Christ are manifest and evident in him to the glory of God.

Christianity is a strong man's Gospel. Christianity, by the grace of God, is calculated to take the weak and fallen and erring and suffering and dying, and by applying the grace and power of God through the soul of man to the need of the individual, lift them up to the "Lamb of God, which taketh away the sin of the world."[3] Blessed be God.

"Down in the human heart,

Crushed by the tempter,

Feelings lie buried that grace can restore,

---

[3] John 1:29.

> Touched by a loving heart,
>
> Wakened by kindness,
>
> Chords that were broken
>
> Will vibrate once more."[4]

I care not how crushed the soul, how bestialized the nature; I care not how sensual, if touched by the Spirit of the living God, he will shed off that which is earthly and sensual and give forth once again the pure note of the living God, heaven's high message, heaven's triumphant song, heaven's high note of living praise to the living God. Blessed be His name.

God is endeavoring by His Spirit in these days, to exalt the souls of men into that high place, that holy life, that heavenly state whereby men walk day by day, hour by hour in the heavenly consciousness of the presence of Christ in the heart of man — all the time.

And the presence of Christ in the souls of men can only produce first, the purity that is in Him. For the "Wisdom that cometh from above, is *first* pure,"[5] bless God. Purity is of God. Purity is of the nature of Christ. Purity is heaven's highborn instinct, filling the soul of man, making him in His nature like the Son of God. Upon that purified soul there comes from God that blessed measure of the Holy Spirit, not only purifying the nature, but empowering him by the Spirit so that the activities of God, the gift of His mind, the power of His Spirit is evident by the grace of God in that man's soul, in that man's life, lifting him by the grace of God into that place of holy and heavenly dominion in the consciousness of which Jesus lived and moved and accomplished the will of God always. Not the earth-consciousness, born of the earth and earthy; but the heaven-consciousness, that high consciousness, that holy consciousness, the consciousness of the living God, of His union with Him, which caused the Christ to walk as a prince indeed. Bless God.

He was not bowed and overcome by conditions and circumstances about Him, but realized that the soul of man was a creative power,

---

[4]   Could not locate the source of this poem.

[5]   James 3:17, paraphrased.

that it was within his soul and common to his nature and the nature of every other man, to protect, accumulate, and possess as sons of God, that through the creative faculty of his soul the desires of his heart might be brought to pass. Blessed be His name.

That is the reason God dared to talk as He did to Moses. That is the reason God dared to rebuke a man when he stopped to pray. That is the reason God said, "Why standest thou here and criest unto me? Lift up the rod that is in thy hand, and divide the waters."[6]

Beloved, your soul will never demonstrate the power of God in any appreciable degree until your soul conceives and understands the real vision of the Christ of God, whereby He knew that through His union with the living God His soul became the creative power through which He took possession of the power of God and applied it to the needs of His own soul and the needs of other lives.

"I am the resurrection, and the life,"[7] bless God. Lazarus was dead. The friends were weeping, but the Christ was there, bless God. Opening His soul to God in a cry of prayer, the Spirit of God so moved within Him that the consciousness of His high dominion in God so possessed Him, that He gave forth that wondrous command, "Lazarus, come forth!"[8] And the dead obeyed the call, and the spirit that had gone on into the regions of the dead returned again, was joined to the body, and Lazarus was restored by the power of God. Blessed be His holy name.

When a boy, I received my religious training in a little Methodist class meeting. I wish there were some old time Methodist class meetings in these modern days, the kind that had the power of God, and the needs of men's souls were met in them, where people could open their hearts and tell of their temptations and their trials and victories and receive counsel from one who guided the class. In such a class meeting, and to such a class meeting, I owe a great deal of the development which God has brought forth in my life.

---

[6] Exodus 14:15-16, paraphrased.

[7] John 11:25.

[8] John 11:43.

In one of these class meetings one day, as I sat listening to the testimonies, I observed that there was a kind of weakening trend. People were saying, "I am having such a hard time. I am feeling the temptations of the world so much." etc. I was not able at the time to tell people what was the difficulty. I was only a young Christian. But when they got through, I observed the old class leader, a gray headed man. He said something like this, "Brethren, the reason we are feeling the temptations so much, the reason there is a lack of the sense of victory, is because we are too far away from the Son of God. Our souls have descended. They are not in the high place where Christ is. Let our souls ascend, and when they ascend into the realm of the Christ, we will have a new note, it will be the note of victory."

Beloved, that is the difficulty with us all. We have come down out of the heavenlies into the natural, and we are trying to live a heavenly life in the natural state, overburdened by the weights and cares of the flesh and life all about us. Bless God, there is deliverance. There is victory. There is a place in God where the flesh no longer becomes a bondage. Where, by the grace of God, every sensuous state of the human nature is brought into subjection to the living God, where Christ reigns in and glorifies the very activities of a man's nature, making him sweet and pure and clean and good and true. Bless His holy name.

I call you today, beloved, by the grace of God, to that high life, to that holy walk, to that heavenly atmosphere, to that life in God where the grace and Spirit and power of God permeates your whole being. More, where not only your whole being is in subjection, but it flows from your nature as a holy stream of heavenly life to bless other souls everywhere by the grace of God.

There was a period in my life when God lifted my soul to a wondrous place of divine power. Indeed, I speak it with all conservativeness when I say that I believe God gave me such an anointing of power as has seldom been manifested in modern life. That anointing remained with me for a period of eight months. One of the evidences of the power of God at that period was that God gave me such a consciousness of dominion to cast out evil spirits that the insane were brought from all quarters of the land, slobbering idiots. In many instances as I approached them, the Spirit of Christ would rise up in me in such dominion that when I got to them I could take hold of them, and looking into their face, would realize that God had given me power to cast it out. Hundreds of times the insane were healed instantly, right on the spot.

I have been a student all my life. Not just a student of letters, but of the things of the soul. God helped me by His grace to take note of and analyze the conditions of my own soul. I noted that when that high consciousness of heavenly dominion rested upon my life, there was one thing that stood uppermost in all my consciousness. That was the vision of the triumphant Christ, the Son of God, as pictured by John in the first chapter of Revelation, where He stands forth in the mighty dignity of an overcomer, declaring,

> I am he that liveth, and was dead; and, behold, I am alive
> for evermore, Amen; and have the keys of hell and of death.[9]

Beloved, I want to tell you that the soul joined to Christ, who exercises the power of God, ascends into the high consciousness of heavenly dominion as it is in the heart of Jesus Christ today, for He is the overcomer, the only overcomer. But yet, when my soul is joined to His soul, when His Spirit flows like a heavenly stream through my spirit, when my whole nature is infilled and inspired by the life from God, I too, being joined with Him, become an overcomer in deed and in truth. Glory be to God.

I am glad that God has permitted man, even at intervals, to rise into that place of high dominion in God, for it demonstrates the purpose of God. It demonstrates that He purposes we should not only rise into the high place at intervals, but that this should be the normal life of the Christian who is joined to God every day and all the time.

Christianity is not a thing to be apologized for. Christianity was the living, conscious life and power of the living God, transmitted into the nature of man until, bless God, man's nature is transformed by the living touch and the very spirit, soul, and being is energized and filled by His life. Thus you become indeed, as Christ intended, a veritable Christ.

---

[9] Revelation 1:18.

That startles some people. But the ultimate of the Gospel of Jesus Christ, and the ultimate of the redemption of the Son of God, is to reproduce and make every man who is bound by sin and held by sensuousness and enslaved by the flesh, like Himself in deed and in truth — sons of God. Not sons of God on a lower order, but sons of God as Jesus was.

Paul declares, "He gave some apostles, some evangelists and some pastors and teachers." What for? "Till we *all* come into the likeness of the measure of the stature of the fullness of Christ."[10] Bless God. Not a limited life, but an unlimited life. The idea of Christ, the idea of God was that every man, through Jesus Christ, through being joined to Him by the Holy Spirit, should be transformed into Christ's perfect image. Glory be to God. Christ within and Christ without. Christ in your spirit, Christ in your soul, and Christ in your body. Not only living His life, but performing His works by the grace of God. That is the Gospel of the Son of God. That is the thing that Paul was not ashamed of. He said,

> I am not ashamed of the gospel of Christ: for it is the power of God unto salvation to every one that believeth; to the Jew first, and also to the Greek.[11]

If any man has a question within his soul of the reality of the baptism of the Holy Spirit, as it has been poured out upon the world in these last ten years, that question ought to be settled in your soul forever by one common test. That test is, that it has raised the consciousness of Christianity to realize what real Christianity is.

If anyone wants to analyze the development that has come into Christian consciousness during the last two hundred years, all they have to do is to begin and follow the preaching of the great evangelists who have moved the world. Think of Jonathan Edwards, who thundered the terrors of God and what hell was like until men grasped their seats and hung on to them, fearing they were falling into hell itself. Men were moved by *fear* to escape damnation. That was

---

[10] Ephesians 4:11,13, paraphrased.

[11] Romans 1:16.

believed to be Christianity. Why, any coward wanted to keep out of hell. He might not have had one idea in his soul of what was the real true earmark of Christianity.

After awhile, others went a step further, and you can note the ascending consciousness. They said, "No, saving yourself from hell and punishment is not the ideal of the Gospel. The ideal is to get saved, so as to go to heaven." And so men were saved in order to get to heaven when they died. I have always had a feeling in my soul of wanting to weep when I hear men pleading with others to become Christians so they will go up to heaven when they die. My God, is there no appeal outside of something absolutely selfish?

Beloved, don't you see that Christianity was unselfishness itself? It had no consideration for the selfish individual. The thing held up above everything else in the world, and the only ideal worthy of a Christian, was that you and I and He Himself might demonstrate to mankind one holy, high beauteous thing of which the world was deficient — a knowledge of God. So Jesus said, "Unto all righteousness"[12] and he wrote it on the souls of men and branded it on their conscience and stamped it on their heart until the world began to realize the ideal that was in the soul of Jesus.

"Unto all righteousness," becoming like Christ Himself, a demonstrator of the righteousness of the living God. That is Christianity, and that only is Christianity, for that was the consecration of the Christ Himself.

The test of the Spirit, and the only test of the Spirit, that Jesus ever gave is the ultimate and final test. He said, "Ye shall know them by their fruits." That is the absolute and final test. "Do men gather grapes of thorns, or figs of thistles?"[13]

So I say to you, if you want to test whether this present outpouring of the Spirit of God is the real thing, the real, pure baptism of the Holy Ghost or not, test it by the fruits that it produces. If it is producing in the world, as we believe it is, a consciousness of God so high, so

---

[12] Matthew 3:15, paraphrased.

[13] Matthew 7:16.

pure, so acceptable, so true, so good, so like Christ, then it is the Holy Ghost Himself. Bless God. No other test is of any value whatever.

I want to tell you, beloved, that the ultimate test of your own of the value of a thing that you have in your heart is the common test that Jesus gave, "By their fruits ye shall know them." "By their *fruits* ye shall know them. Do men gather grapes of thorns, or figs of thistles?"

Men tell us in these days that *sin* is what you think it is. Well, it is not. Sin is what God thinks it is. You may think according to your own conscience; God thinks according to His. God thinks in accordance with the heavenly purity of His own nature. Man thinks in accordance with that degree of purity that his soul realizes. But the ultimate note is in God. The finality is in God.

When men rise up in their soul's aspirations to the place of God's thought, then bless God, the character of Jesus Christ will be evident in their life, the sweetness of His nature, the holiness of His character, the beauty of the crowning glory that not only overshadowed Him, but that radiated from Him. Blessed be God. And the real life of the real Christian is the inner life, the life of the soul.

"Out of the heart," said Jesus, "proceed evil thoughts, fornications, adulteries,"[14] etc. These are the things common to the flesh of man. Out of the soul of man, likewise, proceeds by the same common law the beauty, virtue, peace, power, and truth of Jesus, as the soul knows it.

So he whose soul is joined to Christ may now, today, this hour, shed forth as a benediction upon the world the glory and blessing and peace and power of God, even as Jesus shed it forth to all men to the praise of God.

PRAYER

My God, we bless Thee for the ideal of the Gospel of Christ which Thou has established in the souls of men through the blessed Holy Ghost. God, we pray Thee this afternoon that if we have thought lightly of the Spirit of God, if we have had our eyes fixed on outward

---

[14] Matthew 15:19, paraphrased.

evidences instead of the inward life, we pray Thee to sweep it away from our souls.

May we this day, God, see indeed that the life of God, His inner life, the true life, God's holy life, His practical purpose, that from a race of sinful men, saved through the blood of Christ, cleansed by the power of God, cleansed in the inner soul, in every department of their nature, that the Christ-life is to be revealed, and the Lord Jesus through them is to shed forth His glory and life and benediction and peace and power upon the world. Blessed be Thy precious name.

So my God, we open our nature to heaven today, asking that the Spirit of the living God will thus move in our own soul, that by His grace we shall be so perfectly, truly cleansed of God that our nature will be sweet and pure and heavenly and true, so that we can receive from God indeed the blessed sweetness of His pure, holy, heavenly Spirit, to reign in us, to rule in us, control us, and guide us forevermore. In Jesus' name, Amen.

ivine healing is scripturally correct. It is philosophically sound. It is scientifically true. Healing by the Spirit and power of God is as demonstrable as the action of heat, air, or light. Our person is sensitive to temperature. We would freeze without heat. We would smother for the lack of air, and become pale and devitalized for want of light.

[UNTITLED, SPIRIT, SOUL, AND BODY]

More and more of the medical world is placing reliance on keeping the human body free from obstructions and endeavors to promote free action of all the physical powers. Materia Medicia no longer pretends to heal disease through medicines. They endeavor to build up the resistance of the patient as a means of [illegible]. The school of chiropractic emphasizes the necessity of keeping the nerves of the head, neck, and spine free from pressure through impingements, in order that the currents of vital life may have free course through the veins and nervous system to all parts of the body.

The varied schools of mental science follow a recognized principle of adjusting the mind to its environment and so removing mental strain and congestion, in order that the psychic currents may be directed to the varied parts of the body that need remedying. Observing as they do that unhealthy mental attitudes produce corresponding conditions in the physical, they endeavor to bring the mind of the individual into a state of restfulness and repose.

Each of those systems demonstrate one principle — the necessity of producing harmony in the body. Materia Medica endeavors to remove the difficulties and open the channels of the system through the use of laxatives and stimulants; the chiropractor through the release of the natural vital currents; the mental scientists through stimulating mental action and the control and direction of the mind forces. Each of these methods are classified as scientific. The doctor's method of physical remedy can be truly spoken of as scientific, the chiropractor's method as equally scientific, and the mental scientist's as likewise scientific.

Contention among these varied schools is because of the fact that the knowledge of each is limited. The doctor is sure the chiropractor is a charlatan; the chiropractor is equally sure that the doctor is a dunce and his system out of date; the mental scientist believes he has outgrown both methods and that they are in no way comparable in effectiveness to the mental method.

The real Christian, whose being is attuned with God and in whose consciousness the Christ-life is a divine reality, knows that the life of the spirit of man in contact with the Spirit of God supersedes every other endeavor to harmonize the nature of man and God, and that this harmonization of the Spirit of man and God is the eventual method of producing and maintaining health in the Spirit, in the mind, and in the body. He regards all other methods as superficial and inadequate, in that they fail to touch the [illegible], the point of human difficulty, or to contact the final source of ultimate life and power.

A comprehensive vision of the relationship of man and God is best realized through attention to the prayer of the apostle:

> I pray God your whole *spirit* and *soul* and *body* be preserved blameless unto the coming of our Lord Jesus Christ. Faithful is he that calleth you, who also will do it.
>
> — 1 Thessalonians 5:23-24

In this prayer we have a clear recognition of the entire man, and this prayer could well be construed as highly scientific, in that it touches the three great sciences of physiology, psychology, and pneumatology and climaxes all three in the recognition of a completed science, *ontology, the science of being,* fulfilling the desire of the apostle's heart in the ultimate perfection of the entire man — spirit, soul, and body.

Physiology is the knowledge of the human body and its functions. Psychology is a knowledge of the mind and its powers. Pneumatology is knowledge of the spirit and its activities and forces and its supreme control of the [illegible]. These three, the complete man, body and soul and spirit, manifests ontology. Ontology in its highest manifestation is man — body, soul, and spirit — coordinated and consciously in union with God, the source of life natural and life divine.

Thirty years ago, the doctor whose knowledge was confined to flesh and bones and blood was regarded as the scholar and scientist. Later, the mental scientist came with his knowledge of the human mind. He had knowledge of flesh and bone and blood, as the doctor had, and in addition, knowledge of the mental attitudes essential to producing harmony between the mentality and the body.

The spiritual scientist, the man with Jesus' secret of full salvation — who cannot get his learning from a university, but must seek a higher source of learning and experience for himself the reality of contact with God — possesses a knowledge greater than the doctor, the chiropractor, or the mental scientist and is the only one who has reached the ultimate source of healing and health for the whole man. It is therefore evident that the doctor, whose scientific knowledge is confined to the body, does not rate with the mental scientist, who possesses knowledge of both mind and body. And he in turn is far below the one possessing knowledge of the actions and powers of the spirit upon both the mind and body.

It will be seen at a glance then, that the God-born man, whose spirit is quickened through contact with God, is not a demonstrator of the "power of mind over matter," as is the mental scientist, but he is a demonstrator of the mightier fact of the power of the spirit over both mind and matter!

A spiritual scientist defines the spirit as the part of man which *knows,* the intuitive faculty, the discerning quality, the department of his nature capable of conscious union and understanding of God. The soul is the seat of the affections, desires, emotions, and of the active will, or self. The soul is the servant of the spirit and subject to its control and direction.

Jesus, the discerner of all discerners, the teacher of all teachers, never considered it worthwhile to discuss the method by which man became separated from God. He simply recognized that man was out of harmony with God and that He must be reconciled to God. To this end, He became the "minister of reconciliation."[1] And Christians

---

[1] See 2 Corinthians 5:18-19 and Hebrews 2:17.

everywhere and forever, if they fulfill their Lord's purpose, must likewise ever be "ministers of reconciliation."

"Be ye reconciled to God"[2] is the Christian watchword. Man in each department and manifestation of being must be reunited to God. "Ye must be born anew."[3]

To what extent then, are we expected to be reconciled to God? The Church in general has emphasized the necessity of a reconciliation of the *spirit* of man with God. Reconciliation is spoken of in varied terms, such as to be "born again," "converted," to get "religion" and many other phrases indicating the same experience. Others have taught to exercise faith in Christ for eternal salvation, but it has not been considered necessary that such should manifest in their lives the characteristics of Christ now. Divisions of the Church have taught in such terms as sanctification, holy living, perfect love, holiness, finished work of Christ, that the thought, the speech, and the actions of the individual should harmonize with the thought, the speech, and the actions of Christ.

Others have gone further than either of these and have contended that in order to demonstrate the completeness of Christian experience, Christ should have actual freedom and right of action in the entire spirit, the soul, and the *body* of man and that if this is so, the man would be right through and through. His spirit would be united to Christ in faith and love, his mind would reflect and reproduce the mind of Christ, and if the spirit and mind of man is in harmony with God, his body would likewise be delivered from sickness, even as his soul was delivered from sin. Thus the words of the apostle would become a fact:

> Beloved, I wish above all things that thou mayest prosper and be in health, even as thy soul prospereth.
>
> — 3 John 2

"Even as," means in like manner, to the same degree. The body just as well and prosperous as the soul. "According to your faith be it unto you."[4]

---

[2] 2 Corinthians 5:20.

[3] John 3:7, paraphrased.

[4] Matthew 9:29.

We contend, therefore, that the purpose of Jesus was not to save souls only. His purpose was to save *men* — to save their body from sickness, their soul from sin, their spirit from death. And to this end He gave eternal life to the spirit, peace to the soul, healing to the body, and all are available to every man.

The eventuating purpose of God through Christ is not morality but immortality, man transfigured, transformed, transmuted in feature, character, and substance like Jesus. Relationship to the Lord is not alone a scientific relationship, but an affectionate relationship. God does not ask us for our head only and its knowledge, but for our *heart*, the seat of the affections, the citadel of love.

To be a recipient of the Spirit of Christ is no different from being a recipient of the spirit of your wife or your lover. The affinity of mind and heart must be developed ere a union of human spirits and hearts becomes a possibility. If there is sin, evil, contention, and doubt toward the other in the mind of one, the love of the other does not avail. The purging away of this condition is essential to spiritual union and oneness. It is no different in our relationship with Christ. If sin, selfishness, and disobedience exist and we want to enjoy heart fellowship with Christ, it can only be brought to pass as we turn our backs on our sin and become obedient to His will and learn to walk in fellowship with Him.

The putting away of sin is not merely a phrase, but an absolute essential in order that the heart of Christ and the heart of man may become one in love. It is this relationship that makes possible the transfusion of His life and love through all our being. Healing for the body will be as natural as peace of mind or rest of spirit, and the child of God is thus able to declare that Christ has become his "all in all."

Moses had had his interview with the Lord at the burning bush,

MOSES' REBUKE

and God had definitely commanded him to go to Pharaoh in Egypt and demand the deliverance of the children of Israel. God gave him the signet of His presence with him, his shepherd rod. All the miracles that followed that demand had taken place, and the children of Israel were finally given permission by the king to leave.

They started toward the Red Sea when the king's heart drew back, and I presume he felt he had done an unwise thing. He was losing the services of two and a half, probably four million slaves. In his effort to recall what he had done, he started after them with an army. In the meantime, Moses had gotten down to the Red Sea. On the right and on the left were impassable mountains and Pharaoh and his armies behind him.

The situation from a natural point of view was desperate, and if there was ever a time when a man was seemingly justified in calling on God in prayer, it was then. But I want to show you tonight one of the things I regard as a hindrance in our life for God. Most of us do just exactly what Moses did. When the test comes we stop and cry and as a second thing we stop and pray and put ourselves in a position where we become amenable to exactly the same rebuke that came upon Moses.

Moses started to pray. It is not recorded how long he prayed, or what he said, but instead of God being pleased, He was grieved and said to Moses: "Why standest thou here, and criest unto Me? Speak to the children of Israel that they go forward." I will turn to the Scripture and read the exact words:

> The LORD said unto Moses, *Wherefore criest thou unto me?* speak unto the children of Israel, that they go forward: But *lift thou up thy rod,* and *stretch out thine hand* over the sea, and *divide it:* and the children of Israel shall go on dry ground through the midst of the sea.
>
> — Exodus 14:15-16, emphasis Lake's

God did not even say, "You stretch out your hand, and I will divide the sea." But God said to Moses: "Stretch out *thine* hand over the sea, and divide it." It was not an act for God to perform, but it was an act for Moses to believe for. The responsibility was not with God it was with Moses. A weak Christianity is ever inclined to whine in prayer while God waits for the believer to command it.

In my judgment, that is the place of extreme weakness in Christian character. I feel that very frequently prayer is made a refuge to dodge the action of faith. And just exactly as Moses came down there and began to pray instead of honoring God's word to him by the use of his rod, so many times our prayer becomes offensive to God. Because instead of praying as Moses did, God demands us to stretch forth *our hand*, exercise our rod of faith, and divide the waters.

In many respects it seems to me, this is the most powerful lesson that the Word of God contains on the subject of prayer and faith. Just stop for a moment and think of God throwing the responsibility of making a passage through the sea on Moses. God would not take it. It was for Moses to believe God and act. God commands: "Lift up *thy* rod, and stretch out *thine* hand," not "My hand." He was to lift the rod that God had given to him, the signet of God's presence with him to be used by the hand of Moses.

In the consideration of the whole subject of an Apostolic Church, do you not see the principle in it? The principle of acceptance of responsibility from God.

I want to call your attention now to the New Testament on that line. In the ninth chapter of Luke we have Jesus commanding the twelve disciples:

> Then he called his twelve disciples together, and *gave them* power and authority over all devils, and to cure diseases. And he sent *them* to preach the kingdom of God, and *to heal the sick.*[1]

Moses stood before God, and God gave him the commission to go down to Egypt. Then as an evidence of His presence, He said, "What is it you have in your hands?"

---

[1] Luke 9:1-2.

Moses answered, "A rod."

He said, "Throw it down," and as Moses obeyed it became a serpent.

Then He said, "Take it up," and it was changed to a rod again. This is one of the instances of taking up serpents. God said, "Keep it. It is a signet of My presence with you," and it was so with Moses.[2]

But you see Moses had forgotten as he stood by the Red Sea, that God had given him a sign of His presence with him. Circumstances overpowered him and he commenced to pray and that prayer was an offense to God.

Just as God had done with Moses, so Jesus called the twelve to Him, and *gave them* power and authority over all devils, and to cure diseases, and that was their rod. He sent them to preach the kingdom of God and heal the sick. Suppose they came to the sick, and they commenced to pray and say, "Jesus, You heal this man." They would be in just exactly the same position Moses was when he got down to the Red Sea and prayed, "Lord God, You divide these waters." The two cases are absolutely parallel. God demands the action of the believer's faith in God. *You* stretch out *your* hand and divide the waters.

God has likewise given to *every man* the measure (rod) of faith, and it is for man, as the servant of God, to use the rod that God has given him.[3] In these days there is an attitude of mind that I do not know hardly how to define. It is a mock humility. Rather, it is a false humility. It is a humility that is always hiding behind the Lord and is excusing its own lack of faith by throwing the responsibility over on the Lord. The Word of God, in speaking of this same matter concerning the disciples says, *"They* departed, and went through the towns, preaching the gospel, and healing every where."[4]

Over and over again throughout the New Testament, the Word of God says, "They healed them, the disciples healed them," etc. You see, they had received something from God. They were as conscious of it as Moses was conscious he had received a rod from the Lord. It was theirs to use. It was theirs to use for all purposes. Peter used the

---

[2] See Exodus 4:2-4.

[3] See Romans 12:3.

[4] Luke 9:6.

conscious rod of God to heal the man at the beautiful gate. He did not pray. He did not ask God to heal the man, but he commanded him, "In the name of Jesus Christ of Nazareth rise up and walk."[5] And the man obeyed. That was not intercession. It was a command. It was the faith in Peter's soul that brought the result.

Peter used the rod. The rod in this case was the rod of faith. In whose hands was it? In the hands of Peter and John together, and they used that rod of faith. The Word was spoken through Peter. The command was given through him. Unquestionably, John's soul was in it just as much as Peter's was. By faith in His name, by the faith of the disciples, the power of God was made active, and the lame man was healed.

Beloved, the lesson in my soul is this. There is a place of victory and a place of defeat, but there is a hairbreadth line there. It is the place of *faith in action*. To believe the thing God says and to do the thing that He commands accepting, as the servant of God, the responsibility God lays upon you. Not interceding as Moses did, but as in Peter's case, through the faith that was in his soul, he commanded the power of God on the man. Suppose Peter had prayed, "Oh Lord, You come and heal this man." It would have been his own acknowledgment of lack of faith to do what Jesus told the disciple to do — heal the sick.

In the story of Saul, in 1 Samuel 10, among other things the prophet Samuel says to him:

> The Spirit of the LORD will come upon thee, and thou shalt prophesy with them, and shalt be turned into another man. And let it be, when these signs are come unto thee, that thou do *as occasion serve thee;* for God is with thee.

— 1 Samuel 10:6-7

The lesson I know God wants us to see tonight is this: He endues a man or woman with the authority of God to accomplish the will of God. The power of God is bestowed upon the man. It is not the man that accomplishes the matter. It is the stretching forth of the hand; the dividing of the waters must be in response to the faith of the man. The

---

[5] Acts 3:6.

man is the instrument. "Thou shalt do as occasion serve thee; for God is with thee." That is, you simply go on about your business, and the power of God is present with you to accomplish the desire of your heart.

Returning to the case of Peter, Peter used the faith of God that was in his soul to restore a man who was born lame, and he was instantly restored.

In the case of Ananias and Sapphira, we see Peter using the same power, by the spoken Word, not to restore a man's limbs, but to bring judgment on a liar. When Ananias lied, the Spirit of God fell on him, and he died as an example of sin. His wife likewise died. "Behold, the feet of them which have buried thy husband are at the door, and shall carry thee out."[6]

Man is a servant of God. Man is an instrument through which God works. The danger line is always around this: The weak men have taken to themselves the glory that belonged to God, and they have said, "We did it." They did not do it. God did it, but the man believed God that it would be done.

How closely we are made co-workers with the Lord, "co-laborers together with Him."[7] It is God's divine purpose to accomplish His will in the world through men. God placed a profound respect upon the Body, "the church, which is his body."[8] I want to show you that.

In the tenth chapter of Acts we have that remarkable response to the prayers of Cornelieus when an angel came to him and said,

> [Cornelieus]...thy prayers and thine alms are come up for a memorial before God. And now send men to Joppa, and call for one Simon, whose surname is Peter:...he shall tell thee what thou oughtest to do.[9]

The angel came from heaven. He was a direct messenger of God. Yet the angel did not tell Cornelius the way of salvation. Why did the

---

[6] Acts 5:9.

[7] See 1 Corinthians 3:9.

[8] Ephesians 1:22-23.

[9] Acts 10:4-6.

angel instruct Cornelius to send for Peter? Because Peter was a part of the body of Christ, and God ordained that the power of God, with the ministry of Christ, shall be manifest through the Body. Not through angels, but through the Body, "the church, which is his body."

It is, therefore, the duty of the body to use the Spirit of God to accomplish the divine will of God, the purpose of God. With what strength then, with what a consciousness of the dignity of service, Christians ought to go forth! With what a conscious realization that God has bestowed upon you the authority and not only the authority, but the enduement of the Spirit to cause you to believe God and exercise the faith for the will of God to be accomplished.

Is it any wonder that David said,

> What is man, that thou art mindful of him? and the son of man, that thou visitest him? For thou hast made him a little lower than the angels, and hast crowned him with glory and honour. Thou madest him to have dominion over the works of thy hands; thou hast put all things under his feet.[10]

Man and God working together, co-laborers, co-workers. Blessed be God.

---

[10] Psalm 8:4-6.

nd God blessed them, and God said unto them, Be fruitful, and multiply, and replenish the earth, and subdue it: and have dominion over the fish of the sea, and over the fowl of the air, and over every living thing that moveth upon the earth.

— Genesis 1:28

SATAN'S LIMITED POWER AND LIMITATIONS

Psalm 8:4-8. Two questions are asked in this Psalm. "What is man, that thou art mindful of him?" and "the son of man, that thou visitest him?"(Verse 4.) There is one answer, given in verses 5 through 8.

Consider the first question. "What is man, that thou art mindful of him?"

"For thou hast made him a little lower than the angels." The word "angels" is translated from the Hebrew word *Elohiym*. This is the name of God and is used exclusively in the first five chapters of Genesis and in hundreds of other places in the Old Testament. Man was made a little lower than God. God gave this man dominion over the works of His hands (verses 6-8).

Man was God's understudy.

Man was God's king on the earth.

Man was subject only to God and the law of love.

Note: God gave this man complete power over His creation. He was the boss.

Satan had no power over this creation. He had no power over this man in Eden. Satan was only a bystander.

Satan saw the possibility of gaining the dominion that God had given man for himself. If he could talk man into rebelling against God, the dominion would be his. He knew Adam was a free moral agent. He knew that Adam could choose to be a child of God or become a child of Satan. So he approached the woman and talked her into desiring the forbidden fruit. Genesis 3:6 shows that the woman did not believe that the fruit of the tree was good for food. It was when she saw that it was good for food, pleasant to look at, and good to impart wisdom that she ate.

You see, without a desire there can be no temptation. (James 1:13-14.) Eve was deceived by Satan, but Adam ate the fruit fully knowing better. (1 Timothy 2:14.) At the moment that Adam ate of the forbidden fruit, Satan became the god of this world. At that moment, Satan became the prince of the power of the air. For these titles see Ephesians 2:2; 2 Corinthians 4:4; and John 14:30. All the dominion that God had given to man passed into the hands of Satan. Man legally gave his dominion to the devil.

God is a God of justice. He is fair. He recognized the devil's right to the dominion man had given to him. Though God is bigger than Satan, He cannot stoop to satanic methods in taking the dominion away from Satan. When will the power the devil wields over the creation come to an end? There must be a time element involved as shown by the demons when they spoke to Jesus about tormenting them before the time. (Matthew 8:29.) That is another subject.

Who gave Satan his power and dominion over this creation? Man! God did not give the devil one bit of authority or power. No one gives power unto his enemy unless he is a fool. If God had given the dominion to Satan then He would be guilty of all the acts of Satan.

Man, in turning his dominion over to Satan, found himself in a hopeless and helpless position. He had lost control of his eternal destiny. He needed a Savior.

Let us consider the second question of Psalm 8. "And the son of man, that thou visitest him?"

"For Thou hast made him a little lower than the angels." In taking this Scripture into the New Testament the writer of the book of Hebrews uses for the word "angels," the Greek word *aggelos*. This is the word translated "angels" in the New Testament. Jesus was made a little lower than the angels because He was to suffer death. (Hebrews 2:9.)

To this second Adam God gave the same dominion He gave the first Adam. It is proven by the fact that Jesus had power over the elements

(Matthew 8:26), power over disease (Matthew 8:16-17), and power over death (John 6:39-47). Jesus had power over the creation but also power to undo what man had brought upon himself. It was Jesus' responsibility to break the power of Satan and to set in motion the process which would bring about the redemption of the entire creation. The whole world groaneth until this is accomplished. (Romans 8:22.) Jesus had, and has, dominion over all the power of the enemy. He, through grace, restored to man the right to regain control over his destiny.

Now let the circle represent the dominion God gave to Adam.

ADAM'S DOMINION TO SATAN

It is a limited dominion. Man gave that dominion over to Satan. Within this sphere the devil has the right to move and reign. The devil cannot go beyond that dominion. To do so would be intruding into the pure realm of God's dominion. This the devil cannot do, as God does not give place to the devil. This is one reason that 1 Corinthians 10:13 is in the Book. God will not suffer (let) you to be tempted above that ye are able to take. Satan cannot use supernatural means to tempt. Temptation must remain in the realm of that which is common to man.

Another connotation of 1 Corinthians 10:13 is for here and now. God will not suffer (let) you to be tempted above that ye are able to take. How? Because "greater is he that is in you, than he that is in the world" (1 John 4:4). "I can do all things through Christ." (Philippians 4:13.) To know that gives me strength.

God will make a way of escape from the temptation. How? He has given us a shield of faith that quenches *all* the fiery missiles of the devil. We have the sword of the Spirit.[1] Thus, Satan is a lesser power than the fully-equipped Christian. (Luke 10:19.)

There are two kingdoms operating on the face of this earth. Each has its own army. There is the kingdom of God, headed up by Jesus

---

[1] See Ephesians 6:16-17.

Christ. He is also Captain of God's army. (Hebrews 2:10.) There is also the kingdom of darkness, headed up by Satan.

God, the Father, defeated Satan by operating through His Son, Jesus Christ. As a result, that victory has been handed to the army of God which is the body of Jesus. It is that body's responsibility to maintain that victory. Each individual in that body is responsible for putting on all the armor provided. Each is responsible to maintain that victory in their own lives and help others also to do likewise. Each soldier must be fully armed.

In warfare, the army that takes the initiative has the advantage. Our Captain seized the initiative when He met Satan in the wilderness.[2] He is our victory. We have the advantage. So much so that we are more than conquerors. (Romans 8:37.) That we have the initiative is proven by the fact that the gates of hell cannot prevail against us.[3] No army takes the gates of its city with it when it goes out to war. Satan is on the defensive.

The armor of God given the Christian (Ephesians 6:13-17) is for both offensive and defensive warfare. Offensive, in that we enter the gates of Satan's kingdom and win people to Christ. It is defensive so we can meet Satan's counterattacks. That shield of faith is invincible. God's army is the best equipped and trained that ever was put in the field. It is sad so many Christians do not take their place as active soldiers.

God's army is not ignorant of Satan's devices. (2 Corinthians 2:11.) What are his devices?

He goes about as a roaring lion. (1 Peter 5:8.) A big showoff, a lot of noise, all to frighten, all to try to cover up the fact of his defeat — he is trying to bluff God's people. He roars and the fearful tremble. The devil is looking for those who will give place to him. How do people give place to the devil? By being careless, by taking chances, by breaking the law of love, by being fearful, by neglecting prayer, by not feeding consistently on the "Word," by not maintaining a good confession before men — in short, by not being sober and vigilant. God does not allow the devil to get the advantage over these soldiers. They

---

[2] See Matthew 4:1-11; Mark 1:12-13; or Luke 4:1-13.

[3] See Matthew 16:18.

allow it by not using the equipment God has given them. They allow it by not being alert.

The alert soldier knows that he can keep himself and that the wicked one cannot touch him. (1 John 5:18.) He keepeth himself by being alert and using the equipment provided. The alert soldier knows that God is fully in, with, and back of him. The alert soldier knows that when temptation comes, it is not being allowed of God. God cannot tempt neither can He be tempted (James 1:13). For God to allow the devil to tempt would make God a partaker of the temptation. He cannot be a party to temptation.

Another method of the devil is to come as an angel of light. (2 Corinthians 11:14.) In this method, he comes using the Scriptures to deceive. He also has servants among men who handle the Word of God deceitfully. The true member of Christ's body does not handle the Word of God deceitfully. (2 Corinthians 4:2.) The alert soldier of God measures every teaching by the Word. He searches the Scriptures to see if the teaching being presented is correct. (Acts 17:11.)

Satan is desperate. He knows he has only a short time. (Revelation 12:12.) Within the sphere of influence given to him by man, he can counterattack to try and regain what he has lost to the Son of God. He does not need God's permission to do this. For God to grant such permission would make Him a party to the defense of evil.

God is operating against the army of hell through the body of His Son, the Church. The soldier of God is the salt of the earth. (Matthew 5:13.) Salt prevents the spread of corruption. "Ye are the light of the world" (Matthew 5:14). Light dispels darkness and lights up the true way for men to see and enter.

The soldier of God is one spirit with the Lord. (1 Corinthians 6:17.) The very substance of God indwells him. "Ye in me, and I in you" (John 14:20). He is a new species, a new creation. (2 Corinthians 5:17.) He is a member of Jesus' body, flesh, and bones. (Ephesians 5:30.) He shares in the power and authority of the Head of the body of which he is a member. He has power over all the power of the enemy. (Luke 10:19.)

As a soldier of God he has the finest of equipment. (Ephesians 6:13-17.) It is an invincible armor — a shield of faith that quenches all the fiery darts (missiles) of the devil. The sword of the Spirit, the Word of God, is so powerful the devil cannot stand against it. He flees from it. (James 4:7.) The soldier of God reigns in life now by one, our Lord Jesus Christ. (Romans 5:17.) The soldier of God is one in life now with Jesus Christ.

"Finally, my brethren, be strong in the Lord and in the power of his might" (Ephesians 6:10). Be strong in the grace of God. (2 Timothy 2:1.) The devil's power is limited. His power was broken by our Savior. You are one with Him in destroying the works of the devil. He came to destroy the works of the devil. (1 John 3:8.) Destroy his works every chance you get. How do you do this? By presenting the Word, by casting out devils, by healing the sick — in short, by doing His works. (John 14:12.) The gates of hell cannot prevail against you.

THE POWER OF GOD

I want to read to you one of the best incidents in the Word of God. It is the story of Elijah upon Mount Carmel.

THE SPIRIT OF GOD

And it came to pass, when Ahab saw Elijah, that Ahab said unto him, art thou he that troubleth Israel? And he answered, I have not troubled Israel; but thou, and thy father's house, in that ye have forsaken the commandments of the Lord, and thou hast followed Baalim. Now therefore send, and gather to me all Israel unto mount Carmel, and the prophets of Baal four hundred and fifty, and the prophets of the groves four hundred, which eat at Jezebel's table.

So Ahab sent unto all the children of Israel, and gathered the prophets together unto mount Carmel. And Elijah came unto all the people, and said, How long halt ye between two opinions? If the Lord be God, follow him; but if Baal, then follow him. And the people answered him not a word. Then said Elijah unto the people, I, even I only, remain a prophet of the Lord; but Baal's prophets are four hundred and fifty men. Let them therefore give us two bullocks; and let them choose one bullock for themselves, and cut it in pieces, and lay it on wood, and put no fire under: and I will dress the other bullock, and lay it on wood, and put no fire under: And call ye on the name of your gods, and I will call on the name of the Lord: and the God that answereth by fire, let him be God. And all the people answered and said, It is well spoken.

And Elijah said unto the prophets of Baal, Choose you one bullock for yourselves, and dress it first; for ye are many; and call on the name of your gods, but put no fire under. And they took the bullock which as given them, and they dressed it, and called on the name of Baal from morning even until noon, saying, O Baal, hear us. But there was no voice, nor any that answered. And they leaped upon the altar which was made.

And it came to pass at noon, that Elijah mocked them, and said, Cry aloud: for he is a god; either he is talking, or he

John G. Lake: The Complete Collection of His Life Teachings

is pursuing, or he is in a journey, or peradventure he sleepeth, and must be awaked. And they cried aloud, and cut themselves after their manner with knives and lancets, till the blood gushed out upon them. And it came to pass, when midday was past, and they prophesied until the time of the offering of the evening sacrifice, that there was neither voice, nor any to answer, nor any that regarded. And Elijah said unto all the people, Come near unto me. And all the people came near unto him. And he repaired the altar of the Lord that was broken down.

And Elijah took twelve stones, according to the number of the tribes of the sons of Jacob, unto whom the word of the Lord came, saying, Israel shall be thy name: And with the stones he built an altar in the name of the Lord: and he made a trench about the altar, as great as would contain two measures of seed. And he put the wood in order, and cut the bullock in pieces, and laid him on the wood, and said, Fill four barrels with water, and pour it on the burnt sacrifice, and on the wood. And he said, Do it the second time. And they did it the second time. And he said, Do it the third time. And they did it the third time. And the water ran round about the altar; and he filled the trench also with water.

And it came to pass at the time of the offering of the evening sacrifice, that Elijah the prophet came near, and said, Lord God of Abraham, Isaac, and of Israel, let it be known this day that thou art God in Israel, and that I am thy servant, and that I have done all these things at thy word. Hear me, O Lord, hear me that this people may know that thou art the Lord God, and that thou hast turned their heart back again.

Then the fire of the Lord fell, and consumed the burnt sacrifice, and the wood, and the stones, and the dust, and licked up the water that was in the trench. And when all the people saw it, they fell on their faces: and they said, The Lord, he is the God; the Lord, he is the God. And Elijah said unto them, Take the prophets of Baal; let not one of them escape. And they took them: and Elijah brought them down to the brook Kishon, and slew them there.

—1 Kings 18:17-40

In every land, among every people, throughout all history, there have been occasions when a demonstration of the power of God was just as necessary to the world as it was in the days of Elijah. It is necessary now.

The people had turned away from God. They had forgotten that there was a God in Israel. They were trusting in other gods, just as the people are today. If I were to call you heathen, I suppose most people would be offended, but I want to say that there is no people with more gods than the average American. Men are bowing down to the god of popularity. Men are bowing down to this god and that god. Men are afraid of the opinion of their neighbors, as any heathen ever was in any time in the world. There is practically no Christian, let alone an unchristian, who has the real stamina to stand forth and declare his absolute convictions concerning Jesus Christ, the Son of God. Much less have men with the necessary stamina to declare their convictions as to Jesus Christ, the Savior of mankind.

That is the reason that the modern church has lost her touch with God and has gone into a sleep unto death, a sleep that can only end in spiritual death and the disintegration of the church as she stands. The only power that will revive the church in this land and the world is that which she will receive when she throws her heart open to God as the people of Israel did and says, "Lord God, we have sinned."

The sin she needs to repent of is not the committing a lot of little acts which men call sin (that are the outgrowth of what is in the heart), but the thing that mankind needs to repent of is this — that they have denied the power of God. They have denied to mankind that the Christ of Israel is the Son of God and that He is the Almighty Savior. God's call to the Christian churches today is to come forth from their hiding place, just as Elijah came forth, and meet the king. Declare the ground on which you meet the enemies of God, and meet them in the name of Jesus Christ.

The Christian Church is absolutely, solely, and entirely to blame for the whole existence of metaphysical associations which are covering the earth like a plague of lice. The Church is to blame, for if the Church of Jesus Christ for the last fifty or a hundred years had declared to mankind in the power of the Spirit the Christ of Nazareth as He is, there never would have come into existence the whole tribe of metaphysical societies.

The world today is being taken by the metaphysical associations to such an extent that they are bowing before the metaphysical laws and calling them God. That is human nature and not God. The time has come when the Christian Church has got to give a new demonstration to the world. If metaphysicians, through the operation of natural laws, can produce a certain character and degree of healing, then it is up to the Church of Jesus Christ and the ministry of the Son of God to demonstrate that there is a power in the blood of Jesus Christ to save men and heal men unto the *uttermost* — not half-healed or half the people healed, but I pray and believe that God's time has come for God's challenge to mankind and the challenge of the Christian Church to the world is to come on, and if it is God, let the *fire fall*.

There was no bluffing with the old Israelitish prophets. When the people came, they laid their sacrifices on the altar, and they did not put artificial fire under it. But instead, the soul went down before God. He lifted his heart to heaven and then the fire came down and consumed the sacrifice, that was the evidence that the sacrifice was accepted.

The time has come when God wants the fire to fall and if you, my beloved brother and sister, will pay God's price and make Christ's consecration of yourself to God, we will see God's fire fall. And it will not be destructive either, except that sin and selfishness and sickness will wither under that fire while purity and life and holiness and character will stand forth purified and refined by the glory and the power of the God-fire that comes from heaven. God's fire is creative of righteousness as well as destructive of sin.

Some years ago, when I opened my work in South Africa and the Lord had moved marvelously for about six months, a movement was put on foot to congregate a crowd of Indian Yogi. (The Indian Yogi are a society of people who utterly give themselves up to a demonstration of metaphysical things.) They were Brahman priests, Buddhist priests, Confucian priests, and all kinds of priests and hypnotists. After a time they said, "We would like to have a demonstration."

And I said, "Yes, I would like to have a demonstration also. Come on with your Yogi and your Buddhas and your Confucians and hypnotists.

Let them show their god. Let them heal people if they can. Let it be in the public, and let it be done on the platform of my tabernacle or any other place large enough to accommodate the public. Then when you have finished, we will call on the Christian's God and see what He will do."

Well, they came to the tabernacle to make the demonstration. One man, Professor Henerson, a professional hypnotist, was put forward. He said he was there to demonstrate what he could do through hypnotism. He brought with him as his subject a woman from Germiston who had a locked hip, probably from rheumatics or hip disease. After he had tried and tried privately for months and now publicly before the people, I said, "Stand off."

Calling one of the brethren to pray with me I said, "In the name of the Lord Jesus Christ I command this hip to become unlocked." Instantly she was healed and walked. I want to tell you more of what God did. That was as far as my faith reached, but God met me at that point. As I stood looking at her, I said to myself, *That is the way Jesus did it when He was on the earth and that is the way Jesus does it yet.* It was Jesus who did it.

Well, as I stood looking at her, suddenly something came upon my soul from heaven. It was the anointing of the Spirit of God. I understood then what the blessed old Book talked about when it spoke of the Spirit of the Lord coming upon Elijah[1] and the Spirit of the Lord coming upon Samson[2], etc. Samson, under the power of the Spirit, took the gates of Gaza and carried them off.[3] He took the jawbone of an ass and killed a thousand men with it.[4] These were the things by which God endeavored to teach the world what the Spirit of the Lord is.

Well, as I stood there the Spirit fell upon me, not like the gentle dew of heaven but in power, until my spirit towered up in such strength I did not know how to control it. In my heart I cried out, "My God, what does it mean?" When all at once I discovered the Spirit going

---

[1] See Judges 14:6,19, and 15:14.

[2] 1 Kings 18:46 says the "hand of the Lord" was upon Elijah.

[3] See Judges 16:30.

[4] See Judges 15:15.

out in operation to the spirit of that hypnotist. I said, "Are you the man who has been hypnotizing this woman for two years and grafting her hard-earned money? In the name of Jesus Christ you will never hypnotize anyone else." Grasping him by the coat front, I struck him on the shoulder with my other hand, saying, "In the name of the Son of God come out of him." And it came out. That hypnotic demon was gone out of him. He never hypnotized again but earned an honest living.

God is not the God of the dead. He is the God of the living. And the desire in my soul is that in this city God Almighty may raise up an altar unto the living God, not unto a dead God. Mankind needs an altar to the *living* God, to the God that hears prayer, to the God that answers prayer, and the God that answers by fire. The time has come when God's challenge has gone forth. God is saying, "If there is a Christian, let him pray. If there is a God, let Him answer." God will meet the souls every time you turn to Him and meet Him face to face.

In emphasizing this, the Lord Jesus Christ says to the world, "When ye pray, believe that ye receive, and ye shall have."[5] That is what is the matter. Your blank check is not worth ten cents in your hands. Why? Because you do not believe God. Fill in your check, believe God, and it will come to pass.

The call of Elijah is the call of the present hour. If the Christ is the Christ, get your answer from Him. If Jesus is the Son of God with power on the earth to forgive sins, then as Jesus put it, "Rise up and walk, that ye may know that the Son of man hath power on earth to forgive sins."[6]

Jesus Christ was reasonable enough to meet man's reasoning and inquiries. And the minister of God who is afraid to walk out and believe his God and trust his God for results is no Christian at all.

What does Christianity mean to the world? Is it a hope for the glory land away off in the future? Is that Christianity? Is it a hope that you are not going to fry in hell all the days of your life? No! Christianity is the demonstration of the righteousness of God to the world.

---

5   Mark 11:24, paraphrased.

6   Luke 5:24, paraphrased.

So, brethren, God has given us something to do. He has given us a demonstration to make. If we do not make it, then we have no more right to the claims that we make of being sons of God than other people. If God be God, serve Him; if Baal, then serve him.

COMPASSION

I wonder if you ever settled in your own mind what is the greatest blessing or revelation of the Spirit or power of God. I believe the greatest thing is that Jesus showed the world how to exercise compassion for one another. The law of Moses, that preceded Jesus, was exacting in its demands as all law is. That is the nature of law. And Jesus undertook to reveal the Father-heart to the world. The greatest movement in the soul of God Himself was that movement of compassion for a needy world, which was so great, that the Word says,

> God so loved the world, that he gave his only begotten Son, that whosoever believeth in him should not perish, but have everlasting life.[1]

We are inclined to think, sometimes, that God is careless about the world. Not so.

> For God so loved the world, that he gave his only begotten Son, that whosoever believeth in him should not perish, but have everlasting life. For God sent not his Son into the world to condemn the world; but that the world through him might be saved.[2]

When the multitude had followed Jesus into the wilderness He was moved with compassion for them, for they were like sheep without a shepherd. The disciples said, "Now Lord, let us send them away." Jesus understood men's humanity. He understood the fact that they were hungry, and the heart of the Christ was moved with compassion for them. He said, "No, get them to sit down. All there is in the company is five thousand people, beside women and children. You get them to sit down." When they were seated He took the five loaves and the two fishes, blessed them, brake, and gave to His disciples to give to the multitude.[3]

---

[1] John 3:16.

[2] John 3:16-17.

[3] See Matthew 14:15-21, Mark 6:35-44, Luke 9:12-17, or John 6:5-14.

Jesus taught the world to have compassion. Men have loved to have compassion on the lovable and on the beautiful, but Jesus taught the world to have compassion on the unholy, the sinful, and the ignorant. One day they brought to Him a sinful woman, and they said, "According to our law, she should be stoned." According to the law there was nothing else for her; but the compassion of Jesus covered that soul and He said, "Go, and sin no more."[4]

Someone told me this incident: A lady who lives in the country, a widow, who had one daughter, was laboring for small wages. Her great ambition was to be able to educate her daughter. She had toiled and worked and invested the money in Liberty Bonds, to hold for the education of her daughter. Recently she came down from one of the country towns to Spokane, to make a few purchases for the daughter that would be necessary for the girl's new life at school. She stood at one of the counters of the Crescent Store. She turned her back for a moment and presently discovered that the little treasure was gone. The savings of a whole life, the struggles of a mother's heart!

The endeavor to gratify the one big love of her soul, in the education of her daughter. In spite of the assistance of the officials of the store, she was unable to find any trace of it. At last she sat down and wept bitterly. A lady, the widow of a banker, who saw her, told her to come up on the balcony with her and sit down. Another lady joined them, and the lady who first saw her said, "Now come, we are going to sit down together and believe God on behalf of this soul. We are going to believe that God will move the soul of the person who took that little treasure, until his soul sees that thing like this mother sees it."

Men are learning, blessed be God. And they sat down together to pray for that soul. The mother returned to the country and in the mail following her came a letter, with the little treasure and a little note, saying, "I couldn't keep it. Forgive me, and may God forgive me." Compassion reaches further than law; further than demands of judges. Compassion reaches to the heart of life, to the secret of our being. The compassion of Jesus was the divine secret that made Him

---

[4] See John 8:3-11.

lovable. Religious people are exacting. Good people are exacting, but good folks have to learn to exercise compassion just like others do.

We remember the incident with the disciples and the Samaritans. The Samaritans did not want Jesus and His disciples to come. They said, "We have heard strange stories. How this thing happened, and how that thing happened. How a great amount of swine were drowned, etc."[5] They had heard about the pigs, but they probably had never heard how the widow's son was raised from the dead,[6] how the water had been turned into wine,[7] etc. The disciples loved their Lord, they were exercising His power, they were ministering to the sick, they were endeavoring to alleviate the sufferings of the world; but still that sense of insult was so overpowering, that they said, "Master, shall we call down fire from heaven, to consume them?"[8] My, how the big thing in your soul gets hurt, and how easy it is for us to feel the righteousness of the issue, rather than the compassion of the Son of God. There is no limit to the compassion of Jesus.

Two blind men were crying by the wayside, calling on the Lord to have mercy on them. And He stopped, and asked what they wanted. They answered, "Lord, that we may receive our sight." And He healed them.[9] And if you want the real explanation for His saving men out of their sins and sicknesses, it is in the love of His soul — that divine compassion of God and His desire to help men out of their sorrows and difficulties and back to God.

Jesus' example on the cross is set forever and ever as the very acme and the very soul of the compassion of God, through Christ. After they had pierced His hands and pierced His feet, with His last breath He prayed to God, "Father, forgive them; for they know not what they do."[10] When a man is able to look upon his own murderers and speak such words as these, surely it shows that he speaks beyond that which the human heart is capable of giving, and is speaking only that which the soul of God can give.

---

[5] See Luke 8:30-33.

[6] See Luke 7:12-15.

[7] See John 2:3-10.

[8] Luke 9:54, paraphrased.

[9] See Matthew 20:30-34.

[10] Luke 23:34.

How long should we endure? How long should we endure the mis-
understandings of friends without rebuff? If we consider these things,
surely we see the secret of the life that He endured all the way. And
unto the very end, and also in the very end, He was blessed by God.
His triumph was there. The ignorant crucify you and trample over the
loveliest things of your soul, like they bruised the soul of Jesus. The
triumph is there.

In the divine fullness of the heart of God in Christ, is the revelation
of a divine conception that alone endures, even unto death, and
through which the nature and love of God is revealed to a dying
world. When Jesus was trying to give us balance in the life of God,
He gave us, once more, a beautiful parable — the parable of the
Good Samaritan.

> A certain man went down from Jerusalem to Jericho, and
> fell among thieves, which stripped him of his raiment, and
> wounded him, and departed, leaving him half dead. And
> by chance there came down a certain priest that way.[11]

And one should have expected compassion of a priest, but when he saw
him, he passed by on the other side. And the Levite, the holy man of
the people came down, and he looked upon him, and passed by on the
other side. But the poor Samaritan, the dog in the mind of the Jew,

> When he saw him, he had compassion on him, and went to
> him, and bound up his wounds, pouring in oil and wine,
> and set him on his own beast, and brought him to an inn,
> and took care of him. And on the morrow when he
> departed, he took out two pence, and gave them to the
> host, and said unto him, Take care of him; and whatsoever
> thou spendest more, when I come again, I will repay thee.[12]

He did not do the best thing, but he did the best thing he knew, and
Christ commanded it. How often have you had the loveliest things of
your soul trampled upon? Not by some drunken person, but probably by the one nearest to your heart; probably by the one who ought
to have understood more than any other.

---

[11] Luke 10:30-31.

[12] Luke 10:33-35.

And do you not see the manner in which we wound the soul of Jesus continuously, through our lack of holy compassion? There is a something a man has never divined, and probably that a man never will be able to divine. That subtle something in the nature that can be touched and moved by divine compassion. It takes down the bars of our life and lets the divine love of God flow through our soul.

How often you and I have stood or knelt by the side of the dying and disease smitten and have waited and prayed, ineffectively, until within our own heart something melted, something dissolved, and something richer than tears came from our souls. And by the grace of God, we saw the answer to our prayer before our eyes.

There is such a thing in the world as stigmata. That is, contemplating something so much that it actually becomes a fact in your own being. It is well explained by telling an incident from the life of St. Francis, who had contemplated the cross of Christ with such intensity, and it so moved him, that he said to his followers, "When I am dead, open my body, and you will find the impress of the cross of Christ on my heart." And sure enough, after his death, when they opened his body, there was the impress of the cross of Christ on his heart. There is an inner life; an inworking of God.

The compassion of Jesus was illustrated when He broke up a funeral procession one day as He passed along in that little city of Nain. He was named by these tender terms: the only son of his mother, and she was a widow. When Jesus looked on that procession, something broke loose in His soul. He stepped up to the bier, being moved with compassion, and said: "Young man, I say unto thee, Arise."[13] The sorrows of others moved the soul of Jesus and touched His heart.

Lazarus, His friend, died, and four days later the Lord went there, and hearing that He was approaching the village, one sister came to meet Him. She said to Him: "Lord, if Thou hadst been here, my brother would not have died." The other sister poured out her heart to Him in a similar manner. Eventually, he stood by the grave of His friend. "And Jesus wept." Something terrific was moving in His soul. He said, "God, I thank Thee for Thou hearest Me always." Then He cried with a loud voice: "Lazarus, come forth." And he that was dead came forth.[14]

---

[13] Luke 7:14.

[14] See John 11:1-44.

Once in South Africa, we were praying for a sick lady for a time, without result. Then I said, "I will take my sister and go and pray for her." We prayed again, and there was no victory. A day or two afterwards, we were down in the city in one of the large department stores. As we stood there, the Spirit of the Lord said to me: "Go to her now."

I said to my sister: "As soon as you are through, we will go over and pray for that sick lady." We went and I watched her writhe in pain and agony, until I put my arms about her and cuddled her head close to my heart. And then, presently, something broke loose in my soul. And then in one moment, (I hadn't even started to pray) she was lifted out of her agony and suffering. A divine flood moved her, and I knew she was healed. Then I laid her down on the bed and took my sister's arm, and we went away, praising God.

And yet one more incident. And I want to give you this for your own help and blessing. I knew a man in South Africa, who was an ardent Methodist. He had ten sons, all Methodist (local) preachers; and three daughters, three beautiful daughters; holy women; a wonderful family; one of the most wonderful families I have ever known. The old gentleman had been stricken with disease, and the agony of his suffering was so great that there seemed to be only one way. And that was to drug him into insensibility.

As the years passed, he became a morphine fiend. He told me that he smoked twenty-five cigars, drank two quarts of whiskey, and used a tremendous quantity of morphine every day. Think of it. So the old man, until he was seventy-three years old, was drugged into senselessness most of the time.

I prayed for him, unceasingly, for sixteen hours without result. William Duggin, one of my ministers, hearing of the situation, came to my assistance, and I remember how he stood over him and prayed for him in the power of God. Somehow, there was no answer. I watched that man in convulsions until his daughters begged me just to let them give him morphine and let him die senseless, rather than to see him suffer longer. And I said, "No. I have had your pledge and his too, that life or death, we are going to fight this battle through."

Presently, as I stood there and was watching the awful convulsions, particularly in his old bare feet that were sticking out at the bottom of the bed, this came to my mind: "Himself took our infirmities."[15] And I reached out and got hold of them and held them as in a grip of iron; and that thing, that is too deep for any form of expression that we know, broke forth in my soul. And in a single moment I saw him lie still, healed of God. Many a day after that I have walked with him over this three vast estates, on which there were fifty thousand orange trees and fifty thousand lemon trees, and the old man told me of his love for God and of the richness of His presence, and I had my reward, blessed be God.

If this Church ever succeeds in doing that big thing — that great thing; that unspeakable thing that God purposes that we should do, it can only be when we enter into that divine compassion of the Son of God.

---

[15] Matthew 8:17.

hile ministering at Johannesburg, South Africa, in 19[ ], I received an invitation to preach in the City of Pretoria, Transvaal. Consequently, a series of meetings was arranged for. It was my first visit to Pretoria, and the congregation to whom I ministered were strangers to me. I was entertained at the home of Mr. [name does not appear], Hamilton Street. I arrived about

REMARKABLE MANIFESTATIONS OF THE SPIRIT IN SOUTH AFRICA

three o'clock in the afternoon. About 4:30 a gentleman called and inquired of Mrs. [name does not appear] if an American stranger was at her house. She replied, "Yes. Reverend Lake has just arrived this afternoon from Johannesburg." She told him I was an American and had recently come to Africa. He asked for an interview.

In the course of this interview he told me that he had been secretary to Dr. Leyds and acting Secretary of State for the old Transvaal government under Paul Kruger, the last Dutch president of the Transvaal Republic. He told me that when the Boer War closed, because of what he considered faithfulness to the cause he had represented, he refused to sign the agreement recognizing the authority of the British and in consequence had been blacklisted as an incorrigible.

This prevented him from obtaining employment. His family had been sent to Europe during the war, and he had no money to bring them back. His property and money had all gone in the cause of the Boers, and he was impoverished. He did not have proper clothes to wear, nor sometimes food to eat. He said that notwithstanding these conditions, his soul was consumed with the problems of state and the desire to alleviate the condition of the Boer people and see the people restored to happiness. And in the agony of his soul he had been in the habit of going into one of the mountains for prayer. After several months of this practice, one day the Lord revealed to him that a great deliverance was coming; that a man would arrive in Pretoria from America on a certain date, and could be found at 75 Hamilton Street, at four-thirty P.M.

He said, "This is the date, and I have come in response to the direction of the Spirit, as I received it." He welcomed me as a messenger of the Lord and proceeded to give me the details of the revelation as he had received it. His revelation included political changes that were to transpire, a religious revolution that would grow out of my own work, and many events of national importance, which became historic facts during the next few years.

He further gave detail in prophecy of the European war, and Britain's part in it. This was in August, (1908).

It was only after I had witnessed event after event come to pass, that I became deeply impressed with the real significance of his revelation. He told me that the present meeting I was about to conduct in Pretoria would be marked with extraordinary manifestations of the Spirit. That these manifestations of the Spirit would eventuate in a profound impression of the majesty and power of God upon the minds of the people of South Africa and in later years would create a stimulus of faith in God throughout the world.

Our meeting began at a church on Kerk Street, Pretoria, on Thursday night. At the close of the first service the Spirit of God was deeply manifest upon the people. On Friday afternoon when we assembled, the Spirit of God proceeded to work mightily in the people. Many came to God and confessed their sins. Others who already were Christians sought God with profound earnestness for the real sanctifying power of God in their lives. Some were baptized in the Holy Spirit, their baptism in the Spirit being marked by speaking in tongues under the power of the Spirit, and interpretation of these messages by the Spirit; also blessed healings of greatly diseased people.

The meetings ran practically without cessation from then until the following Wednesday at three A.M. Each service marked a decided increase in the presence and power of God.

On Saturday night the church was packed. All available standing room was occupied with men standing shoulder to shoulder. The majority of those who were standing were men from the Tattersall Racing Club. Most of them were Jews. They included horsemen of all classes — bookies, jockeys, stablemen, race track gamblers, etc.

I was preaching on the subject of the power of God and in a strong spirit was endeavoring to demonstrate that Jesus Christ was the same yesterday, today, and forever, that His power was as great as it ever was, and that the only necessary qualification for touching God for anything was faith in Him. The audience was greatly moved.

At this point, I observed a gentleman with two ladies endeavoring to squeeze through the crowds who were standing in the aisles. I asked the crowd to separate if possible, and permit the ladies to come through and tried to arrange sitting space for them on the steps of the platform. As they approached, I observed that one of the ladies held her arms perfectly stiff and did not move them at all. By instinct I knew at once that she was a rheumatic cripple. As she approached me, I said, "What is the reason you do not move your arms?"

She replied, "My shoulders are set from rheumatics."

I said, "How long have they been like that?"

She replied, "Ten years." I inquired if she had been treated by physicians. She replied, "I have been discharged from three hospitals as incurable."

I said, "What hospitals?"

She answered, "Kimberly, Johannesburg, and Pretoria."

Then I addressed the gentleman who accompanied her, and said, "Do you know this lady?"

He said, "Yes. She is my sister-in-law."

I said, "Do you know her story to be correct?"

He said, "Absolutely." I asked her what she had come for. She replied, "In the hope that the Lord would heal me."

I inquired, "Do you wish me to pray for you for healing?"

She said, "Yes."

Then addressing the noisy crowd of men in the aisles and around the doors, I said, "You men never saw Jesus heal a person in your life. You do not know anything about this matter. You have never witnessed an exhibition of the power of God, and therefore, should be considerate enough to keep still, confess your ignorance of such matters, and learn. This is what I want. Select two of your company, let them come and examine this woman and see if her arms are stiff, as she states." I waited for them to make their selection, and they put forward two men. I have forgotten the name of one of the men at this time, but the name of the other was Mr. Mulluck, a barber, a very intelligent gentleman. His shop was in the market building. I afterward learned he was an American.

They examined the lady critically and found her arms as she had said, quite immovable. Addressing them I said, "Have you finished your examination, and are you satisfied her conditions as stated?"

They said, "We are."

"Then" I said, "stand back, for I am going to pray for this woman, that the Lord will heal her." Placing my hands on her shoulders I commanded in the name of Jesus Christ, the Son of God, that this rheumatic devil that bound the woman be cast out and in Christ's name commanded it to go, rebuking it with all the energy of my soul. The power of God lashed through me like a burning fire, until the perspiration burst from the woman's face. Then taking her by the hands I said, "In the name of Jesus Christ put your arms up." The right arm went up. Then I said, "In the name of Jesus put the other arm up too." She instantly obeyed. Her arms had become free.

As I moved the arm, making the shoulder rotate, I observed that there was a grinding sound in the joint, and addressing the men who had examined her, I said, "You have never heard a dry joint in your life. Come and put your ear to this woman's back, while I make her arm move." As they did so, I moved the arm, and the shoulder joints would grind. The oil had not yet returned to the joints.

In the woman's delight, she threw up her hands and praised God and started for the door. The crowd parted for her and she disappeared, and I did not meet her again for some months.

Another lady arose and came forward, saying, "I wish you would pray for me." I asked her what was the matter, but she did not reply. I bowed my head, saying, "Jesus, show me what is the matter with this woman." Instantly, the Spirit moved my hand down her body from the throat to the stomach, and I prayed for her. She thanked me, and sat down.

Later, I learned that her name was Mrs. Ulyate, and that she had had a cancer of the stomach. I said to her, "When you came for prayer, why did you not tell me what was the matter with you?"

She said, "I was doubtful whether you was a real man of God or not. I said to myself, 'If he is, then the Lord will show him, and I will not have to tell him what is the matter with me.'" She was perfectly healed. I visited with her and enjoyed the association of the family during the years that followed.

At a later time her son, a man of twenty, was healed of total deafness in one ear, the result of an eardrum having been absolutely destroyed in an operation. His healing was instantaneous.

JABBER

On Sunday morning as the service progressed, a gentleman of prominence, who was an employee of the government, came into the meeting. Mr. "J," a man of great stature. As he walked into the church, the Spirit of the Lord fell upon him while walking up the aisle, and he fell prostrate on the floor. Several sons were present in the audience, and Mrs. "J," his wife, was conducting the choir.

The mother, daughter, and sons gathered from their places in the audience and reverently knelt in a semicircle about him while the audience remained in quiet prayer. The Spirit of the Lord dealt marvelously with him, revealing his sins, and Christ unto salvation.

Presently the Spirit fell upon one of the sons, who fell prostrate by the side of the father; then upon another and another, until the whole family lay prostrate under the power of God. When the Spirit of the Lord had lifted somewhat from them, these sons confessed their disobedience to their parents and to God. And the whole family knelt with their arms around one another, melted by the tenderness of the presence and power of God. Confession and repentance on the part of each to the other made the household of one soul.

Words are a poor medium to describe such an event as this. It would have to be seen to be realized. The tenderness and conscious presence of God, the melting power of His mighty Spirit, could only be understood by one who had looked on. No words can tell the story.

Notwithstanding the mighty manifestations of the Spirit, I was anxious that the real working out of the Spirit of God that would remove all character of denominational prejudices, and those elements in man's nature that keeps him from loving and serving God with the broadness in the beauty and grace of holy charity, should be utterly removed from the people's hearts.

JABBER GIRL

As I was preaching during the afternoon, the Spirit fell on a young lady, Miss Jabber, a cousin of the family aforementioned. She fell from her chair prostrate on the floor, where she remained for a considerable time. The young gentleman who accompanied her, and who reverently knelt beside her when she became prostrate, was attracted by her desire to speak to him. She said to him, "Send Mr. Lake to me." I ceased preaching and went to her. I asked her what it was she wanted. She said, "Jesus came and talked to me and told me to tell Mr. Lake not to be discouraged. That the power of God will mightily fall upon this meeting tonight."

About four o'clock P.M. I left the service and went home to rest. I had been on my feet so long without rest or sleep that it seemed as if I could continue no further. I laid down to sleep, saying, "Wake me at seven-thirty for the evening service." I fell into a sound sleep and when it came seven-thirty the family reasoned that I was so exhausted that it would be a shame to wake me and that they would endeavor to get through the evening service without my aid.

However, I awoke at eight and hastened to the church. When I arrived I found that in view of my absence, the church service was being conducted in their former formal manner, instead of the open character of services we had been having. An air of formality pervaded the house. The choir, consisting of about thirty members, were in their places, including the organist, pianist, and director. The choir gallery was arranged with raised steps so that each row of singers sat above the other. The choir chairs were fastened together in sections, but were not fastened to the floor.

When I came into the meeting the pastor who was in charge invited me to preach in his stead. As I preached, my spirit was annoyed by the extreme air of formality that pervaded the meeting, and in my soul I kept praying, "God, do something with this choir. Do something to break up the formality of this service so there may be freedom of the Spirit, that sinners' hearts may be melted and the power of God may descend upon the meeting, and the baptism of the Spirit fall."

As this prayer of my soul continued, the Spirit of the Lord suddenly spoke within me, saying, "Go on with your service. I will take care of the choir."

The anointing of the Spirit came upon me, and I spoke with great liberty in the Lord and was soon so lost in the Spirit that I forgot altogether about the choir, and the formality of the service entirely disappeared. I preached until ten o'clock, when I stepped from the platform and knelt on the floor of the church to pray. An unusual spirit of prayer came upon me. The burden of which was so intense that it caused me to pray out my soul to God in a more than ordinary manner. As I prayed, the Spirit continued to deepen upon me until I was unable to speak in English any longer, and the Spirit caused me to pray in tongues. At such times, the Spirit of the Lord would give me the interpretation of the prayer in English, which would immediately follow the prayer in tongues.

I was lost in prayer, but was conscious of a considerable noise. I did not raise my head or open my eyes until the burden of prayer was lifted from my soul. When I looked up, to my amazement, the audience was standing and at the back of the house many were standing on their seats and all looking toward the choir gallery.

As I turned toward the choir, I saw that the Spirit of the Lord had fallen upon the choir and almost every one of them lay prostrate under the power of the Spirit. When they fell from their seats they pushed the chairs on the row in front of them forward, so that the front legs of the chairs dropped over the edge of the narrow platform. The whole row would turn upside down on top of those who had already fallen prostrate in front.

The deacons of the church came and gathered the chairs off of the prostrate ones as quickly as possible. The unbelievers in the house were startled and frightened at this manifestation, so that they arose and rushed out of the door. I instructed the doorkeeper to turn the key in the door and not permit anyone to come in. The awe of God overshadowed the house. I felt it was not time for unbelievers to be present. God wanted to deal with the church.

I went and sat down in the audience. We remained perfectly quiet in prayer for some time. Then one after another of the prostrate ones began to pray and confess their waywardness and sin to God. There seemed to be but one passion in their soul, to tell out to God the burden of their unbelief, of their sin, their backslidings, and to call on God for forgiveness and restoration and power to overcome. As a soul would thus confess out and pray through into the presence of God, the Spirit of the Lord would raise from them, and they would be permitted to arise. As they did so they were in a perfectly normal state of mind, excepting that the awe of God's presence and power was mightily realized by each.

Many sat and wept. Others sang for joy. Many were baptized in the Holy Spirit. One young man, among the tenor singers, lay on the lower platform. Close to him was his sweetheart, a young lady who was a member of the church. Like the others, he was pouring out the confession of his life to God, and to her, telling of his peculiar sins which were many and vile. Husbands were confessing to wives and wives to husbands, children to their parents, sweethearts to sweethearts, and all to God.

The pianist, Mr. Braun, lay beside the piano stool for possibly an hour helpless and speechless, the Spirit of God working in him. I was moved by the Spirit of God to go to him and pray. As I knelt beside him my hands involuntarily moved to his breast, and laying my hands on his breast, I prayed. I did not know why I did so. I just obeyed the guidance of the Spirit. As I prayed, I was conscious of the Spirit of God flowing through me to him.

I returned to my seat, and in about half an hour he began to pray out his heart to God. When he had finished, he motioned me to come to him. When I reached him he said, "Send my wife to me." I went to the back of the house where his wife sat weeping and brought her to him. She knelt beside him. He put his arms about her and confessed that for three years he had been living in adultery. They wept together for hours. God worked so mightily in them, that at three or four in the morning they returned to their home praising God together.

The next day at ten o'clock he called on me to tell me that the Lord had baptized both him and his wife in the Holy Spirit and that when they were baptized, the Spirit of God came upon both and caused them to speak in tongues and praise God in a spirit of prophecy. His soul was aglow.

He said, "When you prayed for me last night, why did you put your hands on my breast?"

I replied, "I do not know. I simply obeyed the impulse of the Spirit."

He asked, "Did you know I was sick and needed healing?"

I said, "No, I did not know it."

"Well," he said, "I want to show you what the Lord has done." And he opened his clothing and showed me a cancer on the breast, saying, "Three years ago, when I went into adultery this cancer appeared on my body within a few days. I have endeavored to hide it from everyone. Even my wife did not know of its existence, no one but my physician. But look at it now. See how the power of God has withered it?" It had turned brown as if burned by a fire, and in a few days it utterly disappeared.

Among other things, the Spirit of the Lord directed Mr. Braun to make restitution to parties with whom he had had dishonest dealings at different times. One that I especially remember was this: He was employed by the government as a civil engineer on a monthly salary. He had been in the practice at intervals of filling out a report saying that he was sick and unable to attend to his duties and would be gone for some days. He was compelled to confess to his superiors that this was not a fact and that he used this time in recreation.

The thoroughness with which God dealt with each and all of these was very remarkable. Lives were cleansed to the very inmost, every sin, both outward and secret. The Spirit of God had taken possession and natures were changed into the likeness and nature of Jesus Christ.

These meetings were the beginning of a mighty work of God at Pretoria, which continues to this day.

[UNTITLED, POWER OF THE SPIRIT]

he life of a Christian without the indwelling power of the Spirit in the heart is a weariness to the flesh. It is an obedience to commandments and an endeavor to walk according to a pattern that you have not power to follow. But bless God, the Christian life that is lived by the impulse of the Spirit of Christ within your soul becomes a joy and a power and a glory. Blessed be God.

The power in the Spirit of Christ only becomes applicable in our life according to the vision and the application of our thought to our own need. The air is filled with electricity. It is in the skies, it is under the water. There is nowhere you can go to escape from it. Consequently, it is usable everywhere — if you take possession of it. So it is with the Spirit of Christ. The mode, or means, or manner by which the soul of man takes possession of the power of God is through the attitude of the soul and mind of man toward it.

I may live all the days of my life in a quiescent dreamy state, never becoming conscious of the power of God in my life. On the other hand, I can lend my soul and mind to God in active force, until the Spirit of the living God so impregnates my life and flashes from my being that like the Lord Jesus, the evidences and manifestations of that divine life is given to other men.

A little woman, who perhaps is present today, came in from the country last week with a curvature of the spine, so that the back protruded perhaps two inches and the curvature was four or four and half inches long. Of course with such a curve as that in her back, she had lost her power and control. She was in a state of utter [missing pages].

One evening in my own tabernacle, a young girl about sixteen or eighteen, by the name of Hilda Daniels, suddenly became overpowered by the Spirit of God. She arose and stood on the platform beside me. I recognized at once that the Lord had given the girl a message. So I simply stopped preaching and waited while the Spirit of God came upon her and she began to chant in some language I did not know and make gestures like a Mohammedan priest would make when chanting prayers.

Away down in the back of the house I observed a young East Indian, whom I knew. He became enraptured and commenced to walk gradually up the aisle. No one disturbed him, and he proceeded up the aisle until he got to the front and stood looking into the girl's face with intense amazement.

When her message had ceased, I said to him, "What is it?"

He said, "Oh, she speaks my language."

I said, "What does she say?" And he came up on the platform and stood beside me and gave a gist of her message.

"She tells me that salvation comes from God. That in order to save men Jesus Christ, who was God, became man. That one man cannot save another. That Mohammed was a man like other men, and therefore he was only a prophet of God and had no power to save a man from his sins. But Jesus was God, and He had power to impart His Spirit to me and make me like God."

One day I stood at the railway station in Logans Port, Indiana. I was waiting for my train. I observed a group of Italian men, apparently laborers, sitting on a bench. They were going out somewhere to work. As I walked up and down the platform I said, "Oh God, how much I would like to be able to talk to these men about the living Christ and His power to save."

The Spirit said, "You can."

I stepped over to them and as I approached them, I observed myself commencing to speak in some foreign language. I addressed one of the group, and he instantly answered me in Italian. I asked where he was from, and he replied, "Naples." For fifteen minutes God let me tell of the truth of Christ and the power of God to that group of Italian laborers, in Italian, a language I had no knowledge of.

Again and again at intervals, God has permitted such things to occur in my life. But, beloved, that is not the real "gift of tongues" yet. It is a little flash, a gleam, but one day there will come from heaven God's blessed shower that will so anoint the souls of men that they will speak in every language man speaks in, by the power of God. The message of the Christ will be given through these anointed hearts to the nations of the world. Said Jesus, "This gospel of the Kingdom must first be preached to all nations..." etc.[1]

May I refer you once more to history. The Morovian missionaries went to Japan about a hundred years ago. Other missionaries spend long periods trying to acquire the language, but these missionaries, history records, went into a prayer meeting for six weeks, night and day, and came out of that meeting speaking the Japanese languages fluently.

These things only demonstrate to you and me the necessity of keeping the soul open to the ever-growing consciousness of God. Is healing a wonder? No, the marvel is that men have remained blind to the power of God so long. How was it that you and I, raised in Christian homes, reading the Word of God, praying to our Father God, failed to comprehend that the power of God through Christ was able to save a man from *all* his sins and *all* his sicknesses?

Our souls have caught just a little flash, a little larger revelation of the living God through the blessed Word and through the Holy Spirit, the divine power to make it real. But my brother, beyond our soul is the great ocean of God. We are just paddling around on the edge yet.

When I was ready to leave Pullman last week, Thursday, my friends gathered around. Many of them said, "Brother, we never heard anything like it. What a marvelous meeting. What numbers of wonderful healings!" But when I got on the train I sat down and wept. Why? I could remember that back in that town a dozen people had been prayed for who were not healed at all. They were just as worthy perhaps as the ones who were healed. And beloved, if Jesus had been down to Pullman, instead of Brother Lake, they would all have been healed.

There is a place for you and me, way down at the feet of the Lord Jesus Christ, in a humility so deep and true that God can put upon us the real power of God in that holy, heavenly measure that is necessary for the blessing and healing of all men.

Take your umbrellas down. The Spirit is falling. The cry is going up from the souls of men for a new revelation of the power of God through Christ. Bless His name.

---

[1] Matthew 24:14, paraphrased.

Savior? Yes, bless God, Savior from every sin. Do not try to jellyfish your conscience and make yourself believe that you are not sinning, or that there is no sin. No, bless God. There is a power of God so real and true that it will take from your heart every desire for sin and make it so offensive to your soul that your spirit will turn from it. Yea, it will fill you with the Holy Ghost until you raise up a prince and King. Sin gone, sickness gone, the power of God reigning in your life, giving you the glory that was in the face of Jesus, blessed be His name, and putting a song of joy in your heart and the radiant glory of heaven in your life.

Yea, bless God, for this salvation my soul prays, and I pray today that upon this audience the power of God will descend that will open our consciousness to God and take us into the Holy Ghost and reveal the Christ in us, transforming our nature and making us like Him. Not a *little* like Him, but in the measure of the stature of the fullness of Christ.[2] Like Him, like God, like Christ in deed and in truth. God bless you. Amen.

---

[2] See Ephesians 4:13.

SALVATION

ditor's note: This was taken from handwritten notes, apparently written in preparation for the sermon that follows.

THE OFFENSE OF THE CROSS

GALATIANS 5:11

The stumbling block of the cross then is the offence of the cross ceased.

TRANSLATORS

Offence — King James Version

Skalunger — Wycliff

StigmaFerrer — Fenton

ScandalousRoman — Catholic Diary

Scandal — 20 Century

Stumbling Block — American Revised

Stumbling block

Something suddenly trips you.

You stumble, you fall.

Why the scandal of the cross?

The cross was a symbol of justice.

There is no scandal attached to the gallows.

It represents the justice and authority.

The individual stumbles:

Intellectually (sense of propriety outraged);

Emotionally (Emotionally shocked, spiritually stunned);

What about the cross caused the stumbling?

Pilate had posted the inscription over the cross.

"The King of the Jews," but that could not be a stumbling block to any but a Jew.

He wrote in Hebrew, in Latin, in Greek.

When the Jew looked on the cross:

1. It spoke to him of violation of the law.
2. Of moral break down.
3. Of criminality.

Yet, the Galilean preachers were telling the world that the cross of Jesus was the very soul and secret of morality.

And out of the cross flowed a life stream of heavenly virtue and moral force and divine obedience.

And the Jew who only saw a dying culprit was stumbled, offended, intellectually shocked, emotionally displeased, and disgusted.

He looked. He revolted. He said, "Absurd." The more he looked, the surer he was of his correct decision.

The Roman.

And the Roman passes by and looks upon the cross.

To the Roman who knew no law but force.

Who had no consideration for the conquered.

nd I, brethren, if I yet preach circumcision, why do I yet suffer persecution? then is the offence of the cross ceased.

— Galatians 5:11

THE OFFENSE OF THE CROSS

"Offense" the stumbling block of the cross. This word calls for careful consideration. After writing to the Galatians, Paul calls attention to the "offense of the cross." He suggests that those who read his letter would understand what he was saying. The "offense of the cross" was expected. If it was absent there was something wrong.

And remember brethren, if I preach circumcision, then hath the stumbling block of the cross ceased.

We sing: "In the cross of Christ I glory, Towering over the wrecks of time, All the light of sacred story, Gathers round that head sublime." We have almost with astonishment and even with a tendency toward reluctance, come to a phrase like this, "The stumbling block of the cross," or "the offense of the cross." And in meditation I ask you to consider with me the word, the arresting challenge of the word "offense" or "stumbling block." It is very interesting to see how the great translators have attempted to get over the import of the word.

Wycliff's translation employed the word that is now obsolete in our language. We rendered it the "sclaunger" of the cross. That was two words merged. We have divided them into "slander" and "scandal." Cranmer translated it "slaumger." The Geneva Council translated it "slander." The Roman Catholic translated it "scandal." The King James translates it "offense." The English and American Revised Standard versions put it "stumbling block." They were all trying to interpret the word. I am daring to submit for your consideration the Revised Version, as exactly expressing the word — "scandalon," or "stumbling block."

Listen. Something in the way, in the way of progress. Suddenly you trip and stumble and fall. That is the word. I am not quarreling with the word "offense."

What does this mean, "the stumbling block of the cross"? It was something that men stumble over intellectually; stumble over emotionally. It is a stigma attached to the cross.

The cross was well-known throughout the Roman world. The Romans had taken it over from the Venetians for capital punishment. But even in that world it never produced anything in the sense of scandal or upheaval. It was the symbol of *justice*. It was the symbol of punishment for breaking the law. It was the poetic result of wrongdoing against righteousness and justice. Men were not scandalized by the cross.

Then what is Paul talking about? It is the cross of Christ. Yes, but why should it be a scandal? It was the cross of Christ as presented to the world. What was being presented to the world that would make it a scandal? What were those early ministers and preachers declaring about the cross of the Nazarene?

What were they declaring? They were declaring that the cross was the very center of religion, the secret of government, the inspiration of culture. That was what characterized the scandal. Jews from Jerusalem were moving out over all the world. Wherever they went they were telling that the cross of the Nazarene is the center of religion. It is the secret of authority and government. It is the inspiration of true culture to human life. Men laughed. They stumbled over it. Men were against it emotionally, morally, and intellectually.

We can see that there is the same sense in the minds of men today. The cross is still spelling to men a scandal. Men are still intellectually tripped by it. They still revolt against it. The cross is still bearing a stigma.

You and I are called to represent that cross in word and in life, and if we fail to do so, we are failing in loyalty to our Lord and Master.

Will you come patiently with me to the historic scene? Yes, I would remind you of the well-known fact that while Pilate had the superscription written over Jesus, *"This is Jesus the King of the Jews,"* that the wording was not the significant thing. The significant thing was that he had put it in Hebrew, Latin, and Greek. The purpose was that no stranger near the cross should fail to read it. The three languages of the world powers were there.

Now look at the cross. First look at it from the soul of the Jew. Then look at it from the mind of the Roman. Lastly look at it from the person of a Greek.

Now, supposing you could put yourself back of the scene and could see it as a Jew and was aware of the fact that its witnesses were telling that it was the secret of religion. The Jew looking at that cross, what did he see? Disgrace! To the Jew the cross was the place of moral disgrace. "Cursed is every one that hangeth on a tree."[1] Criminals; cursed.

Then for the Jew to be told that that cross was the *center* of religious life, the secret, and the only secret of righteousness for an individual and the world, don't you see intellectually how he stumbled over it; that the cross of the crucified malefactor is the secret of righteousness? *Preposterous!*

Then imagine you are a Roman and look at the cross from that standpoint. The time our Lord was born into this world and exercised His ministry and went to that cross was the only time in human history where a great power had mastered the known world. It had been attempted and never succeeded. It was the period known as *Pax Romana,* Roman peace. While I agree that "war is hell," I declare that that period was worse. Man or woman, boy or girl, did not own his or her own soul under the rule of Rome. Her procouncils were everywhere; her soldiers were everywhere. An example is shown by Pilate, the Roman governor; he had mingled the blood of the Galileans with the Jewish sacrifices.

A Roman comes and looks at the crucified Nazarene, and the Roman is told that that is the throne of an imperial power and imperial empire. That is the King; that is the One and the only One who ever will subdue humanity so that His rule will be universal. I can hear the laughter of Rome at the very suggestion. The Roman suggestion of the cross is that the man there is not only in disgrace, but that the man is *defeated.* It was not a question of morality to them. They had their own laws and jurisprudence, but were not bothered with morality.

Notice this, at that moment on the throne in Rome was a man that was known notoriously. The Roman believed that power was all that

---

[1] Galatians 3:13.

was necessary. And that Galilean, whether He had done anything that was wrong or not, being on the cross could He be a king? If the Jew says, "preposterous" the Roman says, "ridiculous."

Why do the Romans object? Naturally we see why. A defeated man be king! They had a false philosophy of government — the philosophy of force. If you have plundered a man so that he dared not do what he wants to do you have conquered. Rome did not care if my inner heart was in revolt. If they bludgeoned me and I had to do what they said, that is victory. Yes, that is the whole scheme of government; we have not escaped it yet. We still think we can compel a man to be moral. You can restrain him but that doesn't change his heart.

There He was on the cross. What do I see there? The weakness of God! Paul says it is stronger than men.[2] You look at the cross and there is one supreme thing manifested. It is the exhaustion of human power. Man attempting to govern has done all he can. He can do no more. He has taken the criminal and put Him on a cross. He has executed Him. All the armies of Rome can do no more. In a few minutes that malefactor will have left the world. Is that all? They have done their utmost; they are powerless.

Jesus said, "Fear not them which kill the body,"[3] and after that — laughter of the man that thinks he is done for when he kills the body. He faces a rude awakening.

Now for a moment, do not be a Jew or a Roman but a Greek. I am not thinking of the chattering Greek merchant. I am thinking of some chance traveler from Athens. He looked at that cross. If he had looked once, he would never have looked again. A mutilated man was disgusting to the Greek. Greek idealism was looking for the perfection of personality, and there was no room for mutilation in their thought.

It is not a question whether or not this is the result of morality. A broken and mutilated man, the Greek with his esthetic culture turned from it. He would not have looked twice.

Then there passed through the Greek cities, one after another, men who proclaim that the broken, mutilated man of Judea's cross is the

---

[2] See 1 Corinthians 1:25.

[3] Matthew 10:28.

inspiration of culture and of all that is refined and beautiful in life. The Greek intellect stumbled over it. Emotionally, the Greek revolted against it. If the Jew said, "preposterous" and the Roman "ridiculous," the Greek said, "absurd!" Wherever the Gospel was preached, the scandal of the cross became known. The offense of the cross was created.

Why were these things so? What is the real meaning in the Jews' objection of the cross? That it is the center of religion? And to the Romans when they were told it was the secret of government? And to the Greeks when they were told it was the inspiration of culture?

Take the Jew. Why was the Jew scandalized by the cross? Because he had an inadequate sense of sin and was ignorant of the God of his fathers. In the presence of that cross, when told it was the center of religion, he objected because he only saw there the moral delinquency. It was not the curse of the king, but the man who put Him there. "He was made sin."[4] That is the sinner's place, and they did not see it; and men still do not see that it is the only place for sin and that God cannot deliver a man except his sin is put there. The route of religion is the cursing and canceling of sin. Unless sin is cursed and cancelled there is no approach to God.

A man tells me he is disgusted at the cross and that it is the religion of the shambles; that man has never had an adequate sense of sin. A man tells me that he does not go to church; he goes to the country to worship. Worship God through nature while sin is in his heart? Nonsense. Earth is crammed with God and every bush ablaze with Him, but only he who sees takes off his shoes. You cannot worship God while there is still sin in your soul.

There on that bitter cross the God of eternity and the God of Moses was dealing with sin so it would be blighted, blasted, cursed, cancelled, and the way open! And when He cried, "It is finished!"[5] the veil of the temple was rent in twain, and there was a way to the heart of God opened for humanity. They did not see it. Men were ignorant of God. God is holy, yet so full of infinite love that He would bow and bend and stoop, and when sin must be cursed, gathering the curse

---

[4] 2 Corinthians 5:21, paraphrased.

[5] John 19:30.

into His own being and bearing our sins in His own being on the tree, bring deliverance. The cross in religion, to those who are blind and ignorant of God, is still made a scandal and a stumbling block.

Why do the Romans object? A defeated man, dying on a cross, a king! Whoever had heard of such a thing? To the Romans, the man on the cross had no power as He would soon die and it would be all over. I repeat what Jesus said, "Fear not them which kill the body, but are not able to kill the soul..." (Matthew 10:28). After that, then what? His resurrection from the dead. He is God's King. He is going to rule over this world. The secret of His rule is love. His subjects will serve Him because they love Him. He will not bludgeon a man into submission and call it victory while that man is still in rebellion in his heart. Men are afraid of God because of wrong concepts. Let a man meet God in Jesus and he will love God.

To the man with the ideal of bludgeoning power we point to the power of the resurrection. Don't look at the cross and stop there. Look beyond and see the mighty Christ at the right hand of the Father. Listen to the greatest declaration and cry of victory in the history of the world.

> I am the first and the last: I am he that liveth, and was dead; and, behold, I am alive for evermore, Amen; and have the keys of hell and of death
>
> — Revelation 1:17-18

Why did the Greek revolt at the sight of a mutilated man? The soul of the Greek idealism was expressed in the observance of the Olympic Games. It was the perfect person, the perfect personality, the perfect body with its smooth, flowing muscles. The sculpture of ancient Greece displayed this high idealism. Their statues are marvels of perfection that express a high ideal of physical beauty. It is no wonder the Greek would not take a second look at the mutilated man on the cross.

To the man who is looking for physical perfection we would say, "Look at the cross and what it stands for, then look beyond." What will he see? What will the Greek see? He will see one...

> ...clothed with a garment down to the foot, and girt about the paps with a golden girdle. His head and his hairs were white like wool, as white as snow; and his eyes were as a flame of fire; and his feet like unto fine brass, as if they burned in a furnace.
>
> — Revelation 1:13-15

His transfiguration was a foretaste of his beauty. "His face did shine as the sun, and his raiment was white as the light" (Matthew 17:2). Our body shall be like his glorious body. (See Philippians 3:21.)

To the Jew, to the Greek, to the Roman and their counterparts today, we point you to the cross and point out what it means and then take you beyond into the glories that are there and are yet to come to us.

> But we preach Christ crucified, unto the Jews a stumbling-block, and unto the Greeks foolishness; but unto them which are called, both Jews and Greeks, Christ the power of God, and the wisdom of God.
>
> — 1 Corinthians 1:23-24

Christ, the power of God, can change your life. He can make a new creature out of you. Old things will pass away and all things will become new. (See 2 Corinthians 5:17.) Old things are passed away. That is the power of the cross. All things are become new. That is the power of being raised in newness of life in Him. (See Romans 6:4.)

There is the power of His resurrection yet ahead for the physical body. (See Philippians 3:21.) We are to be presented perfect in Christ Jesus, perfect in spirit, perfect in soul, and perfect in body. (See Colossians 1:28 and 1 Thessalonians 5:23.)

James and Peter
Acts 12

Herod killed James with the sword. With the same intent he arrested Peter and put him in jail. In answer to prayer, God delivered Peter. This incident is used often to show that God will deliver some but not others. Some God will heal but not others. What does deliverance or non-deliverance from martyrdom have to do with deliverance from disease? They are two vastly different areas of activity. There is no relationship between them. Jesus said that men would kill you. (See Matthew 24:9 and John 16:2.) He never said disease would kill you. He healed all that came to Him.[6] Martyrdom is partaking of Christ's sufferings.[7] Disease and sickness were not in the category of Christ's suffering that we are to endure.

"Outward attacks and troubles fix, rather than unsettle the Christian, as tempests from without only serve to root the oak faster; whilst an inward canker will gradually rot and decay it." — H. More

Allow God to rid your life of sin and sickness, for they are the inner cankers that destroy life.

---

[6] See Matthew 4:24, 8:16, 12:15, 14:14, 15:30, 19:2, Mark 1:34, 6:13, Luke 4:40, 6:19, 9:11.

[7] See Colossians 1:24 and 1 Peter 4:13.

AS HE IS, SO ARE WE IN THIS WORLD

1 John 4:17

he mind of the world is fixed on the Redeemer. The Old Testament Scriptures, looking up to Christ, are particularly prolific in their description of His life, His sorrows, His sufferings, His death, His sacrifice. All these were the qualities of the Redeemer. All these were endured and exercised by the Redeemer in order to obtain something. That something was *redemption*.

What redemption means is best seen by following the chain of Christ's life from the Crucifixion on — not back of the cross, this side of it. If you want to understand the Redeemer, see Him before the cross comes into view. That is, if you want to understand the Redeemer who obtained the redemption. But if you want to understand the redemption that He obtained, look on this side of Calvary.

The great majority of the Christian world is still weeping at the foot of the cross. The consciousness of man is fixed on the Christ who died, not on the Christ who lives. They are looking back to the Redeemer who was, not the Redeemer who is.

On this side of the cross we see all the marvel of opposites to what we see in the Christ on the other side of the cross. On the other side of the cross we see a man of sorrows and acquainted with grief, bearing our sicknesses, carrying our sorrows.[1] He had nowhere to lay His head.[2] Poverty was one of His characteristics. Nobody every stops to think, or rarely so, that He bore His poverty, and what for? "That through His poverty we might be made rich."[3] He bore our sorrows, what for? That we through His sorrows might be made glad.[4] He bore

---

[1] See Isaiah 53:3.

[2] See Luke 9:58.

[3] 2 Corinthians 8:9, paraphrased.

[4] See Isaiah 35:10 and Psalm 30:11.

our sufferings, for what? That we through His stripes might be healed.[5] He gave His life a sacrifice for sins, for what? That we should know no sin.[6] Then having completed the redemption, or purchasing the redemption, the redemption becomes manifest on this side of Calvary.

I sometimes wish that I could turn the face of the believer the other way. You may observe that I very rarely turn the face of believers to the cross. The world looked to the cross until they passed it. But if they had never passed it, redemption would be no more of a reality than it was before. Redemption becomes a reality as we obtain the redemption. To obtain the fact that the Redeemer purchased is the purpose of the Christian life. On this side of the cross we see the victory, not the suffering, not the humility and dejection and rejection but the *victory*.

We see the first glimmer of that victory when Jesus, who was crucified as a Redeemer, steps forth as the redeemed. The Redeemer, the first-fruits of them that slept,[7] *became* the Redeemer of mankind or the pattern of redemption. He was not the pattern of redemption back there on the other side of the cross. He *became* the pattern of redemption. Paul puts it in such terse terms, "He *became* the author of eternal salvation."[8] Not "was manufactured the author of eternal salvation," not "was born," but *"became* the author of eternal salvation." Why? Because having as the Redeemer entered into the redemption by Himself, "the firstfruits of them that slept," the first Victor, the first example of victory, He became the manifestor, the demonstrator, the revealer, the embodiment of eternal salvation.

On this side of the cross is the victory of His resurrection, the marvel of all victories, the victory over death by which He took death captive. A living man, Himself, He came forth the Conqueror of death itself, having put all things under His feet.[9] What an ascent into triumph! What a change in His consciousness! What a distinction between the Redeemer and the redeemed! No longer subject to death, but triumphing over it. No longer subject to humiliation, but now becoming the exalted One, bless God.

---

5 See Isaiah 53:5.

6 See Hebrews 10:12-18.

7 See 1 Corinthians 15:20.

8 Hebrews 5:9.

9 See 1 Corinthians 15:27, Ephesians 1:22, and Hebrews 2:8.

For in the ascension we see the exaltation of Jesus instead of the man of sorrows, acquainted with grief or sickness. We see the living, triumphant, exultant Son of God ascending to the throne of God, receiving from God the Father what Jesus and the Father considered worthy of the suffering and death and sacrifice and redemption of Jesus Christ. A reward so great that Jesus Himself considered it worth all His sufferings,[10] all His buffetings, His earth career, His humiliation, His sacrifice and death. All to obtain it, the *gift of the Holy Spirit.* (See Acts 2:16-18.)

On this side of the cross we see the distributing of His new life. Not the life that was on the other side, but the life that *is* on this side — the life of triumph, the life of victory, the life of praise, the life of power, the life of glory — exultant, triumphant.

The other night as I lay in bed, I was thinking and praying over some of the things that were passing through my mind concerning Jesus. The scripture of Revelation 1:18 came with new force to me. Where Jesus, not as a humiliated Savior, but as a kingly Conqueror, stands forth with the marvelous declaration that, "I am he that liveth, and was dead; and, behold, I am alive for evermore, Amen; and have the keys of hell and of death."

It seems to me that in all the Word of God there is no such soul of triumph as that. Why, it seems to me as if the very heaven and the earth and all that in them is, ring with that exultant shout of a real Victor — "I have the keys of hell and of death." The enemies of man, taken captive by the Son of God, subject to His dictate. That is the Christ that speaks to my soul. That is the Christ on this side of Calvary. That is the Christ my soul worships.

I am going to tell you a strange thing. I am not much interested in the Christ on the other side of Calvary. Not half so much as I am in the Christ this side of Calvary. Bless God, I love the Redeemer, but I *glory* in His *redemption.*

The marvel of Christianity and the wonder of this scripture that I called your attention to, is that it does not say that "as *He was*" back there, so we are to be in this world. Don't you see, that is where the

---

[10] See Hebrews 12:2.

world fell down, where the Christian life became submerged in a vale of tears and shadows and darkness and poverty and humiliation and suffering. All of which Christian mankind accepted joyfully, because they believed they were exemplifying Jesus Christ and thought they were glorifying Him. They still visioned *not* the Christ that *is*, but the Christ that *was*. The Christ who bore and endured and suffered and died in order to obtain the privilege of the Christ who is, and to become the Christ who is.

Now if I could radically turn your minds tonight clear around from the vision of the Christ before the cross, to the vision of the Christ who *is*, this fact would mean that your souls must ascend in consciousness and union with the overcoming Son of God. Not bowed and bound with the humiliated Savior, but joined in holy glory-triumph with the Son of God who obtained the victory and revealed it and distributes its power and glory to the souls of men.

"As *He is*," not as He *was*, John said, "so are we in this world." Not in the life to come. The glory is not for the life that is coming, but for the life that is now. The victory is not for the future. It is for the *now*. It is not for the good days by and by. It is for the *now*. Not for heaven to come, but for heaven on earth *now*.

Sin, sickness, death under His feet. Hell itself taken captive and obedient to His Word. Every enemy of mankind throttled, bound, chained by the Son of God. Mankind joined with Him by the Holy Ghost in living triumph. Why, if I receive of the Spirit of Jesus Christ, of the Christ who *is*, I receive the spirit of victory and power and might and dominion — of grace, of love, of power, blessed be God, of all the blessed estate of which Jesus Himself is now the conscious Master. All these things He gives to the Christian through imparting to him the Holy Ghost.

The Spirit of the Lord says within my soul, that:

> *The universal sound of praise in which angels and men, all creatures in the earth, the sea, and the sky will eventually join, comes because the consciousness of the overcoming Christ has dawned upon them and possessed their soul.*

Some of the final song, the song of the ages, that song of victory, we find in the fifth of Revelation.

And I beheld, and I heard the voice of many angels round about the throne and the beasts and the elders: and the number of them was ten thousand times ten thousand, and thousands of thousands; saying with a loud voice, Worthy is the Lamb that was slain to receive power, and riches, and wisdom, and strength, and honour, and glory, and blessing. And every creature which is in heaven, and on the earth, and under the earth, and such as are in the sea, and all that are in them, heard I saying, Blessing, and honour, and glory, and power, be unto him that sitteth upon the throne, and unto the Lamb for ever and ever. And the four beasts said, Amen. And the four and twenty elders fell down and worshipped him that liveth for ever and ever.[11]

Should I carry your soul tonight into the place of victory in God, I must carry it into the consciousness of Christ's overcoming life. All His healing virtue, His saving grace, His transforming spirit, all the angelic communion, the heavenly foretaste, the consciousness of the estate of the redeemed, the glory-triumph of Jesus Christ is in the consciousness born from the resurrection and revealed in the revelation, "For as He is, so are we in this world."

Jesus in His earth life, reached forth into that life and kingdom and triumph and exhibited in this world, in a measure, that victory and triumph that His soul knew and visioned. But when the cross came, He entered actually into the life that His soul formerly visioned and knew through the Word of God and the consciousness of God within His heart. And so His ministry in the Spirit is a ministry in the *all power, all consciousness, all knowledge, all grace, all victory, all salvation*. Bless God.

I could lift your soul tonight in the Spirit of God into that glow and glory of the triumphant life. Do you know that it is only as your mind settles back into the humiliation and the suffering and the weakness and the fear and doubting of the dispensation that is past, that you grow weak and sickly and sinful? But only as your soul looks forward and possesses in the present the glorious victory that Jesus acquired

---

[11] Revelation 5:11-14.

and exhibits and enjoys, does it rise out of its sorrows, out of its sins, into that glorious triumph of the children of God.

It would not be pleasant to always have to live with babies and imbeciles, or a lot of half grown-up folks. I want you to sympathize with God. I want you to catch the vision of the ordinary Christian conception. Think of God having to live forever and forever and ever in association with people who were not half big enough to comprehend His will. That is not God's purpose. Jesus Christ undertook the biggest contract that heaven or earth or sea or sky ever knew. He undertook the redemption of mankind and their transformation by the Spirit of the living God into His own likeness and image and stature and understanding, in the grace and power and fullness of His own nature. Jesus Christ is the associate of God, one with Him, and with every son of God. He has purposed that redeemed men, grown up in God, transformed into the very image and likeness and nature and fullness of Jesus Christ, becoming like the Son of God shall be associates of God.

What did God create man for anyway? Answer: "The chief end of man is to glorify God and enjoy Him forever."[12]

God's purpose in the creation of mankind was to develop an association on His own plane. Otherwise, God would have been eternally living with babies or imbeciles. He would have been compelled forever to associate with those who were not able to understand or comprehend His nature or character or the marvel of His being or the wonder of His power.

The wonder of the redemption of Jesus Christ is revealed in the matchlessness of God's purpose to transform man into His very nature and image and fullness. Thereby men, as sons of God become, bless God, the associates of Almighty God, on His own plane of life and understanding.

When my soul saw the vision of God Almighty's marvelous purpose, I felt like falling on my face afresh and crying out, "Worthy is the Lamb that was slain!" For "as He is, so are we in this world." All glory and power that Jesus knows at the throne of God, all the wonders of

---
[12] Westminster Confession of Faith.

His overcoming grace, all the marvel of the greatness of His power is yours and mine to receive through faith in the Son of God, yours and mine to expect through the faith of the Son of God, yours and mine to possess and enjoy and reveal to the glory of God.

HOW TO RECEIVE ETERNAL LIFE

Some Facts About Eternal Life

Portland, Oregon

*I*n the first place, there are three Greek words that are translated "life" in the New Testament. "Psusche," that is the life of a fallen man. It is used to describe life of the animal world. God discriminates. Then "bios," that is manner of life. Then the great big word "zoe," that is eternal life. This latter word is used one hundred and thirty times in the New Testament. Here is the remarkable thing about it, the word "psusche" and the word "zoe" are never used interchangeably.

The Holy Spirit uses "zoe" always in connection with eternal life, the divine life, the life that comes into the spirit of the believer. "Psusche" is never used in that sense. "Bios" is never used in that sense.

If thinking men could just discover what I am giving to you, if our scholars, our great teachers would carefully analyze the thing I am giving you, it would shake the foundation of biology absolutely.

Do you know, brethren, there isn't any chance for a man to be a skeptic if he knows anything about the Bible? Skepticism is simply ignorance gone to seed. But let me say it again, a man is skeptical about a thing that he doesn't know. You are not skeptical about a thing that you do know.

"Oh," a fellow says, "you cannot know anything about that." Well, that is not me. I can and do. I have been studying this marvelous Book for more than forty years. Twenty-seven or twenty-eight years I have been using analytical studies or scientific methods in the study of scriptures. And I have arrived at the place where I absolutely *know* that that Book is not a human production. No human being could produce it.

I want to tell you, men, that the man that believes that Book and gives a little time to analytical studies, knows that he is believing something that no human mind could produce. It is a supernatural book. Someone says, "No man believes in the supernatural now." I want to say that all the sensible ones do believe in the supernatural. It is those little, narrow-minded folks that knock miracles. Big men, real men, men who are thinking through, men whose thumb or finger is upon the pulse of universal consciousness, absolutely *know* that miracles are demanded by universal man.

Do you know that these fellows that have only half thought through, that have walked around the truth and never gone through it, don't know what they are talking about? If you want to master a thing, think through on it. I know it will make your brains sweat, but brain sweat is the sign of genius. Real men sweat in their brains.

Now, eternal life is the biggest problem of the human experience. If I wanted to give a great oratorical address, there isn't any subject that would intrigue me and challenge me like this. Let me show you what I mean.

Over in Job, the oldest book of the Bible, the great, outstanding question back of Job is how to get this thing called eternal life. The problem of Plato was the craving for eternal life. Every one of the old religions came into being because man craved eternal life. Cannibalism came out of the passion in man for eternal life. He laid his offering on the altar, and he said, "If I can drink the blood and eat some of the flesh, I will eat God, and then I will become immortal and live eternally."

The only man that wants to die like the beast is the man that is living below the beast. Real men want to live. Real men rise in rebellion against the very thought that death means extinction.

Gentlemen, I have only begun thinking. I have only begun living. If I could have fifty years more I could do something. But men, I am going to have an eternity, and I am going to associate with all the princes and the queens and all the great men of the ages, and the great women, eternally.

A few years ago people asked me to preach on heaven, and I said, "No I guess not. It is more important that I preach on the present." And I went away, but the thing kept growing on me. I do not know why.

I have always been popular in preaching funeral sermons. Folks want me to come and say pretty things.

By and by one day I said to myself, "I am going to study this heaven business." The result was this, that I made a discovery that heaven was the *center* around which all the ministry of Jesus and the teaching of Jesus revolved.

"I came out from the Father."

"I came into the world."

"I leave the world and go back to my Father."

"In my Father's house are many mansions."[1]

I found out that the book of Revelation has a new heaven and new earth. I found out that God majored on the subject of heaven. The reason is this, that we are eternal beings. You may fiddle around about it all you are a mind to, but you are eternal. You may have philosophical and metaphysical religions, but when it comes down to the real heart of things you will want a religion that is not manmade, and you will want a religion that gives a safe bridge across from time into eternity and makes heaven an absolute surety.

The only man, I said, that wants to die like a brute is the man that has lived lower than a brute. Do you know, men and women, that Christianity is the only religion among all the religions of the world that gives clear conception, a clear teaching about heaven. Why? All the old religions of the world are human religions. What do I mean by that? They are religions that have been born in the mind of a man. Christianity is born in the heart of God the Father.

The eternal life fact is the greatest fact of human experience. Universal man has craved it. Drinking the blood and eating offerings came because the heart craved and outreached for it. It is the parent of all religions. Kings took the names of their gods because they wanted union with God. Man has wanted union with deity through all the ages.

Do you know that Theosophy, that claims to be the consummation of all religions, has as its basic thesis this statement: all men have God in

---

[1] See John 16:28 and 14:2.

them; all men have union with God. That is the basic thesis of Theosophy. That is not true, but Theosophy has gathered all the cry of universal man and attempted with human philosophy to answer that cry.

Jesus came and answered the cry, and Jesus hasn't given us any philosophy. Did you ever think of it? Jesus hasn't given us any metaphysics. Jesus has given us the thing we wanted, and He has given it so we *know* it. You can outgrow, and you will outgrow, any philosophy, any system of metaphysics, any human religion, but you can't outgrow God's life imparted to you. Do you see it? You cannot outgrow real Christianity. It can't be outgrown.

A man said, "Say, Doctor, do you know that So-and-so, who is a Christian, has turned over his church and joined a cult?"

I said, "He is not a Christian man." Friends, I challenge you that no Christian ever received Jesus Christ and then went into a philosophical religion. I have never known it. If you could bring me one case — but you can't, that is all. It is an impossibility, unless the man's mind had broken. Why? Well, I will tell you why. The moment I was born again and the great mighty Holy Spirit came into my life, do you know I reached the ultimate right there? And there has been nothing that challenged me for one minute. I have read everything. I have listened to every man that had anything to offer. I never heard anything but words, beautiful words yes, but they are just words of man. I have found God.

Let me illustrate. Years ago I was giving a series of addresses in Boston. It was when the American Teacher's Association met in Boston. I was advertised for my meeting. Down at the door I had this big word printed. *"Reality."* I was watching the people as they came in. A fine looking man stood looking, then he said, "That is a good word." He said, "Do you know I have been a truth seeker for years."

I said, "You will pardon me, but I have found it."

Just so long as you are seeking, you haven't found. You have found a great deal, but you have not found the "pearl of great price."[2] Let me say to you, men and women, that as long as you are a seeker you are

---

[2] Matthew 13:46.

not a finder. You may be seeking more of the thing that you have, but you are perfectly content with the kind and the quality and the thing that you have. You have found God. You may long to know your Father better, but that is altogether different than being a truth-seeker.

And I said to that man, "I have found it."

He said, "What do you mean?"

I said, "I beg your pardon, but I am the man that is going to speak."

He said, "Do you know, I have been through the whole thing?"

I said, "Through what?"

"Through this church business."

I said, "This is not church business. This is reality. I know what you are talking about, but you are talking about something you don't know anything about. This thing I am talking about is real, and when you have found it you stop searching. You have arrived. To use an Americanism, you have 'got there.'"

Do you understand, men and women, that when you have received eternal life, you have arrived. Let me illustrate: The disciples had been across the Sea of Galilee. They had fed five thousand that afternoon. They had had a marvelous time. They had seen the miracles of God that staggered them. Jesus had gone up into the mountain to pray and told them to get in the boat and go across. They rowed and rowed. The wind was against them and they could not make any headway. In the midst of the storm they saw Jesus walking on the waves. It frightened them. But Jesus drew near and He spoke, and they answered him, and they knew it was Him. Here is what happened. Jesus walked up beside the boat and stepped into it and no sooner than He did, that boat grated on the shore of Capernaum. What does Capernaum mean? It means contentment. The moment that Jesus was in the boat they arrived. That is all.[3]

And I say to you tonight that the moment that Jesus steps over the gunwales of your boat, into your life, you are there. Now Christianity is *life*, not a religion. It is a real life and relationship. It is a union of God and man — not the mass, but the individual. He imparts to us His very nature, His very life.

---

[3] See John 6:5-21.

Now I am going to talk to you on another angle. Before we can fully grasp this it is necessary to go over a little old ground. You see, man was created because God longed for children. God created the world as the habitation of His man, and then He created man "in His own image, after His own likeness."[4] Now the object of man's creation was that God might have children. He was child hungry. You can understand that.

God's heart was the reason for man. Now what kind of a man would it be natural for Him to create if He created a man to be His child? He would create a man in His own class, in His own image, after His own likeness. That would be normal.

Now God is a Spirit. Then man must be a spirit. He has a soul, intellect, affections, and will, but he lives in a body. You say, "What is His conscience?" Consciousness is the voice of man's spirit. It is the spirit speaking. But you say, "Hasn't man a subconscious mind?" No, that is psychological nonsense. The thing we call subconscious mind is simply your own spirit, the real man. Jesus illustrated it. You are cognizant that there is something above your intellect. There is somebody that makes you think when you don't want to. There is somebody above your reason that makes you think when you are tired. And you can watch yourself and after a little while the spirit will separate from your intellect and other faculties, so you will be cognizant.

Your spirit is the mother of faith and the mother of love and the mother of hatred. Joy lives in your spirit. Happiness is in your mind. Happiness depends upon circumstance. Joy depends upon God. Nobody has any joy but the spirit that is in fellowship with God.

Let's go a little farther. Man was created a spirit being. Why? So that God could impart to him His nature. Your spirit is the part of you that receives the nature of God. Your mind can't know God. You cannot know God by study. If you could find God intellectually you would find Him in the laboratory, but you can't find God that way. Scientists have done a lot of loose talking about it. But God is not known by the intellect but by the spirit.

---

[4] Genesis 1:26-27, paraphrased.

You know a lot of things that you cannot give a reason for. They are above your reasoning. Now, your spirit is the part of you that comes in touch with God. Your mind comes in touch with things intellectually. Your spirit is the part of you that comes in contact with God.

Another angle of this. You people who are deeply spiritual have had contacts with God that were above your reason and you could not explain it. Now what part of man is born again? His spirit. That is the part of you that is "Renewed after the image of Him that created him."[5] The new birth is because you have come out of Satan's family into God's family; that is the new birth. There is nothing mysterious about it. It is just as simple as any other fact of human experience. I venture to say this. That the new birth, receiving eternal life, can be classed among the certain sciences. It can be placed on scientific grounds. You do three things and you will receive eternal life as sure as you sit in that chair. I don't care whether you are at the Arctic Circle or the Equator.

Now that is scientific. That is absolutely in the realm of science. Every scholar knows that. A thing is scientific when every single demonstration arrives at a single conclusion. Four plus four are eight. Nine plus nine are eighteen. That is scientific.

You do three things and you are born again as sure as God sits on the throne. That is scientific. I want to tell you that prayer is based on scientific grounds. I have found it out.

In John 10:10, Jesus said:

> I am come that they might have life, and that they might have it more abundantly.

That means have it in profusion; have it without stint or limitation. That staggers you. That is big. That brings us out into the open with it. "I am come that you might have life." His life, God's life, God's nature.

It tells us in Ephesians 2:3 that we "were by nature the children of wrath." It tells us in 2 Peter 1:4 that we become partakers of the divine nature. The biggest thing in the world. What is eternal life? It is the nature of God. Jesus brought that to me.

---

[5] Colossians 3:10, paraphrased.

Why did not God give it before Jesus came? Because God had no legal right to give it. In the first place, man was spiritually dead. He had committed high treason against God. It was necessary that God be vindicated and that man be redeemed. Eternal life, then, is the nature of God, and God gave it to man on legal grounds.

Turn to Romans 5:21:

> That as sin reigned as king in the realm of death, even so might grace reign as king through righteousness unto eternal life through Jesus Christ.[6]

It means that grace is based on righteousness. When God wanted to give eternal life to man, He did it on legal grounds. Had God given eternal life on any other ground it would not be God doing it, because God is just and righteous.

If God had said, "Now I pity the human race; I am sorry for them. I am going to give them eternal life," you could not trust Him any more than the devil. But when He died, He paid the penalty of man's transgression. Then God could legitimately and justly give eternal life to man.

God had a right to give eternal life because He purchased it with His Son's blood. The supreme court of the universe has endorsed Jesus' death and substitutionary sacrifice and accepted it. Then God has a right to give eternal life to us. It is the greatest blessing that ever came to man.

We know we have passed from death unto life. What is God's nature? It is love. Then what is the normal thing for me to do? It is to live. The moment He gives it to me I become a liver. "We know that we have passed from death unto life, because we love the brethren."[7]

Hear this scripture, beloved:

> Every one that loveth is begotten of God, and knoweth God. He that loveth not knoweth not God.[8]

---

6 Paraphrased.

7 1 John 3:14.

8 1 John 4:7-8, paraphrased.

Everyone that loves not, is not born again. There is the touchstone. The moment that you are born again, that moment there comes into your spirit the nature and life of God.

What action does that have on your intellect? That is the greatest fact of the biological study. You take a young fellow sixteen or seventeen years of age, and he has a chum about the same years. They are in the same class in school. They have got the same rating from kindergarten up. And as far as you can see they are just the same. Now one of them receives eternal life — is born again, and he has proper instructions at home and in his church. In three months time the boy that has received eternal life will be ten percent more efficient than his chum. He is from ten to twenty percent more efficient than the boy that has not been born again, and he will hold that ratio if he walks with God.

Why shouldn't it be? Three things happen. First, he has received God's nature and that is reacting on his intellect. That ought to help him some. Second, he has no condemnation. That is gone. And the third thing, he has somebody to rest him all the time. He depends on the strength of another. The other boy can't do it.

Now I want to carry you a step beyond this. You know, men and women, that the children that are born to a Christian man and Christian woman are mentally of a higher order, and they are a finer texture morally than those born of the unsaved. I have proved that beyond a shadow of a doubt.

Another startling thing. You take a man or woman that are not Christians. They have two or three children. Then they are born again, and they have three more children. The last three are mentally superior to the first three. They are more easily managed, and they are more beautiful.

Gentlemen, if this thing was taught in our colleges, ninety percent of our young men and women in our colleges would become Christians. Every intelligent young woman wants to raise the highest grade of children possible, as well as the high type of young men. What man looks forward to raising children that are mentally below what they should be? Every real man wants to give his child the very finest and the best.

I have statistics to prove that out of the four hundred great businesses in the United States, like the sugar and lumber trusts, thirty percent of the men who are managing the greatest industries are sons of clergymen. Out of four hundred, one hundred and twenty are the sons of clergymen who are directing the great business enterprises. Twenty-five percent are the sons of bankers and lawyers, etc., but the sons of clergymen make up thirty percent.

Clergymen's children have the hardest opportunity of any, because the average minister doesn't stay but about seventeen months in a place, and he moves and his children are pulled out of school continually, and yet they have outstripped all the other boys combined. Why? Because the average old-fashioned preacher was born again, and his children grew up in a godly home.

Did you know, men and women, that men like William Jennings Bryant, Beveridge, and others that have given the best things we have had for sixty years, are the sons of Christian men? Did you know that the editors, like the editor of the *Saturday Evening Post*, the *Ladies Home Journal* and the other great papers of this country, are all ministers' sons? They are not all Christians, but their fathers and mothers had eternal life and that eternal life reacted in these children.

I want to tell you that Christianity is not a religion. Christianity is the life of God coming into a man. This is the biggest thing you ever faced in your life, gentlemen. I could pour on you statistics that would carry you off your feet. I know, gentlemen, that Christianity is the life of God in a man. And the greatest crime that is ever committed against our children is to take Jesus away from them. A father that will not give his children Jesus is a criminal in the sight of God and thinking men and women. Listen men. Out on our prairies we raise hogs and cattle and sheep for the eastern market. In our homes we raise children for the devil.

A good farmer would not allow a diseased animal in his herd or his flock, but you allow any kind of a woman to come into your house and fellowship with your children and any kind of a man. He may be as rotten as hell. He may damn your boy, and then you say, "I don't think it is a fair deal that God would damn my boy." You never gave

God a square deal. The biggest thing in all the world is man's union with deity.

I am not preaching religion. I have come down to brass tacks in this thing. This is the biggest thing you ever faced in your life.

Here is the thing, gentlemen. It is your receiving into your spirit the nature and life of God. "But" you say, "how can I do it?" Here is the genius of God. If God had said, "If you are 6'4" or 5'7" you can have eternal life." Or, "If you can pass the high school grades, you can have it." Or, "If you are worth $100,000 you can have it." But He said, "If you believe you can have it."

There are two things that are as natural as breathing: faith and unbelief. Unbelief comes from ignorance and faith comes from the Word of God. Faith is the normal thing in life. Everything in life is based on faith.

You came here tonight believing that you would get back home. You buy a suit of clothes believing that they will meet your need. You marry on faith. You put your money in the bank on faith. Everything about your life is based on faith. Every human relationship is a faith relationship. You have been acting on faith all your life. You say you haven't faculty? You mean you have got a disobedient complex.

What is faith? That you dig into this Book and you come to God like this and you say, "God, as far as I know, that Book is true." You say, "As many as receive Him, to them gave He the right to become the children of God."[9] You say, "Now I want to be Your child. I will take Jesus Christ as my Savior." Then you say, "I must confess Him as my Lord" because it says:

> If thou shalt confess with thy mouth the Lord Jesus, and shalt believe in thine heart that God hath raised him from the dead, thou shalt be saved.[10]

What does God ask? That "If you will take My Son as Savior and confess to the world His sonship, I will give you eternal life." Isn't that the simplest thing you ever heard in your life?

---

[9] John 1:12, paraphrased.
[10] Romans 10:9.

"If you will take My Son to be your Savior, and confess Him before the world as your Lord, I will give you eternal life." That is the easiest thing in the world.

Three things:

You believe that Jesus died and rose for you?

Yes.

Next, You take Him as your Savior?

Yes.

You will confess Him to the world?

Yes.

And as sure as you do it, I will stake my life and everything I have in this world that God will not break His Word. If you will take Jesus Christ as your Savior, and confess Him as Lord, God will give you eternal life.

Someone says, "I don't know whether I have it or not." If you have it, you absolutely know you have. Don't pretend you have it when you don't know. But if you haven't it you can have it where you are tonight, and you say, "The first chance I get I will confess Him as Lord." If you do, God will give you eternal life. You can go to the altar if you like, but there is only one thing you have to do, take Him as your Savior and confess Him as your Lord, and God will take you to be His child. I have seen thousands upon thousands settle it.

SANCTIFICATION AND CONSECRATION

eading Lesson: 1 Thessalonians 5

SANCTIFICATION

Beloved, the thought that is in my spirit tonight is the truth from the words we have just read, the sanctification of spirit and soul and body. Paul says,

> I pray God your whole spirit and soul and body be preserved blameless unto the coming of our Lord Jesus Christ. Faithful is he that calleth you, who also will do it.[1]

Most of us in our reading of the Scriptures have this difficulty, and it is a perfectly natural one, of recognizing body and soul only. And man is generally spoken of as a duality of body and soul. However, the Scriptures do not recognize man as a dual being, but a triune being like Himself.

Therefore, the apostle says:

> I pray God your whole *spirit* and *soul* and *body* be preserved blameless unto the coming of our Lord Jesus Christ.

One difficulty we have in the study of this subject is that in the common translation of our English Bible there is very little distinction made between soul and spirit. It is one of the most difficult things in the world to express the common truths we teach in another language. Paul coined seventeen distinct words in his letter to the Ephesians to express the fine distinctions of soul and spirit.

Paul declares in the book of Hebrews the possibility of divisibility of soul and spirit. He says:

> For the word of God is quick, and powerful, and sharper than any twoedged sword, piercing even to the dividing asunder of soul and spirit, and of the joints and marrow, and is a discerner of the thoughts and intents of the heart.
>
> — Hebrews 4:12

---

[1] 1 Thessalonians 5:23-24.

Beloved, the spirit of man is a great unknown realm in the lives of most men. My judgment is that the spirit lies dormant in most men until quickened by the living Spirit of God and until fertilized by the real Spirit of Jesus Christ. But when touched by the Spirit of God, a quickening takes place. The spirit of man comes into activity and begins to operate within him. It not only discerns things in this life, like the spirit of another, or in another, but it reaches way beyond this present life and becomes that medium by which we touch God Himself and by which we know and comprehend heavenly things.

In my judgment, the spirit of man is the most amazing instrument of God that there is in all the world. We have this declaration in the book of Job concerning man's spirit:

> There is a spirit in man: and the inspiration of the Almighty giveth them understanding.[2]

When a soul comes to God and surrenders his life to Him we say he is converted, and by that we mean changed, born again of God so that the common things which were evident in his life as a fleshly being fell away and were gone, and the spiritual life appeared in him, and in the truest sense he began his walk as a child of God.

I believe a real conversion is the awakening of the spirit of man to the consciousness of the Fatherhood of God through Jesus Christ. In order to be aware of that consciousness of union with God, it is necessary that everything be removed that hides that consciousness and dims the knowledge of God.

Sin is that peculiar thing in the life of man which dims the consciousness of man so he cannot comprehend God. When sin is removed, the veil over the soul of man is gone and the spirit of man looks into the face of God and recognizes that God is his Father through the Lord Jesus Christ. Bless God, the spirit of man ascending into union with God brings into our soul the consciousness that God is our all and in all.

The *soul* of man is that intermediate quality between body and spirit. The soul, in other words, comprehends all the action of our mental

---
[2] Job 32:8.

powers — the natural mind. The soul of man is that which reaches out and takes possession of the knowledge that the spirit has attained and expresses that knowledge through the outer man. The soul of man is the governing power in the constitution of man.

I feel in my heart that one of the things we need to learn very much is this; that the soul of man, not the spirit, has a marvelous power.

If I were to endeavor to define in terms I feel the people would understand, I would speak of the action of the soul of man as that which is commonly spoken of by students as the subconscious. As you read the writings of psychic authors, you will observe the actions and powers they define are not the powers of the spirit in union with God but the action of the soul of man. The soul of man is the real ego. When the Word of God speaks of the salvation of the *soul* it speaks in truly scientific language. For unless the soul, the mind of man, is redeemed from his own self into the Spirit of God that man is, in my judgment, still an unredeemed man.

Sanctification is calculated to apply to the needs of all our nature, first of the spirit, second of the soul, third of the body. Over and over again I have repeated those blessed words of John Wesley in his definition of sanctification. He said: "Sanctification is possessing the mind of Christ, and all the mind of Christ."

The ultimate of entire sanctification would comprehend all the mind of Christ. Christians are usually very weak in this department of their nature. Perhaps less pains have been taken by Christians to develop their mind in God than almost anything else.

We pay attention particularly to one thing only — the spirit — and we do not comprehend the fact that God purposed that the things God's Spirit brings to us shall be applied in a practical manner to the needs of our present life.

I was absolutely shocked the other day beyond anything I think my spirit ever received. A dear lady who professes not only to live a holy life but to possess the real baptism of the Holy Ghost and who discusses the subject a great deal, was guilty of saying one of the vilest things I ever heard concerning another. I said in my own soul, *That individual has not even discerned the outer fringes of what sanctification by the Spirit of God means.* I do not believe there is even an evidence of sanctification in that life. Certainly a mind that could repeat such a damning thing gives no evidence whatever but of a very superficial knowledge of God, very superficial indeed.

It shows us this thing, that people are placing their dependence in the fact that in their spirit they know God, that they have been saved from sin, and are going to heaven when they die; but they are living like the devil in this present life, talking like the devil. It is an abomination. It spells a tremendous degree of ignorance. It shows that that individual does not comprehend the first principles of the breadth of salvation as Jesus taught it to the world — a holy mind, a sanctified spirit.

Beloved, I tell you with all candor, a holy mind cannot repeat a vile thing let alone be the creator of the vile suggestion. It is an unholy mind that is capable of such an act. And I say with Paul, mark such a person. Put your finger on him. Just note it. He can talk, but he does not know God. He does not comprehend the power of His salvation.

But bless God, here is the hope, here is the strength, here is the power of the Gospel of Jesus Christ — that the power of God unto salvation applied to the mind of man sanctifies the soul of man and makes the mind of man like the mind of Christ.

Who could imagine from the lips of Jesus an unholy suggestion that would jar the spirit of another? The mind could not conceive of such a thing. Never could the mind conceive ought from God but the outflow of a holy life, quickening his mind, infilling it with love and purity and peace and power.

Beloved, in our home, in our life, in our office, wherever we are, we leave the impression of our thoughts there. If our thoughts are pure and holy like Christ, people will walk into the atmosphere and instantly discover it.

PRAYER

God, I pray that the power of God will come upon the Christian people, that they may feel, oh God, the necessity of submitting the wicked, accursed, vile mind of man to the living God to be purged and cleansed and remolded, that it may become in deed and in truth the mind of Christ.

If there is any particular place in our lives where as a rule Christians are weak, it is in the consecration of their minds. Christians seem to feel as if they were not to exercise any control over the mind and so it seems to run at random, just like the mind of the world.

Real Christianity is marked by the pureness, by the holiness of the thoughts of man, and if Christianity — the kind you have — does not produce in your mind real holiness, real purity, real sweetness, real truth, then it is a poor brand. Change it right away.

Beloved, there is relief for such; there is a way of salvation. It is in the submission of that mind to the Lord Jesus to be remolded by the Holy Spirit so that that mind becomes the pure channel of a holy nature.

Beloved, surely we who profess to know the living God, who profess to live in union with Him, ought to present to the world that attitude of mind, that pureness of mind, that holiness of mind which needs no recommendation. The people know it, they feel it, they smell it. They know it is the mind of Christ. I love that definition of John Wesley's which says, "Possessing the mind of Christ and *all* the mind of Christ."

PRAYER

Oh God, I ask Thee that Thou wilt help me and the soul of this people to submit our minds to God so that they may be remolded in love and sweetness and purity and holiness, so that in the name of Jesus they are the minds of Christ.

Beloved, we are going a step further — the effect of a pure mind on the body of man and in the flesh of man. Do you know that the sins of vileness in men's lives originate in the mind? A man's life will be of the character of his thought. If he thinks evil he will be evil. If he thinks holy he will be holy. His outward life will be as the inner impulse is. Jesus said,

> From within, out of the heart of men, proceed evil thoughts, adulteries, fornications, murders, thefts, covetousness, wickedness, deceit, lasciviousness, an evil eye, blasphemy, pride, foolishness: all these evil things come from within, and defile the man.

— Mark 7:21-23

They were troubled because Jesus and the disciples were eating and drinking from dishes which were not ceremonially cleansed. Jesus was trying to teach the great lesson of the deep and inner life. He said, "Out of the heart cometh evil things."

"That which goeth into the mouth cannot defile a man," etc.[3]

Beloved, our minds need to be stayed in Christ, kept by the power of God, infilled with the Holy Spirit of Christ so that we reflect His beauty, we show forth His love, we manifest His sweetness, and evidence His power.

Long ago I learned this splendid lesson. One night I was in a strange city and was sick. I wanted somebody to pray for me. A person was present, and they suggested that they would pray. I knelt by a chair on the floor and they put their hands on me, and I arose from that chair with one of the most tremendous passions in my nature, one of the most terrible conditions of sensuousness in me. It was days before I felt that I got back again where I was pure and holy in the sight of God. I did not understand it at the time, but afterward that individual came to me with the confession of the character of their life and I understood then. I received the condition of that nature, and in my receptive attitude I received of the vileness of that person in my nature. It seemed my soul was soiled for days in consequence.

That taught me, beloved, to be careful who laid their hands on me. After that, I waited until the Spirit of the living God indicated in my soul that the person who offered to perform such a ministry was pure.

Isn't it marvelous, beautiful, wonderful to realize that mankind can receive into their nature and being the power and spirit of the living Christ, which contains the purging power to drive forth from the being every particle of evil, every sensuous thing in the thought and nature so that the man becomes what Jesus was. That is what the blood of Jesus Christ is calculated to do. That is what the spirit of Christ is purposed to do in the soul of a man — the cleansing of a nature from the power and dominion of sin.

Beloved, the inflow of holy life into our body *must produce* holiness in the *body,* just as it does in the soul. We cannot even think beautiful

---

[3] Mark 7:18, paraphrased.

thoughts, we cannot think holy thoughts, without them leaving their impression in our nature, in our very flesh.

That same divine power in us dissolves disease, restores diseased tissues. Our flesh is purged by the divine power being transmitted from our spirit, through our soul, into our body.

I have always loved to think of the holy flesh of Jesus, not just His beautiful mind, not just the pure Spirit; but is it not blessed and sweet to contemplate the flesh cleansed and purified until His very body — His hands, His feet, His person — were just as pure by the Spirit of God as His pure soul and His pure Spirit were.

That is why Jesus was the wonderful channel He was. The Spirit of God would flow through Him just as freely, just as fully, just as powerfully as it was possible for it to flow through a holy, purified personality.

I like to contemplate the Lord Jesus on the Mount of Transfiguration and think of the radiant glory that came through His flesh, not just the illumination of His spirit, but the holy glory emanating through His flesh until He became white and glistening, until His clothes were white and His face shown as the light. It is that radiant purity of God that my soul covets. It is that radiant power, evidenced in the pureness of my spirit, my mind, my very flesh that I long for.

So beloved, we see that when something impure, of the character of disease, appears on your flesh and mine and we feel we are being soiled by an unholy touch, in the name of Jesus our spirit reaches up and rebukes that devilish condition, and by the Spirit of the living God we stand, believing that the Holy Spirit of God will flow through the spirit, flow through the soul, through the flesh, and remedy and heal that difficulty that is in the person.

An old Baptist brother was in to see me about his wife. As I sat reasoning with him, I said, "Brother, I would just as soon have my brother commit a sin as to have sickness in his person. One is the evidence of an impure mind, the other is the evidence of an impure body. And the salvation of Jesus was intended to make him pure in spirit, in soul, and in body."

> I pray God your whole spirit and soul and body be preserved blameless unto the coming of our Lord Jesus Christ. Faithful is he that calleth you who also will do it.

There is a stream of life that God permits to flow from your nature and mine to all men everywhere. That blessed stream will be either sweet and pure as the stream that flows from the throne of God, or it will be soiled and foul according to the condition of our nature. The value of the precious blood of Jesus Christ to you and me is that through it that life stream that flows from us may be made holy — that same holy living life-stream that causes the Tree of Life to bloom.

Of all the pictures that the Word of God contains, the one described in the twenty-second chapter of Revelation is the most beautiful:

> He shewed me a pure river of water of life, clear as crystal, proceeding out of the throne of God and of the Lamb. In the midst of the street of it, and on either side of the river, was there the tree of life, which bare twelve manner of fruits, and yielded her fruit every month: and the leaves of the tree were for the healing of the nations. And there shall be no more curse: but the throne of God and of the Lamb shall be in it; and his servants shall serve him: And they shall see his face; and his name shall be in their foreheads. And there shall be no night there; and they need no candle, neither light of the sun; for the Lord God giveth them light: and they shall reign for ever and ever. And he said unto me, These sayings are faithful and true: and the Lord God of the holy prophets sent his angel to shew unto his servants the things which must shortly be done. Behold, I come quickly: blessed is he that keepeth the sayings of the prophecy of this book. And I John saw these things, and heard them. And when I had heard and seen, I fell down to worship before the feet of the angel which shewed me these things. Then saith he unto me, See thou do it not: for I am thy fellowservant, and of thy brethren the prophets, and of them which keep the sayings of this book: worship God. And he saith unto me, Seal not the sayings of the prophecy of this book: for the time is at hand. He that is unjust, let him be unjust still: and he which is filthy, let him be filthy still: and he that is righteous, let him be righteous still: and he that is holy, let him be holy still. And, behold, I come quickly; and my reward is with me, to give every man according as his work shall be. I am Alpha and Omega, the beginning and the end, the first and the last. Blessed are they that do his commandments, that they may have right to the tree of life,

and may enter in through the gates into the city. For without are dogs, and sorcerers, and whoremongers, and murderers, and idolaters, and whosoever loveth and maketh a lie. I Jesus have sent mine angel to testify unto you these things in the churches. I am the root and the offspring of David, and the bright and morning star. And the Spirit and the bride say, Come. And let him that heareth say, Come. And let him that is athirst come. And whosoever will, let him take the water of life freely. For I testify unto every man that heareth the words of the prophecy of this book, If any man shall add unto these things, God shall add unto him the plagues that are written in this book: And if any man shall take away from the words of the book of this prophecy, God shall take away his part out of the book of life, and out of the holy city, and from the things which are written in this book. He which testifieth these things saith, Surely I come quickly. Amen. Even so, come, Lord Jesus. The grace of our Lord Jesus Christ be with you all. Amen.

— Revelation 22:1-21

Beloved, if your life has not been satisfactory, if you have not recognized the holy character that Christ expects from a real Christian, then this call of the Spirit comes to your soul. "The Spirit and the Bride say come." Come up, come into the real life, the high life, the life hid *with Christ* in God.

> I will be within thee a well of water, springing up into everlasting life.[4]

---

[4] John 4:14, parphrased.

THE POWER OF CONSECRATION TO PRINCIPLE

Preface to Second Edition

 uccessful Christian life rests on three essentials:

First: A knowledge of the teaching of the Lord and Saviour Jesus Christ, whose words are the final authority, the bar where every question must be brought for final decision. The words of every other must be measured, and their value determined, by the statements of Jesus Christ. "In him dwelleth all the fulness of the Godhead bodily."[1]

Second: Consecration to do all the will of God as declared by the Lord Jesus.

Third: Recognition of the Holy Spirit as revealer, guide, interpreter, teacher, and empowerer. For without the presence of the Spirit of God in our hearts our consecration would be valueless. We would not be able to live it. And without a knowledge of the teaching of Jesus our consecration would be nonintelligent.

We recommend the use of a Red Letter New Testament to every Christian who truly desires to know what Jesus taught on all subjects.

John G. Lake

SERMON

The great purpose of Jesus Christ in coming to the world was to establish the kingdom of God. The kingdom of God is universal, containing all moral intelligences willingly subject to the will of God both in heaven and on earth, both angels and men. The kingdom of heaven is Christ's kingdom on the earth, which will eventually merge into the kingdom of God. We read of that merging period in the 15th of 1 Corinthians, where it says:

---

[1] Colossians 2:9.

> Then cometh the end, when he shall have delivered up the
> kingdom to God, even the Father; when he shall have put
> down all rule and all authority and power... And when all
> things shall be subdued unto him, then shall the Son also
> himself be subject unto him that put all things under him,
> that God may be all in all.[2]

Now then, in order to establish a kingdom there must be a basis upon which it is to be founded. When the Revolutionary fathers got together in '76 they laid down the Declaration of Independence, the principles upon which American government was to be founded. They laid down as one of the first principles this one: "All men are born free and equal." That every man, by his being born a man, is likewise born on an equality with all others. All men are born free and equal before the law; there is no special privilege.

Next, they considered this as the second principle: That man, because of his birth and his free agency, was entitled to "Life, liberty, and the pursuit of happiness."

Third: That government rests on the consent of the governed.

These were the underlying principles upon which the government was to rest. There was nothing little about them. They did not discuss the doctrines by which these principles were to be made effective, but they laid down the foundational principles upon which was built the greatest system of human government in the world's history.

Now Jesus likewise, when he came to found His kingdom, first enunciated the principles upon which His government was to rest. The eight Beatitudes, as they are given in His official declaration in His Sermon on the Mount, were the great principles upon which His government was to be founded.

A principle is not a dogma, or a doctrine. It is that underlying quality, that fundamental truth, upon which all other things are based. The principles of the kingdom of heaven are those underlying qualities upon which the whole structure of the Christian life rests and the principles upon which the real government of Jesus Christ will be founded and exercised. The eight Beatitudes are the principles of the

---

[2] 1 Corinthians 15:24,28.

kingdom, the Sermon on the Mount is the constitution, and the commandments of Jesus are its laws or statutes.

First, the kingdom is established in the hearts of men. The principles of Jesus Christ are settled in our own spirit. We become citizens of the kingdom of heaven. The aggregate citizenship of the kingdom in this present age constitutes the real Church, which is His body.[3] And throughout the Church age the working of the body is to be apparent in demonstrating to the world the practicability and desirability of the kingdom of heaven, that all men may desire the rule of Jesus in the salvation of men.

It is the purpose of Jesus to make the Church, which is His body, His representative in the world. Just as Jesus came to express God the Father to mankind, and Jesus was necessary to God in order that He might give an expression of Himself to the world, so the Church is necessary to Jesus Christ as an expression of Himself to the world.

Now the first principle that He laid down was this one: "Blessed are the poor in spirit, for theirs is the kingdom of heaven."[4] Usually we confuse this with the other one, "Blessed are the meek,"[5] and we have commonly thought of one who is poor in spirit as being a meek, quiet person — possessing the spirit of meekness. But it is much more than that. The thing Jesus urged upon men was to practice what He had done Himself.

Jesus was the King of glory, yet He laid down all His glory. He came to earth and took upon Himself our condition. "He took not on him the nature of angels; but took on him the seed of Abraham" (Hebrews 2:16). He took upon Himself the condition of mankind, that is, of human nature's liability to sin. Therefore, He was "in all points tempted like as we are, yet without sin."[6] And because of the fact that He took upon Himself our nature and understood the temptations that are common to man, He is "able to succour them that are tempted" (Hebrews 2:18). He understands. He is a sympathetic Christ. Bless God!

---

3 See Ephesians 1:22-23.

4 Matthew 5:3.

5 Matthew 5:5.

6 Hebrews 4:15.

Now see! "Blessed are the poor in spirit." Blessed is he who regards the interests of the kingdom of heaven as paramount to every other interest in the world, paramount to his own personal interest. Blessed is he whose interest in life, whose interest in the world is only used to extend the interest of the kingdom of heaven. Blessed is he who has lost his own identity as an individual and has become a citizen of the kingdom. Blessed is he who forgets to hoard wealth for himself, but who uses all he has and all he is for the extension of the kingdom of heaven. It is putting the law of love of God and one another into practice.

So after Jesus had laid down the things that He possessed, then bless God, He was able to say to us, as He had experienced it Himself, "Blessed are the poor in spirit, for theirs is the kingdom of heaven."

We commonly think as we read the Word of God that some of the teachings of Jesus were accidental or were applied to a particular individual and no one else. So we think of the rich young ruler, who came to Jesus and said:

> Good Master, what shall I do to inherit eternal life? And Jesus said unto him... Thou knowest the commandments, Do not commit adultery, Do not kill, Do not steal, Do not bear false witness, Honor thy father and thy mother. And he said, All these have I kept from my youth up... He [Jesus] said unto him, Yet lackest thou one thing: sell all that thou hast, and distribute unto the poor, and thou shalt have treasure in heaven: and come, follow me.
>
> — Luke 18:18-22

Don't you see, Jesus was applying to that young man that first principle of the kingdom. We have said that young man was covetous and he loved his wealth, etc., and that was keeping him out of the kingdom of heaven. Not so. Jesus was applying one of the principles of the kingdom to that young man's life. He turned away sorrowful. He had not developed to the place where he could do that thing.

There is a apocryphal story that tells us that the rich young ruler was Barnabas. After the resurrection and the coming of the Holy Ghost, Barnabas received from heaven the thing Jesus had tried to impart to him. He forgot all about Barnabas, his own interests and his own desires, and he sold his great possessions and came with the others and laid them at the apostles' feet.[7] "Blessed are the poor in spirit, for theirs is the kingdom of heaven." So Jesus was able, after all, to get the real thing in the heart of Barnabas that He desired in the beginning.

The real miracle of the Holy Ghost at Pentecost was not the outward demonstration of tongues, etc.; but it produced such intense unselfishness in the hearts of all baptized that they each sold their lands and estates and parted the money to every man as he had need. They were moved by God into one family. Their brother's interest was equal to their own. That was "Blessed are the poor in spirit."

The second principle of the kingdom is this: "Blessed are they that mourn: for they shall be comforted."[8] This figure is taken from the old prophets, who when the nation sinned, took upon themselves the responsibility of the nation. They put sackcloth on their body and ashes on their head and in mourning and tears went down before God for days and weeks, until the people turned to God. They became the intercessors between God and man and in some instances in the Word we read where God looked and wondered. He wondered that there was no intercessor. There were no mourners who took upon themselves the responsibility of the sins of the people, who dared to stand between man and God.

We see how wonderfully Moses stood between God and the people. When God said to him after they had made the golden calf, "Let me alone…that I may consume them: and I will make of thee a great nation" (Exodus 32:10). Moses said, "Not so, Lord. What will the Egyptians say, what will be the effect upon Thy great name? Will they not say that their God destroyed them?"[9]

God had said to Moses, "I will make of thee a great nation," but Moses was big enough to turn aside the greatest honor that God could bestow upon a man — to become the father of a race.

---

[7] An exact source for this apocryphal story could not be located. The Apocrypha is non canonical or extrabibilical literature and is not considered inspired by the Holy Spirit. Therefore, the fact that the rich young ruler was Barnabas is unconfirmed.

[8] Matthew 5:4.

[9] Exodus 32:12, paraphrased.

> Not so, Lord. This people have sinned a great sin, and have made them gods of gold. Yet now, if thou wilt forgive their sin… and if not, blot me, I pray thee, out of thy book.
>
> — Exodus 32:31-32, paraphrased.

The prophet became the great intercessor. He took upon himself the burdens and sins of the people, and when he got down to confess he did not say, "Oh! These people are so weak and they do this and that." But when he got down to pray he would say, "Lord God, *we* are unworthy." He was *one* with his people. He was identified with them, as one with them. He was not putting any blame on them. He was big enough to take the whole blame, the entire responsibility, and go down before God and lay the whole matter before God until the blessed mercy of God was again given to the people.

"Blessed are the poor in spirit…Blessed are they that mourn."[10] Blessed is the man who comprehends the purposes of God, who understands his responsibility and possibility, who by God-given mourning and crying, turns the people to God. With his heart yearning for sinners, he becomes a mourner before God and takes the responsibility of fallen men on his own life. He goes down in tears and repentance before God until men turn to God and the mercy of God is shown to mankind.

In the day that God puts the spirit of mourning upon Pentecost, it will be the gladdest day that heaven ever knew. Blessed be His precious name!

Do you know, it always jars me down in the depths of my spirit when I hear people say hard things about churches and sects. That is not our place. Our place is as intercessor — as the one who is to stand between the living and the dead, as those whom God can trust and use to pray down the power and mercy and blessing of God upon this old race.

First we see that the kingdom is based on principles. Principles are greater than doctrines. Principles are the foundation stones upon

---

[10] Matthew 5:3-4.

which all other things rest. Doctrines are the rules, the details by which we endeavor to carry out the things that the principles contain; but the principles are the great foundation stones upon which all things rest.

ABSOLUTE CONSECRATION

Let us turn away from this until we see Jesus at the Jordan, consecrating Himself to His own life work, then we will understand how the Christian is to consecrate himself to carry out the principles.

The Word tells us that when Jesus began to be about thirty years of age, He came down to the River Jordan where John was baptizing and presented Himself for baptism. John looked in amazement on Him and said, "I have need to be baptized of thee, and comest thou to me?" But Jesus said, "Suffer it to be so now; for thus it becometh us to fulfill *all righteousness.*" Unto "all righteousness."[11]

Listen! Hear the declaration to which Jesus Christ was baptized; it was His consecration unto "all righteousness." There was no further to go. It comprehends all there is of consecration and commitment unto the will of God and all there is of good. Unto "all righteousness." Bless God!

So Jesus understandingly permitted Himself to be baptized of John unto "all righteousness." Now listen! You and I have also been baptized. But see! Immediately after He was baptized, something took place. First, the Spirit of God came upon Him as a dove and abode upon Him.[12] Then we read He was led by the Spirit into the wilderness to be tempted of the devil.[13] It was not the devil that led Him into the wilderness. It was the Holy Ghost.

In the 16th of Leviticus, we see one of the beautiful figures which will illustrate that to you. On the day of atonement there were brought two goats. One, the priest laid his hands upon, put a towrope around its neck, then the Levite took the towrope and led it three days into the barren sands of the wilderness, and left it there to die.[14] That is the picture of the *life-death* of Jesus Christ.

---

[11] Matthew 3:14-15.

[12] See Matthew 3:16.

[13] See Matthew 4:1.

[14] See Leviticus 16:7-22.

The Holy Ghost is God's Levite. He put the towrope on the neck of Jesus Christ and led Him likewise three days — a year for a day, God's three days — into the wilderness. What for? To prove out, to test out the real fact of His obedience unto God and whether His consecration was going to stand. So the Spirit, the Holy Ghost, led Jesus into the wilderness.

Now I want you to see something. We are triune beings just as God Himself is triune. You will see the character of the consecration that Jesus made at the Jordan. God is *triune*. He is God the Father, God the Son, and God the Holy Ghost. Man is also *triune*. The Word says,

> I pray God *your* whole *spirit* and *soul* and *body* be preserved blameless unto the coming of our Lord Jesus Christ.
>
> — 1 Thessalonians 5:23, emphasis Lake's

So Jesus, when He went into the wilderness, encountered a peculiar temptation peculiar to each separate department of His being. The Word of God says He fasted forty days and was an hungred. Satan comes to Him and says, "If thou be the Son of God, command that these stones be made bread."[15] But Jesus could not do it. If He had done that, He would have been exercising His own authority in His own behalf and He had committed Himself unto "all righteousness." He only lived to express God, He only lived to express the Father. He said, "The words I speak, I speak not of myself. The work that I do I do not of myself."[16] All He said and all He did and all He was, was the expression of God the Father.

May the Lord give us an understanding of the utterness of what a real baptismal consecration ought to be. When an individual comes and commits himself to Christ once and for all and forever, he ceases to be, he ceases to live in his own behalf, to live for himself any longer, but becomes the utter expression of Jesus Christ to mankind.

So Satan had no power to tempt a man who had made a consecration like that. The hunger calls of Jesus' body, after He had fasted forty

---

[15] Matthew 4:3.

[16] John 14:10, paraphrased.

days, were not enough to turn Him aside from the consecration He had made to God.

The second temptation was one peculiar to the *mind* (soul). He was taken to a pinnacle of the temple, and Satan said, "Do something spectacular, cast yourself down; let the people see You are an unusual person, and that You can do unusual things, and they will give You their acclaim."[17]

Jesus could not do that. There was nothing, bless God, in the mind of Jesus Christ that could tempt Him to be disobedient to the consecration He had made to God, unto "all righteousness." So He turned the temptation aside.

The third temptation was one peculiar to the *spirit*. By a supernatural power Jesus is permitted to see, "All the kingdoms of the world and the glory of them," in a moment of time. Then Satan said unto Him, "All these things will I give thee, if thou wilt fall down and worship me."[18] But Jesus turned him aside. No crossless crowning for the Son of God, no bloodless glory for my Lord. He had come to express God to the world, He had come to demonstrate one thing to you and me. That is, that man relying on God can have the victory over sin and Satan. Bless God! That is the peculiar thing about the life of Jesus Christ that makes Him dear to your heart and mine.

After going on the towrope of the Holy Ghost for three years as the first goat, through the sorrows and trials and disappointments of life — even ministering and blessing — though the world cursed Him, He was able to come as the second goat and present Himself as the sinless, spotless sacrifice unto God at the cross.

If Jesus had fallen down anywhere along the line, if there had been a single instance where He had failed to express God to the world, He could never have been the Savior of the world. *"He became* the author of eternal salvation."[19] He was honored of God in being permitted to die for mankind, having triumphed, having presented Himself the sinless, spotless sacrifice unto God. His blood flowed for all the race. Blessed be His name!

---

[17] Matthew 4:6, paraphrased.

[18] Matthew 4:9.

[19] Hebrews 5:9, emphasis Lake's.

We have seen two things. We have seen the principles of Jesus Christ. We have seen His consecration to carry out those principles. He consecrated Himself utterly unto the mind and will of God. But now we are going a step farther.

EVEN UNTO DEATH

We come to the last night of the Lord's life. He is with His disciples in the upper room. Here comes the final act, the consummation of all His life. There is a phase of this act, I know the Lord has made clear to many.

They sat around the table after they had eaten their supper, Jesus took bread and brake it, saying, "Take, eat: this is My body, which is broken for you,"[20] and yet He was there in the flesh. Now what did it mean? What was its significance?

This: By that act the Lord Jesus Christ pledged Himself before God, before the holy angels, before men, that He would not stop short of dying for the world. There was no limit. He was faithful "even unto death."[21] Just as He had been faithful in life and had lived each day the conscious life-death, dying to every desire of His mind and will and being, He is now going one step further. He is going to be faithful "even unto death."

So He said, "Take eat, this is My body, broken for you." After supper likewise, He took the cup, when He had drunk, saying, "My blood of the new testament."[22]

Now you listen. From time immemorial mankind has been in the habit of pledging themselves in the cup. There is no date that mankind has of its origin. It is so ancient we do not know when the custom began, when men began to pledge themselves in the wine cup, but our Jesus sanctified the custom to God and His Church forever.

---

[20] 1 Corinthians 11:24. [Editor's note: Lake seems to be using Matthew's account of the Last Supper here, but the reference in 1 Corinthians is the only one that includes the words "which is broken for you."]

[21] Matthew 26:38.

[22] Matthew 26:28.

Jesus poured the wine into the cup, took it, and said, "This is my blood of the new testament," and He drank that Himself. That was the pledge of the Lord Jesus Christ. Having laid down the principles of the Gospel of the Son of God, having walked and lived and suffered for three years, now He was going to the very uttermost. There was no further to go. He said, "This is My blood of the new testament," meaning He would give His life for the world.

That is not all. That was His pledge, but after He had drunk, saying, "Drink *ye* all of it."[23] And when they took the cup of which their Lord had drunk, they drank to that pledge. They were made partakers in the same pledge and likewise pledged themselves, "My blood of the new testament." Bless God.

Christianity had character in it. Jesus Christ put character in it. Bless God! "My blood of the new testament." The other day I was going over the list of the apostles as they are given by Hippolytus, one of the early writers, and he tells us that five of the twelve were crucified just as Jesus was. Others died by the spear and sword, and three died natural deaths after enduring tortures. So it meant for them just what it means for their Lord, "My blood of the new testament." We see the degree of faithfulness to which they pledged themselves that night.

We have loved and admired the spirit of the apostles. The spirit of Jesus Christ was so intense in the early Christians, that millions of them gave their lives for the Son of God; multitudes of whom died the death of martyrs and multitudes died in the war to exterminate Christianity. Thirty million! Think of that. It gives some meaning to the saying that "The blood of the martyrs was the seed of the Church."

How often have you and I taken the Lord's cup? Has it meant that to you and me, and does it mean that to you and me now? Beloved, I have no doubt that the sacred cup has touched many lips, perhaps the lips of most of you. If we have been understanding, comprehending Christians, we have realized it meant to us just what it did to the Lord — our everlasting pledge of faithfulness.

There is no place for sin in the Christian's life. There is no place for letting down in the Christian's life. There is no place for weakening in

---

[23] Matthew 26:27.

the Christian's life. Paul said, when they were having a hard time, "Ye have not yet resisted unto blood, striving against sin" (Hebrews 12:4). That was expected of them. They were expected to resist even unto death; so Paul says, "Ye have not yet resisted unto blood." In the Revelation, the Church in Smyrna is commanded, "Be thou faithful *unto* death, and I will give thee a crown of life" (Revelation 2:10).

In this land, after our fathers had signed the old Declaration of Independence they pledged, "Our lives, our fortunes, and our sacred honor," then they went out and gave themselves to eight years of war in order to make it good.

When people make a declaration on principles, it is going to cost them something and it costs them something. After awhile the men in the old Revolutionary Army got where they did not have shoes on their feet, but in the depth of winter they tied straw and rags on their feet. They had stood by principles, they had lived by principles, they were ready to die by principles, and the British tracked them by the blood marks on the snow.

So Jesus Christ, in enlisting an army, put them under a kindred pledge with Himself. He pledged Christians on the same plane with Himself. Just as far as the Lord went, they went "even unto death."

The real purpose of becoming a Christian is not to save yourself from hell or to be saved to go to heaven. It is to become a child of God with the character of Jesus Christ, to stand before men pledged unto the uttermost — "even unto death" — by refusing to sin, refusing to bow your head in shame. Preferring to die rather than dishonor the Son of God.

If the character of Jesus Christ has entered into you and into me, then it has made us like the Christ. It has made us like Him in purpose. It has made us like Him in fact. Bless God! His Spirit is imparted to us. Bless God for that same unquenchable fidelity that characterized the Son of God.

> Be thou faithful unto death, and I will give thee a crown of life.[23]

---

[23] Revelation 2:10.

CONSECRATION PRAYER

My God and Father,

In Jesus' name I come to Thee, take me as I am. Make me what I ought to be in *spirit,* in *soul,* in *body.* Give me power to do right. If I have wronged any to *confess,* to *repent,* to *restore* — no matter what it costs. Wash me in the *blood* of Jesus that I may now become Thy child and manifest Thee in a perfect *spirit,* a holy *mind,* a *sickless body,* to the glory of God. Amen.

 **I,** this day, consecrate my entire life to glorify my heavenly Father by my obedience to the principles of Jesus Christ through the power of the Holy Spirit. All my effort from now on will be directed in an effort to demonstrate the righteousness of God in whatsover I may be engaged.

MY CONSECRATION AS A CHRISTIAN

PRINCIPLE 1

All things earthly that I possess shall not be considered my own, but belonging to my heavenly Father, and shall be held in trust by me to be used and directed by the wisdom of the Spirit of God, as the law of love of men as Christ loved them may dictate.

If at anytime God should raise up men wiser than myself, I will gladly commit my all to their use and turn over all my possessions to them for distribution.

If at anytime in my life I should be engaged in any earthly business and should employ men to aid me in conducting it, I shall reward them justly and equally, comparing their own energy expended with my own after adding a sufficient amount to my own to cover all risk that may be involved in the operation of my business.

I shall consider my employees my equals with rights to the blessings of nature and life equal to my own. I shall not strive to elevate myself to a position of comfort above the rest of my employees and shall direct all my efforts to bring all mankind to an equal plane, where all enjoy the comforts of life and fellowship together.

PRINCIPLE 2

I shall not cease to cry to God and implore Him to deliver mankind from the effects of sin so long as sin lasts, but shall cooperate with God in the redemption of mankind.

I will have seasons of prayer and fasting in behalf of mankind, weeping and bewailing their lost condition and imploring God to grant them repentance unto life as the Spirit of God may lead me.

PRINCIPLE 3

I shall live my life in meekness, never defending my own personal rights, but shall leave all judgment in God who judges righteously and rewards all according to their works.

I shall not render evil for evil or railing for railing, but shall bless all and do good to enemies to return for evil.

By God's grace I shall keep all hardness and harshness out of my life and actions, but shall be gently and unassuming, not professing above what God has imported to me, nor lifting myself above my brethren.

PRINCIPLE 4

I shall consider righteous acts as more necessary to life and happiness than food and drink, and not let myself be bribed or coerced into any unrighteous action for any earthly consideration.

PRINCIPLE 5

By God's grace I will always be merciful, forgiving those who have transgressed against me and endeavoring to correct the ills of humanity instead of merely punishing them for their sins.

PRINCIPLE 6

I shall not harbor any impure thoughts in my mind, but shall endeavor to make my every act uplifting.

I shall regard my procreative organs sacred and holy and never use them for any purpose other than that which God created them for.

I shall regard the home as sacred and always guard my actions in the presence of the opposite sex, so as not to cause a man and his wife to break their vows to one another. I shall be chaste with the opposite sex who are married, considering them as sisters. I shall be careful not to cause them undue pain by playing on their affection.

PRINCIPLE 7

I will always strive to be a peacemaker. First, by being peaceful myself and avoiding all unfruitful contentions and treating all with justice and regarding their rights and their free agency, never trying to force any to my point of view.

If I should offend anyone knowingly, I shall immediately apologize.

I will not scatter evil reports about any person and so try to defame their character, or repeat things that I am not certain of being true.

I will strive to remove the curse of strife among brethren by acting as a peacemaker.

PRINCIPLE 8

I shall not become discouraged when I am persecuted on account of the righteousness mentioned above nor murmur on account of any suffering I undergo, but shall gladly give my life rather than depart from this high standard of life, rejoicing because I know I have a great reward in heaven.

I shall strive to make the above principles the ideal of all the world and give my life and energy to see mankind get the power from God to practice the same.

John G. Lake

MISCELLANEOUS AND PARTIAL SERMONS

[UNTITLED, BASIC BELIEFS]

he gospel of the kingdom reveals a personal, complete redemption as proclaimed by Jesus Christ. It is a triune Gospel, redemption of spirit, soul, and body.

A triune God, redeeming triune man in each department of life from a triune power of darkness — the world, the flesh, and the devil.

Modern Christianity has emerged slowly and gradually from the shadows of the dark ages.

Luther proclaimed the redemption of the spirit, his slogan, "The just shall live by faith,"[1] comprehended a redemptive action of God in the spirit of man, producing a consciousness of life eternal.

John Wesley proclaimed a sanctifying action of God in the mind or soul of man, bringing his thought and habits of mind into conformity with the mind of God. He defines sanctification as, "Possessing the mind of Christ and all the mind of Christ."

The revelation of divine healing is the third link in the purpose of kingdom redemption. The body too must be redeemed from the corruption of disease. Thus healthfulness, holiness, and eternal life become the divine heritage of the kingdom Christian. The salvation of the spirit is essential to eternal life in Christ. A sanctified mind and saved soul was necessary to manifest God in this life and retain intelligence after death, through union of soul and spirit.

The healing and cleansing of the body from disease was not simply another method of recovery from sickness, but is God's way of healing — God's action in the body destroying the effects of sin and completing the preparation of the Christian for the incoming and indwelling of God Himself.

The baptism of the Holy Ghost was God taking literal and conscious possession of the God-saved Christian. From thenceforth, the Christian was actuated and exercised by the predominant all-powerful Holy

---

[1] Romans 1:17, Galatians 3:11, and Hebrews 10:38.

Spirit, the personality of the triune God. The fruits of the Spirit as enumerated in Galatians 5:22-23, are the characteristic of God now being manifested in and by the God indwelt Christian.

The gifts of the Holy Spirit as set forth in 1 Corinthians 12 are the exercising of God in redemptive action in the God-inhabited person. The anointed and indwelt one is set forth first to live the life of Christ; second, to exercise redemptive power by continuing forever to do the sin-, sickness-, and death-destroying works of Christ, and having continued until Jesus comes, was to be immortalized in both spirit and soul and body like Jesus Himself, thus consummating the purpose of God in the Christian by revealing the sons of God. Thus being in nature, character, and substance like Christ, are prepared to assist Him in the control and conquest of the kingdom of Christ on the earth and establish the same.

oncerning old St. Patrick. I am one Protestant minister who loves old St. Patrick. He was one of the mightiest men of God of his age. When they tell you about him banishing the snakes of Ireland, you believe it. They went by the power of God.

He died in the year 465 after Christ. By that time, the Roman Catholic church had begun to spread over the world, and she was corralling the faith of men and bringing them in subjection to the church. Ireland was a long piece from Rome, consequently St. Patrick had a chance to go on in the faith of God. He prayed for the sick and anointed them, and they were healed. But the church changed that practice for the sacrament of Extreme Unction, where the priest comes and bows by the dying man and gives him a wafer and lets him die!

[UNTITLED, ABOUT THE REAL ST. PATRICK]

Editor's note: The following is apparently a portion of a sermon Lake preached at some time.

This is what happens when faith goes out of men's souls. St. Patrick refused to conform to the formula of the church, and he continued to pray the prayer of faith. He was called to account and was tried for his life. On his way he encouraged his soul by such exclamations as, "Christ within me, Christ above me, Christ beneath me, Christ before me, Christ on my right hand, Christ on my left hand, Christ in the eyes of everyone who sees me, Christ in the soul of everyone who knows me," and with such exclamations he continued on his way.

As he went along the road, an old widow was distressed because her cow and two pigs had been stricken with some strange disease. Old St. Patrick turned off the road long enough to heal the cow and the pigs, and then he went on his way, declaring "Christ within me, Christ around me, Christ above me, Christ beneath me," etc.

And this is the story of the snakes. One day he came where a father had just been bitten by a poisonous snake, with his weeping wife and children standing around. And as he stood there his heart rose in God. When presently, somebody called his attention to the snake that had bitten the man, lying on the grass nearby. And going after the thing of hell, he damned it and all its tribe forever, and they went from Ireland to this day.

Two years ago, they invited me in Spokane to give a St. Patrick's address, and I gave such an address as they had never listened to in their life before. I told them of the real St. Patrick.

[Untitled Partial Sermon, The Pillar of Fire]

Editor's note: The first page, or more, of this sermon was missing.

mong these men was Erasmus of Rotterdam, who wrote a book known as the "Praise of Follies."[1] It was a satire on the priesthood and their practices in the Church at that time. The effect of the book was that it set the people to laughing at the priesthood. The Church descended on Erasmus. He ended by landing up against the faggot[2] pile, and he didn't have enough of God to go through. He recanted, the books were collected, a public burning of the books took place, and he went back among the people to be a good boy and keep still.

So God had to bring forth another individual. God couldn't get His purpose accomplished through that man. God's purposes require strength and character. God worked in the heart of another, Martin Luther. One day while going up the stairway of St. Peter's on his bare knees, at Rome, doing penance for his sins, the best thing the world knew at that time to do for sins, suddenly God spoke to him and said, *"The just shall live by faith."*[3]

It was an illumination right out of heaven. It came straight from the throne of God to his heart. He sprang up and said, "If the just shall live by faith, then my works of penance are valueless," and he discarded them. The peace of God came into his heart, and he set

---

[1] Although written in 1509, "The Praise of Follies" was not published until 1511. Erasmus apparently wrote it to amuse his friend, Thomas More, but the book became much more than an amusement. English translations of the text can be found at various sites on the internet.

[2] faggot: A bundle of sticks, twigs, or branches used as fuel. *Webster's Desk Dictionary of the English Language* (NY: Gramercy Books, 1983), p. 321.

[3] Romans 1:17, Galatians 3:11, and Hebrews 10:38.

Europe on fire with *"The just shall live by faith."* The whole Protestant movement was the outcome. The God-fire that swept over Europe was the indication of the presence of God, the pillar of cloud and of fire.[4]

Wherever God is, there is always some kind of a demonstration. The demonstration of His presence in that day was a general revolt from the Roman Church into liberty to worship God according to their conscience. The Church of England, the Lutheran, Presbyterian, and other great bodies were the outcome of the Reformation. There was tumult and war, destruction of life and property. All these things characterized the storm that was in men's hearts. When God moves, there is always something doing. It isn't always a wave of blessed peace that marks God. Rather, it is storm and war and contention. Jesus said,

> Think not that I am come to send peace on earth: I came
> not to send peace, but a sword. For I am come to set a
> man at variance against his father, and the daughter against
> her mother, and the daughter in law against her mother in
> law. And a man's foes shall be they of his own household.[5]

Now there is something behind that condition. It is a stirring of God. It is a moving of God. God begins to move in a family. God gets hold of the son's life or daughter's life or wife's life, as the case may be, and suddenly there is a tumult in the household. They have broken away from the conventional establishment of the home. Perhaps they get Methodistic and pray too loud or they get baptized in the Holy Ghost and speak in tongues or they refuse to take medicine and trust God only, and the household is disturbed. But behind the demonstration is the presence of God in a new degree.

I am thinking of the pillar of fire. Away back seventeen or eighteen years ago, old Hudson Taylor, who the world recognizes as the real prophetic character, during his last years was in China in communion with God, and God revealed this to him and he announced it to the world: That in ten years there would be a war between Japan and

---

[4] See Exodus 13:21.

[5] Matthew 10:34-36.

Russia and Japan would be the victor, notwithstanding that at that time it was all contrary to the opinion of the civilized world.

The second element in his prophecy was this: He said that in Western Europe there will break out a most remarkable revival. It will spread throughout the world. At the close of that revival Jesus Christ will come.

Over in Wales, there began a revival such as the world hasn't seen since the fourth century. There was a stirring among the people. It is commonly believed that it was preached into being and that Evan Roberts preached it into existence. This is not a fact. He was not a vital factor in it. God sent it from heaven. A moving commenced. It didn't commence in one place or one town. It was a stirring of God, a moving of the Spirit throughout the land.

In the common prayer meetings where the people had been meeting week after week, a peculiar thing began to take place. Men began to get a new earnestness in prayer, down in the mines it appeared. People who had not shed tears for twenty years began to shed tears and seek a better place in God. It became general, and spread until the whole nation was in a throb, and thirty thousand people were born to God in a few months. Not with the assistance of preachers, but without them and in spite of them. Sometimes the men God used were men such as no popular minister would have had in his church.

In a room like this, you would find twenty people praying in this corner and twenty people singing at the top of their voice in that corner and twenty people standing up and shouting and praising God in another corner and twenty people conversing over here, and every once in a while a soul would cry out to God and find pardon and peace. The preachers looked on and said, "This is awful, but the people are so happy and are getting saved. If we could just get it fixed up, wouldn't it be glorious revival!"

Together they got to regulating and getting the people to sit still and preachers to preach sermons, etc. And about the time they got it all fixed nice and straight, they regulated the Holy Ghost out of it. The Spirit of the Lord, being grieved, lifted and it was gone. The people were not wise enough and hadn't seen enough of the moving of God and did not understand just to keep out of the way and let the Holy

Ghost work or that men hadn't any right to lay their hands upon the work of God. If the preachers had only known enough to stay at home and stay strictly in bed, I believe with all my soul that that revival would have swept the whole nation and the world, in a way that it has not done.

I want to show you something. The baptism of the Holy Ghost began to be poured out in Wales, and many were baptized in the Holy Ghost and spoke in tongues. In my congregation in Johannesburg, I had three Welshmen who had been baptized in the Holy Ghost and spoke in tongues during that revival in Wales, and they came from different sections of the country. They met in my tabernacle in Johannesburg. They didn't even know what the baptism was and what speaking in tongues meant, but they had been baptized in the Holy Ghost, and for years, it was the evidence of God's fire, it was the pillar of cloud. It was the way God was moving.

Someone, defining a great general, has said, "One who can discern the way that God is moving, and keep out of the way."[6] When men got the Welsh revival generaled to suit themselves, the Spirit of God, being grieved, went disappointed, and the people were left as they were before, excepting for those who had found God.

I have a conviction that there is nothing that comes down from heaven that gets lost, or that evaporates. The things that come down from heaven are the real things, the eternal things, the enduring things. I said to myself in those days, "That descent of the Spirit of God that came down from heaven and swept over Wales is going to land somewhere, and I wish I could be where it lands." I began to pray and the Lord baptized me in the Holy Ghost, and one day as I worked, the Spirit of the Lord said, "Go to Indianapolis, prepare for a winter's campaign, get a large hall. In the spring you will go to Africa." It all came to pass in God's way and God's due time.

Before I went to Africa, indeed it was six months before this incident, one night as I prayed, I was overshadowed by the Spirit of the Lord, and the Lord showed me various places in which I would labor for five years by the illumination that would appear in the heavens. I knew the

---

[6] The source of this quote is unknown.

extent of the work in each place. Among them, and last, was South Africa. That night as I knelt on the floor, I was present in a church in Johannesburg, South Africa, where an acquaintance of mine was pastor. I walked in at the front door of the church and walked to the front, the whole length of the church, and into a little vestry. I looked around the place and took note of everything there, the furniture of the room and all about it. This occurred in my own hometown near Chicago.

In less than a year, I was in that church and pastor of that church. God did the whole thing, and I had nothing to do with it. God having shown with the illumination all over the land the marvelous extent and the character of the work that He was going to do. I had faith to believe that the thing God showed me would come to pass, and I have lived to see it.

There isn't one of us but what longs and hopes and prays for the coming of the kingdom of Jesus Christ. Perhaps it isn't as well defined in our minds as it might be, but the expectation of the man who studies the Word of God is that there is to be a literal kingdom of Jesus Christ in the world, when all the kings of earth will be united under one rulership of the King of kings and Lord of lords — Jesus Himself. That is the day for which the Christian world universal is looking and longing. That was what Tennyson the poet saw and wrote of "The Parliament of Man the Federation of the World."

There is some discussion about the events that will take place between this time and that, but the general consensus of Christian thought in these days marks this outline as the necessary events.

First, the bringing together, or molding together and unifying of the body members of Jesus Christ throughout the world. "That they all may be one."[7] In every church there are those who are the real body members of Jesus Christ. The fact that one is a member of a church and a partaker of its communion and of the communion of the Lord's Supper even, and the other ordinances, is no evidence that your name is written in heaven. But in every church there are those whose names are written in heaven and who have within themselves the witness of the Spirit to that fact. "His Spirit beareth witness with our spirit that we are the children of God."[8]

---

[7] John 17:21.

[8] Romans 8:16, paraphrased.

So the present witness of the Spirit in your own heart is God's guarantee to you that your name is in the Book of Life. The recording angel is the record keeper and the pastors and the preachers and the priests have no control over that book. They can't either put your name on the book or take it off. When all the other records are gone and forgotten, that's the one that will be of importance, that's the Lamb's Book of Life. Bless God! "Whosoever was not found written in the Lamb's Book of Life" had his place among those who suffered condemnation.[9]

There is a moving of the pillar of fire. There are some things that men feel that you can't explain. One of them is that in your spirit there are certain indications of the way in which God is moving. I believe God is moving today in a certain direction. That direction is the bringing together into a spiritual unity the real body members of Jesus Christ. No difference in what church they are, or what country they are in, they are going to unite in the Spirit or be united by the Spirit. There is a dawning, a beginning of a unity in the Spirit of the body in the Holy Ghost, an understanding of the plan of God. We believe that the time has come, God's due time, God's apparent time, made so by the moving of the Spirit for the coming together of the body members of Jesus Christ.

Now I see some poor little saint gets troubled. And says, "What will any preacher say? I will have to cancel my membership in the church where I am a member, and etc." It is not necessary. Your human organization is perfectly harmless. Just leave it alone. It has no important bearing on your heavenly membership in the body of Jesus Christ.

Men's organizations are alright. They are arranged for this purpose, that we can have a better chance to cooperate together for the good of mankind. Some kind of association is necessary. But beloved, there is an association that is all important. It is a spiritual unity with the Lord Jesus Christ. Therefore, everyone everywhere who is one of the body of Jesus Christ will desire to be united with every other member of the body, and God is producing in these days a holy unity, a unity of the Holy Ghost. What its development will be in the days to come nobody can say for a certainty. If these various members of His body

---

[9] Revelation 13:8, paraphrased.

in all the various churches of the world are to be unified into one constructed body, then God will bring them together. God is the attraction. That is the pillar of fire. Everything else will come to that, so we don't need to worry. And the pillar is moving in this direction.

But beloved, the thing for you and me to know is this, "Is the pillar of fire coming our way? Is there anything to mark that God is here?" If I were going to judge, I would say that the pillar of fire has come for the present to Philadelphia. It is Philadelphia's call to the banner of the Lord. It is not spectacular. It may not be apparent to all yet. There are no flaunting banners, but it is God, it is just God. There is an evidence of the presence of God that people haven't been accustomed to seeing before. There is an evidence of the presence of God that people haven't been accustomed to feeling before. God is moving this way.

May I leave a thought in your hearts? God has a purpose, a design. In this blessed work of God we observe, among other things, that in the process of revelation there was a message to the various churches. They were not only the churches at the various places named — Ephesus, Pergamos, Smyrna, Thyatira, Sardis, Philadelphia, and Laodicea — but each of these marked a peculiar dispensation in the Church age.[10]

We will observe in the third chapter of Revelation, that there is one message to the church in Philadelphia, and there we stop and say, "Isn't it strange how God put in some heart of some servant at some time, unknowing perhaps, the thought of naming a city Philadelphia?" But we say, "Brother, he was just some old religious crank; he just admired the name Philadelphia." Probably he was, but God put the admiration in him.

You look over the history of the world, and tell me, does the age make the man, or does the man make the age? Years ago the nation needed a man who was large enough to direct the affairs of this nation and a heart big enough to comprehend the needs of the hour, and looking over all the great minds that others recognized, the Lord went over into the wilds of Illinois, and found an Abraham Lincoln, the most

---

[10] See Revelation 2 and 3.

unlikely man to become a man of note in history, a most unlikely individual. God looked for a head and a heart to match it, big enough for God's need, and He found it there.

Was he born for that purpose? Was the creation of that heart and that mind in the plan of God? Or was it an accident? God don't have accidents. Nothing ever went out of gear in the plan of God. Things were according to God's order. Man sits back and discovers what God is doing and announces himself forthwith as the discoverer. Science discovers the laws by which God works in the world, and then they establish a new god, and they call it "Science." They created nothing, they only discovered that there was such a law, which God made and operated from the eternal ages. So man is always endeavoring to take to himself the glory of what God is doing.

The pillar of fire is coming your way. God is leaving a testimony such as your mind hasn't received before. These are momentous days. In the years to come, you will look back and think of these meetings, in this chapel. Your mind will turn back to these days, as the days of beginning; the beginning of God's moving, or the beginning of your observation of God's moving.

The presence of God brings responsibility. You can't evade it. The pillar of cloud moved, and Moses said, "Come on, you four and a half million people, this is the way," and he followed the cloud, and when the cloud stopped, he stopped.[11] Sometimes it stopped in peculiar places. On one occasion it stopped at Marah, and when they got down to drink, the waters they found were bitter. The people forgot about God and the pillar. They murmured at Moses.[12] Think of Moses with four and a half million people murmuring at him! Brother Atwood and I think it is bad enough when we get a few hundred murmuring at us.

Brother Atwood: Sometimes we can't stand one of them.

Lake: Don't hit too hard, brother, for I have been standing it all day.

Beloved, that was where God stopped, and that was where God worked out His purpose, and His great purpose was that after having

---

[11] See Exodus 13:21.

[12] See Exodus 15:23-24.

demonstrated His power to the people by a miracle performed on the waters, *there,* He brought the purpose to view that He had been after all the time.

> *There* he made for them a statute and an ordinance, and there he proved them, and said, If thou wilt diligently hearken to the voice of the LORD thy God, and wilt do that which is right in his sight, and wilt give ear to his commandments, and keep all his statues, I will put none of these diseases upon thee, which I have brought upon the Egyptians: for I am the LORD that healeth thee.[13]

The miracle on the waters had just turned their faces God-ward, and they found the cloud was there. Moses just took the scolding and went on. So we talk about being "as meek as Moses." He has been the ideal of meekness from that time to this.

> There he made for them a statute and an ordinance, and there he proved them, and said, If thou wilt diligently hearken to the voice of the LORD thy God, and wilt do that which is right in his sight, and wilt give ear to his commandments, and keep all his statutes, I will put none of these diseases upon thee, which I have brought upon the Egyptians: for I am the LORD that healeth thee.

That is the eternal covenant of Jehovah-Rapha, which will stand forever. So God declared Himself the eternal healer. God embodied the covenant in the person of Jesus Christ, and exemplified it through His ministry and demonstrated it through His disciples and bestowed it upon the Church and perpetuated it forever in the nine gifts of the Holy Ghost, for among them is the gift of healings.[14]

God moved that way. God is moving this way tonight. The pillar of fire has stopped here. Have we seen that it was God? The thing we feel isn't an accident on the horizon of our life. It was God. Beyond it was a purpose, God's purpose. God's manifestation and revelation of Himself.

---

[13] Exodus 15:25-26.

[14] See 1 Corinthians 12:28.

Africa has witnessed what Wales did not. It might have come in Wales if God had been permitted to have His way. Africa has witnessed a demonstration of the healing power of God, such as no country in the world has been privileged to see since the days of the apostolic Church. There are incidents in the work in Africa greater than anything recorded in the New Testament, in the way of healing. You observe what a strong statement that is. The multitudes, all that came to them, were healed by Jesus and the apostles, by their personal touch.

In a party of our Brother Saunders, is a native man, Edward Lion, who a few years ago didn't even wear clothes, illiterate, knows nothing whatever of our conception of scholarship. God anointed that man with the faith of God and a measure of the Holy Ghost so intense, that on one occasion when a multitude of sick had been brought and collected in a valley, the power of God came upon him and he went upon the mountainside, stretched out his hands over the sick below, and poured out his heart to God, and in a minute hundreds of them were healed. Healing power fell upon them from heaven. Just as the Holy Ghost sometimes falls on a congregation.

There is no such instance recorded in the New Testament. Jesus promised that the last days should be marked by greater works than He Himself had wrought.[15] But beloved, listen, the knowledge of these things brings upon mankind a new responsibility to God. From the day that man became aware of the moving of God and had a consciousness of the pillar of fire moving this way, all your old standards became back numbers.

God is raising a new standard. Your conviction or condemnation will not be by the old standard of your life any longer. The measurement from this time forth will be by the new light. A moving of God has been going on for years. It has been going on in Aldan. People have smiled, others have mocked. They didn't understand. They murmured at Moses. They didn't see the pillar of fire, nor observe that the cloud had stopped at Marah, but it was there all the time, all the time.

Now you listen. I have been talking to God, and God has been talking to me, and I tell you right now that inside of twelve months there will

---

[15] See John 14:12.

be a moving of God in this community that will startle the people of this community. And the wise man and the wise woman sees God and they forget about their old prejudices and their little environment and they take their eyes off man and off organizations of men and they turn their eyes toward God and move in God's way, and the cloud is moving this way.

Just one thing more and I am done. The pillar of fire has come to Philadelphia, and there will be a moving of God in Philadelphia which will attract the whole nation, and the attention of the whole world, and out of it all God will establish something. The thing that has been in the mind of God all the time, and according to the plan of God, it will be the church of Philadelphia. May I read you about it ere I sit down?

> And to the angel of the church in Philadelphia write; these things saith he that is holy, he that is true, he that hath the key of David, he that openeth, and no man shutteth; and shutteth, and no man openeth; I know thy works: behold, I have set before thee an open door, and no man can shut it; for thou hast a little strength, and hast kept my word, and hast not denied my name. Behold, I will make them of the synagogue of Satan, which say they are Jews, and are not, but do lie; behold, I will make them to come and worship before thy feet, and to know that I have loved thee. Because thou hast kept the word of my patience, I also will keep thee from the hour of temptation, which shall come upon all the world, to try them that dwell upon the earth. Behold, I come quickly: hold that fast which thou hast, that no man take thy crown. Him that over-cometh will I make a pillar in the temple of my God, and he shall go no more out: and I will write upon him the name of my God, and the name of the city of my God, which is new Jerusalem, which cometh down out of heaven from my God: and I will write upon him my new name. He that hath an ear, let him hear what the Spirit saith unto the churches.

— Revelation 3:7-13

It is for you to say whether you will be a member of His Church, bone of His bone and flesh of His flesh, actually so; a member of His body in whom the very heart-pulses of the Messiah will throb. A member of His body, with the very mind of Christ, shall be manifested and demonstrated. That's what it is to be a member of the Church. Note that. A person that will feel the very pulse of the Christ, a soul that will be so absolutely enthused and so controlled by the mind of Jesus that your very walk and your very thought and your very gifts will be a part of the heart-thought of the Christ. That's what it is to be a part of the Church. What Reverend Atwood has brought out tonight is this, that Christ is going to have a Church in which all His characteristics, all His attributes, all His fullness of power is to be manifested.

On the church of Philadelphia is stamped and printed the Brideship. On the church of Philadelphia is to be written the name of the eternal God and Father. On the church of Philadelphia is to be written the name of the New Jerusalem that is coming down from God out of heaven.

So the church of Philadelphia is the spotless bride, and that's why no fault is laid at her door. She is the bride, and there is no fault in the bride. Jesus is going to have the best that earth has brought forth. Then again, on her is written His own new name. And beloved, that very name characterizes the Church of Jesus as a participant in the very Spirit and being of Christ Himself.

John G. Lake

ALPHABETICAL INDEX

TOPICAL INDEX

ABOUT THE AUTHOR

Roberts Liardon is President of Roberts Liardon Ministries, and Founder and Senior Pastor of Embassy Christian Center in Irvine, California. He is also Founder of Spirit Life Bible College and Life Ministerial Association in Irvine.

Roberts Liardon received his call to ministry as an eight-year-old boy. Since then, he has diligently endeavored to follow that call through preaching and teaching God's Word. He has preached in over eighty nations with extensive ministry in Europe, Asia, and Africa.

As a best-selling author, Roberts has expanded his ministry onto the printed page. His books have been translated into over twenty-seven languages and have been circulated throughout the world. Roberts' books reflect his belief that the Church can fulfill its call and bring revival to the nations by combining God's Word with the moving of His Spirit.

As a historian, Roberts possesses a wealth of knowledge regarding the great leaders of three Christian movements — Pentecostal, Divine Healing, and Charismatic. He embarked on his indepth studies as a fourteen-year-old boy and has continued those studies into adulthood. Roberts has established ongoing research through the founding of the Reformers and Revivalist Historical Museum in California.

Through his compilation of *John G. Lake, The Complete Collection of His Life Teachings*, Roberts preserves a treasure of our Christian heritage.

CHURCH HISTORY IS VALUABLE TO US

If you have any materials pertaining to Church history, we would like to know about them. Roberts Liardon Ministries is committed to preserving Christian archives in our Reformers and Revivalists Historical Museum. Memorabilia from our past is very valuable and vital to future Church growth.

We are looking for magazines, letters, books, manuscripts, photographs, audio and videotapes, movies, diaries, scrapbooks, and any other personal items that would portray our Church history. Thank you for desiring to bless the world with your historical treasures. Please contact our research department in California.

ROBERTS LIARDON MINISTRIES INTERNATIONAL OFFICES:

EUROPE
Roberts Liardon Ministries
P. O. Box 2043 • Hove, Brighton
East Sussex, BN3 6JU England
Phone and Fax: 44 1707 327 222

SOUTH AFRICA
Roberts Liardon Ministries
P. O. Box 3155 • Kimberley 8300, South Africa
Phone and Fax: 2753 832 1207

AUSTRALIA
Roberts Liardon Ministries
P. O. Box 439 • Buderim QLD 4556 • Australia
Phone and Fax: 61 754 422108

USA
Roberts Liardon Ministries
P. O. Box 30710 • Laguna Hills, California 92654
Phone: (949) 833-3555 • Fax: (949) 833-9555
or
www.robertsliardon.org

BOOKS BY ROBERTS LIARDON

John G. Lake:
The Complete Collection of His Life Teachings

Breaking Controlling Powers

Smith Wigglesworth Speaks to Students of the Bible

Sharpen Your Discernment

Smith Wigglesworth:
The Complete Collection of His Life Teachings

God's Generals

God's Generals Workbook

A Call to Action

Cry of the Spirit:
Unpublished Sermons by Smith Wigglesworth

Forget Not His Benefits

Haunted Houses, Ghosts & Demons

Holding to the Word of the Lord

I Saw Heaven

Kathryn Kuhlman:
A Spiritual Biography of God's Miracle-Working Power

Religious Politics

Run to the Battle

School of the Spirit

Spiritual Timing

The Invading Force

The Price of Spiritual Power

The Quest for Spiritual Hunger

Also Available:

God's Generals Video Collection
(12 Video Tapes)

Additional copies of this book and other book titles
from ALBURY PUBLISHING are
available at your local bookstore.

ALBURY PUBLISHING
P. O. Box 470406
Tulsa, Oklahoma 74147-0406

In Canada, books are available from:
Word Alive
P. O. Box 670
Niverville, Manitoba
CANADA R0A 1E0